# Multinational Corporations

# The International Library of Critical Writings in Economics

*Series Editor:* Mark Blaug
Professor Emeritus, University of London
Consultant Professor, University of Buckingham
Visiting Professor, University of Exeter

# Multinational Corporations

*Edited by*

## Mark Casson

*Professor of Economics*
*University of Reading*

An Elgar Reference Collection

Published by
Edward Elgar Publishing Limited
Gower House
Croft Road
Aldershot
Hants GU11 3HR
England

Edward Elgar Publishing Company
Old Post Road
Brookfield
Vermont 05036
USA

**British Library Cataloguing in Publication Data**

Multinational corporations. – (The International library of
   critical writings in economics; 1).
   1. Multinational companies
   I. Casson, Mark, *1945*–   II. Series
   338.38

ISBN 1 85278 192 0

Printed in Great Britain by Galliard (Printers) Ltd, Great Yarmouth

# Contents

# Acknowledgements

The editor and publishers wish to thank the following who have kindly given permission for the use of copyright material.

American Economic Association for article: R.N. Batra and R. Ramachandran (1980), 'Multinational Firms and the Theory of International Trade and Investment', *American Economic Review*, **70**, 278–90.

Basil Blackwell Ltd for articles: D.J. Teece (1977), 'Technology Transfer by Multinational Firms: The Resource Costs of Transferring Technological Know-how', *Economic Journal*, **87**, 242–61; E.S. Mansfield, D. Teece and A. Romeo (1979), 'Overseas Research and Development by US-based Firms', *Economica*, **46**, 187–96; J.A. Cantwell (1987), 'The Reorganisation of European Industries after Integration: Selected Evidence on the Role of Multinational Enterprise Activities', *Journal of Common Market Studies*, **26** (2), 127–51; W.H. Davidson and D.G. McFetridge (1984), 'International Technology Transactions and the Theory of the Firm', *Journal of Industrial Economics*, **32** (3), 253–64; D. DeMeza and F. van der Ploeg (1987), 'Production Flexibility as a Motive for Multinationality', *Journal of Industrial Economics*, **35** (3), 343–52; S. Lall (1978), 'The Pattern of Intra-Firm Exports by US Multinationals', *Oxford Bulletin of Economics and Statistics*, **40** (3), 209–22; G.K. Helleiner and R. Lavergne (1980), 'Intra-Firm Trade and Industrial Exports to the US', *Oxford Bulletin of Economics and Statistics*, **41** (4), 297–311.

Cambridge University Press for article: S.J. Nicholas (1983), 'Agency Contracts, Institutional Modes and the Transition to Foreign Direct Investment by British Manufacturing Multinationals before 1939', *Journal of Economic History*, **43**, 675–86.

Frank Cass & Co. Ltd for article: M. Wilkins (1988), 'European and North American Multinationals 1870–1914: Comparisons and Contrasts', *Business History*, **30** (1), 8–45.

Dr L.J. Clegg for his article: (1987), 'The Determinants of Multinational Enterprise: A Comparative Study of the US, Japan, UK, Sweden and West Germany', School of Management, University of Bath.

Croom Helm for excerpts: D.J. Lecraw (1985), 'Some Evidence on Transfer Pricing by Multinational Corporations' from *Multinationals and Transfer Pricing*, A.M. Rugman and L. Eden (eds); J. Johanson and L.-G. Mattson (1988), 'Internationalisation in Industrial Systems – A Network Approach' from *Strategies in Global Competition*, N. Hood and J.-E. Vahlne (eds).

D.C. Heath and Company, Lexington Books, Lexington, Mass. for excerpt: B. Kogut (1988), 'A Study of the Life Cycle of Joint Ventures' from *Cooperative Strategies in International Business*, F.J. Contractor and P. Lorange (eds).

Institute of Comparative Economic Studies, Hosei University, Tokyo for article: A.M. Rugman (1987), 'The Firm-Specific Advantages of Canadian Multinationals, *Journal of International Economic Studies*, **2**, 1–14.

Macmillan, London and Basingstoke for excerpt: M.C. Casson (1985), 'Multinationals and Intermediate Product Trade' from *Economic Theory of the Multinational Enterprise: Selected Papers*, P.J. Buckley and M.C. Casson (eds).

Pergamon Press plc for article: M. Blomström and H. Persson (1983), 'Foreign Investment and Spillover Efficiency in an Underdeveloped Economy: Evidence from Mexican Manufacturing Industry', *World Development*, **11** (6), 493–501.

*Revue Economique* for article: S.H. Hymer (1968), 'The Large Multinational "Corporation": An Analysis of Some Motives for the International Integration of Business', translated from *Revue Economique*, **19** (6), 949–73.

M.E. Sharpe, Inc., New York for article: E.M. Graham (1978), 'Transnational Investment by Multinational Firms: A Rivalistic Phenomenon', *Journal of Post-Keynesian Economics*, **1**, 82–99.

University of Chicago Press for article: E. Helpmann (1984), 'A Simple Theory of International Trade with Multinational Corporations', *Journal of Political Economy*, **92**, 451–71.

University of Pennsylvania for article: I. Horstmann and J.R. Markusen (1987), 'Strategic Investments and the Development of Multinationals', *International Economic Review*, **28**, 109–21.

University of Reading Department of Economics for article: R.D. Pearce (1988), 'The Determinants of Overseas R & D by US MNEs: An Analysis of Industry Level Data', *University of Reading Department of Economics Discussion Papers in International Investment and Business Studies*, No.119.

University of South Carolina for articles: R.W. Moxon (1975), 'The Motivation for Investment in Off-shore Plants: The Case of the US Electronics Industry', *Journal of International Business Studies*, **6**, 51–65; P.J. Buckley and R.D. Pearce (1979), 'Overseas Production and Exporting by the World's Largest Enterprises: A Study in Sourcing Policy', *Journal of International Business Studies*, **10**(1), 9–20; R. Mirus and B. Yeung (1986), 'Economic Incentives for Countertrade', *Journal of International Business Studies*, **17** (3), 27–39; J.J. Boddewyn, M.B. Halbrich and A.C. Perry (1986), 'Service Multinationals: Conceptualisation, Measurement and Theory', *Journal of International Business Studies*, **17** (3), 41–57.

Unwin Hyman Ltd for excerpt: J.H. Dunning (1988), 'US and Japanese Manufacturing Affiliates in the UK: Comparisons and Contrasts' from *Explaining International Production*, J.H. Dunning.

Every effort has been made to trace all the copyright holders but if any have been inadvertently overlooked the publishers will be pleased to make the necessary arrangement at the first opportunity.

In addition the publishers wish to thank the Library of the London School of Economics and Political Science for their assistance in obtaining these articles.

# Introduction

Both the quantity and quality of research on the multinational enterprise (MNE) have increased dramatically over the last few years. Research on the MNE has been instrumental in promoting important ideas in economic theory, such as transaction costs and the related concept of internalization. It has involved the collection of a large amount of firm-level data through sample surveys and questionnaires, and the standardization of industry-level data from different countries. These data have been analysed using multiple regression, cluster analysis and other statistical techniques. Important policy issues have been addressed, such as the consequences of the global integration of markets and the nature of the spill-overs from multinational operations within the host economy.

The rapid growth of highly relevant research is reflected in the selection of papers in this volume, where the emphasis is on relatively recent work at the interface of theory, evidence and policy. An important characteristic of this work is its focus on the MNE as an agent of technology transfer rather than as a conduit for capital flows. This volume therefore highlights the role of the MNE in the creation and exploitation of proprietary technology. The economic performance of the high-technology firm depends crucially on the management of marketing channels and the internal coordination of related production activities. These organizational and institutional issues are also addressed in this volume.

The role of international capital flows between parent and subsidiary, and the financing of the parent firm, are considered in detail in the companion volume, *International Investment*, edited by Peter Buckley. This division of labour between the editors (proposed by the publisher) creates some ambiguities at the margin. A consequence of this is that a few papers appear in the other volume which could just as well appear in this, and *vice versa*. To conserve space, these papers have not been duplicated. The reader should note, in particular, that seminal papers by Horst (*Journal of Political Economy*, 1971) on the pricing strategy of MNEs in segmented markets, by Vernon (*Oxford Bulletin of Economics and Statistics*, 1979) on the 'product cycle' in a new international environment, and by Wolf (*Journal of Industrial Economics*, 1977) on the relation between the geographical and industrial diversification of the firm, all appear in the companion volume.

The selection of papers has also been guided by the principle that material readily available in major books should not be replicated, particularly where these books are likely to be kept in print for the foreseeable future. With a couple of exceptions, no material has been taken from the following basic sources, which should be regarded as complements to, and not substitutes for, the present volume.

Buckley, P.J. and M.C. Casson (1976, second edition 1989), *The Future of the Multinational Enterprise*, London: Macmillan; and New York: Holmes and Meier.
Buckley, P.J. and M.C. Casson (1985), *Economic Theory of the Multinational*

*Enterprise: Selected Papers*, London: Macmillan; and New York: St Martins Press.

Casson, M.C. (1987), *The Firm and the Market: Studies in Multinational Enterprise and the Scope of the Firm*, Oxford: Blackwell; and Cambridge, Mass: MIT Press.

Dunning, J.H. (1988a), *Explaining International Production*, London, Boston and Sydney: Unwin Hyman. (This book partially supersedes the author's important work, *International Production and the Multinational Enterprise*, London, Boston and Sydney: Allen and Unwin, 1981.)

Dunning, J.H. (1988b), *Multinationals, Technology and Competitiveness*, London, Boston and Sydney: Unwin Hyman.

Rugman, A.M. (ed)(1982), *New Theories of the Multinational Enterprise*, Beckenham, Kent, and Totowa, NJ: Croom Helm.

Because of the focus on recent work, the coverage of early work is confined to two theoretical pieces, which have been selected because of their priority in applying important ideas to the analysis of the MNE. The question of priority has proved unnecessarily controversial. The first paper, by Hymer, has been specially translated for this volume. It has its own introduction which explains its importance in relation to subsequent work. The paper shows that Hymer was not only familiar with Coasian internalization theory, but was equally at home with internalization concepts as with the theory of market structure. The fact that the Hymer paper was published in 1968 and the McManus paper in 1972 also underlines the fact that internalization was given a central role in the analysis of the MNE some time before its significance was appreciated by the majority of industrial economists.

No analysis of the MNE is complete without a discussion of the location of production. It is, however, only recently that trade theorists have begun to make creative contributions to the study of MNE. The traditional approach to location and trade, based on a variant of the Heckscher–Ohlin model, is illustrated by the Batra and Ramachandran paper, whilst the consequence of incorporating uncertainty into the analysis of location is considered by de Meza and van der Ploeg. The latter paper shows how, when location analysis is combined with internalization theory, the advantages of the locational flexibility of the MNE can be fully appreciated.

Hymer's emphasis on market structure has proved extremely influential. The papers by Graham, Helpmann, and Horstmann and Markusen illustrate the important part that models of oligopolistic rivalry and monopolistic competition play in the modern theory of the MNE. The last two papers apply principles of contestability and game-theoretic equilibrium to the MNE. In each case the model takes full account of system interdependence, in the sense that it checks rigorously that agents in the MNE's environment behave rationally towards it, and that the MNE itself responds rationally to their reactions.

To understand why multinationals exist it is important to appreciate what the contractual alternatives might be. These alternatives are particularly significant in respect of technology transfer. The alternatives to a wholly-owned foreign subsidiary include a licensing arrangement with an independent host-country firm, a joint venture with an indigenous firm, and – perhaps rather surprisingly – a 'buy back' arrangement relating to the output of an overseas plant whose design embodies the purchaser's technology. The papers by Davidson and McFetridge, Kogut, and Mirus and Yeung evaluate these respective alternatives against the MNE, formulating (and in some cases testing) hypotheses about the conditions which will favour one arrangement rather than another.

Although transaction cost analysis of technology transfer has tended to dominate the literature, a number of important empirical studies address wider issues in the technology field. Particularly significant are studies of the dynamics of learning new technology in the host country. The Teece paper emphasizes the very high costs associated with this learning process. It provides a salutory lesson for those scholars who emphasize the public good nature of technical know-how so much that they equate the marginal costs of technology transfer to zero. The Dunning paper compares the methods of technology transfer used by two source countries – the US and Japan – in the same host country – the UK. This paper summarizes some of Dunning's most important work, including his two major studies of the host-country impact of technology transfer, and demonstrates the practical utility of his 'eclectic paradigm' in analysing issues of this kind. Dunning's paper places considerable emphasis on both the technological and managerial spill-overs of foreign operations on the host economy. Blomström and Persson attempt to measure the magnitude of this impact by relating labour productivity in privately-owned firms to the presence of foreign MNEs in a cross-section of Mexican industries. Mexico provides a suitable case study both because its proximity to the US ensures a high level of US investment in many industries and because of the high quality of Mexican official data.

Successful absorption of foreign technology may allow a host country to become a source country, generating its own indigenous multinationals. There has been some controversy over whether third-world MNEs have the same kind of indigenous technological capability as first-world MNEs. There is case-study evidence which suggests that some of them do, but the systematic study by Wells – an excerpt from which is reproduced here – suggests that typically they do not. Third world MNEs, he claims, have special skills in producing small batches of products 'on demand' for 'niche' markets using standardized or ageing capital equipment. They continue to be comparatively disadvantaged in innovating new 'state of the art' technology.

It is sometimes suggested that in their efforts to appropriate rents from a technological monopoly, MNEs will centralize their R & D close to their headquarters in the interests of preserving secrecy. This particular interpretation of 'appropriability theory' is, however, demonstrably false, in view of the widespread practice of large MNEs in decentralizing R & D. There is considerable evidence that corporate R & D is pulled away from headquarters by the need to synthesize ideas originating in different geographical agglomerations of excellence throughout the developed world. Important empirical work has been done on this fascinating issue, using both firm-level and industry-level data for the US, and firm-level data for Sweden. Three of the major studies are reproduced here.

Technology is not the only area in which secrecy may provide a strategic advantage to the MNE. The internalization of trade may encourage transfer pricing, at the expense of either the source-country or host-country government. In addition, internal markets that are entirely closed to independent firms may constitute a barrier to entry, by widening the range of activities in which an entrant must be self-sufficient, and so indirectly raising the entrant's cost of capital and increasing the amount of technology that he must obtain under licence. For these and other reasons, the trade flows controlled by MNEs have been subjected to considerable scrutiny, and four of the major studies are reproduced here. They show that, amongst other things, intra-firm trade is particularly common in high-technology industries, and also in industries where sophisticated products require comprehensive after-sales service. Strategies for pricing intra-firm exports vary between firms, but it is difficult to assess how far these differences reflect rational responses to different fiscal regimes.

During the 1980s some of the world's leading MNEs have 'globalized' their operations, rationalizing around a nexus of core wholly-owned activities. These core activities are supported by a periphery of more loosely affiliated activities involving joint venture partners and long-term subcontractors. This move has been prompted by trade liberalization – in particular the expansion of free trade areas and the move to levying tariffs on a value-added basis – and has involved a significant relocation of activities, in which off-shore processing has often played an important role. As Hymer foresaw, globalization has also led the major firms into oligopolistic confrontations with each other on a number of fronts. Oligopolists have been drawn into technological competition in which access to agglomerations of expertise is likely to prove crucial for long-term success. These global and dynamic issues are difficult to analyse using conventional tools of analysis, but some progress has been made, as the papers by Moxon, Casson and Cantwell show.

Internalization theory and its application to technology transfer and intra-firm trade is only one strand within the most broadly based transaction cost approach to the MNE. Transaction cost theory also provides a basis for analysing the marketing function, since marketing is specifically designed to reduce transaction costs in arm's length markets. In markets where switching costs are high, continuity of the relationship between buyer and seller is crucial for efficiency. In this context, 'quasi-integration' helps to regulate the negotiation of trades through informal social mechanisms such as reciprocity. In highly interdependent systems, networks of social obligation can provide an effective way of reducing overall transaction costs. These factors seem to be particularly crucial in the international environment. Various aspects of this phenomenon are addressed by Johanson and Mattsson, whilst Nicholas provides an historical perspective on the subject. The importance of marketing skills and proficiency in network management are highlighted in Rugman's study of the firm-specific advantages of Canadian multinationals. Finally, the paper by Boddewyn *et al* shows that the analysis of marketing is particularly crucial for the emerging analysis of multinational operations in the service sector.

Social factors such as reciprocity are important not only in organizing external markets but also in improving the internal markets of the firm. The fact that internal transaction costs are often dubbed 'agency costs' should not obscure the fact that the logic of transaction cost minimization is essentially the same in both intra-firm and inter-firm trade. Since internal transaction costs (agency costs, in other words) can be lowered using social mechanisms, it is natural to postulate that firms based in different societies will adopt different patterns of organizational behaviour and achieve different levels of overall performance. Social factors can also influence attitudes to technological innovation, leading to systematic differences in the pace of technology-based expansion by firms headquartered in different countries. The concluding papers by Wilkins, Negandhi and Clegg address these broad comparative issues from, respectively, an historical, political and economic perspective.

The papers reproduced in this book are drawn from a wide variety of sources, reflecting the diversity of interests and backgrounds amongst scholars who have been attracted to the study of the MNE. Research on the MNE has so far avoided the intellectual sclerosis which has affected some of the more narrow and intensively 'professionalized' sub-disciplines of economics. Interdisciplinary research is alive and well in the MNE field and, so far as its economic content is concerned, there is every prospect that its vitality and relevance will be sustained for some considerable time.

# Part I
# Early Analysis

# [1]

## The Large Multinational "Corporation":

## An Analysis of Some Motives for the International

## Integration of Business

### Stephen II. Ilymer

### Translated from the French by Nathalie Vacherot

### Introduction by Mark Casson

Stephen Hymer is widely recognised as the pioneer of the economic theory of the multinational enterprise (MNE). Most interpretations of his work focus on his thesis (Hymer, 1976) and the papers reprinted in the memorial volume (Hymer, 1979). Controversy has arisen over the relative weight that Hymer attached to internalisation and market structure in explaining the growth of the MNE, and in particular over how successfully Hymer related his own work to that of Coase (1937).

As Acocella (1988) has recently noted, Hymer's most extensive discussion of internalisation is found outside the most familiar sources. In particular, his French-language paper 'The Large Multinational Corporation' (*Revue Economique*, **19** (6) (1968), 949-73), republished in translation here, is a major source for Hymer's views on Coase.

This paper is important because it shows that Hymer developed a Coasian theory of the MNE. In this respect it goes well beyond his thesis (see Dunning and Rugman, 1985). His theory embraces both horizontal and vertical integration, and so clearly anticipates by several years the work of McManus (1972), Buckley and Casson (1976) and others.

This paper also shows that Hymer did not support a dichotomy between the effects of internalisation and market structure of the kind suggested by subsequent writers (for example, Cantwell, 1988). He outlined, instead, a two-way interaction between them. Internalisation within an industry of given size determines the number of firms, and hence industrial concentration and market structure. Market structure feeds back in two ways. It governs the opportunities for further horizontal expansion of the firm within the industry -thus high industrial concentration encourages the firm  to expand through diversification instead.  Secondly, imperfect competition (monopoly, monopsony, bilteral monopoly) at one stage of production induces price distortions within a multi-stage production process (as described by McKenzie, 1951) and so creates an incentive for backward or forward integration.

In this paper Hymer has moved on from the preoccupation with technological advantages which was characteristic of his thesis.  He emphasises instead the role of MNEs in the international division of labour - a theme from classical political economy that he developed at greater length after his conversion to Marxism (which occurred at about the time this paper was published).  His applications of internalisation therefore give more weight than might at first be expected to backward integration into raw materials and much less weight to the way proprietary technology is exploited.  This emphasis on backward integration also reflects increasing awareness of labour problems in the primary sectors of less-developed countries.

Interesting too is the fact that Hymer sees internalisation theory as a general theory of why firms exist.  He does not regard his use of internalisation as an innovation, but merely as an application of established ideas.  The MNE does not require new concepts in order to be understood.  It is simply the international manifestation of institutional forces which have been operating for centuries in national economies.  The process of business integration described by Chandler in the context of the nineteenth century railway revolution is, notes Hymer, the progenitor of the process which continues today in the reduction of barriers to international technology transfer and trade.

Hymer places much more weight than have subsequent writers on capital market imperfections.  According to Hymer, these imperfections explain why shareholders prefer to diversify risks through holding shares in diversified forms.  They also explain why firms reinvest profits, rather than distribute them as dividends and then borrow them back to finance new investment.  Imperfections in financial markets are caused by, amongst other things, indivisibilities in information.  According to Hymer, it is largely because the cost of obtaining information about a firm is independent of its size that large firms can borrow more cheaply than small ones.

The internalisation of financial markets provides a rationale for the multidivisional firm. The board of directors assumes the role of a bank or other financial intermediary. Hymer emphasises the way in which internal markets can be used to reallocate profits for reinvestment between different stages of a multistage production process. He presents an algebraic model to explain how this could be done (modern writers make essentially the same point by showing how under vertical integration investments can be coordinated using long-term internal forward markets).

It is interesting that despite his 'radical' emphasis on market structure and the distribution of income, Hymer's analytical approach is distinctly neoclassical. In analysing the scope of the firm he continually appeals to marginalist principles. Moreover, although he recognises capital market imperfections, he is also clear that capital markets exert an important discipline on the management of MNEs. Management is always constrained by the threat of takeover. Thus while he recognises that the large firm - like the small owner-managed firm - may have a distinct 'personality', quirks in behaviour can be indulged only within very definite limits. There is little emphasis on 'managerial capitalism' here.

Despite its many strengths, however, the paper suffers from some careless presentation, as if it has been written in a hurry, or not revised prior to publication. Only one of the references to Coase appears to be a faithful quotation. One is a composite quotation compiled from two distinct passages, and one extensive quotation appears to be Hymer's own précis - it certainly bears little resemblance to the original.

The French text is stylistically poor, which makes a truthful translation rather cumbersome in places. The discussion also relies rather heavily on metaphors - the 'brain' of the firm, for example - when a more literal description might be more helpful. The equations contain a number of minor errors (possibly uncorrected misprints) which have been corrected here. Finally, and most seriously, the diagrammatic analysis of licensing appears to be wrong. Whilst Hymer's verbal discussion refers to the simultaneous licensing of a number of small producers, his formal model appears to relate to competitive bidding for a single exclusive licence. Comparing Hymer's results with subsequent analysis (Johnson, 1970; Magee, 1977; Casson, 1979, 1987) shows that he has overlooked the fact that licensees selling to overlapping markets must collude if they are to generate sufficient rents for the licensor to maximise his return. It is difficult to say whether his analysis of licensing to a Bertrand monopsonist is correct because the model is not spelt out in sufficient detail. These are, however, only small quibbles with what is, taken as a whole, a remarkably wide-ranging and insightful piece of research.

## References

Acocella, N. (1988) Efficiency and Strategy in the Multinationalisation Process: Towards a More General Theory, paper presented at the International Congress on Internationalisation Theories and the Italian Situation, Rome: Department of Economics, University of Rome 'La Sapienza', October 1988.

Buckley, P.J. and M.C. Casson (1976) *The Future of the Multinational Enterprise*, London: Macmillan.

Cantwell, J.A. (1988) Theories of International Business, *University of Reading Discussion Papers in International Investment and Business Studies* (Series B), No. 122.

Casson, M.C. (1979) *Alternatives to the Multinational Enterprise*, London: Macmillan.

Casson, M.C. (1987) *The Firm and the Market: Studies in the Multinational Enterprise and the Scope of the Firm*, Oxford: Blackwell, and Cambridge, Mass: MIT Press.

Coase, R.H. (1937) The Nature of the Firm, *Economica* (New Series), 4, 386-405.

Dunning, J.H. and A.M. Rugman (1985) The Influence of Hymer's Dissertation on the Theory of Foreign Direct Investment, *American Economic Association Papers and Proceedings*, 75, 228-32.

5

Hymer, S.H. (1976) *The International Operations of National Firms: A Study in Direct Foreign Investment* (Doctoral dissertation, MIT, 1960) Cambridge, Mass: MIT Press.

Hymer, S.H. (1979) *The Multinational Corporation: A Radical Approach* (ed. R.B. Cohen, N. Felton, J. van Liere, and M. Nkosi, with assistance of N. Dennis) Cambridge: Cambridge University Press.

Johnson, H.G. (1970) The Efficiency and Welfare Implications of the International Corporation, in C.P. Kindleberger (ed) *The International Corporation*, Cambridge, Mass: MIT Press, 35-56.

McKenzie, L.W. (1951) Ideal Output and the Interdependence of Firms, *Economic Journal*, **61**, 785-803.

McManus, J. (1972) The Theory of the International Firm, in G. Paquet (ed), *The Multinational Firm and the Nation State*, Toronto: Collier Macmillan, 66-93

Magee, S.P. (1977) Information and the Multinational Corporation: An Appropriability Theory of Direct Foreign Investment, in J.N. Bhagwati (ed) *The New International Economic Order*, Cambridge, Mass: MIT Press.

First of all, what is the nature of the 'thing'? It is designated by countless labels such as direct investment, *International Business, International Firm, International Corporate Group, Multinational Firm, Multinational Enterprise, Multinational Corporation, Multinational Family Group, World Wide Enterprise*, large multinational enterprise, large international unit, or as the French Minister of Foreign Affairs calls it: 'The Giant American Firm'.

Every analysis emphasises two aspects. The first one concerns the modern industrial firm, which is a large bureaucratic network and a place where decisions are taken, and which plays a dominant role in the economy. At the international level, the problem of the multinational firm is the same as that of the large national firm in the economy of a country. Second, though these firms have international activities, they are national by nature, and the fact that they have a nationality complicates the process of decision and their relations with the government. Most of them are American, and the Americans tend to encourage their diffusion and growth. As for the other countries, their feelings towards them are ambiguous. They recognize them but at the same time' they distrust their power.

It is not surprising that the large multinational firm should trigger such a preoccupation, often out of proportion to its actual quantitative importance. It implies two of the main institutions of a modern economy: the "corporation" and the National State, whereas at the same time, at the ideological level, it recalls the most impressive of the words that end with "ism": capitalism, nationalism, imperialism.[1]

The growth of large firms, combined with the state's tendency to bear a growing share of direct responsibility in the economic field, cannot but lead both to tension and harmony. In every country, the problem of a right balance between public and private sections is of crucial importance. When the private sector is of foreign nationality, the search for a compromise becomes very difficult.[2]

From now on, we shall consider things from the firm's point of view and we shall review the reasons for it to become multinational as well as the obstacles it may encounter on the way. In other words, we are going to study the advantages and disadvantages of agreeing with a foreign customer, supplier or competitor, to become its ally, merge with it or take it over. The thinking is straightforward and built on the usual methods of economic analysis. What is new is the fact that the theory of the firm and oligopoly theory have not been applied to the problems of trade and international investment yet.

Although the point is not to study the process of national integration of business from the national state's point of view, the reader should be aware that many of the issues studied from the firm's point of view may be considered from other aspects and analysed to find out their implications in the choice of policies.[3]

## The firm as a tool for saving market costs.

Some firms operate independently; some are linked to others from the same country; lastly, some are linked to foreign firms. Links are varied: ownership and direct control of firms operating on foreign markets, indirect contacts through foreign markets or links of a hybrid nature such as minority participation, licensing agreements, belonging to a cartel, tacit understanding, etc.

What are these links determined by? In other words, what determines the extent of the control by a firm, i.e. the nature and size of the network that links, coordinates, and harmonizes activities that expand in various branches and areas of the world and are as varied as mines, processing industries, wholesale trade, marketing, transport and financial operations?

When it comes to the study of the degree of integration of business and the problem of the size of the firm, the role of economic analysis consists in stating whether there are scale economies or not. The size of the firm results from two opposing tendencies. On the one hand, increasing size leads to increasing profits owing to scale economies; on the other hand, the costs of managing and coordinating numerous units are raised as the firm develops. The firm reaches its optimal size when marginal scale advantages are just overtaken by marginal management costs. As in the game with a rope being pulled from both sides, the forces oppose until reaching an equilibrium. If the equilibrium is reached when the size of the firm involves no more than a small share of total production, competition is perfect in the industry. If, on the contrary, the optimum size of the firm is large compared with the whole industry, the structure of the market is oligopolistic and demand becomes an additional constraint on growth.

Coase's classical analysis of the nature of the firm[4] highlights the determinants of its size. First, he emphasises that:

'...the distinguishing mark of the firm is the supersession of the price mechanism. Outside the firm, price movements direct production, which is co-ordinated through a series of exchange relations on the market. Within a firm, these market transactions are eliminated and in place of the complicated market structure with exchange transactions is substituted the entrepreneur-coordinator, who directs production.'

The great merit of Coases's analysis is that it does not confuse scale economies at the level of the industry and scale economies at the level of the firm. The former have a technological origin and result from the division of labour. As the output increases, it becomes possible to divide stages (of production) and processes (of production) and to draw benefits from specialisation.

As for scale economies achieved by the firm, they result from organisation. The firm is an organism that coordinates activities, and the question of scale economies can be reduced to a problem of efficiency of information. When coordination is effected by the market mechanism, each unit reacts independently to signals received from the market ; when coordination is effected by the firm, each unit transmits the information through the internal network of communication to other units and to a "central brain" which gives orders and dictates adjustment processes to the units.

According to Coase, it is more profitable to coordinate the actions of the cells of the economy through entrepreneurs rather than through markets because markets are imperfect. The choice being between coordination through "management" and coordination through the "market", the size of the firm is determined by the relative efficiency with which each system sustains transactions between economic sectors and by the comparative costs borne in each case. Thus, marketing costs play an essential role in the explanation of the size and the field of action of the firm.

'Thanks to the firm, it gets less and less necessary to specify prices for each of the multiple transactions, for a long-term contract can replace a series of short-term contracts. Instead of negotiating each day the conditions under which factors will be employed and material resources used, an agreement will be reached which covers a long period of time and sets remuneration rates and, at the same time, gives authority to the coordinator to achieve optimal cooperation. In this sense the firm is a tool that saves marketing costs.' (Coase)

One may wonder whether a firm has to use the market to buy the materials and factors of production it needs and to sell its products or if it is better for it to integrate its commercial partner into its own bureaucratic network. The answer to the question depends on the degree of efficiency of the market. If it is a perfect market that guarantees perfect certainty, if the firm can buy whatever it wants, whenever it wants, at a predetermined price, and if it is sure that the price reflects substitution costs, it will tend to use the market. In the opposite situation, it will try to avoid it by appealing to horizontal or vertical integration and by finding another mechanism of coordination. One may believe that the firm weaves its web according to the marginalist principle: it develops until the marginal costs of the rational organisation of production overtake the marginal benefits of eliminating the market.

Labour provides us with an interesting example. It would be very expensive, if not impossible, to hire at each particular time and place the workers for a given task. It saves expense to sign a long-term contract by which the worker accepts within certain limits any task that he is asked to do, while the employer will, for his part, also within certain limits, pay a certain amount of money fixed in advance on the basis of the time worked.  Similarly, it would not be convenient, for example, for a firm operating a steel rolling mill to deal through the market with a firm using a blast furnace every time it needs molten metal.  More regularity to the process is required for coordination to be efficient.

More generally an economy is a large network of processes generated by dividing some products and combining others.  At the first step, raw materials are divided into small amounts shared between numerous customers throughout the economy.  At another step, a firm gathers elements, combines and mixes them in order to get a new product.  This distribution and combination process is expensive and difficult and marketing costs amount to a large share of added value.

In the theory of competition, markets have known prices at which anybody can buy and sell unlimited amounts without any delay.  In practice, it is not so easy:  it is expensive to find customers, fix a price, control quality, and organise transportation and delivery.  Not only is it necessary to spend a lot of time and energy on it, but there is also the serious problem of risk, stemming from the fact that people trading on a market do not know each other, each of them having good reasons for being secretive, bending the truth and even lying.  The firm, when dispensing with the market, reduces this antagonism, liberalises information and provides it with a structure where it can be traded more freely and exactly.

The larger the scope of the firm, the more it tends to avoid markets.  As transactions grow, it can provide them with a reliable framework;  it can buy large quantities and rigorously plan deliveries.  The relative advantage of the market decreases as the firm is growing and profit from control and order is increasing.  A striking example of the scale economies thus made possible is provided by loan operations.  In order to check that a debtor is solvent and that the management of the firm is correct, the creditor needs many pieces of information.  When a financial institution lends money to many small firms, each loan will be negotiated by a subordinate whose information and freedom of action will be limited.  The amount of the loan will tend to be proportional to the amount of information available;  small firms can usually borrow only very small amounts of money and only against secure collateral. A large firm, on the other hand, can provide more information and negotiate with the lender at a higher level of authority. The average cost of the operation is lower and the amount of money lent tends to be higher.

### The large firm has discovered how to discover.

When dealing with scale economies achieved by large firms, one should be aware of the existence of costs incurred by the management and coordination of many activities, in other words by the installation of a network linking the activities in which the firm is involved. In a large firm, a complicated system of communication is necessary to transmit and interpret information. Messages concerning the state of the various markets and processes must reach the management team which must gather data, synthesise the data and take a decision. The "brain" must then transmit the orders to the bottom level and make sure that the whole organisation behaves as it should.[5]

All of this is difficult because a communication network can transmit only a limited amount of information. Messages may be distorted. At any time, the central unit may have a limited capacity for handling information. There must be some lapse of time between the moment when information is received and the moment when the decision is taken. The more abundant the information transmitted to the central unit, the longer the delay. A distinction must be made between a decision requiring complete documentation and a quick decision. If a decision has to be taken quickly, only a small share of the total information available will be used; if more information is required, action will have to be slower. Of course, the "brain" can be enlarged but at the same time, administration costs are increased. The firm has to weigh the pros and cons and choose between expense, attention to detail and speed.

Seventy-five years ago, economists reduced the problem of firm size to the capacity of the entrepreneur - to the organisational abilities of an elite individual who was able to see, know, understand and control everything in his plant. Each firm was a special case: it grew, remained stagnant, and declined reflecting the human being that managed it. Scale economies become negative from quite a small size, for a single man could not control the complexity of information flow associated with a large and complicated system. Firms were small and the hypothesis of perfect competition was realistic. This situation is over now for meanwhile firms have provided themselves with structures that drastically increase their capacities for handling information and thus for organising actities and enlarging their scope. Furthermore, these structures enable them to live longer, far beyond an individual's lifetime.

It may be useful to make a close examination of the advantages of these structures to the firm, for one tends not to be aware of their importance. The institution having reached, under the name of "corporation", its highest degree of development in the US,[6] we shall stick to the American case. The modern type of American "corporation" has been created to take advantage of the possibilities offered by railways and by the flourishing national economy that derived from them in the late XIXth Century. Until then, most firms, small and large, had only one, or very few, local units with a limited scope. They were managed as plants. It was the creation of much larger organisms covering, thanks to the railways, several regions and industrial branches that gave birth to a new form of organisation. The main innovation was the installation at the top of an organisation that was specialised in managing the business and had full control of its large empire. During the 1920s, a new step was made with the appearance of firms with multiple divisions. They had a separate organisation in each branch of production and each division had its own financial, commercial, research and production services. The headquarters secures flexible links with each of the divisions; it makes the programmes, coordinates activities and measures performance. This structure is very flexible, since it makes it easy to add new divisions, and also there is a "brain" in the headquarters consisting of a large team specialised in examining strategic aspects of growth and development.

As a firm, the American "corporation" has so far shown no sign of triggering negative scale economies. The expansion of such a firm is limited in a given period of time. But as time goes by, "corporations" achieve a regular development by solving their organisational problems as they arise, without being dominated and overcome by problems of size. The large multinational firm is even able to enlarge its scope until coordinating at the world-level.

This new kind of commercial organisation was an incentive to the growth of the firm. By learning how to manage a large and complicated activity, the firm became growth-oriented and acquired the capacity to determine its own growth rate. When learning how to plan production, it also learnt how to plan growth.

For instance, in order to sell its output the "corporation" entered directly into contact with the consumer. By doing so, it could forecast the latter's needs and influence them, and learn to manage the growth of demand. As it wanted to have regular supplies, it integrated suppliers in order to control the source of raw materials. By doing so, it enhanced its ability to prospect for materials and became able to discover new sources of supply. When practising the coordination of numerous individuals, it became familiar with methods of interpersonal relations and acquired psychological expertise to cultivate the "human factor" in the firm. Equally, rationalisation of production and the scientifical application of technology made firms integrate research, thus becoming key actors in the development of new technology, instead of behaving only as users. The evolution of organisation which made it possible to absorb technology also gave birth to a conscious and organised technological creation.

Each step made was an adaptation to an old environment, but it led at the same time to the creation of a new environment. By reacting to external conditions, the firm was changing them at the same time. Along with its own evolution, the "corporation" has discovered how to discover.

Lastly, its very size provides the firm with the financial power that enables it to escape the difficulties of financial markets. It has earned itself the profits that ensure its future growth. Instead of distributing profits and borrowing them back through financial intermediaries, it short-circuits capital markets and saves financial costs. By learning how to plan, coordinate and calculate the performance of the divisions of the firm, the headquarters acquires the skill of a financial institution. To a certain extent, the headquarters plays the role of an investment firm managing a portfolio and looking for new uses of savings.

In its evolution, the commercial firm has also found the incentive for its continuing expansion. As the firm was growing, the "brain" played a more and more important role in organisation, given the necessity of efficient coordination. Not only do central services coordinate existing activities, but they also take decisions in the field of expansion. The more developed the organisation and the faster its growth, the larger must be the size of the management team. Thus fast growth provides leaders with better prospects of greater rank and remuneration. A large organisation needs a large headquarters to execute abstract intellectual tasks, but the brain also needs growth and expansion to enrich its substance. Thus, the organisation finds a new factor of propulsion in its new structure; it has to grow, enlarge and create more and more connections.

It has even been alleged that amongst the aims of the firm, growth may sometimes dominate profit maximisation. If a firm has to choose between a higher average rate of profit and a faster rate of growth, it may choose growth. Profit may be sacrificed more than stock holders wish. But it can fail to maximise profits only within certain limits. First, because growth needs profits, and second because there is a threat of takeover. If the leaders of a firm sacrifice too much profit, they jeopardise the financial basis of future growth and risk being fired. It is true that the direction of a firm is in a way protected by the knowledge it has of its own business; its behaviour in a complex situation can, indeed, only be partially known from outside. Thus managers have a certain margin of discretion, and the particular "personality" of the firm, as well as its past, influences its choices of products, places and methods of production. Whether conservative or progressive, broad or narrow, cosmopolitan or regional, the conceptions and tendencies that rule the leaders will determine the rate of growth of the firm and its orientation. Unlike a small firm, a large firm will be able to consider large indivisible projects, while a fast growing firm will refuse opportunities that an older one, with more limited prospects, will accept.

In his classical analysis of the large multinational unit,[7] Byé gives an example that can be quoted here to illustrate briefly the fact that firms do not look like each other. He studies the case of the firm that decides the period during which it will exploit a given natural resource. In the simplest case, which will suffice here, the firm owns a resource it intends to exploit during n years at the rate of $x=X/n$ units a year. Assuming it faces the same demand at each period, the price will depend on the quantity sold each year, i.e. $p = p(X) = p(n)$. The longer the plan, the lower the annual production and the higher the price and the total revenue. The firm has to choose between a higher total revenue spread over a long period and a lower total revenue earned in a few years.

Different firms will make different choices. The conservative firm, having few other possibilities, will tend to take its time. A more dynamic firm having many interesting opportunities, and needing cash, will tend to exploit its resource more intensively in order to get quick profits and to finance diversification. In fact, the large corporation has got itself released from the human limits imposed on the individual entrepreneur, but nevertheless it remains a living organism with its own personality, inertia and history. We are now going to apply the above analysis to the large multinational enterprise. We shall enquire whether, comparatively, multinational firms are a better institution than international markets for stimulating business, transmitting information and fixing prices.

**Firms react to monopoly and to the instability of international markets by direct investment in the production of raw materials.**

The expansion of a business is more difficult beyond national boundaries than inside one country. The firm has to enter a new environment where information is scarce and communication is difficult. It has to learn how to face new problems, for instance, fluctuations in exchange rates and political risks of uncertainty. We are now going to study the various advantages that make it profitable to overcome the inherent risks and costs of operating abroad.

Let us consider a firm using for the first time a raw material produced abroad. If it wanted, it could avoid the difficulties of managing a multinational enterprise by buying the raw materials it needs on the international market, as it buys other things. And yet, very often, firms prefer eliminating the market and integrating the foreign producer into their administrative structure. It happens so often that one tends to admit it too easily without worrying about the reasons and implications of such behaviour.

Like Coase, we assume that the frequency of vertical integration may often be explained by market imperfections. The reason for which firms choose the status of multinational enterprise are the same as those for which they become large-scale firms in one country. They prefer coordination and harmonisation achieved by the administration of a firm to market coordination, for this system saves costs. If markets were perfect and the firm could buy everything it needs at a fixed price determined by competition, then the incentive for direct investment would be very weak. But where markets are imperfect, prices vary, information is scarce and markets are oligopolistic, the system of the multinational enterprise and the suppression of vertical fragmentation becomes a means to reduce inefficiency and waste. In such a case, by having interests abroad and more independence, the firm reduces uncertainty and avoids the dangers of competition.

Let a processing firm face only one of the possible sellers of the raw material it needs. Each seller is large enough to control an important share of total production in the world and therefore has a power of control over prices. If the buyer is nothing more than a small firm, the only thing he can do it to submit to the monopolistic power of the seller. But if the processor is also a large firm and absorbs a great share of the production of raw material, he can take measures against the seller's power. The market structure of this industry is then a bilaterial oligopoly. A small number of processors face a small number of suppliers each of which is big enough to estimate its share of the market and recognise the agents' mutual interdependence.

In such a market, price and quantity will be negotiated and regulated. Firms cannot afford to let the others set prices autonomously. The choice of each party is limited to a small number of possibilities. The raw material seller faces only a few buyers and the buyer only a few suppliers. The price, and thus profits, depend not only on demand and supply, but also on trials of strength. In such a bilaterial oligopoly, tension may be partly overcome by avoiding the use of the market, thus eliminating losses stemming from negotiation.

If there is vertical integration - i.e. firms at each level are under common ownership, and operated as a single unit - conflicts of interest are partly avoided and the determination of price is no longer a problem. the vertically integrated multinational enterprise maximises the total profits of stages A and B together and need not worry about dividing them between the two stages. Vertical integration need not take any account of monopolistic and monopsonistic powers since a vertically integrated firm can dispense with the process of negotiation and avoid the problems that stem from it.

*Market uncertainty* is a second reason for *commercial firms* to integrate internationally. Anyone knows that international raw materials markets are not stable and sellers and buyers are vulnerable to price fluctuations. A firm which buys its raw materials on the market will see its profits fluctuate as scarcity and abundancy alternate on the market. This instability is at least reduced by direct investment. Indeed, there is a negative correlation between profits at one stage and profits at the subsequent stage, i.e. what is won at the first is lost at the second. This is why two firms operating at different stages can make their profits stable by combining them and so insuring themselves against uncertainty. When the price of a material rises, the integrated processor compensates for what he loses as a user by what he earns as a producer and *vice versa* when the price falls. The firm, in other words, has balanced its investments and reduced the risk of owning extremely specialised assets.

A third reason in favour of a multinational system is *financial market imperfections*. Once more, we assume that we are dealing with an industry dominated by large firms. Let us assume that processing firms decide to expand more rapidly in order to meet a growing demand for their goods. For this expansion to be successful, the raw material producer has to expand at the same rate in order to meet the increased demand for raw materials. But this producer may be short of capital and not be able to provide more. Instead of a growth of production along with demand, there will be a shortage, and prices will rise. The rise of prices will cut the profits of the processor and increase those of the supplier of raw materials. It will slow down the rate of growth of the processing industry and increase that of the raw material producer. An equilibrium will eventually occur but it may be at the expense of one side. A simple model may clarify the problem. We shall assume that each firm is financing its expansion only by re-investing its profits. At stage A, the raw material producer saves and invests $s_1$ of his profits whereas the processor saves and reinvests $s_2$ of his. The equations of growth at both stages are shown below. They are almost identical, except that the processors have one more term, which is the cost of raw materials.

$$(1) \quad Q_1^* = \frac{I_1}{K_1} = \frac{s_1}{v_1} \cdot \frac{\pi_1}{Q_1} = \frac{s_1}{v_1} \frac{(P_1 Q_1 - c_1 Q_1)}{Q_1} = \frac{s_1 (P_1 - c_1)}{v_1}$$

$$(2) \quad Q_2^* = \frac{I_2}{K_2} = \frac{s_2}{v_2} \cdot \frac{\pi_2}{Q_2} = \frac{s_2}{v_2} \frac{(P_2 Q_2 - P_1 Q_1 - c_2 Q_1)}{Q_1} = \frac{s_2 (P_2 - P_1 - c_2)}{v_2}$$

| | |
|---|---|
| $Q^*$ | = growth rate |
| $I$ | = investment |
| $K$ | = stock of capital |
| $s$ | = share of re-invested profits |
| $v$ | = capital coefficient |
| $Q$ | = production of the industry |
| $P$ | = price in the industry |
| $c$ | = unit cost of all factors of production other than raw material. |

Units are such that one unit of $Q_1$ is used to produce one unit of $Q_2$, 1 and 2 designating respectively the stages of raw material production and processing. Assuming that $P_2$, the price of the processed material, is given and constant, the formula provides two equations that determine the equilibrium growth rate. (We assume that there are no stocks and that both industries have the same growth rate.) In order to simplify the formula, we assume that capital coefficients are roughly the same in both industries and are equal to 1. The solution is shown in figure 1. We have also assumed that parameters are such that there exists an initial equilibrium for $*Q = *\overline{Q}$ and that profit rates are equal in both industries.

Let us assume now that the processing industry increases $s_2$. In figure 1, the consequence is a growth line II instead of I. Hence the growth rate increases as well as the price of the raw material, but less than it would have done had $P_1$ remained constant. The profit ratio rises at stage A and falls at stage B until a new equilibrium is reached.

Obviously, in such a case, firm A could improve its position if it could reduce the share invested in its own branch and use the funds thus saved to invest in the raw material industry. Vertical integration offers a means of using funds more efficiently.

Such a solution is thus an incentive to vertical integration and a multinational solution. If a single firm owned both stages, it would use efficiently the total profits thus earned, and would divide its financial resources between the two sectors in such a way that the marginal productivity of capital would be equalised between them. Hence firms have a reason to integrate backwards or forwards, namely to raise funds for the firm operating at another stage of production when they find that their partner cannot raise sufficient funds or is reluctant to re-invest his profits. Within the same set of ideas, the unequal access of firms to technology and management techniques is another reason for vertical integration.

If financial markets were perfect, the above situation would not occur. Unequal profit rates would never occur: funds would automatically move from stage 2 to stage 1. Our model is built upon the hypothesis of imperfect financial markets and the self-financing of firms, and it is this particular hypothesis that justifies the particular result.

A fourth reason for vertical integration is *lack of information*. In oligopolistic industries, processes of negotiation are rarely sincere for it is not in the interests of each party to inform the other exactly of everything he knows. The processor prefers that the producer does not know the actual state of demand and the producer prefers not to reveal the actual supply situation. The ability of both parties to plan for the short-term and the long-term suffers as a result. Vertical integration, by gathering separate units into a single multinational firm, makes the circulation of information easier. The processing industry can acquire a better understanding and control over the discovery and exploitation of new sources of supply. The producer of raw materials can plan on the basis of a better knowledge of the present state and future prospects for demand.

In a word, none of the reasons explained above would exist were the markets perfect. If there were many producers, the price would be equal to the marginal cost and any industrialist would regard it as a datum. All firms would have the same access to capital and there would be no need to fund a foreign producer through vertical integration. Even diversification by firms to insure themselves against price fluctuations would be useless. An individual investor would stabilise his portfolio by buying stocks of two or more distinct firms; to do so, he would not have to use the multinational system. It is only when markets are imperfect and firms are large enough to be aware of these imperfections that the administrative structure of MNEs is required in place of market links.

These conclusions are confirmed if we look at the problem from a different perspective, i.e. if we consider it from the point of view of an under-developed country which exports commodities and faces the same kind of problem stemming from the imperfection of the market for its commodities.

Let us consider the case of a country that sells cocoa or coffee, supplied by a large number of very small producers and sold to a highly concentrated processing industry. The oligopsonistic structure of the market (characterised by a small number of buyers) disadvantages producers. Producing countries could probably increase their income by forming a sales cartel to counterbalance the buyers' monopsony. Admitting such a solution is viable, it is not optimal for it implies losses inherent in multi-stage monopoly. In such a case firms cannot integrate backwards through direct investment because there are too many small sellers, but it would not be impossible for some countries to integrate forwards by taking control of certain firms in the customer country that manufactures and sells their materials. Not only would this avoid losses deriving from negotiation but it would also make it possible to plan more rationally. For instance, an industrialist who decides to develop his market includes in his costs the growth of production costs resulting from the increased demand. A great share of this growth constitutes a rent for the producer of the material and, from the point of view of the producer countries, it should be maximised and not reduced to a minimum. Forward integration may be a means of achieving this aim. Besides, unstable prices would cause less trouble. In the absence of integration, the main effect of fluctuations in price stemming from the short-term movements of the inelastic supply and demand curves is a switch of income from the producer to the consumer, which causes uncertainty for both without benefitting either of them. With vertical integration, instability and its financial consequences disappear since the producer and the consumer become a single person. In a word, since firms integrate backwards for these reasons, it may be worthwhile for countries to integrate forwards. In order to solve some of their problems as basic raw materials producers, it may be that LDCs should originate direct investments instead of being contented with being host countries.

**Direct investment in a foreign processing industry protects a firm against competition and helps it maximise the quasi-rents it earns owing to its technological advantages and product differentiation.**

Investment in processing activities abroad follows a well defined cycle most of the time. Firstly, the firm limits its horizon to the region or the country. At this stage, given the proximity of the places where goods are produced and sold, information circulates very fast and easily: producers learn very quickly of market response to their goods and technological innovation is quickly offered to the market.

As time goes by, the national firm develops processes and particular abilities to meet its environment. By doing so, it occasionally happens that it discovers at the same time a technique of production for a new good that can be used somewhere else in the same country or in the rest of the world. At first, the best way to exploit this advantage is to sell the good. Thus, the firm contacts exporters or itself creates a sales structure to prospect foreign markets and sell the goods.

The next step is when the firm realises that it can save transport costs by assembling or manufacturing abroad the good it had so far exported. Frequently, the decision is taken in order to protect the firm against the threat of entry of a foreign producer. Very often, foreign governments put tariffs on imports, which make it profitable to set up a subsidiary.

At this stage, the firm has an alternative: it can sell or rent its advantage to a foreign producer or allow its exploitation by licensing. It can thus escape the troubles and difficulties of multinational activity. The licensing option is pursued only infrequently by large firms. Indeed, using the market in order to sell technology raises many problems that partly explain why the multinational enterprise system is preferred when it comes to exploit on the world scale technological or other advantages.

First, one must be aware that the factors determining the choice are not only economic, but also legal. Multinational enterprises may be formed in order to elude legislation. Indeed,

> 'Exchange transactions on a market and the same transactions organised
> within a firm are often treated differently by Governments or other
> bodies with regulatory powers.' (Coase)

For a firm, taxation, for instance, may depend on its legal status. Under anti-trust laws, strategies such as price discrimination are forbidden when they result from an agreement with a foreign firm but they are not covered by the law if the agreement is made between two subsidiaries of the same MNE. Of course, in certain cases, discrimination may have the reverse effect and favour a direct relation: with regard to foreign currencies, a foreign government may adopt a more indulgent policy for taxes paid outside its national boundaries than for dividends. More examples could be cited.

What we are most interested in, however, are the economic motives for which a firm organises on a multinational basis. First, the advantage the firm owns may be so complex and ill-defined that it is extremely difficult, and sometimes impossible, to sell it. For instance, if the foreign firm needs occasional assistance in the field of management and technology in order to face various problems as they arise, it may prove to be impossible to specify in advance the nature of the help it expects from the American firm and the remuneration it will get for each intervention. On the contrary, it will probably be more efficient to make a long run cooperation agreement based on sharing, with decisions being taken on an administrative basis rather than negotiated each time. The strength of a multinational enterprise stems from the fact that it can trade knowledge internally more quickly than two firms which have to negotiate conditions each time.

Selling an advantage is a source of much more trouble. In order to fix the price charged for the advantage, it is necessary to predict the future use and estimate income. The calculation cannot be but imperfect and errors affect the buyer and the seller in the opposite direction. If the actual income is greater than the expected income, the buyer gains and the seller loses; if, on the contrary, the income does not reach what was expected, the seller will gain and the buyer will lose. In such a case, direct investment is a means of minimising the cost of uncertainty since it implies sharing profits and thus affords a measure of safety.

Besides, both firms may find it very difficult to agree on the evaluation of risk. Their estimates are likely to diverge because each of them has different experience, prospects and power. Each is to a certain extent "unique", with its own capital costs, horizons and risk preferences. A large capital-abundant American firm having a long experience of its own techniques and products will probably be much more optimistic when estimating the value of its advantage; to get this price, it will undoubtedly show much more aggression than a small foreign firm for which the idea is new. Similarly, a local firm, familiar with the market, may have a completely different and more optimistic view about the chances of success than the owner of a patent hesitating whether to launch out into foreign markets.

These problems are difficult to solve even under the most favourable conditions. They are particularly hard to solve in a context of negotiation, given that it is in the interests of each party to disguise information and cheat the other to make a better bargain. The multinational enterprise does not suppress completely these factors since they re-appear under the form of internal tension, but it makes the problem easier to solve.

The owner and seller of a new type of technique or good is interested not only in the present situation, but also in the future outcome. He will wish to insure against the possibility that the buyer uses the information provided to him under a licensing agreement to invent a better technique or product that would compete against the seller's. The seller can prevent this by acquiring ownership and direct control, which enables him at the same time to get indications about future developments. By forming a multinational enterprise the firm enters into direct and immediate communication with the foreign market and so receives a continuous flow of information about local conditions that it can use to develop new products and improve its overall position as seller, buyer and producer.

Lastly, it should be emphasised that in many industries, the concentration of production on a small number of firms is by itself an incentive to vertical integration and the elimination of the market. In such a situation, a firm cannot let the market fix the price; on the contrary, it has to negotiate with the other oligopolists. Direct ownership of a foreign firm is one strategy is can use in the process of negotiation.

To a certain extent, a firm which sells an advantage has a monopoly of this advantage. Direct investment may be necessary to maximise the quasi-rent that comes from it when the number of competing buyers is low. This problem may be illustrated by a simple diagram. In figure 2, VMP is the value of the marginal product of the patent (its marginal physical product multiplied by the price of the good for the production of which the patent is being used). If the buyers are numerous, VMP is also the demand curve for the patent. Competition between a large number of small producers will reduce their supernormal profits to zero and the prices of each factor of production, including the price of the patent, will become equal to the value of their marginal products. VMP being the demand curve (and, to simplify, assuming that the marginal cost of the patent is equal to zero), the owner of the patent will ask a price $\alpha$ for it, the user will produce a volume Q, his marginal revenue product will be equal to zero - i.e. equal to the marginal cost - and the quasi-rent obtained from exploitation of the patent will be a maximum.

If, on the contrary, there is only one or a few buyers for the patent in each country, this analysis is not applicable. The buyer or buyers will not fight with each other in order to reduce their profits to zero, but will adopt a different strategy. Assume for instance that there is one single buyer who behaves like Bertrand's naive monopsonist and tries to maximise his profits given the price fixed by the seller. In this case, he will equate the price of the patent to his *marginal revenue product* (marginal physical product multiplied by marginal revenue) and no longer to the value of the marginal product. For the owner of the advantage, the demand curve is thus no longer VMP but MRP. The optimal price of the patent remains $\alpha$, (it is an arbitrary result coming from the hypothesis of a linear demand curve), but production will now be established at $Q'$. The quasi-rent coming from the patent is reduced by $\alpha(Q - Q')$, whereas profits earned at the production stage rise from zero to $(\beta - \alpha)Q'$. The advantage of becoming the owner of a subsidiary is explained by the loss of total profits resulting from the change from Q to $Q'$. The rise in processing industry profits, under the hypothesis that it is monopolistic, is less than the loss suffered by the patent owner. If he can acquire ownership and direct control of the processing industry, he can re-establish the volume of production at Q and maximise profits. Of course, this is an extremely simplified description of the problem of selling a patent. But more complexity, even if it would reinforce the scope of the demonstration, will not change at all the essential fact that there is an advantage in suppressing bilateral oligopoly.

So far our discussion has underlined the roles of technology and product differentiation, but investment in foreign processing industry may occur even if the firm does not have any kind of advantage. Increased profit resulting from a more perfect collusion may be a sufficient reason for horizontal international integration through the

MNE. A firm belonging to an industry that is highly concentrated inside and outside national boundaries will be in a situation of oligopolistic competition with its national and foreign rivals. The number of firms being reduced, they are very likely to recognise their mutual interdependence and conclude an oligopolistic agreement. As a limiting case, one could imagine that through direct investment, a firm acquires ownership of all the firms that form a given industry and that, having absolute world power, it maximises global profits. The result would be perfect coordination and the largest possible profit. It is a fact, however, that international business integration is far from being complete: several large firms - some from the US and maybe one or two European - are both competing and concluding agreements throughout the world in the context of trade and international investment. The amount of foreign direct investment a firm must do thus depends not only on its competitive position but also on its own combativity and on the combativity of its rivals. An old case, cited by Dunning, that has lost none of the interest of the example shows how negotiation determines market shares:[8]

> '...At the turn of the century, the British tobacco industry was literally 'invaded' by American capital. Restricted in its sales by a high tariff wall imposed on US cigarettes, the American tobacco company acquired the young and prosperous firm of Ogdens Ltd in September 1901, and straight away launched an extensive publicity campaign to sell cheap cigarettes. The Chairman of the US company at the time made no secret of his intentions, viz: 'to obtain a large share of the tobacco trade both of England and the Continent', and he threatened to spend up to £6 million in doing just this. The reaction of the British producers was prompt for within a month of the purchase of Ogden's, thirteen of the leading tobacco companies had amalgamated and formed themselves into the Imperial Tobacco Company with an issued capital of £14$^1/_2$ million. Then followed several months of cut-throat competition between the two concerns.... Eventually a market sharing agreement

was reached in September 1902; Ogden's became part of the Imperial
Tobacco Group, which was given the monopoly of the British and Irish
markets, whilst the United States and its dependencies were to be
supplied by the American Tobacco Company. A new concern, the
British-American Tobacco Co. Ltd. was set up to handle the remainder
of the export business and was allocated factories both in the United
States and in the United Kingdom...'

The international activities of a firm are thus determined as much by trials of
strength as by objective factors such as costs and demand. A firm can agree with others
to divide the market into spheres of influence (for instance, the Americans limiting
themselves to Latin America, Europeans to Asia and Africa, all competing in Canada),
or it can establish tighter cooperative links and share with others the risks of certain
operations, or else it can brutally clash with other firms and create a subsidiary in each
market which has a sufficient size. The restless competitive period does not usually last
long; after a while it is more than likely that a certain stability will be achieved and that
the industry will adopt some formula for sharing the market. At the present time, the
main formulae used amongst large world-scale firms are being tested because of
reductions in trade barriers and the opening of new markets in LDCs. We are now
facing a new kind of struggle for the conquest of markets because each firm is trying to
ensure the basis for its future growth.

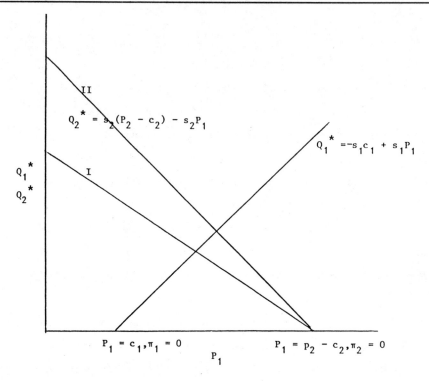

**Figure 1**

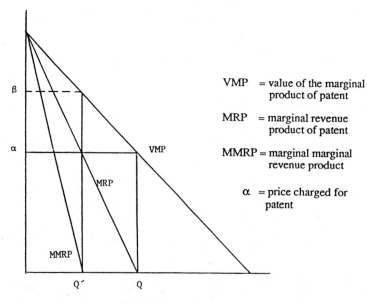

VMP   = value of the marginal product of patent

MRP   = marginal revenue product of patent

MMRP = marginal marginal revenue product

α     = price charged for patent

**Figure 2**

# Footnotes

1   Paul Baran and P. Sweezy, *Monopoly Capitalism*, New York, Monthly Review Press, 1966. John Kenneth Galbraith, *The Affluent Society*, Boston, Houghton Mifflin, 1958; and *The New Industrial State*, Boston, Houghton Mifflin, 1967. Harry Johnson, 'The Political Economy of Opulence', *The Canadian Quandary*, Toronto and New York, McGraw-Hill, 1962.

2   On these different perspectives, see *Foreign Ownership and the Structure of Canadian Industry*, Report of the Task Force on the Structure of Canadian Industry, Ottawa, Queens Printer, 1968. Richard D. Robinson, *International Business Policy*, New York, Holt Rinehart and Winston, 1964. Raymond Vernon 'Multinational Enterprise and National Sovereignty', *Harvard Business Review*, March-April 1967, pp. 156-172.

3   See, for example, Stephen Hymer, 'Direct Foreign Investment and the National Economic Interest'. Peter Russel (ed), *Nationalism in Canada*, Toronto, McGraw-Hill of Canada, 1966, Yale Economic Growth Center Paper No. 108. 'L'impact des firmes internationales', in *La politique industrielle de l'Europe intégré*, Paris. Presses universitaires de France, 1968. C.P. Kindleberger, 'Public Policy and the International Corporation', *International Antitrust*, U.S. Senate. Hearings before the Subcommittee on Antitrust and Monopoly of the Judiciary Committee, Washington, Government Printing Office, 1966.

4   R.A. Coase, 'The Nature of the Firm', reprinted in G.J. Stigler and K.E. Boulding, *Readings in Price Theory*, Homewood (Ill.), Richard D. Irwin Inc. 1952.

5   Leonid Hurwicz, Conditions for Economic Efficiency of Centralized and Decentralized Structures', in: Gregory Grossman (ed), *Value and Plan: Economic Calculation and Organisation in Eastern Europe*, Berkeley, University of California Press, 1960; and 'Optimality and Informational Efficiency in Resource Allocation Processes' in: Kenneth J. Arrow et al., *Stanford Symposium Mathematical Methods in the Social Sciences*, Stanford, Stanford University Press, 1960. N. Chamberlain, *The Firm: Micro Economic Planning and Actions*, New York, 1962.

6   For a brilliant analysis of the evolution of American enterprise, consult: Alfred D. Chandler, *Strategy and Structure*, New York, Doubleday and Co., Inc., 1966.

7   Maurice Byé 'Self-Financed Multiterritorial Units and their Time Horizon' *International Economic Papers*, No.8, New York, Macmillan, 1958.

8   J.H. Dunning, *American Investment in British Manufacturing Industry*, George Allen and Unwin, 1958.

# [2]

## The Theory of the
## International Firm

JOHN McMANUS
Carleton University

Foreign Direct Investment is a rather inappropriate name for the process by which productive activities in different countries come under the control of a single firm. The essence of this phenomenon is not foreign investment, which is an international transfer of capital, but the international extension of managerial control over certain activities. This paper is focused on the international firm as a means of co-ordinating activities in more than one country, and the analysis will ignore the transfer of capital that may or may not be associated with the establishment and operation of an international firm.

Our analysis is intended to explain why foreign direct investment occurs and why it is observed in some activities or industries and not in others. The theory of foreign direct investment that we will develop is based on the existence of economic interdependence among certain activities conducted in various countries. When the value of certain assets in one country is dependent on the actions of foreigners, there will be gains to be made by a co-ordination of the actions of the interdependent parties through which each of them will take into account the international effects of his actions. The more completely each decision-maker within an interdependent group takes

John C. McManus

into account all of the effects of his actions on others in the
group, the higher will be the combined wealth of all of the
members, so long as the costs of co-ordination are less than the
gains from a more efficient allocation of resources. The international firm is one way in which the activities of interdependent
parties in various countries can be co-ordinated; the price
mechanism, perhaps supplemented by contractual arrangements, is another. The theory of foreign direct investment involves the determinants of choice among the alternative means
by which interdependent parties in various countries can act
jointly so as to maximize their total wealth.

Although the analysis we shall present is limited in several
respects — it is static; we assume away international transfers of
capital via the international firm; and we make the usual assumption that the firm's sole objective is to maximize its net pecuniary income — the implications of the theory appear to be
consistent with some of the empirical characteristics of international firms. Another limitation of this analysis of the international firm is that it examines only the conditions under which
the control of productive activities in different countries will be
centralized and has nothing to say about the choice of country
from which an international firm will exercise control. Therefore, there is no direct relationship between the establishment
of an international firm and the flow of foreign direct investment from one country to another. However, our empirical results are based on Canadian data, and for Canada we shall assume, contrary as to the facts but reasonable as an approximation to reality, that all international firms locate their head office
outside Canada. Whenever the control of a Canadian and foreign activity is centralized, we assume that the effect is to raise
foreign direct investment to Canada.

As this discussion of the international firm proceeds, the
reader will find that the term "international" plays no substan-
tive role in the analysis but simply confines the topic to the subject at hand. We could equally well be discussing the interstate
firm, the intercounty firm, or any organization that centralizes
control of productive activities in separate locations. However,
by confining the topic to international firms, we avoid having to
develop a general analysis of the firm itself, and we are able to
take the organization of production within countries as given.
Although our "countries" differ primarily in location, we will
examine some effects of national policies, particularly tariffs
other national differences, such as tastes, legal systems, and tax

policies, can be incorporated within the theory without invalidating its general conclusions.

## 1. SOME EMPIRICAL CHARACTERISTICS OF INTERNATIONAL FIRMS

There are three general observations regarding foreign direct investment in Canada that form a starting point for this analysis of the international firm: there is a substantial variation among industries in the extent to which Canadian production is controlled by foreign subsidiaries; in those industries in which foreign subsidiaries operate, they consistently appear to be the leading producers in terms of their productivity and size; the international firms in Canada have been generally reluctant to issue share capital in their Canadian subsidiaries. As far as we know, there is no theory of the international firm that yields implications consistent with these empirical characteristics of foreign direct investment in Canada.

Many writers have remarked on the great difference in the extent of direct investment in various industries.[1] For a fairly representative sample of sixty-five manufacturing industries in Canada, for which the average percentage of total sales in 1963 made by foreign subsidiaries is 45.8, the standard deviation is 31.3 per cent.[2] The range of the sample includes five industries in which no foreign ownership occurs and two in which no domestically-controlled firms operate. There are four industries of the sixty-five in which foreign subsidiaries accounted for less than 10 per cent of total Canadian sales, and six in which they accounted for more than 90 per cent. These industries are listed in Table 1. The Canadian experience seems to be typical in this respect. It appears that one of the features of the multinational firm is that it is a characteristic way to organize some internationally-joint activities but not others.

There have been various attempts to explain the inter-industry variations of foreign direct investment in Canada. The most widely accepted of these is the view that the establishment of foreign subsidiaries, or branch plants, is a response to tariff barriers, which stimulate the domestic production of commodities that would otherwise be imported.[3] It is argued that foreign firms establish subsidiaries in Canada to supply markets to which they had previously exported. However, the empirical evidence does not confirm the hypothesis that there is a positive relationship between an industry's level of tariff protection and

*John C. McManus* 69

TABLE 1

Industries by Proportion of Total Sales
Made by Foreign Controlled Firms

| Zero | Less than 10% | More than 90% | 100% |
|---|---|---|---|
| 1. Breweries | 1. Distilleries | 1. Rubber Products | 1. Batteries |
| 2. Wineries | 2. Women's Clothing | 2. Commercial Refrigeration and Air-Conditioning Equipment, Office and Store Machinery | 2. Refractories |
| 3. Fur Goods | 3. Sash and Door Planing Mills | 3. Motor Vehicles Parts and Accessories | |
| 4. Coffins Caskets | 4. Publishing, Printing | 4. Electrical Industrial Equipment | |
| | | 5. Petroleum Refineries | |
| | | 6. Plastics, Synthetic Resins, Explosives and Ammunition | |

the proportion of its output under the control of foreign subsidiaries. Many primary manufacturing industries are dominated by international firms although they export a significant proportion of their output. And in secondary manufacturing, there are many industries in which relatively few foreign subsidiaries operate, because their markets are protected by tariffs or transportation costs.[4] For our 1963 sample of sixty-five Canadian industries, the correlation coefficient between the proportion of Canadian production that is foreign-controlled and the level of effective protection[5] is not significantly different from zero at the 80 per cent level of confidence. There is no clear evidence that a relationship exists between the tariff and the incidence of foreign direct investment. We know that an increase in an industry's tariff will stimulate domestic production, but there is no

basis from which to predict whether the increase in production
will be controlled by foreign subsidiaries or by domestic firms.
Similar problems arise with the attempt to associate foreign direct investment with product differentiation,[6] which hypothesis
does not encompass foreign control of primary manufacturing.
For the purpose of a general analysis of the international firm, it
should not be necessary to distinguish between primary and
secondary manufacturing.

The variation in the interindustry incidence of foreign control has also been a problem for those who assert that the existence of foreign subsidiaries is evidence of their technical or administrative superiority over domestic firms. Although it is appealing to find that the best man wins, no evidence has been
presented to show that the extent of foreign control is
significantly correlated with the technological complexity of industrial processes or with the proportion of the total costs of an
industry that are costs of administration. If international firms
arise because of their superiority over domestic firms in certain
identifiable respects, we should expect to find them in industries in which their superiority could be put to the best advantage. However, instead of finding international firms extending
their control internationally to exploit their administrative ability or their technical skills, we find them entering industries
abroad that are the same as, or complementary to, their activities at home. The empirical evidence clearly indicates that the
international extension of a firm's control is specific to the sector in which its production is concentrated or to closely related
sectors.[7] It is unlikely that this specificity in the set of activities
pursued by the international firm would be observed if the firm
were exploiting its superiority in the acquisition or use of general factors of production such as administrative or technological skills. We think a more powerful theory of direct investment
can be found by viewing the international firm as an institutional response to economic interdependence rather than as a
means of transferring factors of production from one country to
another. However, these two interpretations are not mutually
exclusive; both purposes may be served by the international
firm.

The assertion that the international firm exists because of
its technical or administrative superiority finds apparent empirical support from studies that have compared foreign subsidiaries with their domestic competitors in the same industry. All
of these studies have found that foreign subsidiaries are typi-

cally the dominant firms in their industries in the host country. They are consistently larger and more productive, and they pay higher wage rates than domestic firms producing in the same industry.[8] However, there is a problem in interpreting these comparisons because, without a theory of the international firm, the relationship between the ownership of a firm and its costs of production or its size remains unspecified. It is not enough to state, as is often done, that

> . . . the fact is that connections with a parent or affiliated company abroad often involve advantages which either cannot be duplicated by a purely Canadian enterprise, or can be duplicated only at a greater cost to the firm and the public at large. . . . Availability of capital is extremely important, but so too are technology, research, product development, technical and managerial personnel, training facilities, market and supply controls and accumulated experience. . . .[9]

These advantages could, at least in principle, be exchanged between autonomous firms in different countries. Patent rights may be sold to foreign firms, consulting firms will supply experienced research and managerial resources for a price, commercial houses and other middlemen can provide market and supply contacts, and so on. That a foreign firm has advantages over Canadian firms will not necessarily lead it to establish a Canadian subsidiary; it can capture the income to be earned either by directly controlling the exploitation of its advantages in Canada or by selling the right to exploit its advantages to Canadian firms.

In addition, these comparisons of foreign subsidiaries and domestic firms are not conclusive evidence that the subsidiaries are more productive than they would be if their resources were controlled by autonomous domestic firms. In most industries, there is a variation in the size and performance of firms that produce similar outputs. It is possible that international firms have a stronger incentive to gain control over the leading resources in an industry than domestic firms have, so that the differences we observe between their performance and that of their domestic competitors may in some part be due to variations within the industry that would exist regardless of the presence of international firms.

Finally, it is often found that international firms are unwilling to sell shares in their foreign subsidiaries even when there is some pressure from governments or public opinion to do so. Economists have tended to regard this preference for complete ownership as inexplicable[10] or, at best, as an attempt to avoid a relatively insignificant increase in administrative costs. Therefore, they have been willing to advocate that foreign subsidiaries be induced by policy measures to issue share capital in the host country so that domestic wealth holders can enjoy at least minority participation.[11] However, strong resistance is not usually put forth for trivial reasons. The reluctance of international firms to permit minority participation in their subsidiaries provides an important clue to the development of a theory of foreign direct investment. Given the postulate of wealth maximization, the immediate reason for not issuing shares in subsidiaries must be that the total value of the international firm would be reduced. If that were the case, a share of the ownership of a foreign subsidiary would be worth more to the parent firm than its value to an autonomous shareholder. Similarly, the control of the resources of the subsidiary must be worth more to the international firm than its value to an autonomous domestic firm. A theory of the international firm can be developed by pursuing this line of reasoning to identify the conditions under which productive activities in different countries will earn a higher total income if their control is internationally centralized. The analysis that results will explain, at least in part, the interindustry incidence of international firms, the dominant position of subsidiaries within the relevant industries of the host country, and the reluctance of the parent firm to issue shares in its subsidiaries.

## 2. THE THEORY OF THE INTERNATIONAL FIRM

If the international firm is able to pay a higher price than an autonomous domestic firm for the control of certain domestic resources, it is necessary that the value of the domestic resources be dependent upon the actions of the other foreign producers under the control of the international firm. Interdependence among a set of producers in different countries is a necessary condition for the existence of a single firm co-ordinating their actions. The international firm, like any firm, is an organization within which the resources combined in production are allocated by fiat rather than by the decentralized decision-making (subject to market constraints) of the various resource owners involved in production.[12] If the actions of a set of producers in

John C. McManus  73

different countries were completely independent, there would be no gains to be made by centralizing the control of their operations within an international firm. But if a set of autonomous producers in different countries were interdependent, there would be circumstances in which reallocation of their resources would yield a higher total wealth for the group as a whole. Under certain circumstances, such a reallocation might be effected through the establishment of an international firm. If so, the sum of the values of the subsidiaries of the international firm would be higher than it would be if they were operated autonomously.

The wealth-maximizing conditions for the set of interdependent producers can be expressed in terms of the familiar marginal equivalencies. The ratios of marginal physical products of factors of production must be equal for all members of the set using the same factors; rates of transformation among the goods produced by members of the set must be equal for all members producing the same goods; and the ratio of the marginal products of factors of production, some of which may be outputs of other members of the set, must equal the relative opportunity cost of those outputs in terms of the foregone earnings from the production of other goods. If these conditions are satisfied, the set of producers, which must remain arbitrarily circumscribed for the moment, will be producing the maximum output from any given flow of factor services.

In the traditional model of perfect competition, the reaction of the members of the set of producers to market prices automatically leads them to satisfy the marginal conditions for efficient production. The process is automatic in the model because the price mechanism is assumed to operate without cost; therefore, for all of the dimensions of interdependence among the members of the set there will exist price constraints on the behaviour of individual producers. In this model, each producer will automatically take into account all of the marginal gains and losses that his actions impose on other members of the set. Since efficient production is obtained as a result of the free operation of the price mechanism, no other form of co-ordination can lead to a higher wealth for the set of producers being considered.

It may be worth noting at this point that relaxing the assumption of perfect competition would create an incentive for a set of producers to centralize the co-ordination of their actions in some manner. The neo-classical model of perfect competi-

tion assumes that exclusive and freely transferable rights exist
for all resources but that no group of producers is able, for technological or other reasons, to acquire the exclusive right to
trade in any market. The set of producers selling in a competitive market impose "pecuniary" damages on each other by not
taking into account the effects of their decisions regarding their
rate of output on other members of the set; therefore, their autonomous decision-making is inconsistent with maximizing
their joint wealth. If a way can be found to exclude potential entrants from selling in the market, all of the members of the set
can gain by devising some means through which each of them
will take into account the pecuniary effects his actions have on
the others; their gains will be maximized if each member sets
his rate of output so that the net incremental gain he experiences from a small increase in his sales equals the sum of the
net losses the increase imposes on the other members of the
set. The firm is one means by which such a co-ordination of the
actions of interdependent sellers can be obtained.

It is also of interest to the following analysis of the international firm to describe the outcome of the neo-classical
model in terms of the transferability of property rights. To say
that the actions of a set of interdependent producers will be
efficiently co-ordinated by the price mechanism implies that the
resources of these producers will be allocated in the same way
that they would be if all of the resources involved were owned
by a single individual. If the price mechanism is assumed to operate without cost, the rights to use resources must be freely
alienable; therefore, any set of owners combining their resources in production would act in the same way as would a
single owner. All of the effects of an action would be automatically taken into account by the decision-makers involved. In
what follows, it will be important to distinguish between the
firm's co-ordination of the actions of a set of resource owners
and an individual's control over the allocation of those resources for which he owns the right to make decisions.

In order to introduce into the analysis an institution
called the firm, whose function is to co-ordinate the actions of
resource owners, we must bring in the costs of using the price
mechanism, or the costs of transacting. There are several factors
that should be considered here, but it would take us too far
afield to enter into an extensive discussion of transacting costs.
So let us concentrate on one aspect only. We shall treat the
costs of transacting as being equal to the costs that would have

to be incurred by each party to an exchange, in order to measure, in a dimension mutually acceptable to buyers and sellers,
the flows of services or the stock of assets that he is exchanging
with the other party. It is significant that the neo-classical theory
of resource allocation is almost always illustrated in terms of
goods that are easily measurable, and for which each trader can,
at little cost, determine what he is receiving and giving up —
bushels of wheat, number of apples, bales of wool, yards of
cloth, and so on. The illustrations of exceptions to the incidence
of the price mechanism always seem to be less susceptible to
quantification — the smoking factory, pollination of apple blos-
soms, pollution of rivers, congestion of highways, quality of
goods, and so on.

The cost of quantifying the flows of services or assets
being exchanged may be used as a proxy for the costs of transferring a property right from one owner to another. If the cost of
measurement is a rising function of the precision of the measurement, it will not pay traders to determine exactly what the
terms of trade are, and some range of indeterminacy will remain. Traders will incur measurement costs to attain a level of
precision at which the incremental cost of refining the measurement equals the incremental gains from trade that they would
experience by bringing their rates of substitution closer to equality. In general, measurement costs will constrain traders from
satisfying the marginal conditions for neo-classical efficiency
because, within the range of indeterminacy, neither trader will
be willing to pay the cost of enforcing his exclusive right to the
use of the asset or service being exchanged. If a trader cannot
economically measure, to the mutual satisfaction of the parties
to exchange, some range of variation in the flow of a service, he
cannot economically acquire the exclusive right to the use of
the service within that range and will be unwilling to engage in
trade that is not clearly to his advantage. There will be some
forms of exchange that will be almost entirely precluded by
measurement costs, as the many examples of "externalities"
suggest.

The costs of transacting are the costs that are incurred
by the parties to a market exchange to enforce their exclusive
rights to the assets or services being traded. The resources engaged in enforcement or measurement efforts are producing a
more efficient allocation of resources; but because the attain-
ment of efficiency is a costly process, the marginal conditions
for efficient resource allocation will not generally be satisfied. In

the following discussion, we shall reserve the term "efficiency" to describe a wealth-maximizing allocation of resources in the traditional sense, with zero transacting costs. A wealth-maximizing allocation of resources subject to the constraint of transactions costs will be described as economical.

Because of transacting costs, the market is an expensive way to effect some forms of exchange or to constrain some forms of interdependence. Therefore, potential traders, or interdependent resource owners, will seek means to reduce the costs involved in allocating services through market exchange, or in co-ordinating behaviour through the price mechanism. The appositive statements emphasize that to allocate resources means to co-ordinate the behaviour of resource owners and vice versa. For some kinds of interdependence in which transacting costs are relatively high, alternatives to the price mechanism will be sought to reduce transacting costs and increase allocative efficiency. One such alternative is the voluntary contract, an enforceable promise by one party to another as to what he will or will not do through the life of the agreement. The contract has the advantage of reducing the costs of measuring the variations in the effects that one party's actions have upon another, by establishing a rule that defines those actions that would breach the promise and call for compensation to be paid to the damaged party. For some kinds of exchange, the contract is an economical, if inefficient, means by which to co-ordinate the actions of interdependent resource owners.[13]

Under the price mechanism, traders react to the set of relative prices that they observe and attempt to maximize their wealth subject to those constraints. If transacting costs were zero and if markets were perfectly competitive, there would be no opportunities for any trader to gain at the expense of another. However, transacting costs reduce the effectiveness of price constraints on behaviour by creating opportunities for one trader to gain at the expense of others. Exploitation of these opportunities will not be completely prevented by price constraints because of the costs of establishing a mutually satisfactory standard of measurement that could detect, with perfect precision, changes in the flow of services from one trader to another. In a zero transacting-costs world, these changes would automatically be reciprocated by a compensating change in payment by the trader affected. But in a world in which transacting costs impair the ability of traders to constrain their dependence on others, the costs of detecting changes in the flow of services can be so high that the traders will agree to a rule, stipulated in the form of a contract, to facilitate an exchange of services and to limit the opportunities that exist for each of them to gain at the expense of the other. The contract substitutes a discrete, reciprocal adjustment in the terms of trade with respect to certain actions of the traders in place of the continuous adjustments that would be possible if the traders' actions were constrained only by prices.

The costs of effecting exchange through contract are the costs of enforcing the terms of the agreement and the costs of adjusting the terms to unanticipated changes in circumstances. Contractual terms can only be renegotiated, within the life of the contract, to the mutual advantage of both parties. Therefore, the costs of changing the allocation of resources are higher under a contractual arrangement than they would be under the price mechanism. Prices can be changed instantaneously and can be changed to the net disadvantage of some traders. Competition will lead to price changes if the total gain from the change is greater than the total loss; changes in contractual rules can only occur upon termination of the agreement or if the potential losers are fully compensated. Unlike a market price, contracts cannot be made "subject to change without notice."

For some forms of interdependence, the choice between the price mechanism and contracts will not be meaningful because the costs of transacting will make both prohibitively expensive. There are many kinds of potential exchange for which traders could not practically adopt a mutually satisfactory standard whose terms would make contractual promises economically enforceable. As the criteria for determining what actions would fulfil the terms of the agreement become more vague, contractual arrangements becme a less efficient means of co-ordinating the actions of interdependent parties. Some of the allocative problems that we call "externalities" — the smoking factory, the pollution of rivers, the congestion of highways — are not resolved by voluntary contractual arrangements because the costs of enforcing the promises would be too high.

The problem of co-ordination facing a set of interdependent producers in different countries is the same as that facing any group of interdependent individuals; and, if we ignore national differences in law and policy, the alternative means of resolving the problem are also the same. Transactions costs will constrain the degree to which a set of interdependent producers in different countries can attain a maximum joint wealth. Some dimensions of interdependence, those in which transacting costs are relatively low, will be constrained by the price mechanism. For others, the members of the set may chose to constrain their actions by contractual arrangements. Some combination of these two means of constraining the actions of individual producers is the alternative to the establishment of an international firm. The choice facing the set of producers is whether to co-ordinate their actions by relying on decentralized decision-making subject to non-discretionary constraints established through a system of prices and contracts or to co-ordinate their actions by establishing a single authority whose function is to direct the actions of the members by fiat. The members of the set will choose the form of co-ordination that maximizes their joint wealth, subject to the constraint of transactions costs.

It is perhaps worthwhile to repeat here that the firm does not acquire the ownership of the resources that it allocates in production. The transacting costs that prevent an economic exchange of the resources to be combined in production will prevent the firm from transferring the ownership of those resources to itself. If the resources could be economically transferred through the market, the firm would simply act as a broker, facilitating exchange between resource owners but not playing any direct role in co-ordinating their behaviour. However, the firm does not supplement the price mechanism as does a broker; it supplants the price system with direct control over the actions of resource owners.

How does the firm exercise control over the actions of resource owners without acquiring their rights to the use of resources? The owners of resources combined in production under the control of a firm will continue to act in their own self-interest, and will attempt to maximize the value of their individual resources subject to the relevant constraints. There is no reason to suppose that the resource owners acting within a firm are less self-seeking or more co-operative than they would be in any other institutional environment. Given that individual wealth maximization remains as a postulate of analysis, we cannot assert that the firm simply tells resource owners what to do.

Consider again a set of interdependent producers. The members of the set have the choice of co-ordinating their actions by a system of prices and contracts or of co-ordinating them by fiat within a firm. The latter will be chosen if the producers can attain a higher total wealth under centralized control. Given transacting costs, there will exist, within both methods of co-ordination, dimensions of interdependence that will not be constrained efficiently, so that some actions will be taken by individual producers without their taking into account, at the margin, all of the effects that their actions have on the value of the resources of other members of the set. If the choice between the two methods of co-ordination is not a matter of indifference, one of them must yield a more efficient allocation of the resources of the members of the set than the other. Therefore, the actions of the producers will not be the same within the international firm as they would be if the producers acted autonomously. How does the firm induce such changes in behaviour, given that each producer will continue to pursue his own self-interest?

The only way in which the firm can obtain changes in the actions of the set of producers is by changing the constraints facing individual members. For this reason, the firm is said to supersede the price mechanism. If the firm were to retain all of the price and contractual constraints that would exist if the members of the set were to act autonomously, it would be powerless to effect changes in behaviour — the self-interest of the producers would lead them to act in the same way whether they were subsidiaries or not. By reducing or eliminating price and contractual constraints on the relationships among the set of interdependent producers, the establishment of the firm makes the value of the resources of each producer apparently independent of particular relationships with the other members of the set.

The set of producers who choose to combine their resources within a firm will mutually agree to an elimination or reduction of non-discretionary pecuniary constraints as a determinant of their individual decisions so that management control of their actions can be exercised.

The gain from allocating resources by fiat is the increased efficiency that can be obtained through centralized co-ordination of those dimensions of interdependence that cannot be economically constrained by prices and contracts. In other words, the firm is able to reduce the waste that would result from "external effects" among the producers involved if they were to act autonomously. On the other hand, the cost of gaining the power to co-ordinate the actions of the producers is the inefficiency that results from the loss of pecuniary constraints on behaviour. For some activities, the costs of transacting among the set of producers will be so high that the gains in efficiency from an adoption of centralized control will be greater than the losses due to an elimination of a system of prices and contracts. For these activities, the firm will be chosen to co-ordinate production. The establishment of a firm can always "internalize" an "external" effect or reduce a particular marginal inequality but only at the cost of reducing non-discretionary constraints on behaviour and replacing them with management control.

At the present time, we are unable to pursue the analysis further without deriving the equilibrium allocation of resources within the firm. We have shown that the firm will not obtain an efficient allocation of resources because of the constraint of transacting costs, and we have argued that co-ordination of their behaviour by fiat will only be agreed upon by a set of interdependent producers if some of the price and contractual constraints that would otherwise govern their behaviour are removed. To rigorously specify the determinants of the choice between a system of prices and contracts and centralized control by fiat would require that we be able to compare, for a given set of producers, the equilibrium allocation of resources under the two methods of co-ordination. However, we have not been able to specify the minimum level of inefficiency, subject to the costs of management, that will maximize the value of resources when they are allocated by fiat within a firm. Therefore, a general theory of the firm as an institutional alternative to the price mechanism must be relegated to the category of work to be done in the future.[11]

Despite the absence of a fully specified theory of institutional choice, we can say something about the kind of activities, or industries,in which a set of interdependent producers will choose to act as subsidiaries within an international firm. The higher are the gains from the establishment of an international firm, the less efficient is resource allocation subject to price and contractual constraints on the actions of producers. Consider a group of different industries in which domestic producers are dependent on the actions of foreign producers. What characteristics of the industry affect the efficiency with which autonomous domestic producers can economically co-ordinate their actions with the decisions of foreigners through prices and contracts? First, the higher is the cost of measuring the effect a foreign action has upon the value of the resources under the control of domestic producers, the more inefficient will be the international allocation of resources. Second, the stronger is the dependence of the value of domestic resources upon the actions of foreigners, given that the costs of transacting are prohibitively high, the more inefficient will be the international allocation of resources. The higher is the difference in producers' marginal rates of substitution with respect to the unconstrained dimension of interdependence, or the higher are the potential gains from exchange, the less will be the joint wealth of the producers acting autonomously, if no price or contractral constraint exists in a dimension in which domestic and foreign producers are interdependent. The less efficiently the actions of a set of producers can be co-ordinated by a system of prices and contracts, the stronger will be the incentive for the producers to centralize the control of their actions within an international firm.

Let us try to illustrate the determinants of the choice among the alternative methods of co-ordination by drawing some examples from Canadian industries that are dependent upon the decisions of producers in the United States. We will consider three Canadian activities — textile producers, Holiday Inns, and automobile plants — each of which constrains its dependence on decisions made in the United States in a different manner. Textile producers co-ordinate their actions with foreign cotton suppliers principally through the price system; Holiday Inns employ contractual arrangements to organize their international activities; automobile production in this country is co-ordinated with the actions of foreign producers through international firms.

The Canadian textile producer's relationship with the cotton grower in the United States South is co-ordinated through the international market for cotton. For interdependence of this kind, which is experienced through commodity flows, the market serves a co-ordinating function through which cotton growers are induced to take into account, at the margin, the gains or losses that textile producers experience as a result of growers' decisions regarding their rate of production. Of course, the operation of the price mechanism creates a "pecuniary" interdependence among the traders,[15] but if potential competitors cannot be excluded from the market, the pecuniary effects that one firm may suffer as a result of the actions of others cannot be avoided.

The Canadian Holiday Inn chain is an example of an activity in Canada that relies primarily on contracts, rather than mar-

kets, to constrain its dependence on the actions of its counterparts in the United States. Commonwealth Holiday Inns of Canada Limited is a Canadian-controlled firm that arranges for the
use of its trademark and certain other services through a franchise agreement with Holiday Inns of America, Incorporated, a
United States firm. Under the terms of the agreement, the Canadian franchise holder must operate his hotel in accordance with
uniform operational service and maintenance standards, and his
building must conform to minimum standards of construction.
To enforce these terms of the contract, Holiday Inns of America
has a staff of fifteen inspectors. Each Inn is inspected at least
four times a year without prior notice being given.[16]

These contractual stipulations and associated enforcement
efforts are mutually agreed to by the parties to the contract as
a means of constraining their mutual interdependence. The
goodwill capital of the Holiday Inn system is maintained by advertising a certain quality of accommodation and by fulfilling
the expectations of consumers at the various locations of Inns.
Individual Inns in the system are interdependent through the effect that each one can have on the demand for the services of
other Inns. The quality of any one Inn's service will affect the expectations of consumers regarding the quality of service at
other locations. In the absence of an enforced contract, an individual franchise holder within the system could vary the quality
of his service without bearing all of the losses or gains that
would result. The contractual agreement reduces the inconsistency between individual and group maximization of wealth that
would otherwise exist. One conceivable alternative to these
contractual stipulations would be to establish a market in the
quality of Inns in the system. In principle, a price could be set at
which the marginal gain (loss) to any individual Inn from a variation of its service quality equalled the sum of the marginal losses (gains) to the other Inns in the System. In practice, however,
the combination of a public good problem, which offers opportunities for "free riding," with the costs measuring variations in
quality and their effects makes the price mechanism a
prohibitively expensive means of constraining the interdependence among Holiday Inns.

Both the price mechanism and contractual arrangements
serve the same purpose — to maximize the joint wealth of interdependent parties by having each take into account, insofar
as it is economical to do so, the marginal effects of his actions
on others. Through the operation of the price mechanism, cot-

ton growers and textile producers in the United States and
Canada will adjust their levels of output so that the marginal
cost of cotton is equal to its marginal product in textile plants.
Through their market relationship, firms in these two industries
jointly maximize their total wealth, subject to the competitive
conditions that exist in those activities. Holiday Inns in Canada
and the United States are similarly dependent on one another,
but they rely more on contractual agreements as a means of
maximizing their total wealth. A "standard" is established, and
enforcement of the "standard" is a means of attaining a higher
joint wealth than would otherwise be possible, given that the
price mechanism cannot economically constrain all of the dimensions of interdependence among various Holiday Inns.

As we have argued, the international firm is an alternative
means of attempting to maximize the joint wealth of interdependent parties in different countries. To continue with the
previous example, we could imagine that if Holiday Inns of
America found that their contractual relationship with the Canadian Holiday Inns was inconsistent with the highest potential
wealth for the system as a whole, they would purchase the control of the Canadian Inns and centralize the management of operations in Canada and the United States. The firm, through the
allocation of resources by fiat, is one way in which interdependent parties may attempt to maximize their joint wealth.

General Motors of Canada, Ltd., for example, a wholly-
owned subsidiary of its parent in the United States, is dependent on the decisions of General Motors in Detroit in many respects. Advertising by the parent firm in national media in the
United States spills over into Canada and affects the demand for
the Canadian product. Similarly, changes in design and in engineering specifications will have an effect on the costs and/or
revenues of the Canadian subsidiary. However, in principle,
there is no reason why these international effects could not be
traded at arm's length or made the subject of a contractual arrangement between autonomous firms, as we have seen to be
the case with the Holiday Inns. But, in practice, contracts are
relatively difficult to enforce for some forms of interdependence. Consider the problem that General Motors of
Canada, as an autonomous firm, would have in attempting to
draft a 'mutually satisfactory contract with its counterpart in the
United States for advertising expenditures to be made by the
American firm. The Canadian firm would wish to stipulate all aspects of the American advertising program that would affect its

demand curve — type of programming sponsored, regional incidence, the product characteristics to be emphasized, the quality of advertising, and so on. The costs of enforcing a contract
rise as the number of stipulations increase and as the determination of whether or not the terms have been fulfilled becomes
more vague. For some industries, like the automobile industry,
the dimensions of interdependence between two firms in different countries may be so large in number and so difficult to
measure that contractual arrangements between the firms
would be a more expensive means of constraining their interdependence than a centralization of control by the formation of
an international firm.

In comparison, the Holiday Inns are not operated as an international firm because to convert franchise holders into subsidiaries would increase the costs of management — at least,
some of the incentives for individual Inns to be operated so as
to maximize their wealth would be lost — without providing
compensating gains in efficiency. The actions of autonomous
owners of Holiday Inns can be economically co-ordinated by
contractual arrangements; the actions of autonomous automobile plants cannot, and a more expensive means of co-ordination, the firm, is chosen.

In summary, we have argued that the international firm is
one of the methods by which interdependent activities in different countries can be co-ordinated. There are two equivalent
statements of the conditions under which the international firm
will be chosen by interdependent producers in different countries: the producers will choose to centralize control if the international firm is the least expensive way in which to obtain a
given level of efficiency within the joint activity; the producers
will choose to centralize control if the international firm yields
the highest level of efficiency for a given cost of co-ordinating
their joint activity. In other words, resources will be allocated by
fiat between two countries if the sum of the values of resources
in two or more interdependent, productive activities is greater
than it would be if the activities were conducted autonomously.

## 3. SOME EMPIRICAL IMPLICATIONS

The theory of the international firm developed in the section
above appears to be consistent with the three characteristics of
foreign direct investment described in the first section of this
paper. First, we are able to make some progress towards devel-

oping a hypothesis to "explain" the variation in the industrial incidence of foreign control in Canada, without distinguishing between foreign control in primary and secondary manufacturing. The relationship between an industry's tariff protection and the proportion of its total production under the control of international firms can be examined within the context of the costs of co-ordinating the actions of a set of interdependent producers in different countries. Although an increase in a tariff will generally have a positive effect on the price international firms are willing to pay, relative to autonomous domestic firms, for the control of domestic resources in the protected industry, there is no a priori relationship between changes in tariffs and the total inflow of foreign direct investment to the economy. Secondly, we are able to interpret the observation that foreign subsidiaries are consistently the leading producers in the industries of the host country without assuming that the international firm generally possesses superior factors of production. International firms will be willing to pay relatively more than autonomous domestic firms for the control of the leading producers in industries in which some domestic producers can gain a higher wealth if operated as subsidiaries. Finally, the reluctance of international firms to issue shares in their subsidiaries appears to be consistent with wealth maximization for the international firm as a whole. The international firm will wish to sell shares in its returns at the highest possible price, and shareholders will prefer to hold shares in the international firm rather than in its subsidiaries.

The principal conclusion of the theory developed in Section 2 is that the international firm will be chosen as the means of organizing production internationally in those industries in which both the interdependence among producers in various countries and the costs of co-ordinating their actions are relatively high. Although there is no empirical information that directly bears on these aspects of industrial activity, most readers will probably accept the statement that industries vary widely in their dependence on foreign decisions and in the costs of constraining their dependence. If that is correct, it follows that there would be a difference in the proportion of various industries' total production under the control of international firms. Producers in industries that are relatively independent of the influence of foreign producers will have nothing to gain by attempting to more closely co-ordinate their actions with those of foreigners, at the cost of establishing an international firm. Producers in industries whose dependence on foreign

producers is economically constrained by the price mechanism
or contractual arrangements will not choose to form international firms because it would be a more expensive method of
co-ordinating their behaviour. Those industries in which the international firm is the predominant means of international organization will be those in which the allocation of resources internationally would be relatively inefficient if producers in different countries acted autonomously. The international firm is,
like any firm, an alternative to market exchange. But it is not an
alternative to exchange in physical commodities. It is an alternative to exchange in effects that cannot easily be quantitified and
for which the market is, therefore, an expensive means of resolving differences of opinion.

One of the implications of this analysis of the international
firm does yield an empirical test that will permit us to say something about the interindustry incidence of foreign direct investment in Canada. Let us assume that the preferences of Canadians and Americans are identical, so that industries in either
country are not insulated from the effects of actions taken in the
other country by national differences in the reaction of consumers to the same stimuli. For example, we assume that consumers
in either country will react in the same way to a change in the
design of a product or in an advertising campaign, wherever it
originates. Given that assumption, the interdependence among
producers within an industry in either country will be about the
same as the interdependence between groups of producers in
the two countries. For example, the automobile producer in
Ontario will be as dependent on decisions made in Detroit as
will the producer in New York State. In addition, we assert that
the costs of co-ordinating the actions of interdependent
producers will be the same between the United States and Canada as within either country. The costs of communication across
the border are not higher than the costs of intracountry communication, and the costs of effecting market exchange or ar-
ranging contracts will not be significantly altered if the exchange or contract is with a party of the other country.[17]

If the effects of interdependence and the costs of constraining it are the same between the United States and Canada
as within either country, we should expect to find that the incidence of international firms was highest in those industries in
which the concentration of control is relatively high. Within the
United States, industries in which there is a relatively high concentration of control are typically industries in which individual
firms operate a relatively large number of plants in various re-

gions.[18] Given our assumptions about the Canadian – American situation, the gains to individual plants in the United States from a regional integration of their operations will be the same as the gains from continental integration of Canadian plants. There is some evidence that confirms this hypothesis.

In an unpublished dissertation written in 1932, W. H. Carter found that U.S. companies operating subsidiaries in Canada tended to be multiplant firms within the United States:

*Of 398 companies (with Canadian subsidiaries in 1930), I was able to secure data with respect to the number of domestic (U.S.) plants for 358. These 358 companies have 1803 plants in the United States . . . Of the total, 60 per cent had more than one plant, while 30 per cent of the companies had more than five plants each. This is a very much larger number of plants per company than the average in the country. . . . The average number of plants is still larger when we include the number of branches in Canada and other foreign countries. The inclusion of these brings the average to 7.8 branches per company. The typical company, therefore, which establishes branches in Canada is one that operates far more plants than the typical corporation.[19]*

With the available data from the Censuses of Manufactures in the United States and Canada and the statistics of foreign ownership in Canada, we can test the relationship between the degree of foreign control of an industry in Canada and its concentration ratio. For a sample of sixty-five industries in 1963, the estimated correlation coefficient between the concentration ratio of an industry in the United States and the share of total Canadian sales by foreign-controlled firms in the corresponding Canadian industry is $+0.541$, which is significantly different from zero at the 99 per cent confidence level.[20] Unfortunately, this test is not precisely related to the hypothesis developed above. Our hypothesis says nothing about the location of control of an international firm; therefore, the foreign ownership variable should measure the proportion of Canadian output produced by international firms, whether they are held by Canadians or Americans. However, an industrial breakdown of Canadian control of manufacturing industries in the United States is not available.

A more direct test of the theory of foreign direct investment must await the collection of information on the methods by which producers in different industries attempt to constrain their dependence on one another. However, in the absence of better information, casual observation suggests that, within the United States and Canada, the national and international methods of co-ordination are very similar. It appears that the market functions in about the same dimensions across the border as it does within either country. Franchise operations within the United States become franchised in Canada. Firms that license patents within either country are likely to do the same in the other rather than establish a subsidiary. And large multiplant firms in the one country tend to establish subsidiaries in the other.

What role does the tariff play in determining the extent of foreign direct investment in a country? Let us consider first the case for an individual industry. If the tariff has a causal relationship with foreign direct investment, it must have an effect on the *difference* in the price that an autonomous domestic firm and an international firm would be willing to pay for the control of resources in a domestic industry. Since most writers have presumed that tariffs stimulate foreign direct investment,[21] we can ask whether an increase in an industry's tariff would increase the international firm's bid for resources in the industry relative to the bid of domestic firms.

An increase in a tariff does not represent an increase in the costs of transacting between domestic and foreign producers. It affects the terms on which domestic and foreign producers will exchange rights to comodities, but it has no necessary effect upon the costs of transferring rights from one owner to another. However, if the tariff can be avoided by substituting an intrafirm transfer for arm's-length exchange, any increase in the tariff will raise the bid of an international firm relative to the bid of domestic firms for the control of resources in the protected industry.[22] It will be less costly for a parent and a subsidiary to manipulate transfer prices to their mutual advantage than it would be for autonomous traders to do the same thing. Autonomous traders would have two problems not faced by the international firm: the gains from tariff avoidance would have to be distributed among them; opportunities for cheating would arise (as a result of the attempt to manipulate prices) that could only be eliminated if each trader were able to measure the costs of other traders (a variant of the cartel problem would exist). Because the subsidiaries of an international firm would have no incentive to cheat in this way, an integration of traders in different countries is a cheaper way to manipulate prices so as to avoid the effects of the tariff, and the tariff will raise the price international firms are willing to pay for the control of protected domestic resources. Note that the tariff will not necessarily lead international firms to outbid domestic firms for an industry's resources; it will raise the international firm's bid relative to that of domestic firms by some amount.

Although a higher tariff may stimulate foreign direct investment in individual industries, because of opportunities to avoid the tariff through the creation of an international firm, increases in tariffs have no predictable effect on the level of foreign direct investment in the economy as a whole. The structure of tariffs may protect industries of varying dependence on the actions of foreigners, and the effects of an increase in tariff levels on foreign direct investment will depend on whether the effect of the structure is to make the economy's total production more or less dependent on foreign producers.We could easily imagine a tariff structure that stimulated the output of industries that were relatively independent of the decisions of foreign producers and that tended to be under the control of autonomous domestic firms; in that case, an increase of tariff levels would reduce aggregate foreign direct investment by directing resources away from industries in which international firms were the predominant means of co-ordinating production. Examining the international firm in terms of the interdependence among producers in different countries complicates the traditional analysis of the effects of tariffs on total foreign investment, which includes both portfolio and direct investment. There are two independent factors to be considered: the effect the tariff has upon the demand for capital through its protective effect on industries of varying capital intensity, and the effect the tariff has upon the demand for the control of domestic resources by international firms through its protective effect on industries of varying international interdependence. The structure of tariffs would have to be specified in both of these respects in order to determine the relationship between a change in an economy's tariffs and a change in its level of foreign indebtedness.

It was noted in Section 1 that the subsidiaries of international firms tend to be the leading firms within their industries. Although these comparisons of foreign and domestic firms appear to indicate that the former are the more efficient producers, the theory of the international firm suggests another interpretation. In almost all industries we observe a range among the producers in terms of plant size, average labour productivity, and wage rates. In some industries, the leading producers will be operated as subsidiaries because of their relative position in the industry rather than vice versa. If the actions of a foreign firm impose effects upon the producers within a domestic industry that cannot be economically constrained by contractual arrangements, the foreign firm may increase its wealth, depending on the costs of management, by acquiring control of one or more of the producers that it affects. If the effects of the foreign firm's actions in the home country are industry-wide, it will have a stronger incentive to acquire control of the larger producers in the industry in question because the absolute loss due to an inefficient co-ordination of the actions of autonomous firms in different countries will be higher for the larger firms. Therefore, an international firm will be willing to outbid domestic firms by a larger amount for the leading producers in an industry than for the smaller producers, which experience relatively little of the losses due to the effects of unconstrained dependence on the actions of foreign firms. The causal relationship between a producer's relative performance within its industry and its subsidiary or autonomous status is not unequivocally one-way. The difference between the productivity and size of subsidiaries and autonomous firms within the same industry may be interpreted as the sum of two separate effects: the difference in these characteristics that would exist if all of the firms in the industry were domestically controlled, and the gains in productivity and size that result from a more efficient international co-ordination of the actions of the subsidiaries of international firms.

Finally, we are able to cast some light upon the reluctance of international firms to issue shares in their foreign subsidiaries. If we consider the problem of constraining the interdependence between productive activities in different countries, the reason for the parent firm's desire to hold all of the equity in its foreign subsidiaries can be described in familiar terms. The international firm chooses to operate foreign subsidiaries so as to maximize the sum of the values of the international activities under its control. Because of the interdependence among the various operations of an international firm, its subsidiaries will not be managed so as to maximize their particular return, and minority shareholders in a subsidiary will soon discover that it is not being managed in their (the subsidiary shareholders') best interests. In other words, the value of the subsidiary, or any part of it, is higher to the international firm than to an autonomous shareholder. The parent is unwilling to sell shares in its subsidiaries because the price that individuals would be willing to offer is too low. An individual would always be willing to pay a higher price for a share in the income of an international firm than he would be willing to pay for the same share taken in the form of the income to one of its subsidiaries.

## FOOTNOTES

1. For example, Herbert Marshall, Frank A. Southard, and K. W. Taylor, *Canadian-American Industry* (New Haven, 1936), p. 264; and John H. Dunning, *American Investment in British Manufacturing Industry* (London, 1958), pp. 57-8.

2. *Report of the Minister of Trade and Commerce under the Corporations and Labour Unions Returns Act, 1963* (CALURA), Part I, Corporations, Section F (Canada: Department of Trade and Commerce), pp. 45-77. In the Report, a firm is classified as foreign-controlled if over 50 per cent of its voting stock is held by foreigners. Although Section F lists eighty-one manufacturing industries, only sixty-five of these could be matched with comparable industries in the United States, so that American concentration ratios could be used in a test reported below.

3. See H. C. Eastman and S. Stykolt, *The Tariff and Competition in Canada* (Toronto, 1967), p. 105.

4. Marshall, Southard, and Taylor, p. 276.

5. Effective protection estimates taken from James R. Melvin and Bruce W. Wilkinson, *Effective Protection in the Canadian Economy* (Ottawa, 1968), Table III. The sample of industries used is the same as that described in footnote 2 above.

6. Richard E. Caves, "Foreign Investment, Trade and Industrial Growth," The Royer Lectures, University of California, Berkeley (Dec., 1969), mimeo.

7. For example, Donald T. Brash, *American Investment in Australian Industry* (Canberra, 1966), p. 276 and John H. Dunning, *American Investment in British Manufacturing Industry* (London, 1958), pp. 59-82.

8. Brash, *op. cit.*, pp. 170-3; Dunning, *op. cit.*, pp.. 180-3; and André Raynauld, *La Propriété des enterprises du Québec*. Documents of the Royal Commission on Bilingualism and Biculturalism, pp. 119-144.

9. Irving Brecher and S. S. Reisman, *Canada-United States Economic Relations* (Ottawa, 1957), p. 138.

10. Charles D. Kindleberger, *American Business Abroad* (New Haven, 1969), pp. 27-8.

11. *Foreign Ownership and the Structure of Canadian Industry* (Canada: Privy Council, Jan., 1968), pp. 412-13.

12. This description of the firm's function is well established in the literature. For example, D. H. Robertson and S. R. Dennison, *The Control of Industry* ( Cambridge, 1960), p. 73 describes the firm as "islands of conscious power in this ocean of unconscious co-operation"; Ronald H. Coase, "The Nature of the Firm," *Economica*, N.S., IV (1937), pp. 386-405, reprinted in K. Boulding and G. Stigler (eds.), *Readings in Price Theory* (Chicago, 1952), p. 334 states that "the distinguishing mark of the firm is the supercession of the price mechanism"; and Andreas G. Papandreu, "Some Basic Problems in the Theory of the Firm" in B. F. Haley (ed.) *A Survey of Contemporary Economics*, Vol. II (Homewood, Ill., 1952), p. 187 states that "Authoritative co-ordination lies at the heart of the concept of the firm." The following analysis of the international firm owes much to the paper by Coase, as will be apparent to readers familiar with his work.

13. Harold C. Havighurst, *The Nature of Private Contract* (Evanston, 1961), pp. 21, 22, and 33.

14. An attempt to work out a general theory of institutional choice (the firm vs. the price mechanism) can be found in my unpublished Ph.D. dissertation, *The Organization of Production* (University of Toronto, 1971).

15. Compare with Stephen H. Hymer, *The International Operations of National Firms, A Study of Direct Foreign Investment* (unpub. doctoral diss., M.I.T., 1960). Hymer's analysis of foreign direct investment emphasizes the imperfection of market competition in the advantages of the foreign parent as the principal motive for the establishment of foreign subsidiaries (pp. 25, 51). At one point in the thesis, Hymer states the argument more generally: "**The firm internalizes or supersedes the market.** . . . Decentralized decision-making (i.e., a free market) is defective when there are certain types of interactions between firms; that is each firm's behaviour noticeably affects the other firm's." (p. 48) But the point is not developed, and only the pecuniary interdependence among firms is explicitly treated in the thesis.

16. Information taken from the Prospectus of Commonwealth Holiday Inns of Canada Ltd. prepared by Midland–Osler Securities Ltd., Nov. 28, 1968.

17. There are some exceptions. Different legal constraints may make it more expensive to arrange international contracts, and there may be costs involved in international exchange that do not exist in domestic trade. However, the tariff, about which more will be said later, is not a cost of effecting market exchange internationally unless it can be avoided through intrafirm transfers of goods.

18. Joe S. Bain, *Barriers to New Competition* (Cambridge, Mass., 1956), pp. 83-85.

19. W. H. Carter Jr., *American Branch Plants in Canada* (unpublished doctoral dissertation, Harvard, 1932), pp. 167-8.

20. The source of the Canadian data is described in footnote 2 above. The concentration ratio represents the proportion of an industry's shipments in 1963 made by the four largest firms in the industry. The source of this data is United States, Department of Commerce, Bureau of the Census, *1963 Census of Manufacturers*, Report on Concentration in Manufacturing. Gideon Rosenbluth, "The Relation between Foreign Control and Concentration in Canadian Industry," *CJE*, III (1970), pp. 18, 19, finds an estimated correlation between the proportion of foreign ownership and the proportion of a *Canadian* industry's sales made by the largest *eight* firms to be 0.35. Rosenbluth concludes that this relationship between concentration and foreign control is a result of the tendency for foreign parent firms to control the larger firms in each industry, and that "there is no evidence of a tendency to seek out the more concentrated industries." However, both the tendencies to establish foreign control in the relatively large firms and to establish subsidiaries in relatively concentrated industries are consistent with our hypothesis.

21. For example, Brash, *op. cit.*, pp. 36-39; Irving Brecher and S. S. Reisman, *op. cit.*, p. 117; and *Foreign Ownership and the Structure of Canadian Industry*, p. 18.

22. See Thomas Horst, "The Effects of Tariffs on Foreign Direct Investment," *Journal of Political Economy*, (forthcoming).

# Part II
# Marginalist Analysis
# of Location and Trade

# [3]

# Multinational Firms and the Theory of International Trade and Investment

*By* Raveendra N. Batra and Rama Ramachandran*

Despite increased importance of the multinational corporation in the arena of economic activity and political influence, trade theorists have either ignored it or expressed unguarded skepticism at the ability of the conventional trade models to successfully capture and analyze the features of this new phenomenon.[1] The purpose of this paper is twofold: first, by building upon the contribution by Richard Caves, we will show that the traditional trade models can be adapted in a way that preserves most, if not all, of the attributes introduced by international firms.[2] Second, we will conduct a comparative statics analysis to explore the implications of tariffs and taxes for resource allocation and international capital movements. Our results here confirm what has already been well established in myriad empirical studies, that maturation of the international firm has vastly increased economic interdependence among trading countries, and that few nations can eschew the ripples caused by economic policies of other nations.[3]

## I. Assumptions and the Model

The conventional general equilibrium models of international trade and investment, expounded in detail by Murray Kemp and Ronald Jones (1967), rely heavily on the properties of the Heckscher-Ohlin

model. This model is ill-equipped to tackle the specificity of some factors and technology which we consider to be one of the main characteristics of international investments by multinational firms. Almost invariably the multinational firm possesses oligopolistic control over some patents and specific technology which enables it to outcompete local firms in foreign countries. The return to such investments includes not only an adequate return on its capital but also on its inventions, managerial know-how, superior marketing techniques, etc., which it has already developed. While it might have incurred considerable expenses in developing this know-how, the opportunity cost of transmitting such inventions abroad is practically zero, and whatever royalties and fees that are thus received are pure profits.

In this paper we intend to capture these features of the multinational firm by analyzing international investment using the specific factor model of international trade which was popular before 1944 when the contribution by Wolfgang Stolper and Paul Samuelson appeared, and which was recently resurrected by Batra and Francisco Casas, among others. We present below a two-sector model where the multinational capital is specific to one sector while the other sector consists of national and local firms with production activities confined to one nation. The multinational capital, while specific to one sector within each nation, is nevertheless mobile between the same sectors in different nations.[4]

---

*Professor and assistant professor, respectively, Southern Methodist University. We are indebted to George Borts and an anonymous referee for many helpful comments.

[1] See for instance Thomas Horst, and Robert Baldwin and J. David Richardson, p. 264, for expressions of similar opinion.

[2] Actually Caves investigated the implications of the emergence of the international firms in terms of both partial and general equilibrium models. Our analysis builds further upon his general equilibrium system.

[3] See Richard Barnett and Ronald Muller for an eloquent presentation of this view.

[4] See Caves, p. 17. The argument of our paper is based on an assumption that (i) the multinational and local sectors are distinctly defined, and (ii) the multinational sector is a significant part of economic activity in the host country. Regarding (i) there is no problem: Jean Servan-Schreiber points out that in all Europe, the *U.S.*-based firms by the late 1960's produced 80 percent of computers, 95 percent of integrated circuits, 50

The ownership of patents, the availability of special managerial know-how, and the marketing skills are represented by a third factor $S$ in the production function of the multinational firm. Some properties of the specific factor $S$ are noteworthy. Following Harry Johnson, we shall assume that $S$ is measured not in terms of a physical unit but in terms of some intangible abstract unit whose transference by international firms into the host country does not diminish its use in the source country.[5] It is assumed that $S$ is a "state variable" whose value at any instant of time depends on the past efforts at developing the specific skills possessed by the multinational firm. It may be interpreted as an index of Harvey Leibenstein's X-efficiency factor; Leibenstein (1966, p. 412) mentions the nonmarket-

ability of certain inputs as a factor responsible for differing X-efficiency of firms, which is exactly our assumption regarding the role of $S$. As argued by Leibenstein (1966, 1978) and T. Y. Shen, X-efficiency leads to dispersion in the level of productivity of firms at any instant of time. We shall, therefore, assume that $0 < S < \bar{S}$, where $\bar{S}$ is the saturation level at which the marginal product of $S$ is zero. One particular merit of this approach is that the return to the intangible factor $S$ is a pure surplus and captures, in our model, any excess profit earned by multinational firms. In this way, one could incorporate all the features of a world dominated by global firms (excess profits, industry-specific capital and technology, etc.) in a general equilibrium model and still retain the assumptions of perfect competition that considerably simplifies exposition and, in most cases, is the only way in which a general equilibrium analysis can be carried out.[6]

The model developed below will then be based on the following assumptions:

ASSUMPTION 1: *There are two countries, a source country (the home of the multinational firm) and a host country (which is foreign to the global firm); and two sectors, one wherein the multinational firms compete with each other and the other consisting of goods produced by the local firms.*

ASSUMPTION 2: *Labor is the only nonspecific factor and capital is specific to both sectors; the production function of the multinational firms also contains another specific factor that represents patents, technical and managerial know-how, etc.*

ASSUMPTION 3: *All other assumptions of the Heckscher-Ohlin model are retained. Thus perfect competition, linearly homogeneous and concave production functions, full employment, and inelastic factor supplies are also assumed.*

---

percent of semiconductors, and so on. The *U.S.* direct foreign investment is thus concentrated mostly in advanced technology, capital-intensive industries. As regards (ii), the multinational firms perhaps account for less than 10 percent of economic activity in all Europe. The important point, however, is that their assets are growing at phenomenal rates; Barnett and Muller, p. 26, report that by some estimates the direct foreign investment is likely to reach $4 trillion by 1985, or about 54–80 percent of all production assets of the noncommunist countries. Thus, the productive activity of the multinational firms is expected to become a colossus in many host countries; therefore the implications of a distinctive multinational sector is worth exploring. We are also ignoring the phenomena of cross hauling of international investment wherein firms in each country invest and control production facilities in the other country. Despite some recent inroads made by non-American multinational firms, the *U.S.*-based global corporations were by 1969 the biggest suppliers of direct foreign investment. Also a significant portion of direct foreign investment in the United States is in the form of export subsidiary, one that facilitates importing goods, while *U.S.*-based firms set up production facilities abroad. See Sidney Rolfe for further details.

[5] $S$ may be measured in terms of man-hours spent in the conduct of research or in terms of financial capital used in the discovery of patents and so on. Johnson emphasized the point that the know-how and managerial skills have the nature of public goods which have high fixed costs but low marginal costs. C. F. Pratten observes: "From my discussion with officials of companies it was clear that management of national operations of most companies have access to some knowledge of production and marketing techniques, and they can obtain advice from other companies in the same group" (pp. 50–51).

[6] It seems to us that in order to investigate what the emergence of multinational firms means to the world economy, the general equilibrium analysis—as far as it goes—is more appropriate than the partial analysis.

ASSUMPTION 4: *Both the countries are small and take as given the relative prices that are determined in the rest of the world.*[7]

Let $X$ and $Y$, respectively, be the sectors in which the multinational and the local firms produce their products in the source country. The two aggregate production functions are

(1) $\quad X = X(L_x, K_x, S) \quad X^* = X^*(L_x^*, K_x^*, S^*)$

(2) $\quad Y = Y(L_y, K_y) \qquad Y^* = Y^*(L_y^*, K_y^*)$

where $L$ stands for labor, $K$ for capital, $S$ for a specific factor, and the star denotes the variables in the host country. The production functions, which are assumed to be linearly homogeneous and concave, satisfy the following properties: In $X$

(3a) $\quad X_j > 0, \quad X_{jj} < 0, \quad X_{jk} > 0$

$$(j, k = K, L, S; j \neq k)$$

$$X_{LL} X_{KK} - X_{KL}^2 > 0$$

and in $Y$

(3b) $\quad Y_j > 0, \quad Y_{jj} < 0, \quad Y_{KL} > 0 \quad (j = L, K)$

$$Y_{LL} Y_{KK} - Y_{KL}^2 = 0$$

where $X_j$ is the marginal product of the $j$th factor, $X_{jj}$ is the change in the marginal product of the $j$th factor with respect to its own input (i.e., $\partial X_L / \partial L_x = X_{LL}$), and $X_{jk}$ is the change in the marginal product of the $j$th factor with respect to the $k$th input ($j \neq k$); similar properties characterize the function $Y(\cdot)$.

With regard to capital, we assume that $K_x$ and $K_y$ are also specific to each sector; labor is a nonspecific factor and is mobile between two sectors, so that only one wage rate prevails within each country.

The firm wants to maximize global profits after taxes. Generally both the source country and the host country levy corporate income tax. We shall assume, in accordance with current *U.S.* tax practice, that the source country gives limited tax credit for the tax payed in the host country; the maximum tax credit that the corporation can earn is estimated by applying the source-country tax rate to the income earned in the host country. Further assume that the goods produced by the multinationals in the host country are importable goods there and that the host country levies a tariff on its imports. Hence $p^* = p(1 + \tau^*)$ where $\tau^* > 0$ is the host country's tariff rate on its import of good $X$.

The relative price of $X$ in terms of $Y$, $p$ is given by the world market. The firm takes the wage ($w$) and the rental ($r$) rate in both countries as given. Also let $F$ be the expenses incurred by the firm for research and managerial development necessary to maintain its global leadership. The global profits may be computed as follows:

Tax base in host country $= B^*$

$$= (p^* X^* - w^* L_x^*)$$

Tax base in source country $= B$

$$= (pX - wL_x + p^* X^* - w^* L_x^* - F)$$

Tax credit[8] in source country $= C$

$$= (p^* X^* - w^* L_x^*) t$$

Global profit after taxes[9] is given by

(4) $\quad \Pi = B(1 - t) - B^* t^* + C - r^* K_x^* - rK_x$

$$= (pX - wL_x - F)(1 - t)$$

$$+ (p^* X^* - w^* L_x^*)(1 - t^*) - rK_x - r^* K_x^*$$

---

[7] This assumption is reminiscent of Jacob Viner's well-known customs union model where two or three small countries trade with each other at given terms of trade that are determined in the rest of the world.

[8] Batra and Josef Hadar point out that if $t^* < t$, then $t^*$ does not influence the decision of the multinational firm, as $C$ now equals $(p^* X^* - w^* L_x^*) t^* = B^* t^*$.

[9] Actually, following Horst, we should also include the intrafirm exports (or imports), i.e., the exports (or imports) from the parent firm to the subsidiary, in the global profit equation. However, such trade is implicit in our definition. For example, suppose $M$ is the quantity exported by the multinational firms to their subsidiaries in the host country and $D_x$ is the quantity

The marginal (first-order) conditions for profit maximization by the multinational firm require that

$$(5) \qquad pX_L = w_x$$

$$p^* X_L^* = w_x^*$$

$$(6) \qquad pX_k(1-t) = r_x$$

$$p^* X_K^* (1-t^*) = r_x^*$$

Similarly, profit maximization by local firms leads to

$$(7) \qquad Y_L = w_y \quad \text{and} \quad Y_L^* = w_y^*$$

$$(8) \qquad Y_K = r_y \quad \text{and} \quad Y_K^* = r_y^*$$

Mobility of labor in each country ensures that the wage rate is the same in both sectors, so that

$$(9) \qquad w = w_x = w_y \quad \text{and} \quad w^* = w_x^* = w_y^*$$

The rental of capital need not be the same within each country because of limited mobility and industry specificity, but capital stock owned by the international firms is mobile from one country to the other, and this mobility generates an equality between $r_x$ and $r_x^*$. Hence

$$(10) \qquad r_x = r_x^*$$

From equations (5)–(10) we can obtain the factor-market equilibrium conditions which determine the allocation of labor between the two sectors in each country and of the multinational capital between the two countries. From (5), (7), and (9) we have

$$(11) \qquad pX_L(L_x, K_x, S) = Y_L(L_y, K_y)$$

$$(12) \qquad p^* X_L^*(L_x^*, K_x^*, S^*) = Y_L^*(L_y^*, K_y^*)$$

These equations determine the allocation of labor between the two sectors in each country.

From (6) and (10),

$$(13) \qquad p(1-t)X_K(L_x, K_x, S)$$

$$= p^*(1-t^*)X_K^*(L_x^*, K_x^*, S^*)$$

This equation determines the allocation of the multinational capital between the source and the host country.

From full employment of labor in each country,

$$(14) \qquad L_x + L_y = \bar{L}$$

$$(15) \qquad L_x^* + L_y^* = \bar{L}^*$$

and from the constraint imposed by the stock of capital owned by the multinational firms,

$$(16) \qquad K_x + K_x^* = \bar{K}_x$$

where $\bar{L}$, $\bar{L}^*$, and $\bar{K}_x$ are constant. Similarly, since all factors are in inelastic supply, $K_y$ and $K_y^*$ are also constant.

Thus we are able to incorporate the basic attributes of multinational firms in a general equilibrium analysis and use it below to undertake comparative static analysis of the impact of changes in taxes and tariffs. Resource allocation within each country and

---

demanded of $X$, then $M = D_x^* - X^* = X - D_x$. In view of this, global profits (ignoring taxes) become

$$\Pi = (pD_x + pM - w_x L_x - r_x K_x)$$

$$+ (p^* D_x^* - p^* M - w_x^* L_x^* - r_x^* K_x^*) - F$$

which is similar to Horst's definition. Since we have assumed that the production function is linear homogeneous, it is possible to define implicitly (from the product exhaustion rule) the marginal product of the intangible factor, $X_S$ and $X_S^*$,

$$X = X_L L_x + X_K K_x + X_S S$$

$$X^* = X_L^* L_x^* + X_K^* K_x^* + X_S S^*$$

Substituting equations (5)–(8) into (4) would then show that

$$\Pi = p(1-t)X_S S + p^*(1-t^*)X_S^* S^* - (1-t)F$$

The second term represents the addition to pure surplus of the multinational firm from utilizing its expertise for production abroad.

$$(18) \quad \begin{bmatrix} p^*X_{LL}^* + Y_{LL}^* & p^*X_{LK}^* & 0 \\ 0 & -pX_{LK} & pX_{LL} + Y_{LL} \\ p^*(1-t^*)X_{LK}^* & \left\{\begin{matrix} p^*(1-t^*)X_{KK}^* \\ +p(1-t)X_{KK} \end{matrix}\right\} & -p(1-t)X_{KL} \end{bmatrix} \begin{bmatrix} dL_x^* \\ dK_x^* \\ dL_x \end{bmatrix} = \begin{bmatrix} 0 \\ 0 \\ \left\{\begin{matrix} p^*X_K^* dt^* \\ -pX_K dt \end{matrix}\right\} \end{bmatrix}$$

the process of capital movements between the two countries can be determined with the help of six equations given by (11)–(16), containing six variables ($L_x$, $L_y$, $L_x^*$, $L_y^*$, $K_x$, and $K_x^*$) and eleven parameters ($S$, $S^*$, $K_y$, $K_y^*$, $\bar{L}$, $\bar{L}^*$, $\bar{K}_x$, $p$, $t$, $t^*$, and $\tau^*$).

From our assumption that the multinational firms operate in small countries and sell their goods in those countries as well as the rest of the world, the international terms of trade ($p$) can be treated as constant. And with a given $\tau^*$, $p^*$ is also constant. At the present state of the literature dealing with the implications of the multinational firms, this seems to be an appropriate assumption, although a complete analysis should also examine the case where the terms of trade are variable.

## II. Taxes on International Investment

The model can be used to analyze the effects of a change in the corporate income tax. Substituting for $L_y, L_y^*, K_x$ from (14) to (16) into (11), (12), and (13), we get[10]

$$(17) \quad p^*X_L^*(L_x^*, K_x^*, S^*) = Y_L^*(\bar{L}^* - L_x^*, K_y^*)$$

$$pX_L(L_x, \bar{K}_x - K_x^*, S) = Y_L(\bar{L} - L_x, K_y)$$

$$p^*(1-t^*)X_K^*(L_x^*, K_x^*, S^*)$$

$$= p(1-t)X_K(L_x, \bar{K}_x - K_x^*, S)$$

With these substitutions, our model is considerably simplified. The system of equations (17) contains three equations and three unknowns, $L_x^*$, $K_x^*$, and $L_x$. Differentiating these totally we obtain equation (18) shown above, or

$$(18') \quad [A][B] = [C]$$

[10]If $\tau^* = 0$, then $p = p^*$.

where $[A],[B],[C]$ are the three matrices of (18). The determinant of (18) is given by

$$(19) \quad D = -\left[ (p^*X_{LL}^* + Y_{LL}^*)p^2(1-t) \right.$$

$$\times \left( H_x + \frac{1}{p}X_{KK}Y_{LL} \right)$$

$$+ (pX_{LL} + Y_{LL})p^{*2}(1-t^*)$$

$$\left. \times \left( H_x^* + \frac{1}{p^*}X_{KK}^*Y_{LL}^* \right) \right]$$

where $H_x = X_{LL}X_{KK} - X_{KL}^2 > 0$, and similarly for $H_x^*$. In view of our assumptions about the production function, $D$ is positive.

Let us begin our analysis of the income tax on the multinational investment by examining the response of the variables in the host country to a change in the tax rate in that country. With $dt = 0$, the solution of (18) yields

$$(20) \quad \frac{dL_x^*}{dt^*} = \left\{ p^{*2}X_K^*X_{KL}^*(pX_{LL} + Y_{LL}) \right\}$$

$$+ D = -\frac{dL_y^*}{dt^*}$$

$$(21) \quad \frac{dK_x^*}{dt^*} = -\left\{ p^*X_K^*(p^*X_{LL}^* + Y_{LL}^*) \right.$$

$$(pX_{LL} + Y_{LL}) \right\} + D = -\frac{dK_x}{dt^*}$$

Clearly $dL_x^*/dt^* < 0$ and $dK_x^*/dt^* < 0$, and we obtain an eminently plausible result that the international investment tax leads to a decline in the employment of the multinational capital in the host country. Since $d\bar{K}_x$

$=0$, this obviously implies that capital moves back to the source country. As the host country imposes a tax, investment there becomes less attractive because the marginal product of capital net of the tax declines; capital movement back to the source country occurs until the net marginal product of capital in the host country rises to that of capital employed in the source country.

With capital so moving, the marginal product of labor declines in $X^*$ (because $X_{KL}^* > 0$), so that labor moves towards the goods produced by local firms in the host country. That is why $dL_x^*/dt^* < 0$ and hence $dL_y^*/dt^* = -dL_x^*/dt^* > 0$. It also follows that the output of $Y^*$ rises and that of $X^*$ declines.

What happens to factor rewards in the host country? Since $w^* = Y_L^*(L_y^*, K_y^*)$, and $K_y^*$ is constant at any moment of time,

$$\frac{dw^*}{dt^*} = Y_{LL}^* \frac{dL_y^*}{dt^*} < 0$$

so that the real wage rate declines.[11] The reason is that as the marginal product of labor declines in goods produced by the multinationals, demand for labor in $X^*$ declines, creating excess supply of labor in the entire economy, and this forces the real wage to go down to clear the labor market.

This result gains further comprehension from Figure 1 where the real wage rate expressed in terms of $Y^*$ is measured along the vertical axis and labor along the horizontal axis: $BC$ is the negatively sloped demand curve for labor in $X^*$ and $AD$ is the aggregate demand curve for labor, where $AD$ is obtained by a horizontal addition of the demand for labor in $Y^*$ to that demand in $X^*$ at any $w^*$. For simplicity these curves are drawn to be linear. The inelastic supply curve of labor is given by $R\overline{L}^*$, the equilibrium wage by $w_e^*$, labor employed in $X^*$ by $OG$, and that employed in $Y^*$ by $GR$. This is how the initial situation is depicted. Now suppose a tax on the multinational

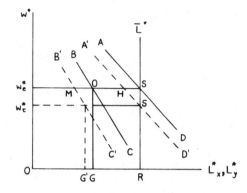

FIGURE 1

investment is imposed by the host country and $K_x^*$ declines; this causes a downward shift of the labor demand curve in $X^*$ to $B'C'$ and of the aggregate labor demand curve to $A'D'$ such that the distance $MQ$ equals the distance $HS$. The equilibrium wage rate declines to $w_t^*$, the employment of labor in $X^*$ declines to $OG'$ and that in $Y^*$ rises to $G'R$. A similar diagram can be used to depict the flight of the multinational capital from the host country.

What about the return to capital? We know that the equilibrium $r_x^* = r_x = p(1 - t)X_K(L_x, K_x, S)$. Therefore,

(22)

$$\frac{dr_x}{dt^*} = p(1-t)X_{LK}\frac{dL_x}{dt^*} + p(1-t)X_{KK}\frac{dK_x}{dt^*}$$

From (18),

$$\frac{dL_x}{dt^*} = -p^* p X_K^* X_{LK}(p^* X_{LL}^* + Y_{LL}^*) + D > 0$$

Substitute this relation and (21) into (22) to obtain

$$\frac{dr_x}{dt^*} = p^2 p^* X_K^*(p^* X_{LL}^* + Y_{LL}^*)$$

$$\cdot \left(H_x + \frac{1}{p} Y_{LL} X_{KK}\right) + D < 0$$

Hence the rental on the multinational

capital declines in both countries. The rentals on the local capital respond differently. For

$$\frac{dr_y^*}{dt^*} = Y_{KL}^* \frac{dL_y^*}{dt^*} > 0$$

Whereas $\quad \dfrac{dr_y}{dt^*} = Y_{KL} \dfrac{dL_y}{dt^*} < 0$

Intuitively, the decline of employment in the multinational firm in the host country leads to a movement of labor to the local sector; this increases the rent of capital in that sector as capital is not free to move between sectors. The fall in demand for labor also leads to a fall in wages. An opposite effect occurs in the source country. The transfer of capital to the source country by the multinational firm leads to an increase in the wage rate and a decline in the rent of local capital in that country.

Consider now the effects of a change in the tax rate on the total profits earned by the multinational firm. Differentiating (4), it can be easily shown that

$$(23) \quad \frac{d\Pi}{dt^*} = (p^*X^* - w^*L_x^*)$$
$$(+)$$

$$-(1-t)L_x \frac{dw}{dt^*} - (1-t^*)L_x^* \frac{dw^*}{dt^*} - \bar{K}_x \frac{dr_x}{dt^*}$$
$$(+) \qquad\qquad (-) \qquad\quad (-)$$

The sign of each of the four terms is shown in parentheses below. The first term is the negative of the total income earned by multinationals in the host country. The second and third terms refer to change in wage payments in the two, assuming that employment is held constant; the two terms have opposite signs. The last term refers to the change in rent earned by the capital of the multinational firm. It is very likely that the first term determines the sign of the expression as the other expressions partially cancel each other; hence an increase in taxes is likely to reduce global profits. If we compute the change in total income (profits plus rent on its capital) earned by multinationals

$$\frac{d\Pi}{dt^*} + \bar{K}_x \frac{dr_x}{dt^*}$$

then it is all the more negative. Thus, the opposition of the multinationals to corporate income taxes is not surprising.

Let us now consider how the tax affects the national income ($I^*$) of the host country:

$$(24)$$

$$I^* = p^*X^* + Y^* - (1 - t^*)(p^*X^* - w^*L_x^*)$$

$$= p^*X^* + Y^* - (1 - t^*)\{ p^*X_K^*K_x^*$$

$$+ (p^*X^* - p^*X_L^*L_x^* - p^*X_K^*K_x^*)\}$$

where $(1 - t^*)(p^*X^* - w^*L_x^*)$ is the income which the multinationals repatriate to the source country. Differentiating (24) and using (6), we get

$$(25) \quad \frac{dI^*}{dt^*} = \left( p^*X^* - p^*X_L^*L_x^* - p^*X_K^*K_x^* \right)$$
$$(+)$$

$$+ t^*p^*X_K^* \frac{dK_x^*}{dt^*} - K_x^* \frac{dr_x^*}{dt^*}$$
$$(-) \qquad\qquad (-)$$

$$+ (1 - t^*)\left[ p^*(X_{LL}^*L_x^* + X_{LK}^*K_x^*) \frac{dL_x^*}{dt^*} \right.$$
$$(-)$$

$$+ p^*(X_{KK}^*K_x^* + X_{LK}^*L_x^*) \left. \frac{dK_x^*}{dt^*} \right]$$
$$(-)$$

Given equation (3),[12] $(X_{LL}^*L_x^* + X_{LK}^*K_x^*)$ and $(X_{KK}^*K_x^* + X_{LK}^*L_x^*)$ are negative. The signs of the other expressions are noted below them in equation (25). $t^*p^*(dK_x^*/dt^*)$ is the only negative term in the equation. If $t^*$ is small, or if initially the host country has no tax so that $t^* = 0$, then the whole expression is unambiguously positive, showing that an introduction of the corporate income tax by the host country raises its net national income. The increase in national income is partly due to an increase in tax

[12]From Euler's equation, $L_x^*X_L^* + K_x^*X_K^* + S^*X_S^* = X^*$. Differentiating partially with respect to $L^*$, we get $X_{LL}^*L_x^* + X_{LK}^*K_x^* = -S^*X_{SL}^*$, which is negative as $X_{SL}^* > 0$ (see the assumption in equation (3)).

collection and partly due to reduction in repatriation of profits by the multinational firm. The reduced repatriation also occurs from a decline in the rent of the multinational firm's capital. Of course, the positive income-augmenting effect of the tax on multinational investment should not be overdone. A large enough increase in the tax rate can drive the entire multinational capital out of the country, and the least amount of loss in real income would then be the tax revenue that would have been earned by a small tax. This suggests that there may exist an optimal $t^*$ which is given by $dI^*/dt^* = 0$.

So far we have discussed the implications of the host country's tax. If, however, the tax was imposed by the source country, the results concerning resource allocation would be reversed; so would the results concerning the real wage rate and the real rental earned by local firms in two countries. However, the rental earned by the multinationals will still decline.

What is the impact of the corporate income tax in either country on the source country's national income which is defined as

$$(26) \quad I = pX + Y + (1-t^*)(p^*X^* - w^*L_x^*)$$

Expanding and substituting as in equation (24) and differentiating, we obtain

$$(27) \quad \frac{dI}{dt^*} = \frac{t}{1-t} r_x \frac{dK_x}{dt^*} + K_x \frac{dr_x}{dt^*}$$
$$\phantom{(27) \quad \frac{dI}{dt^*} = } (+) \qquad\qquad (-)$$

$$- \left( p^*X^* - p^*X_L^* L^* - p^*X_K^* K_x^* \right)$$
$$\phantom{xxxxxxxxx} (+)$$

$$- (1-t^*)\left[ p^*\left( X_{LL}^* L_x^* + X_{LK}^* K^* \right) \frac{dL_x^*}{dt^*} \right.$$
$$\phantom{- (1-t^*)\left[ p^*\right.} (-) \qquad\qquad (-)$$

$$+ p^*\left( X_{KK}^* K_x^* + X_{LK}^* L_x^* \right) \frac{dK_x^*}{dt^*} \left. \right]$$
$$\phantom{+ p^*\left(\right.} (-) \qquad\qquad\qquad (-)$$

If initially there is no corporate income taxation in the source country so that $t=0$,

then $dI/dt^*$ is unambiguously negative. Differentiating (26) with respect to $t$,

$$(28) \quad \frac{dI}{dt} = \frac{t}{1-t} r_x \frac{dK_x}{dt} - (1-t^*)L_x \frac{dw^*}{dt}$$
$$\phantom{(28) \quad \frac{dI}{dt} = } (-) \qquad\qquad\qquad (+)$$

showing that the national income of the source country declines unambiguously.

The results derived in this section emphatically point out the strong degree of economic interdependence that the emergence of multinational firms has brought into existence. In traditional Heckscher-Ohlin trade models, a tax on the international investment in a small-country world simply lowers the earnings on such investments while leaving almost everything else unscathed. For example, there is no change in the distribution of income within each country because such distribution is related only to relative product prices which are constant for small countries. With regard to resource allocation, the outcome is of perfunctory interest for at least that country where complete specialization is assumed—not by choice but by considerations of logical consistency or determinacy.[13] Our analysis, however, shows that the international investment tax policy of one country is bound to affect resource allocation and income distribution in both countries even in a small-country world.

A word may be said about the perennial trade union clamor in the United States for granting lower tax credits on overseas profits of the multinational firms. The workers in either country benefit from an increase in the corporate tax in the other country which will drive the multinational capital away and so increase the real wage rate in the country which did not increase the tax. Although laborers in one country do not

[13]This problem arises in the Heckscher-Ohlin model, because factor rewards are related to the commodity price ratio, provided there is incomplete specialization. Factor supplies come into play only when there is complete specialization. For further details on this point, see Jones (1967). This problem, however, disappears in the specific factor model, because the number of factors exceed the number of goods. See Batra and Casas, for instance.

have the political clout to demand an increase in the tax rate in another country, a reduction in the tax credit given by the source country would be equivalent to an increase in the host country's taxes (as far as multinationals are concerned), thereby benefiting the workers in the source country. The hostility of *U.S.* trade unions to the favorable tax treatment received by multinationals becomes intelligible in the light of our model.

Finally, our analysis suggests that taxes on investment by the multinational firms can be used as a means of granting protection to import-competing industries. Thus to the traditional list of devices of protectionism, such as tariffs, production subsidies and quotas, our analysis adds another tool, namely the international investment tax, that enables a country to encourage production of import-competing industries, provided, of course, that such industries are operated by the local firms.

### III. Income Taxes on Local Firms

The implications of income taxes on the local firms are in sharp contrast to those of international investment taxes analyzed above: There are none. Such taxes simply lower the net rate of return earned by the local firms without causing any change in outputs or factor rewards. Since capital is specific to industries operated by the local corporations, it cannot move elsewhere in response to any taxes; similarly labor employed in local industries does not move to other industries. All that happens is that the local firms are poorer in proportion to the tax.[14]

### IV. Implications of Tariffs

As with international investment taxes, the effects of tariffs turn out to be substantially different from what is known from conventional wisdom. Here again the interdependent nature of the world economies

[14]Thus the effects of taxation on multinational and local firms are dramatically different. This asymmetry is not present in the Heckscher-Ohlin model.

comes to light. Suppose that goods produced by the multinationals in the host country are importable goods there and that the host country introduces a tariff on its imports, so that $p^* = p(1 + \tau^*)$ where $\tau^*$ is the tariff rate. Differentiating equilibrium condition (17) with respect to the tariff rate, we get

$$(29) \qquad [A][B] = [G]$$

where $[A]$ and $[B]$ are the matrices in (18') and

$$(30) \qquad [G] = - \begin{bmatrix} X_L^* d\tau^* \\ 0 \\ X_K^* d\tau^* \end{bmatrix}$$

From (29) we get (assuming for convenience that $t = t^* = 0$),

$$(31) \quad \frac{dL_x^*}{d\tau^*} = \{ X_L^* [ p^2 H_x + p X_{KK} Y_{LL}$$

$$+ p^* X_{KK}^* (p X_{LL} + Y_{LL}) ]$$

$$- X_K^* [ X_{LK}^* (p X_{LL} + Y_{LL}) ] \} + D$$

$$(32) \quad \frac{dK_x^*}{d\tau^*} = \{ (p^* X_{LL}^* + Y_{LL}^*)$$

$$\times (p X_{LL} + Y_{LL}) X_K^* - p^{*2} X_{LK}^* X_L^*$$

$$\times (p X_{LL} + Y_{LL}) \} + D$$

$$(33) \quad \frac{dL_x}{d\tau^*} = \{ (p^* X_{LL}^* + Y_{LL}^*) p X_{LK} X_K^*$$

$$- p p^* X_L^* X_{LK} X_{LK}^* \} + D$$

Here $dL_x^* / d\tau^* > 0$, $dK_x^* / d\tau^* > 0$ and $dL_x / d\tau^* < 0$. In other words, the host country's tariff induces capital to move there, employment of labor rises in $X^*$ and so does its output. In the source country the opposite happens: Capital moves away and employment of labor in $X$ declines and so does its output. At the same time $Y^*$ declines and $Y$ rises, where $Y$ is the importable good sector in the source country. Thus, we reach an unusual conclusion: *The tariff by* one country protects the import-competing industries in both countries. This also implies that tariffs by one country are much more restrictive of international trade than has been noted before. These results make an interesting comparison with those available from the conventional models of international investment where the tariff by a small country protects its own industry while leaving output levels unchanged in the other.

Let us now proceed to the implications of the tariff for real factor rewards. With $w^* = Y_L^*$

$$\frac{dw^*}{d\tau^*} = -Y_{LL}^* \frac{dL_x^*}{d\tau^*} > 0$$

$$\frac{dw}{d\tau^*} = -Y_{LL} \frac{dL_x}{d\tau^*} < 0$$

The wage rate rises in the host country and declines in the source country. Similarly, from $r_x = pX_K$ and $K_x + K_x^* = \bar{K}_x$,

$$\frac{dr_x}{d\tau^*} = p\left[ X_{KL} \frac{dL_x}{d\tau^*} + X_{KK} \frac{dK_x}{d\tau^*} \right]$$

$$= p\left[ \underset{(+)}{X_{KL}} \underset{(-)}{\frac{dL_x}{d\tau^*}} - \underset{(-)}{X_{KK}} \underset{(+)}{\frac{dK_x^*}{d\tau^*}} \right]$$

Thus, a priori nothing can be said about the response of the rental on capital owned by the multinational firms. As regards the return earned by local industries, since $r_y = Y_K$ and $r_y^* = Y_K^*$, we get

$$\frac{dr_y}{d\tau^*} = -Y_{KL} \frac{dL_x}{d\tau^*} > 0$$

and        $$\frac{dr_y^*}{d\tau^*} = -Y_{KL}^* \frac{dL_x^*}{d\tau^*} < 0$$

An intuitive explanation of these results is that a multinational firm shifts capital to the host country when the latter imposes a tariff. This leads to a shift of workers from $Y^*$ to $X^*$. The withdrawal of labor from local industries in the host country leads to an increase in the capital-labor ratio and a fall in the rent of capital in that sector. As for the multinational firm, employment of

capital and labor both increases in the host country and decreases in the source country. Because of the parallel movement of the two factors, the change in its rental is indeterminate.

In short, the implications of tariffs for income distribution in our model are completely different from the standard Heckscher-Ohlin model. There the distribution of income is determined by the Stolper-Samuelson theorem which lays emphasis on the factor-intensity differential in two industries within a country; and the tariff by one country, of course, makes no difference to factor rewards in the other country even when international investment is present.

## V. Tariffs on Goods Produced by Local Firms

If the host country imports $Y^*$ and imposes a tariff, then all the results derived above are reversed. This result contrasts with the similar case, examined in Section III, of the imposition of a tax imposed on the income earned by local firms. There, it may be recalled, the tax simply succeeded in collecting revenue from the local firms without affecting other economic variables.

In order to explore the consequences of the host country's tariff on $Y^*$, simply replace the first equation of system (17) by

$$p^* X_L^* = (1 + \tau_y^*) Y_L^*$$

with $t = t^* = 0$, and then differentiate totally.

It is interesting to note that protection granted to local firms will drive the multinational capital out, and although $r_y^*$ will rise, the real wage rate will decline in the host country. Thus, labor unions' proclivity for protection may turn out to be self-defeating if it is granted to goods produced by local firms.

## VI. Implications of Terms of Trade

Suppose there is an exogenous change in the terms of trade. The implications of this change in the conventional model are quite simple: The output of the relatively more expensive good rises, and so does the real reward of its intensive factor, whereas the real reward of its unintensive factor declines; and all this would occur in both countries. In addition, the effects of tariffs on resource allocation and income distribution are identical to those of changes in relative product prices.

In our model incorporating the phenomenon of the multinational corporation, the results turn out to be dramatically different. Let us assume, without loss of generality, that $t = t^* = \tau^* = 0$ so that $p = p^*$. Differentiating the system (17) totally with respect to $p$, we obtain

$$(34) \quad \frac{dL_x^*}{dp} = \left\{ X_L^* \left[ p^2 H_x + p^2 X_{LL} X_{KK} \right. \right.$$

$$\left. \left. + p X_{KK}^* (p X_{LL} + Y_{LL}) \right] - p^2 X_L X_{KL} X_{KL}^* \right\} \div D$$

$$(35) \quad \frac{dK_x^*}{dp} = \left\{ p X_L X_{KL} (p X_{LL}^* + Y_{LL}^*) \right.$$

$$\left. - p X_L^* X_{KL}^* (p X_{LL} + Y_{LL}) \right\} \div D$$

$$(36) \quad \frac{dL_x}{dp} = \left\{ X_L \left[ p^2 H_x^* + p^2 X_{LL}^* X_{KK} \right. \right.$$

$$\left. \left. + Y_{LL}^* (p X_{KK}^* + p X_{KK}) - p^2 X_L^* X_{KK} X_{LK}^* \right] \right\} \div D$$

All three equations are indeterminate in sign. Therefore, the effects of a change in the terms of trade on resource allocation, capital movements, and hence outputs in the two countries cannot be determined a priori. Similarly the response of factor rewards is also indeterminate.

Reasons for this ambiguity lie in the equation that determines the allocation of the multinational capital between the two countries. Looking at this equation in system (17), it may be observed that relative prices do not enter into this equation, although they do in the equations concerning labor allocation. The movement of capital from one country to the other is then determined by how in each country the price-induced change in labor allocation affects the marginal product of capital employed in the goods produced by the multinational firms. Suppose, for the moment, that $L_x$ and $L_x^*$ both rise in response to the

rise in the marginal value product of labor in $X$ and $X^*$ generated by the rise in $p$. With $X_{KL}$ and $X_{KL}^*$ positive, the marginal product of capital rises in both $X$ and $X^*$, and it is not clear which country exercises the greater pull for the multinational capital.

Indeed if the factors affecting $dK_x^*$ cancel out, so that $dK_x^* = 0$, then $dL_x$ and $dL_x^*$ become determinate. Because then from (35)

$$(p X_{LL} + Y_{LL}) = \frac{X_L X_{KL} (p X_{LL}^* + Y_{LL}^*)}{X_{LK}^* X_L}$$

and using this we obtain

$$\frac{dL_x^*}{dp} = \left\{ X_L^* (p^2 H_x + p X_{KK} Y_{LL}) \right.$$

$$\left. + \frac{X_L X_{KL}}{X_{KL}^*} \left[ p^2 H_x^* + p X_{KK}^* Y_{LL}^* \right] \right\} \div D$$

Thus $dL_x^*/dp$ and similarly $dL_x/dp$ are seen to be positive. If the multinational capital does not move in response to the change in the terms of trade, $L_x$ and $L_x^*$ go up and so do $X$ and $X^*$; $Y$ and $Y^*$ on the contrary decline and we obtain the expected results regarding the price output response.

The same restriction applies if we are interested in obtaining a clear-cut response of factor rewards to the change in $p$. If $dL_x^*/dp$ and $dL_x/dp$ are both positive, then the wage rate rises in both countries, because $dw^*/dp = - Y_{LL}^* (dL_x^*/dp)$ and $dw/dp = - Y_{LL}(dL_x/dp)$ are both positive. Similarly $r_x$ rises but $r_y$ and $r_y^*$ decline, because

$$\frac{dr_x}{dp} = X_K + X_{KL} \frac{dL_x}{dp}$$

$$\frac{dr_y}{dp} = - Y_{KL} \frac{dL_x}{dp}$$

$$\frac{dr_y^*}{dp} = - Y_{KL}^* \frac{dL_x^*}{dp}$$

All these results confirm what has been stated before, that the implications of tariffs on the one hand and those of the terms of trade on the other are dramatically different from each other. This is a novelty that flows from our model that incorporates some features of the multinational industries.

## VII. Conclusions

In this paper we have developed a general equilibrium model that incorporates many features of an international economy where the multinational firms have generated economic conditions which deserve a careful analysis. The framework developed here explains many observed phenomena that the conventional models of international trade and investment are not equipped to tackle. The model stresses the extreme degree of economic interdependence that the institution of multinational enterprise has ushered. All our results corroborate this central theme: that international economic policies pursued by one nation make waves in other nations even in a small-country world where relative prices are determined in world markets, with each nation taking the terms of trade as constant. Some of our results confirming this view are summarized below.

1. An income tax (or profit tax) on the multinational firms by any country drives their capital out and lowers their rate of return on capital stock and possibly on their specific factors, such as technology, managerial know-how, marketing techniques, etc.; the real wage rate declines in the tax-imposing country but rises in the other country. The international investment tax (or subsidy) can also be used for granting protection to import-competing industries —a policy device that requires no intervention in the goods market.

2. The profits tax on the local firms has no effect on other variables in any country; it merely lowers the rate of return on capital earned by the taxed sector.

3. One country's tariff stimulates the output of import-competing industries of not only that country but also of the other country. The real wage rate rises if the tariff is imposed on goods produced by the multinational firms but declines if the local firms are the beneficiaries of protection. The opposite occurs in the other country.

4. The implications of an exogenous

change in relative prices are different from a similar change effected by the tariff. This is an unusual feature of our model and is not present in other conventional models of international trade.

## REFERENCES

**Robert E. Baldwin and J. David Richardson,** *International Trade and Finance,* Boston 1974.

**Richard J. Barnett and Ronald E. Muller,** *Global Reach: The Power of the Multinational Corporations,* New York 1974.

**R. N. Batra and F. R. Casas,** "A Synthesis of Heckscher-Ohlin and Neoclassical Models of International Trade," *J. Int. Econ.,* Mar. 1976, *6,* 21–38.

_____ **and J. Hadar,** "Theory of the Multinational Firm: Fixed Versus Floating Exchange Rates," *Oxford Econ. Pap.,* July 1979, *31,* 258–69.

**R. E. Caves,** "International Corporations: The Industrial Economics of Foreign Investment," *Economica,* Feb. 1971, *38,* 1–27.

**T. Horst,** "The Theory of the Multinational Firm: Optimal Behaviour under Different Tariff and Tax Rates," *J. Polit. Econ.,* Aug. 1971, *79,* 1059–72.

**H. G. Johnson,** "The Efficiency and Welfare Implications of the International Corporation," in Charles P. Kindleberger, ed., *The International Corporation,* Cambridge, Mass. 1970.

**R. W. Jones,** "The International Capital Movements and the Theory of Tariffs and Trade," *Quart. J. Econ.,* Feb. 1967, *81,* 1–38.

_____, "A Three Factor Model in Theory, Trade and History," in Jagdish Bhagwati, et al., eds., *Trade, Balance of Payments and Growth: Essays in Honor of C. P. Kindleberger,* Amsterdam 1971.

**Murray C. Kemp,** *Theory of International Trade and Investment,* Englewood Cliffs 1969.

**H. Leibenstein,** "Allocative Efficiency vs. X-Efficiency," *Amer. Econ. Rev.,* June 1966, *56,* 392–415.

_____, "X-Inefficiency Xists—Reply to an Xorcist," *Amer. Econ. Rev.,* Mar. 1978,

68, 203–11.

C. F. Pratten, *Labour Productivity Differentials within International Companies*, Cambridge 1976.

Sidney E. Rolfe, "The International Corporation," Background Report, XII Congress, International Chamber of Commerce, Istanbul 1969.

W. F. Stolper and P. A. Samuelson, "Protection and Real Wages," *Rev. Econ. Stud.*, Nov. 1941, *9*, 58–73.

Jean J. Servan-Schreiber, *The American Challenge*, New York 1968.

T. Y. Shen, "Technology Diffusion, Substitution, and X-Efficiency," *Econometrica*, Mar. 1973, *41*, 263–84.

Jacob Viner, *The Customs Union Issue*, New York 1950.

# [4]

THE JOURNAL OF INDUSTRIAL ECONOMICS      0022-1821 $2.00

Volume XXXV      March 1987      No. 3

## PRODUCTION FLEXIBILITY AS A MOTIVE FOR MULTINATIONALITY

DAVID DE MEZA AND FREDERICK VAN DER PLOEG*

This paper examines how uncertainty in future operating costs at the time of undertaking long-lived and irreversible capital investment projects may provide an incentive for multinational production. This incentive may be present even if firms are risk-neutral, as long as they face a downward-sloping demand curve. The lower the international correlation between marginal cost shocks and the lower the elasticity of demand, the greater the benefit to establishing plants in different countries. However, even if cost fluctuations are perfectly correlated internationally, there may still be gains from multinational production.

## I. INTRODUCTION

A HORIZONTAL multinational enterprise (MNE) produces the same good in different countries. As Caves [1982, p. 3] lucidly puts it:

> Its existence requires, first, that *locational forces* justify spreading the world's production around so that plants are found in different national markets. Given this dispersion of production there must be some *transactional advantage* to placing the plants (some plants at least) under common administrative control.

The considerations relevant to the second requirement are natural extensions of Coase's [1937] seminal analysis of the nature of the firm. They have been developed in the MNE context by McManus [1972], Buckley and Casson [1976] and Markusen [1984] amongst others. The main idea is that the firm possesses an intangible asset, whose benefits can be made available at little extra cost to a large number of plants, but which cannot easily be sold in the market. Knowledge is the prime example (Caves [1982, pp. 3–15]). As for the locational forces, the most obvious is to economise on transport costs, import tariffs and other impediments to the international movement of inputs and outputs (e.g., Aliber [1970, p. 23]; de Meza [1979], [1980]).

This paper advances an additional locational incentive for horizontally integrated multinational production which does not seem to have been explicitly noted in the literature. When long-lived and irreversible capital investment projects are undertaken, future operating costs will be uncertain. Wage rates and the price of other locally supplied inputs will typically fluctuate in terms of domestic currency and exchange rates may be volatile for reasons unrelated to purchasing power parity considerations. Under these

---

*The authors are grateful to two referees for their constructive comments on a previous version of the paper.

344     DAVID DE MEZA AND FREDERICK VAN DER PLOEG

circumstances, it is impossible to be sure where in the world future production costs will be lowest. Establishing plants in a number of countries then enables the firm to relocate production, at least to some extent, once operating costs are known. Hence, even assuming risk-neutrality, there will be a motive for multinational production. The proposed model is therefore in the spirit of Waugh [1944] and Oi [1961], rather than Markowitz [1959] and Tobin [1958].

This production flexibility argument falls under the locational heading for it offers an explanation as to why plants should be sited in different countries, but not why they should be under common ownership. Standard transaction cost arguments potentially provide the answer to this question. They also underlie the crucial assumption of our model that companies cannot be completely footloose, able to close plants in one country and open them elsewhere at little cost. The reasons are straightforward. If premises are owned by the firm there are the search and transaction costs of buying and selling them. For related reasons, leases for rented property will not normally be of short duration and if they are, a high premium must typically be paid. Additionally, there are the costs of adapting premises for specialised use and installing suitable machinery. Perhaps, most importantly, the hiring and firing costs of attracting or dismissing a complete workforce are considerable.[1]

Insight into the production flexibility argument for multinationality can be obtained by examining the role of contracts designed to insure the company against production cost risk. According to our model, by allowing inter-plant production substitution, cost fluctuations increase expected profit. Hence, a risk-neutral company would not wish to enter into long-term contracts which effectively eliminate output variations. Consider first uncertainty over exchange rate changes. Whatever forward exchange contracts the company holds, the opportunity cost of producing at one location rather than another is obtained by converting costs denominated in terms of local currency into a common currency by means of spot exchange rates. If uncertainty is entirely due to exchange rate fluctuations, then forward exchange contracts, if available, enable the production strategy which maximises expected profit to be followed without subjecting the firm to any profit risk (the hedging strategy in de Meza and von Ungern-Sternberg [1980] can easily be adapted to the present case). The presence of forward exchange markets thus means our results apply in unchanged form to risk-averse firms.

Long-term labour contracts involve different issues. Even if such contracts are enforceable they normally preclude full participation in spot markets. That is to say, newly hired workers have to be paid the same wage as existing

---

[1] This does not mean that, for the fluctuations required in our model, labour is not a variable input. Even if the number of employees is effectively fixed, overtime hours may be flexible. Moreover, natural wastage may mean that reasonably small adjustments in the size of the workforce are relatively cheaply accomplished.

PRODUCTION FLEXIBILITY AS A MOTIVE FOR MULTINATIONALITY     345

workers. This, of course, eliminates the incentive to vary the workforce in the light of prevailing cost conditions. The possibility of taking out long-term labour contracts therefore faces the firm with a trade-off between risk and expected profit. This, of course, does not diminish the incentive for multi-nationality for, unless shocks to marginal cost are very similar in the various countries, the terms of the risk-return trade-off are improved when plants are spread around the world.

The remainder of this paper uses specific functional forms to provide a simple formalisation of the main idea. We abstract from transport costs, import tariffs, profit taxes and so on, in order to highlight the main features of our approach. Similarly, risk neutrality is assumed so as not to confuse the analysis with risk-pooling and risk-spreading behaviour (Caves [1982, pp. 25–29]), although section IV outlines how, in the absence of appropriate futures contracts, risk aversion alters the results. Within the framework of our model, price-taking behaviour is incompatible with multinational pro-duction. However, if the firm faces a downward sloping demand curve then multinational production may be advantageous. The model is therefore consistent with the stylised fact that multinational firms are most prevalent in concentrated markets (see Caves [1982, Chapter 4]). But contrary to commonly held beliefs, there is an incentive for multinational production, even if cost fluctuations are perfectly correlated between countries. This is because the variance of costs may still differ and so plants will not always be subject to the same cost schedules. Profitable inter-plant substitution opportunities then arise.

## II.  THE MODEL

The firm under consideration is a monopolist and faces a linear demand schedule of the form

(1)        $p = \alpha - \beta q, \quad \beta > 0$

where $p$ is the price of the product and $q$ is global production.[2] The cost of operating a plant is the same in each of the two countries in which production can take place and is given by

(2)        $C_i = \tfrac{1}{2}A_1 q_i^2 + (A_2 + u_i)q_i + A_3, \quad A_1, A_2, A_3 \geqslant 0$

where $u_i$ is a random variable with a mean of zero.[3] The fixed costs of $A_3$ are all sunk and marginal cost is thus $(A_1 q_i + A_2 + u_i)$. Since uncertainty enters additively, every unit of output requires a fixed quantity of the random input.

---

[2] This implies an integrated world market, but even if national markets are segmented the results would be little changed.

[3] Although the same good is produced in both countries, the conclusions also hold if the MNE is able to transfer different production processes between plants. The underlying idea can therefore also be applied to vertically integrated MNE's.

346                    DAVID DE MEZA AND FREDERICK VAN DER PLOEG

The fixed costs in opening and operating a plant is a force working to concentrate production in a few plants. That marginal variable cost is rising provides an incentive to spread production amongst a large number of plants. We suppose that the parameters of the cost and demand function are such that the appropriate number of plants to operate is two. Hence, only the location problem, the essence of the multinationality question, needs to be solved.

Given that the firm has a plant in both countries and that there are no transport costs, its profit is given by

(3) $\qquad \Pi = (\alpha - \beta q)q - \sum_{i=1}^{2} [\tfrac{1}{2}A_1 q_i^2 + (A_2 + u_i)q_i + A_3]$

where $q = q_1 + q_2$. After the plants have been installed, the uncertainty is resolved and the MNE selects its profit-maximising levels of output:

(4) $\qquad q = (2\hat{\alpha} - u_1 - u_2)/(4\beta + A_1)$

(5) $\qquad q_1 = [\hat{\alpha}A_1 - u_1 A_1 - 2\beta(u_1 - u_2)]/[(4\beta + A_1)A_1]$

and

(6) $\qquad q_2 = [\hat{\alpha}A_1 - u_2 A_1 - 2\beta(u_2 - u_1)]/[(4\beta + A_1)A_1]$

where $\hat{\alpha} = \alpha - A_2$. According to these three equations, the higher is realised marginal cost in a plant, the less output is produced there and the more is produced in the other plant. Enterprise marginal costs are also raised and so total output falls. That cost fluctuations give rise to both inter-plant output substitution and to variations in total production will be useful in interpreting our later results.

Substituting equations (4)–(6) into (3) and taking expectations yields the expected profit function

(7) $\qquad \mathbb{E}\Pi = [8\beta^2 + 6\beta A_1 + A_1^2](\sigma_1^2 + \sigma_2^2)/[2A_1(4\beta + A_1)^2]$
$\qquad\qquad - 2\beta\sigma_{12}/[A_1(4\beta + A_1)] + K$

where $\sigma_i^2$ is the variance of $u_i$, $\sigma_{12}$ is $\mathrm{cov}(u_1,u_2)$ and $K$ is a constant independent of $\sigma_1^2$, $\sigma_2^2$ and $\sigma_{12}$. To understand equation (7), note that if the levels of production in the two plants were set at certainty-equivalence levels, appropriate when $u_1 = u_2 = 0$, and maintained there whatever the realised value of the random disturbances, expected profit would be independent of mean-preserving increases in uncertainty ($\mathbb{E}\Pi = K$). It is the possibility of making ex-post production adjustments so as to take better advantage of changed cost structures that results in the possibility of expected profits being higher under uncertainty. Thus, the higher the variance in the shocks to marginal cost, the greater the adjustments in total output and in its division between plants. Expected profit is therefore higher. However, the higher the correlation between national cost shocks, the less scope there is for inter-plant substitution and therefore the lower is expected profit.

PRODUCTION FLEXIBILITY AS A MOTIVE FOR MULTINATIONALITY     **347**

The decision where to site the plants must be taken before costs are known. If $\sigma_2^2 = \sigma_1^2$ and $\sigma_{12} = \sigma_1^2$, then (7) shows the expected profits if both plants are located in country 1. It follows that siting a plant in each country rather than placing them both in country 1 raises expected profits if

$$(8) \qquad (8\beta^2 + 6\beta A_1 + A_1^2)(\sigma_2^2 - \sigma_1^2) + 4\beta(4\beta + A_1)\sigma_1(\sigma_1 - \rho\sigma_2) > 0$$

where $\rho \equiv \sigma_{12}/\sigma_1\sigma_2$ is the correlation coefficient between $u_1$ and $u_2$. Similarly, if producing in both countries is to be superior to locating both plants in country 2, it is necessary that

$$(9) \qquad (8\beta^2 + 6\beta A_1 + A_1^2)(\sigma_1^2 - \sigma_2^2) + 4\beta(4\beta + A_1)\sigma_2(\sigma_2 - \rho\sigma_1) > 0$$

holds. Multinational production therefore requires that inequalities (8) and (9) must both be satisfied.

### III.  INTERPRETATION OF THE RESULTS

To get a feel for the working of the model, some special cases will be examined. First suppose that the MNE is a price taker in the output market ($\beta = 0$). From (8) and (9) it follows that if the variance of fluctuations in marginal cost is the same in the two countries, expected profit is independent of plant location and the firm is therefore indifferent between production in country 1 and country 2. If cost variances differ internationally, expected profit is highest when both plants are situated in the high variance location. The reason is that, if demand is perfectly elastic, the profit maximising level of output of each plant is independent of the level of marginal cost in the other plant. Hence, there is no advantage in being able to re-schedule output between the plants and so no benefit from multinational production, for in this model such gains stem entirely from the profitability of inter-plant output substitution. Cost uncertainty does still raise expected profit because of the optimal variation in total output it allows. This source of gain is therefore maximised when both plants are situated in the high variance country, for this gives the greatest opportunity to adjust output in the light of cost fluctuations.

The next case we consider is the opposite extreme of completely inelastic demand. As $\beta$ tends to infinity, inequalities (8) and (9) both tend to

$$(10) \qquad \sigma_1^2 + \sigma_2^2 - 2\rho\sigma_1\sigma_2 = \text{var}(u_1 - u_2) \geqslant 0$$

implying that it is never more profitable to produce in a single country than to diversify.[4] With total output fixed by the vertical demand curve, the only issue is how to allocate production between the plants. When both plants are in the same country they are subject to exactly the same cost shocks and so

---

[4] As $\beta$ tends to infinity, demand shrinks to zero. But increasing $\alpha$ by $(\alpha - p)/\beta$ units for every unit increase in $\beta$ yields an elasticity-reducing pivot in the demand curve at $p$. Since $\alpha$ does not enter (8) or (9), the change in $\alpha$ does not affect our result.

348         DAVID DE MEZA AND FREDERICK VAN DER PLOEG

production will always be divided equally between them (remember marginal cost is rising). But when plants are in different countries there are opportunities for profitable intra-plant substitution. We now turn to the influence of the correlation between cost fluctuations in the two countries. It is clear from (10) that, for vertical demand curves, the incentive for multinational production decreases when the correlation between marginal costs in the two countries increases. Whatever the slope of the demand curve, when the shocks to marginal cost in the two countries are identical ($\sigma_1 = \sigma_2, \rho = 1$), (8) and (9) hold with equality and the firm is indifferent between national and multinational production. In both cases, the firm's expected profits are $\sigma_1^2/(4\beta + A_1) + K$. In effect, as far as economic conditions are concerned, there is really only one country.

The opposite extreme occurs when the shocks to country 1 are the exact opposite to those in country 2 ($u_1 = -u_2$ and thus $\sigma_1 = \sigma_2$ and $\rho = -1$). Inter-plant substitution possibilities are then maximised and, as long as there is some uncertainty, (8) and (9) show that multinationality is always the best strategy whatever the magnitude of the slope of the demand curve. This can be seen directly from the fact that expected profits under multinational production, $E\Pi = \sigma_1^2/A_1 + K$, are clearly greater than expected profits when both plants are located in the same country, $E\Pi = \sigma_1^2/(4\beta + A_1) + K$. Notice that the incentive to engage in multinational production increases as the slope of the demand curve, $\beta$, increases.

More generally, as long as cost fluctuations in the two countries are of equal variance but not identical ($\sigma_1 = \sigma_2$, $-1 \leqslant \rho < 1$) it will always be profitable to diversify production. Furthermore, the incentive to diversify is always inversely related to the correlation coefficient.

When variances differ between countries ($\sigma_1 \neq \sigma_2$) multinational production is possible even if cost fluctuations are perfectly correlated in the two countries ($\rho = 1$). There are then two offsetting influences on locational decisions. Producing only in the country with the highest variance gives the maximum opportunity for profitable variations in total output. But if $\sigma_1 \neq \sigma_2$ cost levels in the two countries will differ in most states of the world, even if $\rho = 1$. So locating in a single country foregoes the gains arising from inter-plant output substitution. The balance of advantage may therefore go either way. However, if shocks are highly correlated, multinational production is more likely to be profitable if demand is fairly inelastic.

### IV. THE INFLUENCE OF RISK AVERSION

So far we have been concerned with the maximisation of expected profit. As noted in the introduction, if complete futures markets are available, our results apply whatever the risk preferences of the firm. In the absence of such markets, and if the firm is risk averse, the variance of profits as well as its expected level matters. But if international cost fluctuations are imperfectly correlated and are not very much larger in one country than the other, multinational production also reduces the variance of profit. Risk-spreading incentives therefore augment production flexibility motives for multi-nationality. However, this particular result is due to the absence of demand uncertainty from the model. The following example shows that foreign production may then raise expected profit at the cost of an increase in risk.

Consider therefore a random shock to the demand curve, $\alpha = \bar{\alpha} + u$, where $\bar{\alpha}$ is known, $\mathbb{E}u = 0$ and $\text{var}(u) = \sigma^2$ and suppose that $u = u_1 = -u_2$ so that $\sigma^2 = \sigma_1^2 = \sigma_2^2 = -\sigma_{12} = \text{cov}(\alpha, u_1) = -\text{cov}(\alpha, u_2)$. This is a simple way to capture the idea that demand and cost fluctuations are closely linked in country 1, but negatively correlated in country 2 as may happen when all sales are made in country 1. Examining the implications for expected profit first, when both plants are located in country 1

$$(11) \qquad \mathbb{E}\Pi = K \equiv (\bar{\alpha} - A_2)^2/(4\beta + A_1) - 2A_3$$

but, when both plants are located in country 2,

$$(12) \qquad \mathbb{E}\Pi = 4\sigma^2/(4\beta + A_1) + K$$

It is therefore better for a risk-neutral firm to engage in off-shore than in home production. When there is demand uncertainty and the firm engages in multinational production,

$$(13) \qquad \mathbb{E}\Pi = 2\sigma^2(A_1 + 2\beta)/(4\beta + A_1)A_1 + K$$

so that multinational production is always more desirable than locating both plants at home. From (12) and (13) it follows that, when $A_1 > 2\beta$ holds, it is better for a risk-neutral firm to produce off-shore rather than engage in multinational production. Note that this is in contrast to the case of demand certainty, since, for this example, the firm always engages in multinational production, even if $A_1 > 2\beta$.

Let us now briefly examine the risk-spreading argument for this example. The profits when the firm locates both plants in country 1 are given by

$$\Pi = (\bar{\alpha} + u)(q_1 + q_2) - \beta(q_1 + q_2)^2 - \tfrac{1}{2}A_1 q_1^2 - (A_2' + u)q_1$$
$$- A_3 - \tfrac{1}{2}A_1 q_2^2 - (A_2 + u)q_2 - A_3$$
$$= \bar{\alpha}q - \beta q^2 - \tfrac{1}{2}A_1(q_1^2 + q_2^2) - A_2 q - 2A_3 + u(q - q_1 - q_2)$$

and in symmetric equilibrium is independent of stochastic shocks to demand or costs. It follows that, for the special case under consideration, locating both plants at home leads to a zero variance of profits. Since the profits under multinational or off-shore production depend on stochastic shocks to demand and costs, variances will then be strictly positive. Hence, a firm that only cares about minimising the variance of expected profits always chooses to produce at home, rather than off-shore or multinationally.

The point is that to avoid risk, the best strategy is to concentrate

350          DAVID DE MEZA AND FREDERICK VAN DER PLOEG

production in country 1, as the positive correlation between revenue and cost fluctuations in that country reduces the variance of profits. But this sacrifices most of the benefits of varying output in the light of realised demand and cost conditions. Minimising risk requires that production is located where the market is, but maximising expected profit favours off-shore or multinational production.

## V. CONCLUSIONS

Most microeconomic analyses of MNE's examine how total output will be divided between plants already established in various countries. The best known of these studies are probably those of Horst [1971], [1973]. The purpose of this paper is to offer an explanation as to why the plants should be located in different countries in the first place. The model makes the distinctive prediction that firms are more likely to be multinational if they face an inelastic demand curve. In addition, our model implies that plants will tend to be located in countries in which cost shocks are imperfectly correlated. This suggests that MNE's will tend to avoid locating all plants in a common currency area or in countries whose currencies are closely tied together. Of course, risk spreading gives an alternative incentive to diversify production. However, in the present model the motivation can exist even if risks are perfectly correlated internationally as long as demand is inelastic and the variance of cost shocks differs between countries. In contrast, conventional risk-spreading incentives for going multinational are consistent with price-taking behaviour, but not with perfect risk correlation. But, as with the risk-spreading model, the production flexibility approach provides a motive for the cross-hauling of foreign direct investment.

DAVID DE MEZA AND FREDERICK VAN DER PLOEG,          ACCEPTED JUNE 1986
*London School of Economics,*
*Houghton Street,*
*London, WC2A 2AE,*
*UK.*

### REFERENCES

ALIBER, R. Z., 1970, 'A Theory of Direct Foreign Investment', Chapter 1 in *The International Corporation. A Symposium*, C. P. KINDLEBERGER (ed.) (M.I.T. Press, Cambridge, Massachusetts).
BUCKLEY, P. J. and CASSON, M., 1976, *The Future of the Multinational Enterprise* (MacMillan, London).
ÇASSON, M., 1979, *Alternatives to the Multinational Enterprise* (Macmillan, London).
CAVES, R. E., 1982, *Multinational Enterprise and Economic Analysis* (Cambridge University Press, Cambridge).
COASE, R. J., 1937, 'The Nature of the Firm', *Economica*, 4 (November), pp. 386–405.

DE MEZA, D., 1979, 'A Theory of Multinational's Choice of Technique and Locational Decisions', *Economics Letters*, 2, pp. 67–71.

DE MEZA, D., 1980, 'LDC Policy Towards Multinational Companies: A Case for Payroll Taxes and Capital Subsidies', *Economics Letters*, 5, pp. 367–370.

DE MEZA, D. and VON UNGERN-STERNBERG, T., 1980, 'Market Structure and Optimal Stockholding: A Note', *Journal of Political Economy*, 88 (2), pp. 395–399.

HORST, T., 1971, 'The Theory of the Multinational Firm: Optimal Behaviour under Different Tariff and Tax Rules', *Journal of Political Economy*, 79, pp. 1059–1072.

HORST, T., 1973, 'The Simple Analytics of Multinational Firm Behaviour', in M. B. CONNOLLY and A. K. SWOBODA, eds., *International Trade and Money*, pp. 72–84 (George Allen and Unwin, London).

MCMANUS, J., 1972, 'The Theory of the International Firm', in G. PAQUET, ed. *The Multinational Firm and the Nation State* (Collier-MacMillan, Don Mills, Ontario).

MARKOWITZ, H. M., 1959, *Portfolio Selection* (Wiley, New York).

MARKUSEN, J., 1984, 'Multinationals, Multi-plant Economies and the Gains from Trade', *Journal of International Economics*, 16, pp. 205–226.

OI, W., 1961, 'The Desirability of Price Instability under Perfect Competition', *Econometrica*, 29 (January), pp. 58–64.

TOBIN, J., 1958, 'Liquidity Preference as Behaviour Towards Risk', *Review of Economic Studies*, 25, pp. 65–86.

WAUGH, F. V., 1944, 'Does the Consumer Benefit from Price Instability?', *Quarterly Journal of Economics*, 58, pp. 602–614.

# Part III
# Market Structure
# and Oligopolistic Reaction

# [5]

EDWARD M. GRAHAM

# Transatlantic investment
# by multinational firms:
# a rivalistic phenomenon?

The spread and growth of multinational corporations over the past two decades raise major public policy questions. Unfortunately, understanding of the economic behavior of the multinational corporation is incomplete. For example, the usual hypotheses of international investment may not be entirely adequate to explain direct investment by European multinational corporations in the United States. Thus, a new hypothesis, based upon rivalistic behavior among firms, is presented and tested.[1] It is concluded that this hypothesis might add some additional explanatory power with policy implications for European direct investment in the United States.

## FOREIGN DIRECT INVESTMENT AND HYPOTHESES TO EXPLAIN IT

Although foreign direct investment and the multinational corporation have been studied extensively for over a decade and a half, a unified, generally accepted theory on why foreign direct investment takes place is lacking. Existing, hypotheses must be viewed largely as partial explanations.

The author is Assistant Professor of Management at MIT. He gratefully acknowledges helpful commentary on earlier drafts of this article by Raymond Vernon, C. P. Kindleberger, and the editors of this journal.

[1] The term "rivalry" (and its linguistic derivatives) is used here to denote competitive conduct among firms within an oligopolistic industry. The term "competition" is not used because, formally, "competition" denotes conduct among firms in a perfectly competitive industry, in which the output decisions of no one firm can affect levels of aggregate supply or price. The essence of oligopoly is that output decisions of each of a number of individual firms can have an impact upon aggregate demand, and hence these individual firms can affect price. Because any of several firms holds the power to affect price, each of these firms must anticipate the future reactions of rival firms to its own pricing and output practices when attempting to set these practices so as to maximize profitability. See Caves (1972, ch. 2) and Klein (1977, chs. 1 and 2).

Although developing nations are host to much foreign direct investment, the major locus of such investment has been the industrialized nations; the hypothesis economists most easily accept to explain this is the investment analogue to the factor proportion theory of international trade. Under this analogue, capital flows from nations in which it is the relatively abundant factor to those in which it is relatively scarce.[2] For this to hold, it must be assumed that the capital-exporting and capital-importing nations possess similar technology and entrepreneurial knowledge, that international investment results in real capital movements, and that factor markets are competitive.

Table 1

## Stocks of Foreign Direct Investment in and by Selected Industrialized Nations

(millions of dollars)

|  | Foreign direct investment by | Foreign direct investment in |
|---|---|---|
| United States (1971) | 78,090 | 13,704 |
| Canada (1967) | 3,728 | 19,166 |
| United Kingdom (1965) | 16,795 | 5,549 |
| Federal Republic of Germany (1970) | 5,775 | 5,861 |

*Source:* United Nations, *Multinational Corporations in World Development* (New York, 1973), Tables 5, 10, 21, and 22.

Despite its intuitive appeal, the factor endowment hypothesis cannot explain why industrialized nations should be both importers and exporters of direct investment capital. (See Table 1.) Additionally, this hypothesis would predict that international portfolio investment should flow from a relatively capital-rich nation such as the United States (during the 1950s and 1960s) into a relatively capital-poor region such as Western Europe. During the decade 1955-65, however, there was a net flow of long-term portfolio investment from Western Europe into the United States. (See Table 2.) This suggests the possibility of imperfect capital markets (Levy and Sarnat, 1970; Stevens, 1972; Ragazzi, 1973; Aho, 1974).

[2]A substantial body of literature has developed on the basis of this hypothesis, dating from Keynes (1924). For a survey, see Dunning (1973).

*JOURNAL OF POST KEYNESIAN ECONOMICS*

Table 2

## U.S. International Long-Term Investment Position*
## Year-end 1958 and 1968, with Respect to Western Europe

(millions of dollars)

|  | 1958 | 1968 | Net change |
|---|---|---|---|
| U.S. private long-term claims on Western Europe | 1,793 | 4,692 | 2,899 |
| European private long-term claims on the United States | 5,698 | 13,244 | 7,546 |
| Net European private long-term claims on the United States | 3,905 | 8,552 | 4,647 |

*Source:* U.S. Department of Commerce, *Survey of Current Business,* October 1969, p. 24; U.S. Department of Commerce, *Balance of Payments Statistical Supplement,* 1963, Table 83.

*Other than direct investment.

    Empirically, perhaps the principal shortcoming of the factor endowment hypothesis is that it fails to suggest a reason for the existence of an industry bias in investment flows. U.S. foreign direct investment in the 1960s and 1970s, however, has been heavily industry specific. (See Table 3.)

    Most foreign direct investment (by value) is of two types: horizontal extension of a firm's activities (producing the same goods elsewhere that are produced at home) or vertical integration backwards (production of raw materials) (Caves, 1971). Foreign direct investment among the industrialized nations of North America and Western Europe tends to be predominantly of the former type, while the latter type is most prevalent in the developing nations.[3] The motivation for vertical foreign direct investment seems relatively self-evident, and thus attention is turned to horizontal direct investment.

    The industry-specific nature of horizontal foreign direct investment has led a number of economists to turn to the framework of industrial organization in order to explain this investment (Hymer, 1976; Vernon, 1966; Caves, 1971; Horst, 1972). The principal hypothesis is that horizontal direct investment results from the possession by certain firms of proprietary intangible assets, such as technological expertise or entrepreneurial

---

[3]And, it might be added, vertical investment is also prevalent in sparsely populated developed nations such as Australia and Canada.

Table 3

Average Yearly Private Investment in Plant and Equipment by U.S. Industry in the United States and by European Affiliates of U.S. Firms in Europe, 1966-74, by Industry

(billions of dollars)

| Industry | (A)<br>Investment in the<br>United States | (B)<br>Investment in<br>Europe | (C)<br>(B) ÷ (A) |
|---|---|---|---|
| All industries | 80.86 | 5.92 | 0.07 |
| Mining and smelting | 2.20 | 0.01 | 0.04 |
| Petroleum | 5.57 | 1.23 | 0.22 |
| Manufacturing | 26.80 | 3.73 | 0.14 |
|   Food products | 2.49 | 0.19 | 0.08 |
|   Paper and paper<br>   products | 1.64 | 0.12 | 0.07 |
|   Chemicals | 3.80 | 0.66 | 0.17 |
|   Rubber and rubber<br>   products | 0.99 | 0.10 | 0.10 |
|   Metals | 4.92 | 0.37 | 0.08 |
|   Machinery, except<br>   electrical | 3.25 | 1.14 | 0.35 |
|   Electrical machinery | 2.10 | 0.30 | 0.14 |
|   Transportation equip-<br>   ment | 2.77 | 0.50 | 0.18 |
|   Other manufacturing | 4.84 | 0.35 | 0.07 |
| Transport, utilities, com-<br>  munications, commerce, and<br>  finance | 45.37 | 0.90 | 0.02 |

*Source:* Calculated by author from data in U.S. Department of Commerce, *Survey of Current Business* (various issues).

skills, that generate economic rents for these firms.[4] If the opportunity cost of exploiting these assets in foreign markets is low relative to the potential return, foreign direct investment results.

Exactly why certain firms should possess intangible assets not easily acquired by other firms is a moot question. In an early work, Stephen Hymer (1976) postulated that monopolistic power enables some firms to

---

[4]The argument is made that, without these intangible assets, a firm would operate at a disadvantage in a foreign market relative to locally based firms. See Kindleberger (1969) and Caves (1971); see also Dunning (1974).

maintain advantages in the form of "superior" knowledge or economies of scale.[5] This postulate assumes the prior existence of monopoly, begging the question of the origin of the monopoly position in the first place. Raymond Vernon (1970, ch. 3) argues that characteristics specific to certain (geographically defined) markets cause firms operating principally within those markets to become more innovative than rivals operating outside those markets. Vernon does not indicate, however, why some firms should be more innovative within a given market. Building upon Hymer's and Vernon's reasoning and a contribution by Harry Johnson (1970), Stephen Magee (1977a; 1977b) argues that the ability of a firm to appropriate a rent from an investment in the creation of new knowledge is the key to whether or not that firm can possess unique intangible assets. The ability to appropriate a rent, by Magee's reasoning, is a function of both the absolute scale of the firm and the market power possessed by the firm.[6] Again, however, little is said about how a particular firm initially achieves this prerequisite scale and market power.

Normatively, industries in which horizontal foreign direct investment based on exploitation of intangible assets occurs must be characterized by an oligopolistic industry structure, resulting from high barriers to entry associated with the high opportunity cost of generating the intangible assets. The possession of intangible assets may enable a firm to achieve a high degree of product differentiation. If the assets are technological in nature, the differentiation may take the form of a technically superior product, while if the assets are entrepreneurial, the differentiation might result from more subjective considerations such as appeals created by advertising.

The alternative of foreign direct investment must be weighed against other alternatives for serving foreign markets, such as exporting or licensing. Richard Caves (1971, pp. 6-9) argues that rents are higher for the direct investment alternative than for other alternatives if the rent-yielding knowledge is primarily manifested by product differentiation rather than by organizational or managerial skills. Raymond Vernon (1970, ch. 3) suggests that exportation is the preferred alternative until foreign competitors are on the verge of developing their own intangible assests for competing with the exporting firm. When foreign competition appears, direct investment becomes necessary for the exporting firm to protest its rents.

[5]Hymer (1976) presented empirical evidence to show that propensity for foreign direct investment to occur was greater in highly concentrated industries than in less concentrated industries. Because empirical evidence demonstrates that economies of scale in production cannot account for levels of industry concentration in the United States (see Scherer, 1970, ch. 4; Jorgenson, 1972), most efforts to develop Hymer's reasoning have tended to emphasize "superior knowledge" or "technology" as the major intangible asset possessed by multinational firms.

[6]Key to Magee's reasoning is the fact that there are significant economies of scale in the creation of new knowledge. For an elaboration, see Magee (1977c).

Empirical tests of industrial organization hypotheses are encouraging. Industries marked by U.S. outbound foreign direct investment are found to be characterized by a high intensity of research and development, extensive product differentiation, and high market concentration (one measure of oligopoly) (Hymer, 1960; Wells, 1969; Hymer and Rowthorne, 1970; Knickerbocker, 1974).

## EUROPEAN DIRECT INVESTMENT IN THE UNITED STATES: A DEFENSIVE PHENOMENON?

Industrial organization hypotheses have been advanced largely as explanations of post-World War II foreign direct investment by U.S.-based firms. During the late 1960s and 1970s, however, there has been large-scale expansion of the multinational activities of European firms, and a significant amount of European horizontal investment has flowed into the United States.[7] (See Table 4.)

Table 4

## Book Value of Stock of Direct European Investment in the United States at Year-end, Various Years

(millions of dollars)

| | | Sector | | |
|---|---|---|---|---|
| Year | Petroleum | Manufacturing | Finance and insurance | Total |
| 1950 | 349 | 669 | 870 | 2,228 |
| 1960 | 1,028 | 1,611 | 1,504 | 4,707 |
| 1965 | 1,478 | 2,167 | 1,724 | 6,076 |
| 1970 | 2,777 | 4,091 | 1,805 | 9,554 |
| 1972 | 3,011 | 4,836 | 3,011 | 11,087 |
| 1974 | 4,714 | 6,109 | 4,423 | 16,756 |
| 1976 | 4,984 | 7,421 | 5,796 | 19,916 |

*Source:* For 1974 and 1976 data, U.S. Bureau of Economic Analysis, "Foreign Direct Investment in the United States," *Survey of Current Business*, October 1977; earlier data from U.S. Commerce Department, *Statistical Abstract of the United States*, 1976.

Conceivably, the determinants of European horizontal foreign direct investment in the United States are corollary to those of U.S. investment in Europe; that is, European firms possess proprietary intangible assets that would yield to these firms rents from direct investment in the United

[7]See Franko (1976) for a survey of European multinationalism.

Table 5

## Sales in Europe by U.S. Multinational Firms and Sales in the United States by European Multinational Firms

(billions of dollars)

|  | (A)<br>Sales by affiliates of<br>U.S.-based companies<br>in Europe (1973) | (B)<br>Sales by a sample of<br>affiliates of European-<br>based companies in the<br>United States (1975) |
|---|---|---|
| All industries | 127.30 | 51.17 |
| Mining and smelting | 0.55 | 0.00 |
| Petroleum | 25.15 | 10.38 |
| Manufacturing | 75.25 | 18.31 |
| Food products | 6.26 | 3.90 |
| Paper products | 2.41 | 0.37 |
| Chemicals, etc. | 13.78 | 6.53 |
| Rubber products | 1.63 | 0.65 |
| Primary and<br>fabricated metals | 6.12 | 1.26 |
| Machinery except<br>electrical | 14.71 | 1.33 |
| Electrical machinery | 8.35 | 2.29 |
| Transportation equipment | 14.07 | 0.10 |
| Other manufacturing | 7.94 | 1.88 |
| Other industries | 13.19 | 4.17 |

*Source:* Column A: U.S. Department of Commerce, *Survey of Current Business*; column B: compiled by the author from data presented in *Across the Board*, the Conference Board, December 1976.

*Note:* Sales figures were used because of the unavailability of disaggregated investment figures.

States.[8] No strong test has been provided for this hypothesis; one argument against it is that there appears to be a positive correlation between industries in which U.S. firms operate in Europe and those in which European firms operate in the United States. (See Table 5.) Intuition suggests that it is unlikely direct cross-investment would occur if the investment were motivated solely by industry-specific intangible assets.

[8]This possibility is explored by McClain (1974) and is favored by Franko (1976).

TRANSATLANTIC INVESTMENT BY MULTINATIONAL FIRMS

An alternative hypothesis is that European direct investment in the United States is defensive in nature.[9] The basic assumption underlying this hypothesis is that the initial entry by a foreign subsidiary into a market is likely to disrupt established patterns of conduct within that market, since the foreign subsidiary engages in pricing and product strategies designed to capture some of the market share from local firms. If the foreign firm brings into local markets special intangible assets, the foreign firm either will be more efficient or will be able to produce a differentiated product preferred by local consumers. Thus, the entry of the foreign firm into a stable oligopoly might disrupt patterns of oligopoly conduct and stimulate rivalrous behavior on the part of local firms, manifested in the home market of the local firms and the home market of the foreign firm.

In the home market of the local firms, rivalry could engender intra-industrial mergers, retaliatory pricing behavior, or aggressive product differentiation. Intraindustrial merger would be an effective response to foreign firm entry if the advantages possessed by the foreign firm were based upon scale.[10] Retaliatory pricing would be a viable strategy if a "limit price" could be found that would deter entry by the foreign firm. Aggressive product differentiation might be an effective strategy in industries where consumer tastes are an important determinant of purchasing decisions; presumably, domestic firms would be more intimately familiar with the tastes of domestic consumers than would foreign firms.

The rivalry could be extended to the foreign firm's home market if: (1) domestic firms themselves possessed or were able to develop intangible assets that would yield rents in this market; or (2) the stability of the home market of the foreign firm could be disrupted. The first case is an extension of the industrial organization hypothesis presented in the first section of this paper, with the difference that in this formulation it is the disruption of the domestic firm's market that stimulates its efforts in the foreign firm's home market. The second case suggests a purely retaliatory defensive move by the domestic firm: if it can threaten the intruder in the latter's home market, the foreign firm might cease its rivalrous strategy in the domestic market.[11]

---

[9] Defensive considerations as possible motivations for international direct investment have been mentioned by a number of authors, including Hymer (1976), Lamfalussy (1963), Kindleberger (1969, p. 26), Hymer and Rowthorne (1970), Caves (1971, p. 16), Sametz (1973), and Vernon (1977). Examples of defensive investment are reported in Graham (1974).

[10] There is evidence to suggest that U.S. entry into European markets has stimulated intra-European merger. See *Third Report on Competition Policy* (Brussels: E.E.C. Commission, 1974).

[11] For a more extensive discussion, see Graham (1974) and McClain (1974).

*JOURNAL OF POST KEYNESIAN ECONOMICS*

## A TEST OF THE RIVALRY HYPOTHESIS

A test is presented here of the rivalry hypothesis. The test is a coarse one, but the results are consistent with the hypothesis.

It is evident that the spread of the activities of U.S.-based multinational firms into Europe has generally preceded the entry of European firms into the United States. Thus, it is assumed here that if rivalrous behavior induces transatlantic foreign direct investment, it is European investment in the United States stimulated by previous entry of U.S. firms into Europe. For the $i$th European firm, investment in the United States in the $j$th industry in the year $t$ would be triggered by direct investment by U.S. firms in the European firm's home market in years prior to $t$. Thus, for industry $j$,

$$(1) \qquad I_{i,t} = \sum_m \sum_k (B_{k,m} I_{k,t-m}) + U_{i,t}.$$

where $I_{i,t}$ is a direct investment in year $t$ in the United States by European firm $i$; $I_{k,t-m}$ is a direct investment in year $t-m$ in the European home market of firm $i$ by U.S. firm $k$; $B_{k,m}$ is a coefficient, positive in value or zero, reflecting the prior probability that firm $i$ will react to firm $k$ after a lag of $m$ years; $U_{i,t}$ is an error term.

If we assume that $B_{k,m}$ is independent of the value of $k$, which would be true if the European firm reacted identically to direct investment in European markets by any U.S. firm or combination of firms, then $B_{k,m} = B_m$ for all $k$ and equation (1) can be written as

$$(2) \qquad I_{i,t} = \sum_m B_m I_{t-m} + U_{i,t}$$

which is a distributed lag equation.

A priori it is difficult or impossible to specify by means of theoretical reasoning the exact form of the relationship implied by equation (2); for example, $B_m$ might be zero for certain $m$. In particular, if there is lead time between the decision of firm $i$ to respond and the actual beginning of investment, $B_m$ might be zero for $m = 0, 1, 2, \ldots, n$ where $n$, the lead time in years, might be highly unpredictable.

Availability of data poses a major problem for those seeking to do empirical research on foreign direct investment. Disaggregated data on foreign direct investment is not published by governmental or international agencies. The data used by this author were gathered at Harvard University by the Multinational Enterprise Project from a sample of 187 U.S. multinational firms and 88 European multinational firms.[12] Working from this data base, the author attempted to construct a few simple models, the most

---

[12]The data base is described thoroughly in Vaupel and Curhan (1973).

uncomplicated of which was to examine the relationship:

$$(3) \qquad\qquad Y_{i,t} = B_{i,t-m} \, X_{i,t-m} + U_{i,t-m},$$

where $Y_{i,t}$ is the number of manufacturing subsidiaries of 88 European multinationals established (or acquired) in the United States in industry $i$ in year $t$; $X_{i,t-m}$ is the number of manufacturing subsidiaries of the 187 U.S. multinationals established in Europe in industry $i$ in year $t - m$.

Table 6 indicates the beta coefficients ($B_{i,\,t-m}$) calculated from equation (3) for years ($t$) 1950 to 1970, lag times ($m$) 0 years to 11 years, and industries ($i$) classified by two-digit SIC code. Statistically significant beta coefficients are found over a range of lag times for several industry groupings, notably food products, chemical products, petroleum refining, primary metals, fabricated metals, nonelectrical machinery, electrical machinery, transportation, and instruments, indicating some sort of lagged relationship between U.S. direct investment in Europe and European direct investment in the United States in those industries. The fact that the lagged relationship differs from industry to industry (and does not exist in some industries) suggested that the lag is not explained by an exogenous factor common to all industries, such as a change in currency exchange rates.

The value of the $R^2$ statistic corresponding to the maximum calculated beta coefficient for each industry in Table 6 was regressed against measures of industry concentration, product differentiation within the industry, and research and development intensiveness of the industry. Bivariate regressions of each of these yield the parameters indicated in Table 7.[13] An intercorrelation matrix of the three "independent" variables is presented in Table 8.

These statistics show that high values of the "maximum $R^2$" statistic are positively associated with high values of measures of industry concentration, product differentiation, and research and development intensiveness in an industry, but that these three variables are not statistically independent of one another. Additional information is gained by a stepwise regression of "maximum $R^2$" as the "dependent" variable and the product differentiation and research and development intensiveness measures as "independent" variables, which indicates that these two variables are surrogate for one another (i.e., high values of "maximum $R^2$" are positively

---

[13]The four-firm concentration ratio was aggregated to the two-digit SIC level by calculating the (value added) weighted average of ratios of each four-digit category within each two-digit category. The product differentiation variable was calculated as the standard deviation of unit values divided by mean unit values of U.S. exports, by SITC category. SITC values were converted into SIC values at the four-digit level. Because the correspondence between SIC and SITC categories is not exact, the conversion was only approximate. Two-digit SIC values were calculated as valued-added weighted averages of four-digit values.

Table 6

# Beta Coefficients Calculated from Lag Equation (3)

| 2-digit SIC industry code | Industry | Lag time M | | | | | | | | | | | |
|---|---|---|---|---|---|---|---|---|---|---|---|---|---|
| | | 0 | 1 | 2 | 3 | 4 | 5 | 6 | 7 | 8 | 9 | 10 | 11 |
| 20 | Foodstuffs and products | .09* | .14* | .61 | .69 | .65 | .70 | .77 | .76 | .88 | .71 | .53 | .75 |
| 21 | Tobacco | — | — | — | — | — | — | — | — | — | — | — | — |
| 22 | Textiles | .15* | .19* | .34* | .38* | .24* | .08* | .19* | -.19* | -.08* | -.26* | -.34* | -.23* |
| 23 | Apparel | — | — | — | — | — | — | — | — | — | — | — | — |
| 24 | Wood and lumber | -.15* | -.15* | .11* | .50 | -.01* | -.13* | -.11* | .15* | .64 | -.09* | -.07* | — |
| 25 | Wooden products, furniture | -.10* | -.10* | -.10* | -.10* | .32* | -.09* | -.07* | -.05* | -.05* | -.05* | -.05* | -.05* |
| 26 | Paper and paper products | -.10* | -.05* | -.24* | -.09* | .14* | .13* | .26* | .23* | .29* | .61 | .47* | .51 |
| 27 | Printing and publishing | -.33* | -.06* | .02* | .39* | .37* | .41* | .44* | .07* | -.04* | -.01* | .04* | .15* |
| 28 | Chemicals, drugs, plastics | -.30* | -.09* | .19* | .42* | .61 | .79 | .86 | .82 | .79 | .89 | .87 | .82 |
| 29 | Petroleum refining | .05* | -.15* | -.15* | .41* | .61 | .49 | .25 | .44* | .34* | .41* | .41* | .01* |
| 30 | Rubber and plastics products | -.02* | -.18* | -.21* | -.23* | .30 | .08* | .33* | -.06* | .09* | .00* | .43* | .55 |
| 31 | Leather products | — | — | — | — | — | — | — | — | — | — | — | — |
| 32 | Stone, glass, clay | -.50 | -.31* | -.35* | .14* | .15* | .00* | .04* | .44* | .20* | .34* | .34* | .34* |
| 33 | Primary metals | -.14* | .03* | -.02* | .27* | .48 | .65 | .36* | .67 | .51 | .67 | .45 | .70 |
| 34 | Fabricated metals | -.11* | -.10* | .18* | .36* | .46* | .64 | .61 | .71 | .63 | .62 | .84 | .62 |
| 35 | Machinery, except electrical | .19* | .41* | .39* | .41* | .58 | .45* | .56 | .41* | .31* | .34 | .27 | .37 |
| 36 | Electrical machinery | -.13* | -.12* | -.16* | .34* | .19* | .43* | .56 | .44* | .54 | .63 | .62 | .73 |
| 37 | Transportation | .20* | .56 | .80 | .49 | .58 | .50 | .26* | .34* | .42* | .22* | .09* | -.15* |
| 38 | Instruments | .00* | -.08* | .05* | .26* | .60 | .43* | .50 | .60 | .91 | .44* | .35* | .17* |

*Coefficients marked by an asterisk are *not* significantly different from 0 in a one-tailed *t* test, 99 percent confidence interval.

*TRANSATLANTIC INVESTMENT BY MULTINATIONAL FIRMS*

Table 7

## Correlation Between $R^2$ and Measures of Industry Concentration, Product Differentiation, and R&D/Value Added

| Variables compared | Beta coefficient | $R^2$ | Significance |
|---|---|---|---|
| $R^2$ and four-firm concentration index | 0.568 | 0.322 | 0.99 |
| $R^2$ and product differentiation | 0.504 | 0.254 | 0.98 |
| $R^2$ and R&D expense/value added | 0.468 | 0.219 | 0.98 |

associated with industries having high measures of both product differentiation and research and development intensiveness, but neither measure adds "explanation" over that accounted for by the other). Further stepwise regression indicates that the industry concentration measure adds "explanation" of the variance in "maximum $R^2$" over that yielded by the research and development or the product differentiation measure.

These results follow from the intercorrelation of the three "independent" measures, as indicated in Table 8. How to interpret the information presented in this table is perplexing. High levels of industry concentration are positively associated with high rates of investment in research and development in the same industries. High rates of investment in research and development are also positively associated with high degrees of product differentiation. High degrees of product differentiation, however, are not positively associated with high levels of industry concentration!

These seemingly paradoxical conclusions might be explained in one of

Table 8

## Beta Coefficients: Intercorrelation Matrix and Three Variables

| | Four-firm concentration index | Product differentiation | R&D/value added |
|---|---|---|---|
| Four-firm concentration index | 1.000 | -0.026* | 0.471 |
| Product differentiation | | 1.000 | 0.596 |
| R&D/value added | | | 1.000 |

*Coefficient not statistically significant at 95 percent confidence level.

three ways. First, the underlying data are highly aggregated, and a distortion of the statistical results might have followed. (The data on U.S. investment activities of European firms cannot meaningfully be disaggregated, and so the high level of aggregation is, for this exercise, a necessary evil.) Second, the measure of product differentiation used here — the standard deviation of unit values of internationally traded products within an industrial category, divided by the mean unit value — might present an inaccurate picture of product differentiation. In particular, if there were many variations on a product of approximately equal price within an industry, the product differentiation would not be recognized by this measure.

Both of these reasons suggest that the apparent paradox of Table 8 is due to statistical error. The third does not. If there exist: (1) some industries that are highly concentrated, highly research and development intensive, and characterized by a low level of product differentiation; (2) other industries that are highly research and development intensive, characterized by a high degree of product differentiation, but have fragmented market structures; and (3) still other industries that are fragmented, non-research and development intensive, and not characterized by product differentiation, the results of Table 8 could follow. The relationships between industry market structure, industry propensities to invest in research and development, and the extent of product differentiation within an industry are not well explored at either the theoretical or the empirical level, and future research should be addressed to these issues.

From the data presented, it would seem that high values of "maximum $R^2$" occur in industries with high measures of industry concentration, independent of the level of product differentiation or research and development intensiveness, but also in industries with high measures of product differentiation and research and development intensiveness, independent of the level of industry concentration. These results are generally consistent with the hypothesis that European direct investment in the United States occurs as a result of rivalistic behavior in oligopolistic industries, stimulated by U.S. direct investment in Europe. The results present some puzzles, however, and fall short of proving the case.

## PUBLIC POLICY CONSEQUENCES OF THE RIVALRY HYPOTHESIS

If the principal hypothesis of this paper is accepted — that is, that direct investment in Europe by U.S. firms has induced direct investment in the United States by European firms — two consequences follow of public policy significance. First, the degree to which international investment will

*TRANSATLANTIC INVESTMENT BY MULTINATIONAL FIRMS*

cause specialization in production to occur between the United States and
Europe will be reduced. Second, patterns of conduct of firms within major
industrial groups will (possibly) be altered.

The first consequence has particular relevance to recent controversy in
U.S. government circles over whether U.S. foreign direct investment reduces labor's share of national income or results in a net "export" of jobs
within manufacturing industries (as the U.S. organized labor movement
generally contends). If U.S. investment in Europe stimulates European
investment in the United States of roughly equal magnitude, the net result
on either labor share of income or levels of employment would be slight.
(This assumes that European investors use production techniques similar
to those utilized by U.S. investors.) To date, European direct investment in
the United States has not been nearly as great as that of the United States in
Europe, although during the 1970s the former has grown more rapidly than
the latter.

If foreign direct investment results in a flow of real capital, then because
U.S. capital exports have not been fully offset by inward direct investment,
labor's share of national income might have been lower than it would have
had no foreign investment taken place. The exact magnitude of the reduction in labor's share of income depends upon the elasticity of substitution
between domestic investment and foreign investment. This elasticity of
substitution doubtlessly varies considerably from industry to industry (and
even from firm to firm within an industry). Consequently, attempts to
demonstrate that aggregate foreign direct investment of the United States
has altered significantly labor's share of national income are moot.[14]

The contention of U.S. organized labor that foreign direct investment by
U.S.-based firms causes a numerical loss of job opportunities is also usually
viewed with skepticism.[15] Unilateral foreign direct investment may lead to
greater specialization of production between investor and host nation, and
hence to a redistribution of resources among industries within both nations. Thus, there will be a reduction of employment within certain industries in the investor nation and expansion of employment in other industries.
In the contracting industries, organized labor naturally would contend that
multinational companies are causing unemployment. Cross-investment

[14]In a report widely cited in U.S. government circles, Peggy Musgrave uses an
econometric model to demonstrate a relative loss of share of income to U.S. labor
resulting from foreign direct investment by U.S. firms. Musgrave, however, assumes that
the primary effect of foreign direct investment is to transfer real capital from the (static)
stock of capital of the United States to overseas stocks of capital. This is equivalent to
assuming that the elasticity of substitution (for a U.S. multinational firm) of foreign
investment and domestic investment is unity (i.e., that one unit of real capital invested
abroad by a U.S. multinational firm results in that firm's investing one less unit of real
capital domestically than would have been the case had the firm not invested abroad), an
unsubstantiated assumption. See Musgrave (1975).

[15]For a presentation of the labor point of view, see Goldfinger (1974).

*JOURNAL OF POST KEYNESIAN ECONOMICS*

between the two nations in the same industries will have the effect of reducing the degree of specialization between those nations, and hence cross-investment will reduce apparent loss of employment within industries. For European direct investment in the United States, this reduction of unemployment may not cheer U.S. trade union officials, because European firms have shown a marked propensity to locate their production facilities in geographic areas of the United States where nonunionized labor can be employed (Faith, 1971; Daniels, 1971).

The effects of foreign direct cross-investment between two markets upon patterns of firm conduct within those markets are complex and do not lead to unambiguously clear policy recommendations. The key issue is the following: does the cross-investment increase rivalry among firms in an oligopolistic industry? As Burton Klein (1977, ch. 2) has observed, rivalistic behavior is likely to result in relatively high rates of technological innovation, changes in market share, and new capital investment, as compared with a low degree of rivalry. Thus, from a welfare point of view, a high degree of rivalry is generally preferable. For the individual firm, however, a low degree of rivalry might be more desirable, especially if that firm were to hold a relatively large market share and if low rivalry were to imply stabilization of the share of the market held by any one firm. In an oligopolistic industry, collective efforts by major firms to "stabilize" conditions are often tantamount to efforts to reduce rivalry within the industry.

At first glance, cross-investment between the United States and Europe would seem to enhance the degree of rivalry. After all, according to the hypothesis advanced in this paper, European direct investment in the United States is a manifestation of rivalistic behavior induced by previous entry into Europe by American firms. This is not, however, a guarantee that rivalry will continue to be the mode of behavior once European and American firms have become established in one another's markets; Stephen Hymer and Robert Rowthorne (1970) have speculated that cross-investment in each others' home markets would eventually lead to tacit collusion among large European and American multinational firms to exploit collectively. their aggregate market power. Hymer and Rowthorne foresee the possibility of future global monopolies in a number of important industries.

While the Hymer and Rowthorne view might be extreme, it is not wholly implausible. U.S. firms operating unilaterally in Europe hold two general advantages over their European rivals: (1) the possession of proprietary intangible assets; and (2) the ability to reduce prices in Europe without having to do so in the United States, an ability that can be used to increase their share of the European market. It was to offset these advantages, as was argued in the second section of this paper, that European firms entered the U.S. market. Once the initial advantages held by American firms have been offset, however, the question arises, will the transatlantic rivalry continue or will an era of tacit collusion among firms on both sides of the Atlantic ensue?

*TRANSATLANTIC INVESTMENT BY MULTINATIONAL FIRMS*

Collusion among major European and U.S. firms is not without historic precedent. Cartelization among firms in Europe in major industries was widespread prior to World War II, and, indeed, in a number of important nations (especially Germany), governments encouraged cartelization.[16] During the 1920s and 1930s, international cartels involving U.S. firms and European firms existed in a number of important industries (Edwards, 1942; Hexner, 1945; U.S. Federal Trade Commission, 1952).

Whether collusive patterns of behavior might again emerge depends on the perceptions among individual firms of the relative gains from continued aggressive rivalry versus a predictable pattern of conduct. If individual firms perceive that the possible (appropriable) gains from continued efforts to create new technology are high, or that the risks associated with allowing a rival firm to develop a technological advantage are great, the prospects are favorable that rivalry will continue. If the perception is commonly held that 'industry barriers to entry are high and that tacit collusion among firms to minimize technological innovation would preserve a jointly appropriable monopoly rent, the worst fears of Hymer and Rowthorne might be realized.

Which direction will be taken in the future by firms in a particular industry is a question that the discipline of economics is not well equipped to answer. Examination of actual behavior of firms within oligopolies reveals that patterns of conduct within an industry can shift from rivalistic to nonrivalistic modes of behavior and back again with the passage of time. The U.S. automotive industry, for example, seems to have been marked by a high degree of rivalry during the early decades of the twentieth century but, beginning sometime in the late 1920s or so, rivalry faded. By the middle 1950s, competition was passive. During the late 1950s, however (if the perception of this author is correct), the intensity of rivalry within the industry began to increase, a phenomenon not unconnected with the success of imported cars in the U.S. market and, later, rising energy prices. It would have been very difficult, a priori, to have predicted these changes within the automotive industry.

In the long run, only the continuous entry of viable new competitors into an industry can reduce tendencies toward collusive conduct. To ensure that established firms, both in the United States and in other advanced nations, are subject to the stimulus of rivalry from new entrants, it is necessary to renew efforts to make the international economic system more open. This is especially so because the development of new industrial firms in the third world can be one source of new entry. If access of these firms to the world's major industrial markets is impeded, the consequence might be not only frustration of efforts by third world nations to develop their internal economies, but also a tendency toward ossification of the industrial sectors of the developed nations.

[16]The literature on the cartelized structure of pre-World War II European industry is enormous. For a partial bibliography, see Hexner (1945) and Plummer (1949).

*JOURNAL OF POST KEYNESIAN ECONOMICS*

# REFERENCES AND BIBLIOGRAPHY

Aho, C. M. "The Effects of Disequilibrium Exchange Rates on Foreign Investment Decisions." Unpublished, 1974.

Caves, Richard E. "International Corporations: The Industrial Economics of Foreign Investment." *Economica*, February 1971, *38* (141), 1-27.

Caves, Richard E. *American Industry: Structure, Conduct, and Performance*. Englewood Cliffs, N.J.: Prentice-Hall, 1972.

Daniels, John. *Recent Foreign Direct Investment in the United States*. New York: Praeger, 1971.

Dunning, John H. "The Determinants of International Production." *Oxford Economic Papers*, November 1973, *25* (3), 289-336.

Dunning, John H. "The Distinctive Nature of the Multinational Enterprise." In John H. Dunning, ed., *Economic Analysis and the Multinational Enterprise*. London: George Allen and Unwin, 1974, pp. 13-30.

Edwards, Corwin D. *Economic and Political Aspects of International Cartels*. Monograph prepared for U.S. Senate Subcommittee on War Mobilization. Washington, D.C.: U.S. Government Printing Office, 1942.

European Economic Commission. *Third Report on Competition Policy*. Brussels, 1974.

Faith, Nicholas. *The Infiltrators*. London: Hamish Hamilton, 1971.

Franko, Lawrence G. *The European Multinationals*. New York: Harper and Row, 1976.

Goldfinger, Nat. "A Labor View of Foreign Investment and Trade Issues." In Baldwin and Richardson, eds., *International Trade and Finance*. Boston: Little, Brown, 1974, pp. 88-103.

Graham, Edward M. "Oligopolistic Reaction and European Direct Investment in the United States." D.B.A. thesis, Harvard Business School, 1974.

Hexner, Ervin. *International Cartels*. Chapel Hill: University of North Carolina Press, 1945.

Horst, Thomas. "The Industrial Composition of U.S. Exports and Subsidiary Sales to the Canadian Market." *American Economic Review*, March 1972, *62* (1), 37-45.

Hymer, Stephen H. *The International Operations of Foreign Firms: A Study of Direct Foreign Investment*. Cambridge, Mass.: MIT Press, 1976. (Ph.D. thesis, 1960.)

Hymer, Stephen H., and Rowthorne, Robert. "Multinational Corporations and International Oligopoly." in Kindleberger, ed., *The International Corporation*. Cambridge, Mass.: MIT Press, 1970, pp. 57-94.

Johnson, H. G. "The Efficiency and Welfare Implications of the International Corporation." In Kindelberger, ed., *The International Corporation*. Cambridge, Mass.: MIT Press, 1970, pp. 35-56.

Jorgenson, Dale W. "Investment Behavior and the Production Function." *Bell Journal of Economics*, Spring 1972, *3*, 220-51.

Keynes, John Maynard. "Foreign Investment and the National Advantage." *The Nation and Athenaeum*, August 9, 1924, *35*, 584-87.

Klein, Burton H. *Dynamic Economics*. Cambridge, Mass.: Harvard University Press, 1977.

Kindleberger, Charles P. *American Business Abroad*. New Haven: Yale University Press, 1969.

Knickerbocker, F. T. *Oligopolistic Reaction and Multinational Enterprise*. Cambridge, Mass.: Harvard University Press, 1974.

Lamfalussy, A. *Investment and Growth in Mature Economies*. London: Oxford University Press, 1963.

Levy, H., and Sarnat, M. "International Diversification in Investment Portfolios." *American Economic Review*, September 1970, *60* (4), 668-92.

Magee, Stephen P. "Multinational Corporations, Industry Technology Cycle, and Development." *Journal of World Trade Law*, July-August 1977, *11* (4), 297-321. (a)

Magee, Stephen P. "Information and Multinational Corporation: An Appropriability Theory of Direct Foreign Investment." In J. Bhagwati, ed., *The New International Economic Order*. Cambridge, Mass.: MIT Press, 1977, pp. 317-40. (b)

Magee, Stephen P. "Multinational Corporations and International Technology Trade." 1977. (Mimeographed.) (c)

McClain, David S. "Foreign Direct Investment in United States Manufacturing and the Theory of Direct Investment." Ph.D. thesis, MIT, 1974.

Musgrave, Peggy. *Direct Investment Abroad and the Multinationals: Effects on the United States Economy*. Report prepared for Subcommittee on Multinational Corporations, U.S. Senate Committee on Foreign Relations. Washington, D.C., August 1975.

Plummer, Alfred. *Industrial Combines in Modern Industry*. London: I. Pitman and Sons, 1949.

Ragazzi, G. "Theories of the Determinants of Direct Foreign Investment." *IMF Staff Papers*, July 1973, *20* (2), 471-98.

Sametz, A. N. "The Foreign Multinational Company in the U.S." Unpublished, 1973.

Scherer, F. M. *Industrial Market Structure and Economic Performance*. Chicago: Rand McNally, 1970.

Stevens, G. V. G. "Capital Mobility and the International Firm." In Machlup et al., eds., *International Mobility and Movement of Capital*. New York: Columbia University Press, 1972.

U.S. Federal Trade Commission. *The International Petroleum Cartel*. Monograph prepared for the U.S. Senate Subcommittee on Monopoly. Washington, D.C., August 22, 1952.

Vaupel, J. W., and Curhan, J. P. *The World's Multinational Enterprises*. Cambridge, Mass.: Harvard University Press, 1973.

Vernon, Raymond. "International Investment and International Trade in the Product Cycle." *Quarterly Journal of Economics*, May 1966, *80* (2), 190-207.

Vernon, Raymond. *Sovereignty at Bay*. New York: Basic Books, 1970.

Vernon, Raymond. *Storm over the Multinationals*. Cambridge, Mass.: Harvard University Press, 1977.

Wells, Louis T. "Test of a Product Life Cycle Model of International Trade." *Quarterly Journal of Economics*, February 1969, *83* (1), 152-62.

# [6]

# A Simple Theory of International Trade with Multinational Corporations

## Elhanan Helpman

*Tel-Aviv University and Massachusetts Institute of Technology*

Using the idea that firm-specific assets associated with marketing, management, and product-specific R & D can be used to service production plants in countries other than the country in which these inputs are employed, I develop a simple general equilibrium model of international trade in which the location of plants in a differentiated product industry is a decision variable. The model is then used to derive predictions of trade patterns, volumes of trade, the share of intra-industry trade, and the share of intrafirm trade as functions of relative country size and differences in relative factor endowments.

## I. Introduction

The role of multinational corporations in the conduct of foreign trade has grown over time and has reached very large proportions. In the United States, for example, at the all-manufacturing level, multinational corporations accounted in 1970 for 62 percent of its exports ($22 billion out of $35 billion) and 34 percent of its imports ($10.5 billion out of $31 billion) (see U.S. Tariff Commission 1973, p. 322). It is therefore not surprising that the ramifications of their existence

I wish to thank Richard Caves for insightful discussions during my work on this project, as well as my wife Ruth for patiently listening to long lectures on the subject of this paper. Helpful comments on a previous version were provided by Eitan Berglas, Torsten Persson, Lars Svensson, and José Scheinkman. This is a revised and much simplified version of Harvard Institute of Economic Research Discussion Paper no. 961. The first version was written when I was a Visiting Professor in the Department of Economics at Harvard University.

[*Journal of Political Economy*, 1984, vol. 92, no. 3]

are of major concern to international trade experts. Nevertheless, there exists no well-articulated theory that explains the conditions for their emergence or predicts under these conditions a structure of trade that comes close to observed trade patterns.

Existing general equilibrium theories of international trade have been developed without explicit treatment of the multinational corporation. The discussion of direct foreign investment in Caves (1971) (and the work that followed from it) is an exception. There are many treatments of the multinational corporation in a partial equilibrium framework (see Caves 1982, chap. 2), but they shed only limited light on a central problem of trade theory, namely, the explanation of trade patterns. We are in need of a theory that describes conditions under which firms find it desirable to shift activities to foreign locations and that is able to predict the pattern of trade that emerges under these conditions. Foundations of such a theory are proposed in this paper, with the following important features: (*a*) there are differentiated products, economies of scale, and monopolistic competition; and (*b*) there exist inputs (e.g., management, marketing, and R & D) that can serve product lines without being located in their plants.

In this paper the theory deals with single product firms. I deal with horizontal and vertical integration in Helpman (1983*b*). Firms maximize profits and make, therefore, cost-minimizing location choices of product lines. This feature brings about the emergence of multinational corporations as a result of the tendency of factor rewards to differ across countries. Here the emphasis is on one source of pressure on relative factor rewards—differences in relative factor endowments. Transport costs and tariffs are assumed away, so that production facilities are not established in order to save transport costs or in order to produce behind tariff walls. Other reasons for multinationality, such as tax advantages of various forms, are also not considered.

Apart from describing in a general equilibrium system conditions under which firms choose to become multinational, the theory provides an explanation of trade patterns in which the multinational corporations play a central role. There is intersectoral, intra-industry, and intrafirm trade. The last trade component has become of major importance in recent years (see U.S. Tariff Commission 1973, chap. 3; Buckley and Pearce 1979).

In order to bring out as clearly as possible the value added of the theory, simplifying assumptions are used throughout. The next section provides a description of the basic model. The structure of an equilibrium in an integrated world economy is described in Section III. Then, in Section IV, the features of the integrated world equilibrium are used in order to describe the relationship between factor endowments and trade patterns. The behavior of the volume of trade is analyzed in Section V and the behavior of the shares of intra-industry and intrafirm trade is analyzed in Section VI. The last section is devoted to concluding remarks.

## II. The Basic Model

For the purpose of the current study I employ a two-sector modified version of the now standard model of international trade in differentiated products. Preferences are assumed to be identical everywhere and representable by a homothetic utility function $u(Y, U_x)$, where $Y$ is the consumption level of a homogeneous product and $U_x = u_x(\cdot)$ is the subutility level attained in the consumption of differentiated products. The function $u_x(\cdot)$ depends on the specification of preferences for a differentiated product; they can be, for example, of the Dixit and Stiglitz (1977) type or of the Lancaster (1979) type (see Helpman [1983a, sec. 8] for a description). In both cases a demand function facing a producer of a single variety can be derived; in the Dixit-Stiglitz case this demand function is of the constant elasticity type (assumed to be larger than one), while in the Lancaster case its elasticity depends on commodity prices and the number of varieties available to consumers (and this elasticity is always larger than one).

It is assumed that there are two factors of production: labor, $L$, and a general purpose input, $H$, whose special role in the production of differentiated products will be explained below. The homogeneous product is produced by means of a standard linear homogeneous production function with the associated unit cost function $c_Y(w_L, w_H)$, where $w_i$ is the reward to factor $i$. A producer of the homogeneous product has to employ all inputs in the same location. In a competitive equilibrium the price of the homogeneous product, taken to be the numeraire, equals unit costs:

$$1 = c_Y(w_L, w_H). \tag{1}$$

The structure of production of differentiated products is more complicated. A firm that wants to produce a given variety has to hire the general purpose input $H$ and adapt it at a cost in order to make it suitable for the production of this variety. Once adapted, the input becomes a firm-specific asset in the sense used by Williamson (1981), and it is tied to the entrepreneurial unit. However, this firm-specific input can serve many plants and it need not be located within a plant in order to serve its product line. In particular, it can serve plants that are located in different countries (see Hirsch [1976] for a similar assumption). Inputs that fit this description are management, distribution, and product-specific R & D. The importance of this type of asset in the operation of multinational corporations is described in

454                                          JOURNAL OF POLITICAL ECONOMY

Caves (1982, chap. 1). Clearly, in practice, combinations of inputs are required in order to generate such assets; here this aspect is simplified by assuming that only $H$ can serve this purpose.

Let $l(x, h_X)$ be the quantity of labor required to produce $x$ units of a variety of the differentiated product in a single plant when $h_X$ units of $H$ have been adapted for its particular use. A possible form for this function is $l = f_p + g_1(x, h_X)$, where $f_p > 0$ and $g_1(\cdot)$ is positively linear homogeneous. Here $f_p$ generates a plant-specific fixed cost and the variable cost component exhibits constant returns to scale. More generally, I assume that $l(\cdot)$ is the inverse of an increasing-returns-to-scale production function in which $h_X$ is essential for production. Let also $g(w_L, w_H, h_X)$ be the minimum costs required in order to adapt $h_X$ to the desired variety, where $g(\cdot)$ is associated with a nondecreasing-returns-to-scale production function. Then the firm's single plant cost function is

$$C_X(w_L, w_H, x) = \min_{h_X} [w_L l(x, h_X) + g(w_L, w_H, h_X) + w_H h_X].$$

This function obviously has the standard properties of cost functions associated with increasing-returns-to-scale production functions. One can also define cost functions for larger numbers of plants. The point worth noting, however, is that the firm or corporation has fixed costs that are corporation specific but not plant specific (they consist of hiring $h_X$ and adapting it), it has plant-specific fixed costs, and it has plant-specific variable costs. The assumption that $l(\cdot)$ is the inverse of an increasing-returns-to-scale production function implies that it pays to concentrate production in a single plant unless there are transportation costs or differences across location in product prices. Since impediments to trade are not considered in this paper, the single plant cost function described above is relevant for what follows. All varieties have the same cost structure.

It is assumed that there is Chamberlinian-type monopolistic competition in the differentiated product sector. Hence, as is well known, in this case firms equate marginal revenue to marginal costs and free entry brings about zero profits in every firm. In a symmetrical equilibrium these two conditions can be written as:

$$px = C_X(w_L, w_H, x) \tag{2}$$

and

$$R(p, n) = \theta(w_L, w_H, x), \tag{3}$$

where $p$ is the price of every variety of the differentiated product; $R(\cdot)$ is average revenue divided by marginal revenue, and it measures the degree of monopoly power (it is a constant under the Dixit-Stiglitz

MULTINATIONAL CORPORATIONS 455

specification of preferences); $n$ is the number of varieties available to consumers; and $\theta(\cdot)$ is average costs divided by marginal costs, using $C_X(\cdot)$, and it measures the degree of returns to scale in the production of differentiated products (see Helpman 1981).

The formal conditions of industry equilibrium (1)–(3) that were described above are identical to the conditions used in existing models of trade in differentiated products (see Helpman 1983a). The important difference lies in the interpretation of the technology available to corporations in the differentiated product industry. As in most trade theory I will assume that factors of production do not move across national borders. However, because of the technology available in the differentiated product industry, the firm-specific asset $h_X$ can serve product lines in plants that are located in countries other than the country in which $h_X$ is located, and the specificity of $h_X$ implies that arm's-length trade in its services is an inferior organizational form to an integrated firm (see Klein, Crawford, and Alchian 1978). This is precisely the feature that brings about the emergence of multinational corporations. We will call the country in which $h_X$ and the entrepreneurial center are located the parent country of the corporation and the country in which the subsidiary is located the host country.

## III. Equilibrium in an Integrated World Economy

As a first step toward the study of international trade between economies of the type described in the previous sections, I describe in this section the symmetrical equilibrium of an integrated world economy. The features of the integrated world economy will then be used to identify patterns of cross-country distributions of the world's endowment of labor and the $H$ factor, which generate certain trade patterns and volumes of trade. This particular link provides valuable information because differences in factor endowments can be associated with differences in relative country size and differences in relative factor endowments, two variables that play a major role in empirical studies. We will study trade patterns and volumes of trade for a fixed-size world economy.

In a symmetrical equilibrium of an integrated world economy factor prices are the same everywhere, and all the corporations that operate in the sector that produces differentiated products have a similar structure; every corporation produces one variety, but there is no overlap in varieties produced by two different corporations: they employ the same quantity of the $H$ factor and the same quantity of labor; they charge the same price for every variety and produce the same quantity of each one of them. Free entry into the industry brings profits down to zero. The number of corporations $n$ is treated as a continuous variable. This is a reasonable approximation when $n$ is a large number.

Apart from (1)–(3) the equilibrium conditions consist of equilibrium conditions in factor markets and in commodity markets. The equilibrium conditions in commodity markets depend on the specification of preferences, and we will not present them because no use is made of them in what follows (for an example see Helpman 1981). It is only important to remember that the upper tier utility function $u(Y, U_x)$ is homothetic. The equilibrium conditions in factor markets are:

$$a_{LY}(w_L, w_H)y + A_{LX}(w_L, w_H, x)n = L, \qquad (4)$$

$$a_{HY}(w_L, w_H)y + A_{HX}(w_L, w_H, x)n = H, \qquad (5)$$

where $a_{iY}(w_L, w_H) = \partial c_Y(w_L, w_H)/\partial w_i$, $i = L, H$, is the cost-minimizing input of factor $i$ per unit output of the homogeneous product; $A_{iX}(w_L, w_H, x) = \partial C_X(w_L, w_H, x)/\partial w_i$, $i = L, H$, is the cost-minimizing input of factor $i$ in a representative corporation in the differentiated product industry, and $L$ and $H$ are the total quantities of labor and the $H$ factor available. The quantity $A_{HX}(\cdot)$ consists of $h_X$ plus any other quantity of $H$ that might be required as an input in the process that converts $h_X$ into a firm-specific asset. Condition (4) assures equilibrium in the labor market, and (5) assures equilibrium in the $H$ market. Conditions (1)–(5) plus an equilibrium condition in commodity markets (e.g., that the demand for $Y$ equal its supply) determine the equilibrium values of factor rewards ($w_L$ and $w_H$), the price of differentiated products ($p$), the output level of a single variety of the differentiated product ($x$), the output level of the homogeneous good ($y$), and the number of corporations in the differentiated product industry ($n$), which equals the number of varieties available to consumers.

For what follows I make the natural assumption that in this equilibrium the homogeneous product is labor intensive relative to the differentiated product; that is,

$$\frac{a_{LY}}{a_{HY}} > \frac{A_{LX}}{A_{HX}}.$$

Under this assumption the equilibrium distribution of employment across sectors can be described by means of figure 1. The vector $O\overline{E}$ represents the endowment of factors of production, the vector $OQ$ represents employment in the differentiated product industry, while $OQ'$ represents employment in the homogeneous good industry. The line $BB'$ represents an equal factor cost line; its slope equals relative factor rewards. It is tangent to an isoquant of the homogeneous good

MULTINATIONAL CORPORATIONS      **457**

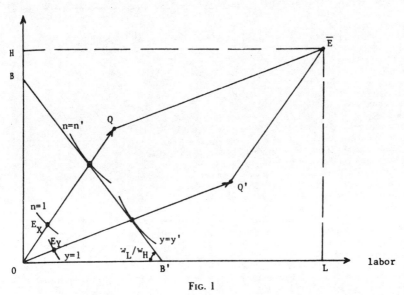

FIG. 1

at its intersection point with $OQ'$. At the intersection of $BB'$ with $OQ$ the equal factor cost line is also tangent to an isoquant, but one of a different nature. This isoquant can be recovered from the cost function by means of the set $\{(L_X, H_X) \mid \exists(w_L, w_H) > 0 \text{ such that } (L_X, H_X) = [A_{LX}(w_L, w_H, x), A_{HX}(w_L, w_H, x)]\}$. This is the collection of inputs that makes possible the production level of a single corporation, and it can be represented by a regularly shaped isoquant, labeled $n = 1$ in figure 1. Now draw an entire family of isoquants by a radial expansion and contraction of this single corporation isoquant. Every isoquant in this family represents a different number of corporations, equally sloped on a ray from the origin. Thus, at the intersection of $BB'$ with $OQ$ there is an isoquant belonging to this family that is labeled $n = n'$. Because of its definition this isoquant is tangent to $BB'$.

Finally, observe that using the single corporation isoquant we can calculate the number of corporations that can operate in equilibrium with inputs represented by a point on $OQ$ by dividing the distance of the point from the origin by $\overline{OE_X}$. In a similar way the output of the homogeneous good that is obtained in equilibrium by an input combination represented by a point on $OQ'$ can be calculated by dividing the distance of the point from the origin by $\overline{OE_Y}$. This completes the description of the integrated world equilibrium that is necessary for what follows.

458                                    JOURNAL OF POLITICAL ECONOMY

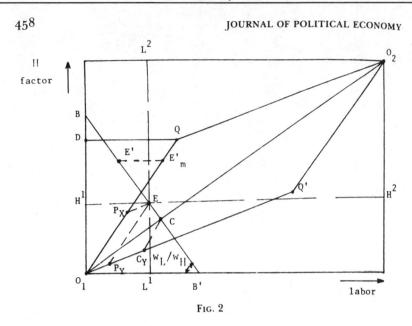

FIG. 2

## IV. The Pattern of Trade

In the standard Heckscher-Ohlin two-country, two-good, two-factor model in which there are no factor intensity reversals and preferences are homothetic and identical across countries, the set of endowment allocations can be divided into two subsets. In the interior of one subset there is factor price equalization and no specialization in production, and every country exports the good whose production makes relatively intensive use of the factor with which the country is relatively well endowed. In the interior of the other subset every country pays a lower reward to the factor of production with which it is relatively well endowed and a higher reward to the other factor of production, at least one country specializes in the production of the good which is a relatively heavy user of its cheaper factor of production, and the pattern of trade is the same as in the former subset. If figure 2 (which is a box-diagram reproduction of fig. 1 with $O_j$ representing the origin for country $j$) were to describe feasible allocations across countries for a standard Heckscher-Ohlin type economy, then the set with factor price equalization would be represented by $O_1QO_2Q'$ and the other set by its complement.[1]

[1] See Dixit and Norman (1980, chap. 4), who also deal with a case in which there is factor intensity reversal.

The pattern of trade that emerges in the present model is much richer than described above. It is useful to describe it by starting with intercountry factor allocations in the set $O_1QO_2Q'$ of figure 2. Because of the symmetry in structure it is sufficient to analyze endowment points above the diagonal $O_1O_2$; this way country 1 is the $H$-factor-rich country while country 2 is the labor-rich country. Allocations in this set were analyzed in Helpman (1981).

Take, for example, the factor endowment point $E$ in figure 2. This point describes an allocation $(L^1, H^1)$ of labor and the $H$ factor to country 1 and an allocation $(L^2, H^2)$ of labor and the $H$ factor to country 2. It is straightforward to see that with this world structure there is an equilibrium with factor price equalization whose cross-country aggregation looks the same as the integrated world equilibrium described in the previous section. In this equilibrium corporations based in one country have no incentive to open subsidiaries in the other country in order to locate product lines there. Assuming that under these circumstances all operations of a corporation are concentrated in the parent country, the output level of the homogeneous product in country $j$ and the number of corporations in the differentiated product industry in that country can be solved from the following factor market equilibrium conditions:

$$a_{LY}y^j + A_{LX}n^j = L^j, \qquad (6)$$

$$a_{HY}y^j + A_{HX}n^j = H^j. \qquad (7)$$

Here the input-output coefficients in the homogeneous product sector and labor and $H$-factor use per corporation in the differentiated product industry are taken from the equilibrium of the integrated world economy, because factor prices, product prices, and output per variety are the same in both cases. This is indeed an equilibrium if the solution of $(y^j, n^j)$ from (6)–(7) is nonnegative for $j = 1, 2$. But this is, of course, the case for every point in $O_1QO_2$, as is demonstrated by the broken-line parallelogram drawn from the particular $E$ in figure 2.

Now observe that because profits are zero all income is factor income. Hence, by drawing through $E$ a line $BB'$ whose slope is $w_L/w_H$, we show the cross-country income distribution. Relative incomes can be read off as follows: Let $C$ be the intersection point of $BB'$ with the diagonal $O_1O_2$. Then the relative income of country 1 is $\overline{O_1C}$ divided by $\overline{CO_2}$. In fact, by a proper choice of units, $\overline{O_1C}$ represents the income level of country 1 and $\overline{CO_2}$ represents the income level of country 2. Since both countries have the same spending pattern, country 1 consumes a proportion $s^1$ of the world's output $y$, where $s^1$ is its share in world income. Hence with a line through $C$ parallel to $O_1Q$ its consumption of the homogeneous product can be represented by $\overline{O_1C_Y}$, where $C_Y$ is the intersection point of this line with $O_1Q'$. Since production $y^1$ is represented by $\overline{O_1P_Y}$, country 1 imports the homogeneous product. Finally, since trade is balanced, this means that country 1 is a net exporter of differentiated products.

I have shown that in the set of factor allocations $O_1QO_2$ the intersectoral pattern of trade is the same as in the Heckscher-Ohlin model. Here, however, there is also intra-industry trade in differentiated products. Country $j$ produces $n^j$ varieties of the differentiated product and it exports them to its trading partner. Hence, the pattern of trade that emerges is the same as in the models of trade in differentiated products that were developed in recent years. To summarize, for factor endowments in the set $O_1QO_2$ free trade generates no incentive for the formation of multinational corporations. The structure of trade is the same as in recent models of trade in differentiated products; the intersectoral trade pattern is explained by differences in relative factor endowments while intra-industry trade is explained by monopolistic competition in differentiated products.

The theory proposed in this paper takes on interest because it can identify and analyze the implications of circumstances in which corporations find it profitable to establish subsidiaries abroad. This theory associates multinational corporations with the ability of firms to exploit cross-country differences in factor prices by shifting activities to the cheapest locations. Generally speaking, this theory can be applied to differences in factor prices that result from many different sources. However, in what follows it is applied to potential differences in factor rewards that arise from differences in relative factor endowments.

It is clear from conventional theory and from the previous discussion that factor endowment points above $O_1QO_2$ lead to unequal factor prices *if* firms have to employ all factor inputs in the same country. Suppose that under these circumstances the $H$ factor is cheaper in country 1 and labor is cheaper in country 2. Now consider what happens when a corporation need not employ all labor and $H$ at a single location; for simplicity also assume that no labor is used in the process that adapts $h_X$ to the particular variety produced by the corporation. Clearly, under these circumstances corporations wish to choose country 1 as their parent country and they wish to open subsidiaries in country 2. These desires reduce the demand for labor in country 1 and increase it in country 2, and they increase the demand for the $H$ factor in country 1 and reduce it in country 2. An equilibrium is attained when either factor prices are equalized or country 1 becomes the parent country of all corporations (with unequal factor prices all $H$ producing differentiated products are located in the $H$-cheap country). When factor price equalization obtains, there are many equilibrium configurations with various degrees of foreign in-

MULTINATIONAL CORPORATIONS                          461

volvement of the corporations in the differentiated product industry, just as there are many configurations in the factor price equalization set $O_1QO_2$. In the latter case, factor price equalization is achieved without invoking the possibility that corporations can decentralize their activities geographically. In the case under current examination factor price equalization can be achieved *because* companies can decentralize their activities geographically. There are many ways in which the decentralization can be made consistent with equilibrium. The rule to be adopted below is to consider equilibria in which foreign labor employment is as small as possible, which amounts to considering equilibria with the smallest number of multinational corporations.[2]

Start by considering factor allocations that are in the set $O_1DQ$ of figure 2. I argue that endowment points in this set lead to equilibria with factor price equalization and the emergence of multinational corporations (I maintain in the figure the assumption that labor is not used in the adaptation process). Clearly, for endowment points in this set there are no equilibria in which factor prices are equalized, and every firm employs its factors of production in a single location. Hence, multinational corporations have to emerge. The only question that remains, therefore, is whether their emergence brings about factor price equalization. Take, for example, the endowment point $E'$ in figure 2. If all the resources of country 1 are employed in the production of differentiated products and its corporations employ in the foreign country the amount of labor $\overline{E'E'_m}$, where $E'_m$ is the intersection point with $O_1Q$ of a horizontal line drawn through $E'$, then the aggregate world equilibrium corresponds to the equilibrium of the integrated world economy. In this discussion $E'$ is the endowment point and $E'_m$ is the employment point. The existence of international corporations enables the employment point to differ from the endowment point. The distance $\overline{O_1E'_m}$ represents the number of corporations that are based in country 1 ($n^1$) and the distance $\overline{E'_mQ}$ represents the number of corporations that are based in country 2 ($n^2$) (the total number is the same as in the integrated world equilibrium). More precisely, since $y^1 = 0$ and $y^2 = y$, the number of corporations that are based in country $j$, $n^j$, and the employment of labor in country 2 by subsidiaries of country 1–based multinationals, $L^f$, are obtained from the following factor market clearing conditions:

$$A_{LX}n^1 = L^1 + L^f, \quad a_{LY}y + A_{LX}n^2 = L^2 - L^f, \tag{8}$$

$$A_{HX}n^1 = H^1, \quad a_{HY}y + A_{HX}n^2 = H^2. \tag{9}$$

[2] This choice can be justified as a long-run equilibrium of a dynamic adjustment process in which it is costly to shift plants abroad.

462                                      JOURNAL OF POLITICAL ECONOMY

However, the number of varieties produced in country $j$ does not equal $n^j$; the number of varieties produced in country 1 is smaller than $n^1$ and the number of varieties produced in country 2 is larger than $n^2$. The precise difference depends on the size of the labor force $L^f$ employed by subsidiaries. In fact the number of varieties produced in country $j$, $M^j$, $j = 1, 2$, is

$$M^1 = n^1 - \frac{L^f}{A_{LX}}, \quad M^2 = n^2 + \frac{L^f}{A_{LX}}.$$

To summarize, we have seen that endowment points in the set $O_1DQ$ lead to an equilibrium with factor price equalization and the emergence of multinational corporations. Under my assumption about locational tendencies of corporations, in this set country 1 specializes in the production of differentiated products and it serves as a base for the multinational corporations. Country 1 imports the homogeneous product, and there is intra-industry trade in differentiated products. Part of the intra-industry trade is carried out by multinationals. It is also easy to see that the set $O_1DQ$ can be divided into two subsets such that in one subset country 1 is a *net exporter* of differentiated products and in the other subset country 1 is a *net importer* of differentiated products. Finally, there exists intrafirm trade whose nature is discussed below.

The existence of intrafirm trade is, of course, well documented in the empirical literature (see, e.g., U.S. Tariff Commission 1973, chap. 2; Buckley and Pearce 1979). This takes the form of imports of the parent firm from its subsidiaries as well as exports of the parent firm to its subsidiaries. Much of this trade stems from vertical integration with which one cannot deal satisfactorily by means of the framework employed in this study, but which can be dealt with in a proper extension (see Helpman 1983$b$). However, there is one genuine component of intrafirm trade that is well represented by this model, namely, the invisible exports of the parent to its subsidiaries of services of the $H$ input. Observe that because of the zero-profit condition (2) labor costs are lower than the revenue obtained from sales. This means that the multinational corporation is making "profits" in its subsidiary, because the subsidiary hires labor only in the host country. This means that the profits of the subsidiary are just sufficient to cover the costs of the $H$ input, which is hired in the parent country. The difference between revenue and labor costs of all subsidiaries is $\mu p x - w_L L^f$, where $\mu = L^f / A_{LX}$ is the number of multinational corporations. This can be considered to be either profits repatriated by the parent firms or payments by the subsidiaries for services rendered by the parent firms. From an economic point of view the second interpretation is the appropriate one. Hence, $\mu p x - w_L L^f$ represents intrafirm trade.

In order to proceed with the analysis of trade patterns figure 3

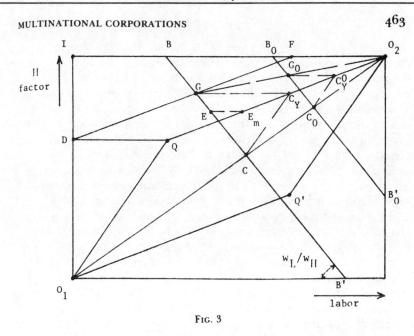

Fɪɢ. 3

reproduces the basic features of figure 2 and contains a further division of the set above $O_1QO_2$. Now consider endowment points in the parallelogram $O_2QDF$. Following the discussion of endowment points in the set $O_1DQ$ it is clear that endowment points in $O_2QDF$ lead to equilibria with factor price equalization and multinational corporations that are homomorphic to the integrated world economy equilibrium. Thus, if $E$ is the endowment point, then $E_m$ is a feasible employment point when the techniques of production of the integrated world equilibrium are used, and $\overline{EE_m}$ represents labor employment of country 1–based multinationals in country 2. It is also clear from figure 3 that endowment points in the set $DIF$ can have no equilibria with factor price equalization, for in order to use the integrated world equilibrium production techniques country 1 has to employ in country 2 a quantity of labor larger than total employment required in the differentiated product industry. This cannot take place, because only in this sector can corporations shift activities to other countries. Hence, for endowment points in the set $DIF$, all corporations that produce differentiated products are based in country 1 and all product lines are located in country 2.[3] Country 1 exports services of the $H$ input and imports all the differentiated products from country 2. It may import or export the homogeneous product.

---

[3] This is necessarily so when production is homothetic. It seems that the reverse pattern of specialization is possible in the absence of homotheticity.

Returning to endowment points in the set $O_2QDF$, observe that there are two possible patterns of trade depending on the location of the endowment point. For the endowment point $E$ and the employment point $E_m$, country 1 imports the homogeneous product as well as varieties of the differentiated product that are produced by its subsidiaries, and it exports the other varieties as well as services of the $H$ input. The only part of this assertion that requires elaboration is that country 1 imports the homogeneous product. This can be seen as follows. Let $BB'$ be the equal cost line that passes through $E$. Then its intersection point with the diagonal $O_1O_2$, that is, point $C$, represents each country's income level. Draw through $C$ a line parallel to $O_1Q$ and let $C_Y$ be its intersection point with $O_2Q$. Then $\overline{O_2C_Y}$ represents the consumption level of the homogeneous product in country 2 while $\overline{O_2E_m}$ represents the output level of the homogeneous product in country 2. Hence, country 2 exports the homogeneous product and country 1 imports it. It is clear from figure 3 that the same pattern of trade emerges for all endowment points on $BB'$ that belong to $O_2QDF$.

Now consider endowment points in $O_2QDF$ that lie on $B_0B_0'$. For the distribution of income represented by this line the consumption of the homogeneous product is represented by $\overline{O_2C_Y^0}$ (constructed in the same way as above). It is clear, however, that only at endowment points below $G_0$ does country 2 export the homogeneous product, while at endowment points above $G_0$ country 1 exports the homogeneous product. At point $G_0$ (as well as at point $G$) there is no trade in the homogeneous product. Generally, at endowment points that are in $O_2QDF$ but below $GO_2$, the pattern of trade is as the one described for point $E$. On the other hand, at endowment points that belong to $O_2QDF$ but are above $GO_2$, country 1 exports the homogeneous product as well as services of the $H$ input and some varieties, while country 2 exports only varieties that are produced by subsidiaries of country 1–based multinationals. A further division into subsets in which country 1 is a net exporter or a net importer of differentiated products is also possible.

We have identified five sets of endowment distributions relevant for the study of trade patterns ($O_1QO_2$, $O_1DQ$, $O_2QDG$, $O_2GF$, and $DIF$). In four of them the equilibrium requires the existence of multinational corporations. Overall, they represent a rich collection of trade patterns with features that seem to fit reality better than those provided by existing trade theories.

## V. The Volume of Trade

I have described in the previous section possible trade patterns and how they are related to the distribution of the world's endowment of

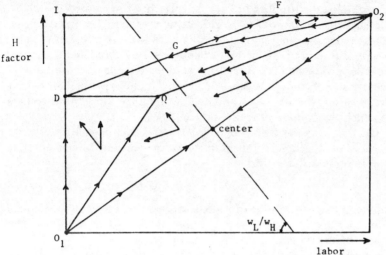

FIG. 4

factors of production. As is clear from the partition of the endowment set into subsets in which certain patterns of trade obtain (see fig. 3), the pattern of trade depends on two factors: (*a*) relative country size in terms of GNP and (*b*) the difference in relative factor endowments. For example, if country 1 is relatively small and has a relatively high endowment of the *H* factor, then the endowment point is in $O_1DQ$, there exist multinational corporations that are based in country 1, country 1 exports differentiated products and invisible *H* services to its subsidiaries, and it imports differentiated products and the homogeneous good. Differences in relative factor endowments and the relative sizes of the countries are observable economic variables of major interest. I provide, therefore, in this section a description of the effects that these two variables have on the volume of trade. These findings are summarized by figure 4 in which the arrows indicate directions in which the volume of trade increases.

Start by considering endowment points in the set $O_1QO_2$. In this region there are no multinational corporations. The volume of trade is defined in the usual way as the sum of exports, where the summation is over countries and sectors. Because of balanced trade, this is equal in a two-country world to twice the exports of one of the countries. In this set country 1 exports only differentiated products, so that the volume of trade is:

$$V = 2pxs^2M^1 \quad \text{for } E \in O_1QO_2, \tag{10a}$$

466                                              JOURNAL OF POLITICAL ECONOMY

where $M^1$ is the number of varieties produced in country 1 and $s^2$ is the share of country 2 in world income. Hence, for fixed relative country size the volume of trade increases with the number of varieties produced in the $H$-factor-rich country, and for a fixed number of varieties produced in country 1 the volume of trade increases with the relative size of country 2. Since $M^1$ is fixed on lines parallel to $O_2Q$, the arrows inside the set $O_1QO_2$ and on $O_2Q$ in figure 4 describe directions in which the volume of trade increases.

On the diagonal $O_1O_2$ we have $M^1 = s^1M$, where $M = n$ is the number of varieties produced in the world economy. Upon substitution into (10a) this yields:

$$V = 2pxMs^1s^2 \quad \text{for } E \in O_1O_2, \tag{10b}$$

implying that the volume of trade is largest when the countries are of equal size and is smaller the more unequal the size of countries. This is also described by the arrows in figure 4.

On the line $O_1Q$ we have $pxM^1 = s^1Z$, where $Z$ is world income and spending and $M^1 = n^1$. Hence, upon substitution into (10a):

$$V = 2Zs^1s^2 \quad \text{for } E \in O_1Q \tag{10c}$$

and the volume of trade rises the more equitable is the world's distribution of income. In figure 4 country 1 is of smaller size than country 2 at endowment points on $O_1Q$ (which is, of course, not always the case); therefore the volume of trade increases in the northeastern direction as indicated by the arrow. The behavior of the volume of trade in the set $O_1QO_2$ described above is a generalization of propositions 5 and 6 in Helpman (1981).

For endowment points in $O_1DQ$ country 2 exports the homogeneous good and $M^2$ varieties of the differentiated product. Some of the varieties it exports are produced by country 2–based firms while $\mu$ of them are produced by subsidiaries of country 1–based multinational corporations. The same trade pattern exists in $O_2QDG$, except that in this set all the varieties exported by country 2 are produced by country 1–based multinationals (i.e., $M^2 = \mu$). This means that the volume of trade can be represented as follows:

$$V = 2(y^2 - Y^2 + pxs^1M^2) \quad \text{for } E \in (O_1DQ) \cup (O_2QDG). \tag{11}$$

For endowment points in $O_1DQ$ the homogeneous product is produced only in country 2, so that $y^2 = y$. Also, since $Y^2 = s^2y = (1 - s^1)y$, upon substitution into (11) we obtain:

$$V = 2s^1(y + pxM^2) \quad \text{for } E \in O_1DQ. \tag{12}$$

This means that when the relative country size is given the volume of trade increases with the number of varieties produced in country 2,

MULTINATIONAL CORPORATIONS $4^{6}7$

whereas when the number of varieties produced in country 2 is given, the volume of trade increases with the relative size of country 1, as shown in figure 4.

At endowment points in the set $O_2QDG$ all the varieties exported by country 2 are produced by subsidiaries of country 1–based multinationals; that is, $M^2 = \mu$. Also $Y^2 = s^2y$ and $s^2Z = y^2 + w_L\mu A_{LX}$, where $Z = pxn + y$. Combining these with (11), we obtain:

$$V = 2[(1 - s^1)pxn + px\mu(s^1 - \theta_{LX})] \quad \text{for } E \in O_2QDG, \quad (13a)$$

where $\theta_{LX}$ is the share of labor costs in the production of differentiated products. Hence, when the relative country size is given the volume of trade increases with the widening of the difference in relative factor endowments (with $\mu$) if and only if the share of country 1 in world income exceeds the share of labor costs in the differentiated product industry. The arrows in $O_2QDG$ that indicate the increase in the volume of trade in the northwestern direction (see fig. 4) are drawn on the assumption $s^1 > \theta_{LX}$ (which always holds for endowment points close to $O_2$). It is also clear from (13a) that given $\mu$ the volume of trade decreases as the relative size of country 1 increases. However, $\mu$ is constant on lines parallel to $O_2Q$. Therefore, the volume of trade increases in the southwestern direction as indicated by the arrows drawn in region $O_2QDG$ and on $DG$. Finally, on $O_2G$ we have $M^2 = \mu$, $y^2 = Y^2 = s^2y$, and $s^2Z = y^2 + w_L\mu A_{LX}$, which yield upon substitution into (11):

$$V = \frac{2s^1s^2px(Z - y)}{w_L A_{LX}} \quad \text{for } E \in O_2G, \quad (13b)$$

implying that the volume of trade declines the more unequal countries are in relative size. This is indicated by the arrows drawn on $O_2G$.

It remains to consider endowments in $O_2GF$. In this region country 2 exports only differentiated products produced by subsidiaries of country 1–based multinationals, and the volume of trade is

$$V = 2pxs^1\mu \quad \text{for } E \in O_2GF, \quad (14)$$

implying that for given $\mu$ the volume of trade rises with the relative size of country 1 and that for given relative country size it rises with $\mu$. On $O_2F$ $\mu$ is proportional to $s^2$, which makes the volume of trade larger the closer the endowment is to $F$ (because on $O_2F$, $s^1 > s^2$). These features are also represented by arrows in figure 4.

In summary, figure 4 represents a fairly detailed description of the relationship between factor endowments and the volume of trade. It shows that in some sense the larger the difference in relative factor endowments the larger is the volume of trade. On the other hand, relative country size has an ambiguous effect on the volume of trade.

## VI. Intra-Industry and Intrafirm Trade

In this section I investigate the dependence of the shares of intra-industry and intrafirm trade on cross-country differences in relative factor endowments. In all cases, except for region $O_1QO_2$, the investigation is restricted to fixed relative sizes of the two countries.

The volume of intra-industry trade is defined as the total volume of trade minus the sum over all sectors of the absolute value of the difference between imports and exports. In the current model this reduces to

$$V_{i-i} = 2px \min (s^1M^2, s^2M^1). \tag{15}$$

The definition of the volume of intrafirm trade is more complicated. Exports of the parent firms of services of the $H$ factor are undoubtedly part of this volume of trade. The problem arises with the treatment of the finished differentiated products. If parent firms serve as importers of the finished products manufactured by their subsidiaries, then this appears in the data as intrafirm trade, and similarly if subsidiaries serve as importers of the differentiated products manufactured by parent firms. In some cases the treatment of these flows of goods as intrafirm trade has no economic justification because it is more the consequence of bookkeeping practices than a true economic calculus. In the present model there is no natural choice—much depends on the implicit assumptions about the marketing technology. I choose, therefore, to define intrafirm trade as trade in the services of the $H$ factor. Hence,

$$V_{i-f} = px\mu - w_L L^f = a\mu, \tag{16}$$

where $a = w_H A_{HX} > 0$.

For endowment points in $O_1QO_2$ we have $s^1M^2 < s^2M^1$, so that using (10a) and (15) we calculate the share of intra-industry trade to be

$$S_{i-i} = \frac{s^1M^2}{s^2M^1} = \frac{s^1n^2}{s^2n^1} \quad \text{for } E \in O_1QO_2. \tag{17}$$

This is shown in Helpman (1981, proposition 4) to be a declining function of the difference in relative factor endowments. The share of intrafirm trade is zero at endowment points that belong to $O_1QO_2$ because in this region there are no multinational corporations.

Using (12), we obtain:

$$S_{i-i} = \frac{px \min (s^1M^2, s^2M^1)}{s^1(y + pxM^2)} \quad \text{for } E \in O_1DQ. \tag{18}$$

Since one can show that $M^1/M^2 > s^1/s^2$ on $O_1Q$, then for a given relative country size the share of intra-industry trade rises with the difference

MULTINATIONAL CORPORATIONS 469

in relative factor endowments as we start moving the endowment allocation along an equal income line from a point on $O_1Q$ in the northwestern direction. If country 1 is small enough, however, this share reaches a maximum and declines with further redistributions that increase the gap in relative factor endowments. This means that with the emergence of multinational corporations the share of intra-industry trade may be positively or negatively related to differences in relative factor endowments. Using (16), the share of intrafirm trade in $O_1DQ$ can be represented by

$$S_{i-f} = \frac{a(\mu/2)}{s^2 p x M^1 + a\mu} \quad \text{for } E \in O_1DQ, \tag{19}$$

where $s^2 p x M^1 + a\mu$ is the volume of exports from country 1. Therefore, for given relative country size a widening of the difference in the $H$ to $L$ ratio between country 1 and country 2 increases the share of intrafirm trade (because it increases $\mu$ and reduces $M^1$).

For an endowment point in $O_2QDG$ we have $M^2 = \mu$, so that (15), (16), and (13a) imply:

$$S_{i-i} = \frac{px \min (s^1\mu, s^2 M^1)}{(1 - s^1) p x M + p x \mu (s^1 - \theta_{LX})} \quad \text{for } E \in O_2QDG, \tag{20}$$

$$S_{i-f} = \frac{a(\mu/2)}{(1 - s^1) p x M + p x \mu (s^1 - \theta_{LX})} \quad \text{for } E \in O_2QDG. \tag{21}$$

Assume $s^1 > \theta_{LX}$ in this region. Then, for a given relative country size, starting from $O_2Q$ the share of intra-industry trade rises with increases in the difference between the $H$ to $L$ ratio in country 1 and country 2, and it may reach a maximum and decline afterward. This pattern is similar to that in $O_1DQ$. The share of intrafirm trade, on the other hand, is larger the larger the difference in relative factor endowments (given relative country size).

In region $O_2GF$ country 2 exports only differentiated products. Therefore, because of balanced trade, at endowment points that belong to it $s^1\mu > s^2 M^1$. Using this relationship as well as (14), (15), and (16), we find that on lines in $O_2GF$ that represent constant relative country size, the share of intra-industry trade declines with increasing differences in relative factor endowments and the share of intrafirm trade is constant.

The broad picture that emerges from this analysis is that for given relative country size the share of intrafirm trade is larger the larger the difference in relative factor endowments, but that in the presence of multinational corporations no clear-cut relationship exists between the share of intra-industry trade and differences in relative factor endowments.

470                                              JOURNAL OF POLITICAL ECONOMY

## VII. Concluding Comments

I have developed in this paper a general equilibrium theory of international trade in which multinational corporations play an essential role. This theory can identify and analyze the implications of circumstances in which corporations find it profitable to become multinational. These corporations are well-defined economic entities, they possess firm-specific assets, they engage in monopolistic competition, and they play an active role in foreign trade. The theory explains the simultaneous existence of intersectoral trade, intra-industry trade, and intrafirm trade. Despite the relative richness of the theory it needs further extensions and elaborations in order to deal with the wide range of problems that are at the heart of international economics. An extension of the current theory to horizontally as well as vertically integrated corporations is presented in Helpman (1983b). This extension generates more realistic patterns of resource allocation without altering the fundamental properties of trade patterns that were derived in the current study. In particular, integrated multinational corporations end up having production facilities in parent as well as in host countries, and the existence of vertical integration brings about intrafirm trade both in $H$ services and in intermediate inputs. This realism is achieved at a substantial cost in terms of the complexity of the theory of the firm. Nevertheless, I believe the benefit-cost ratio to be larger than one. The current theory can also explain cross-country penetration of multinational corporations as a result of impediments to trade (such as transport costs or tariffs). This is evident from the fact that the establishment of a new plant for the same variety requires additional fixed costs but saves the costs associated with trade impediments and does not require the hiring of new $H$ factors. Hence, for sufficiently high impediments, cross-country penetration is expected.

## References

Buckley, Peter J., and Pearce, Robert D. "Overseas Production and Exporting by the World's Largest Enterprises: A Study in Sourcing Policy." *J. Internat. Bus. Studies* 10 (Spring/Summer 1979): 9–20.
Caves, Richard E. "International Corporations: The Industrial Economics of Foreign Investment." *Economica* 38 (February 1971): 1–27.
―――. *Multinational Enterprise and Economic Analysis.* Cambridge: Cambridge Univ. Press, 1982.
Dixit, Avinash K., and Norman, Victor. *Theory of International Trade.* Cambridge: Cambridge Univ. Press, 1980.
Dixit, Avinash K., and Stiglitz, Joseph E. "Monopolistic Competition and Optimum Product Diversity." *A.E.R.* 67 (September 1977): 297–308.
Helpman, Elhanan. "International Trade in the Presence of Product Differentiation, Economies of Scale and Monopolistic Competition: A Chamber-

MULTINATIONAL CORPORATIONS                                     471

lin-Heckscher-Ohlin Approach." *J. Internat. Econ.* 11 (August 1981): 305–
40.
————. "Increasing Returns, Imperfect Markets, and Trade Theory." In
*Handbook of International Economics,* vol. 1, edited by Ronald W. Jones and
Peter B. Kenen. Amsterdam: North-Holland, 1983. (*a*)
————. "Multinational Corporations and Trade Structure." Mimeographed.
Cambridge, Mass.: M.I.T., December 1983. (*b*)
Hirsch, Seev. "An International Trade and Investment Theory of the Firm."
*Oxford Econ. Papers* 28 (July 1976): 258–70.
Klein, Benjamin; Crawford, Robert G.; and Alchian, Armen A. "Vertical
Integration, Appropriable Rents, and the Competitive Contracting Pro-
cess." *J. Law and Econ.* 21 (October 1978): 297–326.
Lancaster, Kelvin. *Variety, Equity, and Efficiency.* New York: Columbia Univ.
Press, 1979.
U.S. Tariff Commission. *Implications of Multinational Firms for World Trade and
Investment and for U.S. Trade and Labor.* Washington: Government Printing
Office, 1973.
Williamson, Oliver E. "The Modern Corporation: Origins, Evolution, Attri-
butes." *J. Econ. Literature* 19 (December 1981): 1537–68.

# [7]

INTERNATIONAL ECONOMIC REVIEW
Vol. 28, No. 1, February, 1987

## STRATEGIC INVESTMENTS AND THE DEVELOPMENT
## OF MULTINATIONALS*

By Ignatius J. Horstmann and James R. Markusen[1]

### 1. INTRODUCTION

Recently, the activities of multinational enterprises (MNE) have been the focus of considerable policy debate. This interest has spawned a number of empirical studies which seek to identify factors associated with the across-industry variation in the fraction of production carried out by MNE's.[2] These studies emphasize the importance of two factors: (i) firm specific assets such as advertising expenditures, research facilities and the like, and (ii) the degree of tariff/transportation costs. Specifically, these studies find that a greater fraction of production is organized in MNE's (as opposed to domestic producers) as the costs due to firm specific assets and transportation become "important". What "important" means in this context is unclear.

In spite of the empirical interest in this issue, the theoretical literature has remained virtually silent. To be sure, a number of studies have assumed a technology which incorporates the above two elements and analyzed either gains from trade issues (Markusen [1984]) or questions of the pattern of production and trade (Helpman [1984]) in the presence of MNE's. However, invariably these studies simply assume the existence of MNE's and that the assumed technology is sufficient to support the given production configuration.[3]

This paper, in contrast, presents a model in which the pattern of MNE-non-MNE (domestic) production arises as an equilibrium phenomenon. It provides conditions on a widely assumed production and transportation technology sufficient to result in either a mixed MNE-domestic production pattern on the one hand or a solely domestic production pattern on the other. Further, it generates a predicted pattern of production which is supported by the body of empirical work.

* Manuscript received May, 1985; revised April, 1986.

[1] The authors would like to thank participants in seminars at M.I.T., Toronto, Boston College, Stockholm, Sussex, and the N.B.E.R. Summer Institute for helpful comments and suggestions.

[2] Even a partial list of the many empirical studies would be rather lengthy, not to mention a description of their results. Caves [1982] provides an extensive and up-to-date bibliography, as well as an analysis and synthesis, of the various contributions.

[3] Exceptions are in Rao and Rutenberg [1979] and Buckley and Casson [1981]. These authors derive MNE activity endogenously. In their models, however, there is no possibility for production by domestic producers. Therefore, the only question is whether or not the MNE should export or open a branch plant. There are no explanations for the assumption that the MNE meets local demand rather than an independent domestic producer.

110                    I. J. HORSTMANN AND J. R. MARKUSEN

To be precise, the paper considers the case of a horizontal MNE; that is, an MNE which operates plants producing identical products in several countries. The technology of production, much like the papers of Markusen [1984] and Helpman [1984], is assumed to involve certain firm specific activities like research, organizational activities and marketing.[4] These activities give rise to multiplant scale economies that give an MNE a cost advantage over potential domestic producers. Branch plant production (MNE activity) is then encouraged by the existence of international transportation costs. Counter-balancing this are plant scale economies that lead (ceteris paribus) to centralized production and the serving of foreign markets through exports. The model predicts that as an equilibrium phenomenon, MEN production occurs if firm specific and export costs are large relative to plant scale economies. The latter, which are ignored by most of the MNE literature, are important not only in a cost sense, but also in determining the ability of the MNE to deter entry in the host country. The latter in turn bears on the (potential) MNE's decision to enter rather than simply export to the host country.

## 2.  A DYNAMIC MODEL OF MULTINATIONAL ACTIVITY

Let $X$ denote the good in question. To begin producing $X$ a firm must incur the once-for-all sunk cost of $F$ (firm-specific cost) and a per-plant sunk cost, $G$ (plant-specific cost). The marginal cost of producing $X$ is constant for each plant and equal to $c$. The consequences of increasing marginal cost are discussed at the end of Section 3. Should a home-country firm export $X$ to the host country, it incurs an additional per unit export cost of $s$, a constant. Producers of $X$ are assumed to maximize the present value of their profits $(V_t)$ and can borrow at a constant rate, $r$, to cover sunk costs.

Demand for $X$ by an individual consumer at time $t$ is assumed to depend only on the price at $t$, $p_t$. Market demand at $t$, therefore, depends only on $p_t$ and the number of consumers at $t$. It is represented by the relationship $p_t = D(X_t, t)$. A consequence of this is that instantaneous revenue net of variable costs for a firm producing an amount $\hat{x}_t$ depends only on $\hat{x}_t$ and $X_t$ and so can be represented by the relationship $R_t = R(\hat{x}_t, X_t, t)$. Demand is assumed to be such that $R(\cdot)$ is continuously differentiable and concave in $\hat{x}_t$.

At $t = 0$ it is assumed that firms already exist in the home country who are producing $X$ and, therefore, have incurred the firm-specific cost, $F$ and at least one plant-specific cost, $G$. Host-country demand is assumed to be too small initially to support any domestic production of $X$. All demand for $X$ is met by home-country exports to the host country. Over time the host country labor force and so demand for $X$ grow at some exogenously given rate. The model, thus, roughly parallels the situation faced by many U.S. firms serving Canada,

---

[4] This assumption is a simple way of capturing the more general notion of the existence of a distinction between a plant and a firm (i.e., a group of plants under joint control). This notion is obviously crucial to any discussion of MNE activity.

Europe and Third World countries in the first half of the twentieth century.

To focus attention on the entry problem in the host country (i.e. on the origins of MNE activity), we make two simplifying assumptions. First, there is only one home-country firm that can provide $X$ (either through exports or a host-country branch plant) to the host country. Second, we assume "segmented markets" such that $X$ can be exported from the home country to the host country but no $X$ can be profitably exported back to the home country. (e.g. the home country has achieved a steady-state equilibrium). This, combined with the technology assumption, means that all firms make their entry decisions based solely on host-country demand.

Given these assumptions, it is trivial to provide conditions under which an MNE chooses to operate a host-country branch plant rather than to export if never threatened by entry from local host-country producers. The interesting aspect of MNE's, however, is that an MNE branch plant and not a local host-country firm provides $X$ to the host-country market. A model of MNE's must provide an analysis of the incentives for organizing production in this fashion.

To this end, we assume the existence of a large number of host-country producers with access to the same technology as the MNE. Thus a domestic firm can provide $X$ to the host country by incurring the once-for-all cost, $F$, and a per-plant cost, $G$. The marginal cost of producing $X$ is constant and equal to $c$, the MNE marginal cost. Of course the domestic firm does not incur the export cost, $s$ (nor would an MNE branch plant). The entry market is assumed to be competitive so that entry occurs by a domestic producer as soon as the present value of profits is zero.[5] In addition, it is assumed that costs and host-country demand are such that, should the MNE delay investment in the host country until the time that would be optimal were there no potential entrants, at least one local host-country firm would have entered the market. This assumption serves to rule out equilibria which are only trivially different from the no-entry equilibrium. In particular, should all host-country demand for $X$ over some period of time be met by an MNE branch plant, this represents direct substitution of MNE production for local firm production and not just adverse exporting conditions. The focus, therefore, is on patterns of production which are equilibrium outcomes reflecting genuine competition between the MNE and local host-country producers.

Finally, it is assumed that, at each $t$ for which there is more than one firm providing $X$ to the host country, output for each firm is given by that firm's respective single-period Cournot equilibrium output. In addition, since investment by the MNE involves irreversible decisions, its investment strategy takes account of all future equilibrium output allocations as well as future entry decisions.[6]

---

[5] This would be the perfect Nash equilibrium outcome if there were a continuum of potential entrants.

[6] That is, the results provided here are the perfect Nash equilibrium outcomes of a game between an MNE and a continuum of potential entrants in which the strategy spaces are an output each period and an enter/no enter decision.

The analysis of the equilibrium pattern of production will proceed along two lines. The first will consider a case in which host-country demand never grows large enough to support more than one plant in the host-country (either a potential entrant's plant or an MNE branch plant). This will be done in the next section. The second will consider a case in which host-country demand can support at most two plants. These two cases are exhaustive in the sense that, given the assumptions of the model, they cover situations in which the MNE is either able (the first case) or unable (the second case) to prevent all entry into the host-country market. As will be seen below, this element plays an important role in determining the relationship between costs and the pattern of MNE/domestic production.

### 3. MULTINATIONAL V LOCAL PRODUCTION: THE PREEMPTION CASE

This section considers the case in which host-country demand grows large enough relative to costs to support at most one host-country plant. In particular, in addition to the restrictions defined in the preceeding Section, it is assumed that the values $F$, $G$ and $s$ and the function $D(X_t, t)$ are such that the following two conditions hold.

(i) $\int_t^\infty R(x_d^c, \tau)e^{-r(\tau-t)}d\tau - F - G \geq (\leq)0$ as $t \geq (\leq)t_1$, where $R(\cdot)$ is revenue net of variable costs for a potential entrant and $x_d^c$ is the entrant's equilibrium output when competing against MNE exports.[7]

(ii) $\int_t^\infty R(x_h^c, \tau)e^{-r(\tau-t)}d\tau - G < 0$   $\forall t$

where $x_h^c$ is the equilibrium output of a firm with a single host-country plant competing against another firm with a single host-country plant, MNE exports equal zero.

Together these assumptions imply that the MNE can preempt all entry into the host-country market by opening a branch plant at some $t < t_1$.

As the following proposition indicates, an MNE in this situation will always choose to preempt entry. All host-country demand in this case will be met by MNE branch plant production.

PROPOSITION 1. *For any $F$, $G$, $s > 0$ and functions $D(X_t, t)$ satisfying* (i) *and* (ii), *there exists an interval $[t_1 - \Delta, t_1]$ such that the value to an MNE of investing (opening a host-country branch plant) at any $t$ in the interval is larger than that of not investing in this interval.*

PROOF. Were the MNE not to invest in this interval, then it would be preempted from later entry by a local host-country producer. Its profits at $t_1$ would be $V_{t_1}^e = \int_{t_1}^\infty [R(x_e^c, \tau) - sx_e^c]e^{-r(\tau-t_1)}d\tau$ with $x_e^c$ giving its Cournot equilibrium level of exports at each $t \geq t_1$. By investing on or before $t_1$, the MNE can preempt entry. Its profit should it invest at $t_1$ and preempt entry would be $V^m_{t_1} = \int_{t_1}^{\infty} R(x^m_h, \tau)e^{-r(\tau - t_1)}d\tau - G$ with $x^m_h$ being the MNE branch plant's monopoly output at each $t \geq t_1$. By definition, this must be larger than $V^c_{t_1} = \int_{t_1}^{\infty} [R(x^c_e, \tau) - sx^c_e]e^{-r(\tau - t_1)}d\tau + \int_{t_1}^{\infty} R(x^c_d, \tau)e^{-r(\tau - t_1)}d\tau - G$, the sum of the entrant's and MNE's Cournot profits should the MNE not preempt. From the definition of $t_1$, $V^c_{t_1} = \int_{t_1}^{\infty} [R(x^c_e, \tau) - sx^c_e]e^{-r(\tau - t_1)}d\tau + F > V^e_{t_1}$. This implies that $V^m_{t_1} > V^e_{t_1}$ or the profits from preempting at $t_1$ exceeds the profits of not preempting. Further since $V^m_{t_1}$ is continuous in $t$, the profits from preempting at $t \in [t_1 - \Delta, t_1]$ is at least as large as not preempting. Q. E. D.

Thus, the MNE always has an incentive to operate a host-country branch plant prior to entry by any local host-country firm (even if this implies investing prior to $t_1$). The incentive comes strictly from the ability to credibly preempt entry by opening a plant with costs identical to that of the entrant's plant. By preempting entry (i.e. investing prior to $t_1$), the MNE becomes a monopolist for all future periods. It earns profits each period strictly larger than the sum of profits for the entrant and itself in the Cournot equilibrium that would result should it not preempt entry. The MNE, therefore, operates a host-country branch plant and so captures all of the rents available in the market rather than just a share of them.

Two points about Proposition 1 are worthy of note. First, as long as (i) and (ii) are satisfied, the relationships among $F$, $G$ and $s$ are not crucial. It is only important that $s > 0$. One might, therefore, view Proposition 1 as a formalization of the early notion that MNE branch plants exist because of the existence of host-country "tariff walls". To the extent that s represents tariff costs, the MNE in this case "jumps the tariff wall" by operating a host-country branch plant. It is important to note, however, that this occurs not simply because of the tariff but because of the threat of entry from firms "protected" by the tariff.

Second, the assumption that at most one plant can profitably operate in the host-country is in some sense crucial in the above analysis because of the assumption that marginal cost is constant. That is, should more than one plant be able to operate profitably in the host country, the existence only of MNE branch plants could still obtain as long as the MNE possessed some way of preempting entry credibly each time it were threatened. Increasing marginal costs would accomplish this since a two-plant MNE would credibly produce more output than a one-plant MNE. The MNE, therefore could delay entry forever simply by adding an additional plant each time entry were threatened.[8]

If the MNE cannot credibly preempt all future entry (or if it can but this is

---

[8] Of course, it would have to be shown that such a strategy would be less costly than one that would allow some entry. This provides an additional complication not present in the above analysis. One would expect, for instance, that complete preemption would not occur for all values of $F$, $G$ and $s$.

very costly) its equilibrium behavior is less straightforward. To gain some insight into the problem in these circumstances, the next section considers the model of Section 2 when multiple entry can occur.

4. MULTINATIONAL V LOCAL PRODUCTION: THE
INCOMPLETE PREEMPTION CASE

In the preceding section, because at most one plant could operate profitably in the host country, the MNE could preempt entry simply by opening a branch plant prior to $t_1$. Were more than one plant able to operate profitably, however, complete preemption would not be possible. The MNE could still preempt one entrant by opening a branch plant but, because of the constant marginal cost assumption, it could not credibly preempt more than one entrant by a proliferation of branch plants.[9] This presents a new problem for the MNE. By incurring the cost $G$ (i.e. by operating a host-country branch plant) the MNE once again obtains returns from the lowered production costs for $X$ (it avoids $s$) as well as from reduced competition from other firms (it preempts one entrant that would otherwise compete against MNE exports). Unlike the previous case, however, the MNE cannot appropriate all of the returns from the reduced costs and competition. This incomplet appropriability makes it possible that MNE branch plant operation is no longer an attractive alternative to a simple exporting strategy. Clearly, this depends on the size of the variable returns from branch plant operation and the degree of appropriability. As is shown below, the magnitude of these values is determined by the relative magnitudes of the cost parameters, $F$, $G$ and $s$.

In order to explore these issues while maintaining some degree of simplicity, we suppose that, in the model of Section 2, cost parameters and host-country demand are such that, in the face of MNE exports, at most two plants can operate profitably in the host-country. To make this notion precise we define potential entry times, $t_i$, analogous to $t_1$ in Section 3. Because of the increased number of possible production configurations, there are two sets of these entry times. The sets are distinguished by whether an MNE branch plant exists or not. Should the MNE choose to export for all $t$, then times $\hat{t}_1$, $t_3$ are defined such that:

---

[9] We assume that, if the MNE operates more than one plant, it coordinates its output decision across plants so as to maximize the sum of plant profits. Given this and the constant marginal cost assumption, MNE output is independent of the number of plants. This implies that all entry and output decisions by local producers are independent of the number of MNE branch plants beyond one. Since each branch plant results in a cost to the MNE of $G$ this implies it will operate at most one plant. Clearly, were the MNE to operate its branch plants as Nash competitors, this result would not hold. Unless the MNE can licence production to independent host-country producers, however, we see no way that it can credibly commit to operating plants as Nash competitors. Further, in this model the existence of "special firm costs" rules out licencing as an alternative.

STRATEGIC INVESTMENTS BY MULTINATIONALS                    115

(iii)    $\displaystyle\int_{\hat{t}_1}^{t_3} R(x_d^c, \tau)e^{-r(\tau-\hat{t}_1)}d\tau + \int_{t_3}^{\infty} R(x_{2d}^c, \tau)e^{-r(\tau-\hat{t}_1)}d\tau - F - G$

$$\geq (\leq)0 \text{ as } t \geq (\leq)\hat{t}_1$$

where $x_{2d}^c$ is the Cournot equilibrium output of a local host-country firm competing against another local host-country firm and MNE exports.

(iv)        $\displaystyle\int_{t_3}^{\infty} R(x_{2d}^c, \tau)e^{-r(\tau-t_3)}d\tau - F - G \geq (\leq)0 \text{ as } t \geq (\leq)t_3 .$

Clearly $\hat{t}_1$ and $t_3$ are the times at which local host-country firms would choose to enter given the MNE continues to export. It is assumed that should the MNE delay investment until after $t_3$, the exporting strategy dominates a strategy of operating a branch plant.

The second set of times is defined for the case in which the MNE operates a branch plant (and so exports are zero). Define $\bar{t} < t_3$ as the time at which the MNE invests in the host-country. (Note $\bar{t} > t_3$ is ruled out by the above; that is, from (iv) the MNE will not invest if it has not done so by $t_3$.) Then times $\bar{t}_1$ and $t_2$ are defined such that

(iii′)    $\displaystyle\int_{\bar{t}_1}^{\bar{t}} R(x_d^c, \tau)e^{-r(\tau-\bar{t}_1)}d\tau + \int_{\bar{t}}^{\infty} R(x_h^c, \tau)e^{-r(\tau-\bar{t}_1)}d\tau - F - G$

$$\geq (\leq)0 \text{ as } t \geq (\leq)\bar{t}_1$$

(iv′)     $\displaystyle\int_{t_2}^{\infty} R(x_h^c, \tau)e^{-r(\tau-t_2)}d\tau - F - G \geq (\leq)0 \text{ as } t \geq (\leq)t_2 .$

$\bar{t}_1$, therefore, is the time at which an entrant would enter given the MNE delays investment until some $\bar{t} > \bar{t}_1$. $t_2$ is the time at which an entrant would enter given the MNE invests prior to $\bar{t}_1$ (i.e. $\bar{t} < \bar{t}_1$). A comparison of (iv) and (iv′) makes it clear that $t_2 < t_3$. Again, it is assumed that, for any $t > t_2$, entry by a second local host-country firm is unprofitable.

Which of the above production configurations results in equilibrium depends upon the relative magnitudes of $F$, $G$ and $s$. A sufficient condition for the existence of an MNE branch plant is that there exists a $t = \bar{t} < t_3$ such that

(1)                    $R(x_h^c, \bar{t}) - rG = R(x_e^c, \bar{t}) - sx_e^c .$

This is simply the condition that would define the switch time for the MNE from exports to branch plant production given one local producer and given the MNE ignores the possibility of entry at $t_3$. Since the returns to exporting should the MNE ignore entry are at least as large as the returns to exporting should it take account of entry and MNE investment prior to $t_3$ preempts any future entry, (1) defines the optimal switch time whether the MNE accounts for entry or not. If (1) holds for some $\bar{t}$, therefore, the MNE will invest at $\bar{t}$ if it has not already done so.

Essentially, condition (1) is a statement about the relationship between cost parameters and the size of the returns due to the reduced production costs from

MNE branch plant production. As $G$ becomes small relative to $s$, then the returns to the MNE from being a more efficient competitor compensate for the costs of investment and the MNE operates a branch plant.

For any $t < \bar{t}$, cost reduction considerations alone are not sufficient to induce the MNE to operate a branch plant. Nonetheless, it may choose to do so because of the gains that accrue to entry preemption. Whether or not this happens depends on how much of these gains the MNE can appropriate. The following proposition provides conditions under which the degree of appropriability is sufficiently large as to induce the MNE to open a branch plant prior to entry by any host-country producers.

PROPOSITION 2. *If there exists a $\bar{t}$ defined by (1) and such that $\bar{t} < t_2$, then there exists an interval $[\bar{t}_1 - \Delta, \bar{t}_1]$ such that investment by the MNE at any $t$ in the interval yields profits at least as large as those from investment at $\bar{t}$.*

PROOF. The proof proceeds much as that for Proposition 1. In particular, were the MNE not to invest at $\bar{t}_1$ its profits would be given by

$$V_{\bar{t}}^c = \int_{\bar{t}_1}^{\bar{t}} [R(x_e^c, \tau) - sx_e^c]e^{-r(\tau-\bar{t}_1)}d\tau + \int_{\bar{t}}^{\infty} R(x_h^c, \tau)e^{-r(\tau-\bar{t}_1)}d\tau - Ge^{-r(\bar{t}-\bar{t}_1)}.$$

If it invests at $\bar{t}_1$, profits are $V_{\bar{t}_1}^m = \int_{\bar{t}_1}^{t_2} R(x_h^m, \tau)e^{-r(\tau-\bar{t}_1)}d\tau + \int_{t_2}^{\infty} R(x_h^c, \tau)e^{-r(\tau-\bar{t}_1)} d\tau - G$. Since the MNE is a monopolist over the interval $(\bar{t}_1, t_2)$ should it invest at $\bar{t}_1$, $V_{\bar{t}_1}^m$ must be greater than $V_{\bar{t}_1}^c = \int_{\bar{t}_1}^{\bar{t}} [R(x_e^c, \tau) - sx_e^c]e^{-r(\tau-\bar{t}_1)}d\tau + \int_{\bar{t}_1}^{\bar{t}} R(x_d^c, \tau) \cdot e^{-r(\tau-\bar{t}_1)}d\tau + \int_{\bar{t}}^{\infty} R(x_h^c, \tau)e^{-r(\tau-\bar{t}_1)}d\tau - G$. Use of the definition of $\bar{t}_1$ implies that $V_{\bar{t}_1}^m > V_{\bar{t}_1}^c = \int_{\bar{t}_1}^{\bar{t}} [R(x_e^c, \tau) - sx_e^c]e^{-r(\tau-\bar{t}_1)}d\tau + F$. Then $V_{\bar{t}_1}^m > V_{\bar{t}_1}^c > V_{\bar{t}}^c$ as long as $F > \int_{\bar{t}}^{\infty} R(x_h^c, \tau)e^{-r(\tau-\bar{t}_1)}d\tau - Ge^{-r(\bar{t}-\bar{t}_1)}$. That this inequality must hold follows from the definition of $t_2$ and the fact that $\bar{t} < t_2$ implies $\int_{\bar{t}}^{\infty} R(x_h^c, \tau)e^{-r(\tau-\bar{t}_1)}d\tau - G < F$ (and so $\int_{\bar{t}}^{\infty} R_\tau(x_h^c, \tau)e^{-r(\tau-\bar{t}_1)}d\tau - Ge^{-r(\bar{t}-\bar{t}_1)} < F$.) Continuity of $V_{\bar{t}_1}^m$ in $t$ proves the result for $t \in [\bar{t}_1 - \Delta, \bar{t}_1]$.      Q. E. D.

The implications of this proposition as regards the relationship between costs parameters, appropriability and MNE branch plant production can be seen if one considers the relationship between cost parameters and the values $\bar{t}$, $t_2$ and $t_3$. From (1), it is clear that $\bar{t}$ is independent of the firm-specific cost, $F$. $t_2$, on the other hand, is a function of both $F$ and the plant-specific cost $G$. It is such that, if $F$ is increased and $G$ decreased by equal amounts, $t_2$ is unchanged. Finally, $s$ can always be made sufficiently large that the Cournot equilibrium level of exports is zero. Together, these results imply that, for any constant $\bar{t}_2$ and $t < \bar{t}_2 \leq t_3$, $F$, $G$ and $s$ can be varied such that (1) holds. This would be accomplished by increasing $F$ and $s$ relative to $G$. Proposition 2 then implies that, in such a case, the MNE would operate a branch plant prior to entry by any local producers. The reason for this is that, while the instantaneous returns from investment prior $\bar{\imath}_1$ do not alone justify it (i.e. $\bar{\imath}_1 < \bar{\imath}$), investment prior to $\bar{\imath}_1$ allows the MNE to appropriate monopoly profits over the interval $(\bar{\imath}_1, t_2)$. The fact that $G$ is small relative to $s$ implies that the instantaneous losses from investment are small, while the large $F$ guarantees that the period of monopoly returns $(\bar{\imath}_1, t_2)$ is large enough to more than offset these losses. The fact that $F$ and $s$ are large relative to $G$, then, guarantees the right mix of appropriability and returns from investment.

A prediction of this model, then, is that in a cross-section study of industries at various points in their investment time series, multinational activity is more likely to be observed in industries in which firm-specific and export costs are large relative to plant-specific costs. These are industries in which an MNE branch plant is likely to exist since the MNE will be first to invest in the host country. This in contrast to the complete preemption case in which MNE activity is essentially independent of the relationship among $F$, $G$ and $s$.

The above argument obviously can be reversed in the sense that, for any $t < t_2$, one can raise $G$ and lower $F$ and $s$ such that $t_2$ is unchanged but (1) is violated. Then the results of Proposition 2 would no longer hold. Moreover, since $F$ and $G$ can be adjusted in the same fashion to leave $t_3$ unchanged, the same could be done for any $t \leq t_3$. In such $s$ case, the returns from MNE branch plant operations due to avoidance of $s$ never, by themselves, justify the expenditure of $G$. Only if the MNE can appropriate enough rents from reduced competition will it then pay to operate a branch plant. Conditions sufficient to guarantee that this is not the case can be derived; they are presented in the following proposition.[10]

PROPOSITION 3.   *If $F = 0$, $G > 0$ and $R(x_h^c, t) < 2R(x_{2h}^c, t) \forall t$, then there exists an $\varepsilon > 0$ such that for all $0 < s \leq \varepsilon$.  MNE exporting dominates branch plant operations for all $t$.*

The proof of this proposition is fairly lengthy and contained in the Appendix. The intuition for the result, however, is fairly simple. The fact that $s$ is small guarantees that (1) is violated for all $t \leq t_3$, so that the returns to the MNE from switching from exporting to branch plant production do not justify the cost, $G$. $R(x_h^c, t)$ gives the instantaneous returns to the MNE should it operate a branch plant prior to $t_3$ and so preempt the second entrant. For small $s$, $R(x_{2h}^c, t)$ is approximately the instantaneous return from exporting (i.e., the returns should the MNE not preempt the second entrant). The condition that $R(x_h^c, t) < 2R(x_{2h}^c, t)$ guarantees that the MNE does not appropriate enough of the rents from preemption to offset the losses from switching to branch plant production. Therefore, the MNE chooses to export for all $t$.[11]

---

[10] In the proposition $x_{2h}^c$ is the Cournot equilibrium output for a host-country plant competing against two other host-country plants, MNE exports equal zero.

[11] It should be noted that this result holds for $s$ strictly positive. For $s = 0$ the result is trivial. Further, since $V_t$ is not continuous in $s$ (it has a discontinuity at $s = 0$) the condition $R_t(x_h^c) < 2R_t(x_{2h}^c)$ is necessary for the result to hold since limiting arugments are invalid at $s = 0$.

I. J. HORSTMANN AND J. R. MARKUSEN

Proposition 3, then, provides the predictions complementary to those from Proposition 2. In a cross-section of industries, MNE activity is likely not to be observed in those industries in which firm-specific and export costs are small relative to plant-specific costs. Again, this is on the assumption that there is incomplete preemption.

Before concluding, a few words would seem in order concerning the interpretation of the results in this and the preceeding section. While a comparison of $G$ and the variable returns to the MNE from switching to branch plant operations are important in determining its investment decision, this does not tell the complete story. In section 3, for instance, an MNE branch plant will exist even if $F$, $G$ and $s$ are such that a monopolist not threatened by entry would never operate one. The other important issue, there, is the gains from entry preemption. This section and Section 3 are related in that, in both sections, the MNE investment decision depends upon how much of these gains the MNE can appropriate. In Section 3, the ability of the MNE to preempt all entry guarantees that it appropriates all of the rents in the market. Therefore, the relative magnitude of $F$, $G$ and $s$ are unimportant. In this section, because preemption is incomplete, MNE rent appropriation is incomplete as well. The MNE investment decision then depends on the magnitude of rent appropriation relative to the returns from switching to branch plant operations. The relative sizes of $F$, $G$ and $s$ now are important in determining these magnitudes. The model of this section predicts that $F$ and $s$ large relative to $G$ provides the right degree of appropriability and returns to switching to induce MNE branch plant operations. A wealth of empirical results support this prediction.

## 5. CONCLUSIONS

The purpose of this paper was to construct a model which allowed the existence or non-existence of MNE to arise as an equilibrium phenomenon. We showed that this could be done in an empirically relevant way by combining three elements: firm-specific costs plus tariff/transportation costs which together create incentives for MNE branch-plant production, and plant scale economies which create an incentive for centralization and serving foreign markets through exports. Our general result based on both strategic and non-strategic (cost) considerations is that MNE will tend to be found in industries in which firm-specific and tariff/transportation costs are large relative to plant scale economies.

*University of Western Ontario, Canada*

### APPENDIX

This appendix provides a proof of Proposition 3. Before proceeding with the proof, a concept not contained in the text must be introduced. This is the notion of an *s*-economy. Clearly, the equilibrium levels of individual firm output and so $\hat{t}_1$ and $t_3$ depend on the value of $s$. Therefore, a demand specification and values $F$, and $G$ which satisfy (iii) and (iv) for one value of $s$ may not for a higher (lower) value of $s$. To deal with this, an $s$-economy is defined as one in which demand is given by $p_t = D(X_t, t, s)$ and such that, for $F = 0$ and some $G > 0$, (iii) and (iv) hold for all $s$. Further, it is such that, if the MNE has not operated a branch plant by $t_3$, it never will. Revenues net of variable costs in a given $s$-economy are defined by the function $R_s(\cdot)$.

It is also necessary to define a limit economy in this context. This is the economy which fulfills (iii) and (iv) given $s = 0$. Revenues net of variable costs in this economy are defined by the function $R_0(\cdot)$. A sequence of $s$-economies is said to converge to the limit economy if, as $s$ approaches zero, the equilibrium outputs of each firm at each $t$ converge to those in the limit economy (i.e., $R_s(\cdot)$ is continuous in $s$). It is assumed in what follows that this is the case. (If the demand specification in the limit economy were given by $p_t = f(x_t, t)$, then demand specifications in the $s$-economies of the form $p_t = k(s)f(x_t, t)/[k(s) + s]$ would satisfy this convergence property.)

Since $R_s(\cdot)$ is bounded above by $R_0(\cdot)$ and $x_e^c$ approaches $x_h^c$ as $s$ goes to zero, it is always possible to make $s$ sufficiently small that, for any $G > 0$, (1) is violated for all $t < t_3$. Therefore, if the MNE has not invested by $\hat{t}_1$, its only reason to invest is to preempt entry at $t_3$. Moreover, in this case, the MNE will want to invest at $t_3$ (or as close to $t_3$ as possible). The following lemma shows that if the MNE has not invested by $\hat{t}_1$, then there is sufficiently small $s$ such that it does not pay the MNE to preempt entry at $t_3$.

LEMMA 1. *Given the assumptions of Proposition 3 and given a value of $s = \bar{s}$ such that (1) is violated for all $t \leq t_3$, then there exists a half-open interval $(0, \hat{s}]$ such that, for all $s \in (0, \hat{s}]$, profits to the MNE from investing at $t_3$ are less than profits from not investing at $t_3$.*

PROOF. Consider an arbitrary $s$-economy. Were the MNE to invest at $t_3$, its profits would be given by $V_{t_3}^c = \int_{t_3}^{\infty} R_s(x_h^c, \tau)e^{-r(\tau - t_3)}d\tau - G$. Were it not to invest at $t_3$, profits would be given by $V_{t_3}^e = \int_{t_3}^{\infty} [R_s(x_e^{2c}, \tau) - sx_e^{2c}]e^{-r(\tau - t_3)}d\tau$ where $x_e^{2c}$ is the equilibrium level of MNE exports at eact $t$ given competition from two host-country firms. From the definition of $t_3$,

$$G = \int_{t_3}^{\infty} R_s(x_{2d}^c, \tau)e^{-r(\tau - t_3)}d\tau.$$

Therefore, no investment dominates investment as long as

$$V_{t_3}^e - V_{t_3}^c = \int_{t_3}^{\infty} [R_s(x_e^{2c}, \tau) - x_e^{2c} - R_s(x_h^c, \tau) + R_s(x_{2d}^c, \tau)]e^{-r(\tau - t_3)}d\tau > 0.$$

If a sequence of $s$-economies converging to the limit economy is taken, then, by definition, $x_c^{2e} \to x_{2h}^c$ and $x_{2d}^c \to x_{2h}^c$ as $s \to 0$. Then, no investment dominates

investment on this interval $(0, \hat{s}]$ as long as $\lim\limits_{s \to 0} V_{t_3}^e - V_{t_3}^c = \int_{t_3}^{\infty} [R_0(x_{2h}^c, \tau) +$
$R_0(x_{2h}^c, \tau) - R_0(x_h^c, \tau)]e^{-r(\tau - t_3)}d\tau > 0$. By assumption, $2R_s(x_{2h}^c, t) > R_s(x_h^c, t) \forall t$
proving the result. Q. E. D.

Lemma 1 guarantees that, as long as $s \in (0, \hat{s}]$, if the MNE hasn't invested before $t_3$, it will not pay to do so at $t_3$. Define by $s'$ the value of $s$ given by min $[\hat{s}, \bar{s}]$. Then lemma 1 guarantees that, for any $s \in (0, s']$, if the MNE invests, it does so on or before $\hat{t}_1$. The next lemma shows that for $s$ sufficiently small, this is not profitable either.

LEMMA 2. *Given the assumptions of Proposition 3, there exists an $\varepsilon > 0$ such that, for all $0 < s \leq \varepsilon \leq s'$, profits to the MNE from investing at $\hat{t}_1$ are less than profits from not investing at $\hat{t}_1$.*

PROOF. Given the definition of $s$, should the MNE not invest at $\hat{t}_1$, it never will. Its profits in this case are given by

$$V_{\hat{t}_1}^e = \int_{\hat{t}_1}^{t_3} [R_s(x_e^c, \tau) - sx_e^c]e^{-r(\tau - t_1)}d\tau + \int_{t_3}^{\infty} R_s(x_e^{2c}, \tau) - sx_e^{2c}]e^{-r(\tau - t_1)}d\tau.$$

Were the MNE to invest at $\hat{t}_1$, its profits would be

$$V_{\hat{t}_1}^m = \int_{\hat{t}_1}^{t_2} R_s(x_h^m, \tau)e^{-r(\tau - i_1)}d\tau + \int_{t_2}^{t_3} R_s(x_h^c, \tau)e^{-r(\tau - i_1)}d\tau$$
$$+ \int_{t_3}^{\infty} R_s(x_h^c, \tau)e^{-r(\tau - i_1)}d\tau - G.$$

From the definition of $\hat{t}_1$, $G = \int_{\hat{t}_1}^{t_3} R_s(x_h^c, \tau)e^{-r(\tau - t_1)}d\tau + \int_{t_3}^{\infty} R_s(x_{2d}^c, \tau)e^{-r(\tau - i_1)}d\tau$.
Then, again, if a sequence of $s$-economies converging to the limit economy is taken, no investment dominates investment for $s \in (0, \varepsilon]$ if

$$\lim\limits_{s \to 0} V_{\hat{t}_1}^e - V_{\hat{t}_1}^m = \int_{t_3}^{\infty} 2R_o(x_{2h}^c, \tau) - R_o(x_h^c, \tau)]e^{-r(\tau - t_2)}d\tau$$
$$+ \int_{t_2}^{t_3} R_o(x_h^c, \tau)e^{-r(\tau - t_2)}d\tau > 0.$$

By assumption, however, $2R(x_{2h}^c, t) > R(x_h^c, t) \forall t$ proving the result. Q. E. D.

## REFERENCES

BUCKLEY, P. J. AND M. CASSON, "The Optimal Timing of Foreign Direct Investment," *Economic Journal*, 91 (1981), 75–82.

CAVES, RICHARD E., *Multinational Enterprise and Economic Analysis* (London: Cambridge University Press, 1982).

EATON, B. CURTIS AND RICHARD LIPSEY, "The Theory of Market Preemption: The Persistence of Excess Capacity and Monopoly in Growing Spatial Markets," *Economica*, 46 (1979), 149–158.

HELPMAN, ELHANAN, "A Simple Theory of International Trade with Multinational Corporations," *Journal of Political Economy*, 92 (1984), 451–471.

HORSTMANN, IGNATIUS AND JAMES R. MARKUSEN, "Licensing Versus Direct Investment: A Model of Internalization by the Multinational Enterprise," University of Western Ontario Working Paper (1986).

MARKUSEN, JAMES R., "Multinationals, Multi-Plant Economies, and the Gains from Trade," *Journal of International Economics*, 14 (1984), 205–226.

RAO, R. AND D. RUTENBERG, "Preempting an Alert Rival: Strategic Timing of a First Plant by Analysis of Sophisticated Rivalry," *Bell Journal of Economics*, (1979), 412–428.

# Part IV
# Technology Transfer:
# Contractual Alternatives

# [8]

THE JOURNAL OF INDUSTRIAL ECONOMICS                0022-1821 $2.00
Volume XXXII                    March 1984                    No. 3

## INTERNATIONAL TECHNOLOGY TRANSACTIONS
## AND THE THEORY OF THE FIRM*

W. H. Davidson and Donald G. McFetridge

### I. INTRODUCTION

THE THEORY of the firm, as conceived by Coase [6] and developed by Williamson ([23], [24], [25], [26]), holds that the firm and the market are alternative methods of organizing exchange and that the choice between intrafirm and market exchange will be based on their relative costs. Arrow [2] has argued that market exchanges of information will be particularly costly relative to intrafirm exchanges. This insight has been cited by a number of authors to explain the prominence of multinational firms in high-technology industries (Caves [5]; Vernon [20]; Teece [17], [18]; Buckley and Casson [3]; Magee [12]; Casson [4]; and Dunning [8]).

This paper employs the theory of the firm in an attempt to define more precisely the circumstances under which it is advantageous to internalize international transactions involving technology. The hypotheses which emerge from our analysis are tested using a sample of 1,376 internal and arm's-length (market) transactions involving high-technology products carried out by 32 U.S.-based multinational enterprises between 1945 and 1975.[1] We find that there are systematic differences in the characteristics of intrafirm and market technology transactions. These differences are largely consistent with those implied by the theory of the firm.

### II. THE CHOICE OF TRANSACTION MODE: IMPLICATION OF THE
### THEORY OF THE FIRM

Differences in the respective costs of intrafirm and market transactions are the result of differences in the incentives of the transacting parties (Williamson [23, p. 113], [24, p. 29]; McKean [15, p. 124]; McManus [16, p. 344]). Each party in a market transaction has an incentive to attempt to appropriate a larger fraction of the gain from trade. Each party will expect the other to use whatever opportunities are available to turn the terms of trade in their favour.

* This paper is based on research supported by the National Science Foundation and the Harvard Multinational Enterprise Project. The authors wish to thank Greg Hammett and Luis Leigh for research assistance and Keith Acheson, Steven Ferris and Ed Hughes for their advice and comments.

[1] In this paper all transactions between unaffiliated firms are regarded as market transactions. Two firms are unaffiliated if neither holds more than five per cent of the equity of the other. A transaction is defined as internal if one of the firms involved holds at least 95 per cent of the equity of the other. Transactions between firms, one of which holds between 5 and 95 per cent of the equity of the other are not analyzed in this paper. A full description of the data can be found in Vernon and Davidson [22] or in Davidson [7].

The participants in an intrafirm transaction have different incentives. The incomes of firm members will not, in general, depend on the outcomes of transactions carried out within the firm. As a consequence, the parties in an intrafirm transaction will have less incentive to engage in activities designed to redistribute the gains from trade.

While firm membership weakens the relationship between an individual's income and the outcome of the intrafirm transactions in which he participates, it also weakens the relationship between his income and his productive activity. Individual firm members will therefore find the consumption of leisure (shirking) and other non-pecuniary benefits less costly in terms of income foregone than would participants in a market transaction (Alchian and Demsetz [1, pp. 778–81]; McManus [16, pp. 343–45]).

Behaviour of this nature can be reduced by the expenditure of resources to monitor the activities of firm members. Monitoring will be carried to the point at which its marginal cost is equal to the marginal output loss it prevents. Intrafirm exchange will be less costly than market exchange whenever the value of resources saved by reducing redistributive activity exceeds the sum of the values of output lost due to shirking (given optimal monitoring) and the resources devoted to monitoring.

Williamson [24, pp. 21–27]; [25, pp. 248–54] suggests that the extent to which redistributive activity can be reduced by the internalization of exchange will be greater: (a) the more costly it is to measure the qualities of the goods or services involved; (b) the greater is the degree of uncertainty regarding the environment within which the transaction is to take place; and (c) the greater is the extent to which the transaction is supported by durable transaction-specific assets.[2]

In addition, the net advantage of internalization will decline with the value of the intrafirm transactions contemplated. The formation of a firm will involve shirking and monitoring costs regardless of the amount of intrafirm exchange it facilitates. The smaller are the potential gains from intrafirm trade, the less likely it is that savings from reduced redistributive activity will offset losses in output due to shirking and the diversion of resources to monitoring.[3]

### III. DETERMINANTS OF THE MODE OF TECHNOLOGY TRANSFER

The extent to which a technology transaction is likely to be burdened by high measurement (verification) costs, uncertainty and the need to make transaction-specific investments will be greater: (a) for newer technologies;

[2] In an earlier version of this paper we used the term "irreversible commitments" to describe a situation in which it is costly for either or both parties to turn to alternative traders should their arrangements prove unsatisfactory. For further discussion see Klein, Crawford and Alchian [10, p. 307] and Williamson [26, pp. 10–12].

[3] McManus [16, p. 346] deals with the limiting case in which there is no interdependence among firm members and thus no intrafirm exchange. The formation of a firm will involve shirking and monitoring costs with no offsetting benefits and will thus be wealth-reducing.

INTERNATIONAL TECHNOLOGY TRANSACTIONS 255

(b) for technologies which represent a more significant advance on the state of the art; (c) for technologies with fewer previous transfers; (d) for technologies with fewer and more distant substitutes; and (e) the smaller is the amount of past transfer activity of the parties involved.

For widely used technologies which are close to "existing practice" it is less costly to verify assertions regarding their characteristics and there will be less uncertainty surrounding their application.[4] Verification costs and uncertainty will also be lower if the technology involved is an imitation rather than an innovation and if either or both parties have a record of past transfer activity from which inferences of reliability can be drawn.

The extent to which one or both of the transacting parties must make investments which are specialized to the transaction, and is therefore vulnerable to the opportunism of the other party, will be greater the newer, more radical and less widely used is the technology involved.

The advantages of internalization will be less likely to outweigh its costs the smaller in value and/or the less frequent are the transactions contemplated.[5] The transacting parties are less likely to expect the repetition of transfers of technologies which are distantly related to the transferor's principal line of business.

The number of transfers which are expected to occur in the future will increase with the amount of new technology the transferor is expected to produce. The anticipated flow of new technology should, in turn, be greater the larger is the fraction of the transferor's resources devoted to scientific research and development.

The value of a technology, that is, the stream of rents it can command, will be smaller the closer and the greater in number are the substitutes for it. The smaller is the value of the stream of rents involved, the less there is to be gained by reducing the incentive of the transacting parties to redistribute them, that is, by internalizing the transaction.

Vernon [21, p. 81] has argued that the post-war period has been characterized by increasing international competition in the development of new technologies. If this were the only secular factor in operation we should observe that, other things being equal, there is a trend toward market technology transactions over the sample period.

The relative cost of an intrafirm transfer will also depend on the mode of transfer which has been adopted in the past. If the transferor already has an affiliate in the receiving country, the fixed cost of internalization is a sunk cost. Since it is with the small incremental cost of the internal transfer with which the market alternative is then compared, the presence of an affiliate increases the likelihood that subsequent transfers will be internal.

---

[4] See Magee [12, pp. 328–29]. Williamson [25, p. 254] has also suggested that the uncertainty surrounding a transaction will decline as the industry in which the transacting parties are located matures.

[5] This point has also been made by Caves [5, p. 7].

256          W. H. DAVIDSON AND DONALD G. MCFETRIDGE

Finally, the mode of transfer chosen will also depend on the characteristics of the receiving country. We do not discuss these characteristics or test for their effect in this paper. Instead, we examine and report on a number of alternative means of holding country effects constant. There include: (1) employing the past relative frequency of internal transfers to each receiving country as an additional variable in the model; (2) allowing the intercept term to vary across countries or groups of countries; and (3) estimating the model for individual countries, or relatively homogeneous groups of countries.

### IV. THE MODEL: ITS SPECIFICATION AND ESTIMATION

The determinants of the probability of internal transfer suggested by the discussion of Section III are summarized in equation (1). Variable definitions together with the expected signs of the partial derivative of the dependent variable with respect to each independent variable follow.

(1) $\quad\quad P_i = f(t_i,\ C_i,\ A_i,\ T_i,\ N_i,\ M_i,\ B_i,\ E_i,\ R_i,\ F_i)$

where $P_i$ = probability that the $i$th transfer will be internal;

$\quad t_i$ = year in which the $i$th transfer is made;

$\quad C_i$ = proportion of transfers to the country receiving the $i$th transfer during the preceding five years which have been internal, $f_C > 0$;

$\quad A_i$ = age of the technology, in terms of number of years since its U.S. introduction, at the time of the $i$th transfer, $f_A < 0$;

$\quad T_i$ = number of transfers of the technology prior to the $i$th transfer, $f_T < 0$;

$\quad N_i$ = dummy variable equal to one if the $i$th transfer is of a technology which is a radical advance on the state of the art, zero if it is an incremental advance, $f_N > 0$;

$\quad M_i$ = dummy variable equal to one if the $i$th transfer is of an innovation, zero if it is of an imitation, $f_M > 0$;

$\quad B_i$ = dummy variable equal to one if the $i$th transfer is of a technology assigned to the same U.S. three digit SIC code as the transferor, $f_B > 0$;

$\quad E_i$ = number of prior transfers made by the firm making the $i$th transfer, $f_E < 0$;

$\quad R_i$ = R&D: Sales ratio of the form making the $i$th transfer, $f_R > 0$;

$\quad F_i$ = dummy variable equal to one if the firm making the $i$th transfer had an affiliate in the receiving country in the year prior to the transfer, zero otherwise, $f_F > 0$.

Since each transaction must fall into either the market or the intrafirm category, the dependent variable in this model is a binominal random variable, $Y$, which takes on values of zero and one for market and intrafirm transactions respectively. The probability $P_i$ in equation (1) is thus the expec-

INTERNATIONAL TECHNOLOGY TRANSACTIONS 257

tation of $Y$ conditional on the values of the independent variables. If (1) is written as a linear function and the $i$th value of the $j$th independent variable is written as $X_{ij}$, the population regression model is:

$$(2) \qquad Y_i = E(Y_i) + \varepsilon_i = P_i + \varepsilon_i = \sum_{j=1}^{J} b_j X_{ij} + \varepsilon_i$$

As Goldberger [9, p. 249] and others have noted, (2) does not constrain $P_i$ to lie between zero and one. It is also characterized by heteroskedastic residuals.

An alternative which constrains $P_i$ to lie between zero and one and which stabilizes the variance of $\varepsilon_i$ is to write (2) as a logistic function. Thus

$$(3) \qquad E(Y_i) = P_i = 1 \bigg/ \left[ 1 + \exp\left( - \sum_{j=1}^{J} c_j X_{ij} \right) \right]$$

The $\hat{c}_j$ values are then obtained by the maximum likelihood method. To assist in the interpretation of the $\hat{c}_j$ reported in Section $V$, we note that by differentiating (3) with respect to $X_j$ and substituting we obtain

$$(4) \qquad \frac{dP}{dX_j} = c_j P(1 - P)$$

The change in the probability of an internal transfer resulting from a given change in $X_j$ is a function of $c_j$ and the probability of internal transfer itself. The marginal effect of $X_j$ on $P$ can be calculated for any given $P$. It reaches its maximum value at $P = 0.5$.

If, as is often the case in this study, the $X_j$ are in logarithmic form, differentiating (3) with respect to $X_j$ and substituting yields

$$(5) \qquad X_j \frac{dP}{dX_j} = c_j P(1 - P)$$

In this case the change in $P$ resulting from a given percentage change in $X_j$ is a function of $P$ and reaches its maximum at $P = 0.5$. A measure of the maximum effect on $P$ of a given percentage change in $X_j$ can be obtained by multiplying reported $\hat{c}_j$ values by 0.25.

Finally, the likely changes (or percentage changes) in the $X_j$ will differ for $j = 1, \ldots, J$. To indicate the effect on $P$ of equally likely changes in the $X_j$ we report estimates of the standardized coefficients of the $X_j$ which we refer to as $d_j$ coefficients. The coefficient $d_j, j = 1, \ldots, J$ can be interpreted as the effect on $P$ of a one standard deviation change in $X_j, j = 1, \ldots, J$ evaluated at $P = 0.5$.

Logit estimates of the $c_j$ were obtained from a sample of 1,376 international transfers of 221 significant new product innovations and 359 imitations undertaken subsequent to U.S. introduction by 32 U.S.-based multinationals

258                   W. H. DAVIDSON AND DONALD G. MCFETRIDGE

during the period 1945–75.[6] The 32 firms from which new product transfer information was obtained are listed in Vernon and Davidson [22, pp. 83–86] and in Davidson [7, pp. 206–7]. Significant innovations and imitations are those which met the minimum standards for technological novelty and accumulated U.S. sales described in Davidson [7, p. 16].

### V. EMPIRICAL RESULTS AND THEIR INTERPRETATION

Five sets of estimates of the $c_j$ in equation (3) are reported in Table I. The first set is based on the full sample with all continuous independent variables in logarithmic form and employs the fraction of internal transfers during the preceding five years to the country receiving the $i$th transfer to standardize for country effects.

The second set differs from the first only in that there is no logarithmic transformation of any of the independent variables. The third set is the same as the first except that the existing affiliate variable, $B$, is omitted.

The fourth set differs from the first in the manner in which country characteristics are held constant. In this case estimates are based on a subsample which includes only transfers to Canada and western Europe. The intercept is allowed to differ between Canada and western Europe and this difference is reflected in the coefficient of the Canada dummy, CDA.

The fifth set differs from the fourth in that it is estimated using a subsample which includes all transfers to non-communist countries. In this case the intercept term is allowed to take on a different value for each of three countries or groups of countries, Canada, western Europe and the balance of the non-communist world. The differences between the Canada and western Europe intercepts is given by the coefficient of the Canada dummy, CDA, while the difference between the respective intercepts of western Europe and the balance of the non-communist world is given by the coefficient of the rest of the world dummy, ROW.

The results are generally robust with respect to changes in specification and sample size.[7] Only one variable, the innovation/imitation dummy, $M$, takes on a sign which is not in accord with our theoretical expectations. All other

---

[6] Estimates of the parameters of the logit model were obtained using the AQD package at Harvard Business School. See Schlaifer [19, pp. 232 36].

[7] The results of a classification analysis performed using Equation (1), Table I are:

|  | Predicted | | |
| --- | --- | --- | --- |
| *Actual* | *Market* | *Intrafirm* | *Total* |
| Market | 293 | 179 | 472 |
| Intrafirm | 107 | 797 | 904 |
| Total | 400 | 976 | 1376 |

Percentage correctly classified = 79.2
A transaction is assigned to the "intrafirm" category if $\hat{P} > 0.5$

coefficient estimates are not only of the expected sign but, with the exception of the coefficients of age and the radical/incremental dummy in equation (4), also are different from zero at significance levels under 5 per cent (one tail test).

The results imply, first, that the possibility that a given transaction will be internal depends on the characteristics of the receiving country. Specifically, equations (1) ⋯ (3) imply that the probability that the $i$th transfer will be internal increases with the fraction of previous transfers by all sample firms to the receiving country which were internal. Equations (4) and (5) imply that, other things being equal, the probability of an internal transfer is greater in the case of Canada than Western Europe and greater in the case of Western Europe than in the balance of the non-communist world.

Second, the probability of an internal transfer is greater if the transferor had an affiliate in the receiving country in the year prior to the transfer. When the existing affiliate variable is omitted (column 3, Table I), explained variation falls but remains statistically significant. Inferences regarding the other parameters of the model remain unchanged. Thus, while the existing affiliate variable is clearly important to the model, it does not appear to be the source of any misleading inferences as to the marginal effects of the other independent variables.[8]

Third, the probability of internal transfer is higher the newer and more radical is a technology and the fewer the occasions upon which it has been transferred. These results confirm those obtained in other investigations of the technology transfer process. A negative relationship between the age of a technology and the probability of internal transfer has been observed in a bivariate context by Mansfield and Romeo [13, pp. 738–39].[9] Wilson [27, p. 177] found a negative relationship between product complexity and the propensity to engage in arm's-length licensing arrangements. Finally, Teece [17, p. 84] found that the cost advantage of an internal over a market transaction was greater for technologies which had no prior commercial application.

Changes in prior transfer activity have a greater effect on the probability of internal transfer than do changes in the age of a technology. In the case of equation (1), Table I, for example, the $d$ estimates imply that, beginning from $P = 0.5$, a one standard deviation increase in the logarithm of age reduced $P$ by 0.09 while a one standard deviation increase in the logarithm of the number of prior transfers reduced $P$ by 0.14.

A fourth inference which may be drawn from our results is that, although the relationship is statistically weak, an imitation is more likely than an innovation to be transferred internally. The argument that verification costs will be lowered and that there will be less scope for opportunistic behaviour during the transfer of imitations is not supported by these results.

Fifth, the probability that a transfer will be internalized is greater the larger

[8] The percentage of transactions classified correctly falls to 76.2.
[9] A similar finding is reported by Mansfield, Romeo and Wagner [14, pp. 54–55].

TABLE I
ESTIMATES OF EQUATION (3)

| Variable | Equation 1 | | Equation | | Equation 3 | | Equation 4 | | Equation 5 | |
|---|---|---|---|---|---|---|---|---|---|---|
| | $\hat{c}$ | $\hat{a}$ | $\hat{c}$ | $\hat{a}$ | $\hat{c}$ | $\hat{a}$ | $\hat{c}$ | $\hat{a}$ | $\hat{c}$ | $\hat{a}$ |
| const. | -0.1824 (0.7912) | — | -3.365 (0.600) | — | 0.4332 (0.7529) | — | 1.810 (1.110) | — | 0.3156 (0.7853) | — |
| $t$ | 0.2246 (0.0574) | 0.587 | 0.1925 (0.0559) | 0.503 | 0.1910 (0.0551) | 0.534 | 0.2667 (0.0779) | 0.681 | 0.2560 (0.0569) | 0.664 |
| $t^2$ | -0.0042 (.0013) | -0.460 | -0.0034 (0.0014) | -0.373 | -0.0030 (0.0012) | -0.351 | -0.0046 (0.0019) | -0.477 | -0.0041 (0.0013) | -0.443 |
| $C$ | — | — | 1.679 (0.226) | 0.209 | — | — | — | — | — | — |
| ln $C$ | 2.528 (0.316) | 0.224 | — | — | 3.458 (0.295) | 0.327 | — | — | — | — |
| $A$ | — | — | -0.0267 (0.0147) | -0.078 | — | — | — | — | — | — |
| ln $(A+1)$ | -0.2641 (0.1364) | -0.091 | — | — | -0.3268 (0.1303) | -0.120 | -0.2048 (0.1918) | -0.071 | -0.3029 (0.1371) | -0.104 |
| $T$ | — | — | -0.1023 (0.0209) | 0.172 | — | — | — | — | — | — |
| ln $T$ | 0.4235 (0.0993) | -0.143 | — | — | -0.4882 (0.0950) | -0.177 | -0.5282 (0.1420) | -0.166 | -0.4083 (0.0998) | -0.133 |

| | (1) | (1) β | (2) | (2) β | (3) | (3) β | (4) | (4) β | (5) | (5) β |
|---|---|---|---|---|---|---|---|---|---|---|
| $N$ | 0.3131 (0.1565) | 0.060 | 0.4154 (0.1546) | 0.079 | 0.1754 (0.1483) | 0.036 | 0.3932 (0.2237) | 0.071 | 0.2840 (0.1556) | 0.054 |
| $M$ | −0.2017 (0.1466) | −0.041 | −0.1675 (0.1473) | −0.034 | −0.1644 (0.1397) | −0.036 | −0.4762 (0.2078) | −0.094 | −0.2537 (0.1461) | −0.051 |
| $B$ | 1.196 (0.160) | 0.237 | 1.185 (0.158) | 0.235 | 1.061 (0.154) | 0.225 | 1.375 (0.249) | 0.266 | 1.256 (0.160) | 0.249 |
| $E$ | — | — | −0.0122 (0.0033) | −0.150 | — | — | — | — | — | — |
| $\ln(E+1)$ | −0.3321 (0.0860) | −0.171 | — | — | −0.3007 (0.0819) | −0.165 | −0.2705 (0.1249) | −0.134 | −0.3625 (0.0862) | −0.187 |
| $R$ | — | — | 18.25 (4.90) | 0.123 | — | — | — | — | — | — |
| $\ln R$ | 0.5790 (0.1284) | 0.135 | — | — | 0.5828 (0.1212) | 0.145 | 1.038 (0.186) | 0.231 | 0.5771 (0.1264) | 0.135 |
| $F$ | 1.587 (0.167) | 0.298 | 1.585 (0.168) | 0.298 | — | — | 1.455 (0.232) | 0.279 | 1.685 (0.164) | 0.319 |
| CDA | — | — | — | — | — | — | 1.467 (0.373) | 0.234 | 1.380 (0.362) | 0.181 |
| ROW | — | — | — | — | — | — | — | — | −0.4830 (0.1454) | −0.097 |
| $R^2$ | 0.444 | | 0.443 | | 0.363 | | 0.478 | | 0.441 | |
| $n$ | 1376 | | 1376 | | 1376 | | 776 | | 1357 | |

is the fraction of the transferor's resources devoted to scientific R&D and if the technology involved lies within the transferor's principal line of business.

Sixth, the greater is the number of prior transfers of all technologies conducted by the transferor, the lower is the probability that a subsequent transfer will be conducted internally.

Seventh, given the characteristics of the technology and of the parties to the transfer, the probability of an internal transfer has changed over time. The quadratic specification reported in Table I implies that the probability of an internal transfer rose until 1970 and fell thereafter. This is consistent with the contention that there has been an increase in international competition in high technology industries in recent years.[10]

## VI. CONCLUSIONS AND SUGGESTIONS FOR FUTURE RESEARCH

In this paper we have analyzed the factors which determine whether a technology will be transferred internally between affiliated firms, or through an arm's length licensing arrangement. While we have had some success in isolating the factors which influence this decision, much remains to be done.

First, technology transfer joint ventures, in which the transferor holds between 5 and 95 per cent of the equity of the receiving firm have yet to be analyzed. The theory of the firm can assist in explaining both when joint ventures will be used and the form they will take.[11]

Second, Williamson [25, p. 253] has noted that what we have called transactions may be carried out under any one of a number of distinct types of contractual arrangements. Other investigators have noted that, given explicit contractual provisions, so-called market arrangements vary widely in duration and in the implicit standards of co-operation (MacMillan and Farmer [11, pp. 280–82]). A complete analysis would establish the circumstances under which each of the possible arm's length technology transfer arrangements is chosen.

Third, there are other methods by which the characteristics of technology receiving countries might be taken into account. Both the economic and social characteristics of receiving countries and the policies of their governments

---

[10] This increase in international competition has reduced the relative cost of market transactions, first, by increasing the ease with which the qualities of a given technology can be verified. Second, it has reduced the extent to which either party in a technology transaction will be "locked in" and thus vulnerable to the opportunism of the other. Third, it has resulted in a more rapid bidding down of the rents to new technologies thereby reducing the incentive to engage in redistributive behaviour. The finding of Mansfield, Romeo and Wagner [14, p. 55] that "marginally profitable" technologies are less likely to be transferred on an intrafirm basis is consistent with this line of reasoning.

[11] We have something under 400 additional observations on transfers in which the transferor owns between 5 and 95 per cent of the receiving firm. Most of these observations involve ownership percentages between 48 and 52 per cent. (Davidson [7, p. 80]. While the theory of the firm should be of assistance in predicting when joint ventures will be observed and what form they will take, our view is that the joint venture decision can and should be analyzed separately from the choice between purely intrafirm and purely market transactions.

INTERNATIONAL TECHNOLOGY TRANSACTIONS 263

toward technology transfer are potentially measurable. In subsequent papers we hope to examine their impact on the mode of transfer adopted.

*W. H. Davidson,*
*The Colgate Darden School of Business*
  *Administration,*
*The University of Virginia,*
*Charlottesville, Virginia,*
*22906, U.S.A.*

*D. G. McFetridge,*
*Faculty of Social Sciences,*
*Department of Economics,*
*Carleton Unviersity,*
*Loeb Building,*
*Ottawa,*
*Canada, K1S 5B6*

ACCEPTED NOVEMBER 1982

## REFERENCES

[1] ALCHIAN, ARMEN A. and HAROLD DEMSETZ, "Production, Information Costs and Economic Organization", *American Economic Review*, 62, No. 5 (December 1972), pp. 777–95.

[2] ARROW, K. J., "Economic Welfare and the Allocation of Resources for Invention" in *The Rate and Direction of Inventive Activity: Economic and Social Factors* (NBER, Princeton, Princeton U. Press, 1962), pp. 609–26.

[3] BUCKLEY, P. J. and MARK CASSON, *The Future of the Multinational Enterprise* (London, MacMillan, 1976).

[4] CASSON, MARK, *Alternatives to the Multinational Enterprise* (London, MacMillan, 1979).

[5] CAVES, R. E., "The International Corporation: The Industrial Economics of Foreign Investment", *Economica* 38, No. 149 (February 1971), pp. 1–27.

[6] COASE, RONALD, "The Nature of the Firm", *Economica*, 4, No. 16, 1937, pp. 386–405; reprinted in G. J. Stigler and K. S. Boulding, eds., *Readings in Price Theory* (Homewood, Irwin, 1952), pp. 331–51.

[7] DAVIDSON, W. H., *Experience Effects in International Investment and Technology Transfer* (Ann Arbor: UMI Research Press, 1980).

[8] DUNNING, JOHN H., "Alternative Channels and Modes of International Resource Transmission", in Tagi Sagafi-nejad, Richard W. Moxon and Howard V. Perlmutter, eds., *Controlling International Techology Transfer: Issues, Perspectives and Policy Implications* (New York, Pergamon, 1981).

[9] GOLDBERGER, ARTHUR S., *Econometric Theory* (New York, Wiley, 1964).

[10] KLEIN, B., R. G. CRAWFORD and A. A. ALCHIAN, "Vertical Integration, Appropriable Rents and the Competitive Contracting Process", *Journal of Law and Economics*, 21, No. 2, (October 1978), pp. 297–326.

[11] MACMILLAN, KEITH and DAVID FARMER, "Redefining the Boundaries of the Firm", *The Journal of Industrial Economics*, 27, No. 3, (March 1979), pp. 277–85.

[12] MAGEE, STEPHEN P., "Information and the Multinational Corporation: An Appropriability Theory of Foreign Direct Investment", in J. N. Bhagwati, ed.,

264                 W. H. DAVIDSON AND DONALD G. MCFETRIDGE

*The New International Economic Order: The North–South Debate* (Cambridge, MIT Press, 1977).

[13] MANSFIELD, EDWIN and ANTHONY ROMEO, "Technology Transfer to Overseas Subsidiaries by U.S.-Based Firms", *Quarterly Journal of Economics*, 94, No. 4 (December 1980), pp. 737–50.

[14] MANSFIELD, EDWIN, ANTHONY ROMEO and SAMUEL WAGNER, "Foreign Trade and U.S. Research Development", *Review of Economics and Statistics*, 61, No. 1 (February 1979), pp. 49–57.

[15] McKEAN, ROLAND N., "Discussion", *American Economic Review*, 61, No. 2, (May 1971), pp. 124–25.

[16] McMANUS, J. C., "The Costs of Alternative Economic Organizations", *Canadian Journal of Economics*, 8, No. 3 (1975), pp. 334–50.

[17] TEECE, D. J., *The Multinational Corporation and the Resource Cost of International Technology Transfer* (Cambridge, Ballinger, 1976).

[18] TEECE, D. J., "The Multinational Enterprise: Market Failure and Market Power Considerations", *Sloan Management Review*, 22, No. 3 (Spring 1981), pp. 3–17.

[19] SCHLAIFER, ROBERT, *User's Guide to the AQD Collection* (Boston, Harvard Business School, 1978).

[20] VERNON, R., *Sovereignty at Bay: The Multinational Spread of U.S. Enterprises* (New York, Basic, 1971).

[21] VERNON, R., *Storm Over the Multinationals* (Cambridge, Harvard University Press, 1977).

[22] VERNON, R. and W. H. DAVIDSON, "Foreign Production of Technology-Intensive Products by U.S.-Based Multinational Enterprises" (Working Paper, Graduate School of Business Administration, Harvard University, Boston, 1977).

[23] WILLIAMSON, O. E., "Vertical Integration of Production: Market Failure Considerations", *American Economic Review*, 61, No. 2 (May 1971), pp. 112–23.

[24] WILLIAMSON, O. E., *Markets and Hierarchies: Analysis and Antitrust Implications* (New York, The Free Press, 1975).

[25] WILLIAMSON, O. E., "Transaction-cost Economics: The Government of Contractual Relations", *The Journal of Law and Economics*, 22, No. 2 (October 1979), pp. 233–61.

[26] WILLIAMSON, O. E., "Vertical Integration and Related Variations on a Transaction Cost Economics Theme" (Paper prepared for presentation at an International Economics Association Conference on "New Developments in Market Structure", Ottawa, Canada, May 10–14, 1982.

[27] WILSON, ROBERT W., "The Effect of Technological Environment and Product Rivalry on R&D Effort and Licensing of Inventories", *Review of Economics and Statistics*, 59, No. 2 (May 1977), pp. 171–78.

# 10
# A Study of the Life Cycle
# of Joint Ventures

*Bruce Kogut*

Joint ventures, like any form of organization, undergo a cycle of creation, institutionalization, and, with high probability, termination. The additional complexity of a joint venture is that its creation is the product of two or a few existing organizations which, by right of equity ownership, jointly—though not necessarily equally—may exercise control. Of course, if the partners had nonconflicting goals, the management dilemma of a joint venture would be no greater than the problems inherent in any subsidiary–corporate headquarters relationship. But joint ventures are often, though not exclusively, created due to competitive motives, either between the partners or relative to other firms. Herein lies the irony, namely, that the competitive conditions that motivate the creation of a joint venture may also be responsible for its termination.

The relationship between the motivations to create and to terminate implies the need to analyze issues of stability from the perspective of the life cycle of a joint venture. Recent work in organizational theory has shown, for example, that the early history of an organization molds the patterns of behavior into relatively inert institutional structures. Similarly, the motivations of the partners to cooperate mold the institutional structure of the joint venture and influence their future behavior.

This chapter seeks to develop a few theoretical perspectives on the creation and termination of joint ventures. The first section presents data on the mortality of joint ventures. The second describes three theories of joint ventures from the perspectives of transaction cost economics, strategic behavior, and organizational ecology. The subsequent section reviews the literature on joint venture stability and relates previous findings, where possible, to the three theoretical perspectives. In addition, a few representative hypotheses are statistically tested. In the fourth section, a case history of an international joint venture is analyzed from the perspectives of the three theories. The final section presents a set of conclusions.

I would like to acknowledge the helpful criticism on an earlier draft by Erin Anderson and John Kimberly, as well as the research assistance of Bernadette Fox. The research for this chapter has been funded under the auspices of the Reginald H. Jones Center of the Wharton School of the University of Pennsylvania through a grant from AT&T.

## Descriptive Statistics of Joint Venture Mortality

Because there has been little cross-sectional research on mortality rates of joint ventures over time, this section reports mortality rates according to age, function, industry, and country. Information on joint ventures was taken from the publication *Mergers and Acquisitions.* A questionnaire was sent to one of the parent companies of 475 joint ventures. Despite a response rate of 55.5 percent, only 148 questionnaires were usable due to either refusal to give pertinent information, the decision not to invest following the published announcement, or a misclassification by the respondent of nonequity contracts as a joint venture. Only ventures located in the United States were used so as to eliminate the effects of government regulations in other parts of the world. A domestic venture is between only U.S. partners; an international venture includes at least one non-U.S. firm. By looking only at ventures located in the United States, differences in business and political conditions can be reduced as influences on stability.

As seen in table 10–1, instability rates peak in years 5 and 6 for the sample of all joint ventures, though this trend is more pronounced for international ventures. Rates of termination by acquisition (whether by the partners or by a third firm) appear slightly more stable than those by dissolution. Studies on business failure rates, in general, show dissolution rates to be roughly 10 percent a year for small start-ups (Reynolds, 1986). While the mortality rates are not much different than what we find for joint ventures, the difference is that these ventures are started and owned by existing firms with the requisite financial resources.

In table 10–2, mortality rates are lower for production, financial service, and development of new products. However, statistical tests that correct for age of the

## Table 10-1
## Hazard Rates for Joint Ventures by Acquisition and Dissolution as a Percentage of Those at Risk

|  | *Age* | | | | | | |
|---|---|---|---|---|---|---|---|
|  | *1* | *2* | *3* | *4* | *5* | *6* | *> 6* |
| Domestic joint ventures terminated | 5.6 | 13.5 | 5.1 | 12.7 | 10.4 | 8.3 | 25.9 |
| Dissolved | 4.2 | 7.5 | 1.7 | 3.6 | 10.4 | 5.6 | 14.8 |
| Acquired | 1.4 | 6.0 | 3.4 | 9.1 | 0 | 2.7 | 11.1 |
| International joint ventures terminated | 3.9 | 5.4 | 10.8 | 4.2 | 20.0 | 24.0 | 12.6 |
| Dissolved | 2.6 | 2.7 | 3.1 | 2.1 | 14.3 | 12.0 | 6.3 |
| Acquired | 1.3 | 2.7 | 7.7 | 2.1 | 5.7 | 12.0 | 6.3 |
| Both international and domestic joint ventures terminated | 4.7 | 9.3 | 8.1 | 8.7 | 14.7 | 14.8 | 20.9 |
| Dissolved | 3.4 | 5.0 | 2.4 | 2.9 | 12.0 | 8.2 | 11.6 |
| Acquired | 1.3 | 4.3 | 5.7 | 5.8 | 2.4 | 6.6 | 9.3 |

**Table 10-2**
**Mortality Rates by Function**

| | Total | | Alive | | Dissolved | | Acquired | |
|---|---|---|---|---|---|---|---|---|
| | *Number* | *Percentage* | *Number* | *Percentage* | *Number* | *Percentage* | *Number* | *Percentage* |
| Research | 7 | 4 | 3 | 42.9 | 4 | 57.1 | 0 | 0 |
| Development of existing products | 28 | 1 | 15 | 53.6 | 5 | 17.9 | 8 | 28.6 |
| Development of new products | 50 | 3 | 30 | 60.0 | 12 | 24.0 | 8 | 16.0 |
| Production | 69 | 4 | 40 | 58.0 | 16 | 23.2 | 13 | 18.8 |
| Marketing and service | 72 | 4 | 37 | 51.4 | 19 | 26.4 | 16 | 22.2 |
| Financial service | 10 | | 6 | 60.0 | 4 | 40.0 | 0 | 0 |
| Natural resource development | 24 | 1 | 12 | 50.0 | 8 | 33.3 | 4 | 16.7 |

**Table 10-3**
**Mortality Rates by Industry**

| | Total | | Alive | | Dissolved | | Acquired | |
|---|---|---|---|---|---|---|---|---|
| | Number | Percentage | Number | Percentage | Number | Percentage | Number | Percentage |
| Resources | 19 | 12.8 | 10 | 52.6 | 7 | 36.8 | 2 | 10.5 |
| Paper and allied products | 4 | 2.7 | 3 | 75.0 | 1 | 25.0 | 0 | 0 |
| Chemicals and allied products | 27 | 18.2 | 16 | 59.3 | 6 | 22.2 | 5 | 18.5 |
| Petroleum and coal products | 4 | 2.7 | 1 | 25.0 | 2 | 50.0 | 1 | 25.0 |
| Rubber and miscellaneous plastic products | 3 | 2.0 | 2 | 66.7 | 0 | 0 | 1 | 33.3 |
| Primary metal industries | 7 | 4.7 | 3 | 42.9 | 0 | 0 | 4 | 57.1 |
| Fabricated metal products | 4 | 2.7 | 3 | 75.0 | 0 | 0 | 1 | 25.0 |
| Machinery, except electrical | 18 | 12.2 | 12 | 66.7 | 2 | 11.1 | 4 | 22.2 |
| Electrical and electronic equipment | 16 | 10.8 | 11 | 68.8 | 4 | 25.0 | 1 | 6.3 |
| Transportation equipment | 4 | 2.7 | 2 | 50.0 | 1 | 25.0 | 1 | 25.0 |
| Instruments and related products | 6 | 4.1 | 2 | 33.3 | 3 | 50.0 | 1 | 16.7 |
| Other manufacturing industries | 7 | 4.7 | 2 | 28.6 | 1 | 14.3 | 4 | 57.1 |
| Communications | 3 | 2.0 | 1 | 33.3 | 0 | 0 | 2 | 66.7 |
| Utilities | 3 | 2.0 | 1 | 33.3 | 2 | 66.7 | 0 | 0 |
| Wholesale trade | 2 | 1.4 | 2 | 10.0 | 0 | 0 | 0 | 0 |
| Financial services | 9 | 6.0 | 2 | 22.2 | 6 | 66.7 | 1 | 11.1 |
| Real estate and construction | 5 | 3.4 | 4 | 80.0 | 1 | 20.0 | 0 | 0 |
| Other services | 7 | 4.7 | 3 | 42.9 | 2 | 28.6 | 2 | 28.6 |
| Total | 148 | 99.9 | 80 | 54.1 | 38 | 25.7 | 30 | 20.2 |

**Table 10-4**
**Mortality Rates by Country of Joint Venture Partner**

| | Total | | Alive | | Dissolved | | Acquired | |
|---|---|---|---|---|---|---|---|---|
| | Number | Percentage | Number | Percentage | Number | Percentage | Number | Percentage |
| United States | 70 | 47.3 | 33 | 47.1 | 22 | 31.4 | 15 | 21.4 |
| Britain | 9 | 6.1 | 4 | 44.4 | 2 | 22.2 | 3 | 33.3 |
| Japan | 23 | 15.5 | 15 | 65.2 | 2 | 08.7 | 6 | 26.1 |
| Scandinavia | 8 | 5.4 | 4 | 50.0 | 4 | 50.0 | 0 | 0 |
| Switzerland | 3 | 2.0 | 1 | 33.3 | 1 | 33.3 | 1 | 33.3 |
| Germany | 10 | 6.8 | 7 | 70.0 | 1 | 10.0 | 2 | 20.0 |
| France | 4 | 2.7 | 1 | 25.0 | 3 | 75.0 | 0 | 0 |
| Netherlands | 3 | 2.0 | 3 | 100.0 | 0 | 0 | 0 | 0 |
| Belgium | 5 | 3.4 | 3 | 60.0 | 1 | 20.0 | 1 | 20.0 |
| Malaysia | 1 | .7 | 1 | 100.0 | 0 | 0 | 0 | 0 |
| Canada | 12 | 8.1 | 8 | 66.7 | 2 | 16.7 | 2 | 16.7 |
| Total | 148 | 100.0 | 80 | 54.1 | 38 | 25.7 | 30 | 20.2 |

venture show only that ventures including marketing and after-sales service have significantly higher mortality rates. (The nature of these tests is described in the next section.) Particularly interesting is the difference in how ventures terminate according to function. Development of new products shows a higher rate of dissolution than acquisition, which makes sense given the risk attached to development. But development of existing products shows a tendency to terminate by acquisition, presumably because the development risk is lower and partners may differ in their valuations placed on the product.

In table 10–3, mortality rates are given for ventures by industry as defined by SIC codes. Because of the lower number of cases in some industries, it is difficult to infer mortality trends. However, when the ventures are aggregated into services, manufacturing, and resources, the statistical tests show a significantly higher mortality rate for services.

Table 10–4 presents data by the second partner's country. Again, it is important to caution against inferences without controlling for age. The Japanese joint ventures tend to be younger, which explains why the statistical tests do not show a significantly higher probability of termination. Interestingly, the Japanese ventures show a high rate of termination by acquisition when compared to the total sample. Of these six acquisitions, five were by the Japanese partner. When grouping the ventures into international and domestic categories, the tests show a higher probability of termination for international ventures, when correcting for age effects.

## Theoretical Explanations

The central thesis of this chapter is that the reasons for the termination of a joint venture frequently lie in the motives responsible for its creation. There are many possible explanations for the creation of joint ventures. Many of these explanations, however, are variants of three theoretical perspectives, namely, transaction costs, strategic behavior, and organizational behavior. Though all three of these are complementary, they differ also in important ways.

Transaction cost economics has been developed by a number of scholars working on the determinants of the firm's boundaries. The most influential statement of transaction-cost economics is associated with Williamson (1975, 1985). His argument is that institutional design reflects efforts to *minimize* the sum of production and transaction costs. Production costs are simply the costs usually associated with the transformation process, with factors including the costs of inputs, the degree of scale economies, and the efficiency of the productive technology. Transactions costs are less well specified, but represent the costs of monitoring efforts, of investing in ways to bond performance, and of cheating. Since it is difficult to observe these costs, Williamson proposes instead to focus on the conditions that are likely to lead to high transaction costs. He lists three: asset specificity (or the degree to which assets are dedicated to transacting with a particular economic partner), uncertainty (which represents the difficulty of predicting and observing cheating), and frequency (which influences whether there is sufficient volume to justify a fixed investment in establishing an organizational solution). All of these conditions are necessary; none is sufficient.

There have been few attempts to extend transaction costs to joint ventures, with the notable exception of Stuckey (1983), and Buckley and Casson (chapter 2). One approach is to analyze the unique organizational properties of a joint venture and the transaction hazards to which they are addressed. What sets a joint venture apart from other organizational forms is that the parties share ownership of the assets and derived revenues and, thus, share monitoring and control rights, which (even if not exercised) are still valuable. There are, thus, two issues: (1) joint investment in ownership and (2) control and monitoring rights. Joint investment addresses the issue of creating incentives to perform, for what better incentive is there than requiring both parties to put up the capital or capitalized assets? Joint investment is, thus, a form of *mutual hostage positions* which mitigate the incentives to shirk or to behave contrary to fiduciary responsibility. Along with ownership comes the right to monitor and control, though to what extent is frequently the subject of negotiation. Of course, complete ownership also provides these benefits, but due to obstacles to merger and to differentiated abilities among the partners, both parties are forced to venture outside (see Buckley and Casson, chapter 2).

Unlike transaction-cost theory, strategic-behavior explanations rest, not on predicting that a joint venture will be chosen if it represents the minimum-cost institution, but if it maximizes profits. As Contractor and Lorange point out in chapter 1, the motives for strategic behavior are plentiful, from defensive arrangements which hurt other competitors to collusive arrangements to enhance market power, perhaps at the expense of buyers. To many researchers, strategic-behavior and transaction-cost–economics are compatible approaches, for once two firms decide to collude, many of the issues of bilateral bargaining discussed by Williamson are also relevant to the design of the collusive agreement.

Though compatible, the two approaches differ in terms of predicting institutional choice. Consider the following example of a firm that sources components outside for internal assembling into a product sold as a final good. A firm implicitly calculates the degree of asset specificity, uncertainty, and frequency; it decides that the sum of the transaction and economic costs favors a buy decision. Unexpectedly, consumers suddenly insist on, and are willing to pay a premium for, greater quality of components. Asset specificity, frequency, and uncertainty have not changed their values.

Transaction-cost economics would predict no change in the buy decision; strategic behavior implies a move toward a make decision because the importance of quality has increased and the downstream assembler is under greater incentives to appropriate the rents. One way to handle this problem is to rig the analysis to look like a cost-minimizing issue. For example, it could be posited that the downstream firm compares the revenue stream under internal manufacture to that under outside purchase, calls this difference an opportunity cost, and then proceeds to minimize the sum of transaction, economic, and opportunity costs. But if this solution is to be permitted, then every situation can be reduced ad hoc to comply with transaction costs. For the point of view of what is of analytical interest, it is empirically and theoretically important to separate out reasons of appropriability of revenue streams derived from strategic positioning in a particular product market from reasons of minimizing costs. What is the point of a theory if there is no variance to be explained?

Another explanation for joint ventures is derived from organizational theory and stresses cooperative motivations. The basis of this perspective is that firms can be conceived as organizations embodying different skills. To the extent that these skills are embedded in complex organizational routines, the transfer of organizational skills through the market or through a license may be impeded. Moreover, since organizational knowledge is very likely to be what Polanyi (1967) calls "tacit," the transfer of organizational knowledge can only be carried out if the organization is itself replicated.

This perspective has a straightforward implication for joint ventures. If a firm desires to sell a portion of its technological competence, it may do so by a spot market, by a license agreement, by acquiring or being acquired by another party, or by a joint venture. Let us rule out acquisitions by assuming that the technology being transferred is only a small portion of the total value of the firm. A common mechanism by which to transfer technology but still control its use is the licensing agreement. But if the knowledge is organizationally bound, a license may be an inadequate mechanism by which to transfer tacit knowledge. In this case, a joint venture serves as a vehicle that better allows for the transfer and imitation of complex and tacit organizational routines.

As discussed in the later sections, the three theoretical perspectives on the motives for joint venture creation have direct implications for the causes of instability. Both transaction-cost and strategic-behavior explanations view joint ventures as derived from a competitive dynamic, vis-à-vis either the parties to the venture or other competitors. It stands to reason, therefore, that changes in the parameters influencing the competitive positioning of the partners may lead to destabilizing their cooperation. An organizational-knowledge argument, however, views termination as the completion—successful or not—of the attempt to transfer complex technological routines. In this case, termination is planned.

## Perspectives on Joint Venture Stability

Most studies that have analyzed joint venture stability have concentrated on the competitive dynamics between the partners to the neglect of the competitive nature of the industry and of the completion of technology transfer. Partner competition is, however, consistent with transaction-cost and strategic-behavior theories of joint venture creation, for it stands to reason that changes in the values of the parameters found to influence joint venture creation should influence stability. To isolate the factors that influence joint venture stability requires analyzing the stability of the cooperative and competitive incentives among the partners. Changes in the environment, of strategies, and of bargaining power over the life of the venture can affect dramatically the longevity of cooperation.

The importance of partner conflict has been confirmed by several studies. Franko (1971) analyzed joint venture instability in terms of strategic change, as proxied by whether the U.S. partner reorganized its international activities. Stopford and Wells (1972) looked at conflicts between the desire of a U.S. multinational to control the joint venture as a subsidiary and the desire of the country partner to maximize local profits. Hladik (1985) found a similar pattern in her analysis of whether an overseas venture carried out exporting.

The most detailed studies of partner-conflict explanations for joint ventures have been carried out by Killing (1982, 1983) and two colleagues, Schaan (1985) and Beamish (1985). These studies are especially relevant to transaction-cost explanations, since their focus is principally on the governance properties of joint ventures. Killing argues that since dual control is inherently problematic, ventures dominated by one of the partners are more likely to be stable. Based on a sample of thirty-seven ventures, Killing finds support for his thesis, though statistical tests were not provided. In summarizing his Ph.D. thesis work, Beamish (1985) qualifies Killing's results by showing that ventures where the local partner is dominant or shares control reveal higher rates of instability in LDCs. Schaan (1985) was able to specify more clearly the link between dominant control and performance. Through a study of ten joint ventures in Mexico, he concluded that satisfactory performance is more likely to the degree to which parents fit control mechanisms to their criteria for success, presumably because otherwise there is likely to be confusion over how each partner can exercise power to achieve its objectives without infringing upon its partner's authority.

No matter what the initial agreement on control and ownership may have been at the start of a venture, environmental and strategic changes over time may shift the relative bargaining power among the partners. Harrigan (1985), in particular, has stressed motives of strategic behavior as an explanation of joint venture creation and stability. See also chapter 12. Among other factors, she proposes that partner asymmetries, the durability of the advantages each partner brings, and the existence of exit barriers tend to stabilize ventures. Empirical tests in chapter 12 show some support for the influence of asymmetry on stability.

These studies suggest several possible explanations for joint venture instability. Since many of these explanations are of managerial and scholastic curiosity, I have gathered a number of hypotheses from the aforementioned authors and tested them against a sample of 148 joint ventures. Based upon this data, a few hypotheses prevalent in the literature may be tested. Killing states clearly two hypotheses:

Hypothesis 1: Dominant joint ventures are more stable than shared-control joint ventures (Killing, 1982, 1983).

Hypotheses 2: Joint ventures formed between firms that differ significantly in size are less stable because many additional problems arise (Killing, 1983, p. 123).

While it is not possible with the available data to specify many of Harrigan's suggestions, the following statements can be tested:

Hypothesis 3: "Concentrated settings will be more attractive settings for joint ventures because firms operating within oligopolies can focus on mutually desirable goals with greater ease" (Harrigan, 1985, p. 124).

Hypothesis 4: Ventures with a partner having market access are more stable because access is a more durable advantage than technology (Harrigan, 1985, pp. 59, 83).

The hypotheses are tested by using a partial likelihood model. This model treats the influence of the explanatory variables (or covariates) as influencing linearly the log of the hazard function. The method works, not by comparing ventures that terminated to those that did not, but by the order of terminations and censorship (that is, ventures still existing when last observed). Effectively, estimates on the covariate coefficients are derived by a procedure that compares ventures that terminated early to those terminating later.

The specification of Killing's hypotheses are straightforward. Because, as noted earlier, ownership and control theoretically and, as Killing's data shows, in practice are correlated, stability should be higher for ventures when one partner has majority control. The ratio of the asset size of the larger partner to that of the smaller is a fair approximation for hypothesis 2. Hypothesis 3 uses an eight-firm concentration ratio at the four-digit SIC code level; unfortunately, such data are only available for manufacturing industries. (Tests using four-firm concentration ratios did not alter the results substantially.) Hypothesis 4 is specified by a dummy variable indicating whether the venture includes a marketing and distribution activity. Hypotheses 1 and 2 are related to transaction-cost–theory explanations; numbers 3 and 4 bear a greater relevance for strategic-behavior theories.

Table 10–5 provides a list of the variables, their sources, expected signs, and the results. A positive coefficient means that a variable acts to increase the likelihood of termination; a negative coefficient means a decrease in the likelihood of termination. As a control for industry conditions, a dummy variable is included; it takes a value of one if industry shipments at the four-digit SIC level are greater than the median, while it takes a value of zero otherwise.

The results do not support the hypotheses. Majority share is correctly signed but highly insignificant. (When replaced by a dummy variable for whether the

**Table 10-5**
**Summary of Variables and Results**

| Hypothesis | Variable | Source | Expected Sign | Partial Likelihood Estimate |
|---|---|---|---|---|
| 1 | Majority share owner | Questionnaire | – | –.25 (–0.62) |
|  | Shipment growth | Unpublished data from U.S. Dept. of Commerce | – | –.46 (–1.28) |
| 2 | Relative size | Moody's | + | –.0001 (–.85) |
|  | Shipment growth | See above. | – | –.51 (–1.49) |
| 3 | Concentration | Bureau of Census 1977, 1982 | – | .01 (1.69*) |
|  | Shipment growth | See above. | – | –.51 (–1.59) |
| 4 | Marketing activity | Questionnaire | – | .56 (1.73*) |
|  | Shipment growth | See above. | – | –.56 (–1.76*) |

\* = significant at .10 or better

venture had a partner who had dominant equity, the results remained the same.) Hypothesis 2 carries the reverse sign as predicted, but is also insignificant. The sign reversal is not surprising, for it could be argued logically that the greater the difference in asset sizes between the partners, the more likely it is that one firm will dominate; thus, by Killing's contention, the venture should be more stable. Hypothesis 3 is contradicted, as the higher the degree of concentration, the more likely it is that the venture will terminate; the relationship is significant at .10. This result also contradicts Kogut's (1986a) hypothesis that the higher the concentration rate, the higher the entry barriers and the more likely any venture's survival. The result may imply that in concentrated industries, the competitive incentives for the partners to defect increases. Hypothesis 4 is also contradicted. Ventures with marketing activities are more likely to terminate. The Shipment growth variable is correctly signed in all the estimations, but significant only in the fourth regression.

These results should be viewed as discounting any simple statement on the causes of joint venture instability. At the same time, some of these relationships may be confirmed when other important influences are considered. There is a danger, in other words, of specification error.

Some current work suggests, in fact, that joint venture stability is influenced jointly by competitive incentives among the partners and competitive changes in industry structure. In recent work, Kogut (1986a) found that the likelihood of termination is decreased when partners to the venture have other ongoing agreements. Mutual forbearance, to use Buckley and Casson's terminology, is enhanced when disrupting the venture may affect other transactions. This result supports the transaction-cost explanation of hostage positions stabilizing economic relationships. Moreover, it was found that whereas ventures located in growing industries are more likely to survive, those located in industries that are becoming more concentrated and to which both partners belong are more likely to terminate. This result is consistent with transaction-cost argument, but is particularly pertinent to strategic-behavior argument.

Whereas the statistical tests given in Kogut (1986a) confirm the influence of competitive dynamics between the partners and within the industry on joint venture stability, they do not examine terminations due to completion of the transfer of organizational knowledge. Nor do these tests provide rich insight into the origins of shifts in bargaining power among the partners. For this purpose, the following section examines a case history of a joint venture in terms of the reasons for its establishment and reasons for its demise.

## A Life History of a Joint Venture

In 1983, the Honeywell Corporation and L.M. Ericsson signed a multifaceted agreement for the sale of a telecommunication switch and for joint development of technology. In January 1987, it was publicly announced that their joint research venture had been terminated and acquired by Ericsson. While the factors influencing the creation and termination of the venture are many, the following analysis concentrates on the motives and concerns of the two partners, the process of institutionalization, and the influences on stability.

In the early 1980s, the Honeywell Corporation was involved in the production of control equipment and systems and, to a lesser but still significant extent, in the manufacture and sale of information systems products and services. The control business had been the primary business of Honeywell since its founding. The information systems businesses, on the other hand, had been acquired from other firms (such as General Electric and RCA) during the 1960s and 1970s. Honeywell's aggressive acquisitions placed it in the second tier of the industry, with IBM occupying the premier position. However, its computer investments had come at a cost and had not earned the profitability of its other businesses.

In the late 1970s, Honeywell recognized the possibility to consolidate its control and information systems businesses by linking the two by a smart private branch exchange (PBX). The convergence of its two major product groups is the key to a major new strategy to offer "intelligent buildings" which integrate telecommunications, data processing, and system controls. Honeywell was searching for a stable and long-term source of supply of PBXs.

In the 1970s, L.M. Ericsson had captured the leading share of the non–United States public digital switching market and was a major provider of telecommunication services and products, including cable and cellular radio products. Despite its international strength, its U.S. position was weak and consisted mostly of the cable sales from L.M. Ericsson Inc. (Its U.S. joint venture, of which it owned 50 percent and Anaconda—which ARCO had acquired—owned the other 50 percent.) Ericsson was, therefore, looking for an entry into the U.S. private telecommunications market, which promised substantial growth following deregulation and recent product innovations. Ericsson hoped to build a large market for its MD-110 PBX. A sale to a major customer would provide critical market share to support the costs of entry and software development to adapt the MD-110 to the demands of the U.S. market.

Whereas an agreement for Ericsson to supply Honeywell with the MD-110 would meet the goals of both parties, there were critical areas of instability that would persistently endanger a simple supply contract. Honeywell, for its part, would be dedicating significant resources to interface with the MD-110 switch. What would happen if L.M. Ericsson developed a different line or divested the business? For Ericsson, Honeywell would be incorporating the PBX into its products and, thus, drawing away potential customers. More importantly, Honeywell's further development of the software and hardware to interface with its equipment would enhance its abilities to develop and manufacture its own PBX. How could Ericsson guarantee that it is not giving up technology to a competitor?

The critical decision was made to solve these problems before the agreement was signed. The cooperative framework was divided into four separate agreements. One agreement established the pricing for a long-term supply of the MD-110. Two other agreements provided for a sale of technology from Ericsson to Honeywell and a licensing provision by which Honeywell can choose itself to manufacture the PBX. Thus, the fears concerning loss of technology and future supplies were assuaged. The sale of technology is particularly interesting, for it implies that Ericsson recognized that it could not protect its technology. By selling the technology, the future cooperation is left unencumbered over the use and leakage of the proprietary knowledge. If the parties cannot agree on the pricing of the technology, then without adequate protection, cooperation on the long-term supply is itself destined to fail.

The fourth agreement established the Honeywell Ericsson Development Company (HEDC) as a 50:50 joint venture (in the legal form of a partnership) in order to develop software for the adaptation of the MD-110 to the U.S. market. The partnership not only shared the fixed costs and risks of developmental work, but also served the important function of bringing together the research efforts of both parties, thereby creating personal trust and team learning between Ericsson and Honeywell.

The use of multiple clauses to the agreement fits well with transaction-cost arguments. The licensing contract eliminated some of Honeywell's dependence on a single source for a critical component. The technology agreement resolved an issue that would otherwise be destabilizing. Finally, the joint venture served not only to share development costs, but to enhance the cooperation between the firms.

The joint venture was also critical to the successful transfer of knowledge between the firms. Both firms had started development efforts prior to the agreement. Much of this knowledge was being produced by engineering teams which had not yet codified the work in process. By bringing the engineering teams together and then circulating some of the people back to the partner organizations, the requisite know-how was transferred between the two firms.

Since the central task of HEDC was to develop software applications and transfer the products back to the partner firms, the institutional structure of the venture mirrored these objectives. The venture was controlled through three organizational entities: the board of directors consisting of 3 executives from each firm; the executive board consisting of 2 executives from each; and a project planning board consisting of 3 executives from each and including the project planning manager of the joint venture. Over time, the executive board was dropped as redundant. The board of directors met twice a year and was chaired by a Honeywell executive since the venture itself was headed by a former Ericsson manager. It had the primary task of overseeing progress and ascertaining whether the venture was progressing on what was called the "project road map." This road map was a careful statement incorporated into the agreement which laid out the research projects and objectives for the venture. The project planning board was the critical linchpin between the venture and the market planning groups in the partner organizations. A concern raised in the negotiations was whether the venture might stray from the partner strategies. The function of the project planning board was to keep the development activities of HEDC in line with the partners' marketing objectives.

Over the first year and a half of operations, HEDC grew to over 160 engineers and successfully tested the first major development project: the integration of voice and data signals. However, several problems inherent in the beginning of the venture began to emerge. First, since Ericsson and Honeywell already had established facilities in the United States, HEDC was split between Anaheim and Dallas, the former close to Ericsson's operations, the latter to Honeywell's. Because of the geographic isolation, separate projects were allocated to each location, though visits were frequent and coordination was closely maintained. Second, whereas both firms wanted integrated voice/data communication capabilities, the other projects were not always of equal importance to the partners. This difference was especially evident regarding a packet switch which was more valuable to Ericsson's efforts in promoting electronic mail.

In late 1985, Honeywell chose to reduce drastically its cost commitment to the venture and some fifty engineers were released to their parent organizations. As a result, HEDC consolidated its operations to its Anaheim location. Despite the dismissal, the projects remained largely on track. Still, in late 1986, Honeywell decided to pull out entirely, leaving HEDC to become a wholly owned part of Ericsson's U.S. operations. (Ericsson had acquired a 100 percent ownership of L.M. Ericsson Inc. the previous year.)

Though terminated, the venture could hardly be considered a failure. Both the supply and technology agreements remain in force, even though Ericsson and

Honeywell occasionally confront each other as competitors in the PBX market. Moreover, the venture succeeded in adapting the switch to the U.S. market and transferring the software know-how of both firms to each other. In this sense, termination reflected the completion of the limited objectives of the original agreement. Finally, through the acquisition of HEDC, Ericcson obtained an ongoing research facility critical to its plans for further product development and adaptation.

The Honeywell and Ericsson agreement illustrates three important issues. First, a joint venture is frequently only a part of a multiplicity of contracts between the partners. To understand the joint venture, it is necessary to analyze it from the perspective of the total relationship, if not from its position in the wider cooperative network of the partners.

Second, the history of the venture suggests that there was a possible shift of bargaining power in the course of the relationship. Initially, Ericsson was in possession of a switch that had already been proven outside the United States and of proven capabilities in leading developments in digital communication technologies. Honeywell offered the clout of a large-purchase contract and some software application know-how. But, over the course of time, Honeywell acquired growing familiarity in the development of the relevant technologies. On the other hand, the disappointment of Ericsson's other businesses in the United States increased the importance of Honeywell as a potential customer for other products and, possibly, as a partner in other areas. However, the incentives for Honeywell to contribute its marketing strengths to a venture with Ericsson diminished once the requisite technology had been transferred.

The shift in bargaining power raises a third issue concerning whether it was a missed opportunity for Ericsson to restrict the agreement. Like Honeywell (but to a far lesser extent), Ericsson also acquired firms in information systems, and it was to the information systems division that a considerable amount of investment was allocated for the purpose of entering the U.S. market. From the vantage point of hindsight, it is interesting to speculate on whether a broader coalition with Honeywell in return for the contribution of its technology would not have advanced Ericsson's information systems strategy. The timing for this coalition is past. Honeywell is currently joining its information systems businesses in a joint venture with other partners, and Ericsson has signed an agreement with DEC for development efforts located in Stockholm. On the other hand, the stability of the wider Honeywell–Ericsson agreement may reflect the decision to limit cooperation. In this sense, the endurance of their cooperation represents a successful response to both transaction-cost hazards and the requirements of technology transfer, as well as the avoidance of the turbulence involved in coordinating strategies in the information technologies market.

## Conclusion

Both theory and empirical studies point to the importance of competitor incentives for the formation and termination of a joint venture. Ventures are a means to resolve competitive conflicts inherent in economic relationships or to affect the competitive positioning of firms relative to rivals, including buyers and suppliers. But ventures motivated on the basis of competition are vulnerable to changes in the bargaining power of the partners and in the competitive structure of the market. Whereas the design of the venture and overall partner relationship can mitigate competitive incentives, the sources of destabilizing pulls are often inherent in the original motivations to establish the venture.

This perspective casts a sobering light on the cooperative motivations for a joint venture. A joint venture is indeed a pooling of assets under the joint ownership and control of a few partner firms. But though cooperative in intent, joint ventures are troubled by the enduring influence of competitive rivalry on stability. To the extent that firms are committed to each other through other agreements, the design of the overall relationship between the partners can attenuate the incentives to terminate. But, it would be foolhardy to view a joint venture as anything but the institutional cooperation between firms within a larger competitive context.

Joint ventures play, however, another role outside of resolving or affecting competitive factors; namely, such ventures are vehicles by which knowledge is transferred and by which firms learn from each other. The Honeywell–Ericsson agreement is a fine example of cooperation for the objectives of sharing the costs of knowledge generation and of transferring complex knowledge. Imitation is frequently the goal of a joint venture, and when imitation is complete, the sign of success is termination. In this sense, it would be a mistake in the efforts to pinpoint the competitive sources for joint venture creation and termination to swing the pendulum too far and obscure the cooperative merits.

## Bibliography

Beamish, P.M. 1985. "The Characteristics of Joint Ventures in Developed and Developing Countries." *Columbia Journal of World Business,* Fall: 13-20.

Berg, S., and Friedman, P., 1977. "Joint Ventures, Competition, and Technological Complementarities." *Southern Economic Journal,* 43 (3): 1330-37.

———. 1981a. "Impacts of Domestic Joint Ventures on Industrial Rates of Return." *Review of Economics and Statistics,* 63: 293-98.

———. 1981b. "Impacts of a Pooled Cross-Section Analysis, Domestic Joint Ventures on Industrial Rates of Return." *Review of Economics and Statistics,* 63.

Duncan, L. 1982. "Impacts of New Entry and Horizontal Joint Ventures on Industrial Rates of Return." *Review of Economics and Statistics,* 64: 120-25.

Franko, L.G. 1971. *Joint Venture Survival in Multinational Corporations.* New York: Praeger.

———. 1976. *The European Multinationals.* London: Harper & Row.

Hannan, M.T., and Freeman, J.H., 1976. "The Population Ecology of Organizations." *American Journal of Sociology,* 82: 929-64.

———. 1984. "Structural Inertia and Organizational Change." *American Sociological Review,* 49: 149-64.

*Study of Life Cycle of Joint Ventures* • 185

Harrigan, K.R. 1985. *Strategies for Joint Ventures.* Lexington, Mass.: Lexington Books.

Hladik, K.J. 1985. *International Joint Ventures: An Economic Analysis of U.S. Foreign Business Partnerships.* Lexington, Mass.: Lexington Books.

Killing, J. 1982. "How to Make a Global Joint Venture Work." *Harvard Business Review,* 60 (3): 120–27.

———. 1983. *Strategies for Joint Venture Success.* New York: Praeger.

Kimberly, J.R. 1975. "Environmental Constraints and Organizational Structure: A Comparative Analysis of Rehabilitation Organizations." *Administrative Science Quarterly,* 20: 1–9.

Kimberly, J.R., and Miles, R.H., (eds.). 1981. *The Organizational Life Cycle.* San Francisco: Jossey-Bass.

Kogut, B. 1986a. *Cooperative and Competitive Influences on Joint Venture Stability under Competing Risks of Acquisition and Dissolution.* Working paper. Reginald H. Jones Center, The Wharton School, University of Pennsylvania, Philadelphia.

———. 1986b. "On Designing Contracts to Guarantee Enforceability: The Case of East-West Trade." *Journal of International Business Studies,* 17: 47–62.

———. 1987. "Joint Ventures: Theoretical and Empirical Perspectives." Mimeo.

McKelvey, B. 1983. *Organizational Systematics: Taxonomy, Evolution, Classification.* Berkeley, Calif.: University of California Press.

Nelson, R., and Winter, S., 1982. *An Evolutionary Theory of Economic Change.* Cambridge, Mass.: Harvard University Press.

Polanyi, M. 1967. *The Tacit Dimension.* New York: Doubleday.

Reynolds, P.D. 1986. "Organizations: Predicting Contributions and Survival." Mimeo.

Schaan, J.L. 1985. *Managing the Parent Control in Joint Ventures.* Presented at the Fifth Annual Strategic Management Society Conference, Barcelona, Spain.

Stinchcombe, A.L. 1965. "Social Structure and Organizations." In J.G. March (ed.), *Handbook of Organizations.* Chicago: Rand McNally.

Stopford, M., and Wells, L., 1972. *Managing the Multinational Enterprise.* New York: Basic Books.

Stuckey, A. 1983. *Vertical Integration and Joint Ventures in the Aluminum Industry.* Cambridge, Mass.: Harvard University Press.

Williamson, O.E. 1975. *Markets and Hierarchies: Analysis and Antitrust Implications.* New York: Free Press.

———. 1985. *The Economic Institutions of Capitalism.* New York: Free Press.

# [10]

## ECONOMIC INCENTIVES FOR COUNTERTRADE

### Rolf Mirus* and Bernard Yeung**
*University of Alberta*

### Abstract

This paper examines countertrade using standard economic theory. We show that in many circumstances countertrade is a rational response to transaction costs, information asymmetry, moral hazard-agency problems, and other market imperfections. This paper also integrates countertrade into international business theories. Some preliminary hypotheses, that may be empirically testable after refinement, are developed.

As reports of countertrade arrangements have become frequent, academic interest has increased. Many popular explanations have been advanced, among them shortage of foreign exchange, balance of payments difficulties, exercise of monopsony power, and imposition of trade barriers. It has also been alleged that countertrade is an inefficient form of international trade and that it represents a retrograde development. Most of these arguments have not been established theoretically, nor have they been tested empirically.

Countertrade does not usually take the ancient form of barter and its existence does not imply the decline of international business into

---

*Rolf Mirus is Professor of International Business and Finance at the University of Alberta. He holds a doctorate in economics from the University of Minnesota and his research interests are in the area of international financial markets and managements.

**Bernard Yeung is Assistant Professor of International Business and Finance at the University of Alberta. He holds a Ph.D. in International Business from the University of Chicago, and his major research interest is in applying economic theory to international business phenomena.

Both authors are currently involved in a project to transfer management education to China under the auspices of the Canadian International Development Agency.

This paper was presented at the Administative Sciences Association of Canada Montreal Conference (May 1985). We would like to thank the conference reviewers for their comments.

We are grateful to our colleagues, Giovanni Barone-Adesi, Randy Chapman, Ted Chambers and Colin Hoskins, for their helpful comments. We also acknowledge the valuable suggestions of three anonymous referees.

Received: June 1985; Revised: November 1985 & February 1986; Accepted: February 1986.

bartering, but rather a complicated contractual exchange of economic resources, either contemporaneously or intertemporally. At the same time, countertrading parties normally have the option of diverting their resources into money-mediated trade elsewhere. It is therefore evident that a more thorough understanding of countertrade requires an examination of the trading parties' incentives for bypassing money-mediation. This paper undertakes such an examination through the application of economic theory.

The results suggest that countertrade is a rational economic response to differential transaction costs, information asymmetry, incomplete markets (in particular, the lack of forward and future markets), and political and ownership constraints that lead to principal-agency problems. In other words, countertrade occurs in situations where the superiority of market-mediated transactions is not well established; it may even lead to transactions that would otherwise not occur. In consequence, countertrade is not generally inefficient; indeed it often promotes rather than inhibits the growth of international business.

Our analysis also points out that countertrade involves a class of international transactions that can be viewed as vertical or horizontal integration of economic activities while ownership remains separate. Therefore, countertrade can be seen as a hybrid of joint venture, franchising, vertical integration, and foreign direct investment, under political and ownership constraints. The contribution of this paper is that it shows countertrade as an integral part of the theory of international business.

In section two, we provide an elementary conceptualization of countertrade contracts. Section three explains "intertemporal" countertrade, often referred to as "buy-backs" in the literature and section four discusses simple barter ("contemporaneous" countertrade). These two sections give rise to five simple hypotheses which may become suitable for empirical verification after some further refinement. Finally, in the fifth section we briefly extend our analytical result to the case of counter-purchase.

## CONCEPTUALIZATION OF THE COUNTERTRADE PROBLEM

Countertrade involves "simple barter", "buy-back", and "counter-purchase". This paper suggests economic incentives for the first two types of countertrade and argues that some of the results may also be applicable to counter-purchase.[1] In the following, we present the motivation for our analysis.

Diverse and complex as the actual forms are, countertrade is characterized by a significant substitution of payment in kind for payment in an international money. To explain countertrade satisfactorily, the economic motivation for this preference needs to be uncovered. Two observations may help in this context. First, countertrade involves the exporter's and the importer's resources which usually have alternative uses. The opportunity costs of these resources are not less than their prices in money-mediated market transactions, and presumably countertraders would cover at least these opportunity costs. For both parties to a countertrade there must then exist compatible economic incentives in order to forego ordinary market alternatives. Second, countertrade is often conducted in tightly controlled and/or less developed economies. In these economies, a competitive price system, pure profit motive, and private ownership of the means of production (especially foreign) are often absent. Also, market imperfections are the norm and business skills are often scarce, while foreign investors face many restrictions and a lack of information about the business environment. Were it not for these factors, countertrade would perhaps be displaced by money-mediated transactions in the form of commodity trade, factoring, forward sales, foreign direct investment and other forms of internalization. Based on these two lines of thought, we develop our analysis.

## INTERTEMPORAL BUY-BACK[2]

Intertemporal buy-back is the most prevalent form of countertrade (Walsh 1984). It usually involves the export of a technology package, frequently amounting to the provision or construction of an entire plant combined with start-up operating assistance. The buyer pays the technology supplier by delivering a share of the output in the future. There are some unique aspects to technology and capital packages that are significant in this context. First, they are ambiguously defined bundles of goods and their quality is difficult to judge ex ante for anyone except the supplier. Second, physical capital usually requires continuous maintenance; the effort devoted to this is also difficult to observe for outsiders. Third, most physical capital and technology is in the form of highly specialized assets and can only be altered slowly and/or at high costs. Investment in capital and technology is mostly provided by the final user due to these market imperfections.

A firm motivated by a desire to integrate horizontally or vertically, or to benefit from firm-specific advantages, would want to apply its capital and technology in production abroad. However, due to high ownership costs and political constraints, it may be prevented from assuming ownership. In this situation, the imperfections intrinsic in markets for capital and technology are not overcome by internalization, resulting in the divergence of the economic interests of the user and supplier of capital and technology. This problem is aggravated by the information asymmetry between the user and the supplier. We argue that buy-back is a rational contractual resolution to market imperfections and is, in fact, a substitute for internalization in three kinds of situations.

### Buy-back as a Double Coincidence of Wants

In the simplest case, where the quality of the capital/technology package is unimportant, buy-back is simply the result of a double coincidence of wants. This notion is best illustrated by the following scenario. A firm is searching for access to a needed raw material and has a firm-specific advantage in its mining and processing. This firm may be bothered by the absence of long-term futures and forward markets for the raw material in question. It would normally respond by backward integration to assure itself of a reliable source of supply. Of course, there may exist other benefits in this integration. When the resource exists in an environment where ownership is impossible (e.g., in the People's Republic of China) or perceived as prohibitively expensive (e.g., in South Africa), the usual response of vertical integration is precluded.

For the owner of the resources the alternatives to countertrade are to allow foreign ownership and receive tax income, or to buy the technology package and develop the market for output. The first alternative may not be better than countertrade if there is a preference for ownership or control. The second alternative can also be inferior to countertrade, as there are costs of market penetration and uncertainty concerning future sales. In addition, it may be difficult to determine a money price acceptable to both the buyer and the seller. Offering output in return would lower market penetration costs, especially for the inexperienced producer, although less learning benefits would be gained. In addition, this tactic establishes a much needed long-term continuous forward sale with obvious economic advantages. There may thus be powerful economic incentives for countertrade. The market development need of the resource-owner and the backward integration motive of a foreign firm constitute a double coincidence of wants that obviates the need for money. Generalizing from these considerations, we hypothesize the following:

> H1: Intertemporal buy-back of natural resources is more likely the more expensive forward purchase of input supply by the user, the more expensive (or prohibitive) foreign ownership, the more advantageous vertical integration to the capital owner, and the more costly market penetration/development for the owner of the natural resources.

It is desirable to examine the nature of the capital and technology involved in the development of the original resources and the production of the commodity. If this capital/technology package is homogeneous and has a competitive market, the pure motives for countertrading are forward sales, savings in market development cost (by the owner of the resource) and backward integration (by the capital/technology supplier). Countertrade is merely the result of a double coincidence of wants. If the package is heterogeneous so that potential suppliers have differential provision costs (these may include management and maintenance costs), countertrade gives further advantages to the resource owner. The heterogeneity property means that a standard price for the package may not be readily available (to the owner of the resource), nor are the differential costs usually observable at reasonable expense, especially for less developed countries. Through countertrade the resource-owner avoids a cost accounting problem: no explicit mutual agreement on the price of capital is needed. The resource-owner is then protected against overstatement of capital costs. Moreover, the moral hazard problem of shirking behavior by the capital/technology supplier is avoided because the capital supplier is compensated by what his technology produces. Lastly, the countertrade scheme ensures that the most efficient capital supplier, the one who is able to extract the highest expected net economic benefits from the final output, is the most competitive bidder. Thus, most economic rent can be extracted. Since all these advantages are also available in a revenue-sharing contract, the prime motive for countertrade must still be convenient forward sale, i.e., savings in marketing cost.

This explanation of countertrade hinges on the double coincidence of wants: the internalization need of the foreign firm encountering high ownership costs and the desire by the owner of the local resources for production and market development. It appears that this is the only way to explain the simplest case, where heterogeneity of capital and technology is not important to the buyer, as there is no fundamental economic conflict between the buyer and seller and countertrade is used for no other purposes. This explanation, however, may also be extended to the more complicated cases analyzed below.

### Buy-back as an Incentive Contract - Output with a Quality Dimension

In the presence of ownership constraints, where the final user of the capital and technology is not the supplier of the package, there is no guarantee that the recipient and the supplier of the package have compatible economic interests. Generally, it is not in the supplier's interest to provide quite the technology the recipient desires, and the behavior of the former is not observable (ex ante, at least). This gives rise to a subtle principal-agency problem.[3] In this subsection we show that when the output has a distinct quality aspect, which is determined by the quality of the production technology, countertrade is an incentive compatible contract that allows both parties to achieve their objectives: integration for the technology-supplier and the transfer of quality technology for the recipient.

The quality attribute of a capital and technology package is often unidentifiable to anyone but the supplier. When a capital/technology transfer takes place, a problem is caused by the fact that the capital/technology recipient has inferior information about its quality. The supplier will have an incentive to overstate (undersupply) the quality of the capital/technology he provides, as long as the supply cost increases with quality and/or his revenue increases with the claimed quality; this represents a typical principal-agency problem. Conceivably, when profits are the only objectives for the supplier and the recipient, a revenue-sharing contract that resolves the problem can be constructed.[4,5]

If the technology recipient's desire is not just profits from the final output but also the quality of the technology transferred, another dimension is added to the principal-agency problem. The quality decision made by the supplier is fundamentally unobservable (at least, ex ante) to the recipient and cannot be controlled directly. In particular, under an ordinary revenue-sharing contract, the supplier has the freedom to choose both the quality and quantity of output; the resultant quality in technology transfer may not satisfy the recipient's demand.

By writing a contract that gives the supplier, in return for the technology, a fixed quantity of output for a specified number of years, the recipient has a means to influence the supplier's provision of quality.[6] The assumption is that the distinct quality attribute of the output is determined, in a monotonic manner, by the quality of the capital/technology input. Usually, the price of the output varies with its perceived quality. In this situation the supplier's decision on quality is dependent on its stipulated quantity return. If quantity and quality are substitutes (complements) from the supplier's point of view, a decrease (an increase) in its quantity return will induce more supply in quality. Therefore, the quantity-sharing contract is a desirable incentive contract for the recipient to offer whenever the supplier's decisions on quantity and quality are not independent.[7]

A caveat is that with this type of contract the supplier has no incentive to conceal its quality decision, either ex ante or ex post. First, a statement of the quality provision is not required in the contract. Second, the supplier's actual payoff depends only on the actual input in quality. On the other hand, the supplier does have an incentive to misrepresent the functional relationship between its quality decision and its quantity return. We conjecture that this problem is not material if a hedonic market price function for the output is observable ex ante. The quantity buy-back contract may also have the favourable signalling effect mentioned in Murrell (1982). Of course, the countertrade arrangement does not displace further monitoring requirements in technology transfer. Still, it is reasonable to propose the following hypothesis:[8]

> H2: When technology transfer with a quality dimension is involved, countertrade (in buy-back form) is more likely the more unobservable the quality dimension, the less available services for monitoring supply performance, the stronger the recipient's desire for quality, and the more explicit and stronger the relationship between the quality decision of the supplier and its quantity return.

The significant implication, of course, is that foreign exchange shortage has nothing to do with this type of arrangement. It is the very nature of markets for technology, information asymmetry coupled with ownership constraints, that explain the phenomenon: countertrade is an incentive contract that ensures the transfer of desirable quality technology and post-installation service performance. In this type of contract, the recipient influences the supplier's decision on the quality of the technology and capital transferred by stipulating a quantity of final output in return. The crucial assumption that leads to the incentive compatibility is the relationship between the quality of the technology and capital input on the one hand, and per unit value of the final output on the other. Without this relationship, our result does not obtain.

### Buy-back as an Incentive Contract - A Differentiated Product Used as an Input by the Technology-Supplier.

Buy-back is an incentive contract in the more complicated case whereby a firm contracts to provide a production facility to another accepting in return some of the output for use in further production. We assume that the output is production process-specific, so that other firms would find it costly and time-consuming to adjust their production process to make use of the good. It would be equally difficult for the original firm to find a replacement for the input. An example would be the recent construction of an engine production plant in the German Democratic Republic by VW. As compensation the company receives every year during a specified period a fixed quantity of the engines produced. In comparison with the previous case, the complexity of the situation increases due to a time inconsistency problem and a double information asymmetry problem.

A time inconsistency problem exists because of the putty-clay nature[9] of the project and prohibition of ownership. Assuming the motives of the technology-supplier include the diversification of sourcing, cost reduction, and collection of economic rents on its firm-specific advantage, the normal solution would be to internalize the market by means of foreign direct investment. This choice is not feasible if there are restrictions on, or high cost associated with ownership. In such a situation, a contractual arrangement between the technology-buyer and supplier becomes necessary. The technology-buyer would face significant risks if a plant were purchased and some of its output in subsequent periods were sold back to the technology-supplier. As market transactions these would be separated and sequential in nature. By the putty-clay feature of the project, the current seller of the technology would be the sole future customer for the product. In later periods, he has the incentive and ability to monopsonistically depress the price of the output, or to increase the price of the management and production services provided. In anticipation of being "locked-in and ripped-off," the technology-buyer might want to cut short the local commitment. A similar fear may also exist on the technology-supplier's side. He may worry that, in the later periods, the plant owner (the technology recipient) may suddenly monopolistically inflate the price of the output. Given that a steady supply of this output at a predetermined price is vitally important to him, he may then want to cut short his technology and capital commitment in the construction of the plant. These circumstances, in a non-cooperative Nash game setting, would result in an equilibrium of less/lower technology being coupled with lower amounts of (local) labor as compared to the internalization outcome. In the extreme, it is possible that no plant would be built. In short, in this particular case the time inconsistency of the decisions necessitates a credible contract that ties the value of technology to the value of future output. For both parties such a contract should be an improvement over the non-cooperative Nash outcome.

When a contract is specified in terms of prices, however, there is still the double information asymmetry problem. The problem arises from the fact that the valuation of the output, which is tied to the value of its marginal physical productivity in further production, is much better known to the technology-supplier. From the perspective of the technology recipient this creates the possibility that the supplier will understate the value of the output in contract negotiations that try to specify a mutually agreed money-price. The net cost of the output to the technology-supplier is the price he pays for the local participation. This price will be positively related to the agreed money-price of the output. Therefore, the technology-supplier will have an incentive to understate his valuation of the output. The supplier can also inflate the value of other management and production services and, at the same time, undersupply the promised provisions. The technology recipient may be hard pressed to assess the quality, reliability and, thus, the value of the technology. On the other hand, because of the lack of a competitive local factor market,[10] the technology-supplier may have an information disadvantage as regards the shadow price and the productivity of local participation. The supplier may be suspicious that the local partners inflate their factor cost schedules (practicing monopsonistic pricing). Hence, a severe double "informational-asymmetry-moral-hazard" problem exists.

A contract that specifies physical quantities can first of all overcome the problem of quantity-quality substitution referred to in the previous case. It thus satisfies the recipient's desire for state-of-the-art technology. But even when quality is not an issue, a quantity contract will conceivably induce the supplier to reveal his valuation of the product by furnishing technology to the extent that the marginal revenue from extra technology is equated to its marginal cost. Similarly, the recipient has no incentive to waste labour resources or to put less than the best effort forward. In this fashion, the countertrade contract is an institutional choice that overcomes difficulties that, in all likelihood, prevent a market solution. At the same time, there is good reason for the two parties to contract to exchange technology for output because this is the original motive for the transaction. Viewed in this light, the observed practices are a substitute for foreign direct investment and are the direct result of the high costs of ownership.[11]

Finally, it appears that countertrade, in the present case, is efficiency-improving. There are four possible relationships between the technology supplier, who wants to internalize a firm-specific advantage, and the technology recipient, who wants a local industry: (i) no deal, (ii) the non-cooperative Nash equilibrium, (iii) a monetary contract equilibrium, and (iv) a countertrade equilibrium. Our analysis suggests that countertrade is the most Pareto-efficient among the last three equilibria. Countertrade then materializes if it is more Pareto-efficient than the no deal situation. If this is indeed the case, countertrade is efficiency-improving and creates trade. This argument also applies to the previous case (case (b)).As a tentative hypothesis we would argue that:

> H3: Given informational asymmetry, the more costly is ownership, the more likely is this type of countertrade. Also, it follows that the more "putty-clay" the nature of a plant (i.e., the more "lock-in" and "rip-off" is

possible), the more likely is this type of countertrade contract.

Our analysis of buy-back has thus progressed from a simple situation of double coincidence of wants to the present complicated case. Buy-back arises as a rational economic resolution to market imperfections caused by high ownership costs[12] (or politically motivated ownership constraints) and information asymmetry. It is not necessarily an inefficient form of international trade, nor is it inevitably a reflection of a shortage of foreign exchange. Countertrade is simply a substitute for other more standard forms of internalization under the conditions outlined. In this sense, our analysis links countertrade to the existing theory of international business.

## CONTEMPORANEOUS COMMODITY EXCHANGE

Simple barter is of a one-time, simultaneous exchange of often unrelated commodities. Again, it is troubling to accept foreign exchange shortage as a general explanation for the occurrence of this type of international transaction when countries such as the Soviet Union or the German Democratic Republic are involved. These are nations with relatively good international credit standing that should have little trouble raising the necessary import/export financing for such one-time deals, even on a more or less ongoing basis. Indeed, a nation that has successfully arranged a barter trade could have instead used the good "exported" in the barter deal as collateral for a foreign exchange loan so as to finance the very same imports. Moreover, countries that experience the most severe credit problems do not seem to be the most active in seeking countertrade deals.[13] It would appear that there must have been a political decision that is at the root of some of the observed countertrade: the decision not to access financial markets. It is idle to speculate why one would forego borrowing but perceived loss of independence or loss of face might be possible motives. In the following, we suggest two different reasons for countertrades.

It appears that foreign exchange shortage or rationing and other forms of capital control can explain some countertrade when we focus on the Western suppliers. When an exporter has identified a customer and an order is likely, the fact that foreign exchange is rationed in the importer's country implies a time-consuming foreign exchange allocation process, so much so that uncertainty surrounds not only the conclusion of a contract but also its value. In this setting, the supplier may accept payment in terms of a marketable commodity to move the deal forward in time. This will be more likely the longer the expected waiting time and the higher the uncertainty of being able to conclude a money-based contract.[14] In a very real sense, countertrade here is akin to selling an account receivable (i.e., factoring). Moreover, in this context, countertrade may actually be seen as an officially sanctioned way of bypassing a black market for foreign exchange.[15] We, therefore, tentatively hypothesize the following:

> H4: Given regulatory difficulties in currency exchanges, simple barter is
> more likely to occur the greater the uncertainty, the longer the expected

waiting time for the foreign exchange allocation and the lower the implicit marketing cost of the countertrade goods.[16]

The nature of some observed countertrade transactions suggests further possible rationales. When, for example, VW sells compact cars to the German Democratic Republic in return for canned hams, the impression gained is that the GDR wants to sell a temporary excess supply. Such situations tend to have a low probability of recurrence. In the normal course of events, (additional) exports of this product would saddle the seller with extra search and transactions costs (in either direct sale or indirect sale through a marketing agent). By availing itself of VW's familiarity with Western markets, cars-plus-marketing services are obtained for ham, while the benefit of learning from the experience of direct sale is foregone. From the countertrader's point of view, two necessary imports, in this example cars and marketing services, can apparently be more cheaply obtained bundled together[17] and the shared savings may exceed the loss due to the foregone learning benefit from direct sales experience. The other side of the deal is that the Western firm gets a bundle: a product and reduced uncertainty regarding future market access. Payment consists of its own goods and marketing services. The Western exporter stands to gain whenever the sum of the net (of marketing cost) gain of the goods accepted and the long-run benefit of more certainty in future market access is not less than the cost of its exports. From that perspective, countertrade is economically more efficient than the same trade conducted in terms of money, and it is conducted to save search and transaction costs. The scenario reveals that countertrade is an exchange of bundled goods and services according to comparative advantage. This cost-benefit analysis leads to the following tentative hypothesis.

> H5: Simple barter is more likely the lower the benefit of learning from direct sales experience, the higher the cost of direct sale of a stochastic commodity surplus with low probability of recurrence, and the lower the implicit cost of marketing services for the Western supplier.

Our assessment of simple barter would lead to the conclusion that the often stated reason giving rise to the practice, that is foreign exchange shortage, is at best a partial and somewhat, superficial explanation. The deeper causes must be sought in government policy choices regarding access to financial markets and bureaucratic delays inherent in maintaining overvalued exchange rates. In this light, countertrade appears to be a form of uncertainty resolution from the Western supplier's point of view.

In addition, given the specialized nature of marketing skills and the comparative advantage of Western firms in market knowledge, countertrade may be a reflection of high transactions and search costs faced by a trader in Eastern Europe (or elsewhere) when trying to dispose of occasional surplus production. These observations amount to bringing observed countertrades into the fold of the theory of the firm. It shows that the firm rationally responds to market conditions: countertrade may be more Pareto-efficient than ordinary trading modes; it helps markets function.

## COUNTER-PURCHASE

There is now need to discuss counter-purchase and to assess the extent to which our explanations also apply to this case. In a typical counter-purchase arrangement, a seller, usually from the Western world, is partially paid in terms of trade credits that must, subject to a time and an availability constraint, be used for purchase from a prespecified list of goods. (Part of the payment may be made in convertible currencies.) While these trade credits are sometimes negotiable, nonfulfillment of a counter-purchase commitment usually invokes a penalty clause, such as a reduction in the trade credits. The essential feature of counter-purchase is the exchange of goods delivered now for goods delivered in the future. From this perspective, counter-purchase is similar to simple barter (contemporaneous exchange of goods), albeit more complicated. Some of our results in the previous section should apply to counter-purchase.

First, making payments in terms of credits that can only be used for future purchases from a prespecified list of local products is essentially a form of exchange control. Hence, the relationship between exchange control and simple barter applies to counter-purchase and a firm will accept counter-purchase requirements if the price is sufficiently attractive. Second, given that Western firms not infrequently have specialized marketing skills or easier access to them, a counter-purchase requirement can be viewed as a form of forward purchase of the Western firm's marketing skills by the local countertrader. The conceptualization of barter as an exchange of bundled goods and services based on comparative advantage is then also applicable to counter-purchase.

Counter-purchase, however, is not identical to simple contemporaneous exchange of goods. Even though the economic incentives may be similar, there are usually other complications. Counter-purchase is, by definition, intertemporal and hence has a forward selling aspect. There is also more uncertainty in counter-purchase because some of the goods on the shopping list may not be available. Moreover, the timing of the purchases is uncertain. The nature of counter-purchase arrangements may facilitate gaming behavior or, possibly, be a result thereof. On the surface our analysis thus appears generally applicable to counter-purchase but, given the unique features noted, explanations for this trading practice warrant further research.

## CONCLUSION

We have attempted to explain observed countertrade transactions using the standard tools of economic analysis. While this may be a narrow view, some headway had been made toward moving the discussion from the descriptive to the analytical. For example, we found that contemporaneous countertrade can be the result of attempts to save search costs and transaction costs. Alternatively, it can be viewed as a form of factoring a future receivable.

In the case of intertemporal countertrade, which almost inevitably involves the transfer of complex technology, the root of countertrade is to be found in the high cost of foreign ownership which makes more severe the problems of information asymmetry, of moral hazard, and of decisional time inconsistency. Countertrade is revealed as a contractual resolution to these problems, and it is also a rational substitute for foreign direct investment. As a cost-saving arrangement and, sometimes, as an efficiency-improving, incentive-compatible form of contracting, countertrade is neither an inefficient form of trade nor, as is commonly alleged, is it detrimental to the growth of international business.We conclude that countertrade arrangements may be a rational response of economic agents to environmental constraints and market imperfections; that they do not necessarily represent inefficient economic exchange. Obviously, we do not claim that our analysis has comprehensively explained all manifestations of countertrade, nor do we assert that countertrade can only be explained by the tools of positive economics. Nevertheless, our approach should be seen as a first step towards a more rigorous and general analysis of countertrade. Suggestions for further work include refinement of our hypotheses for empirical testing and formalization of the arguments.

## NOTES

1. Counter-purchase is not a major focus of this paper because we do not have a satisfactory general explanation for it. Interested readers may consult a recent paper by John Parsons (1985) that discusses counter-purchase extensively. In general, his analysis is very close to ours.

2. We originally differentiated buy-back according to the degree of standardization of output and analyzed it accordingly. A referee pointed out that the heterogeneity of production technology is the really crucial factor in our analyses. We subsequently revised our discussion of buy-back and gratefully acknowledge the reviewer's insightful comment. See also footnote 7.

3. A review of this problem is provided in MacDonald (1984).

4. Solutions to the problem are discussed in Ross (1973), MacDonald (1984) and articles cited therein.

5. Up to now, the relationship between the quality of the output and that of the technology does not play a crucial role. The argument is applicable to standard output with negligible quality attributes.

6. Analytically, a regressive quantity-sharing contract has the same effect on the firm's quality/quantity choice behavior as a fixed quantity contract.

7. If the output is standard but input productivity is affected by the quality of the technology, the technology supply is a function of the price of output. Either a revenue-sharing rule or an output-sharing rule can influence the technology supply and there is no presumption as to which of these will be the outcome. Conceivably, the output-sharing rule (buy-back) is sometimes, and only sometimes, the outcome. This points out that the relationship between the quality of the output and that of the technology is only one of the sufficient conditions for buy-back, not a necessary one. On the other hand, the unidentifiable quality attribute of the technology is neither a sufficient nor a necessary condition for buy-back.

8. The analysis in this subsection can be illustrated by a formal mathematical model. To preserve the non-mathematical nature of this paper, this is not provided.

9. By assumption the output is not readily useful to other producers.

10. This is an assumption that is realistic for many socialist countries and for some developing countries.

11. As we do not yet have a formal proof of its general validity, this point is conjectural. We also speculate that the buy-back provision contributes to the overall credibility of the countertrade contract.

ECONOMIC INCENTIVES FOR COUNTERTRADE  39

12. Note that this cost can be the intrinsic internalization cost and/or the cost of political risk exposure. Psychological and economic costs of rendering ownership control arise for the original resource-owner.

13. Recently, there is evidence that some Latin American countries are also actively seeking countertrade.

14. Just as the currency of invoice is negotiable and acceptance of local currency can garner a contract, "invoicing" in goods may hasten a sale.

15. When the currency value deviates from the true market value, the money prices of trading commodities do not necessarily reflect the true market prices. From this perspective, countertrade is a way to adjust the relative prices at which goods are traded when their nominal prices do not reflect their real values. See Adrian E. Tschoegl (1985), p. 2.

16. This point includes Weigand's (1980) argument as a subcase.

17. This bundling suggests some market imperfections. Increased competition and specialization tends to unbundling in competitive markets unencumbered by regulation. The offshore financial markets are a case in point.

## REFERENCES

Akerlof, George A., The Market for Lemons: Quality Uncertainty and the Market Mechanism, *Quarterly Journal of Economics*, 84, 1970, pp. 488-500.

Calvet, A.L., Foreign Direct Investment Theories and Theories of the Multinational Firm: A Canadian Perspective. In K.C. Dawan, Hamid Etemad and Richard W. Wright, eds., *International Business: A Canadian Perspective*, p. 281. Don Mills, Ontario: Addison-Wesley, 1981.

Culpan, Refik, Emerging Countertrade Practices, The Case of Brazil, Academy of International Business, Annual Meetings, Cleveland, October 1984.

Dennis, Robert D., The Countertrade Factor in China's Modernization Plan, *Columbia Journal of World Business*, 17, 1, Spring 1982, pp. 67-75.

Kaikati, Jack G., Marketing Without Exchange of Money, *Harvard Business Review*, November-December 1982, pp. 72-74.

Librowicz, Michel and Serruya, Michel, Countertrade, A Partial Solution to the Liquidity Crisis, Academy of International Business, Annual Meetings, Cleveland, October 1984.

MacDonald, Glenn M., New Directions in the Economic Theory of Agency, *Canadian Journal of Economics*, Vol. 1, No. 3, August 1984, pp.415-440.

Murrell, Peter, Product Quality, Market Signalling and the Development of East-West Trade, *Economic Inquiry*, Vol. 20, No. 4, October 1982, pp. 589-603.

Parsons, John E., A Theory of Countertrade Financing of International Business, Finance Department, Sloan School of Management, Massachusetts Institute of Technology, Working Paper 1632-85, March 1985.

Rosen, Sherwin, Hedonic Prices and Implicit Markets: Product Differentiation in Pure Competition, *Journal of Political Economy*, Vol. 82, No. 1, February 1974, pp. 34-55.

Ross, Stephen A., The Economic Theory of Agency: The Principal's Problem, *American Economic Review*, 63, 1973, pp. 134-139.

Tschoegl, Adrian E., Barter, *Lloyd's Bank Review*, 1985.

Walsh, James I., Countertrade Megatrends: Where Are We Now? How Did We Get Here? And What Next?, Academy of International Business, Annual Meetings, Cleveland, October 1984.

Weigand, Robert E., Barters and Buy-Backs: Let Western Firms Beware!, *Business Horizons*, Vol. 23, No. 3, June 1980, pp. 54-61.

——————, International Trade Without Money, *Harvard Business Review*, November-December 1977, pp. 28-42.

# Part V
# Technology Transfer: Resource Costs and Spillover Benefits in the Host Country

# [11]

*The Economic Journal*, **87** (*June* 1977), 242–261
*Printed in Great Britain*

# TECHNOLOGY TRANSFER BY MULTINATIONAL FIRMS: THE RESOURCE COST OF TRANSFERRING TECHNOLOGICAL KNOW-HOW*

## I. INTRODUCTION

The essence of modern economic growth is the increase in the stock of useful knowledge and the extension of its application. Since the origins of technical and social innovations have never been confined to the borders of any one nation, the economic growth of all countries depends to some degree on the successful application of a transnational stock of knowledge (Kuznets, 1966). In other words, the economic growth of every nation is inextricably linked to the successful international transfer of technology. Nevertheless, economists have been remarkably slow in addressing themselves to the economics of international technology transfer. The result is that "at both the analytic and factual level very little is known about the international transfer of knowhow" (Reynolds, 1966).

This paper addresses itself to this need. The starting-point is Arrow's suggestion that the cost of communication, or information transfer, is a fundamental factor influencing the world-wide diffusion of technology (Arrow, 1969).[1] The purpose of the paper is to examine the level and determinants of the costs involved in transferring technology. The value of the resources which have to be utilised to accomplish the successful transfer of a given manufacturing technology is used as a measure of the cost of transfer. The resource cost concept is therefore designed to reflect the ease or difficulty of transferring technological know-how from manufacturing plants in one country to manufacturing plants in another.

## II. TECHNOLOGY TRANSFER AND THE PRODUCTION OF KNOWLEDGE

The literature on technological change recognises that it takes substantial resources to make a new process or product feasible (Mansfield, 1968). However, it is common to assume that the cost of transferring the innovation to other firms is very much less, so that the marginal costs of successive application is trivial compared to the average cost of research, development, and application. This paradigm is sometimes extended to international as well as domestic technology transfer (Rodriguez, 1975).[2] Buttressing this view is a common belief that

* The findings described in this paper resulted from research undertaken for my Ph.D. dissertation, "The Multinational Corporation and the Resource Cost of International Technology Transfer" (Cambridge, Mass.: Ballinger, 1976). The trenchant comments of Professor Edwin Mansfield were much appreciated during all phases of the study. My particular gratitude goes to the participating firms, without whose co-operation this paper would not have been possible. I should also like to acknowledge the financial support provided for this study by the National Science Foundation, under a grant to Professor Edwin Mansfield of the University of Pennsylvania.

[1] Arrow asks: "If one nation or class has the knowledge which enables it to achieve high productivity, why is not the other acquiring that information?...The problem turns on the differential between costs of communication within and between classes" (or nations). P. 33.

[2] "Transmission of technology between countries is assumed costless. Thus, it is possible for the

technology is nothing but a set of blueprints that is usable at nominal cost to all. Nevertheless, it has been pointed out that generally "only the broad outlines of technical knowledge are codified by non-personal means of intellectual communication, or communication by teaching outside the production process itself" (Berrill, 1964). The cost of transfer, which can be defined to include both transmission and absorption costs, may therefore be considerable when the technology is complex and the recipient firm does not have the capabilities to absorb the technology. The available evidence is unfortunately very sketchy. From the case studies of Mueller and Peck, Arrow inferred that transfer costs must be high (Arrow, 1962). From the Hall and Johnson study of the transfer of aerospace technology from the United States to Japan, it is not clear that this is true (Hall and Johnson, 1970). Robinson believes that economists' views on transfer costs are exaggerated (Robinson, 1973) while Mansfield and Freeman take the opposite view (Freeman, 1965; Mansfield, 1973). The lack of compelling evidence is apparent, and the appeals for further research (Mansfield, 1974; UNCTAD, 1970) seem to be well founded.

### III. THE SAMPLE

The domain of this study is the transfer of the capability to manufacture a product or process from firms in one country to firms in another. Consequently the transfers can be considered as horizontal,[1] and in the design phase.[2] Data on 26 fairly recent international technology transfer projects were obtained. The proprietary nature of much of the data meant that sampling costs were high, which in turn severely limited the size of the sample that could be collected. All 26 transfers were conducted by firms which were multinational in the scope of their manufacturing activity, although they varied considerably in sales value (10–20 billion U.S. dollars) and R & D expenditures (1·2–12·5% of sales value). All had headquarters in the United States. The transferees were on the average much smaller and less research-intensive. In 12 instances they were wholly owned subsidiaries of the transferor, in 8 instances the transferor and transferee were joint ventures partners, in 4 instances transfers were to wholly independent private enterprises, and the remaining 3 were to government enterprises. Table 1 shows that 17 of the projects fall into a broad category which will be labelled "chemicals and petroleum refining." The remaining 9 projects fall into a category which will be labelled "machinery".[3] Table 1 also indicates the wide geographical dispersion of the transferees.

---

country which owns the technology to operate a plant in a foreign country without any transfer of factors." P. 122.

[1] Horizontal transfer refers to the transfer of technical information from one project to another. It can be distinguished from vertical transfer, which refers to the transfer of technical information within the various stages of a particular innovation process, e.g. from the basic research stage to the applied research stage.

[2] For the distinctions between materials transfer, design transfer, and capacity transfer, see Hayami and Ruttan (1971).

[3] Chemicals and petroleum refining thus embrace ISIC categories (United Nations, 1968), 351, 353, and 356, while "machinery" embraces categories 381, 382, and 383.

Table I

Twenty-six Technology Transfer Projects: 3 Digit ISIC Category and Transferee Location

| Location | "Chemicals and Petroleum Refining" | | | "Machinery" | | | Total |
|---|---|---|---|---|---|---|---|
| | 351: industrial chemicals | 353: petroleum refineries | 356: plastic products | 381: fabricated metal products machinery and equipment | 382: machinery except electrical | 383: electrical machinery, appliances, and supplies | |
| Canada | 1 | 1 | 0 | 1 | 0 | 0 | 3 |
| Northern and Western Europe | 3 | 1 | 0 | 0 | 4 | 1 | 9 |
| Australia | 0 | 0 | 1 | 0 | 0 | 0 | 1 |
| Japan | 3 | 0 | 0 | 0 | 1 | 0 | 4 |
| Eastern Europe | 2 | 0 | 0 | 0 | 0 | 0 | 2 |
| Latin America | 2 | 1 | 0 | 0 | 0 | 1 | 4 |
| Asia (excluding Japan) | 1 | 0 | 0 | 0 | 0 | 1 | 2 |
| Africa | 1 | 0 | 0 | 0 | 0 | 0 | 1 |
| Total | 13 | 3 | 1 | 1 | 5 | 3 | 26 |

IV. DEFINITION OF TECHNOLOGY TRANSFER COSTS

An economic definition of transfer cost is developed below. The emphasis is on the resources which must be utilised to transfer technological know-how. Of course royalty costs or rents must be incurred merely to secure access to the technology, but these costs are not the focus of attention of this paper.[1] In order to appreciate the import of the definition that will be presented, a distinction must first be made between two basic forms in which technology can be transferred. The first form embraces physical items such as tooling, equipment, and blue prints. Technology can be embodied in these objects. The second form of technology is the information that must be acquired if the physical equipment or "hardware" is to be utilised effectively. This information relates to methods of organisation and operation, quality control, and various other manufacturing procedures. The effective conveyance of such "peripheral" support constitutes the crux of the process of technology transfer, and it typically generates the associated information flows. It is towards discovery of the cost of transfer of this "unembodied"[2] knowledge that the attention is directed.

Technology transfer costs are therefore defined as the costs of transmitting and absorbing all of the relevant unembodied knowledge. The costs of performing the various activities which have to be conducted to ensure the transfer of the necessary technological know-how will represent the cost of technology transfer.[3] Clearly, a great many skills from other industries (e.g. design engineering) will be needed for plant design, plant construction, and equipment installation. However, not all of these skills will have to be transferred to ensure the success of the project. As defined, the costs of transfer clearly do not include all of the costs of establishing a plant abroad and bringing it on stream.

The definition of transfer costs presented at the conceptual level can be translated into operational measures by considering the nature of a given project activity. At the operational level the subset of project costs identified as transfer costs fall into four groups. The first group is the cost of pre-engineering technological exchanges. During these exchanges the basic characteristics of the technology are revealed to the transferee, and the necessary theoretical insights are conveyed. The second group of costs included are the engineering costs associated with transferring the process design and the associated process engineering[4] in the case of process innovations, or the product design and production engineering[5] in the case of product innovations. If the technology has already

---

[1] Many observers equate the cost of technology with royalty fees (Mason, 1973; Gillette, 1973). Royalty costs are considered in the dissertation from which this paper was taken.

[2] Unembodied knowledge is the term used here to denote knowledge not embodied in capital goods, blueprints, and technical specifications, etc.

[3] All of the relevant costs are included, irrespective of which entity initially or eventually incurs them.

[4] Process engineering for continuous flow technology involves the compilation of flow diagrams, heat balances, control instrumentation, etc. It can be distinguished from detailed engineering which involves the translation and elaboration of the process engineering into a manufacturing facility.

[5] Production engineering for a specified item can be divided into two phases: production design and process planning. Production design is the modification of the functional design in order to reduce manufacturing costs. (Functional product design is the design of a product to fulfil certain specifications and requirements.) Given the design, process planning for manufacture must be carried out to specify,

been commercialised,[1] transmission may simply involve transferring existing drawings and specifications with the minimum of modification. However, the process of absorption may be more difficult, requiring the utilisation of considerable consulting or advisory resources. "Engineering" costs not falling into the specified categories[2] are excluded from transfer costs. The excluded engineering costs are essentially the plant or detailed engineering costs, net of advisory or consulting costs. This residual is assumed to correspond with routine drafting costs. Routine drafting is generally performed by technicians under the supervision of engineers. Drafting skills do not have to be transferred for the viability of the project to be assured. Accordingly, drafting is not considered to represent a transfer activity.[3]

The third group of costs are those of R & D personnel (salaries and expenses) during all phases of the transfer project. These are not the R & D costs associated with developing the underlying process or product innovations. Rather, they are the R & D costs associated with solving unexpected problems and adapting or modifying the technology. For instance, research scientists may be utilised during the transfer if new and unusual technical problems are encountered[4] with the production inputs. These R & D costs are generally small or non-existent for international transfers falling into the "design transfer" category.

The fourth group of costs are the pre-start-up training costs and the "excess manufacturing costs". The latter represent the learning and debugging costs incurred during the start-up phase, and before the plant achieves the design performance specifications. It is quite possible that no marketable output will be produced during the initial phases of the start-up. Nevertheless, normal labour, materials, utilities, and depreciation costs will be incurred, together with the costs of the extra supervisory personnel that will inevitably be required to

---

in careful detail, the processes required and their sequence. The production design first sets the minimum possible costs that can be achieved through the specification of materials, tolerances, basic configurations, methods of joining parts, etc. Process planning then attempts to achieve that minimum through the specification of processes and their sequence to meet the exacting requirements of the design specifications. The accepted end-point for production design is manifested by the drawing release. Process planning takes over from this point and develops the broad plan of manufacture of the part or product. A distinction can also be drawn between process planning and the layout of the physical facilities. Some process planning will take place during the layout phases of the design of a production system, Process plans can be regarded as inputs to the development of a layout. (*McGraw-Hill Encyclopedia*. 1960.)

[1] An innovation is said to have been commercialised if it has already been applied in a facility of economic size which is essentially non-experimental in nature. Thus pilot plant or prototype application is not considered to represent commercialisation.

[2] These categories are (*a*) process or design engineering costs and related consultation for process innovations or (*b*) production engineering expenses for product innovations; and (*c*) costs of engineering supervision and consultation (salaries plus travel and living) for the plant engineering.

[3] Drafting costs can be considered an implementation cost rather than a transfer cost, the implication being that if the host country does not have these skills, the viability and cost of the project is unlikely to be affected. The advisory and consulting costs, on the other hand, represent transfer costs since these activities are necessary if the technology is to be adjusted to the local circumstance and requirements. Clearly, if an existing plant was to be duplicated in its own environment, consulting costs could be expected to go to zero, whereas routine drafting would still have to be performed.

[4] Referring to process technologies, it is possible that differences in feedstocks amongst various locations may create problems that only research scientists can effectively handle. Similarly, changes in atmospheric conditions or water supply could have unexpected consequences for some highly complex processes.

assist in the start-up. The operating losses incurred during initial production are very often a close approximation to excess manufacturing costs.[1]

### V. TRANSFER COSTS: DATA AND HYPOTHESES

1. *The Level of Transfer Costs*

The above definition was used to calculate the transfer costs for 26 projects. The results are presented in Table 2. The costs are given in absolute dollars, and then normalised by total project costs.[2] For the sample as a whole, transfer costs average 19% of total project costs. Clearly, the data do not support the notion that technology is a stock of blueprints usable at nominal cost to all. Nevertheless, there is considerable variation in the sample data, with transfer costs ranging from 2% to 59% of total project costs. The number of factors influencing transfer costs is undoubtedly very great,[3] but some factors are likely to have a more pervasive influence than others. The discussion to follow is restricted to hypotheses for which statistical testing is feasible, given the available data. Two groupings of testable hypotheses can be identified: characteristics of the technology/transferor, and characteristics of the transferee/host country.

2. *Technology/Transferor Characteristics*

A critical factor in the transfer of technology is the extent to which the technology is completely understood by the transferor. The number of manufacturing start-ups[4] or applications which the transferor has already conducted with a specific technology can be used as an index of this knowledge.[5] An increase in the number of applications is likely to lower transfer costs since with each start-up additional knowledge about the technology is acquired. Since no two manufacturing start-ups are identical, each start-up provides the firm with the opportunity to observe the effects of different operating parameters and differences in equipment design. Each application can be regarded as a new experiment which

---

[1] An important consideration is the extent to which excess manufacturing costs correctly reflect technology transfer costs rather than the costs of discovering and overcoming the idiosyncrasies of a new plant. One way to confront this issue is to consider the level of excess manufacturing costs when an absolutely identical plant is constructed in a location adjacent to an existing plant. Further, assume the second plant embodies the same technology as the first plant, and the labour force from the first is transferred to the second for the purpose of performing the manufacturing start-up. The assumption is that under these circumstances excess manufacturing costs in the second plant will be zero, or very nearly so. The correctness of this assumption was corroborated by a subsample of project managers subsequently questioned about this matter. The postulated circumstance would be identical to shutting down the first plant and then starting it up again. Some excess manufacturing costs might be incurred during the initial hours of operation if the plant embodies flow process technology. (For the projects in the sample the average duration of the manufacturing start-up was 8·2 months.) However, these costs are unlikely to be of sufficient magnitude to challenge the validity of classifying excess manufacturing costs as a component of technology transfer costs.

[2] Total project costs are measured according to the inside boundary limits definition commonly employed by project accountants. Installations outside the plant perimeter are thereby excluded.

[3] For a broader view of the spectrum of hypotheses, see the author's Ph.D. dissertation.

[4] Manufacturing start-ups are synonymous with the number of applications of the technology. If a new plant is built for each application, it would also by synonymous with the number of plants that are built which utilise the technology.

[5] Corporations engaged in technology transfer ventures not grounded on their own technology are known to have encountered massive transfer problems and costs.

yields new information and new experience.[1] Transfer will be facilitated the more fully the technology is understood. Besides these engineering economies, additional applications provide expanded opportunities for the pre-start-up training of the labour force. Clearly, if identical or similar plants exist elsewhere,

Table 2

*Sample Data on the Resource Costs of Technology Transfer: 26 International Projects*

| Chemicals and Petroleum Refining | | Machinery | |
|---|---|---|---|
| Transfer costs: dollar amount (thousands) | Transfer costs: dollar amount / total project cost | Transfer costs: dollar amount (thousands) | Transfer costs: dollar amount / total project cost |
| 49 | 18 | 198 | 26 |
| 185 | 8 | 360 | 32 |
| 683 | 11 | 1,006 | 38 |
| 137 | 17 | 5,850 | 45 |
| 449 | 8 | 555 | 10 |
| 362 | 7 | 1,530 | 42 |
| 643 | 6 | 33 | 59 |
| 75 | 10 | 968 | 24 |
| 780 | 13 | 270 | 45 |
| 2,142 | 6 | | |
| 161 | 2 | | |
| 586 | 7 | | |
| 877 | 7 | | |
| 66 | 4 | | |
| 2,850 | 19 | | |
| 7,425 | 22 | | |
| 3,341 | 4 | | |

then experienced operators from these plants can be used to assist the start-up in the new plant. In addition, untrained operators can be brought into existing plants for pre-start-up training.

The second variable to be considered is the age of the technology. The age of the technology is defined as the number of years since the beginning of the first commercial application of the technology[2] anywhere in the world, and the end[3] of the technology transfer programme. The age of an innovation will determine the stability of the engineering designs and the transferor's knowledge of the manufacturing procedures. The older the technology, *ceteris paribus*, then the greater have been the opportunities for interaction between the development groups and the manufacturing and operating groups within the firm. Problems

[1] The first application represents first commercialisation of the technology. This will result in the creation of a set of basic engineering drawings and specifications. Duplication and alteration of these for subsequent start-ups will involve a modest cost compared to the initial cost of constructing them.

[2] If there is more than one key innovation embodied in the technology, then the date of commercial application of the most recent key innovation is the reference date.

[3] Age is defined up to the end of the transfer programme since any knowledge about the technology acquired up to this point is potentially useful for the transfer. For the very first start-up, age will be the length of the transfer minus the development overlap.

stand a better chance of already being ironed out, and the drawings are likely to be more secure. Further, since technology is not embodied in drawings alone, there is a great deal of uncodified information – the relevant "art". This kind of knowledge is carried by the supervisors, engineers, and operators. As the age of the technology increases, more individuals in the firm have the opportunity to acquire this non-codified information, and hence are potentially available to assist in the transfer. There will, however, be some point after which greater age will begin to increase the cost of transfer. When the length of stay of corporate personnel begins to be outstripped by the age of technology, then the non-codified dimensions of design knowledge may be lost to the firm.[1]

It is necessary to distinguish the cost reductions resulting from additional start-ups from the cost reductions resulting from greater age of the technology. For continuous flow technologies, additional applications of an innovation in entirely new plants will allow experimentation with scale and with the basic parameters of the design. This will generate a greater understanding of the technology. On the other hand, greater age, given the number of applications or start-ups, generally permits experimentation only with operating parameters, the design of the plant remaining fixed throughout.

The third technology variable to be considered is the number of firms utilising the technology, or one that is "similar and competitive". This is taken to represent the degree to which the innovation and the associated manufacturing technology is already diffused throughout the industry. The greater the number of firms with the same or similar and competitive technology, then the greater the likelihood that technology is more generally available, and can therefore be acquired at lower cost.[2]

These technology variables and the attendant hypotheses begin to take on some extra significance when viewed together. Taken singly they define the technology to only a limited degree. Together, they hypothesise, *ceteris paribus*, that the most difficult and hence costly technology to transfer is characterised by very few previous applications, a short elapsed time since development, and limited diffusion. Technology displaying such characteristics can be termed "leading-edge" technology. "Leading-edge" technology is likely to be in a state of flux; the engineering drawings will be constantly altering, thus frustrating the transfer. In comparison, state-of-the-art technology is hypothesised, *ceteris paribus*, to involve lower transfer costs since the engineering drawings are more likely to be finalised and the fundamentals of the technology stand a better chance of being more fully understood.

[1] In the limit, the firm could terminate its utilisation of a particular technology, and the non-codified information associated with it could be gradually lost for ever as the technology becomes historic. Further, the drawings associated with technology that is very old may suffer from so many small alterations that the very essence of even the codified technology may become quite obscure. Since none of the technology transfer projects in the sample were historic in the above sense, the relevant range of the hypothesised age–transfer cost function involves an inverse relationship between the age of the technology and the cost of transfer.

[2] An identification problem may exist here because more firms may have applied the technology because the transfer cost is low.

### 3. Transferee and Host Country Characteristics

The technical and managerial competence of the transferee will be presented as an important determinant of the ease with which technology can be absorbed. The years of manufacturing experience of the transferee in a given 4-digit ISIC industry (United Nations, 1968) is used as an index of the extent to which managers, engineers, and operators have command over the general manufacturing skills of an industry. A firm skilled in the manufacture of a group of products is likely to have less difficulty absorbing a new innovation in that industry group than is the firm which has had no previous experience manufacturing products in a particular industry group (Rawski, 1975). Older enterprises, with their skilled manufacturing personnel, seem more likely to be able to understand and apply codified knowledge to the manufacture of a new product, or the utilisation of a new process.[1]

Another variable to be considered is the size of the transferee. Although less compelling, the reasoning behind the hypothesis that transfer costs decline with firm size is that larger firms generally have a wider spectrum of technical and managerial talent which can be called on for assistance during the transfer. A small firm may be technically and managerially quite competent yet unable to absorb new technology easily because of the extra demands placed on its scarce managerial and technical manpower. Consultants may have to be engaged by the smaller firms to perform tasks that are typically handled internally in larger firms.

A third variable considered is the R & D activity of the transferee. When unusual technical problems are unexpectedly encountered, an in-house R & D capability is likely to be of value. Oshima has argued that the R & D capability of Japanese firms facilitated the low-cost importation of foreign technology by Japanese firms (Oshima, 1973). The R & D to sales ratio of the transferee is taken as an index of its R & D capability, and an inverse relationship between this and transfer cost is postulated.

The final variable considered is designed to reflect the level of development of the host country infrastructure, which is hypothesised to be a determinant of the cost of transfer. For example, the level of skill formation in the host country will influence the amount and type of training that the labour force will require. Similarly, if the new venture is to acquire its inputs domestically, the quality of the inputs available will undoubtedly influence the level of start-up costs. There are many other considerations of similar kind which could be discussed. However, the high degree of cross-sectional collinearity between indices of development (Kuznets, 1966) makes the identification of separate effects statistically difficult. However, GNP *per capita*, a measure of productive capacity, can

---

[1] According to Rawski, recent experience of the People's Republic of China shows that during at least some phases of industrialisation, production experience may be a key determinant of the level and fungibility of industrial skills. Rawski notes that "with their skilled veteran workers and experienced technical persons, old industrial bases and old enterprises find it easier to tackle complicated technical problems than new enterprises and new industrial bases. With these advantages, it is the established centers which are best able to copy foreign equipment samples, to extract useful information from foreign technological publications, and to apply it to current domestic problem areas." (Rawski (1975), p. 386.)

be expected to capture some of the above considerations, and it will be used in this study as an index of economic development. A negative relationship between transfer cost and GNP/*per capita* is postulated.[1]

## VI. DETERMINANTS OF THE COST OF INTERNATIONAL TECHNOLOGY TRANSFER: TESTS AND RESULTS

### 1. *The Model*

The basic model to be tested is

$$C_i = f(U_i, G_i, E_i, R_i, S_i, N_i, P_i, Z_i), \tag{1}$$

where $C_i$ is the transfer cost divided by the total project cost for the $i$th transfer; $U_i$ is the number of previous applications or start-ups that the technology of the $i$th transfer has undergone by the transferor;[2] $G_i$ is the age of the technology in years; $E_i$ is the number of years of manufacturing experience that the recipient of the $i$th transfer has accumulated; $R_i$ is the ratio of research and development to sales for the recipient of the $i$th transfer, calculated for the year the transfer commenced; $S_i$ is the volume of sales, measured in millions of dollars, of the recipient of the $i$th transfer; $N_i$ is the number of firms identified by the transferor as having a technology that is identical or "technically similar and economically competitive" to the technology underlying the $i$th transfer; $P_i$ is the level of GNP *per capita* of the host country (International Bank, 1973); $Z_i$ is the random error term for the $i$th transfer. The expected derivatives are:

$$\frac{\partial C_i}{\partial U_i} < 0, \quad \frac{\partial C_i}{\partial G_i} < 0, \quad \frac{\partial C_i}{\partial E_i} < 0, \quad \frac{\partial C_i}{\partial R_i} < 0, \quad \frac{\partial C_i}{\partial S_i} < 0, \quad \frac{\partial C_i}{\partial N_i} < 0, \quad \frac{\partial C_i}{\partial P_i} < 0.$$

Since one of the best tests of any hypothesis is to look for the convergence of independent lines of evidence, the testing of this model will proceed in two phases. First, cross-section data on 26 completed projects is utilised in a linear version of the model estimated by ordinary least-squares procedures. Secondly, cost estimates provided by project managers for comparable projects are pooled to test a more specific non-linear version of the model.

### 2. *Statistical Tests: Phase 1*

The model to be tested is

$$C_i = \alpha_0 + \alpha_1 \bar{U}_i + \alpha_2 G_i + \alpha_3 E_i + \alpha_4 R_i + \alpha_5 S_i + \alpha_6 N_i + \alpha_7 P_i + Z_i, \tag{2}$$

where $\bar{U}_i$ is a dummy variable taking the value 1 if the transfer represents the first manufacturing start-up, and zero otherwise. $\bar{U}_i$ is used rather than $U_i$ for empirical reasons, since the first start-up is often of critical importance. The sample was dichotomised because of the large differences between continuous flow process technology, and product technology. One category includes chemicals and petroleum refining and the other includes machinery (see Table 1).

---

[1] The sample did not include countries where high GNP statistics were grossly dependent on oil revenues.

[2] The number of previous manufacturing start-ups was significant in Phase 1 only when it was included as a dummy variable taking the value 1 if there had been no previous manufacturing start-ups of this technology by the transferring firm, and zero otherwise.

The results in Table 3 indicate that in chemicals and petroleum refining $\bar{U}_i$, $N_i$, and $E_i$ are significant at the 0·05 level and carry the expected signs. In the machinery category the variables $N_i$, $G_i$, and $E_i$ all carry the expected signs and are significant at the 0·05 level. $N_i$ and $E_i$ are thus significant in both industry

Table 3

*Regression of Coefficients and t Statistics in Regression
Equations to Explain C (The Cost of Transfer)*

| Independent variable | Chemicals and petroleum refining | | Machinery | |
|---|---|---|---|---|
| | Equation (1)* | Equation (2)* | Equation (1)* | Equation (2)* |
| Constant | 12·79 | 13·42 | 16·67 | 65·98 |
| | (6·82) | (6·98) | (8·27) | (6·60) |
| Novelty dummy variable $\bar{U}$† | 6·73 | 6·11 | — | 1·62 |
| | (1·92) | (1·75) | | (0·15) |
| Number of firms variable | −0·37 | −0·39 | −1·29 | −1·26 |
| | (−2·06) | (−2·22) | (−2·28) | (−1·95) |
| Age of technology variable (years) | — | — | −2·43 | −2·35 |
| | | | (−3·53) | (−2·51) |
| Experience of transference variable (years in 4-digit ISIC) | −0·09 | −0·08 | −0·84 | −0·85 |
| | (−1·66) | (−1·42) | (−3·37) | (−2·95) |
| Size of transferee variable (thousands of dollars of sales) | — | −0·0009 | — | — |
| | | (−1·18) | | |
| Number of observations | 17 | 17 | 9 | 9 |
| $R^2$ | 0·56 | 0·61 | 0·78 | 0·78 |
| F | 5·66 | 4·73 | 6·00 | 3·22 |
| Significance level of F | 0·01 | 0·02 | 0·04 | 0·12 |

\* Omitted coefficient indicates variable dropped from the regression equation.
† Note 2, p. 251.

groupings, strongly supporting the hypothesis that transfer costs decline as the number of firms with identical or "similar and competitive" technology increases, and as the experience of the transferee increases. However, $R_i$ and $P_i$ were not significant in any of the equations, and although $S_i$ carries the expected sign and approaches significance in one of the regressions it is not possible to be more than 85 % sure that the sign is correct or that the coefficient is different from zero.[1]

[1] Multicollinearity does not appear to be a serious problem in any of the equations. Correlations amongst pairs of the independent variables were never significant at the 0·05 level. The stability of the regression coefficients further suggests that multicollinearity is not a serious problem. Dummy variables were introduced to test for the effects of the organisational relationship between transferor and transferee (affiliate/non affiliate, public enterprise/private enterprise), but they were not found to be statistically significant determinant of transfer costs. Application of a forward step by step procedure did not reveal a preferred subset of variables. However, it is possible that the correct model is the simultaneous equation model $Ci = f(N_i, ...)$, $N_i = f(C_i, ...)$. To eliminate simultaneous equation bias it would be desirable to use a two-stage procedure. A predictor of $N$ could first be obtained by regressing $N_i$ on arguments other than $C_i$. This could then be used as an argument in the transfer cost regression. It was not possible to obtain a good predictor of $N$ using the available cross-section data, so this procedure was not employed. Consistency was sacrificed for efficiency. It is therefore possible that simultaneous equation bias remains in the model. Therefore, the estimates of the parameters may not be consistent.

The results therefore generally support the hypotheses advanced earlier, but there are differences in the size of coefficients as well as in the specification of the equations between the industry groups. In particular, the novelty variable $\bar{U}_i$ is significant in chemicals and petroleum refining, but insignificant in machinery. The converse is true for the age variable $G_i$. The reason may be that there exists relatively less latitude for production experimentation with continuous flow process technology than with product technology. Once the plant is constructed, the extent to which the design parameters can be changed is rather minimal because of the degree of interdependence in the production system. In comparison, many product technologies allow greater design flexibility. Innumerable small changes to the technology are very often possible without massive reconstruction of the plant. It is also of interest that the coefficient of the experience variable $E_i$ is considerably larger in machinery than in chemicals and petroleum refining. This is consistent with other findings that reveal important learning economies in fabrication and assembling (Tilton, 1971).

### 3. *Statistical Tests: Phase II*

The above analysis is handicapped by the small sample size and the very high costs of adding additional observations. Limited variation in exogenous variables coupled with the problem of omitted variables can imply difficulties with bias and identification. For the projects in the sample, a procedure was therefore devised to hold the missing variables constant while generating large variation in the exogenous variables. The respondent firms were asked to estimate how the total transfer costs would vary for each project if one particular exogenous variable happened to take a different value, assuming all other variables remain constant. The responses were taken into account only if the exercise generated circumstances within the bounds of an executive's experience. Given these limitations, the change specified was quite large in order to provide a robust sample. Generally the actual value of a selected variable was hypothesised first to halve and then to double. The estimated impact on transfer costs was noted. The exercise was performed for the following independent variables: the number of applications or start-ups that the technology has undergone; the age of the technology; the number of years of previous manufacturing experience possessed by the transferee in a given four-digit industry; the research and development expenditures to sales ratio for the transferee; the size (measured by sales value) of the transferee. For each variable this exercise generated at most three observations (including the actual) or transfer costs for each project. Pooling across projects produces enough observations for ordinary least-squares regression analysis.

The estimation procedure is commenced by assuming that the shape of the cost function can be represented by the following relatively simple but quite specific equation

$$C_j = V e^{\phi / X_j}. \tag{3}$$

$C$ is the estimated transfer cost as a percentage of total project cost, $X$ represents the value of various independent variables, $j$ refers to the $j$th observation.

With this specification, the transfer cost for a project asymptotically approaches a minimum non-zero value as the value of each $X$ increases. That is, as $X$ goes to infinity, $C$ goes to $V$. Therefore $V$ is the minimum transfer cost with respect to the $X$ variable. However, there is no maximum cost asymptote for the range of the data. The expression for the elasticity of transfer cost with respect to $X$ is given by

$$\frac{-X}{C}\frac{dC}{dX} = \frac{\phi}{X}. \tag{4}$$

Thus for a specified value of $X$, the elasticity of transfer cost with respect to $X$ is determined by $\phi$. Hence the elasticity depends only on $\phi$ and $X$. In order to estimate the function, the log of the arguments in (3) are taken:

$$\log C_j = \log V + \frac{\phi}{X_j}. \tag{5}$$

Dummy variables are used to pool the observations across projects. Inclusion of dummy variables allows the minimum cost asymptote to vary from project to project. It is assumed that $\phi$ is constant across projects. These assumptions provide a pooled sample with intercepts which vary across projects.

Ordinary least-squares regressions of $\log C_j$ on the dummy variables and $1/X_j$ then proceeded for five different $X$ variables, and for five data sets. These were: total transfers; transfers within the chemical and petroleum refining category; transfers in the machinery category; transfers of chemicals and petroleum refining technology to developed countries; and transfers of chemical and petroleum refining technology to less developed countries.[1] The Chow test (Chow, 1960) of equality between sets of coefficients in two linear regressions revealed that the separation of the sample along industry lines was valid, except for the research and development variable. However, there was no statistically valid reason for disaggregating the chemical and petroleum refining subsample according to differences in GNP *per capita* in the host countries.

The results of the estimation are contained in Table 4. The high $R^2$ values are partly because the large across-project variation in costs is being captured by the project dummies. The intercept term was always highly significant and the coefficients on all the dummies were significantly different from each other. All of the coefficients are significantly greater than zero at the 0·20 level and the age of the technology, the number of manufacturing start-ups, transferee size and experience achieve at least the 0·05 significance level in one or other of the subsamples. In several cases the coefficients are highly significant, providing strong statistical support for the hypotheses that have been advanced. The number of previous applications once again has a sizeable impact. Diffusion and manufacturing experience are particularly important in the machinery category.

The calculation of elasticities allows interpretation and comparisons of estimated effects. Average or point elasticities for some typical sample values of $X$ are presented in Table 5. These estimates suggest that in the chemicals and petroleum-refining category, the second start-up could lower transfer costs by

---

[1] A purely arbitrary classification was used where less developed countries were defined as those with GNP/*per capita* less than $1,000.

34 % over the first start-up, other variables held constant. The corresponding change for conducting a third start-up is 19 %. The other elasticities can be interpreted similarly.

Table 4

*Estimated values of $\phi$ (obtained from regressing $\log C_j$ on $\log V + \phi/X_j$) together with corresponding t-statistics, sample size, degrees of freedom, and coefficient of determination $R^2$*

| Variable | $\phi$ | t-statistic | Sample size | Degrees of freedom | $R^2$ |
|---|---|---|---|---|---|
| Start-ups | | | | | |
| Chemicals and petroleum refining | 0·46 | 4·23 | 45 | 25 | 0·92 |
| Machinery | 0·19 | 1·76 | 20 | 10 | 0·91 |
| Age | | | | | |
| Chemicals and petroleum refining | 0·04 | 1·29 | 47 | 30 | 0·89 |
| Machinery | 0·41 | 2·19 | 21 | 13 | 0·94 |
| Experience | | | | | |
| Chemicals and petroleum refining | 0·007 | 0·85 | 52 | 33 | 0·78 |
| Machinery | 0·57 | 6·08 | 23 | 14 | 0·91 |
| Size | | | | | |
| Chemicals and petroleum refining | 0·008 | 1·17 | 54 | 35 | 0·88 |
| Machinery | 0·081 | 5·18 | 17 | 10 | 0·99 |
| R & D sales | | | | | |
| Total sample | 0·06 | 1·58 | 59 | 30 | 0·90 |

## VII. DIFFERENCES BETWEEN INTERNATIONAL AND DOMESTIC TECHNOLOGY TRANSFER

Although this is primarily a study of international technology transfer, it is apparent that many of the characteristics of international technology transfer are also characteristic of the technology transfer that occurs within national borders, but there are differences. For instance, distance and communication costs very often differentiate international from domestic transfers. Although the communications revolution of the twentieth century has enormously reduced the barriers imposed by distance,[1] the costs of international communication are often significant.[2] Language differences can also add to communication costs, especially if the translation of engineering drawings is required. The experience of Polyspinners Ltd at Mogilev in the Soviet Union (Jones, 1973) is ample testimony to the extra costs that can be encountered.[3] International differences in units of measurements and engineering standards can compound the problems encountered (Meursinge, 1971). Additional sources of difficulty are rooted in

---

[1] Facsimile equipment exists which can be used to transmit messages and drawings across the Atlantic instantaneously.

[2] One of the participating companies indicated that travel, telegraph, freight, and insurance added about 10% to the total cost of a project established in New Zealand.

[3] The project manager estimated that documentation alone cost £500,000, and the translation a similar amount.

the cultural and attitudinal differences between nations, as well as differences in the level of economic development and the attendant socioeconomic structure.

It is of interest to know the magnitude and determinants of the "international component" of the transfer cost. Unfortunately, foreign and domestic transfers

Table 5

*Arc or Point Elasticity of Transfer Costs With Respect to Number of Start-ups, Age of Technology, Experience, Size and R & D/Sales of Transferee*

| Independent variable | Chemicals and petroleum refining | Machinery |
|---|---|---|
| | Arc elasticity | |
| Number of start-ups | | |
| 1–2 | 0·34 | 0·14 |
| 2–3 | 0·19 | 0·08 |
| 3–4 | 0·13 | 0·05 |
| 9–10 | 0·05 | 0·02 |
| 14–15 | 0·03 | 0·01 |
| Age of technology (years) | Point elasticity | |
| 1 | 0·04 | 0·41 |
| 2 | 0·02 | 0·20 |
| 3 | 0·01 | 0·14 |
| 10 | 0·00 | 0·04 |
| 20 | 0·00 | 0·02 |
| Experience of transferee (years) | Point elasticity | |
| 1 | 0·007 | 0·57 |
| 2 | 0·003 | 0·28 |
| 3 | 0·002 | 0·19 |
| 10 | 0·001 | 0·06 |
| 20 | 0·000 | 0·03 |
| Size of transferee (millions of sales dollars) | Point elasticity | |
| 1·0 | 0·008 | 0·081 |
| 10 | 0·001 | 0·008 |
| 20 | 0·000 | 0·004 |
| 100 | 0·000 | 0·001 |
| 1000 | 0·000 | 0·000 |
| R & D/Sales of transferee (%) | Total sample point elasticity | |
| 1 | 0·06 | |
| 2 | 0·03 | |
| 3 | 0·02 | |
| 4 | 0·01 | |
| 5 | 0·01 | |
| 6 | 0·01 | |

are rarely identical in scope or in timing, and so it is not possible to gather comparative data on implemented projects at home and abroad. It was therefore found necessary to rely on estimates provided by the firms involved in international transfers. For the projects in the sample, project managers were asked to estimate the dollar amount by which transfer costs would be different if the international transfers in the sample had occurred domestically, holding firm and technology characteristics constant. The procedure was designed to highlight the effects of country characteristics such as differences in language, differences in engineering and measurement standards, differences in economic infrastructure and business environment, and geographical distance from the transferor. The international component of the transfer cost for the projects in the sample could be obtained by subtracting the estimated transfer cost from the

Table 6

*International Component\* of Transfer Cost*

| Chemicals and petroleum refining | | Machinery | |
|---|---|---|---|
| Dollar amount (thousands) | As % of actual transfer cost | Dollar amount (thousands) | As % of actual transfer cost |
| 3·03 | 6·07 | 35·55 | 17·88 |
| 0·00 | 0·00 | −399·37 | −110·93 |
| −12·81 | −1·87 | 50·06 | 4·93 |
| 43·90 | 31·00 | 830·70 | 14·20 |
| 0·00 | 0·00 | −4·59 | −0·02 |
| 5·17 | 1·42 | 226·80 | 14·82 |
| 132·75 | 20·63 | 0·67 | 1·99 |
| 0·00 | 0·00 | −134·40 | 13·87 |
| 342·00 | 43·84 | 34·98 | 12·95 |
| 0·00 | — | | |
| 0·00 | — | | |
| 0·00 | 0·00 | | |
| −10·77 | −6·66 | | |
| −50·16 | −8·52 | | |
| 0·00 | — | | |
| 637·32 | 72·60 | | |
| −1·33 | −1·99 | | |
| 1,723·81 | 60·48 | | |
| 1,370·25 | 18·45 | | |
| 524·25 | 15·69 | | |

\* Amount of actual transfer costs attributable to the fact that transfer was international rather than domestic. (Accordingly negative values indicate that firms estimated that transfer costs would be higher had the transfer been domestic.) In general, these numbers were derived from taking the weighted average of estimated changes in the various identifiable components of transfer costs.

actual transfer cost. The data, contained in Table 6, reveal that the difference in cost is not always positive. This indicates that in at least some of the cases, the international transfer of an innovation was estimated to cost less than a comparable domestic transfer. This may seem paradoxical at first, given that international technology transfer generally augments the transfer activities that have to be performed.[1] An analysis of the determinants of the international component of transfer costs may yield an explanation.

Several hypotheses are presented and tested. The first is that the difference is

[1] The source of the apparent paradox may be differences in labour costs. Nevertheless, the identification of the transfer for which international transfer costs less than domestic transfer is an issue of importance.

large and positive when the technology has not been previously commercialised. National boundaries are often surrogates for cultural and language barriers, differences in methods and standards of measurement, and distance from the home country. During first commercialisation of a product or process, there are generally enormous information flows across the development-manufacturing interface. The hypothesis is that placing a national boundary at this interface can complicate matters considerably, and escalate the costs enormously. The second hypothesis is that transfers to government enterprises in centrally planned economies will involve higher transfer costs. Transferors can expect numerous delays and large documentation requirements (Jones, 1973). The third hypothesis is that the less the diffusion of the technology, measured as before by the number of firms utilising the innovation, the greater the positive differential associated with international technology transfer. The fourth hypothesis is that whereas, in general, low levels of economic development are likely to add to transfer costs because of inadequacies in the economic infrastructure, this may be more than offset, in some circumstances, by low labour costs. Labour costs can have a substantial impact on excess manufacturing costs, especially in relatively labour intensive industries. Since machinery manufacture is relatively labour intensive, the hypothesis is that the GNP *per capita* in the host country is positively related to the transfer cost differential in this classification, but is negatively associated with the differential in the chemicals and petroleum refining category.

To test these hypotheses it is assumed that

$$D_i = \alpha_0 + \alpha_1 d_i + \alpha_2 \bar{U}_i + \alpha_3 N_i + \alpha_4 P_i + Z_i,$$

where $D_i$ is the "international component" as a percentage of actual transfer cost for the $i$th transfer. $d_i$ is a dummy variable which takes the value 1 if the recipient of the $i$th transfer is a government enterprise in a centrally planned economy, and zero otherwise. The other variables carry the same definitions as previously. The expected derivations are:

$$\frac{\partial D_i}{\partial d_i} > 0, \quad \frac{\partial D_i}{\partial \bar{U}_i} > 0, \quad \frac{\partial D_i}{\partial N_i} < 0;$$

$\partial D_i / \partial P_i \gtrless 0$ according to the industry category (the partial is postulated positive for the machinery category, and negative otherwise). Least-squares estimates of the $\alpha$'s were obtained, the results being:

Chemicals and petroleum:

$$D_i = 0.285 + 3.84 d_i + 4.46 \bar{U}_i \quad (n = 17, r^2 = 0.71).$$
$$(0.91) \quad (5.01) \quad (4.89)$$

Machinery:[1]

$$D_i = -8.59 \quad -1.39 N_i + 0.005 P_i \quad (n = 9, r^2 = 0.94).$$
$$(-1.96) \quad (-5.98) \quad (3.90)$$

---

[1] $U_i$ was omitted from the machinery regression since none of the actual transfers in this category were to government enterprises in centrally planned economies.

The hypotheses are to some extent borne out by the data, but the small sample size must counsel caution in the interpretation of these results.[1] In chemicals and petroleum, the results indicate that transfers to government enterprises, and transfers before first commercialisation, involve substantial extra costs. Furthermore, both $N_i$ and $P_i$ are significant in the machinery category, despite the small number of observations, yet they are insignificant in chemicals and petroleum refining, where there are more than twice as many degrees of freedom. Apparently, the level of host country development and the degree of diffusion of an innovation have no bearing on the international–domestic transfer cost differential in the chemicals and petroleum grouping. This calls for an explanation. The diffusion variable $N_i$ is taken to indicate the degree to which the requisite skills are generally available. The statistical results suggest that the relevant skills for highly capital intensive industries, such as chemicals and petroleum refining, are more easily transferred internationally than are the requisite skills in the machinery category.[2] Furthermore, $P_i$ was not significant in chemicals and petroleum refining, suggesting that costs of transfer are independent of the level of economic development in this category. This is consistent with speculation that international transfer is no more difficult than domestic transfer when the underlying technology is highly capital intensive. The perceived reluctance of multinational firms to adapt technology to suit the capital-labour endowments of less developed countries could well be rooted in the desire to avoid escalating transfer costs to unacceptable levels.

### VIII. CONCLUSION

The resources required to transfer technology internationally are considerable. Accordingly, it is quite inappropriate to regard existing technology as something that can be made available to all at zero social cost. Furthermore, transfer costs vary considerably, especially according to the number of previous applications of the innovation, and how well the innovation is understood by the parties involved. It is equally inappropriate, therefore, to make sweeping generalisations about the process of technology transfer and the costs involved. For instance, technology transfer in chemicals and petroleum refining displayed relatively low transfer costs, presumably because it is possible to embody sophisticated process technology in capital equipment, which in turn facilitates the transfer process.

The analysis of the determinants of technology transfer costs provided some interesting findings with development implications. The success of the more experienced enterprises, indicated by lower transfer costs, points towards economic models which emphasise the accumulation of skills, rather than fixed

---

[1] If the second observation on $D_i$ in the machinery category is excluded, and the regression results recomputed, the estimates of the coefficients exhibit considerable instability and the "goodness of fit" deteriorates. The estimated equation is

$$D_i = -4\cdot96 \quad -0\cdot66 N_i + 0\cdot003 P_i \quad (n = 8, \, r^2 = 0\cdot45).$$
$$\quad\;\; (1\cdot14) \quad (2\cdot40) \quad (1\cdot94)$$

These estimates are nevertheless significant at the $0\cdot05$ level for a one-tail test.

[2] This is consonant with the views expressed by several project managers in the chemical industry. It was asserted that technology could be transferred with equal facility to almost anywhere in the world, including less developed countries, assuming host government interference is held constant.

assets or capital, in facilitating the technology transfer process. This seems consonant with the findings of several economic historians (Rosenberg, 1970; Rawski, 1975).

The results also provide some managerial implications for the multinational firm. Consider the costs associated with separating production from development (Arditti, 1968). The results indicate that the international transfer of technology is most likely to be viable when production runs are long enough to allow second sourcing. The especially high cost of transfer before first application favours the development location, at least for production of initial units. However, transfer costs will be lowered once the first production run has been commenced, and international transfer then becomes more likely, a finding consistent with the product cycle model (Vernon, 1966). However, inter-industry differences are important, and the costs involved in separating first production from development did not prove to be an insurmountable transfer barrier for an important subset of the sample projects.

A second implication is that since transfer costs decline with each application of a given innovation, technology transfer is a decreasing cost activity. This can be advanced as an explanation for the specialisation often exhibited by engineering firms in the design and installation of particular turnkey plants,[1] a characteristic particularly noteworthy of the petrochemical industry.

A third set of managerial implications relate to the criteria which might be used for the selection of a joint venture or licensing partner to utilise the innovating firms' technology abroad. While the manufacturing experience, size, and R & D to sales ratio of the transferee were identified as statistically significant determinants of transfer costs for the sample, there was also evidence to suggest that, *ceteris paribus*, any firm moderately matured in these dimensions is a good candidate to absorb the technology at the minimum possible transfer cost. It is not clear, therefore, that super giant firms have any advantage in this respect over moderately sized firms. Nor is it clear that highly research intensive firms have more than a slight cost advantage in absorbing technology over firms with a minimal commitment to research and development activity. However, manufacturing experience is important, especially for transferring machinery technology. In addition, there is evidence that transfers to governments in centrally planned economies involve substantial extra costs, perhaps because of high documentation requirements, or differences in language and managerial procedures.

Technology transfer by multinational firms is clearly a complex matter. Collection and analysis of proprietary data has provided some helpful insights. Few issues have been settled although many have been raised. Further analytic research and more extensive data collection is required if our understanding of international technology transfer is to be improved.

D. J. TEECE

*Stanford University, California*

*Date of receipt of final typescript: November 1976*

---
[1] Turnkey plants generally embody state-of-the-art technology.

REFERENCES

Arrow, K. (1969). "Classificatory Notes on the Production and Transmission of Technological Know-ledge." *Amercian Economic Review; Papers and Proceedings*, vol. 52 (May), pp. 29–35.

—— (1962). Comment in Universities-National Bureau Committee for Economic Research. *The Rate and Direction of Inventive Activity*. Princeton: Princeton University Press.

Arditti, F. (1968). "On the Separation of Production from the Developer." *Journal of Business*, vol. 41 (July), pp. 317–28.

Baranson, J. (1967): *Manufacturing Problems in India: The Cummings Diesel Experience*. Syracuse, N.Y.: Syracuse University Press.

Berrill, K. (ed.) (1964). *Economic Development with Special Reference to East Asia*. New York: St Martins Press.

Chow, G. C. (1960). "Tests of Equality between Sets of Coefficients in Two Linear Regressions." *Econometrica*, vol. 28 (July), pp. 591–605.

Freeman, C. (1965). "Research and Development in Electronic Capital Goods." *National Institute Economic Review*, no. 34, vol. 34 (November), pp. 1–70.

Gillette, R. (1973). "Latin America: Is Imported Technology Too Expensive?" *Science*, vol. 191 (6 July), pp. 4–44.

Hall, G. R. and Johnson, R. E. (1970). "Transfers of United States Aerospace Technology to Japan." In *The Technology Factor in International Trade* (ed. R. Vernon). N.Y.: National Bureau of Economic Research.

Hayami, Y. and Ruttan, V. (1971). *Agricultural Development and International Perspective*. Baltimore: Johns Hopkins.

International Bank for Reconstruction and Development (1973). *World Bank Atlas*. Washington, D.C.: I.B.R.D.

Jones, D. (1973). "The 'Extra Costs' in Europe's Biggest Synthetic Fiber Complex at Mogilev, U.S.S.R." *Worldwide Projects and Installations*, vol. 7 (May/June), pp. 30–5.

Kuznets, S. (1966). *Modern Economic Growth: Rate, Structure, Spread*. New Haven: Yale University Press.

Mansfield, E. (1974). "Technology and Technical Change." In *Economic Analysis and the Multinational Enterprise* (ed. J. Dunning). London: Allen and Unwin.

—— (1968). *The Economics of Technological Change*. New York: Norton.

—— (1973). "Discussion of the Paper by Professor Griliches." In *Science and Technology in Economic Growth* (ed. B. R. Williams). New York: John Wiley.

Mansfield, E., Rapoport, J., Schnee, J., Wagner, S. and Hamburger, M. (1971). *Research and Innovation In the Modern Corporation*. New York: W. W. Norton.

Mason, R. Hal (1973). "The Multinational Firm and the Cost of Technology to Developing Countries." *California Management Review*, vol. 15 (Summer), pp. 5–13.

Meursinge, J. (1971). "Practical Experience in the Transfer of Technology." *Technology and Culture*, vol. 12 (July), pp. 469–70.

*McGraw-Hill Encyclopedia of Science and Technology* (1960). Vols. 4, 10, pp. 639–44. New York: McGraw-Hill.

Oshima, K. (1973). "Research and Development and Economic Growth in Japan." In *Science and Technology in Economic Growth* (ed. B. R. Williams). New York: John Wiley.

Rawski, T. (1975). "Problems of Technology and Absorption in Chinese Industry." *American Economic Review*, vol. 65 (May), pp. 363–88.

Reynolds, L. (1966). Discussion. *American Economic Review*, vol. 56 (May), pp. 112–14.

Robinson, E. A. G. (1973). "Discussion of the Paper by Professor Hsia." In *Science and Technology in Economic Growth* (ed. B. R. Williams). New York: John Wiley.

Rodriguez, C. A. (1975). "Trade in Technical Knowledge and the National Advantage." *Journal of Political Economy*, vol. 93 (February), pp. 121–35.

Rosenberg, N. (1970). "Economic Development and the Transfer of Technology: Some Historical Perspectives." *Technology and Culture*, vol. 11 (October), pp. 550–75.

Teece, D. (1976). *The Multinational Corporation and the Resource Cost of International Technology Transfer*. Cambridge: Ballinger.

—— (1977). "Time–Cost Tradeoffs: Elasticity Estimates and Determinants for International Technology Transfer Projects." *Management Science*, vol. 23 (April).

Tilton, J. (1971). *International Diffusion of Technology: The Case of Semiconductors*. Washington, D.C.: Brookings Institution.

United Nations (1968). *International Standard Industrial Classification of all Economic Activities*. United Nations Statistical Papers, Series M., Number 4. New York: United Nations.

UNCTAD (1970). "The Transfer of Technology." *Journal of World Trade Law*, vol. 4 (September/October), pp. 692–718.

Vernon, R. (1966). "International Investment and International Trade in the Product Cycle. *Quarterly Journal of Economics*, vol. 80 (May), pp. 190–207.

*Chapter Eight*

# US and Japanese Manufacturing Affiliates in the UK: Comparisons and Contrasts

## INTRODUCTION

This chapter compares and contrasts some aspects of the role of US manufacturing affiliates in the UK in the early 1950s, with that of their Japanese counterparts in the early 1980s. In so doing, it identifies some of the more important country-of-origin differences in the reasons for investing in the UK, in ownership patterns and organizational structure, and in economic impact; and also changes which have occurred both in the international economic scenario and in the character of multinational hierarchies over the intervening three decades. Finally, it relates these issues to recent advances in the theory of international production and in particular the eclectic paradigm set out in this book.

## DATA SOURCES AND METHOD OF ANALYSIS

In the early 1950s, the present author undertook a survey of some 205 US manufacturing subsidiaries in the UK.[1] These affiliates accounted for between 90 and 95 per cent of the output of all US-owned manufacturing offshoots. The survey covered all aspects of their operations, including their organizational form and locus and patterns of decision making; and analyzed, in some detail, their impact on the UK economy. Each of the subsidiaries was visited and interviews conducted with one or more senior executives. Not all the executives were prepared to give information about the structure and mechanism of their decision-making, but 150 were, and the data on US-owned subsidiaries used in this book were derived from this source.

Nearly 30 years later, the author undertook a similar survey of Japanese manufacturing affiliates.[2] Some 26 of these were identified and visits paid to 22 of them. Once again, information was sought, and for the most part obtained, of the ways in which decisions were taken, both within these subsidiaries and between the subsidiaries and their parent companies. In this survey, however, rather more attention

220                                    *Explaining International Production*

was paid to the reasons for their presence in the UK; moreover, the presentation of the results was set within the framework of the eclectic paradigm of international production.[3]

In the course of this chapter, we shall identify several differences between the reasons for and effects of US and Japanese direct investment in the UK. At the outset, however, it must be admitted that it is difficult to identify the extent to which such differences that do emerge are specifically due to the country of origin of the affiliates, and how far they reflect other distinguishing features between the two groups of firms, e.g. size, industrial composition, ownership patterns and, perhaps most important of all, the 30 years' difference in the timing of the surveys.

At the end of the day, the attribution of similarities and differences to one or more causes must be a matter of judgement. Data simply do not permit any econometric evaluation of the explanatory variables. But, as we hope the chapter will demonstrate, we can get a long way by examining the features of two groups of firms, their motives for investing in the UK, the very different economic and cultural background from which they originate, and the major differences in the economic environment facing inward investors in the 1980s from in the 1950s. It is these and similar questions we take up in the next section.

## THE EXTENT AND PATTERN: THE FACTS

In December 1953, US manufacturing affiliates employed about 3 per cent of the total labour force in UK manufacturing industry and accounted for about 4 per cent of all manufacturing costs. Since the corresponding figures of 1981 (Business Statistics Office) were 10 per cent and 15 per cent respectively, it can be seen that US direct investment in UK industry was considerably less significant than it is today. Nevertheless, it already had a long history. Since 1929 at least (when the first US *Census of Overseas Assets* was conducted), the UK had consistently remained the second largest recipient of US direct investment in manufacturing (after Canada) and, in the 1950s, was by far and away the most favoured location in Europe.[4]

Thirty years later, Japanese manufacturing MNEs were just beginning to make their presence felt in the UK. In June 1983, there were only 26 Japanese manufacturing affiliates (compared with at least 250 US subsidiaries in 1953). They employed 5,375 (compared with over a quarter of a million in US subsidiaries in 1953) - a minute fraction, just 0.05 per cent of the total manufacturing labour force, and only 0.5 per cent of the employment in all foreign manufacturing affiliates. Their corresponding share of UK and foreign affiliate manufacturing sales were 0.08 per cent and 0.40 per cent. In the main, Japanese manufacturing investment in the UK is of very recent origin. The first postwar manufacturing affiliate - YKK Fasteners - was not set up until 1969,[5] and it is only since 1979 that the scale of Japanese participation has become at all noticeable.[6]

Table 8.1 *Percentage Distribution of Employment of United States and Japanese Manufacturing Affiliates by Selected Industrial Sectors*

| | US (1953) | | Japanese (1982) | |
|---|---|---|---|---|
| | Employment | % | Employment | % |
| Chemicals | 31 300 | 12.7 | 106 | 2.0 |
| Electrical goods | 13 600 | 5.5 | 4 059 | 75.6 |
| Non-electrical engineering | 77 000 | 31.3 | 698 | 13.0 |
| Vehicles | 56 000 | 22.7 | 0 | 0.0 |
| Precision instruments | 16 200 | 6.6 | 324 | 6.0 |
| Textiles and clothing | 3 900 | 1.6 | 42 | 0.8 |
| Others | 48 200 | 19.6 | 146 | 2.7 |
| | 246 200 | 100.0 | 5 375 | 100.0 |

*Source*: Dunning (1958 and 1986a).

The industrial structure of the two groups of foreign affiliates shows both differences and similarities. The differences are illustrated in Table 8.1. While more than half (54 per cent) the employment in US affiliates in 1953 was within the engineering and motor vehicles sector, no less than 80 per cent of the labour force of Japanese affiliates in 1983 was in consumer and industrial electronics. The chemical sector accounted for 12.7 per cent of employment of US affiliates and 2 per cent of Japanese affiliates.

However, in spite of these differences, there is one important similarity between the two groups of affiliates: they both strongly favour the more technologically advanced and faster growing sectors of UK industry, and those producing branded consumer goods with a high income elasticity of demand. In 1953, for example, 43.8 per cent of employment in all UK firms was in the traditional sectors of metal manufacturing, textiles, food, drink and tobacco, woodwork, and paper and printing, which accounted for only 14.5 per cent of employment of US affiliates. In 1983 less than 10 per cent of employment of Japanese subsidiaries was in these industries; of the rest, more than three-quarters was in the consumer electronics sector alone.

## THE EXTENT AND PATTERN: THE EXPLANATION

In our 1958 study, little attempt was made to explain the extent and pattern of US participation in UK industry in terms of any general theory of foreign direct investment (FDI) or international production. It was, however, noted (pp. 19–20 and 78) that the sectors in which the concentration quotient of US affiliates was greater than 1,[7] were those in which their parent companies had first evolved innovatory management and/or entrepreneurial advantages, and that these, in turn, reflected the particular country specific ESP characteristics of the US relative to the

UK economy.[8] The specific ownership (*O*) advantages of US firms identified in the 1958 study (see p. 78 ff.) were (1) their ability to innovate
particular kinds of goods and services; (2) their managerial and marketing
skills in producing and selling these goods and (3) their capacity to exploit
large-scale and fairly homogeneous markets. On the one hand, because of
its high wage costs, the US had the incentive to produce labour-saving products and to engage in capital or technology intensive production methods;
on the other, its large and reasonably homogeneous home market and the
high income of its consumers generated patterns of demand which, when
emulated by other countries, gave US firms a powerful competitive edge
over their international rivals.

The nature of the *O* advantages of Japanese firms over UK firms in the
1980s is similar in some respects and different in others. It is similar in that
the advantages arise from the possession of individual rent earning assets,
rather than those to do with cross-border transaction cost minimizing
activities.[9] Since the end of the Second World War, Japan has been seeking to catch up with the USA and Europe in its manufacturing capabilities.
To break into foreign markets dominated by its international competitors,
its firms had either to produce new products, which, because of their
limited innovatory capabilities they found very difficult to do; or to tempt
consumers to switch their purchases to their own products, e.g. by lower
price, superior design, quality and reliability, which, in fact, was the
strategy chosen by Japanese firms. Nowadays, the particular *O* advantages
of Japanese MNEs, especially in consumer goods industries, is self-
evident. By efficient work organization, use of latest equipment, and a
rigorous and comprehensive system of quality control - of both
intermediate and final products - they have captured markets from their
competitors. In addition, as might be expected from late entrant firms into
the product cycle, the Japanese have sought to differentiate their products.
This they have done (especially in the motor vehicle industry) mainly by
providing ancillary equipment, normally reserved for up-market products. Coupled with aggressive marketing tactics, Japanese MNEs have
created distinct *O* advantages in the production of fairly standardized and
mature products, which has often enabled them to out-compete their
Western rivals in UK markets.

The main difference, then, between the *O* advantages of US affiliates in
the 1950s and Japanese affiliates in the 1980s is that the former rested on
the innovating capacities of the investing companies and on the more successful application of management and marketing skills; while the latter
arise from quality control, product differentiation and cost advantages, an
emphasis on good industrial relations, and efficient procurement policies.[10]
The pharmaceutical and vehicles sectors in the 1950s in which the US affiliates were particularly dominant, were recipients of the first kind of advantage; the consumer electronics and the vehicle sectors in the 1980s, of the
latter. Looking to the future, however, there is some reason to suppose that
Japanese MNEs in both consumer and industrial electronics are beginning
to generate innovatory advantages of their own. Certainly, like the parent
companies of the US affiliates in the 1950s, they are among the most
technologically progressive and fastest growing companies in Japan.[11]

## THE GEOGRAPHICAL DISTRIBUTION: THE FACTS

The location of Japanese foreign direct investment stake in UK manufacturing in the 1980s is very different from its US counterpart in the 1950s. Outside North America, which attracted 27 per cent of the Japanese cumulative foreign investment stake in March 1983, Asia accounted for 33 per cent, Latin America 20 per cent and Europe only 7 per cent. By contrast, in 1955, the US direct investment stake in foreign manufacturing facilities was mainly concentrated in Canada (45 per cent), Europe (30 per cent) and Latin America (15 per cent).

Within Europe, the UK has always been the preferred location for US MNEs, though, since 1955, other European countries have increased their share of new manufacturing investment. In 1983, Japanese participation in European industry was rather more widely spread, with Spain accounting for 35 per cent of the employment in manufacturing affiliates, Belgium 17 per cent and the UK 13 per cent. However, in the last five years, the growth of new investment has been most pronounced in the UK, and, by the end of 1984, the UK had overtaken Spain as the leading employee of Japanese manufacturing affiliates in Europe.

Within the UK, the concentration of Japanese affiliates in the less prosperous regions is even more marked than that of their US predecessors. Table 8.2 sets out some details. Within these regions, while Wales has been particularly favoured by Japanese affiliates, Scotland ranked highest for US investors. This probably reflects the different industrial composition of the two groups. In the rest of the UK, Japanese affiliates have been especially drawn to expanding towns and cities of the Midlands (e.g. Milton Keynes, Telford and Northampton); by contrast, in the 1950s, US affiliates strongly favoured a South East location, and especially the Outer London area.

## THE GEOGRAPHICAL DISTRIBUTION: THE EXPLANATION

The initial *raison d'être* for both kinds of inward investment has been to service local markets - and sometimes adjacent markets as well - previously supplied by the parent company. The literature suggests that the location of such import-substitution investment will be influenced mainly by market size and character, the prospects for growth, production costs, transport costs, investment and other incentives, tariffs and other artificial barriers to trade, and performance and other requirements imposed by host governments. In the 1950s, the shortage of US dollars restricted American exports both to European and some Commonwealth countries. The reaction by American exporters was to service these markets from production affiliates in the UK; in the 1980s, the appreciation of the yen, and voluntary restrictions on Japanese exports to Europe, have been the most important inducements for Japanese firms to relocate their production.

Table 8.2 *Percentage Distribution of Employment of US, Japanese Manufacturing Affiliates and all UK firms by Broad Geographical Area*

|  | US (1953) % | All UK (1953) % | Japanese (1983) % | All UK (1979) % |
|---|---|---|---|---|
| *Regions of above average unemployment* | | | | |
| Northern England | 10.6 | 28.6 | 10.0 | 26.6 |
| Wales | 2.8 | 4.4 | 68.0 | 4.5 |
| Scotland | 12.1 | 10.1 | 9.1 | 9.4 |
| South West England | 6.5 | 9.8 | 5.4 | 6.9 |
|  | 32.0 | 52.9 | 92.5 | 47.4 |
| | | | | |
| *Regions of average or below average unemployment* | | | | |
| Midlands | 10.1 | 16.5 | 0.2 | 16.7 |
| South East England | 47.0 | 25.2 | 5.4 | 32.9 |
| East Anglia | 10.9 | 5.3 | 1.9 | 3.0 |
|  | 68.0 | 47.0 | 7.5 | 52.6 |

*Source*: Dunning (1958 and 1986a).

*NB*: In the later 1980s, the problem of Japanese employees in the Midlands has risen dramatically with the Sumitomo acquisition of the Dunlop operations in Birmingham; as has that in Northern England with the establishment in 1985 of Nissan at Washington in Tyne & Wear.

In consequence, both US and Japanese affiliates exported a substantial part of their output – 36 per cent in the former case and 31 per cent in the latter. However, whereas the strategy of the US firms towards the export of their UK affiliates was largely defensive, and/or preparatory to investment in individual recipient markets, that of the Japanese has been part and parcel of an aggressive integrated strategy in which *ab initio* Europe was regarded as the target market, but with that market mainly to be supplied from a single production base.[12]

Within Europe, both American and Japanese investors favoured the UK, first and foremost, for language reasons; and next because of the similarities (relative in the Anglo-Japanese case) of commercial, legal and educational systems in the investing and host countries. Size of the domestic market was a stronger pull in the case of US investors than that for Japanese investors. Indeed, in the latter case – particularly in the major sector of involvement, i.e. consumer electronics – local demand conditions appeared to be less important as a locational choice than production opportunities as, in most cases, the UK plant is intended to serve the European market.

Within the UK, government attempts to steer new industry to the regions of above average unemployment or those dominated by older or less dynamic sectors, was as strong an influence on the locational decisions of Japanese affiliates in the 1980s as it had been 30 years earlier for American affiliates. In general, the evidence suggests that foreign owned firms are more likely to respond to government persuasion and incentives than are domestic firms (Dunning and Yannopolous in Dunning, 1981). Perhaps, the only major endogenous locational factors which have assumed more significance since the 1950s are road and air communications and cross-border telecommunication and data transmitting facilities. Within the two groups of firms, the importance attached by Japanese companies to the attitude and motivation of labour, makes them avoid regions with a heritage of industrial conflict; the age and sex structure of employment in Japanese affiliates is also different than that of their US predecessors,[13] even within particular industrial sectors.

## THE FORM OF INVOLVEMENT

In our 1958 volume, little attention was given to the modality of resource transfer, such as the licensing versus foreign direct investment choice of exploiting $O$ specific assets. In the Japanese study, we asked quite specifically why the hierarchical rather than the contractual route was chosen. The reasons given by the management of consumer electronic affiliates were threefold: (1) to ensure full quality control over both intermediate and final products, (2) to rationalize markets (and eventually production) in Europe and (3) to benefit from co-ordinating economies stemming from a common parentage. In the case of other sectors, the reasons for FDI were more varied, but the protection of property rights in the case of the process (notably the chemical) sectors, and the perceived need to control market access, were the two most commonly cited.

Thirty years previously, the characteristics of market failure making for US investment exhibited both similarities and differences. Earlier, we suggested that the $O$ advantages of US MNEs *vis-à-vis* their UK competitors, reflected the particular pattern of resource endowments in the home country, which helped create intangible assets, and which, because of structural imperfections (e.g. patent laws) became the privileged possession of individual US firms. Where the transaction costs of transferring these assets or their rights to UK firms were higher than those within the same US firm, then the transfer was internalized. Our reading of the rationale for foreign direct investment by US firms in the 1950s is that the markets for $O$ advantages based on product or process innovations were internalized, partly because of lack of technological capacity (including support skills) in the UK, and partly to exploit firm economies of scale and scope. By contrast, those based on marketing efficiency were internalized to protect quality control, e.g. of selling and after-sales servicing; those and those resting on the managerial professionalism, philosophy and dynamic entrepreneurship were generally tacit and uncodifiable, and required face-to-face contact for their efficient transfer.

In the case of both groups of investors, it would appear unlikely that the UK was chosen because of favourable conditions for internalizing market distortions generated by host governments.

## ORGANIZATIONAL AND OWNERSHIP PATTERNS[14]

The way in which parent enterprises control decision-taking in their affiliates tells us something about the nature of the hierarchical relationships within MNEs, and especially whether the affiliate is viewed as an independent entity, or as part of a co-ordinated network of international activities. In the latter case, one would expect the *O* advantages of MNEs to be more of a *transaction cost*-minimizing kind rather than those resting on the privileged possession of a particular asset, which enable new or better products to be supplied or the same product at lower prices.

Table 8.3 summarizes some similarities and differences between the extent to which the management practices of US and Japanese affiliates were (or are) influenced and controlled by their parent companies. The following points may be highlighted: First, in general, Japanese affiliates in the 1980s would seem to exercise closer influence and control over general managerial philosophy and style than did their US counterparts in the 1950s. This is partly a function of type of activity, pattern of ownership and age of affiliate,[15] but, perhaps most significantly, the more holistic approach adopted by the Japanese to decision taking. The attention paid to encouraging the right work ethic, group behaviour and team support, requires an integrated organizational policy, the control and monitoring of which must be centralized. Hence, for example, in an area in which Japanese influence and control are *prima facie* quite loosely exercised (wages and industrial relations) the managing director of the affiliate is likely to require that the policies of the personnel manager towards recruitment, work organization and standards, discipline, wage and incentives, promotion, and industrial relations are fully consistent with the overall philosophy and strategy of the company, that is to produce a high quality defect-free product at a competitive price. By contrast, the goal of US managerial control in the 1950s was more to ensure that American product and production innovations and marketing methods were smoothly and economically transferred to a UK environment; and more generally, that in all branches of management and decision taking a degree of professionalism was injected.[16] The greater importance attached to inculcating the Japanese approach to management, and the higher costs of decentralizing decision taking within Japanese MNEs,[17] is shown by the fact that whereas the chief executive of 30 per cent of US subsidiaries in the 1950s was a US expatriate, the corresponding figure for Japanese subsidiaries in the mid-1980s was 85 per cent.

Second, linguistic and cultural differences between home and host countries also explain why in many functional areas, the Japanese influence and control is greater than was that of the Americans.

*US and Japanese Manufacturing Affiliates in the UK* 227

Basically, one can identify three sets of communication channels in which the affiliates of MNEs may be involved: (1) between themselves and their parent or other home based companies; (2) between different groups within themselves (e.g. management and workers, technical and sales staff, etc.); and (3) between themselves and their local suppliers, customers, competitors and government. In order to avoid misunderstandings, due *inter alia* to language and/or different ways of gathering, monitoring and presenting information, e.g. accounting data, it is not surprising that most heads of finance departments in Japanese affiliates are Japanese nationals; and that, usually, Japanese production managers and chief technicians are appointed to ensure a free exchange of knowledge and ideas between themselves and their counterparts in Japan or heads of R&D departments. By contrast, efficient face-to-face communication within subsidiaries and between the subsidiaries and local firms, customers, labour unions, industrial associations and government bodies, requires not only a full understanding of the local language, but of culture, business customs and psychology and commercial law. This is why a UK national usually heads both the personnel and procurement departments. Accepting this, however, special attention is given to training these managers in the Japanese way, while there is usually a senior Japanese expatriate on the staff of these departments.

In the case of US subsidiaries in the 1950s, these constraints were not as severe; and it was in the area where the parent company considered indigenous management lacking in the requisite skills, experience or initiative that US expatriates were most likely to be in charge. Examples included sales, production management and marketing; accounting and finance to a lesser extent; and personnel and industrial relations very rarely.

Third, while both groups of affiliates claimed that they conformed to local customs and norms, there is a good deal of evidence that, in somewhat different ways, they have actively influenced these. Some illustrations are given in a later section of this chapter. For the moment, we would point to some differences in personnel and wages policies. Most US subsidiaries in the 1950s adopted an aggressive style to labour recruitment and were willing to pay well above the local average wage to attract the right kind of labour; they also gave substantial incentives to encourage productivity (Dunning, 1958, p. 254ff.). By contrast, Japanese affiliates are highly sensitive to local criticism of their labour policies. They make every effort not to poach from other firms; they have broadly conformed to nationally agreed wage levels; and tend to offer few bonuses or monetary incentives. Their distinctive impact is shown in the area of hiring policy, where they seek to recruit employees, able and willing to work as part of a team; the adoption of a more open and consultative style of industrial relations; and the provision of first class working and social conditions. The facts that most of their workforce – in the consumer electronics sector at least – is semi-skilled female labour and is normally recruited in areas of high unemployment has no doubt made it easier for them to adopt a more paternalistic stance towards,

Table 8.3    *Comparative Managerial Influence and Control Exerted by US and Japanese Parent Companies over UK Affiliates*

| Area of management | US affiliates (c. 1953) | Japanese affiliates (c. 1983) |
|---|---|---|
| Overall managerial strategy | Moderately reflects that of US parent company (though varies between sectors). US nationals or expatriates mostly a minority on board of directors of affiliates. | Strongly influenced and moderately controlled by parent company. Chief Executive of affiliate normally a Japanese national. Japanese nationals or expatriates comprise majority of local board of directors. |
| Product policy | Truncated range of products supplied by parent companies. Minor modifications and adaptations to UK customer requirements. | Affiliates supply only one major product line which, when adapted to local needs, is of the same quality as that produced by parent companies. Product policy decided centrally. |
| Production methods | Less automated, particularly in ancillary e.g. mechanical handling equipment. Otherwise broadly comparable to US plants. | Mainly same as in Japanese parent companies but in some cases scaled down to suit lower volumes produced. |
| Procurement policy | Left mainly to UK personnel managers, but stricter tolerances and standards required cf. those demanded by UK owned firms. | Especial attention paid to quality control circles and inspection and testing procedures. Strongly influenced and controlled by payment company. very rigorous quality control procedures. |

| | | |
|---|---|---|
| Wages and salaries | Loosely controlled; tendency to pay well above average rates; many incentives and bonuses. | Moderately influenced and loosely controlled. Pay slightly above average rates. Few incentives. Time rates disliked. |
| Industrial relations | Loosely influenced and controlled, but bargaining conducted at plant level. Majority of affiliates unionized; some just one union. | Expected to conform to overall managerial philosophy; hiring and firing policy decided centrally. No, or only one, union preferred. |
| Marketing | Strongly influenced and controlled by parent company. Marketing methods mainly replicate US practices. A lot of attention given to sales promotion and after sales servicing. | Destination of output decided and controlled by parent company. Most output sold to separate marketing affiliates. Nothing especially noticeable in marketing methods, except Japanese are tough negotiators over price, and salesmen maintain more face-to-face contact with clients than is normal UK practice. |
| Research and development | Strongly influenced and controlled by parent company. Some r & d in UK mainly to do with machinery design, product and materials adaptation. Some development research in industrial instruments, pharmaceuticals and vehicles. | Strongly influenced and controlled by parent company. Little R & D in UK, but some product design related research starting in CTV sector. |
| Accounting and financial control | Moderately influenced, especially in new methods of production planning and budgetary control. Accounting usually standardised on US lines. | Strongly controlled by parent company. Usually a Japanese is in charge of this managerial area. |

230                              *Explaining International Production*

and be more demanding of, their workers; this, however, is in marked contrast to the friendly and relaxed style of management which was a conspicuous feature of American affiliates 30 years earlier.

Fourth, the innovatory activities of both groups of affiliates were decided upon by their parent companies; as were major items of capital expenditure. Because, from the start, most Japanese affiliates in the UK were set up as part of a regional strategy, their export markets were generally closely controlled from headquarters or from regional sales offices elsewhere in Europe. This was not so in the case of US affiliates whose foreign markets were mainly determined by the availability of foreign exchange. Both groups also tended to replicate their parent companies' production methods as far as they could; of the two, probably the US subsidiaries were forced to make the most adaptations, mainly because differences in market characteristics and the cost of factor inputs between the US and the UK in the 1950s were greater than those between Japan and Europe in the 1980s.[18]

Fifth, compared with their Japanese counterparts, US subsidiaries were given rather more freedom to introduce new products or to modify existing products; however, there was less insistence on the quality standards of the parent company being met. In this latter area, there is absolutely no compromise by the Japanese. Moreover, the strict adherence to standards and inspection procedures is practised at every stage of the value-added chain, including procurement and after-sales servicing. Though, for example, US firms maintained quite strong relationships with their suppliers in the 1950s, this never quite matched that of the Japanese in the 1980s. Moreover, where US affiliates bought (and still buy) comparatively few inputs from their parent companies in 1982, Japanese subsidiaries bought more than half their components from this source. Quite apart from quality and price considerations (and, again, it should be remembered that, in the 1950s, US wages were three times that of UK wages, while, in the early 1980s, Japanese wages were only 1¼ to 1½ times those of UK workers), there was a serious shortage of dollars in the 1950s, while there were fewer obvious gains to be derived from the economies of bulk purchase and/or the common ownership of inter-related activities, as is currently the case with internalized Anglo-Japanese transactions.

In summary, differences in types of activity, the stages of the product cycle, management styles, strategy and objectives and between the Anglo-Japanese and Anglo-American cultural, legal and economic environment, explain most of the variations in the way the two groups of affiliates were, and are, administered and managed.

Sixth, similar factors also explain the greater preference of Japanese MNEs for 100 per cent-owned UK subsidiaries than their American counterparts. In mid-1983, only 5 of the 26 Japanese manufacturing affiliates were less than 100 per cent owned, and only one of the nine electronics subsidiaries. In 1953, 73 per cent of US affiliates were wholly owned and the balance were joint ventures. This higher propensity for the internalized use of *O* specific advantages of Japanese firms is explained, partly by the nature of the advantages, partly by the higher transaction costs between Japan and the UK compared with that between the US and the UK, and partly by the greater emphasis on transaction cost minimization by Japanese firms. Taking this latter point first, the fact that some Japanese affiliates are intended to service the regional European market – sometimes in conjunction with other European affiliates to supply a different group of products – suggests that the expected gains through product and market rationalization may well have been a stronger motive for their initial investment in the UK than in the case of US subsidiaries in the 1950s, which were primarily set up to replicate a truncated range of products produced by their parent companies. There was also very little parent-affiliate or intra-affiliate trade in inputs in the 1950s, and no competition in the markets served. Hence the opportunities for exploiting the economies of common governance were limited.

As regards the other *O* advantages, our reading is the Japanese believe that (1) the risk of dissipation or misappropriation of idiosyncratic knowledge (particularly in the knowledge-intensive processing industries), (2) the additional costs of controlling the quality of the end product and (3) the avoidance of haggling between licensor and licensee about the value of the technology transferred, encourage the internalized transfer of knowledge and information.

Part of the reluctance of the Japanese to conclude contractual arrangements with UK firms almost certainly stems from their very recent involvement in the UK economy. By contrast, no less than 47 per cent of the employment in US manufacturing in the 1950s was in those which were first set up before 1914.[19] It may then be reasonable to presume that at least the original *O* advantages provided by these firms may have been disseminated to, or copied or learnt by, their indigenous competitors. However, of the 59 US affiliates established between 1940 and 1953, all but 11 were 100 per cent owned; these were mainly in industrial good sectors in which products were new, or in consumer good sectors, where both quality control and after sales service were perceived as vital ingredients for success.

## ECONOMIC IMPACT

We now compare and contrast some of the more important economic consequences of US and Japanese direct investment for the UK economy.

The distinctive impact of inward direct investment arises partly from the nature (and price) of the intangible assets transferred, partly from the control exercised over these and local resources, and partly from the way in which transaction-specific *O* advantages are exploited. The impact will obviously vary according to type of investment (cf., e.g. import substitution and rationalized investment), the domestic economic structure and policy framework within which the foreign subsidiaries operate, and the extent to which they are integrated into the local economy. The impact may be both direct, through the operation of the affiliates themselves, and indirect, through spillover and linkage effects on other parts of the host economy, and on UK economic policy.

In this chapter, we have selected five impact areas for review. These are: (1) productivity and efficiency, (2) linkages with local suppliers, (3) technology transference, (4) market structure and (5) the balance of payments.

## Productivity and Efficiency

Both US and Japanese manufacturing affiliates recorded lower labour productivities than those of their parent plants, but considerably above those of their UK competitors. In 1982, the average (physical) output per head of factory workers of seven Japanese affiliates producing colour television (CTV) sets was 75 per cent of that of their parent companies; that of the other affiliates was 90 per cent. Thirty years earlier, of some 128 US affiliates willing to reveal details, 25 per cent asserted the average labour productivity (of all workers) in their UK subsidiaries was substantially lower that of their American parents, 49 per cent that it was slightly lower, 23 per cent that it was about the same and 3 per cent that it was higher (Dunning, 1958, p. 149). In both groups, there was a substantial range of productivity differences, e.g. 40 per cent to 100 per cent in the case of Japanese affiliates and less than 60 per cent to over 100 per cent in the case of US subsidiaries. Many of the reasons given for these differences were also the same: that the parent plants produced larger volumes of output, used more sophisticated equipment, made fewer product modifications, used their machinery and equipment more intensively, and experienced more satisfactory supply conditions than their UK equivalents.

In the case of Japanese affiliates, lack of experience was more frequently voiced as a contributory factor to lower UK productivity, while their US counterparts were inclined to complain more about labour attitudes and the shortage of certain types of skills (e.g. industrial engineers, adequately trained foremen and good salesmen). Neither Japanese nor US affiliates appeared to encounter serious difficulties with UK organized labour; the latter, however (but not the former), found some resistance to the installation of labour-saving machinery. Some of these differences reflects industry specific factors; and some, changes in the economic and industrial climate between the 1950s and the 1980s.[20] But others mirror the different approaches of the two groups of firms to improving labour productivity. While the US affiliates tended to favour monetary incentives, the Japanese preferred to inculcate a work ethic and spirit geared to high productivity and product quality.

In 1954, US affiliates recorded an average labour-productivity of 32.8 per cent above that for all UK manufacturing industry:[21] This ranged from 9.9 per cent in scientific, surgical and photographic instruments to 71.4 per cent in tools and cutlery. Data for Japanese affiliates in 1982 suggest that the differences were less marked; in the electronics sector, for example, output per man year was around 15–20 per cent above that of UK firms, and in the other sectors 20–25 per cent above. Part of the reason for these differences is that most Japanese affiliates are of very recent origin and the learning effect is still at work. More impressive performances are recorded in factories now run by the Japanese affiliates which were previously under UK or Anglo-Japanese ownership.[22]

The reason for the productivity differences revealed are basically to do with the superior $O$ advantages of the two groups of firms vis-à-vis their UK competitors. Some are common to both groups, e.g. more advanced machinery and production methods, less material wastage, better use of factory space, and so on. But others are more country-of-origin specific. The Japanese, for example, put their success down to more efficient work organization, the scrupulous attention given to quality control and testing procedures, a better trained, more co-operative and committed work force, fewer defects in supplies, lower inventories and lower rework levels.[23] By contrast, the Americans attribute their success in the 1950s to their innovatory ability, to their more automated production methods (and greater experience in same), to better trained (and more professional) management and to more aggressive marketing.

### Linkage Effects: Impact on Suppliers

One of the most remarkable similarities revealed by the two surveys was the reaction of both US and Japanese affiliates to the quality, price, and delivery timetables of their locally purchased inputs.[24] Indeed, almost all the criticisms of UK suppliers by US subsidiaries and the perceived impact of the latter's purchasing demands on the former were reiterated (with even more fervour) by Japanese firms 30 years later! Whether it is an inherent feature of foreign companies to castigate local suppliers and claim a beneficial impact on their performance we do not know, but we were a little surprised that so little change had apparently taken place in the perceived capabilities of the supplying sectors over the intervening 30 years. We believe that part of the explanation is that US and Japanese affiliates bought, or buy, from different suppliers, and part that the purchasing requirements of the two groups of firms reflected the fact that their end products were at different stages of the product cycle. For, whereas the US affiliates were making completely new demands on UK suppliers and, in consequence, found them lacking in experience vis-à-vis their US counterparts; Japanese companies producing basically similar products to their UK competitors found the existing quality, price and delivery timetables of the materials, components and parts below the standards they required. We now look into this and related questions in a little more detail.

*Extent of subcontracting*  In 1954, US subsidiaries bought out between one-half and two-thirds of their gross output, mainly from UK firms. In 1983, the respective figure for Japanese affiliates was 68 per cent, but only 42 per cent of this latter amount (29 per cent of the value of sales) was procured from UK firms.[25] The marked difference in the origin of supplies may appear surprising as many of the products of Japanese firms were already being supplied in the UK by their competitors, which was not the case with US firms 30 years earlier. However, whereas, in the mid-1950s, an overvalued dollar and higher US wage costs made most US imports uncompetitive, in the early 1980s, in spite of the rising value of the yen, the prices of many inputs in Japan were still below their UK equivalents. One other difference between the two groups was that there was much closer and more rigorous quality control exercised by Japanese affiliates over their supplier's products; and it was more common for the parent companies of the former to operate central purchasing departments and to buy components on behalf of their European affiliates. This difference partly reflects the younger age,[26] and the smaller relative size of Japanese affiliates;[27] and partly the more closely integrated procurement policies pursued by Japanese companies.[28]

*Impact on local suppliers*   Both groups of subsidiaries asserted that they provided their local suppliers with more information, technical and management assistance than their UK counterparts. While the Japanese like to stress that they treat their suppliers as part of their own family, 30 years earlier, at least one US affiliate claimed a similar relationship (Dunning, 1958, p. 201). Dissatisfaction on quality of inputs, prices and delivery dates were also voiced by both US and Japanese affiliates. As a consequence, their reject rates tended to be greater than those of their UK competitors, and were only reduced as a result of assistance given to the suppliers.

In the course of both surveys, we visited the major suppliers of the affiliates for their views. These too told a common story, but with a few important differences. Most suppliers agreed, for example, that their US and Japanese customers were stricter in their demands for close tolerances, adherence to specifications and delivery dates. They were also uniformly more willing than the average UK firm to supply detailed information in the form of specification, blueprints, drawings, designs, etc. In general, it was thought that Japanese firms were more prepared to give advice on product design, equipment, production methods, work organization and pricing than their US counterparts, who were often afraid of being accused of interference. In particular, there was widespread agreement – even among the very large UK suppliers – that their Japanese customers had helped upgrade their quality control, inspection and testing procedures; and, in some cases, had forced them to reappraise their production philosophy.[29] Certainly, as compared with their dealings with their UK customers, domestic suppliers found the relationship with their Japanese counterparts less distant and more co-operative and stable.[30]

All but one of the 20 suppliers considered in our survey said that they were regularly visited by their Japanese customers;[31] and about one-half thought that Japanese firms had the edge on their UK counterparts, especially in the frequency of visits paid by managers, design and production engineers, and technicians. Much more than in the case of their American counterparts, Japanese parent companies were brought in to advise on the suppliers' production problems. They were also universally regarded − and much more so than their US counterparts − as extremely prompt payers of bills.

On the other hand, there was some criticism that foreign owned customers made insufficient allowance for differences in the supply conditions in the UK, cf the US and Japan; and the fact that it was not always economic (*inter alia* because of the size of the order placed) to install the equipment necessary to meet the tolerances set by the parent companies. In the case of suppliers to Japanese affiliates in particular, standards were regarded as unnecessarily or unreasonably rigorous; while US subsidiaries were accused of being inconsistent in their orders, and treating the supplier as a stopgap until they could build up capacity to manufacture for themselves. This criticism was not directed at Japanese affiliates, whose long-term commitment to their suppliers was generally appreciated. Indeed 90 per cent of the suppliers appeared to be satisfied with their dealings with Japanese firms.

**Technology Transfer**

We have referred to the different kinds of $O$ advantages possessed by US MNEs in the 1950s and Japanese MNEs in the 1980s. It might therefore be expected that the type of technology transferred to the UK would also be different. This is, in fact, the case. The main contribution to US MNEs in the 1950s was to make available new products and production technology in (1) high income consumer goods and (2) technology- and/or capital-intensive producer goods. This mainly consisted of automated or quasi-automated manufacturing methods and, in the case of some new products, e.g. computers, new manufacturing techniques altogether. But no less important were the transfer of more professional managerial practices, especially in the area of sales and marketing, and financial and personnel management.[32] By contrast, Japanese MNEs, being late entrants into most of the sectors in which they are now international investors, have had to compete through improvements in product design and reliability, and leading in second or third generation technological advances, e.g. automated printed circuits in the production of CTVs; and it is these $O$ advantages which they are transferring to their foreign affiliates, and, through competitive pressure, are forcing indigenous companies to copy or acquire.

However, when questioned on this point, most UK and other foreign owned CTV companies alleged that, with one exception, it was competition from Japanese companies, rather than the presence of Japanese affiliates in the UK, that had forced them to reappraise their product, production and marketing strategies. Thirty years earlier, the competitors of US MNEs asserted that it was the fact the former were producing in the UK which stimulated them to introduce new products and/or production methods.[33] The one exception that UK competitors of Japanese firms were ready to concede was that, by example and personal contact in the UK, they had learnt much from the Japanese about the holistic approach to work practices, quality control and inspection procedures. Though it was argued there is little new in these procedures, the idea of treating each stage of production as an integral part of the whole process, the belief that the value-added chain is only as strong as its weakest link, and the attention paid to educating workers (via quality control circles and the like) to accept the zero-defect concept is something which the Japanese have put into practice with considerable success; and which, *via* the normal commercial routes, e.g. visits to Japanese factories, dissemination of views at seminars, conferences and workshops,[34] is gradually being adopted by both suppliers and competitors.

As far as the transfer of technological *capacity* or the technology of innovation is concerned, there is very little R&D done by Japanese affiliates in the UK, but some is planned in the future. By contrast, 56 per cent of the US manufacturing affiliates in the 1950s were undertaking some applied or developmental research; and 19 per cent some basic research. While most research activity was geared towards the adaptation of products and/or materials formulae, or scaling down of production methods, a few subsidiaries − particularly the larger and well established − did undertake some product and materials research on behalf of their parent companies. Some illustrations of the types of technological expertise transferred by US firms to the UK (and also in reverse) are given in Dunning (1958, pp. 190−1 and 313).

### Market Structure

The 1958 study revealed that, of the 246,000 people employed by US manufacturing affiliates in the UK, 87 per cent within industries in which either the affiliate was the dominant (and in some cases the sole) producer, or where it (or they) was (were) among the largest of a small number of producers (Dunning, 1958, p. 157). The study suggested that the effect of the presence of US affiliates on market structure was a mixed one, and this was confirmed in a later report by Steuer (1973). In some cases, the penetration by US firms was seen to lead to an increase in concentration ratios; in other cases a reduction (Dunning, 1958, p. 154 ff.). There were examples of US affiliates both breaking up monopolies and encouraging a more oligopolistic market structure; but overall, there was little evidence to sustain the argument that, as a result of their presence, the competitive structure of UK industry had been adversely affected. This is not to deny that US affiliates sometimes engaged in restrictive practices, but, in so far as the industries in which they were strongly represented had been investigated by the Monopolies Commission, they were (and have since been) given a relatively clean bill of health (Dunning, 1958, 1981 Chapter 7).

The penetration of Japanese firms has led to more (or more effective) competition in most sectors,[35] although, in some cases, e.g. in the CTV industry, their presence has mainly been at the expense of Japanese imports. However, as with their US counterparts, they have fostered some rationalization among competitors; again the CTV sector is a good case in point.

As a whole, Japanese affiliates in the CTV sector accounted for 35 per cent of the UK production in 1983,[36] so it is fair to infer that they compete in a monopolistic competitive veering towards an oligopolistic market structure. In the case of the non-electronics affiliates, in 11 out of 13 cases the structure was oligopolistic veering towards the monopolistic, with the Japanese affiliate usually being either the largest or the second largest firm in the sector. Competitors to both US and Japanese firms readily admit their policies and strategies have been affected by the foreign presence. However, whereas the main competitive edge of Japanese firms was perceived to be in the areas of (1) product design, (2) purchasing standards and techniques, (3) management style and philosophy, (4) in-house cost and quality control and testing procedures and (5) personnel relations, that of US affiliates 30 years earlier was thought to be in (a) sales and marketing techniques (an area in which UK competitors to Japanese firms claimed they had the edge), (b) production and financial control techniques, (c) automated and semi-automated production methods and (d) some wage incentive and industrial-relations schemes. But the important point to note is that, in both groups, although the emphasis given to particular functional areas may differ, there was, or is, a common belief in the responsibility of management, both to manage professionally and to encourage all those with a stake in the firm to accept its objectives. Our study on Japanese companies in the UK concluded there is very little uniquely innovatory about the products or processes of Japanese affiliates; simply that they more effectively put into practice the best of management – and particularly production management – practices known for several years.

## Balance of Payments

Our 1958 study did not make a full balance of payments assessment of the presence of US affiliates in the UK. As we did not ask for information about imports, little can be inferred from the fact that, in the mid-1950s, US subsidiaries exported a higher proportion of their output than their UK counterparts in almost every industrial sector. Only, if one were to assume that such output was totally in place of imports, might one categorically conclude that the UK balance of payments had been improved.[37] The Steuer investigation (Steuer *et al.*, 1973) did, however, attempt to make some assessment for all foreign firms in the mid-1960s and concluded that, assuming the most likely counterfactual situation, inward investment had marginally benefited the UK balance of payments.[38]

Our 1985 study found that Japanese affiliates recorded a net deficit on their current balance of payments account in 1983 (i.e. exports – imports + dividends and royalties). Obviously, the net *effect* of their presence depends on the alternative position assumed; if one postulates that, in their absence, everything now produced in the UK by them would have been imported (either from Japan or another European country), then clearly their contribution is strongly positive. By contrast, if one assumes the output gap would have been taken up by UK competitors (a somewhat dubious assumption, bearing in mind had not they come to the UK, Japanese companies would have located elsewhere in the EEC) it would have been substantially negative. We believe that the most likely scenario is somewhere between these two extremes, veering towards the former, with the balance of payments effects of Japanese direct investment being marginally positive (the same conclusion as that reached by Steuer with respect to all FDI 20 years earlier).

However, neither the Steuer nor our most recent study took account of the indirect or spillover effects of inward investment. Moreover, it is likely as Japanese affiliates become more established in the UK, that their export–import ratio will markedly increase.[39] At the time of our field research, however, and in contrast to their US counterparts, it was their hefty import bill from their home countries which considerably weakened their contribution to the UK balance of payments.[40] However, unlike the 1950s and 1960s, the impact of inward foreign direct investment in the UK balance of payments is not a matter of political concern.

## CONCLUSIONS

This chapter has revealed certain time- and country- (or origin-) specific differences in the industrial composition of inward direct investment into the UK, its ownership patterns and organizational structure and the nature of its impact on the UK economy. While both US investment in the 1950s and Japanese investment in the 1980s were mainly import substituting, rather than resource-based or rationalized in character, the perceived asset advantages of the two groups were different and strongly reflected the comparative country-specific advantages of the home countries. Both the reasons for internalizing the use of these advantages and those for setting up production units in the UK were basically similar: in the former case, to protect against the erosion of rent earning property rights, to ensure quality control of intermediate and end products, and to counteract a possible loss of markets by international competitors; and, in the latter, to circumvent import barriers and/or appreciating exchange rates in the home country. Only in the case of Japanese firms is there some suggestion that they have invested in the UK as part of a regional strategy, and with a view to eventually exploiting some of the *O* advantages of common governance. Were we to examine the contemporary nature of US direct investment in the UK, we suspect that we would see the *O* advantages of the parent firms are much more to do with their capacity to minimize transaction costs across national boundaries, particularly within the EEC.[41]

The impact of the two groups of investors reflects both similarities and differences in their *OLI* configuration. As stated at the beginning of this chapter, while US MNEs in the 1950s were essentially transferring

US and Japanese Manufacturing Affiliates in the UK
239

innovatory advantages to their UK affiliates, their Japanese counterparts in the 1980s were exporting the advantages of an imitator, whose competitive edge rested on the introduction of differentiated products (including qualities of reliability and consistency) and greater productive efficiency. It is these which Japanese companies have transmitted so effectively to the UK, in a way which has taken not only markets away from indigenous companies but some of the earlier innovating US subsidiaries as well.

## NOTES

1  The results of which were published in J. H. Dunning: *American investment in British manufacturing industry* (London: Allen & Unwin, 1958); hereafter referred to as Dunning (1958).
2  See J. H. Dunning: *Japanese participation in UK industry* (London: Croom Helm, 1986); hereafter referred to as Dunning (1986).
3  An analysis of the applicability of the paradigm to understanding the determinants of Japanese direct investment in UK manufacturing industry is set out in Chapter 3 of Dunning (1986).
4  In 1955, 57.7 per cent of all US manufacturing investment in Europe was in the UK, a slight decline on the 1951 figure of 58.1 per cent.
5  A handful of manufacturing affiliates existed before the Second World War but these were all liquidated during the War.
6  Latest (March 1988) figures published by the Invest in Britain Bureau suggest that at the end of 1987 there were 55 Japanese factories, then producing in the UK, with a total employment of 18,000. Another 28 Japanese firms have announced their intention to manufacture in the UK.
7  Defined as the share of the total employment of US manufacturing affiliates accounted for by a particular sector, divided by the corresponding share of employment in all UK firms.
8  Pages 21–4 of Dunning (1958) give examples of new products and production methods originating from the US in the 40 years prior to the First World War, and suggests reasons for the reluctancy of UK manufacturers to adopt and exploit the basic inventions of the period. For a more detailed analysis of country specific *O* advantages as determinants of international production see Dunning (1981), Chapter 4, and Swedenborg (1981).
9  For an elaboration of the difference between these two kinds of advantages, see Chapter 3 and Dunning (1988), Chapter 2.
10  In the terminology of Vernon (1974), US MNEs investing in the UK were mainly innovation-based oligopolies, while the Japanese investors, at least in the product areas in which they were involved in the UK, are mature or even senescent oligopolies.
11  In 1981–82 their R&D/sales ratio worldwide was 3.1 per cent, nearly twice the average for all Japanese manufacturers.
12  To begin with, however, Japanese subsidiaries tend to supply the UK market with locally produced goods; and then as output increases to service continental European markets in place of Japanese exports. In the case of US affiliates in the 1950s, the majority had been supplying European markets since before the Second World War (see Dunning 1958, pp. 291–98).
13  In the consumer electronics sector, for example, the Japanese employ proportionately more female school-leavers than their US counterparts 30 years earlier.

14  These issues contained in this section are explored in more depth in Dunning (1986b).

15  Influence and control tends to be greater the more idiosyncratic the *O* advantages are, the younger the age of the affiliate and the greater the equity participation of the parent company.

16  In our 1958 study, it was shown that top management in US subsidiaries were younger and better educated and trained than their counterparts in UK owned firms.

17  Cf. US subsidiaries in the 1950s. This is partly due to country-specific factors, and partly to differences in the decision taking skills required to transmit and implement the *O* advantages of Japanese firms. See particularly Chapter 4 of Dunning (1986).

18  The main market of the majority of Japanese companies in the 1980s.

19  Of these 31 affiliates, 15 were joint ventures.

20  Noticeably the much higher rate of unemployment in the 1980s.

21  Value-added per man year. See p. 181, Dunning (1958). Data were obtained directly from US subsidiaries and compared with that of UK firms in the same industry, as published in the *Census of Production*.

22  For example, within a year of the start of its operations at Lowestoft, Sanyo was producing 500 TV sets monthly per person compared to 286 when Phillips owned the plant.

23  According to Reitsperger (1982) rejects traceable to human error in Japanese managed CTV companies in the late 1970s were one-tenth of those in UK managed companies. One year after Toshiba began operations it was achieving a 95–8 per cent success rate in its first-time testing of CTV products produced; at the time of the Rank Toshiba joint venture the corresponding success rate was nearer 50 per cent.

24  See Chapter 7 of Dunning (1958) and Chapters 6 and 7 of Dunning (1986a).

25  We suspect this figure has risen in the last five years, while over the last 30 years (and particularly the last 15 years) the proportion of imports of US manufacturing subsidiaries has risen.

26  For example, the evidence suggests that the ratio of local to imported sourced components tends to increase quite dramatically in the first five years of a CTV affiliate's life in the UK.

27  The average output of CTV sets produced by a Japanese affiliate in the UK was 12 per cent of that of their nearest equivalent Japanese plant; for other affiliates it averaged 27 per cent. In 1954, nearly half the employment in US subsidiaries was in plants whose output was at least 25 per cent that of the parent companies.

28  Most Japanese affiliates assert they do not 'buy British' because of uncompetitive prices, unsatisfactory quality, or the failure of suppliers to keep to delivery schedules. However, there may be other benefits of a centrally controlled purchasing policy which could explain the very high propensity of Japanese affiliates to purchase their Japanese inputs from their parent companies or sister affiliates. Moreover, 'alleged' poor quality of UK components may be used as a rationale for any failure of the Japanese affiliates to keep to the local sourcing targets set by the UK government.

29  As the executive of one electronics subsidiary said, 'The Japanese have helped us to promote a philisophy of "things should get better every day" and to pay attention to detail; and to inculcate into each worker on the shop floor a sense of responsibility not to accept anything less than his best'.

30  In particular, Japanese affiliates make a special effort to build up long-term relationships with their suppliers. We did not find this feature so evident in

## US and Japanese Manufacturing Affiliates in the UK 241

the case of US affiliates. Once again, this reflects differences in the purchasing customs of Japanese and US parent companies.

31 Normally twice to three times a year.

32 As described in Chapter 9 of Dunning (1958).

33 See especially Chapter 7 of Dunning (1958). Again, these differences partly reflect the different stages of the product cycle the two groups of affiliates were in when they first invested in the UK, and the exchange rates existing at the time.

34 And not least through the Consumer Electronics Working Party of the National Economic Development Office.

35 We obtained some data in respect of some 27 product groups. In 23 of these, it was perceived that the Japanese presence had led to more competition, and in 4 to less competition. In 15 the concentration ratio had fallen and in 12 it had increased. In 15 product groups, both competition had intensified and concentration had fallen.

36 With no one producer accounting for more than 10 per cent of UK production.

37 At the same time, as one knows (from US data) that US affiliates imported only a very small amount of their inputs from the US in the late 1950s, while there were few sister affiliates elsewhere in Europe, there is no reason to suppose that their propensity to import was out of line with their UK competitors.

38 See Chapter 4.

39 This, in fact, is what has happened in the case of the two CTV subsidiaries set up prior to 1980.

40 We do know, for example, that in 1957, US subsidiaries imported less than 5 per cent of their gross sales from America; while in 1982 Japanese affiliates imported 35 per cent of their sales from Japan.

41 Hence the greater preference of US MNEs in the 1970s cf. those in the 1950s for full ownership of their UK affiliates.

# [13]

*World Development*, Vol. 11, No. 6, pp. 493–501, 1983.
Printed in Great Britain.

0305-750X/83 $3.00 + 0.00
© 1983 Pergamon Press Ltd.

# Foreign Investment and Spillover Efficiency in an Underdeveloped Economy: Evidence from the Mexican Manufacturing Industry

MAGNUS BLOMSTRÖM
*University of Gothenburg and Institute for International Economic Studies, Stockholm, Sweden*

and

HÅKAN PERSSON
*University of Umeå, Sweden*

**Summary.** – In this paper we consider the question whether differences in technical efficiency of Mexican plants in part derive from spillover efficiency associated with foreign direct investment. We use labour productivity as a measure of technical efficiency, and relate this to capital intensity, labour quality and scale of production. We measure the degree of competition by different concentration indices and the final factor determining efficiency is the presence of foreign subsidiaries. If there is a positive relation between efficiency of domestic plants and the foreign participation of various industries we conclude that there is a spillover of technical efficiency. The empirical evidence from the study indicates that this is the case.

## 1. INTRODUCTION

When analysing the effects of foreign investment on host economies it is common to distinguish between two broad sets of effects, namely direct and indirect effects. If foreign investment, for instance, raises productivity in the host country and this increase is not wholly appropriated by the investor, other groups in the host country get some direct gains from the investment. These direct gains can accrue to domestic labour in the form of higher real wages, to consumers by way of lower prices and/or to government through higher tax revenues. Beyond this, direct investment may also result in indirect effects on the host economy. By indirect effects we mean external effects or spillovers.

The spillovers can be of different kinds. They may influence both the industrial structure of the host economy and the conduct and performance of domestically-owned firms. In fact, many economists claim that one of the most significant contributions of foreign investment is likely to come from external effects (see e.g. Meier, 1976), but since they are normally difficult to measure, few empirical estimates appear in the literature.

In this paper we concentrate on one particular aspect of foreign investment – its influence on the technical efficiency of host country firms. Since multinational corporations (MNCs) usually represent advanced technologies, one question which arises is whether this technical knowledge in one way or another is being transferred to domestic plants owing to the mere presence of MNCs. This type of transfer of technology will thus be an indirect effect of foreign investment, and we will refer to it

* Morgan Åberg has been very helpful during the work on this paper. We are also indebted to Lennart Hjalmarsson, Jorge Katz, Charles P. Kindleberger, Sanjaya Lall, Constantine Vaitsos, Stefan de Vylder and an anonymous referee for valuable comments on an earlier draft, and to Eduardo Jacobs, CIDE, Mexico City, for making some of the data available. Financial support from the Swedish Agency for Research Cooperation with Developing Countries (SAREC) is gratefully acknowledged.

as a spillover efficiency benefit if it leads to an increase in efficiency of domestic firms.

To the best of our knowledge, only two available econometric studies deal with spillover efficiency of foreign investment, and neither is applied to an underdeveloped economy. One study is of Australia (Caves, 1974) and the other of Canada (Globerman, 1979). Both find some support for the spillover benefit hypothesis. However, in both studies there are some problems connected with lack of data. On the four-digit level Globerman, who has the most comprehensive data, uses a sample of 49 manufacturing industries. (At the same level of aggregation we use a sample of 215 manufacturing industries.) Some variables are also missing which forces him to use proxies.

In line with the two studies mentioned, we take labour productivity as a measure of technical efficiency. We relate this to capital intensity, labour quality and scale of production. We measure the degree of competition by different concentration indices and the final factor determining efficiency will be the presence of foreign subsidiaries. As in Caves (1974) and in Globerman (1979) we conclude that there is a spillover of technical efficiency if there is a positive relation between labour productivity of domestic plants and the presence of foreign firms in various industries. We thus restrict our analysis to intra-industry spillovers and concentrate on their existence, not their magnitude or nature.[1]

The reason for choosing Mexico is twofold. First of all the foreign presence in the Mexican economy is considerable. About 35–40% of the manufacturing output is produced by foreign firms. The other reason is that this country has a wide experience in industrialization problems and has had a rapidly growing industrial sector. This has had the result that parts of the industry, including those domestically owned, are today highly developed. For instance, during the 1970s, Mexico was a rapidly growing exporter of technology (see Ablin, 1979). One question is whether this development of the Mexican industry is in some way linked to the presence of foreign firms in Mexico.

The remainder of the paper proceeds as follows. In the next section we give a short discussion on the nature of spillover efficiency. Section 3 describes the data, and Section 4 the model, used. In Section 5 the empirical results are presented and, finally, Section 6 draws the main conclusions.

## 2. THE NATURE OF SPILLOVER EFFICIENCY BENEFITS

Foreign investment can give rise to indirect gains for the host economy through the realization of external economies. Generally these benefits are referred to as 'spillover' effects, which indicates the importance of the way in which the influence is transmitted. Although the purpose of this paper is restricted to ascertaining whether such spillovers exist, something should be said about the potential ways in which they may occur. Presumably the most important channel is via competition. Although MNCs may suffer from some disadvantages *vis-à-vis* the domestic entrants, e.g. as far as legal rights and the different language and cultural background are concerned, it is likely that they enjoy other and more important advantages in overcoming such barriers to entry as capital requirements, risks, and research and development intensity. It is therefore also likely that MNCs have better possibilities to enter markets where the barriers to entry for new firms are high (see Gorecki, 1976) and that foreign entry may increase competition and force domestic firms to adopt more efficient methods.

Another source of gain to the host economy is the training of labour and management, or investment in human capital, which may then become available to the economy in general. This type of spillover efficiency should be more important in underdeveloped countries than in developed ones since such a factor of production is in short supply there. In Mexico, for instance, many managerial people in large locally-owned firms once started their career in a MNC, and management practices may in this way be substantially improved in domestic firms.

A third possible source of spillover efficiency benefits is that MNCs may speed up the transfer of technology. For both process and product technology such a transfer is a central activity of MNCs, and this may stimulate domestic firms to hasten their access to a specific technology, either because they would not have been aware of the technology's existence, or because they would not have felt it profitable to try to obtain the technology in this manner. Particularly in technologically backward countries this may hasten the time when domestic producers have access to a technology.

Inter-industry influences should, naturally, also be taken into account, but such influences are more difficult to measure in statistical material like ours. The impact made by foreign firms in the host economy on its suppliers, by insisting that they meet standards of quality control, delivery dates, prices, etc., should be important. Brash (1966) provided an early discussion on this when he studied the impact made by General Motors in Australia on its suppliers. This aspect is especially important in larger and more industrialized underdeveloped countries like Mexico, because of their legislation requiring domestic content, but here we are left with very little empirical work. There is, however, no reason to assume that inter-industry influences work in opposition to influences within industries.

## 3. THE SAMPLE

The empirical data for this study comes from the Mexican 1970 Census of Manufactures supplemented by data broken down by ownership in different industries. Ownership in the statistical material is divided into three categories: state ownership, domestic private ownership and foreign ownership. Those plants of which at least 15% of the shares are foreign-owned are there defined as 'foreign'.[2]

The state-owned plants, however, are excluded from this study for several reasons. One is that state companies may have other goals than the privately-owned ones. They may accept lower productivity if that could contribute to higher employment or have a favourable effect on the geographical decentralization of the industry. Another reason, working in the opposite direction, is that state-owned companies may have more power in negotiations with foreigners, and this may favour them. A separate study of the state-owned plants is then necessary, but this should be the topic of another paper.

The level of aggregation is the four-digit level. Of the existing 230 individual four-digit industries, 15 had to be discarded, because of lack of information. For the remaining 215 industries, divided between domestically-owned private and foreign-owned plants, the following variables were used: number of plants, employment, wages, assets, gross production, value-added and gross investment. The following data, not separated by ownership, were also used: size distribution of plants (measured in gross production), average man-hours per year and the division between blue-collar and white-collar workers. All information is for 1970.

## 4. THE MODEL

The basic thought behind our statistical model is as follows: if there is a positive relation between the productivity level in the domestically-owned plants in an industry and the share of foreign plants in the same industry (*ceteris paribus*), the foreign investment does raise the productivity in domestically-owned plants through spillover efficiency. In assuming this we closely follow the assumption behind the models of Caves and Globerman. However, since foreign companies cluster around high technology and marketing activities, it can be argued that the opposite causal relationship may be present. Perhaps our model reflects industrial characteristics other than spillover effects? In order to answer these questions further research must be done, but for the moment we have to accept the reasoning behind the Caves and Globerman models.

The dependent variable in our model should thus be a productivity measure for the domestically-owned plants. Naturally we would like to construct this as the ratio of net output to an index of total factor inputs, but the available data did not permit this. Like Caves and Globerman we therefore have to use a partial measure of productivity namely labour productivity. This is constructed as the ratio of total value-added in domestically-owned private manufacturing plants to the total number of employees in the same plants ($VL^d$).

To be able to test our spillover hypothesis we need to take care of other factors influencing value-added per employee. We analyse five such factors. The first, and most important, is the capital intensity in the Mexican plants ($KL^d$). We expect a positive relation between labour productivity and capital intensity. Looking at the studies of Caves and Globerman neither of them was able to get data on the domestic capital stock, so they had to use proxies. Globerman, for example, used the corresponding information from the US industry as a proxy. For the Mexican economy, however, data on the capital stock are available, so we define our capital intensity variable $KL^d$ as the ratio of total assets (book value) to the total number of employees in the domestically-owned plants.[3]

Another factor that may influence the dependent variable is the quality of the labour force. Higher quality, in the sense that for example the education level is higher, will probably raise value-added per employee. To avoid simultaneity problems we have to reject the possibility of using the usual measure of labour quality in productivity studies – average wages. Instead we use the ratio of white-collar workers to blue-collar workers in different industries as a proxy. However, we do not have this ratio for the domestically-owned part of an industry only, but for the industry as a whole (including state-owned and foreign-owned plants). Using this ratio (denoted $LQ_1$) in our regressions, we would expect a correlation between foreign presence in an industry and the labour quality, since it is known that the labour quality, defined in this way, is higher in an average foreign plant than in an average domestic one. We therefore construct a new variable, $LQ_2$, defined as the error term, $e$, in the regression $LQ_1 = a + bFS + e$ ($FS$ is the foreign share of employees in an industry). The error term shows how much of the dependent variable is not explained by the $FS$ variable, and we thus have a proxy for labour quality in the Mexican industry.[4]

Since our dependent variable is expressed in value terms, we also need to analyse the importance of the market situation in an industry. Two industries, with the same technical efficiency, may show different value-added per employee because of a monopoly situation in one of the industries. In studies of industrial economics the concept of concentration is clearly associated with three factors that are all considered to be very important determinants of competition. The factors are the number of firms in an industry, the inequality of market shares and coalition potentials. In their comparison of 11 different measures of industrial concentration, Vanlommel *et al.* (1977) find that the best individual concentration index to capture these three important factors is the Herfindahl index ($H$), and we will therefore use that index as our concentration measure.[5] From the point of view of theoretical considerations we would expect a positive correlation between the concentration level and the dependent variable, value-added per employee.

Labour productivity may also differ across plants because of scale economies, so we need to know whether Mexican plants exhibit any diseconomies of scale. In large-scale cross-section statistical analyses the measurement of scale economies has been a difficult exercise in the absence of specific engineering data. Several indirect measures for scale economies have been constructed, each of which suffers from certain disadvantages (see e.g. Caves *et al.*, 1975; and Cory, 1981). The basic assumption in those studies is that the unit production cost curves are J-shaped, or at least approximately so, over a significant range of output levels beyond minimum efficient scale ($MES$). If we then could construct a measure of a $MES$-

plant, and compare the average privately-owned plant in an industry with the $MES$-plant, we would at least get a rough indicator of the presence of scale economies.

Statistical studies of the US economy assume that the larger plants in an industry exhaust available economies of scale. Generally, the average size of the larger plants that account for 50% of an industry's output has been used as a $MES$ proxy. Globerman notes, however, that this argument is reasonable only when considering large industrial countries. In countries with small domestic markets, such as Canada, the use of '50% of output' as a rule seems inappropriate. This supports the use of $MES$ estimates derived from US industries. He therefore obtains his estimates of $MES$ plants for the Canadian industry by calculating the average size of the largest plants accounting for 50% of value-added in comparably defined US industries.[6]

Mexico, like Canada, is a country with a small domestic market.[7] This means that we should not calculate $MES$ plant from the largest plants supplying the top 50% of that market. Lacking data on comparable US industries, we construct a somewhat different $MES$ estimate. We assume that minimum efficient scale equals the largest plants of each industry in Mexico.[8] It turns out that these plants generally account for less than 50% of industry output although there are exceptions. Comparing gross production of the largest plants in an industry with gross production of an average privately-owned Mexican plant will give us an indicator of whether Mexican plants suffer from diseconomies of scale. We thus construct the scale variable ($SCALE^d$) as the ratio of the average gross production in domestic privately-owned plants in an industry to our estimated '$MES$' plant.

Ideally we would like to express our dependent variable in per hour productivity, but such a variable is not possible to construct from our data. Anyway, we need to analyse whether the average amount of hours per employee in different industries will influence our estimations. Data available on the four-digit level show average effective work days during 1970 in different industries (including state- and foreign-owned plants). Since there is no *a priori* belief that the effective work day should vary because of ownership, we can use these data as a proxy (called $AD$) for the Mexican plants. The variable $AD$ will thus correct for the possibility that systematic differences in overtime, strikes, holidays, etc. will generate different value-added per employee.

Finally, we need a variable for the proportion of foreign participation in different industries. According to our test hypothesis we are interested in the existence of a correlation between the productivity in domestically-owned private plants in an industry and the foreign participation in that industry. If we find a significant positive correlation, we cannot reject the hypothesis that spillover efficiency, in the way we have defined it, is present. The *FS* variable was defined as the foreign share of employment in each industry.[9] We can thus list our independent variables one by one:

$KL^d$ = the ratio of total assets (book value) to the total number of employees in the domestically-owned private plants

$SCALE^d$ = the ratio of the average gross production in domestically-owned private plants in an industry to our estimated '*MES*' plant

$LQ_1$ = the ratio of white-collar workers to blue-collar workers for the industry as a whole (including state- and foreign-owned plants)

$LQ_2$ = the error term '*e*' in the regression $LQ_1 = a + bSF + e$

$H$ = Herfindahl index

$AD$ = average effective work day during 1970 in an industry as a whole (including state- and foreign-owned plants)

$FS$ = share of employees in an industry employed in foreign plants.

## 5. STATISTICAL RESULTS

The equation we want to estimate is thus as follows:

$$VL^d = f(KL^d, H, SCALE^d, AD, (LQ_1, LQ_2), FS)$$

where $VL^d$ is value-added in domestically-owned private plants divided by total employees in these plants. The method of estimation used is the ordinary least squares, and the results obtained from different linear estimations are shown in Table 1.[10] The form of the equation used is additive and we estimate the coefficients of the various independent variables.

Following the independent variables in the table from left to right we find that, with the assumption of normally distributed errors, the capital-intensity variable registers a positive coefficient that is significantly different from zero at the 0.01 level. We also see that this factor explains most of the variance of the dependent variable. That means that most of the intra-industry differences in labour productivity are explained by differences in capital intensity, and this is not surprising.

Neither the concentration level in an industry nor the scale factor, however, has a significant influence on the dependent variable in our estimations, even though their coefficients are correctly signed. The variance of the concentration index, $H$, is small and $H$ is highly correlated with the intercept. Excluding the intercept makes $H$ significant at the 0.01 level, and excluding the concentration variable does not change the results very much [equation (3)].

More surprising is that the scale variable never carries a significant coefficient, even though it is correctly signed. An alternative

Table 1. *Regression results for the determinants of productivity: 215 industries*

| Equations | Constant | $KL^d$ | $H$ | $SCALE^d$ | $LQ_1$ | $LQ_2$ | $FS$ | $R^2$ |
|---|---|---|---|---|---|---|---|---|
| (1) | 0.0546 (0.0179) | 0.5328 (0.0476) | 0.0098 (0.0347) | 0.0280 (0.0587) | 0.0810 (0.0333) | – | 0.0563 (0.0302) | 0.5533 |
| (2) | 0.0710 (0.0163) | 0.5328 (0.0476) | 0.0098 (0.0347) | 0.0280 (0.0587) | – | 0.0810 (0.0333) | 0.0871 (0.0283) | 0.5533 |
| (3) | 0.0745 (0.0107) | 0.5327 (0.0475) | – | 0.0319 (0.0569) | – | 0.0799 (0.0330) | 0.0889 (0.0275) | 0.5532 |
| (4) | 0.0771 (0.0096) | 0.5423 (0.0442) | – | – | – | 0.0791 (0.0330) | 0.0859 (0.0269) | 0.5525 |
| (5) | 0.0722 (0.0164) | 0.5588 (0.0469) | 0.0002 (0.0335) | 0.0255 (0.0593) | – | – | 0.0823 (0.0286) | 0.5407 |

Standard error in parentheses.

scale measure constructed in the same way but based on capital instead of gross production, does not change this result.[fn] Nor does the omission of the variable in the regression [equation (4)] make much difference. Since there are no serious problems of collinearity here, one explanation of this result is perhaps due to the fact that the model is improperly specified. We mentioned above our problems in constructing a *MES* plant for the different industries. Possibly we would get more reliable results here if we were to use *MES* plants defined on US industries.

The labour quality measure $LQ_1$ is constructed in such a way that *a priori* we can say that it is correlated with the foreign presence in an industry. The simple correlation coefficient between the two variables is 0.45. Using the $LQ_1$ variable we therefore find [equation (1)] that some of the variance of the dependent variable which is explained by the foreign presence is now explained by labour quality [compare equation (2)]. This has been 'corrected' in equation (2) by using the alternative labour quality variable $LQ_2$, and we then see that the level of significance of the *FS* variable has improved. Anyway, the labour quality variable $LQ_1$ registers a significant positive coefficient at the 0.05 level.

As regards the average effective work day, *AD*, it turned out to be highly correlated with the intercept and was therefore excluded and is not shown among the results.

Finally we turn to the variable that this study is actually about, the *FS* variable. According to our spillover hypothesis we expect a positive coefficient in front of it if intra-industry spillover efficiency exists, and as can be seen from the table we cannot reject this hypothesis. Behind the results of equation (1) it should be clarified that there is a high level of co-linearity between $LQ_1$ and *FS*. Together with the 'corrected' labour quality measure $LQ_2$ the *FS* variable is significant at the 0.01 level [equations (2)–(4)]. The omission of the labour quality variable [equation (5)] does not change the $R^2$ value much or influence the efficiency of the other parameters.

In comparison with the results from the studies of Caves and Globerman, we thus find a much stronger support for the spillover efficiency hypothesis. This may be explained by the fact that we are studying an underdeveloped economy, but not necessarily so. On the one hand, it can be argued that the differences in productivity between foreign and domestic plants must be much higher in an underdeveloped country like Mexico than in Canada or Australia, and this may specifically make the contribution from the transfer of technology more important there. On the other hand, it is the existence of such large differences that has been one of the most important arguments in the development literature when saying that this type of spillover effect might not occur, and if it does, it is only the 'modern' part of the underdeveloped economy that benefits from it.

Since our data include the entire manufacturing industry, and not only the 'modern' sector, we cannot say anything about whether it is the entire industry, or only parts of it, that have benefited from those investments. In order to investigate this matter at a deeper level, more detailed research has to be done.

In comparison with the studies of Caves and Globerman, our sample contains more variables and more than four times as many observations, which, of course, increases reliability. Our results should thus be interesting not only in terms of fairly industrialized underdeveloped economies but more generally regarding spillover efficiency from foreign investment.

We wind up this section with a discussion of how protection might affect the results. We use a concentration index to measure the degree of *domestic* competition, but this index does not take *foreign* competition into account. A high value-added per employee may therefore be a result of protection rather than efficiency. Since there are no protection data available for the entire manufacturing industry in Mexico, we were unable to include this among our independent variables. However, Ten Kate and Bruce Wallace (1977) give the rate of effective protection for 93 four-digit industries 1970, and although the inclusion of this rate among our independent variables considerably reduces the degree of freedom, it may provide some useful information.

Equation (1) in Table 2 shows the rate of effective protection among the independent variables and apparently this variable does not have any effect at all on the dependent variable. The interpretation of this is that the rate of effective protection seems to have no direct influence on value-added per employee in domestic plants.

On the other hand there is a weak correlation between the rate of effective protection and foreign participation in an industry. The simple correlation coefficient between the protection variable and *FS* is 0.19. This suggests that foreign presence, at least to some extent, is dependent on the existence of protection, but

Table 2. *Regression results for the determinant of productivity: 93 industries*

| Equations | Constant | $KL^d$ | H | $SCALE^d$ | PROTECTION | FS | $R^2$ |
|---|---|---|---|---|---|---|---|
| (1) | 0.0679 (0.0255) | 0.5715 (0.0589) | 0.0766 (0.0578) | −0.1183 (0.0904) | 0.0000 (0.0000) | 0.0612 (0.0418) | 0.6119 |
| (2) | 0.0683 (0.0242) | 0.5720 (0.0579) | 0.0765 (0.0575) | −0.1187 (0.0895) | − | 0.0616 (0.0411) | 0.6119 |

Standard error in parentheses.

there is no evidence that a high effective protection causes high value-added in the protected industries. *MNC*s may therefore be a partial 'substitute' for the world market's competitive pressure. The fact that the foreign share variable has no strong influence on the dependent variable in equation (1) can be explained by the industry sample used. The omission of the protection variable in equation (2), where we use the same industry sample, does not affect the efficiency of the foreign share variable.

## 6. SOME COMMENTS

The empirical evidence from this study shows that we are not able to reject the hypothesis that the labour productivity in domestically-owned private plants in an industry in Mexico is associated with the presence of foreign subsidiaries in that industry. According to the model our results thus indicate the existence of spillover efficiency benefits from the foreign-owned plants to the domestically-owned ones.

Two qualifications must however be made here. First of all, we shall emphasize that inter-industry spillovers are excluded from this study. It would not be inappropriate to assume that for example local suppliers in other industries to a given foreign plant may be heavily affected. However, there is no reason to assume that inter-industry influences work in opposition to influences within industries. Secondly, it is very important to distinguish between technical efficiency and technological development. It is possible that a considerable presence of foreign subsidiaries retards the more fundamental process of local technological development in the host country. Lall has shown, for example, that production efficiency may be improved at the expense of basic design and development activity, with the latter being continuously imported from abroad by foreign and local firms (Lall, 1980).

Elsewhere it has been shown that the search for new theories on development that was so important during the 1960s and 1970s to overcome the simplistic thoughts of the modernization theorists, today is blocked much because of the absence of empirical knowledge (Blomström and Hettne, 1983). This is true not least concerning the technological development process in underdeveloped countries. Here the pioneering work by Jorge Katz on technical progress in Argentina which shows the existence of a fairly rapid development of domestic technology there, is very important and opens up new, interesting research areas (see e.g. Katz, 1978). One of these is the role of the multinationals in this process, and further research into the relationship between the presence of foreign corporations and local generation of technology in the Third World is needed.

## NOTES

1. Thus, no conclusions about the overall effects of foreign investment are possible from this study. An overall assessment should not only include the total effects on local technological development (including inter-industry spillover efficiency), but also effects such as employment creation, net income generation, balance-of-payment effects, and so on. Nor are we treating the 'appropriateness' of the technological transfers.

2. Obviously it would be interesting to look into the joint-venture question, but this is not possible with the data at hand.

3. Our measure of capital intensity is affected by the number of shifts worked, and the proper measure of capital intensity relates to the flow of capital services instead of the stock. Since the Mexican data does not provide us with any information on shift work we have to assume that the rate of shift work is the same across industries.

4. Denote labour quality of domestic industries by $LQ_1^d$ and of foreign-owned industries by $LQ_1^f$. We then have

$$LQ_1 = FB \, LQ_1^f + (1 - FB)LQ_1^d$$

where *FB* is the ratio of blue-collar workers in foreign plants in an industry to the total blue-collars in that industry. But it follows from the above definition of *FS* that

$$FS = FB\alpha + \beta$$

where $\alpha$ expresses the ratio of blue-collars to total employees in an industry, and $\beta$ is the ratio of white-collar workers in foreign plants in an industry to total employees in that industry. But $\beta$ is small and $\alpha$ has little variance, and it is then reasonable to postulate a linear relation between $LQ_1$ and *FS*.

5. The Herfindahl index has been calculated in the following way:

$$H = \sum_{i=1}^{n} \left(\frac{x_i}{X}\right)^2,$$

where $x_i$ represents the employment of the *n* individual plants and *X* represents the total employment of the industry.

An index on the absolute concentration level in an industry, $CR_4$, which shows the proportion of the industry's employment accounted for by the four largest plants, was also calculated. As expected, this index was highly correlated with the share of foreign plants in an industry (see Appendix). It is well known that the foreign plants in Mexico show larger sizes.

6. For discussion of the use of '50% of output' as the cut-off point between suboptimal and optimal capacity, see Cory (1981).

7. Even though Mexico has almost 70 million inhabitants, its internal market is relatively small due to underdevelopment. Canada, for example, with a population of 24 million people, has nearly three times as high a GNP as Mexico. It is not, however, the domestic market that actually interests us, but the total market (including the export market). Since we are using data from 1970, we can assume that the export markets for the Mexican plants were not so important, because of the import-substitution policy that had been followed. Many Mexican industries were protected from foreign competition, which excluded them from the world market.

8. In the Mexican Census of Manufactures each four-digit industry is divided into size groups of plants. There are 14 such size classes. However, in order to maintain confidentiality, there are no data published on classes containing less than three plants. In such cases, two (or more) classes are aggregated into one. For our purpose we choose the class containing the largest plants within each four-digit industry.

9. An alternative measure for foreign participation was constructed as the foreign share of gross production in each industry. The simple correlation coefficient between the two measures was, however, very high (0.95), and since productivity is being explained, it seems more plausible to use an input rather than an output measure. Furthermore, the estimations with the employment measure gave a somewhat higher $R^2$ value. The alternative measure did not change the results in any significant way.

10. See Appendix for a correlation matrix.

11. The simple correlation coefficient between the two alternative scale factors is also very high (0.94).

## REFERENCES

Ablin, E., 'Technology exports from developing countries: afterthoughts in the light of the Argentine case', paper submitted to the Nordic Symposium on Development Strategies for Latin America and the New International Economic Order (Lund: September 1979).

Blomström, M. and B. Hettne, *Third World Contributions to a Theory of Development* (London: Zed Press, 1983).

Brash, D. T., *American Investment in Australian Industry* (Cambridge, Mass.: Harvard University Press, 1966).

Caves, R. E., 'Multinational firms, competition, and productivity in host-country markets', *Economica,* Vol. 41 (1974), pp. 176–193.

Caves, R. E., J. Khalilzadeh-Shirazi and M. E. Porter, 'Scale economies in statistical analyses of market power', *Review of Economics and Statistics,* Vol. 57, No. 2 (1975), pp. 133–140.

Cory, P. F., 'A technique for obtaining improved proxy estimates of minimum optimal scale', *Review of Economics and Statistics,* Vol. 63, No. 1 (1981), pp. 96–106.

Globerman, S., 'Foreign direct investment and "spillover" efficiency benefits in Canadian manufacturing industries', *Canadian Journal of Economics,* Vol. 12, No. 1 (1979), pp. 42–56.

Gorecki, P. K., 'The determinants of entry by domestic and foreign enterprises in Canadian manufacturing industries: some comments and empirical results', *Review of Economics and Statistics,* Vol. 58, No. 4 (1976), pp. 485–488.

Katz, J., 'Technological change, economic development and intra and extra regional relations in Latin America' (Buenos Aires: IDB/ECLA Research Programme in Science and Technology, Working Paper No. 30, 1978).

Lall, S., 'Developing countries as exporters of industrial technology', *Research Policy,* Vol. 9 (1980), pp. 24–52.

Meier, G. M., *Leading Issues in Economic Development* (Oxford: Oxford University Press, 1976).

Ten Kate, A. and R. Bruce Wallace, 'La protección efectiva en México 1970', *Investigación Económicas* (UNAM, México), No. 1 (Nueva época) (1977), pp. 205–264.

Vanlommel, E., B. de Brabander and B. Liebaers, 'Industrial concentration in Belgium: Empirical comparison of alternative seller concentration measures', *Journal of Industrial Economics*, Vol. 26, No. 1 (1977), pp. 1–20.

## APPENDIX

Table A1. *Simple correlation coefficients for independent variables*

|                | $KL^d$ | $LQ_1$ | $H$  | $CR_4$ | $SCALE^d$ | $FS$  | $FS_A$ |
|----------------|--------|--------|------|--------|-----------|-------|--------|
| $KL^d$         | 1.00   |        |      |        |           |       |        |
| $LQ_1$         | 0.34   | 1.00   |      |        |           |       |        |
| $H$            | 0.19   | 0.01   | 1.00 |        |           |       |        |
| $CR_4$*        | 0.24   | 0.15   | 0.58 | 1.00   |           |       |        |
| $SCALE^d$      | 0.41   | 0.00   | 0.30 | 0.15   | 1.00      |       |        |
| $FS$           | 0.38   | 0.45   | 0.23 | 0.47   | −0.04     | 1.00  |        |
| $FS_A$†        | 0.33   | 0.44   | 0.18 | 0.48   | −0.10     | 0.95  | 1.00   |

*$CR_4$ is an index on the absolute concentration level in an industry which shows the proportion of the industry's employment accounted for by the four largest plants.
†$FS_A$ is an alternative measure for foreign participation constructed as the foreign share of gross production in each industry.

# 3

## Small-Scale Manufacturing as a Competitive Advantage

Since much of the research on multinationals from the advanced countries has emphasized their technological advantages, it should not be surprising to discover that technical know-how also provides many foreign investors from the developing countries with competitive advantages that enable them to survive abroad. The latter's technological advantages are of a very special kind; they reflect the investors' home markets and give the firms considerable potential for contributing to the development process in the poorer countries.

### Small-Scale Markets

One particular feature in developing countries that gives firms in this study an edge abroad is the small size of the markets for most manufactured goods. Entrepreneurs in developing countries have a special propensity to respond to that characteristic.

If firms in the developing countries simply import manufacturing technology commonly used in the industrialized countries, the factories are likely to be too large for their market. In 1959, for instance, Sri Lanka turned to the Soviet Union for help in establishing iron and steel works. The first plant was to be a rolling mill. The smallest rolling mill the Russians had built had a capacity of 60,000 tons of steel per year. (Even this plant was very small by the standards of industrialized countries; the average steel mill elsewhere produced some one million tons per year.) But total Sri Lankan demand was only 35,000 tons. Moreover, this demand was for a wider variety of products than the Russian mill could supply and the export potential was poor. In spite of the scale problem, the Sri Lankans, like many other developing countries, acquired the large-scale technology instead of turning to, say, India for small, manually operated rolling mills.[1] As a result, Sri

Small-Scale Manufacturing                                          20

Lanka utilized only about a quarter of its installed capacity for rolled
steel products in 1973 and continued to import rolled steel products,
largely of kinds not produced by the existing plant.

Faced with small markets for many products, entrepreneurs in developing countries can increase profits if they can adapt technology to
small-scale manufacture. In most cases, they start with technology from
an industrialized country and adapt it later. Of 52 Indian parent firms
interviewed, 42 reported that they obtained their original technology
abroad, but 47 also reported that over half of their technology was
"indigenous" by the time of the interview (table 3.1). One Indian firm
that processes edible oil illustrates the pattern. It began operations in
India in 1917 with copra crushing equipment imported from the United
States. By 1976, it was using entirely Indian equipment. The local
equipment was not slavishly copied from the earlier imported machinery; it was changed in response to Indian conditions. In many
cases, locally adapted technology was eventually exported to foreign
subsidiaries, as is apparent from the fact that "Indian machinery" was
the source of know-how in most of the foreign investments for which
data were available.

A manufacturing process might be scaled down in various ways.
When larger plants consist primarily of duplicate pieces of equipment,
such as spinning and weaving plants, little innovation is required. Some
of the small-scale plants observed in this study simply used fewer
pieces of equipment than large-scale plants. In other cases, adaptation
to small scale means the substitution of batch processing for mass
production. Packages Limited of Pakistan manufactures paper containers
in short runs, and a Philippine firm manufactures pharmaceutical products in batches. Sometimes assembly lines are dropped and semifinished
products are moved in batches from work station to work station, such
as in several flashlight battery manufacturers in Indonesia. On occasion,
labor may be substituted directly for machines. Thus, steel auto bodies
may be fashioned by hand to avoid the high fixed cost of dies. To
facilitate manual work, some products are redesigned. Jeepney bodies
in the Philippines, for example, were designed with simple bends instead
of the curves typical of auto bodies in richer countries. Similarly, a
Hong Kong firm redesigned appliances to use fewer molded plastic
parts. The adaptation of the manufacturing process to small scale may
sometimes involve a completely different technology, such as the use
of fiberglass instead of steel for auto bodies. In some cases, factories
for small-scale manufacture use machinery that has been especially

Small-Scale Manufacturing 21

**Table 3.1**
Sources of technology of Indian parent firms and their foreign manufacturing subsidiaries (1977)

| Sector | Source of parents' original technology | | | Source of foreign subsidiaries' technology | | | Source of parents' 1977 technology | |
|---|---|---|---|---|---|---|---|---|
| | India | Foreign collaboration | Imports of foreign machinery | India | Japan | Other foreign countries | At least 50 percent indigenous | Mostly imported |
| Paper and cardboard | 1 | 2 | 2 | 7 | | | 5 | |
| Chemicals, soaps, and drugs | 2 | 1 | 3 | 8 | | 1 | 4 | 2 |
| Edible oils | 1 | 2 | 1 | 9 | | | 4 | |
| Automobile ancillary | 1 | 5 | 3 | 7 | 1 | 1 | 8 | 1 |
| Foods, beverages, and confectionery | 1 | 3 | 1 | 5 | | 3 | 3 | 2 |
| Construction | | | 3 | 3 | | | 3 | |
| Miscellaneous light ancillary | 1 | 5 | 3 | 12 | | 1 | 9 | |
| Heavy industry | | | 3 | 4 | | | 3 | |
| Textiles | 3 | 2 | 3 | 4 | 1 | 3 | 8 | |
| Total | 10 | 20 | 22 | 59 | 2 | 9 | 47 | 5 |

Source: Interviews conducted by Carlos Cordeiro.

designed for lower output levels. A carpet maker in the Philippines uses 16-inch looms; many U.S. firms use 200-inch looms. Some factories rely on multipurpose machines to manufacture at small volumes. Thus, parts for various products may be made on standard lathes or bent with simple equipment. One firm planning for a capacity of 20,000 refrigerators per year chose multipurpose equipment for the production of cabinets. The machines could be adjusted for various models of refrigerators and for other appliances. Sometimes workers may be used, much like multipurpose machines, for a number of tasks in the production process.[2]

It is exactly these kinds of small-scale technology that were exported by many of the firms in this study. Information from Lecraw's work in Thailand bears out the point.[3] Capacity utilization is one way to confirm the small scale of developing country firms. Multinationals from the advanced countries on the average operated at only 26 percent of their capacity, whereas foreign investors from other developing countries operated at 48 percent. The role of scale is verified when the outputs of the plants of various nationalities are compared. The size of an average plant owned by an industrialized country parent was more than twice the size of an average plant owned by a developing country parent within the same industry.

In another study, Lecraw compared a group of foreign investors from Southeast Asian countries with multinationals from wealthy countries. He calculated index numbers to measure relative size for each industry, with the largest firm in the industry assigned the number 100. The size of the subsidiaries from Southeast Asian parents averaged 46; the counterparts from the industrialized countries averaged 109.[4]

A study of Taiwan's exports of capital equipment provided additional support for the contention that firms in developing countries innovate small-scale technology.[5] It demonstrated that Taiwan's advantage in such exports appears in the sale of equipment for small-scale plants.

In the interviews for this study, managers were asked how the sizes of their home plant and their subsidiaries would compare to the size of typical plants in an industrialized country. The typical answer was "smaller." The following data illustrate the sizes of the subsidiaries of firms that were interviewed. Hong Kong managers reported, as evidence, the number of looms for five overseas subsidiaries to be 3,000, 1,920, 440, 250, and 200. One Argentine firm indicated that it had 169, 240 and 168 looms in its three Brazilian mills.[6] Hong Kong firms reported the number of spindles for seven spinning subsidiaries to be 110,000,

Small-Scale Manufacturing                                                 23

**Table 3.2**
Average investment in manufacturing subsidiaries in Indonesia (1967–1976)

| Home of investor | Average total investment ( × $1,000) |
| --- | --- |
| Chinese in Hong Kong, Singapore, and Taiwan | 2,722 |
| Other Southeast Asian countries | 960 |
| Other developing countries | 3,935 |
| Japan | 5,687 |
| United States | 2,403 |
| United Kingdom | 1,189 |
| Other industrialized countries | 2,063 |

Source: Calculated from data on realized projects from the Indonesian Investment Board.

100,000, 40,000, 23,000, 16,000, 14,000, 10,000, 10,000.[7] Two Indian firms reported 30,000 and 20,160 spindles in their subsidiaries. The Argentine firm had 14,700, 29,800, and 11,500 spindles in its foreign factories.[8] by the standards of the industrialized countries, these are almost all small plants.[9]

More evidence of the comparatively small size of factories owned by foreign investors from developing countries was provided by foreign investors in Nigeria and Indonesia. In Nigeria, textile plants owned by nationals from other developing countries were, in most cases, smaller than the subsidiaries owned by European, American, or Japanese parents.[10] In Indonesia, factories for flashlight batteries show a similar pattern. A Singapore-owned factory (with Taiwanese technicians) had a capacity of 12 million batteries per year on a one-shift basis. In contrast, an American-owned factory in Indonesia could produce more than 65 million batteries in the same period.[11]

Aggregate data are more difficult to analyze but tend to support the same conclusions. Consider Indonesia, for which a great deal of information was available about investors of various national origins. The Indonesian data suggest that there might not be any consistent differences between the subsidiaries of parents from developing countries and those from advanced countries (table 3.2). However, the overall figures are misleading. A disproportionate number of developing country subsidiaries are for food processing, and they are among the largest projects of developing countries. When one examines the capital investment by industry, a more consistent pattern emerges. Out of 8 two-digit SIC (Standard Industrial Classification) industries with both developing country and industrialized country investors, the average developing country subsidiary has a smaller investment in 6 industries. (The exceptions are in "food, beverages, and tobacco" and in "stone, glass and similar products," which contain only 2 developing country projects.) In the textile and paper products industries, the average developing country subsidiary is considerably less than half the size of its competitors from industrialized countries. In the remaining cases, the difference is at least 30 percent. When the industries are broken down to the three-digit level, the results are similar. Out of 14 industries with 2 or more subsidiaries of each type of parent, the average subsidiary of a parent from another developing country is smaller in 11 cases. The exceptions are all in food and beverages, where market size is probably not a major constraint in the choice of technology.

There is a substantial risk that differences in capital-labor ratios of the two types of investors could cause the figures to be misleading, as factories with smaller total investment may actually have larger output. To account for this possibility, the plants were compared in terms of capacity of production. Unfortunately, output data were not available for Indonesia. If the employment figures were also smaller for the developing country subsidiaries, then one could feel confident in claiming that the plants were indeed smaller. Unfortunately, the data are not thoroughly convincing. In 15 of the 22 three-digit SIC industries, firms from other developing countries had fewer employees than their advanced country competitors; but the remaining 7 had more.

Although the analysis of such data lends some support to the contention that foreign investors from developing countries have smaller subsidiaries than advanced country firms, a completely convincing case cannot be built without output data. Fortunately, data reported from other countries and the interviews provided strong support for the contention that the two types of investors do build plants of very different sizes.

To be sure, the small-scale technologies used in the foreign subsidiaries of developing country parents were not always those in use in the home plants at the time the investments were made. As wage rates have risen in Hong Kong, for example, labor-intensive machinery appropriate to conditions in Hong Kong a few years earlier has been replaced with more automated equipment, and some of the old machinery has been exported to various affiliates. A complete plant was, for instance, moved to Ghana for textile manufacture. In 1979, a Brazilian bicycle manufacturer had a large-scale factory at home but established a small-scale subsidiary in Bolivia. Managers pointed out that the capacity of the new Bolivian plant was comparable to that of the parent company in Brazil only ten years earlier. Although the Brazilian firm's small-scale technology was outdated at home, in the small Bolivian market it was quite appropriate[12] and not easily available from the advanced countries where such techniques had been long forgotten.

### Characteristics of Small-Scale Technology

The most striking characteristic of the technology developed by firms in response to small markets is its labor intensity. India's small-scale sugar mills, for example, employ about three times the workers and a half or a third the capital for the same volume as a mill from an advanced country.[13]

The pattern is similar for the firms examined in this study. Capital-labor ratios for subsidiaries of parents from developing countries with those of subsidiaries of parents from industrialized countries offer the simplest kind of comparison.[14] In Indonesia, the first group uses, on average, only $8,500 of capital for each worker employed; the second group uses $16,300. (Table 3.3 breaks down the data further by nationality of investor.) The striking differences do not result from any special characteristics of Chinese firms, which are very important in Indonesia. It is apparent that investors from developing countries, Chinese or not, use more labor-intensive techniques than do investors from the advanced countries.

Such gross comparisons of capital-labor ratios are quite dangerous, as the observed differences could result from differences in industries in which the various investors are found. Developing country firms might be attracted to industries that are inherently more labor-intensive than those that attract firms from the advanced countries. A breakdown of investment by industry, therefore, allows a more careful comparison of firms originating from different countries. When the original Indonesian industry classifications are used, eight two-digit industries contain subsidiaries of parents from both developing and industrialized countries, and in all eight, the capital-labor ratios of the plants with parents from other developing countries are lower than those of their counterparts from the industrialized countries. In only one case (food and beverages) was the ratio for developing country firms more than 65 percent of the ratio for subsidiaries of firms from the industrialized

Small-Scale Manufacturing                                          26

**Table 3.3**
Capital-labor ratios in manufacturing subsidiaries in Indonesia (1967–1976)

| Home of investor | Average capital-labor ratios (× $1,000/worker) | Median capital-labor ratios (× $1,000/worker) |
|---|---|---|
| Chinese in Hong Kong, Singapore, and Taiwan | 8.3 | 4.9 |
| Other Southeast Asian countries | 8.2 | 4.5 |
| Other developing countries | 10.4 | 9.4 |
| Japan | 18.8 | 14.1 |
| United States | 16.9 | 10.5 |
| United Kingdom | 19.9 | 10.6 |
| Other industrialized countries | 13.2 | 8.6 |

Source: Calculated from data on realized projects from the Indonesian Investment Board.

countries. At the three-digit level, the average investors from other developing countries are more labor-intensive in 13 out of the 14 industries that have two or more of each group of firms. The exception again is in food products, where market size provides little constraint on scale.

The results might not arise from differences in technology but from differences in investments for building, working capital, or other assets. The figures for investment in machinery per employee, however, show a pattern similar to that for total investment per worker. The developing country firms invest less in machinery for each job created (table 3.4). These differences are only slightly less striking than the differences in overall capital-labor figures. In five of the eight industries, a comparison of the value of machinery per worker for the firms from other developing countries and the firms from industrialized countries indicates less difference than do the figures for total capital invested per worker.

An understanding of why the two measures differ slightly is not critical at this point, but the differences should not be surprising. Total investment reflects building and working capital as well as machinery. One might argue that a labor-intensive factory would require a larger building to house the greater number of workers. The observed results could arise from either of two sources. One possibility is that investors from developing countries spend less on building than do their industrialized counterparts. Another possible explanation of the pattern

Small-Scale Manufacturing                                           **27**

**Table 3.4**
Machinery investment per worker in manufacturing subsidiaries in Indonesia
(1967–1976)

| Home of investor | Average machinery investment (× $1,000/worker) |
| --- | --- |
| Chinese in Hong Kong, Singapore, and Taiwan | 4.42 |
| Other Southeast Asian countries | 2.92 |
| Other developing countries | 4.89 |
| Japan | 8.14 |
| United States | 5.37 |
| United Kingdom | 5.34 |
| Other industrialized countries | 7.14 |

Source: Calculated from data on realized projects from the Indonesian Investment Board.

is that the developing country firms invest less in working capital. The fact that the Indonesian data show fixed assets as a slightly higher percentage of total investment for the investors from developing countries suggests that this might indeed be the case. One could argue that labor-intensive factories need more working capital than would capital-intensive plants because of the need to meet regular wage bills. One could also argue that such factories can run with smaller inventories and thus need less working capital. On this point, one can only speculate, particularly since the Indonesian data come from official application forms in which working capital could only be estimated. My own guess is that firms from developing countries invest less in buildings and have a slight tendency to underestimate the required working capital when they apply for investment permits.

The main point, that the labor intensity of technology used by foreign investors from developing countries is high, is strongly supported by rather sophisticated analysis of Thai data.[15] Since output data were available for that country, Lecraw was able to estimate production functions for 12 four-digit industries. The results effectively demonstrate that foreign investors from other developing countries use more labor-intensive technology than either Thai firms or foreign investors from industrialized countries.

Another major difference that distinguishes the projects of foreign investors from developing countries from those of local firms in their host countries and those of the multinationals from the industrialized countries is flexibility. Flexibility was emphasized quite explicitly by the manager of a Hong Kong textile firm with subsidiaries in Indonesia and Malaysia, who said that the operations "have to be flexible to weave many kinds of textiles and spin many kinds of yarn. We don't make something and then sell it." The implication was that advanced country multinationals make a small variety of products and then devote their efforts to convincing consumers to accept the standardized versions, while his firm responds to market niches by providing a wide range of products.

Since one specialized model or version of a product is unlikely to have a sufficiently large market in developing countries to keep typical machines fully occupied, machines are designed or chosen for their flexibility. Thus, Packages Limited of Pakistan carefully studied the downtime involved in product changeovers for various kinds of European machinery used for making paper packages and used these studies to select equipment that minimizes the costs of short runs of many products. Similarly, a Hong Kong appliance maker selected sheet metal working equipment that can be used to produce various models of both stoves and refrigerators. The manager of a Hong Kong textile firm with spinning facilities in Indonesia explained that using "small package spindles" was more labor-intensive than the usual spindles, requiring more loading and unloading, but was "more flexible." A manager from a Southeast Asian pharmaceutical firm that makes as many as 400 products at home and 50–100 products in the company's foreign subsidiaries reported that the plants "must use the same equipment for many products."

In their efforts to design flexible plants, firms from developing countries occasionally build a special kind of excess capacity into their factories. The plant design includes extra machines required to produce special models or versions of the basic products, even though those machines may stay idle much of the year. The Hong Kong textile manager just quoted explained that he did "not expect every piece of equipment to be used all the time." Packages Limited had a simple machine for making paper cups that was used only occasionally, since the principal customer for paper cups, the Pakistani national airline, did not order enough to keep the machine fully occupied. Nevertheless, paper cups and similar products were needed to fill out the company's line and keep other machinery busy.

In some cases, the design of a flexible, small-scale plant depends largely on knowing well equipment available from a large number of suppliers in the industrialized countries. A German machine for one step may be combined with an Italian one for the next operation. A few firms in the developing countries have made the large investment required to learn about a wide range of such equipment. They not only have collected specifications but have tried the equipment for reliability and know the availability of spare parts. Once acquired, such knowledge is useful in other small markets.

The special knowledge possessed by some companies from developing countries is quite extensive. One firm I interviewed had drawn up a list of suppliers for various pieces of equipment. The list covered a wide range of European suppliers and included the capacity and cost of the equipment and the set-up time required to adjust the equipment to other kinds of output. The supplying firms were evaluated according to their delivery and service records; the machines, according to their needs for maintenance. This was invaluable information for competition with firms in other countries.

To meet the special needs of small-scale manufacture, a number of developing countries have manufactured their own machinery. When special machinery from the home country was used by the firms interviewed, it was usually made by the firm that operated it, not by specialist machinery manufacturers. Typically, a firm started at home with all, or almost all, imported equipment. As the company replaced imported machinery or expanded, the experience gained by its technicians enabled it to supply more of the technology and machinery internally.[16] Eventually, some of this machinery was used abroad. For instance, the original plant of Packages Limited in Pakistan began with equipment acquired in Europe. Spare parts, however, were expensive by the time they reached Pakistan, and lead times in acquiring them were such that repairs could not be made quickly. Moreover, some of the original European equipment was second-hand and quite old; parts for this machinery were not easily available even in Europe. Since local shops were unable to make needed parts quickly and reliably, the firm established its own machine shop and foundry. The shop had excess capacity as long as it supplied only spares, so the shop operators began to experiment with modifications to the original machinery that might improve its performance. Such modifications in some cases increased flexibility by generally decreasing set-up time. Gradually, the shop began to copy the imported machines, but with modifications that were useful for short runs of many products. Eventually, the shop was producing a number of machines largely of its own design, with special features in response to local problems. As Packages Limited ventured outside of Pakistan, it provided its foreign affiliates with machinery of its own manufacture.[17]

Since U.S. studies have discovered the importance of a close link between the user of capital equipment and the supplier for successful innovation,[18] it should perhaps not be surprising that the adapted equipment in developing countries is so often made "in-house." If innovations were undertaken by firms that are first and foremost machinery manufacturers, they would probably be involved in some of the investments uncovered in this study. To sell innovative machines abroad, little-known machinery manufacturers from developing countries might well have to take equity positions in facilities that would use the machinery. The infrequency of foreign investments by firms that were primarily machinery manufacturers suggests that they have not been as innovative as some of the equipment users who felt pressing needs for changes in the machinery.

Investors from developing countries obtain a considerable amount of their equipment from their home nations. For this study, data were available on the source of machinery for 151 subsidiaries; 122 subsidiaries imported machinery from their home country (or, occasionally, another developing country). A study of Taiwanese firms found that more than 30 percent of their foreign investment in nontrade activities was made up of Taiwanese machinery.[19] The Indians are particularly likely to use equipment from home. Given the Indian government requirements that Indian firms use Indian machinery overseas, the finding is not surprising. Firms from other developing countries bring a quarter of their machinery from their home countries. Although this fraction is smaller than the fraction of home machinery used by investors from the advanced countries, it is still a large number given the small amount of machinery manufactured and exported by developing countries. Table 3.5 shows the sources of various foreign investors in Thailand.

A striking fact that appears in table 3.5 is that a quarter of the machinery of developing country investors is made in Thailand, which is more than even local investors use. Thus, the foreign investors have a high propensity to use local machinery as well as local materials in Thailand. My impression from interviews is that locally produced machinery is usually made to order to designs supplied by the parent.

Machines newly manufactured at home or in the host country and carefully selected new machinery from the industrialized countries do

Small-Scale Manufacturing 31

**Table 3.5**
Source of machinery in manufacturing firms in Thailand (1962–1974)

| Home of investor | Source of machinery (%) | | | | | | Total (%) |
|---|---|---|---|---|---|---|---|
| | United States | Europe | Japan | India | Other developing countries | Thailand | |
| United States | 51 | 25 | 16 | 0 | 0 | 8 | 100 |
| Europe | 20 | 57 | 13 | 0 | 0 | 10 | 100 |
| Japan | 6 | 4 | 80 | 0 | 0 | 10 | 100 |
| India | 4 | 10 | 8 | 45 | 8 | 25 | 100 |
| Other developing countries | 7 | 8 | 30 | 5 | 25 | 25 | 100 |
| Thailand | 30 | 27 | 26 | 2 | 25 | 13 | 100 |

Source: Donald Lecraw, "Choice of Technology in Low-Wage Countries," unpublished doctoral dissertation in business economics, Harvard University, 1976. Original data from Thai Investment Board and interviews.

not exhaust the sources of small-scale equipment for foreign investment by firms from the developing countries. Second-hand machinery provides an important alternative.[20] In most cases, such machinery was produced in an industrialized country, but when the market there was smaller or before technological change had increased the optimal scale for the high-wage country.[21]

The interviews for this study identified a large number of subsidiaries that operated some second-hand machinery. Machinery formerly used in Hong Kong, for example, has been located all over Southeast Asia and as far away as West Africa.

In most cases, old machinery is more labor-intensive and flexible than new equipment. In the textile industry, for instance, spinning equipment of 1950 vintage has roughly half the output per man-hour of 1968 equipment.[22] To be sure, occasionally newer machinery is more flexible; recent innovations in electronic controls for carpet weaving have increased flexibility, according to the manager of one firm interviewed. Although applications of electronics to machinery may make this kind of case more common, in the late 1970s it seemed that "old" usually implied "flexible."

In sum, foreign investors from developing countries obtain their equipment from a range of sources, but regardless of the source, the machinery that is selected is usually flexible, labor-intensive, and suited for relatively small-scale manufacture.

## Low Overheads

Low overheads give many developing country firms a strength that supports their ability to manufacture at small volumes with low unit costs. The savings in overhead costs derive largely from the low salaries that such firms pay to managers and technicians and partly from the small expenditures on buildings.

Hong Kong-based foreign investors in one study reported that they consider lower costs for managerial and technical staff as their most important advantage over other multinationals.[23] The possible contribution to competitive position of low expatriate salaries is suggested by a study of U.S.-based multinationals that reported that expatriate costs represented 4 to 20 percent of the pretax profits of all international operations.[24] Since the number of expatriates in a subsidiary is not proportional to the size of sales, the costs would be an even larger percentage of profits for small operations in developing countries.

The salaries paid to managers and technicians of the foreign subsidiaries of firms from developing countries appear strikingly low compared to those paid by a multinational from an industrialized country. An Indian firm reported paying a department head between $350 and $700 a month at home, with no significant premiums for overseas assignments. A Hong Kong textile firm reported salaries for its engineers in Indonesia of about $1,000 to $1,200 per month, considerably less than that of a U.S. or European engineer stationed in Southeast Asia. Many of the managers and technicians from developing countries do not take their families with them on overseas assignments, even when the assignment is a year or more. This is especially true for Pakistani and Taiwanese firms. The result is more savings for the firm.

Two additional characteristics of compensation for managers are, in some cases, important in saving overheads for the firms in this study. In a number of Hong Kong enterprises, managers receive a significant part of their income in the form of a bonus, which is large only if the subsidiary does well. For such firms, the fixed costs associated with expatriate managers are comparatively low. In addition, the managers are, in many cases, relatives of the owners of the parent firm. For Chinese firms particularly, the relatives would be drawing a certain amount of income out of the enterprise even if they were not managing a foreign subsidiary. Thus, their incremental cost to the enterprise is small.

Why developing country investors spend less than multinationals from advanced countries on building and operate in more cramped quarters is less apparent, but this fact has been observed before.[25] The traveler in the developing world can hardly avoid being struck by the attractive, modern buildings of the advanced country multinationals. In many cases, they are virtual carbon copies of plants at home. In Indonesia, the Jakarta Coca-Cola bottling plant is, for example, hardly distinguishable from a Coca-Cola bottling plant in a medium-size U.S. city, even down to having windows for pedestrians to watch the automatic bottling equipment.[26] The plant is spacious and attractive and expensive. On the other hand, the Singapore-based F&N bottling plant in Jakarta is clean, sturdy, and seemingly quite adequate to the task but simple and somewhat crowded. Some of the Chinese-owned plastic sandal factories in Indonesia are more austere. Many operate from little more than rudimentary sheds, jammed with workers, inventory, and equipment. The manager may have only a tiny cubicle in a corner, filled with files and papers. Data on buildings in Mauritius and the Philippines indicate the same pattern.[27]

The reasons for the different approaches to building probably lie in the role that image plays in the marketing strategies of firms from different areas. For certain multinationals from rich countries, such as Coca-Cola, image is important, and buildings play at least some part in maintaining that image. As will later become apparent, image is second to price and cost in the strategies of most foreign investors from developing countries.

The savings that can accrue from low overhead add up. The Thai data show adminstrative expenses to be only 5 percent of sales for foreign investors from developing countries. For the traditional multinationals, they amount to 14 percent.[28]

## Exploiting the Advantages

The firm that ventures abroad from a developing country has two principal types of competition: firms indigenous to the country in which they are investing and multinationals from the industrialized nations. If the advantage of the firm from another developing country lies in small-scale manufacture, a potential indigenous competitor would have to develop similar skills or work out some kind of arrangement to obtain the skills from a foreign enterprise. To develop the skills at home, the potential competitor must incur costs similar to those already incurred by the foreign firm. If the equipment is designed and produced by the firm, the development costs are likely to be high. If the technology involves the gathering of machinery from a number of countries, the expenses involved in searching out such sources will be significant. If the machinery is second-hand, the task is to find reliable sources. Even when the potential competitor is knowledgeable about suppliers, the risks associated with purchase appear great, and the variance in performance of second-hand equipment is large.[29] The search for a reliable dealer is likely to involve some costly mistakes. Moreover, in most cases, the firm that has experience with small-scale technology has lower costs that have resulted from using technology over a period of time. A potential competitor must incur the costs of acquiring experience before it can be on equal footing with the foreign firm. Whatever the nature of the costs required of the potential indigenous competitor, they are almost certainly greater than those involved in transferring the foreign firm's skills to the potential competitor's country.

Small-Scale Manufacturing                                    **35**

A multinational from the United States, Europe, or Japan could, it would seem, apply its formidable skills to scale down production and develop technology that is most suitable for developing countries. Through its large network, the multinational enterprise could spread the development costs over many plants. In fact, multinationals have usually not devoted their resources to down-scaling. Rather, they have preferred to concentrate on advanced technology or on marketing skills that enable them to avoid worrying about production costs. Most see their comparative advantages in fields other than small-scale manufacture. Even if they were to develop the know-how and experience, as some have attempted (such as Philips of The Netherlands),[30] they would still be saddled with high overhead costs not assumed by the investor from a developing country.

The strategies of a number of multinationals from the advanced countries have been just the opposite. Some familiar firms have built or preserved a competitive advantage in their international businesses by integrating operations across national boundaries. In some cases, such integration has allowed the enterprises to obtain low production costs through sheer scale of manufacture. In Europe, Ford Motor Company has, since the 1960s, designed its automobiles so that certain components are common to models offered in different markets. Common components are produced for all of Europe in large, specialized plants in one or two places. The German and British operations, for example, trade certain engines and transmissions that they produce in large volumes. Another approach in the search for economies of scale is to specialize plants by models of the final product rather than by parts. Volkswagen, for example, has produced the "Safari" in Mexico ("The Thing" in the U.S. market) for several of its overseas markets, even though some of those markets have plants that produce other models of Volkswagen.

In some truly exceptional cases, similar integration strategies appear from time to time among firms from the developing countries. A Peruvian firm, Pan Americana, produced television programs in several countries. The same programs could be used in different markets; moreover, there were opportunities to obtain certain kinds of talent cheaply in one country and other kinds in other countries. To take advantage of the opportunities, Pan Americana operated in Argentina, Puerto Rico, Venezuela, and cities of the continental United States with a large Spanish-speaking population. The international business ground to a halt only when the Peruvian government restricted the firm's activities and eventually acquired control. Similarly, Televisa, a large Mexican television firm, established operations in Los Angeles and elsewhere in the United States.[31] The firm is able to use the same programs in Mexico and for the Latin American community in Los Angeles.

In conventional manufacturing, no developing country firms were encountered that had integrated operations across borders. Rather than attempting to emulate firms from the richer countries, the developing country investors stuck by their skill in small-scale manufacture. The reader should not, however, be misled. The factories are neither primitive nor tiny. They are not the rural, almost handicraft industries of Ghandi. And, as will become apparent, running them demands a great deal of management and technical skill.

# 4

## Local Procurement and Special Products as Competitive Advantages

Although adaptation of technology to the small scale required for developing countries is widespread among Third World firms, it hardly exhausts their innovative activities. Other technological developments have given certain enterprises from developing countries advantages that they can exploit abroad, and these advantages stem from special conditions in the firms' home countries.

### Use of Local Resources

One such condition is the chronic balance of payments difficulties that have plagued many developing countries. Their governments have responded, in many cases, with severe controls on imports, sometimes to discourage local consumption and sometimes to encourage local manufacture of what had been imported. The resulting high prices for imported products has encouraged local entrepreneurs to begin manufacturing many goods that had previously come from abroad. Such controls provided the incentive for the creation of many of the parent firms in this study. But the influence of import controls has not stopped with the establishment of a factory to manufacture a final product that had been imported, for the factory itself faces a need to import materials and components.

In the advanced countries, where manufacturing technologies have usually originated, the design of end products reflects the wide availability of high-quality materials and special items in the industrialized markets. Special steels, custom-made threaded parts, and an unending array of other special materials and components are readily obtainable and of predictable quality as a result of the scale of demand from industrial firms and the skills available in the richer countries.

In developing countries, a local manufacturer needing specialized inputs has a problem. The producer may need steel products, but if there is a steel plant in the country, its output is likely to be of the most widely demanded sorts. Special steels must come from abroad. Similarly, regular nuts and bolts may be readily available from local suppliers, but special threads and shapes are difficult to come by locally. Moreover, with little competition, local suppliers often produce materials and components of low or unpredictable quality. Imports may be available, but the policies designed to discourage foreign exchange expenditures and promote industrialization are likely to make them very expensive.[1] Moreover, the lead times for foreign orders (or for special manufacture locally, for that matter) are likely to be long.

To diminish the need for special inputs associated with technology imported from the industrialized countries, firms in the developing world might search out ways to substitute locally available inputs. Indeed, they do. The importance of this task is pointed out in a study showing that most of the R&D of Indian firms (even the largest) "originated in the problem of manufacturing standard products out of the non-standard raw materials. . . ."[2] Packages Limited, a Pakistan firm interviewed for this study, had an extensive program of developing local materials. The firm replaced imported adhesives, lacquers, linseed oil, and alum with substitutes that it manufactured locally. Further, the company helped local firms to develop adequate quality soapstone, chalk, and silicate for its plant.[3]

Once firms have learned to substitute locally available materials and components for specialized inputs, they can use that know-how in other developing countries where manufacturers would face similar problems. For example, in cooperation with The Technology Consulting Centre, a Ghanaian entrepreneur came up with a paper glue made from cassava starch and alkali extracted from plantain peels. After capturing a large part of the Ghanaian market for glue, the firm reached an agreement to manufacture the product in the Ivory Coast, where cassava and plantains are also abundant.

Latin American firms also have innovated to make use of local raw materials. A Brazilian steel firm has led in the development of a technology to use charcoal instead of coking coal in the steel reduction process. The innovation was designed to reduce the firm's dependence on special metal-grade coal that was not available in Brazil.[4] Similarly, a Mexican firm has developed (with U.S. involvement) an efficient direct reduction technology that uses gas. The Brazilian and Mexican firms are now transferring technology to other developing countries that do not have a local supply of coking coal.

The advantages of firms from developing countries in this kind of innovation appear not to be limited to nations with strict import controls or even to innovations made at home and exported. The long lead times and difficulty in obtaining special inputs from abroad seem to have left their mark on a number of firms even in the open economies of East Asia. For example, when a paint manufacturer from an Asian island joined with a U.S. multinational for the manufacture of paint in a Southeast Asian country, a conflict developed quite early. The U.S. partner had provided a technician whose job was to supervise the chemicals used in the plant. The Asian partner suggested that local minerals could be used; the technician from the United States insisted that they could not. The dispute finally led to the dismissal of the technician and his replacement by a national of the Asian partner's country. Local minerals, after suitable reformulation of the mixtures, proved quite satisfactory and clearly met the tough quality standards demanded by the U.S. firm whose brand name was being used (and jealously protected by the U.S. partner).

Other examples indicate a related but not identical advantage held by the firm that has innovated at home when it has faced a similar problem abroad. The experience of innovating at home seems to provide managers with the flexibility to find substitute materials in other countries, even if those substitutes differ from what the firm uses at home. Thus, an Indian firm had its Indian labs develop processes for its Mauritius subsidiary to use Mauritius coral sand for cement manufacture. An innovative paper manufacturer from one developing country has experimented abroad with local raw materials that are quite different from what the firm used at home. Thus, the firm that has learned to make paper from rice stalks finds it relatively easy to substitute another plant in some other tropical country for imported softwoods from temperate countries. The critical step seems to be the one that carries the firm away from the materials used in the standard technologies available from the industrialized countries.

Innovations designed to use local materials are so desired by other developing countries that firms are occasionally actively courted by foreign governments or firms to provide their know-how. A Philippine firm, for example, owns an apparently successful technology for producing paper from a mixture of pulpwood that contains a high percentage of tropical hardwoods to substitute for pulp from temperate softwoods. Although many other developing countries have, for some time, been searching for ways of using commercially unattractive woods

Local Procurement and Special Products                                    40

from their tropical forests for paper manufacture, it seemed that the
Philippine firm held a lead over many competitors. Although it had
not by 1979 sold its technology or invested in other developing countries,
it had been contacted by representatives of other countries seeking the
know-how.

Although multinationals from advanced countries may, on occasion,
substitute locally available inputs for the inputs to which they are
accustomed, Thai data suggest that foreign investors from developing
countries use local materials much more frequently.[5] Factories in Thailand belonging to parents from other developing countries imported
only 39 percent of their raw materials; subsidiaries of multinationals
from the advanced countries imported 76 percent. Even Thai-owned
manufacturers had large imports: 65 percent of their materials. The
differences among the various kinds of investors could not be explained
by differences in the industry mix.

Although local competitors are likely to face pressures for innovation
similar to those faced by factories belonging to parents from other
developing countries, firms from the richer developing countries benefit
from the advantage that comes with having already faced and dealt
with the problems. Some have already incurred the costs of developing
solutions that can be used directly in poorer countries. Even when the
specific knowledge needed for a certain foreign country has not been
developed, perhaps because of the special nature of local materials,
the firm from a more industrialized developing country has an advantage
over a local firm, since it is likely to have had enough experience with
similar innovations to do the incremental development of new
innovations.

Although multinationals from advanced countries could, and sometimes do, carry out such innovations,[6] there are several reasons why
they do not often do so. First, their personnel are typically experienced
in the markets of the industrialized countries where such innovations
are not necessary. Further, even if the "mind set" of managers were
to be changed, it is not clear that the pressures to adapt would be as
great for the advanced country multinationals. If the multinational faces
less price competition (as this study will suggest is typical), then there
is less pressure on managers to innovate to save money.[7] Moreover,
the multinational from an advanced country is more likely than developing country firms to be manufacturing its inputs in affiliated factories elsewhere. With captive sources at its disposal, the multinational
enterprise as a whole may have lower relevant costs than would a

developing country firm that must obtain inputs abroad from unaffiliated enterprises. For the advanced country multinational, the relevant costs are the marginal costs of additional output from its affiliated plants, while the developing country competitor is likely to have to pay full costs. In addition, the multinational might well have some preference for importing from its affiliates to gain the option of manipulating transfer prices on the materials.[8] It may, for example, want to extract profits from a local partner or escape local exchange controls. The desire on the part of the firm from a developing country may be similar, but it cannot exercise that option if it does not have controlled sources of inputs overseas. Finally, advanced country firms are particularly likely to emphasize brand name (as will be evident later) and thus be concerned with producing a product of very standardized quality. Local inputs, with their varying standards, are likely to pose particular problems for such firms.

## Ethnic Products

Some interesting investments identified in the research were based on another, rather special kind of advantage. These subsidiaries were established primarily to serve a local community that was related to an ethnic group of the investor's home country. Such projects form a small percentage of the total foreign investments of firms from developing countries but nevertheless account for a significant number of the "upstream" investments, those aimed at industrialized countries. For example, a Hong Kong firm bought a building in Sydney to house a Chinese restaurant and newspaper. Indian firms own Indian restaurants in Britain (at least two) and the United States (at least four).[9]

Many of the "ethnic investments" are within the developing countries and include projects such as the Singapore manufacturers that make Chinese biscuits and noodles in Indonesia and the plant owned by an Indian manufacturer to produce gripe water in Kenya.[10] One group of atypical plants in Indonesia belonging to developing country investors has already been mentioned: food processing facilities. Their advantages did not lie in small-scale or labor-intensive production, according to comparisons with plants owned by advanced country investors, but largely in their ability to produce products for the local Chinese community.

The success of firms that produce ethnic products overseas is a simple matter. It reflects an ability of those firms to manufacture and market products that appeal to people whose tastes are well known to the manufacturer. In some cases, the investing firms bring brand names that are familiar to the local community as well as products that are already known. In fact, such firms account for some of the exceptions to the generalizations made later about the unimportance of product differentiation in the marketing strategies of firms from the developing countries.

In contrast to most of the foreign investors discussed thus far in this book, the competitive edge of the producers of ethnic products seems less likely to be in process than in product. Nevertheless, one still wonders whether Kenyans even know the technology of manufacturing Indian gripe water.

**Other Innovations**

Simple generalizations fail to describe all the innovations of multinationals, whether they come from industrialized countries or from developing countries. As a rule, the Europeans innovated to save capital and raw materials, which were scarce in those economies, but consider the strength of German pharmaceutical firms which seems to have arisen in part from the large market created by the German government's early entry into a national health scheme. Firms in the developing countries have also had a rich history of innovations, not just those suggested by small-scale markets and scarce or expensive inputs. Nevertheless, the innovations have usually been in response to special conditions in the home market.

The early innovation of rice equipment in Thailand provides an example of the variety of innovations by firms in developing countries. Although the original plants for the steam milling of rice were established by westerners, by the last quarter of the nineteenth century local Chinese had gained a great deal of strength. First, they bought western mills, initially hiring foreigners to run them. Soon the Chinese-owned firms began to make their own machinery, originally from sketches of British equipment. About 1890, they pioneered a process for producing white rice that was eventually copied by Europeans.[11] The location of innovation, of course, reflects the importance of rice in the diets of Southeast Asia.

# Part VI
# Organization and Location
# of R & D

# [15]

*Economica* **46**, 187–196

## Overseas Research and Development by US-Based Firms

By Edwin Mansfield, David Teece and Anthony Romeo

*University of Pennsylvania, Stanford University, University of Connecticut*

### Introduction

In recent years, the overseas research and development activities of US-based firms have become the focus of controversy. Some observers view such activities with suspicion, since they regard them as a device to "export" R and D jobs, or as a channel through which American technology may be transmitted to actual or potential foreign competitors.[1] Others, particularly the governments of many developing (and some developed) countries, view them as highly desirable activities that will help to stimulate indigenous R and D in these countries. Indeed, the United Nations Group of Eminent Persons recommended that host countries require multinational corporations to contribute towards innovation of appropriate kinds, and to encourage them to do such R and D in their overseas affiliates.[2] Although the amount of controversy in this area might lead one to believe that the nature of existing overseas R and D activities of US-based firms has been studied quite thoroughly, this is far from the case. The unfortunate truth is that economists have devoted little or no attention to even the most basic questions concerning these activities.[3] In this paper, we try to fill part of this gap.

### I. Overseas R and D Expenditures: 1960–1980

How big are the overseas R and D expenditures of US-based firms, now and in the past, and how big do firms expect them to become by 1980? To help answer this question, we constructed a sample of 55 major manufacturing firms, this sample being divided into two parts. The first subsample, composed of 35 firms, included major US-based firms in the chemical, petroleum, electrical equipment, metals and machinery, drugs, glass, food and paper industries. The second subsample, composed of 20 firms, included major manufacturing firms in the southern New England and Middle Atlantic states. Table 1 shows the percentage of R and D done overseas by these firms, during 1960–1974 (for the first subsample) or 1970–1974 (for the second subsample), as well as the estimated value of this percentage in 1980. In each subsample, about 10 per cent of the total amount spent on R and D by these firms was carried out overseas in 1974. Based on the 35-firm subsample, it appears that this percentage grew substantially during the 1960s and early 1970s.[4] Based on the estimates provided by the firms in the sample, this growth will continue, but at a reduced rate, during the rest of the 1970s; by 1980 they estimated that about 12 per cent of their R and D expenditures will be made overseas.

Because of the importance in the innovation process of close communication and cooperation among R and D, marketing, production and top management, Vernon (1974) and others have argued that a firm's R and D activities will tend to be centralized near its headquarters. Why then do these US-based firms spend

188                    ECONOMICA                    [MAY

TABLE 1

PERCENTAGE OF COMPANY-FINANCED R AND D EXPENDITURES CARRIED OUT
OVERSEAS, 1960–1980: 55 FIRMS

|  | 1960* | 1965† | 1970‡ | 1972† | 1974 | 1980§ |
|---|---|---|---|---|---|---|
| 35-firm subsample: | | | | | | |
| Weighted mean | 2 | 6 | 6 | 8 | 10 | 10 |
| Unweighted mean | 2 | 4 | 5 | 7 | 8 | 8 |
| Standard deviation | 3 | 7 | 7 | 8 | 10 | 8 |
| 20-firm subsample: | | | | | | |
| Weighted mean | — | — | 4 | — | 9 | 14 |
| Unweighted mean | — | — | 5 | — | 8 | 11 |
| Standard deviation | — | — | 7 | — | 10 | 14 |

\* Data were not available for 4 firms in the 35-firm subsample.
† Data were not available for 1 firm in the 35-firm subsample.
‡ Data were not available for 1 firm in the 35-firm subsample and 1 firm in the 20-firm subsample.
§ Data were not available for 9 firms in the 35-firm subsample.
*Source*: see Section I.

about 10 per cent of their R and D dollars overseas? There are a variety of possible reasons, including the presence of environmental conditions abroad that cannot easily be matched at home, the desirability of doing R and D aimed at the special design needs of overseas markets, the availability and lower cost of skills and talents that are less readily available or more expensive at home, and the greater opportunity to monitor what is going on in relevant scientific and technical fields abroad. In our sample, practically all of the firms doing R and D overseas say that the principal reason is to respond to special design needs of overseas markets. In their view, there are great advantages in doing R and D of this sort in close contact with the relevant overseas markets and manufacturing units of the firm.

## II. FACTORS INFLUENCING THE PERCENTAGE OF A FIRM'S R AND D EXPENDITURES CARRIED OUT OVERSEAS

What determines the percentage of its R and D that a firm conducts overseas? Given the fact that overseas laboratories seem to be so closely geared to the special design needs of foreign markets (and the firm's overseas plants), we would expect that the percentage of a firm's R and D expenditures carried out overseas would be directly related to the percentage of the firm's sales that is derived from abroad. Firms with relatively small foreign markets would be expected to spend relatively little on overseas R and D. Further, we would expect that the percentage of a firm's R and D expenditures carried out overseas would be more closely related to the percentage of its sales from foreign subsidiaries than to its percentage of sales from exports. This is because much overseas R and D is in support of foreign manufacturing operations.[5]

Holding constant the percentage of a firm's sales that come from abroad, we would expect that the percentage of a firm's R and D expenditures that is carried out overseas would be directly related to the firm's size. Economies of scale require that R and D laboratories be a certain minimum size if they are to be relatively efficient. If it is going to establish an overseas laboratory, the firm must have a big enough prospective market (in the area served by this laboratory) to support a laboratory of minimum economic scale. If the percentage of a firm's sales that comes from abroad is held constant, the probability that this prospective market will be of the requisite size is an increasing function of the absolute size of the firm.

Further, we would expect that, holding constant both the firm's sales and its percentage of sales coming from abroad, there would be inter-industry differences in the percentage of a firm's R and D expenditures carried out overseas. For example, we would expect this percentage to be relatively high in the pharmaceutical industry because some firms, according to industry sources at least, have moved a substantial amount of R and D abroad to avoid Food and Drug Administration regulations. Also, foreign regulations sometimes require that R and D be done locally. Because of these regulatory considerations, as well as other factors discussed below, we might expect the drug firms in our sample to carry out a relatively high percentage of R and D overseas.

In addition, we would expect that, if the firm's sales, its percentage of sales coming from abroad and its industry are held constant, there will be differences over time in the percentage of a firm's R and D carried out overseas, owing to changes in the profitability of locating R and D overseas rather than in the United States (as well as bandwagon effects).[6] In general, during the period covered here, we would expect these effects of time to be positive, since cost differentials and other factors favoured the expansion of overseas R and D.

To test these hypotheses, we carried out two sets of computations. First, we pooled the 1970 and 1974 data for the 35-firm subsample, and regressed each firm's percentage of R and D expenditures carried out overseas on its percentage of sales from abroad, its sales, an industry dummy variable, and a time dummy variable. The results are

$$(1) \quad A_{it} = -1.13 + 0.73T_t + 0.15Q_{it} + 0.004S_{it} + 16.10D_i, \quad (\bar{R}^2 = 0.50;$$
$$\qquad\quad (0.44) \quad (0.34) \quad (1.81) \quad (3.09) \quad (5.41) \qquad n = 51)$$

where $A_{it}$ is the percentage of the $i$th firm's R and D expenditures carried out overseas in year $t$ (1970 or 1974), $T_t$ is a dummy variable that equals 1 if $t$ is 1974 and 0 if $t$ is 1970, $Q_{it}$ is the percentage of the $i$th firm's sales derived from abroad in year $t$, $S_{it}$ is the $i$th firm's sales (in millions of dollars) in year $t$, and $D_i$ is a dummy variable that equals 1 if the $i$th firm is in the drug industry and 0 otherwise.[7] Each regression coefficient's $t$-ratio is given in parentheses.

Second, we pooled the 1970 and 1974 data for the 20-firm subsample, and regressed each firm's percentage of R and D expenditures carried out overseas on the same variables as in equation (1), except that we split the percentage of sales from abroad into two parts—the percentage of sales from foreign subsidiaries, and the percentage of sales from exports—and we redefine the industry dummy to include both chemicals and drugs, not drugs alone.[8] The results are:

$$(2) \quad A_{it} = 2.79 + 4.40T_t + 0.322F_{it} - 0.539E_{it} - 0.00162S_{it} + 4.52C_i,$$
$$\qquad\quad (1.16) \quad (1.91) \quad (4.47) \quad (2.32) \quad (1.13) \quad (1.76)$$
$$\qquad\qquad\qquad\qquad\qquad\qquad\qquad (\bar{R}^2 = 0.54; n = 39)$$

where $F_{it}$ is the percentage of the $i$th firm's sales from foreign subsidiaries in year $t$, $E_{it}$ is the percentage of the $i$th firm's sales from exports in year $t$, and $C_i$ is a dummy variable that equals 1 if the $i$th firm is in the drug or chemical industries and 0 otherwise.

The econometric results generally are in accord with our hypotheses. As expected, equation (1) shows that there is a direct and statistically significant relationship between a firm's percentage of sales derived from abroad and its percentage of R and D expenditures carried out overseas. And when sales derived from abroad are disaggregated in equation (2), a firm's percentage of sales from foreign subsidiaries has a highly significant positive effect on its percentage of R and D expenditures carried out overseas, while its percentage of sales from exports has a significant negative effect, which suggests that these firms' exports may be more R and D-intensive than their domestic sales.[9] With regard to our hypothesis that $A_{it}$ would be directly related to $S_{it}$, the results of equation (1) bear this out, but in equation (2), $S_{it}$ does not have a statistically significant effect (and its regression coefficient has the wrong sign). As expected, most of the industry and time dummies are statistically significant.[10]

### III. OVERSEAS R AND D: MINIMUM ECONOMIC SCALE AND RELATIVE COST

As noted above, many governments, particularly of developing countries, favour the establishment in their nations of overseas R and D laboratories by US-based firms. One factor influencing the practicality of establishing a laboratory of a certain type in a particular overseas location is the extent of economies of scale in such laboratories. If the minimum economic scale for a laboratory of this type is quite large, a firm must be prepared to shift considerable R and D resources abroad if the laboratory is to be competitive.[11] Despite the fact that data concerning the minimum economic scale of R and D laboratories of various types would be of value to many kinds of microeconomic studies, practically no information is available on this score. In this section, we present the estimates (obtained from 27 members of the 35-firm subsample) of the annual R and D expenditures for an overseas laboratory of minimum economic scale. Although these estimates should be treated with caution, they are of considerable interest, since they seem to be the first systematic evidence on this topic.[12]

The results, shown in Table 2, indicate that the minimum economic scale tends to be quite substantial in most industries. On the average, for a single product line it was estimated that the expenditures per year for an R and D facility of minimum economic scale would be about $1 million in pharmaceuticals and glass, about $2 million in electrical equipment and petroleum, and about $5 million in chemicals. However, the minimum economic scale seems to vary considerably, depending on the responsibilities of the laboratory. It is less for a laboratory that performs either research or development than for one that performs both, and less for a laboratory that deals with a single product line than for one that deals with several product lines. For a laboratory that is concerned entirely with minor product changes, the average estimated expenditure per year for an R and D facility of minimum economic scale is only about $500,000 per year—and in some industries it is substantially less. In interpreting the results in Table 2, the dispersion among the estimates is almost as interesting as the averages. The estimates in each industry vary enormously, reflecting the fact that the minimum economic scale of an R and D laboratory depends on the specific type of work to be done, as well as the fact that opinions differ on this score even among experts.[13]

TABLE 2

ESTIMATED ANNUAL R AND D EXPENDITURE FOR OVERSEAS LABORATORY OF MINIMUM ECONOMIC SCALE, 1975: 27 FIRMS ($million)

| Industry* | Single product line | | | | Several product lines | | | |
|---|---|---|---|---|---|---|---|---|
| | Research | Development | Minor product changes | Research and development | Research | Development | Minor product changes | Research and development |
| **Chemicals (n = 7)** | | | | | | | | |
| Mean | 2·42 | 3·27 | 0·72 | 4·57 | 2·50 | 2·46 | 1·39 | 3·31 |
| Range | 1·0–5·0 | 0·1–14·0 | 0·03–2·0 | 0·46–20·0 | 1·5–3·5 | 0·26–6·0 | 0·24–3·5 | 0·16–6·7 |
| **Petroleum (n = 6)** | | | | | | | | |
| Mean | 1·64 | 1·46 | 0·28 | 2·30 | 2·60 | 2·23 | 1·18 | 3·40 |
| Range | 0·25–3·0 | 0·25–3·0 | 0·15–0·50 | 0·40–5·0 | 0·40–5·0 | 0·40–4·5 | 0·25–3·0 | 0·6–7·5 |
| **Drugs (n = 2)** | | | | | | | | |
| Mean | 3·25 | 0·50 | 0·12 | 1·00 | 6·00 | 1·30 | 0·35 | † |
| Range | 1·5–5·0 | 0·5–0·5 | 0·10–0·13 | 0·50–1·5 | 5·0–7·0 | 0·60–2·0 | 0·19–0·50 | † |
| **Electronics and electrical equipment (n = 5)** | | | | | | | | |
| Mean | 1·00 | 1·15 | 0·40 | 2·00 | 2·42 | 3·95 | 0·77 | 6·75 |
| Range | 0·8–1·2 | 0·36–2·0 | 0·20–0·50 | 1·25–2·75 | 1·0–5·0 | 0·54–8·0 | 0·51–1·0 | 1·25–10·0 |
| **Glass (n = 2)** | | | | | | | | |
| Mean | 0·70 | 0·85 | 0·42 | 1·38 | 0·73 | 1·53 | 0·71 | 1·88 |
| Range | 0·1–1·3 | 0·4–1·3 | 0·08–0·75 | 0·50–2·25 | 0·20–1·25 | 0·80–2·25 | 0·16–1·25 | 1·0–2·75 |
| **Total (n = 27)** | | | | | | | | |
| Mean | 1·58 | 1·82 | 0·47 | 3·00 | 2·62 | 2·83 | 1·23 | 4·10 |
| Standard deviation | 1·34 | 2·78 | 0·45 | 4·10 | 1·87 | 2·76 | 1·30 | 3·68 |

* *n* is the number of firms that provided estimates.
† An estimate was obtained from only one firm.
*Source*: see Section I.

According to many observers, one major reason why US-based firms have carried out R and D overseas is that costs have tended to be lower there. However, very little information has been published concerning the extent of this cost differential, and how it has varied over time. To help fill this gap, we obtained data from the 35-firm subsample concerning the ratio of the cost of R and D inputs in Europe, Japan and Canada to those in the United States in 1965, 1970 and 1975.[14] The results, shown in Table 3, indicate that there was a very substantial cost differential in 1965: on the average, the cost of R and D inputs seemed to be about 30 per cent lower in Europe, 20 per cent lower in Canada and 40 per cent lower in Japan than in the United States. And although there was some increase in R and D costs relative to those in the United States during 1965–1970, the cost differential remained quite substantial in 1970.

TABLE 3

MEAN RATIO OF COST OF R AND D INPUTS IN SELECTED OVERSEAS LOCATIONS TO THAT IN THE UNITED STATES, 1965, 1970 AND 1975.*
35-FIRM SUBSAMPLE†

| | Location | | |
| Year | Europe‡ | Japan | Canada |
| --- | --- | --- | --- |
| 1965 | 0·68 | 0·56 | 0·82 |
| 1970 | 0·74 | 0·60 | 0·86 |
| 1975 | 0·93 | 0·90 | 0·96 |

* Note that there are many costs of communication and coordination in a multinational network of laboratories. See Mansfield (1974).
† Usable data were obtained from 19 firms. Many of the rest had no overseas R and D experience.
‡ There are considerable differences within Europe in the level of R and D costs. According to a number of firms in our sample, costs tend to be relatively low in the United Kingdom and relatively high in West Germany.

However, between 1970 and 1975 the situation changed drastically. Owing in part to the depreciation of the dollar relative to other currencies between 1970 and 1975, the cost differential was largely eliminated for many firms. On the average, the cost of R and D inputs was estimated to be about 10 per cent lower in Japan, and about 5 per cent lower in Europe and Canada, than in the United States in 1975. Of course, this helps to explain the fact (noted in Section I) that the percentage of R and D carried out overseas was expected to increase less rapidly between 1974 and 1980 than in the period prior to 1974. Since the cost differential between overseas and domestic R and D was smaller, it is quite understandable that firms would expect this percentage to grow less rapidly than in earlier years.[15]

## IV. OVERSEAS R AND D: NATURE OF WORK AND RELATION TO DOMESTIC R AND D

Some observers, as we have seen, are suspicious of overseas R and D because they fear that it may be a channel through which American technology may "leak out" to foreign competitors. The extent to which such a leakage is likely to occur depends in part on the nature of the work being carried out in the overseas laboratories of US-based firms. For example, if such work is focused largely on the modification and adaptation of products and processes for the local market, there is less need to transfer much of the firm's most sophisticated technology overseas than if the work is focused on major product or process developments intended for a worldwide market. Based on information obtained from 23 firms in our sample, it appears that these firms' overseas R and D activities tend to focus on development rather than research, on product and process improvements rather than on new products and processes, and on relatively short-term, technically safe work.

Specifically, on the average the percentage of overseas R and D going for basic research is about 6 percentage points less than the percentage of domestic R and D going for basic research; the percentage of overseas R and D going for applied research is 10 percentage points less than the percentage of domestic R and D going for applied research; while the percentage of overseas R and D going for development is 16 percentage points greater than the percentage of domestic R and D going for development. Moreover, about three-fourths of these firms' overseas R and D expenditures are aimed at product or process *improvements* and *modifications*, not at entirely new processes or products. This percentage is much higher than for all domestic R and D.

Firms seem to differ considerably in the extent to which they have integrated their overseas R and D with their domestic R and D.[16] Worldwide integration of overseas and domestic R and D exists in almost one-half of the firms (with overseas R and D) in our sample, according to the firms. On the other hand, about one-sixth say that they attempt no such integration, and the rest say that some limited integration is attempted.

Finally, of how much value is overseas R and D to a firm's US operations? Policy-makers are interested in this question because it must be considered in any full evaluation of the effects of overseas R and D (and foreign direct investment) on America's technological position *vis-à-vis* other countries. Unfortunately, practically no evidence exists on this score. To shed a modest amount of light on this question, we obtained estimates from 27 firms in our sample concerning the percentage of their 1975 overseas R and D expenditures with no commercial applicability to their US operations. The results indicate that, on the average, about one-third of these firms' overseas R and D expenditures have no such applicability. Also, we asked each firm to estimate the amount that it would have to spend on R and D in the United States to get results of *equivalent value to its US operations* as a dollar spent overseas. The results, which are only rough, indicate that, on the average, a dollar's worth of overseas R and D seems to result in benefits to these firms' US operations that are equivalent to about 50 cents' worth of R and D carried out in the United States.

## V. CONCLUSIONS

Overseas R and D expenditures by US-based firms topped the billion-dollar mark in the early 1970s. In 1974 they amounted to about one-tenth of total domestic company-funded R and D expenditures, and the firms in our sample reported that they expected them to amount to a larger proportion of their domestic R and D expenditures by 1980.[17] When compared with the total R and D expenditures in various host countries, their size is perhaps even more striking. In the early 1970s about one-half of the industrial R and D performed in Canada and about one-seventh of the industrial R and D performed in the United Kingdom and West Germany was done by US-based firms.[18]

Yet despite the magnitude and importance of these overseas R and D activities, little is known about their purpose, nature or effects. Indeed, the very existence of such activities is ignored in all current econometric studies carried out to estimate the effects of R and D on US productivity growth. Our purpose in this paper has been to present some basic information concerning the size, nature, minimum economic scale and relative cost of overseas R and D. The limitations of these findings should be recognized. In particular, our results pertain to a sample of 55 firms, and some of the data obtained from the firms were necessarily rough. None the less, we believe that these results, although only a first step, shed substantial new light on this topic.

## ACKNOWLEDGMENTS

The work on which this paper is based was supported by a grant to Edwin Mansfield from the Division of Policy Research and Analysis of the National Science Foundation. Of course, the views expressed here are not necessarily those of the Foundation. We are grateful to the more than 50 firms that provided us with data concerning their overseas R and D activities. Some of the results were presented in papers given by Mansfield at Johns Hopkins, Vanderbilt and Yale Universities, and at the National Science Foundation, as well as the 1978 annual meeting of the American Economic Association.

## NOTES

[1] For discussion of this point of view, see David (1974) and Conference Board (1976).

[2] United Nations (1974). *The Impact of Multinational Corporations on Development and on International Relations.* New York, p. 70.

[3] Caves (1974), Hufbauer (1974), Mansfield (1974) and Stobaugh (1974) have pointed out the need for work concerning this and related aspects of international technology transfer. For some interesting case studies, see Ronstadt (1975). Also, see Mansfield, Romeo and Wagner (1979) for some related findings regarding international technology transfer.

[4] The Conference Board (1976) has estimated the total overseas R and D expenditure of US-based multinational firms in 1971–1973. According to its estimates, overseas R and D constituted about 9–10 per cent of total R and D expenditures carried out by US firms during these years. This agrees quite well with our results for 1972 and 1974. The proportion of firms in our sample with no overseas R and D is somewhat lower than that reported by the Conference Board for firms of comparable size, but this may be due to different industry mix, the later year, or sampling error. The US Department of Commerce (undated) has estimated the total overseas R and D expenditure of US firms in 1966. According to its figures, overseas R and D constituted about 7 per cent of all R and D expenditures carried out by US firms in 1966 (see Conference Board, 1976). This agrees reasonably well with our result for 1965. In 1978 the National Science Foundation published data for 1976 which indicated that overseas R and D constituted about 7 per cent of all R and D expenditures by US manufacturing firms.

[5] Suppose that a firm's desired R and D expenditures in a given year equal

$$R = a_u S_u + a_f S_f + a_e S_e$$

where $S_e$ is its export sales during the relevant year, $S_f$ is its sales through foreign subsidiaries, $S_u$ is its sales from domestic plants to domestic customers, $a_u$ is the proportion of sales to domestic customers that it wants to devote to R and D, $a_f$ is the proportion of sales through foreign subsidiaries that it wants to devote to R and D, and $a_e$ is the proportion of export sales that it wants to devote to R and D. If only the R and D in support of foreign subsidiaries is done overseas, it follows that the proportion of its R and D expenditures carried out overseas equals

$$P = \frac{a_f F}{a_u U + a_f F + a_e E}$$

where $F$ is the proportion of its sales from foreign subsidiaries. $U$ is the proportion of its sales to domestic customers, and $E$ is the proportion of its sales that are exports. Under these circumstances, it can be shown that $\partial p/\partial F$ is always positive, but whether or not $\partial p/\partial E$ is positive depends on whether or not $a_u > a_e$. Of course, this model is a polar case, but it illustrates the point in the text.

[6] In terms of the highly simplified model in n. 5, the $a$'s are a function of time. (Also, as indicated previously in the text, they are a function of the firm's size.)

[7] Other industry dummies were tried in equation (1), but $D_i$ was the only one that was statistically significant. The reason why $n$ is less than 70 is that data could not be obtained concerning the percentage of sales from abroad for all firms in both years.

[8] The reason for this redefinition is that none of the firms in this subsample is really an ethical drug fim. (There are several such firms in the other subsample.) The closest we could come to ethical drugs is the chemical firms, some of which do some work in the drug area (broadly defined).

[9] This result concerning $E_{it}$ would be expected if $a_e > a_u$ in n. 5, and if the extremely simple model given there were valid. However, although it may be a reasonable approximation to regard some firms' overseas R and D as being entirely in support of foreign subsidiaries, this is far from the case in other firms.

[10] The industry dummy is much larger and more highly significant in equation (1) than in equation (2) because, as pointed out in n. 8, none of the firms in equation (2) is really an ethical drug firm. Because of sampling variation, the estimate of $D_i$ in equation (1) is probably too large. One of the drug firms in our sample carried out an unusually large percentage of its R and D overseas.

[11] By minimum economic scale we mean the smallest scale that realizes all, or practically all, of the relevant economies of scale.

[12] Freeman *et al.* (1965) have presented some relevant data concerning the electrical equipment industry. Eight members of the 35-firm subsample could not provide estimates, sometimes because they had no experience on which to base such estimates.

[13] These figures help to explain why, holding other factors constant, smaller firms in equation (1) tend to carry on a smaller percentage of their R and D overseas than bigger firms. But they should not be interpreted as saying that smaller firms are squeezed out completely. The estimates in each industry vary enormously. In most industries, at least some of the respondents felt that research and development could be carried out effectively with an annual budget of $500,000, and that minor product changes could be carried out with one of about $100,000. Although these levels of expenditure are hardly trivial, they are within the reach of many firms other than the billion-dollar giants.

Needless to say, these results in no way contradict the finding by many economists that small firms and independent inventors continue to play an important role in the inventive process. Their contribution is frequently in the earlier stages of the inventive process, where the costs are relatively low. Further, according to some observers, costs tend to be lower in smaller organizations, and the figures in Table 2 reflect the perceptions of large firms. For some relevant discussion, see Mansfield *et al.* (1977).

[14] The relative cost of R and D inputs is the ratio of the annual cost of hiring an R and D scientist or engineer (together with the complementary amount of other inputs) in various overseas locations to do the sort of work carried out there to the annual cost of hiring a comparable R and D scientist or engineer (together with the complementary amount of other inputs) to do the same sort of work in the United States. Each firm was asked to estimate this ratio for each year. Many of the estimates were based on studies the firms seem to have carried out in recent years on this topic.

[15] If very significant differences exist between the productivity of US and overseas R and D personnel, they may offset the observed differences in the relative costs of inputs. About 80 per cent of the firms in our sample regarded the productivity of their R and D personnel in Canada, Europe and Japan to be no lower than those in the United States. Thus, this factor cannot offset the observed difference in the relative cost of R and D inputs in the great majority of firms in our sample.

[16] By integration, we mean that the firm's worldwide R and D is viewed as a whole, and laboratories are given worldwide missions, if this seems desirable.

[17] In early 1977, the United States Treasury put into effect a new regulation (1.861-8) that, according to some observers, may increase the amount of R and D done overseas by US-based firms. Since the forecasts in Table 1 were made before this new regulation was announced, they do not take this factor into account. Also, they do not take account of recent changes in exchange rates, which may have tended to discourage overseas R and D.

[18] See Conference Board (1976, p. 86).

## REFERENCES

CAVES, R. (1974). Effect of international technology transfers on the U.S. economy. *The Effects of International Technology Transfers on U.S. Economy*, Washington, DC: National Science Foundation.

CONFERENCE BOARD (1976). *Overseas Research and Development by U.S. Multinationals, 1966– 1975*. New York: Conference Board.

DAVID, E. (1974). Technology export and national goals. *Research Management*, **17,** 12–16.

FREEMAN, C., HARLOW, C. and FULLER, J. (1965). Research and development in electronic capital goods. *National Institute Economic Review*, **34,** 40–91.

HUFBAUER, G. (1974). Technology transfers and the American economy. In *The Effects of International Technology Transfers on U.S. Economy*. Washington, DC: National Science Foundation.

MANSFIELD, E. (1974). Technology and technological change. In *Economic Analysis and the Multinational Enterprise*, (J. Dunning, ed.). London: George Allen and Unwin.

—— *et al.* (1977). *The Production and Application of New Industrial Technology*. New York: W. W. Norton.

——, ROMEO, A. and WAGNER, S. (1979). Foreign trade and U.S. research and development. *Review of Economics and Statistics*, forthcoming.

RONSTADT, R. (1975). R and D abroad: the creation and evolution of foreign R and D activities of U.S.-based multinational enterprises. Unpublished DBA thesis, Harvard University.

STOBAUGH, R. (1974). A summary and assessment of research findings on U.S. international transactions involving technology transfers. *The Effects of International Technology Transfers on U.S. Economy*. Washington, DC: National Science Foundation.

US DEPARTMENT OF COMMERCE (undated). *U. S. Direct Investments Abroad, 1966*, Part II. Washington, DC: US Government Printing Office.

VERNON, R. (1974). The location of economic activity. In *Economic Analysis and the Multinational Enterprise* (J. Dunning, ed.). London: George Allen and Unwin.

# [16]

## ORGANIZATION AND EVOLUTION OF FOREIGN R & D IN SWEDISH MULTINATIONALS

BY

LARS HÅKANSON*

## Introduction

Superior, firm-specific technology confers competitive advantages that facilitate and induce the penetration of foreign markets through exports and local production (Hymer 1960/1976; Caves 1971). As developed in the 'oligopolistic theory of foreign direct investment', this thesis is certainly corroborated in the history of the large corporations that today dominate the Swedish industrial economy. Many of these companies were founded to pursue and exploit unique technical capabilities, based on domestic inventions and development of imported technology.

Although sheer size and geographical diversification may in time create new types of competitive advantages, most multinationals remain dependent on an efficient supply of new technology to maintain competitive strength. Research and development (R & D) are usually thought to be a principal means by which firms create new technical capabilities and commercial opportunities. As a growing literature testifies, the manner in which multinationals organize and perform the task of technological renewal is a matter of considerable interest not only to corporate planners, but also to policy-makers in home and host countries.

Of course, new technology can only in part be generated internally. An important purpose of R & D is to maintain a sufficient 'technological level' in order to quickly detect and respond to technical changes in the environment. The relative emphasis given to internally generated and externally acquired technology, i.e. 'technologi-

cal strategies' (Freeman 1974: 255 ff, Thomas 1975), varies greatly between firms and industries. This diversity is reflected in the amount, nature and organization of R & D in different firms and environments.

During recent years, the exploration of such differences and their determinants has come to include the question of the *location* of R & D facilities in multinational corporations, especially R & D in foreign subsidiaries. Unfortunately, empirical data are patchy and most available analyses are based on American multinationals, whose conditions and behaviour may differ from those of corporations with headquarters in smaller countries.

In a study of Canadian foreign investors, Cordell (1973) found that increasing shares of R & D tended to be transferred to the most 'active' market area—the United States. He suggests that the situation for Swedish firms vis-à-vis the European Common Market may be similar to that of Canadian firms vis-à-vis the United States, and that the following 'iron law' might hold:

> When a company in a relatively smaller country expands its international operations into a significantly larger market it finds, over time, that it pays to locate not only production but support and managerial functions in the larger offshore market area. (Cordell 1973: 26)

This paper explores the merits and implications of this hypothesis, as applied to R & D in Swedish multinationals. Following a brief discussion of the economic significance of R & D in foreign subsidiaries, a number of theoretical propositions emerging from the literature are examined in light of a recent Swedish study (Håkanson 1980).

* Dr. Lars Håkanson, Dept. of Geography and Institute of International Business, Stockholm School of Economics, Box 6501, S-113 83 Stockholm, Sweden.

HÅKANSON

## The economic significande of R & D in foreign subsidiaries

Multinational corporations perform and control a major share of world industrial R & D.

In 1978, some 70 per cent of total R & D in Swedish industry were performed by manufacturing groups with production abroad, companies with only domestic manufacturing and foreign-owned subsidiaries accounted for 25 and 5 per cent, respectively. Thus, multinational corporations control roughly three quarters of Swedish industrial R & D.

> The picture hardly changes if a more restrictive definition of multinationality is employed. In 1975, the 20 largest Swedish multinationals (as measured by employment abroad) alone accounted for around 60 per cent of industrial R & D costs (SCB 1977: 9 f). Private industrial R & D, in turn, account for close to two thirds of total scientific and technical R & D in Sweden (SCB 1979).

In view of such figures – although the Swedish case is somewhat on the extreme side – Government concern over the technical dominance exercised by multinational corporations is hardly surprising, especially at a time when international recession and structural change make technical progress seem the panacea of economic problems. The particular concern with the location of R & D, viz. R & D in foreign subsidiaries, rests on a number of more or less well founded fears, hopes and assumptions.

## R & D in technology transfer

Technical innovations are characterized by the context and purpose for which they were originally developed. Only rarely will it be possible, with retained efficiency, to apply new technologies in new contexts and for new purposes without some degree of modification. Development and adaptation are integral parts of the transfer process (Bradbury 1978).

Successful technology transfer enhances the skills and capacity of the receiving unit. The characteristics of the transfer process varies with the *types* of skill and capacity being acquired or augmented. On this basis, three 'types' or 'stages' of technology transfer may be distinguished:

First, an elementary but economically very significant transfer of technology takes place through international trade in capital goods, many of which 'embody' new technologies that a buyer may immediately utilize. Such transfer is often aided by training programs and service facilities provided by the seller. A second stage in the transfer process entails the capacity to produce a new product, or to utilize a new process. Characteristically, the requisite skills and knowledge can only imperfectly be conveyed by blueprints, manuals and other easily transferable documents, but must be supplemented by personal communication, demonstration and 'learning-by-doing'. Moreover, successful application often requires adaptations to local conditions, such as smaller scale of production, local market characteristics or the price and quality of available inputs. Such activities, if performed locally, may, in time, lead to an independent indigenous capacity for development and innovation, the third stage of the transfer process.

Conceivably, foreign R & D units may be instrumental at all three stages. However, the economic significance of their activitites differs, depending on the types of transfer in which they are involved. Whereas development associated with the introduction of new products in foreign customer industries may be of mutual benefit to home and host countries, conflicts of interest – real or imagined – may arise from the transfer of production technologies and the build up of innovative capacity in foreign subsidiaries. Specifically, such developments may be associated with diversion of investment, production capacity, employment and exports from home to host countries. However, the functional interdependencies and locational linkages between marketing, production and R & D in multinational corporations are complex, and the assessment of net costs and benefits is still a matter of controversy.

## The organization of multinational R & D

The work performed by industrial R & D departments includes a wide range of activities, from basic research without clearly specified applications to more or less 'routine' development in support of on-going production. In small and medium-sized corporations, and corporations active in technologically stable industries, all R & D-related functions are usually performed in one central department. With growth, diversifi-

48

cation and geographical extension the amount and heterogenity of R & D increase, inducing the organizational differentiation of such functions. The location and organizational status of specialized R & D units can be adapted to their specific requirements in terms of control, coordination and contact linkages. Hence, corporations often find it advantageous to decentralize R & D along product lines and/or the 'level of technology' (Harmann & Stock 1976: 331 ff., Terpstra 1977).

In diversified firms, organization of R & D by product lines may be motivated by the heterogenity of the technologies employed, but may also facilitate interaction with production and marketing. Moreover, such decentralization is often a logical consequence of a (product) divisional structure and the allocation of profit responsibility to divisional management. Above and within product divisions, functional characteristics of R & D provide a further basis for differentiation, roughly corresponding to the 'ideal phases' of the 'R & D cycle', i.e. basic research, applied research, development and adaptation (Figure 1).

Of course, an ideal typology of this kind only very crudely captures the complexity of the actual phenomenon. In reality, the transition between the various stages is apt to be fluid. Moreover, other differentiating principles, such as organization by scientific discipline, process type or individual projects, frequently supplement (and sometimes supersede) the functional division of R & D (Schwetlick 1973: 115 ff).

However, functional specialization of R & D does seem to coincide with several organizationally relevant variables, e.g the area of application of R & D results, the economic significance of costs and potential returns as well as the interrelationship with other corporate functions. Moreover, the locational influences and orientation of functionally specialized R & D units differ (Malecki 1980).

## The locational evolution of multinational R & D

The R & D activities of multinational corporations have typically evolved from the technical departments of the mother companies. Hence, most R & D is performed in the vicinity of the corporate head office and major producing units in the country of origin (Pavitt 1971, Mansfield 1974, Creamer 1976). This tendency is reinforced by the need for prompt and frequent contacts with officials in other functional areas, promoting the efficiency of R & D and strengthening top management control. Typically, such contacts involve the communication of unstructured information and are associated with negotiations, persuasion, common problem solving etc. Since direct personal contacts are usually required, it may be advantageous to geographically concentrate the officials involved. Intra-organizational contact patterns, in combination with the historical, social and economic linkages that tie head offices to their original locations, thus account for the development of corporate 'core areas' and the geographical concentration of 'high-order', non-routine corporate functions (Ahnström 1973, Vernon 1974, Mansfield 1974, McNee 1974).

However, in the process of growth and internationalization, internal as well as external forces induce corporations to geographically dis-

Figure 1. Functional characteristics of R & D

| R & D Function | Time Horizon | R & D Focus | Area of Application | Dominating Functional Linkages |
|---|---|---|---|---|
| Technical support/ technology transfer | Short/imme- diate range | Adaption | National/ plant specific | Production |
| Development | Medium range | Product improvement | Regional/ market specific | Marketing |
| Development applied research | Medium/long range | New product development | Global/ product specific | Production/ marketing |
| Basic research | Long range | New texhnicla capabilities | Global/firm specific | External scientific communities |

perse some of their R & D, also to foreign countries. As a rule, locational decentralization is accompanied by organizational and functional specialization, the nature of which determines the size and locational orientation of R & D facilities. The functional characteristics of R & D units located abroad reflect, in turn, the motives and forces that induce the establishment of such units.

## Technical support laboratories

The most common motive for setting up R & D facilitites abroad is to help transfer technology from the parent to foreign subsidiaries (Ronstadt 1978, Cordell 1973).

The task of such units is to adapt products and processes to local conditions, and to perform similar services to local customers. Initially, such technical service functions are usually performed by the parent organization. However, especially in the case of unstandardized technology, the amount and complexity of technical service functions are often sufficient to motivate the creation of the corresponding technical capacity abroad.

Since the bulk of technical service tasks is specific to particular plants, markets and customers, 'transfer technology units' are commonly administratively and locationally linked to manucaturing affiliates on major markets (Ronstadt 1977). However, technical support units are sometimes set up to serve a number of subsidiaries over a wider geographical area, in effect operating as an extension of the technical service departments of the mother company.

Transfer technology units probably make up the majority of all foreign R & D establishments and account for a significant share of the total R & D that multinationals perform in host countries. However, far from all host country R & D is directed to the adaptation of products and processes to foreign market conditions.

## Product development abroad

A survey comprising 45 American multinationals indicated that, on average, 30 per cent of the R & D costs incurred abroad referred to applied research, double the corresponding share of the parent companies (Creamer 1976). Similarly, data collected in a survey of Swedish manufacturing subsidiaries abroad indicate that foreign R & D include a considerable amount of advanced development and research. Close to half of the R

& D costs incurred abroad referred to improvements of existing products and processes, but development of new products and processes and long-range research accounted for 40 and 10 per cent, respectively. (The percentage distribution is in fact similar to that of domestic industry).

The establishment of more advanced development abroad is a response to a variety of factors and considerations. They include the wish to employ foreign technical expertise, to monitor the technical activities of foreign competitors, and, occassionally, to productively utilize profits tied in foreign subsidiaries. In certain industries, climate and other environmental conditions may be important, in others, the nature of local demand. In general terms, however, capacity for new product development is a sequel to the spontaneous growth and evolution of foreign subsidiaries.

Foreign manufacturing units, originally established as mere market outlets, in time acquire their own technical, managerial and marketing expertise. In consequence, their bargaining power in internal negotiations, e.g. regarding the allocation of R & D investments, will tend to increase. Hence, technical support laboratories tend to expand and evolve into more advanced R & D, i.e. development of new and improved products for foreign markets. Furthermore, the accumulated experience of R & D, production and marketing may create a 'unique' technical capability within the group, sometimes formally recognized by the allocation of global development responsibility for a certain line of production (Ronstadt 1978).

Of course, foreign R & D units are frequently acquired in the course of take-overs and mergers. The decision whether to disband or retain and possibly expand such units depends on the degree to which their competence and activities duplicate those of existing laboratories. As a rule, the acquisition of foreign R & D facilities is incidental to other objectives, such as improving market access or increasing production capacity. Sometimes, however, foreign acquisitions are a means to diversify production and strengthen the technical basis of the corporation. In either case, the considerations governing such decisions are likely to be similar to those concerning the establishment and expansion of R & D in existing subsidiaries.

The evolution of foreign R & D units along the lines suggested above may entail changes in their

50

ORGANIZATION AND EVOLUTION OF FOREIGN R & D

organizational status. However, development laboratories usually remain locationally linked to major manufacturing plants. In this respect they differ from R & D units engaged in long range research and development work not related to existing product lines.

*Research centers*
Although basic and applied research account only for a small portion of total industry R & D, some large multinationals devote substantial resources to such activities. As a rule, research laboratories are located in the home country, but some corporations — including some large Swedish ones — have established 'research centers' also at foreign locations.

The functional properties and organizational status of corporate research centers limit their interaction with other corporate functions. Indeed, it may often be an advantage to limit such interaction, less research laboratories become enmeshed in day-to-day technical problems. Their location is therefore relatively independent of other corporate units. Instead, locations can be selected that permit easy access to universities and other research institutions, from which staff is recruited and with which frequent contacts are maintained. The principal motive for setting up research in foreign countries is to facilitate the recruitment of foreign specialists and to establish a contact network with foreign research organizations. A specific factor in the case of Swedish multinationals is the domestic income tax structure that makes it virtually impossible to offer internationally competitive net salaries to highly qualified technical and scientific expertise.

## International division of labour and R & D coordination

Although R & D may be "the last activity of the firm to be organized on an international basis" (Terpstra 1977:26), whether through the establishment and evolution of technology transfer units or as an incidental consequence of foreign acquisitions, international growth is generally accompanied by increasing amounts of R & D at foreign locations.

As the number of foreign R & D units increases, so does the need to coordinate their activities. Such coordination may be necessary to avoid duplication of effort and uneconomical

product differentiation, but may also bring scale economies and other synergetic advantages (Granstrand & Fernlund 1978, Terpstra 1977).

However, as pointed out by Fischer and Behrman (1979:29), "... the introduction of geographic distance, market variations, and language and cultural differences of personnel" amplify the problems of coordination and control. In addition, the controversial issue of parent-subsidiary coordination "... excacerbates the original dilemma of autonomy-control/centralization-decentralization associated with R & D."

As always, the potential benefits of coordination must be weighed against the costs of creating and managing appropriate information and control systems. However, by utilizing modern communication technologies and designing suitable organizational structures, it may be possible to realize an efficient balance between geographic decentralization and central coordination (Papo 1971, Potter 1971, Hanson & Van Rumker 1971, Granstrand & Fernlund 1978).

Typically, the allocation of R & D tasks to foreign subsidiaries reflects international specialization and rationalization of production. Specialized manufacturing and R & D units occur in diversified corporations, reflecting organizational decentralization along product lines. However, such units are found also in specialized manufacturing groups, where concentration of production of certain models or components to specialized units permits the exploitation of scale economies not only in production but also in other functional areas, e.g. purchasing, design and development. In Swedish multinationals, this process has been facilitated by the liberalization of trade, especially the establishment of free trade within the European Communities. Subsidiaries, originally established to serve local national markets have been able to serve larger market areas, inducing specialization and concentration. Moreover, these tendencies accede to host country political demands for local production and exports. (Cf SCB 1980:15 ff.)

On the one hand, international division of labour may entail and facilitate the geographic decentralization of R & D; on the other, it tends to strengthen the interdependencies between subsidiaries in different countries, increasing the need for central control and coordination and limiting local autonomy (Fischer & Behrman 1979).

HÅKANSON

## Foreign R & D in Swedish multinationals

*Aggregate trends*
In 1978, some 40 Swedish multinationals carried out R & D in foreign countries – three times the number in 1965. On average, foreign subsidiaries accounted for 16 per cent of corporate R & D, but shares fluctuated widely between industries and firms. In the machinery industry, foreign affiliates accounted for close to 40 per cent, and this sector alone accounted for nearly half of all foreign R & D. The total costs of R & D outside Sweden are estimated at 500 million kronor, 11 per cent of total domestic R & D in industry.

Between 1965 and 1978, the R & D costs of Swedish foreign subsidiaries increased by an annual average of 19 per cent. Until the middle of the 1970's, the growth rate abroad was considerably higher than in Sweden. During 1974–78, following the sale of a number of R & D intensive subsidiaries to foreign interests, the calculated growth rate declined to that of the domestic average. Similarly, during the first half of the 1970's foreign R & D costs increased more rapidly than the value of foreign production, the ratio increasing from 0.7 to 1.0 per cent, a level maintained in 1978.

However, the comparisons may be confounded to the extent that the movements of current exchange rates do not accurately reflect changes in the costs of R & D in different countries. The result of a recent OECD study (1979) suggests that during the first part of the 1970's – with the exception of the United Kingdom – cost levels for R & D in major industrial countries have tended to converge to the level of traditionally high cost countries, such as the United States and Sweden. By implication, the increasing share of foreign R & D costs in Swedish firms may only partially reflect a corresponding shift in the volume of R & D.

Average R & D intensity in the foreign subsidiary sector is considerably lower than in domestic industry. In 1974, the differences were the least in the pulp and paper, machinery and transportation industries. Subsidiaries in these industries are also characterized by high export propensities, indicating the connection between specialization of production and foreign R & D.

Virtually all foreign R & D is found in industrialized countries. In 1978, Western Europe accounted for nearly three quarters, United States and Canada for one fifth and other industrialized countries (Australia, New Zeeland and South

Africa) for most of the remainder. Moreover, in these areas R & D intensity and shares of R & D devoted to long range research and development of new products and processes are considerably higher than in the rest of the world.

*Determinants of foreign R & D*
As quoted above, aggregate data give little support to the notion of an "inexorable 'iron law'" forcing the transfer of R & D from Sweden to larger markets abroad. However, aggregate data frequently conceal significant trends and differences at the level of individual industries and corporations.

Specifically, prior expectations suggest that the propensity to perform R & D abroad increases with successive stages of corporate growth and development. Corporations with large R & D employment, wide geographic spread and long history of operations in foreign markets are more likely to allocate R & D to foreign units, than are smaller firms during the initial stages of growth and internationalization.

In addition, foreign R & D shares may be related to the growth strategies of individual corporations, i.e. the relative emphasis of foreign expansion and domestic diversification. On the one hand, a high share of foreign production is likely to be associated with strong internal demands and external pressures to locate R & D abroad; on the other, diversified production may facilitate the allocation of R & D and manufacturing to specialized units.

The absence of suitable time series renders the direct analysis of corporate trends impossible. Instead, the following analysis relies on cross-sectional data relating to some 60 Swedish foreign investors in 1978. The data were collected by the Industrial Institute for Social and Economic Research in a survey of all Swedish corporations with more than 50 employees, having (majority-owned) manufacturing subsidiaries abroad. (Cf. Swedenborg 1979.) The corporations included in the analysis represent roughly 40 per cent of the population by numbers, but account for more than 90 per cent of production and employment. Hence, the sample is strongly biased towards larger corporations. However, it includes a sufficient number of smaller firms to allow a meaningful analysis.

*Foreign R & D in 'types' of corporations*
As a first step in the analysis, corporations were classified along three dimensions: 'growth

ORGANIZATION AND EVOLUTION OF FOREIGN R & D

stage', degree of internationalization and diversification. 'Growth stage' is, of course, closely related to size, but also to the geographical extension of corporate activities. Four measures were used: number of employees, corporate sales, and the number of sales and manufacturing subsidiaries abroad. (For details, see Håkanson 1980: 250 ff.) The so called Herfindahl's index was computed as a quantitative measure of diversification (cf. Swedenborg 1979: 98 f). Three indices of internationalization were used: domestic share of sales and employment and foreign subsidiaries' share of production. By means of principal component analysis and computation of factor scores, a composite measure of each of the three underlying dimensions was devised (Table 1).

Following visual inspection of a graphic plot of observations, factor scores close to zero were—somewhat arbitrarily—selected as basis for dichotomization. Six classes of corporations were distinguished (Table 2).

Table 2. Classification of Swedish mul'inationals.

| | | 'Late growth stage' (40) Diversification | | 'Early growth stage' (29) Diversification | |
|---|---|---|---|---|---|
| | | Low | High | Low | High |
| Internationalization | Low | MNF1 (5) | MNF4 (8) | | MNF6 (10) |
| | | | | MNF5 (19) | |
| | High | MNF2 (6) | MNF3 (21) | | |

(40) = number of observations

Table 1. Swedish multinationals: correlation of factor scores and manifest classification variables.

| Classification variables | Factor 1 | Factor 2 | Factor 3 |
|---|---|---|---|
| No. of foreign manufacturing subsidiaries | 0.781 | 0.034 | 0.135 |
| No. of foreign sales subsidiaries | 0.759 | 0.136 | −0.011 |
| Corporate sales | 0.759 | 0.528 | −0.280 |
| Employment | 0.809 | 0.433 | −0.320 |
| Domestic share of sales (per cent) | −0.654 | 0.444 | −0.026 |
| Foreign share of production (per cent) | 0.701 | −0.586 | 0.029 |
| Domestic share of employment (per cent) | −0.613 | 0.601 | 0.116 |
| Degree of diversification | 0.564 | 0.334 | 0.724 |
| Eigenvalue | 4.032 | 1.502 | 0.740 |
| Share (per cent) | 50.4 | 18.8 | 9.3 |
| Cumulative share (per cent) | 50.4 | 69.2 | 78.4 |

Factor 1 was taken as a measure of size and 'stage of growth'. It is strongly correlated with the number of foreign subsidiaries, corporate sales and employment. However, the measure is correlated also with diversification and internationalization. Factor 2 indicates (with reversed sign) the degree of internationalization. Factor 3 is strongly correlated only with diversification.

Production and R & D are heavily concentrated to a small number of industrial giants. Six multinational groups, characterized by moderate levels of diversification and internationalization (MNF1), account for more than 40 per cent of employment and for more than half of the R & D costs (Table 3). Diversified, highly internationalized corporations (MNF3) account for one third of overall R & D, but for almost half of that performed abroad. The smaller corporations in the sample (MNF5 + MNF6) account for only insignificant shares of R & D in Sweden as well as abroad.

Table 3. R & D in six groups of Swedish multinationals.

| Group | No. of corporations | Share of R & D costs (%) Total | In Sweden | Abroad |
|---|---|---|---|---|
| MNF1 | 5 | 51.0 | 55.6 | 23.6 |
| MNF2 | 6 | 5.8 | 2.7 | 23.7 |
| MNF3 | 19 | 34.9 | 32.6 | 48.7 |
| MNF4 | 7 | 6.3 | 7.0 | 2.1 |
| MNF5 | 18 | 1.1 | 1.0 | 1.8 |
| MNF6 | 9 | 1.0 | 1.1 | 0.2 |
| Total | 64 | 100.0 | 100.0 | 100.0 |

As expected, the relative share of foreign R & D is related to the degree of internationalization (Table 4). The average for the domestically oriented large corporations (MNF1 + MNF4), 6.2 per cent, is significantly lower than that of the

53

HÅKANSON

**Table 4.** Foreign R & D in six groups of Swedish multinationals.

| Group | No. of corpora-tions | Share of R & D costs incurred abroad (%) x̄ | s | R & D intensity abroad[a] x̄ | s |
|---|---|---|---|---|---|
| MNF1 | 5 | 9.1 | 9.9 | 0.5 | 0.6 |
| MNF2 | 6 | 25.8 | 30.9 | 0.9 | 0.9 |
| MNF3 | 18 | 19.4 | 17.7 | 1.1 | 1.3 |
| MNF4 | 6 | 3.8 | 3.5 | 0.4 | 0.4 |
| MNF5 | 12 | 5.2 | 12.1 | 0.2 | 0.3 |
| MNF6 | 9 | 4.2 | 7.2 | 0.9[b] | 2.2[b] |
| Total | 56 | 12.0 | 17.7 | 0.7[c] | 1.2[c] |

x̄ = average, by corporation
s = standard deviation

a) R & D costs incurred abroad as percentage of foreign production
b) 8 corporations
c) 55 corporations

internationalized ones (MNF2 + MNF3), 21.0 per cent. (Throughout, significance was computed by Welch approximate t-test with a significance level of five per cent.) However, no significant differences can be detected between diversified and more specialized firms.

A similar pattern appears when foreign R & D costs are related to the value of foreign production. R & D intensity abroad is higher in the large internationalized firms (MNF2 + MNF3) than in the domestically oriented ones (MNF1 + MNF4), but does not appear to be influenced by diversification.

The data indicate remarkably small differences between large corporations at an advanced stage of growth (MNF1 – MNF4) and the smaller ones (MNF5 + MNF6). The former's average R & D intensity abroad is almost double that of the latter, but the difference is not statistically significant. However, one corporation with foreign R & D costs in the order of 500 000 kronor accounts for the high average (and standard deviation) in group MNF6. If this corporation is excluded, average R & D intensity abroad is almost six times higher in the large corporations, and the difference significant at 0.5 per cent.

*Regression analysis*
The analysis reported above generally supports the argument that foreign R & D tends to in-

crease with size and corporate development, especially the degree to which expansion has occurred abroad. However, only weak statistical associations could be detected due to the small number of observations and the large variances within each group of corporations. In order to further explore the determinants of foreign R & D, the hypotheses outlined above where combined in the following formalized model:

$$Y = f(S, I, D, R_T, R_N \ldots) \qquad (1)$$

The dependent variable (Y) denotes the relative amount of R & D performed abroad. It is assumed to be positively related to corporate size/ stage of development (S), to the degree of internationalization (I) and diversification (D). Since the overall amount of R & D work, especially work not directly related to existing production, determines the feasibility of organizational and locational decentralization, foreign R & D are assumed to be positively associated with the absolute amount of R & D performed by the corporation ($R_T$), particularly to that share which is devoted to new product development ($R_N$).

Foreign share of R & D (Y) was measured by the relative proportion of R & D costs incurred abroad. For the independent variables, two alternative specifications were utilized. In the first case, the three first independent variables (S, I, and D) were measured by the corresponding (mutually uncorrelated) latent variables defined in the principal component analysis (Factor 1, ... 3; cf. Table 1). In the second case, manifest variables were utilized, i. e. employment, foreign share of production and degree of diversification according to Herfindahl's index. The amount of R & D ($R_T$) was measured by total R & D costs, and the share of new development ($R_N$) by the corresponding costs for development of new products and processes.

In the absence of clear hypotheses as to the relevant form of the assumed relationships, simple additive association was tested by means of stepwise linear regression (OLS), yielding the following estimates:

*Regression no 1*
No. of observations: 47    $R^2 = 0.41$    F = 10.34

$Y = 5,36 + 10.760^{+++}S - 4,274^{+}D + 0.207^{++}R_N$
      (4.47)           (1.72)          (2.50)

ORGANIZATION AND EVOLUTION OF FOREIGN R & D

where S   = FACTOR1 ('stage of corporate development')

D   = FACTOR2 ('diversification')

$R_N$ = R & D costs relating to new products and processes

*Regression no 2*

No. of observations 47   $R^2 = 0.46$   F = 12.68

$Y = -5.70 + 0.001^{+++}S + 21.74^{++}I + 0.156^{++} R_N$
$\phantom{Y = -5.70 +} (3.44) \phantom{S +} (2.09) \phantom{I +} (2.07)$

where S   = number of employees

I   = foreign share of corporate produc- ·tion

$R_N$ = R & D costs relating to new products and processes

Significance at 10−, 5− and I per cent is indicat ed by +, ++, +++, respectively.

The results of both estimates are compatible with the assumption that the propensity to perform R & D abroad increases with corporate size and with the amount of R & D devoted to the development of new products and processes. Contrary to expectation, regression no. 1 does not indicate that the degree of internationalization significantly influences the foreign share of R & D, that, instead, appears to be negatively related to diversification. The result cannot be explained by a possible negative correlation between these variables, since the factor scores are, by definition, mutually uncorrelated. However, FACTOR1 is a composite measure and positively correlated with internationalization (Table 1). When S is measured by employment alone, as in regression no. 2, foreign R & D shares are positively related to the share of foreign production abroad. In this case, diversification does not reach the ten per cent level of significance required for inclusion in the final estimate.

## Conlusion

In spite of the fact that location of R & D is apt to be influenced by a wide range of strategic considerations, impossible to capture in simple quantitative models, a few conclusions seem to emerge.

Empirical data, based on the Swedish experience, support the argument that the historical

evolution of corporate systems is associated with direct foreign investment not only in production, but also in other corporate functions, including R & D. The propensity to locate R & D abroad seems to be related not only to corporate size and geographical extension, but also to the amount of R & D resources devoted to new product development. The size of R & D employment influences the degree of organizational and functional specialization and, hence, the feasibility of geographically decentralized operations.

High shares of foreign R & D are assumed to reflect international rationalization of production, i. e. concentration of manufacturing to specialized subsidiaries serving several national markets. Contrary to expectation, such international division of labour does not seem to be influenced by diversification; specialized corporations appear to have had equally strong inducements and possibilities to allocate production of components and product types to specialized foreign units.

However, it seems reasonable to assume that the degree of corporate centralization/subsidiary autonomy differs. Foreign affiliates that are the sole manufacturers of a specific product, based on specific technical competence, tend to have relatively great autonomy in setting R & D priorities and in the design of R & D projects. Development and manufacture of products and components that are part of common systems require considerably tighter coordination. Empirical study of the interdependencies − and politically relevant changes−that ensue on 'global rationalization' are much needed.

## References

*Ahnström, L.*, 1973: *Styrande och ledande verksamhet i Västeuropa: En ekonomisk-geografisk studie* (Stockholm: Ekonomiska Forskningsinstitutet vid Handelshögskolan i Stockholm).

*Bradbury, F. R.*, 1978: Technology Transfer, in F. Bradbury *et al.* (Eds.), *Transfer Processes in Technical Change* (Alphen aan den Rijn: Sijthoff & Noordhoff), pp. 107−118.

*Caves, R. E.*, 1971: International Corporations: The Industrial Economics of Foreign Investment, *Economica* (new series), Vol. 38, pp. 1−27.

*Cordell, A. J.*, 1973: Innovation, the Multinational Corporation: Some Implications for National Science Policy, *Long Range Planning*, Vol 6, No. 3. pp. 22−29.

*Creamer, D.*, 1976: *Overseas Research and Development by United States Multinationals 1966−1975. Estimates of Expenditures and a Statistical Profile* (New York: The Conference Board).

## HÅKANSON

Fischer, W. A. & Behrman, J. N., 1979: The Coordination of Foreign R & D Activities by Transnational Corporations, *Journal of International Business Studies*, Vol. 10, No. 3, pp. 28–35.

Freeman, C., 1974: *The Economics of Industrial Innovation.* (Harmondsworth: Penguin).

Granstrand, O. & Fernlund I., 1978: Coordination of Multinational R & D: A Swedish Case Study, *R & D Management*, Vol. 9, No. 1. pp. 1–7.

Hanson, W. T. & Van Rumker, R., 1971: Multinational R & D in Practice: Two Case Studies, *Research Management*. Vol. 14, No 1, pp. 47–54.

Hartmann, W. D. & Stock, W., 1976: *Management von Forschung und Entwicklung* (Berlin: Akademie-Verlag).

Hymer, S. H. 1960/1976: *The International Operations of National Firms: A Study of Direct Foreign Investment* (Cambridge, Mass.: MIT Press).

Håkanson, L., 1980: *Multinationella företag: FoU-verksamhet, tekniköverföring och företagstillväxt. En studie av svenska storföretag och utlandsäga företag i Sverige* (Stockholm: Statens Industriverk 1980: 4, Liber förlag).

Malecki, E. J., 1980: Corporate Organization of R and D and the Location of Technological Activities, *Regional Studies*, Vol. 14, No. 3, pp. 219–234.

Mansfield, E., 1974: Technology and Technological Change, in J. H. Dunning (Ed.), *Economic Analysis and the Multinational Enterprise* (London: George Allen & Unwin), pp. 147–183.

McNee, R. B., 1974: A Systems Approach to Understanding the Geographic Behaviour of Organizations, Especially Large Corporations, in F. E. I. Hamilton (Ed.), *Spatial Perspectives on Industrial Organization and Decision-making* (London: Wiley), pp. 47–75.

OECD, 1979: *Trends in Industrial R & D in Selected OECD Member Countries 1967–75* (Paris: Organisation for Economic Co-operation and Development).

Papo, M., 1971: How to Establish and Operate Multinational Labs, *Research Management*, Vol. 14, No. 1, pp. 12–19.

Pavitt, K., 1971: The Multinational Enterprise and the Transfer of Technology, in J. H. Dunning (Ed.), *The Multinational Enterprise* (London: George Allen & Unwin), pp. 61–85.

Potter, B. V., 1971: Effective Information and Technology Transfer in Multinational R & D, *Research Management*, Vol. 14, No. 1, pp. 20–27.

Quinn, J. B., 1969: Technology Transfer by Multinational Companies, *Harvard Business Review*, Vol. 47, Nov.– Dec., pp. 147–161.

Ronstadt, R. C., 1977: *Research and Development Abroad by U S Multinationals* (New York: Praeger).

Ronstadt, R. C., 1978: International R & D: The Establishment and Evolution of Research and Development Abroad by Seven U. S. Multinationals. *Journal of International Business Studies*, Vol. 9, No 1, pp. 7–24.

SCB 1977: Industrier med stor verksamhet i utlandet 1975, *Statistiska meddelanden*, Ser. F 1977: 10.

SCB 1979: Forskningsstatistik 1977–1979. Teknisk och naturvetenskaplig forskning och utveckling inom industri, myndigheter, institut, organisationer och fonder, *Statistiska meddelanden*, Ser. U 1979: 25.

SCB 1980: Svenska internationella företag, *Statistiska meddelanden*, Ser. F 1980: 2.

Schwetlick, W., 1973: *Forschung und Entwicklung in der Organisation industrieller Unternehmen* (Berlin: Erich Schmidt Verlag).

Swedenborg, B., 1979: *The Multinational Operations of Swedish Firms: An Analysis of Determinants and Effects* (Stockholm: Industriens Utredningsinstitut).

Terpstra, V., 1977: International Product Policy: The Role of Foreign R & D, *Columbia Journal of World Business*, Vol. 12, No. 4, pp. 24–32.

Thomas, M. D., 1975: Economic Development and Selected Organizational and Spatial Perspectives of Technological Change, *Economie appliquée*, Vol. 28, No. 2–3, pp. 379–400.

Vernon, R., 1974: The Location of Economic Activity, in J. H. Dunning (Ed.) *Economic Analysis and the Multinational Enterprise* (London: George Allen & Unwin), pp. 89–114.

# [17]

## "THE DETERMINANTS OF OVERSEAS R & D BY US MNEs; AN ANALYSIS OF INDUSTRY LEVEL DATA"

by

### Robert D. Pearce

## 1. Introduction

A number of pieces of work now exist which seek to delineate, and empirically test, the factors that influence the extent to which US MNEs have undertaken R & D overseas. The dominant conceptual approach embodied in these studies has been to see the MNEs' decision making on R & D as an attempt to achieve an optimal balance between forces tending to draw R & D into a centralised location (presumed, in these studies using data on US MNEs, to be in the home country) and those tending to pull it away from the center into other decentralised locations. Most of these pioneering studies (the exception is the work of Mansfield, Teece and Romeo, 1979) utilised US industry level data for 1966 to formulate their dependent variable. In this paper we set out to update this approach using information for 1982, derived from the most recent benchmark survey of US direct investment abroad (US Department of Commerce, 1985). We also derive all the independent variables included in our tests from this same data source, thus attaining a level of internal consistency not available to earlier researchers, though, as a compensating disadvantage, we are not able to derive a proxy for the potentially important (see section 2.5) R & D economies of scale.

A second and potentially very rewarding approach, uniquely exemplified so far by the work of Hewitt (1980,1983), places the evolution of foreign R & D in MNEs into a more broadly based scenario. Overseas R & D is perceived as emerging with the overseas operations of the MNEs, but in ways which vary according to the basic motivation (or orientation) of the MNE and according to its means of organising its global operations. Whereas the approach balancing 'centripetal versus centrifugal' forces may be seen as implying an attempt to balance these in a way that optimises a clearly defined efficiency-based objective function, Hewitt sees his approach as embodying no such optimising presumption. Rather Hewitt views the 'satisficing' or 'behavioural' approach as providing the foundation for his scenario. Since the data used here does not permit tests which could encompass the various dimensions of

2

Hewitt's scenario (indeed his own tests were somewhat constrained by data availability), we do not discuss his model in depth in our survey of hypotheses in section 2. However certain facets of his model, and several of his tests, do relate constructively to the approach we develop, and are incorporated as appropriate.

In section 2 of this paper we review the various influences which previous work has suggested may contribute to the decision on location of R & D by MNEs, either by pulling R & D away to peripheral sites or by supporting a tendency to keep it centralised at a dominant laboratory. In addition, where appropriate, we introduce the variables included in our own analysis to test these influences. The results of our tests are reported in section 3 and conclusions outlined in section 4.

Our tests use a full sample of 30 manufacturing industries, and, following the precedent of Lall discussed in detail in section 2.2, we also derive subsamples of 9 engineering industries[1] and 14 process industries [2].

The dependent variable for our tests is **ORDR** (overseas R & D ratio) i.e. 'R & D[3] of overseas affiliates as a percentage of total group R & D'.


2 .  **Hypotheses**

2.1  **Level of Overseas Sales and Production**

If R & D economies of scale (see section 2.5) are widely considered to be the most powerful centripetal force operating to discourage the geographical dispersion of R & D, then the overseas spread of sales and production takes pride of place as its centrifugal equivalent. As the work of Ronstadt (1977; 1978) and Behrman and Fischer (1980) has indicated effective foreign production and marketing by MNEs does tend to require R & D back-up, either to *adapt* existing products or processes to new requirements, or to *derive* distinctive new products or processes to accommodate particularly idiosyncratic characteristics of those markets or producing locations. Where other influences (notably economies of scale and adequate intragroup communications) permit it is logical to suggest that R & D back-up for overseas operations would be most effectively located in conjunction with the units to be supported. The internationalisation of production and sales by MNEs therefore plays a central role in all empirical studies of the determinants of the industrialisation of their R & D.

In their analysis of a sample of 35 US firms Mansfield, Teece and Romeo (1979) found a statistically significant positive relationship between 'percentage of firms R & D expenditure carried out overseas' and 'percentage of sales derived from abroad'. For an alternative 20 firm sample [4], Mansfield, Teece and Romeo found 'percentage of firms R & D expenditures carried out overseas' to be significantly positively related to 'percentage of firms sales from foreign subsidiaries' (i.e. overseas production), but significantly negatively related to 'percentage of sales from exports'. They suggest (1979, p. 190) that the negative result for exports is compatible with a situation where 'exports may be more R & D intensive than domestic sales' and where the R & D support of exports is carried out at home. This negative result for exports was confirmed by Hirschey and Caves (1981) using US industry level data.

In their regression analysis based on industry level data Hirschey and Caves (1981) also found a significant positive relationship between their dependent variable 'foreign R & D spending as a percentage of total R & D spending by US MNCs' (i.e. DISPER) and 'ratio of sales by foreign affiliates of US MNCs to worldwide sales'. Hirschey and Caves extend the familiar line of argument at this point, however, by suggesting that if overseas R & D is mainly undertaken to support the operations of individual affiliates, any one affiliate is more likely to obtain R & D back-up the greater the level of its sales. Thus, for a given overall level of internationalisation of sales, they suggest (1981,p119) 'we expect that the more concentrated are [overseas] sales among a few affiliates, the more favourable the opportunity to found an efficient-scale R & D facility abroad, and the higher will be DISPER. In addition to the advantages of efficient scale in R & D, a few large overseas R & D facilities should be easier to organise and manage from the parents headquarters'. The variable CENTRAL is derived, measuring 'foreign affiliates exports to destinations other than the US divided by total sales by foreign affiliates'. If this variable distinguishes between MNEs that service a given total overseas market from a large number of small dispersed facilities

4

and MNEs that service a similar market from a small number of large facilities then it would be predicted that CENTRAL would be positively related to DISPER. This prediction is significantly verified in the empirical tests.

Another interesting extension of the analysis pursued by Hischey and Caves (1981,pp121-2) is to take account of the nature of intragroup trade, and its influence on the location of R & D. Though their own results, and those of Mansfield,Teece and Romeo, suggest that servicing foreign markets through exports does not stimulate foreign R & D they suggest that it may be necessary to qualify this view when the exports are intermediate goods transferred to foreign affiliates for further processing before sale. In such circumstances converting intermediate goods into final products suitable for a local market may require R & D capability in the foreign affiliate. A positive relationship is then predicted between the dependent variable DISPER and 'the percentage of exports by US MNCs shipped to their foreign affiliates'. The relationship was found to be positively signed, but did not approach significance.

By contrast Hirschey and Caves expect 'percentage of exports by foreign affiliates of US MNCs shipped to US parent companies' to be negatively related to DISPER. It is argued that such 'sales to US parents usually consist of inputs for further processing and sale as final products. The foreign affiliated output constitutes one link in a chain of processes and any R & D needed for the chain takes place at home with the results transferred to foreign locations'. The predicted negative sign emerges, and is (marginally) significant. Hewitt (1970) includes in his tests a variable XUSI (export to US intensity) ie 'majority owned foreign affiliates exports to the US divided by total foreign sales'. Hewitt suggests that the higher is XUSI the more likely is it that an industry's foreign subsidiaries have been granted world product mandates. The sign of the relationship between XUSI and the propensity to perform R & D abroad is left unpredicted by Hewitt, since it is not clear if the mandated producing subsidiary will incorporate associated R & D work. This will depend on whether such R & D is most effectively located near production or near the main target market for that production (assumed to be the US). Of course the line of argument favoured by Hirschey and Caves for their comparable variable would predict a negative sign for XUSI. In fact

5

Hewitt's tests produce a significant positive sign on XUSI, which encourages the tentative conclusion (1980, p. 324) that XUSI does reflect the degree of product mandating, and that such mandates do pull R & D into the host country.

Lall's (1979) approach to his internationalisation variable (FS - the foreign spread of each industry, measured by 'the sales of overseas affiliates of US firms as a percentage of total domestic sales of each industry') is to see it as reflecting the degree of **experience** of internationalisation of activity, with the implication that higher FS suggests the existence of conditions likely to allow the firm to overcome the coordination problems of decentralised R & D.[5]

In his tests Lall found FS to be positively related to 'propensity to conduct R & D overseas', for his full 28 industry sample. The relationship was also significantly positive for the 12 'process' industries in the sample; it was significantly negative for the nine 'engineering' industries, and insignificantly negative for seven 'other' industries. The positive relationships are compatible with Lall's arguments (see section 2.2) about 'delinking'. Thus 'greater foreign experience and spread help US MNCs to overcome the centralising tendencies that normally govern research activity' (1979, p.326). The fact that this is most strongly true for process industries is in line with Lall's view that 'delinking' is most feasible in those industries. The absence of the positive relationship in engineering industries is interpreted as suggesting that 'greater foreign spread and experience is...unable to counterbalance the centralising tendencies that affect R & D location in these industries' (1979, p.328), which again is compatible with the predictions of the 'delinking' hypothesis. The emergence of the negative relationship in the engineering industries subsample is, however, less easy to explain. One possibility is that overseas production needs more R & D support (of a sufficiently advanced nature not to be easily decentralised ie 'major applied research' in Lall's formulation) than comparable domestic production, so that increasing FS implies (ceteris paribus) increases in total research not matched by increases in overseas research. Lall observes that 'engineering MNCs do undertake substantial amounts of R & D in every place they place a plant, but most of this seems to be devoted to minor technological work and to be concentrated in older technologies'.

6

We incorporate five variables in our tests to cover the hypotheses outlined in this section.

**OPR** (overseas production ratio) ie 'overseas production as a percentage of total group sales'.

**ER** (export ratio) ie 'exports of parent company as a percentage of total group sales'.

**FMER** (further manufacturing export ratio) ie 'exports of parent company to overseas affiliates for further manufacturing as a percentage of total parent exports'.

**HOME** (US market orientation of overseas affiliates) ie 'sales of overseas affiliates to US as a percentage of total sales of overseas affiliates'.

**CENT** (centralised supply of overseas markets) ie 'exports of overseas affiliates to other non-US destinations as a percentage of all sales of overseas affiliates except those to US'.

### 2.2    R & D Intensity

In his empirical work Lall (1979) investigates the relationship between the propensity to perform R & D overseas by US MNEs and the overall R & D intensity (RD) of their industries. Central to the argument here is Lall's belief that 'the extent to which R & D can be shifted abroad depends on the "linkages" between R & D and other activities in the NME'. It is a further crucial hypothesis then that it is the extent to which **major applied research** can be separated from the managerial and marketing functions in the MNE that is the main factor determining the strength of these linkages.

The more **basic** types of scientific research are not expected to be particularly closely linked to other functional areas of the firms operations, and Lall does not expect this type of research work to notably influence his empirical results since 'there are no *a priori* grounds for expecting its linkages to differ significantly between industries' (1979 p.323). By contrast **minor development work**, consisting 'mainly of translating given technologies into practical use, and of tailoring them to specific material and marketing needs in each production unit', is seen as inextricably linked with location of production and as not having any close links with head office strategic planning decisions. The need for such development work will differ between industries, probably being most prevalent in engineering industries, where detailed design is an integral part of the production process. Because such adaptive R & D is likely to be undertaken, to some extent, in the vast majority of overseas and domestic subsidiaries Lall suggests that 'it may result in a high absolute value of foreign R & D, as well as high R & D in relation to sales, but not in a high **propensity** to undertake foreign R & D' (1979 p.323). For this reason Lall indicates that the linkage between adaptive R & D and production cannot account for inter-industry differences in the propensity to perform R & D overseas.

Having delineated major adaptive research as the point of focus for his analysis of linkages Lall perceives important differences between groups of industries, the basic premise being that these R & D functions can be more easily 'delinked' in process [6] industries than in engineering[7] ones.

It is Lall's hypothesis that in the process industries firms have greater freedom to seek the ideal locations for particular parts of their applied research work. The characteristics pulling this R & D away from centralised locations in those process industries may be pure cost effectiveness influences, or the more indefinable(and unquantifiable) agglomeration factors (see section 2.6) which impart self-reinforcing reputations to particular areas for particular types of work. The relative freedom to seek such locations for applied research in process industries stems, according to Lall, from the relative weakness of certain linkages in these industries. Thus in process industries the product rarely needs to be 'tailored' to the requirements of individual customers, so that close monitoring of, and reaction to, main markets is not a major factor drawing R & D units into contact with these markets. Lall also suggests that in these industries new product development can often be delinked quite effectively from research into new production processes, again creating scope for optimal diffusion of applied R & D. Following from the argument that the more committed to R & D and innovation a firm is the more it will pursue the course of optimising its activity in this area by incorporating efficient overseas locations in its R & D network, Lall hypothesises that in process industries 'a greater degree of research intensity should lead to a higher propensity to undertake R & D abroad' (1979, p234). In line with this hypothesis the

8

process industries emerge in Lall's empirical work as the only industry subgroup where research intensity and propensity to undertake R & D abroad are positively related. However, though statistically significant, R & D intensity is a relatively weak influence on propensity to undertake R & D in these industries[8].

By contrast with the process industries Lall perceives that in the case of the engineering industries there is a stronger need for a continuous interaction between all the major functions related to innovation, and between these functions and those in procurement, production, management and marketing. These strong linkages are seen to reflect the special roll in the engineering industries' innovation process of the improvement and testing of new products and designs, in conjunction with leading customers. This makes it 'more difficult to separate such functions as exploring the needs of major customers, bringing scientific and technical skills to bear on these needs, getting rid of bottlenecks in successive stages of production, ensuring an adequate supply of new components of various kinds, marketing the product and reacting to "feed back" from the users' (1979, p323). The argument is then that, in engineering industries, the greater is the need for innovation-oriented major applied research the greater will be the overall research intensity and the greater the tendency to centralise R & D in the US. Thus a negative relationship is hypothesised between R & D intensity and propensity to perform R & D overseas. This prediction is strongly verified by Lall's results[9].

Hewitt also found a significant negative relationship between overall industry level R & D intensity and propensity to perform R & D overseas. Though an explanation for this exists within his broadly based model of the evolution of overseas R & D, Hewitt also acknowledged (1980, pp324-5) the possibility of a more direct explanation. Thus to the extent that higher values of R & D intensity reflect higher proportions of more expensive 'original' (or basic) R & D relative to cheaper 'adaptive' R & D, and to the extent that basic R & D is the type most likely to be centralised, the negative sign would be predicted. Hirschey and Caves (1981,p120) take a contrasting view, predicting a positive relationship between their variable BASIC ('proportion of research reported by the US industry that is classified as basic, rather than applied or

9

developmental') and the propensity to perform overseas R & D. Thus they expect that after controlling for other important influences (notably R & D economies of scale and the pull of overseas production facilities and markets) those industries which have the greatest focus on basic R & D will have the greatest tendency to locate R & D abroad, in search of 'access to foreign scientific communities and institutions where relevant research is underway'. Though taking the predicted positive sign the relationship was never significant.

Our tests using the 1982 US Benchmark data include the variable **IRDI** (industry R & D intensity) i.e. 'total R & D expenditure of MNEs as a percentage of total sales of MNEs', to test the hypotheses introduced in this section.

## 2.3    Royalties

Lall (1979,p322) includes amongst the independent variables in his regression analysis ROYALTY, i.e 'royalties and fees earned abroad by US MNCs as a percentage of their R & D in the US', intended as a measure of their propensity to rely on licensing as a means of exploiting their technology.

This may be positively related to the propensity to perform R & D overseas for three reasons.

(1)   Since there does exist an active market in the sale of licences by US MNEs it is feasible that some foreign R & D may be undertaken to make these technologies more marketable by adapting them to non-US conditions. In effect the US MNEs may be entrusting the foreign licensing of their technology to their overseas affiliates, who, as a result of their own experience of technology adaptation, may be able to carry out the transfer most effectively. Thus Lall indicates that the more a US industry uses licensing as a means of exploiting its technology (as measured by the variable ROYALTY) the more it is likely to promote overseas R & D to support the marketing of this technology in foreign countries.

(2)   Reversing the causal connection from (1), however, 'a larger R & D establishment abroad may, by producing a greater stock of readily transferable technology, promote a greater use of licensing' (Lall, 1979, p.322).

## 10

(3) Both high licensing and high overseas R & D may be related to a third factor, namely the age of the technology in question. Studies of licensing in MNEs have demonstrated that this is most common for the older and more stable technologies. It is also these more mature technologies which are most amenable to the expansion of R & D abroad, since they retain fewer 'linkages' with the more centralised head office functions than the more recently innovated ones. In this way, Lall suggests, licensing abroad and foreign R & D may grow together, without being causally related.

In Lall's study ROYALTY is always positively related to the dependent variable, but this result is only strongly and persistently significant in the engineering subsample. The strong results for engineering industries may be seen as compatible with Lall's 'linkage' approach. Thus if 'linkage' influences do cause innovative activity in these industries to be particularly strongly centralised, then when the stage of licensing is reached a relatively large amount of adaptive work may still need to be done to make the technology suitable for the environments to which it is to be applied. Where possible, however, it will be attempted to carry out this adaptive activity in support of licensing in the environment to which it is to be applied.

In our empirical analysis the variable formulated to test these hypotheses is ROYUN i.e. 'royalty receipts of MNE parents from unaffiliated foreigners as a percentage of parent R & D expenditure'.

It should be noted that ROYUN improves on Lall's comparable variable ROYALTY (in a manner which Lall would have preferred [1979,p325] but could not implement with his available data ), since it focuses on royalty earnings from unaffiliated foreigners, and excludes intra-group royalty payments.

## 2.4    Nature of products

The propensity to perform R & D overseas differs substantially between industries. Much of this difference may be attributable to those industry characteristics included as independent variables in the multiple regressions carried out in the various studies (e.g. internationalisation of markets and production). Nevertheless it is expected that in some cases industry or product characteristics not explicitly quantifiable may influence the internationalisation of R & D.

Thus Hirschey and Caves included in their multiple regression a dummy variable taking a value of one for industries producing durable goods, and found this to be (marginally) significantly positive. This result reflects the suggestion (Hirschey and Caves, 1981, p120) that 'durable goods tend to have more complex configurations than other goods, and we might expect more R & D to be needed to modify or adapt them to local markets abroad. Both industrial and household goods may frequently need adaptation to different physical conditions of use or different relative values of labour time and relative factor costs in foreign markets. Also, the sheer complexity of capital goods means that more adaptation could be done'.

Mansfield, Teece and Romeo (1979) tested for, and found, a significantly above average propensity to perform overseas R & D in pharmaceuticals. This may have reflected a number of factors. Host country governments may have a particularly pronounced tendency to insist on MNEs doing local R & D in this industry. Pharmaceutical firms themselves may have found it particularly desirable to do local R & D as the most effective means of ensuring adequate compliance with local health authority drug regulations. Also it was suggested that, at least when the Mansfield, Teece and Romeo survey was carried out, US pharmaceutical firms may have moved a substantial amount of R & D abroad to avoid Food and Drug Administration regulations. A further possibility is that pharmaceuticals may be an industry where an unusually high proportion of the more attractive 'agglomeration sites' for R & D (see section 2.6) are outside the US.

It may be considered to be an implication of Lall's 'linkages' approach, outlined above, that firms in process industries would have a greater proportion of their R & D overseas than otherwise similar firms in engineering industries. To test for this difference we incorporate in our regressions using the full sample of 30 industries the variables

**ENG**,a dummy variable taking a value of 1 for engineering industries

**PROC**, a dummy variable taking a value of 1 for process industries.

12

## 2.5   Economies of scale in R & D

An idea that pervades most of the thinking on decentralisation of R & D and, though difficult to incorporate in tests directly, underlies much of the empirical analysis, is that of economies of scale in R & D facilities.  It is often assumed that the implementation of additional, geographically dispersed, R & D facilities will only be considered as efficient when the first, or parent, laboratory had achieved a 'critical mass' which makes full use of all its resources.

The incorporation of expensive equipment in a laboratory may encourage the focusing of all R & D in this unit until this equipment is being optimally utilised[10]. Another factor which may contribute to the role of economies of scale is the need for R & D workers to comprise balanced teams of specialists.  This may place upward pressure on the minimum efficient scale of use of the laboratory, firstly by requiring a large team in order to encompass all the relevant specialist areas of expertise, and secondly to fully employ outstanding specialists in the use of their unique and distinctive talent.

It may be a plausible speculation that, once a MNE has implemented some decentralised R & D facilities the relevance of economies of scale on the further evolution of this system may decline.  Or, put another way, the optimal level of use of a laboratory may be less when it is part of a decentralised system of such facilities than it would be if it were the sole unit.  If the factor setting a substantial minimum efficient scale of use for a laboratory is an expensive and high capacity piece of equipment then, once sister laboratores **do** exist, full use of this equipment could be achieved by making it accessible to assist the work of other units, rather than by expanding the work of the unit in which it is housed up to its optimal capacity.  Similarly if a high level of use of a laboratory is considered necessary to fully employ a particular scientist in the type of work at which he or she may be an outstanding specialist, then this becomes less relevent if that person can spend time assisting decentralised laboratories.  Thus we are arguing that if a major factor encouraging large centralised R & D facilities, and mitigating against geographical decentralisation, is certain distinctive high capacity units of physical or human capital then this becomes a less crucial influence if these can be

13

shared with sister R & D facilities. However, the effective implementation of this escape from R & D economies of scale as a vital centralising influence depends not only on the existence of decentralised laboratories, but also on an effective communications network, and mood of mutually supportive cooperation, between the dispersed units[11]. Thus the fact that access to a centrally located piece of equipment could benefit a decentralised laboratory, and usefully expand the creative use of that equipment, may only be perceived where knowledge of the ongoing work and capabilities within the dispersed network is effectively diffused and assimilated. The same point, of course, applies to the realisation of the value of visits to other laboratories by leading centrally based specialists.

Even if we can argue that the concept of minimum efficient scale in R & D may become a less relevant influence within a well developed and effectively coordinated globally dispersed network of R & D facilities, it remains plausible that it may well be a notable constraining factor operating to deter the emergence of such networks. For this reason it would still appear relevant to attempt to incorporate it in empirical tests of the decentralisation of R & D in MNEs.

In fact direct measures of economies of scale in R & D have not been available in a form suitable for inclusion in the tests so far performed. Though they could not incorporate them in their regression tests Mansfield, Teece and Romeo (1979) did derive useful estimates from their sample of firms for 'annual R & D expenditure for an overseas laboratory of minimum economic scale in 1975'. Minimum economic scale was found to vary substantially between industries. It was also predictably influenced by the type and scope of the laboratories responsibilities. Thus Mansfield, Teece and Romeo found it to be less for a laboratory performing either research or development than for one combining both, and also less where the laboratory deals with a single product line than where it encompasses a wider product range. Again as would be expected Mansfield, Teece and Romeo were able to verify the relatively low cost of efficient overseas R & D concerned entirely with the implementation of minor product charges (1979,p190)[12].

14

Hirschey and Caves (1981, pp118-9) created a proxy measure to indicate scale economies in R & D in their tests of industry level data.  As predicted this was found to be significantly negatively related to the percentage of R & D performed overseas. Hewitt's tests of his scenario for the evolution of foreign R & D in MNEs included two estimates of R & D scale economies (Hewitt, 1980, p320).  Neither was found to be at all related to the propensity to perform R & D overseas.  Hewitt found this compatible with the relatively small role played by R & D economies of scale in influencing R & D abroad in his 'behavioural' view of the influences on such decisions.

It should be noted that though several of the studies of the determinants of overseas R & D were forced to forego the direct incorporation of an independent variable to measure R & D economies of scale, the potential relevance of the concept frequently underlies the articulation of the hypotheses relating to variables that are included (e.g. see Pearce, 1986).

As we noted in section 1 it is not possible to create a reasonable proxy for R & D economies of scale from the data source used in our tests.

## 2.6    Agglomeration factors

It is felt by many observers that a factor limiting the dispersion of R & D operations in several industries is the existence of research communities which have an established reputation as a dynamic focal point in their industry's creative activity.  It is felt that these closely knit research/development communities, which incorporate and link private and public (e.g. university) facilities, are likely to generate an atmosphere of creative stimulus which is likely to provide notable external benefits to any firm locating major operations within them.  An alternative consideration, which may be starting to impinge on decision making is that firms may benefit from locating some R & D activity away from such recognised agglomeration sites, in order to avoid the 'bandwagonism' of such communities, and to seek new independent perspectives.

Clearly these agglomeration factors may contribute to the centralisation of a substantial part of a firms R & D *somewhere*, but not necessarily in its home country. This has made it difficult to incorporate these influences in the tests of R & D diffusion by MNEs so far carried out.  It may be hoped, however, that some hypotheses relating to these agglomeration factors could eventually be derived and tested given a large multidimensional (i.e. divided by parent nationality and industry) firm level data base, and utilising informed judgements as to where an industry's strongest research agglomeration sites might be. Thus if, for sake of illustration, it was suggested that Europe was relatively strong compared to the USA in research agglomeration sites in chemicals (see Lall, 1979, p. 321), then if tests were run for a sample of chemical firms it would be expected that, after allowing for all other relevant influences, European firms would have a lower propensity to overseas R & D (agglomeration influences keeping R & D at home) than US firms (agglomeration influences pulling R & D abroad). Similarly advocation of the USA as superior to Europe in research agglomeration sites in electronics would lead to the prediction that, again after allowing for all other potential influences, European electronics firms would have a higher propensity to overseas R & D than US electronics firms.

We may also suggest the possible existence of a firm-level 'agglomeration dynamic'. It may be considered plausible that certain of a firms R & D institutions, perhaps especially those in the home country, may develop an ongoing momentum which places a claim on a major part of the firms technical budget and creates psychological barriers to taking the decision to set up ('cold') new facilities in new locations. Thus established facilities may be a 'hothouse' environment where current work is continually stimulating new offshoot ideas to provide the basis for the next generation of work. Then a new overseas facility with a new team, strangers to each other and to the physical support facility, will have to establish their roots 'cold', before the various branches of their output begin to emerge. However, once new institutions are implemented they are likely to create their own dynamic, as indicated by Ronstadt's (1977, 1978) evidence on the changing function of overseas facilities. This would support the empirical supposition of a relationship between the level of overseas production and overseas R & D, with overseas production providing the need for local technology transfer units, which then evolve to embrace more advanced functions. Thus overseas production could be quite well established before overseas R & D starts, but then R & D may grow faster than production as the 'agglomeration dynamic' of the R & D facility generates the capability to encompass more expensive types of R & D.

## 3.    Results

The results of multiple regressions seeking to test the hypotheses outlined in section 2 are presented in tables 1 to 3.   These results should, of course, be treated with due caution bearing in mind the limited degrees of freedom, especially in the tests of the subsamples, and the potential for collinear relationships between certain independent variables[13].

The performance of OPR in our tests is very much in line with the hypotheses outlined in section 2.1, and with results of earlier researchers.   In the full sample of 30 industries OPR is consistently significantly positively related to ORDR.   For the nine engineering industries the relationship between OPR and ORDR is negative, though only significant in equation 2.4.   This result essentially replicates Lall's result for engineering industries and may be explained in terms of his 'linkages' approach in a manner outlined in section 2.1.   Again in line with Lall's hypothesis and results our tests find a (usually significant) positive relationship between OPR and ORDR for the 14 process industries.

In the regressions for the full 30 industry sample ER is never significant.   Perhaps worthy of some scrutiny, however, is the change of sign from negative in equations 1.1 to 1.3 to positive in equations 1.4 and 1.5.   The crucial influence here, we hypothesise is the absence from the latter two equations of the variables covering other aspects of the MNEs' trade orientation, especially those (HOME and CENT) relating to the export orientation of overseas affiliates.   In fact ER is highly correlated with HOME (simple correlation coefficient 0.421) and CENT (simple correlation coefficient 0.723).   The link between these variables reflects the extent to which firms in industries tend to adopt strategies of supplying the global market for particular products from a limited number of locations (likely to produce high values of both ER and CENT) or to specialise stages of production in particular locations generating substantial intra-group trade in components etc. (likely to produce high values of ER, HOME and CENT).   In

Table 1
**Regressions using full sample of industries - dependent variable ORDR**

| | 1.1 | 1.2 | 1.3 | 1.4 | 1.5 |
|---|---|---|---|---|---|
| OPR | 0.33798*<br>(2.0293) | 0.37231**<br>(2.3776) | 0.35941**<br>(2.3488) | 0.24450*<br>(1.8635) | 0.29779**<br>(2.3985) |
| ER | 0.40732<br>(0.64600) | 0.25238<br>(0.61817) | 0.14488<br>(0.39902) | -0.20008<br>(-0.58157) | -0.25441<br>(-1.0934) |
| FMER | 0.00144<br>(0.01074) | 0.00993<br>(0.07640) | -0.03365<br>(-0.31427) | | |
| IRDI | -0.40849<br>(-0.47124) | -0.48830<br>(-0.60920) | | | |
| ROYUN | 0.26683<br>(1.7249) | 0.28441*<br>(1.9470) | 0.29378*<br>(2.0506) | | |
| HOME | -0.17871<br>(-0.78838) | -0.19805<br>(-0.96162) | -0.21254<br>(-1.0534) | | |
| CENT | -0.13227<br>(-0.70858) | -0.09673<br>(-0.62873) | -0.08803<br>(-0.05827) | | |
| ENG | -0.13804<br>(-0.02797) | | | 2.1150<br>(0.55277) | |
| PROC | 2.2131<br>(0.74383) | | | 3.8178<br>(1.3628) | |
| $R^2$ | 0.4008 | 0.3791 | 0.3687 | 0.2540 | 0.1983 |
| F | 1.486+ | 1.919+ | 2.238++ | 2.128+ | 3.340++ |

\* significant at 10%  \*\* significant at 5%
\+ significant at 25%  ++ significant at 10%

18

## Table 2
### Regressions using engineering industries sample - dependent variable ORDR

|        | 2.1 | 2.2 | 2.3 | 2.4 |
|--------|-----|-----|-----|-----|
| OPR    | (-0.33375)<br>(-1.3854) | -0.46741<br>(-1.8100) | -0.31498<br>(-1.0900) | -0.49308*<br>(-2.9200) |
| ER     | -1.0530**<br>(-3.2898) | -1.1608**<br>(-3.6181) | -1.0773*<br>(-2.8119) | 0.21983<br>(0.40492) |
| IRDI   | -0.89256<br>(-1.7562) | -1.3590<br>(-2.1504) | -0.96967<br>(-1.4254) | -1.4777**<br>(-3.6657) |
| ROYUN  | -1.1323<br>(-2.0646) | -1.5381*<br>(-2.4345) | -1.1436<br>(-1.8142) | -1.8355**<br>(-4.0629) |
| FMER   |  | 0.15347<br>(1.1601) |  |  |
| HOME   |  |  | 0.05386<br>(0.21913) |  |
| CENT   |  |  |  | -0.59120*<br>(-2.5388) |
| $R^2$  | 0.7740 | 0.8440 | 0.7776 | 0.9282 |
| F      | 3.425+ | 3.246+ | 2.097 | 7.759++ |

| *  | significant at 10% | ** | significant at 5%  |
|----|--------------------|----|--------------------|
| +  | significant at 25% | ++ | significant at 10% |

## Table 3

**Regressions using process industries sample - dependent variable ORDR**

|  | 3.1 | 3.2 | 3.3 | 3.4 |
|---|---|---|---|---|
| OPR | 0.60003** (2.7319) | 0.58490** (2.5033) | 0.46915* (2.0837) | 0.57652* (1.9715) |
| ER | 0.84233 (1.5078) | 1.0394 (1.3613) | 1.2778* (2.1164) | 0.93019 (1.0474) |
| IRDI | -1.1759 (-0.81395) | -1.9360 (-0.80014) | -1.0830 (-0.79551) | -1.0661 (-0.61282) |
| ROYUN | 0.25556 (1.5628) | 0.26517 (1.5297) | 0.29154* (1.8704) | 0.26235 (1.4522) |
| FMER |  | 0.11350 (0.40325) |  |  |
| HOME |  |  | -0.72145 (-1.4683) |  |
| CENT |  |  |  | -0.04214 (-0.13270) |
| $R^2$ | 0.5167 | 0.5264 | 0.6193 | 0.5178 |
| F | 2.406+ | 1.778+ | 2.603+ | 1.718+ |

\*     significant at 10%     \*\*     significant at 5%
\+     significant at 25%

20

equations 1.4 and 1.5 it may be that ER is acting as a proxy for the general orientation of MNE activity, and, in particular, reflecting a tendency (indicated in equations 1.1 to 1.3) for higher export orientation in overseas affiliates to lead to lower values of ORDR. With HOME and CENT included in the equations an insignificant tendency for higher parent company export orientation to generate some supportive R & D overseas is suggested.

For engineering industries (see table 2) ER is significantly negatively related to ORDR in three of the four equations. An explanation for this result could be that exports in engineering industries need particularly extensive R & D support (perhaps reflecting the frequently customised nature of the demand in these industries) thus increasing total industry R & D, but that this R & D is done in the parent country due to the centralising linkage influences in these industries suggested by Lall, thus lowering ORDR. However, when CENT is included in equation 2.4 it is found to be significantly negatively related to ORDR, whilst ER becomes insignificantly positive. This suggests that we cannot rule out the possibility that, when negative, ER was acting as a proxy for CENT (reflecting the general tendency to export orientation) and reflecting its negative relationship with ORDR. For the process industries (see table 3) ER is consistently positively signed and significant in equation 3.3. This suggests that in these industries some overseas R & D tends to be generated to support exports.

The variable FMER is formulated to test the hypothesis that a given value of ER is more likely to generate overseas R & D the more important in these parent company exports are goods intended for further processing by overseas affiliates. Though usually positively signed FMER never approaches significance.

The basic hypothesis relating to the variable HOME is that, for a given OPR, the production of overseas affiliates is less likely to generate R & D the more it is intended for export to the US. One circumstance causing a high value of HOME would be if the overseas affiliates were mainly involved in processing local raw materials before export to the US. In such cases a small amount of process adaptive R & D might be needed to make an essentially standardised technology amenable to local conditions, but this would be quite a rare and inexpensive occurence. A high value of HOME would also be found where industries have adopted the procedure of locating certain stages of production at overseas facilities, exporting components or assembled products back to the US. In such cases the technology is likely to be defined by the parent, which coordinates the process, and locations selected as amenable to the requirements of the technology, so that local R & D is not implied. Though usually taking the hypothesised negative sign HOME is never significant in the tests.

It will be recalled that the original articulation of CENT derives from Hirschey and Caves hypothesis (see section 2.1) that a given value of OPR is more likely to generate R & D if the overseas production is centralised in a small number of sites, increasing the likelyhood that these locations would be large enough to justify and support R & D work (ie an extension of the R & D economies of scale argument). High values of CENT are then interpreted as implying that a given overseas market is supplied through exports from a small number of relatively large producing units, rather than by widely dispersed smaller units in most of the local markets. This line of argument predicts a positive relationship between CENT and ORDR. In fact, though only significant in the engineering sample (equation 2.4), CENT is consistently negatively signed. Thus the more oriented are MNEs overseas subsidiaries to exporting (to other non-US locations), the smaller is the overseas share of R & D. Again we may suggest as an explanation that high export orientation implies that the overseas subsidiary has been *selected* to play a specialised role in the MNEs global operations (eg performing a particular stage in a production process, producing a component for assembly elsewhere, or producing a final product for a wider market), but that it has been selected because it is recognised as a suitable location to utilise existing technology, ruling out local R & D. Broadly then it seems that the results for both HOME and CENT tend to confirm the view that overseas R & D is most likely to support overseas producing operations aimed at serving local markets.

Our results for the relationship between industry level R & D intensity (IRDI) and ORDR are consistently negative, though only once (in engineering subsample equation 2.4) significant. A justification for a pervasively negative relationship was (as we noted in section 2.2) suggested by Hewitt in terms of the preponderant type of R & D.

22

Thus if high values of IRDI mainly reflect the relative dominance of expensive basic research, and if this is also the type most difficult to decentralise, then IRDI and ORDR should be negatively related. As we outlined in detail in section 2.2 Lall predicts a negative relationship between IRDI and ORDR in engineering industries, and a positive one in process industries. Thus our results confound this prediction by producing negative signs for both groups, though the relationship does have a stronger statistical significance in the engineering group.

Our variable ROYUN seeks to test Lall's hypothesis (see section 3.3) that in order to effectively licence their parent company technology abroad US MNEs utilise the adaptive expertise of their overseas R & D facilities, thus predicting a positive relationship between ROYUN and ORDR. ROYUN takes the predicted positive sign in the full sample of industries and for the process industries subsample, but is negatively signed for engineering industries. Though Lall's tests had produced a positive relationship between royalty earnings and overseas R & D for his engineering subsample, our negative relationship may be compatible with his reasoning for these industries, suggesting that significant adaptive work may be necessary to make engineering technology suitable for a licensors needs but that for linkage reasons (or simply due to the lack of suitable extant overseas facilities in these industries) this licensing support R & D is done at home.

In our analysis of the full sample of 30 industries we included dummy variables for engineering industries (ENG) and process industries (PROC). With dummies for the 'other' industries omitted the coefficients on ENG and PROG reflect the difference between ORDR in these industries and 'other' industries, net of the influence of other variables included in an equation. Though never significant the coefficients on ENG and PROC in table 1 support the view that the technological characteristics of process industries are more amenable to the international decentralisation of R & D in MNEs than those in engineering industries.

## 4    Conclusions

The pioneering researchers into the determinants of overseas R & D by MNEs have made very useful progress in outlining viable approaches to the issue and in delineating the nature of the important factors influencing decisions. The data available to date has, however, constrained the ability to fully test all the dimensions entering into the hypotheses derived. A multidimensional firm level data base, encompassing the variables discussed earlier, and also permitting the investigation of differences between industries and between MNE's country of origin, would represent an ideal step forward.

The ground breaking empirical studies have, in the main, found it easier to address those influences likely to draw R & D away from centralised locations than to test directly those considered likely to pull R & D into these locations (e.g. economies of scale in R & D, agglomeration influences). A partial exception to this generalisation is found in the work of Lall who makes a focus of his discussion the importance of various communication links as a potential centralising influence. Lall then makes these linkage hypotheses testable as factors determining the degree to which the (empirically more accessible) decentralising influences can operate. In the main Lall's approach proved to be an empirically rewarding refinement of the mainstream tests.

The predicted influence of overseas production as a centrifugal force drawing R & D towards overseas facilities is substantially verified in the tests reported, though engineering industries emerge as an exception to this for reasons perceived to relate to communications or linkage influences. Exports from the parent country are found to be a stronger independent influence on R & D location than perhaps might have been expected, though this influence seems to vary in a manner that merits further investigation. Predominantly in line with prediction are results that suggest that MNEs overseas producing units aimed at their local markets are more likely to generate decentralised support R & D than export oriented overseas facilities. Finally parent companies attempts to license their technology overseas often seem to generate supporting R & D overseas, presumably to make the technology more suitable to new environments or more accessible to its foreign licensors.

24

**FOOTNOTES**

1. Construction, mining and materials handling machinery; office and computing machines; other non-electrical machinery; household appliances; radio, TV and communications equipment; electrical components and accessories; other electrical and electronic equipment; instruments and related products.

2. Grain mill and bakery products; beverages; other food and kindred; industrial chemicals and synthetics; drugs; soap, cleaners and toilet goods; agricultural chemicals; other chemicals and allied products; tobacco manufactures; textile products and apparel; paper and allied products; printing and publishing; rubber products; miscellaneous plastics products.

3. The R & D covered includes any performed for the MNE or affiliates *by* others, but not work performed by the MNE *for* others (e.g. US government). In fact 97.7% of the R & D performed *for* manufacturing MNEs covered was carried out *by* their own facilities, i.e. only 2.3% was subcontracted.

4. For details of these samples see Mansfield, Teece and Romeo (1979, p187).

5. In his tests Hewitt (1980) found a strongly significant positive relationship between 'the average age of US foreign subsidiaries in each manufacturing industry' and the industry propensity to perform R & D overseas. This suggests that the longer have the MNEs operated abroad the more clearly have they come to perceive the potential advantages of moving away from an initial position of R & D centralisation, and the more aware they will have become of their own ability to organise decentralised activities. This relevance of gradually emerging perceptions is interpreted by Hewitt (1980,p323) as one of the results in his study which recommends a 'satisficing' approach to the modelling of the globalisation of MNE R & D.

6. The 12 'process' industries distinguished by Lall are grain mill products; beverages; other foods; paper; drugs; soaps; industrial chemicals; plastics; other chemicals; rubber; textiles; printing and publishing.

7. The 9 'engineering' industries distinguished are farm machinery; industrial machinery; office machinery; electronic and other non-electrical machinery;

25

household and industrial electrical equipment; radio and TV; other electrical machinery; transportation equipment; instruments.

8. Lall is also concerned about the extent to which this result for R & D intensity can be interpreted independently of its highly collinear relationship with FS (proportion of production carried out overseas) which is a much stronger positive determinant of the propensity to overseas R & D in process industries. In general, given the limited data available, Lall faced serious problems of multi-collinearity. Attention is paid to these in the presentation and interpretation of results.

9. A significant negative relationship was also found between R & D intensity and propensity to perform overseas R & D for Lall's seven 'other' industries. This was, however, less influential than for the engineering industries group. The seven 'other' industries are, primary metals; fabricated metals; aluminium; other metals; lumber wood and furniture; stone, clay and glass; miscellaneous.

10. Thomas (1983,p31) provides illustrative examples of the need to optimise the use of expensive capital equipment as a motive for centralised R & D.

11. See Lall (1979,pp320-1)

12. See also Behrman & Fischer (1980,pp73-7)

13. The most obvious problem of this type indicated by the theory of MNEs could emerge from a relationship between OPR and IRDI. The simple correlation between these variables is 0.370, but this does not appear to unduly distort the regression results.

26

**BIBLIOGRAPHY**

Behrman J N and Fischer W A (1980) *Overseas R & D Activities of Transnational Companies* Cambridge, Mass: Oelgeschlager, Gunn and Hain.

Hewitt G K (1980) "Research and Development Performed Abroad by US Manufacturing Multinationals" *Kyklos*, Vol. 33 Fasc 2 pp308-26.

Hewitt G K (1983) "Research and Development Performed in Canada by American Manufacturing Multinationals" in Rugman A M (ed) *Multinationals and Technology Transfer - The Canadian Experience* New York : Praeger pp36-49.

Hirschey R C and Caves R E (1981) "Internationalisation of Research and Transfer of Technology by Multinational Enterprises" *Oxford Bulletin of Economics and Statistics* Vol42 No 2 pp115-30.

Lall S (1979) "The International Allocation of Research Activity by US Multinationals" *Oxford Bulletin of Economics and Statistics* Vol 41 No 4 pp313-31.

Mansfield E, Teece D and Romeo A (1979) "Overseas Research and Development by US-based Firms" *Economica* Vol 46 No 182 pp187-96.

Pearce R D (1986) "The Internationalisation of Research and Development by Leading Enterprises: An Empirical Study" University of Reading Discussion Papers in International Investment and Business Studies, no 99.

Ronstadt R C (1977) *Research and Development Abroad by US Multinationals* New York : Praeger.

Ronstadt R C (1978) "International R & D : The Establishment and Evolution of R & D Abroad by Seven US Multinationals" *Journal of International Business Studies* Vol 9 No 1 pp7-24.

Thomas L J (1983) "The Centralized Research Organization" in Brown J K and Elvers L M (eds) *Research and Development : Key Issues for Management* Conference Board Report No 842. New York: The Conference Board

US Department of Commerce, Bureau of Economic Analysis (1985) *US Direct Investment Abroad : 1982 Benchmark Survey Data* Washington : US Department of Commerce.

# Part VII
# Intra-Firm Trade

# [18]

## THE PATTERN OF INTRA-FIRM EXPORTS BY U.S. MULTINATIONALS*

*By* SANJAYA LALL

### I. INTRODUCTION

This paper reports on an attempt to explain inter-industry differences in the pattern of intra-firm exports (exports from parent MNCs to affiliates abroad) by U.S. manufacturing firms in 1970. The growth of intra-firm exports of manufactures in the past two decades has been noted with interest in the literature, though much of this interest has centred on the possibilities of transfer price manipulation by MNCs.[1] No serious effort has, to my knowledge, yet been made to examine the economic factors which account for the wide inter-industry differences observed in the propensity to use intra-firm rather than unrelated-party (or 'open market') trade, despite the significance of these differences for understanding MNC strategy and for formulating policies to deal with the potential dangers of transfer price manipulation.[2]

Two factors place handicaps in the way of such an examination. First, there is little theory which deals specifically with this problem; conventional trade theory, which does not distinguish betwen inter- and intra-firm trade, certainly offers little guidance. The study of vertical integration in industrial economics comes closest to analysing the factors that account for the pattern of intra-firm trade, but we need to supplement it with considerations specific to the operations of MNCs, where 'vertical integration' in the form of common ownership already exists and where the international nature of the phenomenon adds a new set of influences. Second, and more significantly, data on intra-firm trade are scarce, and those that are published are highly aggregated.[3] Thus a detailed investigation which deals with specific products, arguably the ideal level of analysis, cannot be undertaken.

The present study suffers from both handicaps, and its limitations must be acknowledged at the start. It is, however, hoped that what does emerge is of interest, and that this preliminary attempt will lead to further investigation. We proceed as follows: section II describes some relevant characteristics of intra-firm exports for the U.S.; section III discusses factors that may be expected to account for inter-industry differences in intra-firm trade; section IV describes the variables; and section V gives the results of the empirical tests.

### II. INTRA-FIRM EXPORTS BY U.S. MNCs

In an earlier paper (Lall (1973)) I traced the growth of intra-firm trade by U.S. firms from 1962 to 1970, and noted difficulties in comparing figures for different

---

* I am very grateful to Gerry Helleiner and John Knight for helpful comments on an earlier draft.
  [1] See, for instance, Lall (1973).
  [2] The relevance of these considerations for policy-makers in less-developed countries is discussed at greater length in Lall (1978).
  [3] See U.S. Tariff Commission (1973).

years created by changes in sample coverage (of the parent MNCs as well as of the definition of affiliates). The massive study conducted by the U.S. Tariff Commission (1973), which contains by far the most comprehensive data on intra-firm trade by industry, and is the source of data used in this paper, also faced similar problems. It had to rely on data from a sample of 298 MNCs, extrapolated, on the basis of a 1966 survey of all MNCs, to provide estimates for the whole universe of MNCs for 1970. It also had to interpolate items of information suppressed by source agencies for reasons of confidentiality.[4] Furthermore, it confined its estimates of intra-firm trade to MOFAs (majority-owned foreign affiliates) of U.S. firms, leaving out minority-owned affiliates which may account for substantial trade with parent companies. It did not provide a breakdown of the destination of intra-firm exports, of their composition, of the nature of the firms indulging in such exports, all of which are relevant to explaining their industrial distribution.[5] Nevertheless, these are the best data available, and we have to make do with them.

Of total U.S. manufactured exports of $31.7 billion in 1970, MNCs accounted for $21.7 billion or 68 per cent. Of this latter sum $8.8 billion (41 per cent of MNC exports and 28 per cent of total U.S. exports) was exported to MOFAs and 'charged on the books of parent MNCs'.[6] However, some of the exports were undertaken on behalf of other U.S. firms. By themselves, MNC exports to MOFAs totalled $7.7 billion (35 per cent of MNC and 24 per cent of U.S. exports) in 1970:[7] in the rest of this paper we shall concentrate on these intra-firm exports.

Appendix 1 sets out the detailed figures on 1970 intra-firm exports of U.S. MNCs by industry. Such exports are expressed as two percentages, both of which form the dependent variables in regressions described below: IFX, or intra-firm exports as a percentage of total exports by MNCs, and IFP, intra-firm exports as a percentage of production by MOFAs receiving those exports. There is a substantial variation in propensities to use intra-firm channels to export from the U.S., both between two-digit industries and, within the two-digit level, between three-digit industries. For industries like soaps, plastics, chemical combinations, instruments and office and calculating equipment, intra-firm trade accounts for well over half of total exports by MNCs; for others, like beverages, industrial chemicals, primary metals, electrical equipment or timber and wood products it accounts for under 20 per cent. Given the quantitative significance of U.S. intra-firm trade and its inter-industry variations, it is surprising that no attempt has been made to analyse its economic determinants.

There are several interesting facts which are relevant to a study of this phenomenon that are not shown by the Tariff Commission figures nor discussed in its study.

First, the destination of intra-firm exports. A study for 1965 shows that of total intra-firm exports of $4.6 billion, 35 per cent went to Canada alone and

---

[4] See U.S. Tariff Commission (1973) pp. 267–70.

[5] Some indications of these are provided by Bradshaw (1969) for an earlier period, and are mentioned below.

[6] U.S. Tariff Commission, p. 361. This figure is mentioned here because earlier studies used this definition of intra-firm exports.

[7] *Ibid.*, p. 367. If we combine intra-firm exports from MOFAs, the total comes to $18.5 billion, 49 per cent of the total exports of MNCs plus MOFAs.

another 36 per cent to Europe.[8] If we make an allowance for Australasia and South Africa, the share of developed countries may reach 80 per cent; less-developed countries accounted for less than a quarter of the total.

Second, the same study shows that, in 1965, 49 per cent of total intra-firm exports were goods 'for resale without further manufacture' and another 7 per cent were 'exports sold for parents' account on a commission basis',[9] making the total share of finished goods for resale 56 per cent. Goods 'for further processing and assembly' comprised another 36 per cent, capital equipment 5 per cent and unallocated 3 per cent. A very large part of intra-firm exports was, therefore, simply finished products being channelled through affiliates in order to serve third parties; intermediate goods, which were used in affiliates' manufacturing, comprised only slightly over a third of the total.

Third, of the total intra-firm exports of goods by manufacturing MNCs for resale and on commission basis, some 53 per cent was channelled through manufacturing affiliates and the remainder through other (mainly distribution) affiliates.[10] Thus, manufacturing affiliates served significantly as sales and service outlets for their parent companies, quite apart from engaging in their main industrial activity. These affiliates also absorbed a large share of intra-firm exports of intermediate goods for their own use (49 per cent of the total).

Fourth, a major reason for the growth of intra-firm exports (and reimports) by certain U.S. firms in recent years has been the granting of special duty drawbacks on items which were sent abroad for processing and then finished and marketed in the U.S.[11] This provision (items 807.00 and 806.30 of the U.S. Tariff Schedules) allows import duty to be paid only on the value-added component of foreign manufacture rather than on the full value of the imported goods, giving a great incentive to the industries concerned to set up facilities abroad to use cheap semi-skilled labour and so extend intra-firm trade. Thus, such industries as metal fabrication, electronic equipment, automobile parts, textiles and apparel and instruments have benefited significantly from these schedules, and the growth of their intra-firm trade may to some extent be traced to them.

The Tariff Commission's study does not differentiate between different kinds of intra-firm exports or between sales and manufacturing affiliates. Nor does it try to assess the impact of tariff provisions in stimulating particular industries' growth of intra-firm trade. The figures it provides thus amalgamate a variety of different factors. They contain exports of finished goods which are marketed by manufacturing and distribution affiliates. They contain intermediate products which are used in production by manufacturing and other affiliates, and the resulting output is sold in host countries, other foreign countries, or exported back to the U.S. To explain the propensity to use intra-firm exports, therefore, we must look for determinants which encompass all these factors.

---

[8] Bradshaw (1969), Table 14.
[9] *Ibid.*, Table 1.
[10] *Ibid.*, Table 6.
[11] U.S. Tariff Commission (1970).

212                    BULLETIN

### III. Determinants of Intra-firm Export Behaviour

The reasons for undertaking intra-firm exports are rather similar to the conventional economic reasons for undertaking vertical integration, and we may fruitfully start our search for explanations by looking at this literature.[12]

Vertical integration refers to the tendency of a firm or an industry to internalise, by bringing under common ownership, production or marketing functions directly connected to its own activity. The choice of a parent MNC to sell, and so of the affiliate to buy, a product internally rather than to trade with third parties, represents a similar decision to internalise a transaction—with one major difference. Vertical integration in general describes the act of merging of ownership (or the taking over of one firm by another), while the internalisation of trade by MNCs refers to the choice between external and internal markets of firms which are already under common ownership and control.

The fact of foreign investment as such may also be viewed as the 'internalisation' of the markets for certain intangible advantages. The literature on MNCs postulates that the expansion of firms abroad occurs in response to, and in an attempt to internalise the benefits arising from, the possession of certain 'monopolistic advantages' such as advanced technology, product differentiation, skills of various sorts, access to capital and so on.[13] The fact that internalisation is preferred to open market sales of these advantages is taken to reflect imperfections in what may broadly be labelled 'information' markets. These imperfections raise the cost of transacting open market sales, because of the difficulties inherent in fully appropriating the gains from the possession of superior 'information' in open markets, and result in 'market failure'.[14]

The choice of MNCs to resort to intra-firm trade may also be viewed as a response to market failure in commodity markets, which renders recourse to external transactions either impossible or relatively costly. However, the imperfections which cause failure in information markets, and so lead firms to resort to direct investment rather than to the sale of their intangible advantages, are not the same as, though they may sometimes be related to, imperfections causing failure in commodity markets. Failure in information markets may be closely related to failure in commodity markets when the commodities involved embody new information (i.e. when they are produced with new technology). In such cases, the reasons for investing abroad (technological superiority) will be close to the reason for internalising trade (highly 'specific' products not available on open markets). In other conditions, however, the reasons for the two will be quite different. Several of the following set of reasons for resorting to intra-firm trade are not strong reasons for undertaking foreign investment (we shall remark on the similarities between the two later). To start with, therefore, it seems justified to keep the two phenomena separate.

[12] See Stigler (1951), Adelman (1955), Oi and Hunter (1965), Blair (1972) and Porter and Spence (1977).

[13] See Kindleberger (1969), Caves (1971), Dunning (1973, 1977), Hirsch (1976), Buckley and Casson (1976) and Magee (1977).

[14] For an elegant theoretical analysis of transaction costs and market failure see Arrow (1971).

INTRA-FIRM EXPORTS BY U.S. MULTINATIONALS **213**

The conventional theory of vertical integration[15] provides a number of plausible reasons for the internalisation of commodity trade. We have selected those which seem relevant to intra-firm trade, and added some by drawing on the specific experience of MNCs. The first factor discussed below applies to intra-firm exports of finished products, and is analogous to explanations of forward integration. The others apply mainly to export of intermediate products, and are analogous to explanations of backward integration.

(1) *Marketing requirements.* An MNC may prefer to rely on affiliates for the sale of finished products abroad for various reasons: first, the desire to control distribution facilities, where these are exceptionally profitable; second, the existence of a need for a great deal of specialised after-sales service, maintenance and updating (because of the possibilities of pooling technical resources with manufacturing affiliates this may lead MNCs to use such affiliates to act also as pure sales outlets); third, the need for assimilating and communicating information to and from consumers on their requirements, designs, plans, and so on; and, fourth, the need where relevant for keeping direct representation in order to maintain government contacts, monitor or influence policy, or win large orders.

(2) *Specificity of product.* The more specific is an intermediate input to the firm concerned, the more will it tend to rely on internal rather than external supplies. 'Specificity' refers to such characteristics as uniqueness (high-technology products made by the MNC, not available on open markets), high quality (precision, performance or high tolerance, available externally only at high cost or after considerable search) and suitability to demanding or variable requirements (available externally only after close relationships with suppliers are established).

(3) *Risk and uncertainty.* Even for non-specific intermediate commodities the risks of disruption, delay, price changes, quality variation and the like can clearly lead firms to rely on internal sources of supply. For MNCs, the strength of this inducement will depend on the political and economic state of international markets as well as on conditions in particular host countries in which they happen to be located.

(4) *Unexploited capacity and scale economies.* A parent MNC which has spare capacity or unexhausted plant economies of scale would prefer to use its own facilities to supply affiliates rather than let them go to open markets. A firm may do this even when the cost of internal trading to the enterprise as a whole is higher than that of buying externally, if it feels obliged (owing to political, strategic or trade union pressures) to use its existing facilities in its home country.

(5) *'Divisibility' of production processes.* Certain industries use processes which can economically be divided, and parts of them relocated in cheap-labour areas abroad.[16] Where these cheap-labour areas do not possess their own firms capable of undertaking the task, or where the MNCs concerned prefer to set up

[15] Two recent textbooks, Jacquemin and de Jong (1977) and Howe (1978) provide simple and concise treatments; for a more theoretical analysis see Porter and Spence (1977).
[16] The viability of such relocation depends on several factors, such as the nature of the process (continuous-process chemical manufacture would be difficult to divide), the weight-to-value ratio of the goods involved, transport costs to the cheap labour areas, the nature of production skills required, the importance of labour in total costs, and scale economies.

their own affiliates to capitalise on technological advantages (the best example being the semi-conductor industry), the internalisation of the cost advantage will lead to the growth of direct investment together with that of intra-firm trade. In cases where local firms in cheap-labour areas *can* undertake the job efficiently, of course, the MNC may realise the cost advantage by subcontracting (and so increase inter- rather than intra-firm trade).[17] For U.S. firms, slightly less than half of such activity has taken place through direct investment and intra-firm trade.[18]

(6) *Home government policy.* The policies of the home (i.e. U.S.) government may influence the extent of intra-firm trade, reducing it, on the one hand, by requiring parent companies to use domestic installed capacity to supply affiliates, or increasing it, on the other, by permitting or even encouraging the transfer abroad of 'divisible' processes (as defined above). There is little evidence that the first has been practised; the second, however, is, as we saw in section II, an important element of U.S. policy. The provisions of Tariff Schedules 807.00 and 806.30 have promoted the growth of intra-firm exports by industries whose processes are 'divisible', though there is good reason to believe that these exports would have grown even in the absence of such provisions.[19]

(7) *Host government policy.* The policies of host governments with respect to foreign investment, imports and domestic purchasing can influence the extent of intra-firm exports. This is particularly true of less-developed countries which, on the one hand, create a high initial dependence on imported (often intra-firm) inputs by attracting foreign investments into highly protected activities, and, on the other, seek to reduce the import content of production over the longer run by forcing foreign firms to use local inputs. Thus, the distribution of MNC affiliates over countries at different levels of industrial development and with different policies will affect their propensities (and abilities) to indulge in intra-firm trade.

(8) *Transfer pricing.* MNCs may wish to increase the extent of intra-firm trade simply in order to enlarge the scope for using transfer-prices to remit profits or evade taxes.[20] This inducement is likely to be stronger for operations in LDCs than in developed countries, but it may also operate for the latter.

These are the factors which we expect to influence the pattern of intra-firm exports by different U.S. industries. It is apparent that some of them (like specificity of product) are closely related to factors (technological superiority) which also account for foreign investment, while others are not so closely related. As with most such investigations, the empirical testing falls far short of theoretical requirements, but the next section shows what we have been able to accomplish with the material at hand.

[17] See Helleiner (1973).

[18] U.S. Tariff Commission (1970), pp. 6–7.

[19] *Ibid.*, pp. 230–31. It is in fact likely that the profitability of moving divisible processes abroad led powerful MNCs to influence U.S. government policy, rather than the other way round; see Helleiner (1977).

[20] This factor applies to trade in finished as well as intermediate products. It is, however, probably a more powerful inducement to intra-firm exports of intermediate products, because the risk of getting 'caught out' is less here than for finished products. See Lall (1973).

## IV. The Variables

The variables used for empirical testing are given below; the sources of data are described in Appendix 2. The *dependent* variable is intra-firm exports at the industry level, deflated by two sets of figures:

*IFX:* intra-firm exports for each industry expressed as a percentage of total MNC exports for that industry. This variable shows the propensities of parent firms in each industry to use internal rather than external outlets for their exports.

*IFP:* intra-firm exports for each industry expressed as a percentage of sales of affiliates receiving these exports. This variable shows the propensity of subsidiaries to purchase from internal rather than external sources. The two formulations of the dependent variable are designed to capture propensities from both sides of the intra-firm transaction.

The *independent* variables are:

*RD:* research and development expenditures as a percentage of industry sales in the U.S. This variable, measuring the technological intensity of each industry, is intended to capture the innovational cause of 'specificity' of products. The higher is RD and the more specific a product, the greater is the expected incidence of intra-firm exports.

*VAL:* value-added per employee, the 'Lary measure' of the flow of physical capital and skill services, for each industry in the U.S. This variable partly captures the skill element in each industry that may contribute to product 'specificity', and partly it captures an element of capital intensity, which in turn may contribute to scale economies in each sector. This measure suffers from the handicap that it catches a number of influences, such as market power, not related to skill or capital-intensity, but it does have the advantage that it is easy to calculate.

*SALES:* a dummy variable to denote the marketing requirements of each industry, taking the value of 1 when after-sales service requirements were high and 0 when they were low. The need for after-sales service was worked out from figures provided by Bailey (1975) who gives 'marketing-support' (mainly advertising and market research) costs separately from 'selling-related' (field service, technical support and other kinds of after-sales activities) for a number of U.S. industries. Where selling-related costs were more than double the marketing support costs, and when the industry spent a relatively high amount on sales and technical services, the industry was deemed to have high after-sales service requirements.

*AD:* advertising as a percentage of sales, a further indicator, but a negative one, of the need for specialised after-sales service. It is postulated that highly advertised goods (in the U.S.) are mass-produced commodities sold directly to consumers, and so require little specialised follow-up by skilled personnel who need to be controlled by the producer. Products where a great deal of design and information exchange goes on between producer and buyer, and where the need for marketing *via* affiliates is higher, naturally need lower levels of advertising. Thus, *AD* is expected to be negatively related to the dependent variables.

*TAR:* a dummy variable taking the value 1 when the industry used Tariff Schedules 807.00 and 806.30, and 0 when it did not. This variable captures the influences of both the 'divisibility' of production processes and of home government policy: since the two go so closely together, we cannot separate them here.

*FA:* foreign assets as a percentage of domestic assets of each U.S. industry, a measure of the foreign spread of each sector. We argued above that the reasons which make for greater foreign investment (the 'internalisation' of intangible monopolistic advantages) were not the same as, though they may sometimes be similar to, those that make for the internalisation of commodity trade. The extent of foreign investment may, however, be used as a proxy variable to catch four different types of influences on intra-firm exports. First, it can reflect the existence of intangible advantages (like efficient and immediate communication between parent and affiliate) that lead to greater intra-firm trade by increasing the relative cost of collecting information on external markets. Thus, the more international an industry, the more 'specific' its trade may become for those products where intra-firm information becomes relatively cheap to gather. Second, a greater international spread may expose an industry to greater social, political and economic risk, and so may lead it to rely more on internal sources of supply. Third, some industries may invest abroad to keep a direct presence in countries where such representation is necessary to win contracts, adapt designs, and exert political influence. Thus, greater foreign spread may reflect greater marketing requirements, which in turn may reflect the existence of highly 'specific' products. Fourth, it may act as a proxy for inducements to indulge in transfer-price manipulations. The more widespread an industry's operations, the more the opportunities to benefit from tax, tariff and other differences between countries, and the greater the incentives to use intra-firm trade (to allow tax minimisation on global profits by changing the prices assigned to such trade).

Despite all our efforts, a number of potential influences on intra-firm exports could not be captured at all, or were only unsatisfactorily captured by the proxy variables. Thus, such factors as risk and uncertainty, excess capacity, scale economies or the geographical distribution of MNC trade,[21] are inadequately represented in our empirical tests. The inability to take these factors into account is a serious gap in this study, but with the data available it is practically impossible to test a more comprehensive model. Furthermore, the high level of aggregation of the data must certainly conceal large variations within industry groups, but there is no way of correcting for this.

The data provided by the Tariff Commission (1973) are collated in such a way as to give 32 observations for IFX and 30 for IFP. Two- and three-digit industries are combined in the sample; however, where a three-digit industry (e.g. drugs) is used, the relevant two-digit category (chemicals) is dropped. This procedure is unexceptional as long as the extent of aggregation for the industries in the final sample is not dissimilar or misleading. The table in Appendix 1, which shows the

---

[21] It may be argued that policies of LDC governments cannot affect intra-firm exports significantly, since only about 20 per cent of total U.S. intra-firm exports go to LDCs. However, they may well be important for particular industries—we cannot tell.

sample industries (all the two-digit ones without three-digit breakdown, e.g. paper, rubber etc., were used), indicates that our procedure is likely to be correct.

## V. The Results

The statistical procedure used was ordinary least squares linear regression. A set of logarithmic formulations was also tried, but did not give noticeably better results. We do not report their results. Table 1 sets out the main results, showing three equations for the dependent IFX and four for IFP.

Table 1

*Determinants of Inter-industry Differences in U.S. Intra-Firm Exports, 1970*

| Dependent | RD | (RD)² | AD | FA | VAL | TAR | SALES | Constant | R² |
|---|---|---|---|---|---|---|---|---|---|
| 1. IFX | 0.361ᵃ (2.47) | — | — | — | 0.08ᶜ (1.53) | — | — | 14.07 | 0.20 |
| 2. IFX | — | — | | 0.119ᵃ (3.34) | 0.301 (0.77) | 16.25ᵇ (1.93) | — | 7.18 | 0.30 |
| 3. IFX | | — | | 0.110ᵃ (3.61) | — | — | — | 20.77 | 0.28 |
| 4. IFP | — | — | — | 0.102ᶜ (1.70) | | 22.53ᵇ (1.74) | 43.17ᵃ (2.87) | 40.34 | 0.49 |
| 5. IFP | — | — | −0.53ᵇ (−1.98) | — | — | 18.17ᶜ (1.38) | 57.90ᵃ (4.55) | 65.06 | 0.49 |
| 6. IFP | 2.22ᵃ (2.65) | −0.02ᵇ (−1.73) | −0.615ᶜ (−1.53) | — | — | 28.20ᵇ (2.01) | — | 49.50 | 0.42 |
| 7. IFP | 2.30ᵃ (2.77) | −0.02ᵇ (−1.95) | — | — | — | 36.52ᵃ (2.72) | — | 30.17 | 0.40 |

R² corrected for degrees of freedom; *t*-values in brackets. One-tail tests used.
ᵃ Denotes significant at 99 per cent;    ᵇ 95 per cent;    ᶜ 90 per cent.

Multicollinearity problems existed among some of the independent variables, and should be noted at the outset. RD was highly correlated with the dummy SALES (simple correlation coefficient of 0.77) suggesting that high-technology industries also have to provide heavy after-sales service and maintain large sales-related staff. Both SALES and RD were also significantly correlated with FA (0.51 and 0.63 respectively) indicating that technological advantage, and the need to follow up the sales of high-technology products with affiliate servicing, constitute important factors in promoting foreign investment.[22] VAL was correlated with AD (0.65), indicating a relationship between value-added and advertising-based market power. The other variables had relatively low correlation coefficients. The results shown exclude cases with severe collinearity problems.

The results are, in general, interesting and, given the nature of the data, not as poor as may have been feared. The model works better for IFP than for IFX: the determinants identified here are more significant when intra-firm exports are calculated as an input into affiliate sales rather than as proportions of total MNC exports. The independent variables are able to explain nearly half of the variation in IFP and somewhat less than a third for IFX. This is a moderately successful

[22] A similar point is made in a theoretical analysis of the determinants of foreign investment by Hirsch (1976).

preliminary attempt, but factors which we could not account for clearly are of significance in determining intra-firm exports.

The explanatory variables which perform best are RD, FA, TAR and SALES. Of these, RD is uniformly positive and always highly significant.[23] However, it is possible that at very high levels of technology the relationship may be reversed, for two reasons. First, the industry may, according to product cycle theory,[24] export innovative products at the beginning of the cycle to unrelated buyers because it has not yet started foreign production; or, second, because economies of scale in R & D are so large that it is uneconomical to invest abroad. To test for this possibility, a quadratic formulation was tried (equations 6 and 7); it gave significant results, supporting the hypothesis than an inverse U-shaped relationship exists between IFP and RD.

The extent of foreign investment, as measured by FA, is positively and significantly related to both dependent variables. It has a much stronger effect on IFX than on IFP: this may be because IFP already contains a measure of the international spread of the industry (foreign sales) in the denominator. The results indicate that the more internationally diversified industries have a higher propensity to use intra-firm exports, but because FA captures the effect of several possible influences we cannot establish the exact causation more clearly.

TAR has a strong, positive and significant effect on both dependent variables, confirming the influence of economic pressures forcing industries with 'divisible' processes to expand intra-firm trade, and of U.S. tariff policy in encouraging such expansion. Curiously enough, TAR has a very low correlation coefficient with FA (0.09), probably because the volume of capital investment involved in offshore processing is relatively low in relation to total foreign investment.

The after-sales service dummy SALES has the most powerful positive effect on IFP. It is also positive for IFX but usually fails to reach significance (not shown in Table 1). As noted above, SALES is collinear with RD and FA, but its coefficient in relation to IFP is higher and more significant than either of these variables. As far as intermediate goods exports are concerned, SALES may be picking up the influence of technology on product specificity. However, as far as finished goods exports go, the indications are that the need to control the after-sales function provides a strong incentive to channel exports, particularly of high-technology products, through affiliates.

AD has the predicted sign and reaches significance for the dependent IFP; providing some grounds for arguing that heavily promoted goods may be efficiently marketed through unrelated dealers. VAL barely reaches significance for IFX and behaves erratically for IFP (not shown): whether this is due to its misspecification as a proxy for skill and scale factors, or to the unimportance of these factors themselves in affecting intra-firm trade, is difficult to say.

[23] Buckley and Pearce (1977) find, in a study of 156 MNCs from several countries, that nationality and industry groups make significant differences to the propensity to use intra-firm exports (neither of these is relevant to our study), and that high-technology firms have higher intra-firm exports than low-technology ones (which confirms our findings).
[24] Vernon (1966). Vernon's theory is posed in terms of products, but Magee (1977) argues that it may also apply to whole industries.

Despite the extent of unexplained variation and despite the level of aggregation of the data, it appears that the pattern of intra-firm trade is amenable to rational economic explanation. The forces which make for vertical integration within countries also seem to make for the internalisation of commodity trade between countries. The use of better measures of risk and uncertainty in internal markets, of host government policy, excess capacity and scale economies, and the use of more disaggregated data for the dependent variables, should greatly improve the performance of our model.

## VI. Concluding Remarks

Our attempt to explain the pattern of U.S. intra-firm exports has met with some success. The usefulness of the tools of industrial economics in clarifying the phenomenon bears out the validity of this approach (now increasingly popular[25]) in analysing problems in international trade and capital movements more generally. The factors which, in our model, affect the pattern of intra-firm exports are: technological intensity, the extent of foreign investment, the 'divisibility' of production processes and the need for after-sales service.

There remain clear gaps in the present empirical investigation. We need to focus on specific products rather than on industries. We need to add variables to account for risk, scale economies, capacity utilisation and host government policy. And we need longer coverage over which to study the problem. All these, however, require much more detailed data than are presently published by the U.S.; other capital exporting countries provide far less than the U.S. government does.

*Institute of Economics and Statistics,*
*Oxford University*

[25] See Caves (1971) and Dunning (1973).

# APPENDIX 1

*Intra-Firm Exports of U.S. MNCs by Industry, 1970*

($ million)

| Industry | Total exports | Intra- firm exports | IFX (%) | IFP (%) | Industry | Total exports | Intra- firm exports | IFX (%) | IFP (%) |
|---|---|---|---|---|---|---|---|---|---|
| *Food products* | 1,062 | 362 | 34 | 5 | *Non-electrical machinery* | 3,795 | 1,674 | 44 | 15 |
| Grain Mills | 227 | 106 | 47 | 8 | Farm machinery | 392 | 192 | 49 | 20 |
| Beverages | 58 | 11 | 19 | 1 | Industrial[a] | 1,694 | 457 | 27 | 12 |
| Combination | 40 | 9 | 23 | n.a. | Office[b] | 576 | 431 | 75 | 17 |
| Other | 737 | 236 | 32 | 5 | Computing | 399 | 298 | 75 | 17 |
| *Paper* | 609 | 150 | 25 | 7 | Other | 734 | 296 | 40 | 20 |
| *Chemicals* | 2,342 | 845 | 36 | 7 | *Electrical machinery* | 2,060 | 575 | 28 | 8 |
| Drugs | 361 | 138 | 38 | 5 | Household[c] | 157 | 39 | 25 | 5 |
| Soaps and cosmetics | 130 | 70 | 54 | 3 | Equipment | 978 | 151 | 15 | 7 |
| Industrial | 1,198 | 181 | 15 | 9 | Electronic | 734 | 210 | 29 | 8 |
| Plastics | 318 | 279 | 88 | 12 | Other | 191 | 175 | 92 | 12 |
| Combinations | 114 | 114 | 100 | n.a. | *Transport equipment* | 6,750 | 2,748 | 41 | 17 |
| Other | 221 | 63 | 29 | 8 | *Textiles, Apparel* | 244 | 97 | 40 | 6 |
| *Rubber* | 383 | 148 | 39 | 6 | *Lumber, wood furnishing* | 352 | 40 | 11 | 10 |
| *Primary and fabricated metals* | 2,237 | 278 | 12 | 4 | *Printing, publishing* | 144 | 36 | 25 | 6 |
| Primary | 976 | 51 | 5 | 6 | *Stone, clay, glass* | 267 | 86 | 32 | 6 |
| Fabricated (excluding aluminium, brass and copper) | 554 | 131 | 24 | 4 | *Instruments* | 848 | 522 | 62 | 18 |
| Aluminium | 627 | 56 | 9 | 2 | *Other manufacturing* | 625 | 146 | 23 | 3 |
| Other | 80 | 40 | 50 | 6 | ALL MANUFACTURING | 21,718 | 7,707 | 35 | 10 |

*Source:* U.S. Tariff Commission (1973), pp. 367, 374.

*Notes:* IFX: Intra-firm exports as percentage of total exports by MNCs.

   IFP: Intra-firm exports as percentage of total MOFA sales (i.e. local sales plus exports, including exports to U.S.).

   n.a.: data not available.

   Two-digit industries are in italics.

   [a] Data for MOFA production of industrial and 'other' were shown jointly by the Tariff Commission; it was assumed that the IFP for latter was higher because of IFX figures.

   [b] Data for MOFA production of office and computing equipment were shown jointly; it was assumed that same IFP applies to both.

   [c] Data for MOFA production of household and other electrical machinery were shown jointly; latter was assumed to have much higher IFP than former because of IFX figures.

# APPENDIX 2

*Data Sources*

All the data on intra-firm exports, foreign production and assets are taken from the U.S. Tariff Commission (1973). Advertising data are gathered from the *Statistical Abstract of the United States 1972*, Comanor and Wilson (1974), and (after adjustment) from Bailey (1975). Value added figures were taken from the *Statistical Abstract*. Information on use of tariff schedules 807.00 and 806.30 was taken from the U.S. Tariff Commission (1970). The after-sales service dummy was constructed on the basis of data given in Bailey (1975); some interpolations had to be made for missing industries. R & D figures were taken, with a few interpolations, from the National Science Foundation, *Research and Development in Industry 1973*, **Washington, D.C.,** 1975.

INTRA-FIRM EXPORTS BY U.S. MULTINATIONALS **221**

## REFERENCES

Adelman, M. A. (1955), 'Vertical Integration and Market Growth', reprinted in Yamey (1973).

Arrow, K. J. (1971), 'Political and Economic Evaluation of Social Effects and Externalities", in M. D. Intriligator (ed.), *Frontier of Quantitative Economics*, Amsterdam: North-Holland.

Bailey, E. L. (1975), *Marketing-Cost Ratios of U.S. Manufacturers*, New York: Conference Board.

Blair, J. M. (1972), *Economic Concentration*, New York: Harcourt, Brace, Jovanovich.

Bradshaw, M. T. (1969), 'U.S. Exports to Foreign Affiliates of U.S. Firms', *Survey of Current Business*, May, pp. 34–51.

Buckley, P. J. and Casson, M. (1976), *The Future of the Multinational Enterprise*, London: Macmillan.

Buckley, P. J. and Pearce, R. D. (1977), 'Overseas Production and Exporting by the World's Largest Enterprises—a Study in Sourcing Policy', University of Reading, Discussion Papers in International Investment and Business Studies, no. 37.

Caves, R. E. (1971), 'International Corporations: the Industrial Economies of Foreign Investment', *Economica*, pp. 1–27.

Comanor, W. S. and Wilson, T. A. (1974), *Advertising and Market Power*, Cambridge (Mass.): Harvard University Press.

Dunning, J. H. (1973), 'The Determinants of International Production', *Oxford Economic Papers*, pp. 289–336.

Dunning, J. H. (1977), 'Trade, Location of Economic Activity and the MNE: a Search for an Eclectic Approach', in B. Ohlin *et al.* (ed.), *The International Allocation of Economic Activity*, London: Macmillan.

Helleiner, G. K. (1973), 'Manufactured Exports from Less-Developed Countries and Multinational Firms', *Economic Journal*, pp. 21–47.

Helleiner, G. K. (1977), 'Transnational Enterprises and the New Political Economy of U.S. Trade Policy', *Oxford Economic Papers*, pp. 102–16.

Hirsch, S. (1976), 'An International Trade and Investment Theory of the Firm', *Oxford Economic Papers*, pp. 258–70.

Howe, W. S. (1978), *Industrial Economics: an Applied Approach*, London: Macmillan.

Jacquemin, A. P. and de Jong, H. W. (1977), *European Industrial Organisation*, London: Macmillan.

Kindleberger, C. P. (1969), *American Business Abroad*, New Haven: Yale University Press.

Lall, S. (1973), 'Transfer-Pricing by Multinational Manufacturing Firms', *Oxford Bulletin of Economics and Statistics*, pp. 173–95.

Lall, S. (1978) 'Transfer-Pricing and LDCs: Some Problems of Investigation', *World Development* (forthcoming).

Magee, S. P. (1977), 'Information and the Multinational Corporation: an Appropriability Theory of Direct Foreign Investment', in J. N. Bhagwati (ed.), *The New International Economic Order*, Cambridge (Mass.): MIT Press.

Oi, W. Y. and Hunter, A. P. (1965), 'A Theory of Vertical Integration in Road Transport Services', reprinted in Yamey (1973).

Porter, M. E. and Spence, A. M. (1977), 'Vertical Integration and Different Inputs', University of Warwick, Research Paper 120.

Stigler, G. J. (1951), 'The Division of Labour is limited by the Extent of the Market', *Journal of Political Economy*, pp. 185–93.

U.S. Tariff Commission (1970), *Economic Factors Affecting the Use of Items 807.00 and 806.30 of the Tariff Schedules of the United States*, Washington, D.C.: GPO.

U.S. Tariff Commission (1973), *Implications of Multinational Firms for World Trade and Investment and for U.S. Trade and Labor*, Washington, D.C.: GPO.

Vernon, R. (1966), 'International Investment and International Trade in the Product Cycle', *Quarterly Journal of Economics*, pp. 190–207.

Yamey, B. S. (1973), (ed.), *Economics of Industrial Structure*, Harmondsworth: Penguin.

# [19]

# OVERSEAS PRODUCTION AND EXPORTING BY THE WORLD'S LARGEST ENTERPRISES: A STUDY IN SOURCING POLICY

**PETER J. BUCKLEY***
*University of Bradford Management Centre*

**R. D. PEARCE***
*University of Reading*

**Abstract.** The sourcing policy of a multinational enterprise is the result of the firm's decisions as to which of its production facilities shall service its various final markets. We can thus speak of an international network linking production to markets. Critical determinants of this policy are the firm's size, industry characteristics, and influences deriving from the firm's nationality of ownership. We suggest that research intensity is an important influence on sourcing policy, particularly through its effect on the firm's internal exports.

■ The decisions of Multinational Enterprises (MNEs) about location of production and exporting have been, in recent years, the subject of intense policy interest. This paper presents some evidence on the methods by which 156 of the world's largest enterprises service foreign markets.

**INTRODUCTION**

A MNE can service an overseas market either by exporting to that market from a production base located in the parent country, or from a third country subsidiary, or it can set up production facilities in the market itself.[1] The sourcing policy of a MNE is the result of the firm's decisions as to which of its production facilities shall service its various final markets. We can thus speak of an international network linking production to markets. Our data enable us to analyze sourcing policy in some detail and to identify the existence of regularities in behavior across MNEs according to industry, country of ownership, and size of firm.

More specifically, we wish to test a particular hypothesis which is derived from the theoretical explanation of MNE behavior put forward by Buckley and Casson.[2] Buckley and Casson suggest that there are strong incentives for firms to grow by eliminating external markets in intermediate goods by internalizing those markets within the firm. When international markets are internalized, we observe multinational firms whose internal transfers of goods and services are exports or imports for the nation-states between which the goods and services are transferred. There are powerful reasons for believing that the incentives to internalize intermediate goods markets are most strong in areas where research inputs and proprietary technology are an important part of the production process. Consequently, we wish to test the extent to which the firms' internal exports can be said to be technology flows embodied as intermediate goods transferred internationally within the firm.

There are several important reasons for the belief that a high degree of R&D intensity will be linked with internal exports. These reasons derive from the fact that the incentive to internalize (international) markets is greater at higher levels of R&D. Five major influences can be determined. First, the longer gestation period involved in the production of research intensive goods means that, in the absence of adequate external futures

* Dr. P. J. Buckley is Lecturer in International Business at the University of Bradford Management Centre, U.K. He has published articles in the field of International Investment and is coauthor, with Mark Casson, of *The Future of the Multinational Enterprise* (Macmillan, 1976).

** R. D. Pearce is Esmee Fairbairn Research Assistant in International Investment at the University of Reading. He has published articles and books in cooperation with Professor John H. Dunning.

The authors would like to thank Mark Casson and an anonymous referee for comments on an earlier draft and Michelle Foot for computing assistance.

9

markets, the firm can coordinate production and avoid costly time lags in a way which external markets cannot match. Second, knowledge, the product of R&D, represents a natural monopoly. Sale of such knowledge on the open market often leads to a situation of bilateral monopoly, which is an inherently unstable situation. Indeed, often the value of knowledge is at least partially dependent upon secrecy. Such proprietary knowledge is of great importance among the firms we are considering. Third, knowledge can be considered as a public good *within* the firm (that is to say, the return on its worldwide exploitation is high relative to the cost of its utilization). Fourth, an internal exploitation of the fruits of R&D allows discriminatory pricing to be used—increasing the returns by charging different affiliates differing amounts. This practice cannot normally be utilized on the open market. Finally, there are difficulties and high costs of transferring knowledge *between* organizations which do not arise *within* an organization; in addition, prices (transfer prices) remain under the sole control of the transferor. For these reasons we would expect R&D intensive firms to have more incentive to internalize markets and therefore to have a greater amount of internal exports.

Consequently, this paper has two purposes: (1) to examine the determinants of sourcing policy and (2) to test the hypothesis that the firm's internal exports are strongly related to its R&D intensity, which therefore exerts an influence on sourcing policy.

**THE DATA**  Our study uses information on the sourcing behavior of 156 of the world's largest enterprises in 1972. These data were compiled during a recent study of the world's largest industrial companies.[3] The 156 companies were classified into 11 Nationality of Ownership groups and 17 industry groupings. The sample consists of firms from the largest 500 United States-owned and top 200 non-United States-owned firms who completed a questionnaire which included the following questions:

1. What percentage of your world wide sales for 1972 was accounted for by your foreign affiliates or associated companies? Here, sales should include all goods produced and sold abroad by affiliates and associates, but exclude finished goods imported from the parent company for resale (i.e., without any further processing or packaging).

2. (a) What percentage of the total sales of your domestic operations were exported in 1972?
   (b) Of this total (i.e., all exports = 100) how much was exported to affiliate or associated companies?

By applying these percentage figures to the absolute value of worldwide sales in 1972 (of these enterprises) obtained from *Fortune* magazine,[4] we obtained the following data for each company:

a  Total worldwide group sales
b  Total foreign production
c  Total parent company production
d  Total parent company exports
e  Total parent company intragroup exports
f  Total parent company extragroup exports.[5]

The firms are categorized by geographical origin of the parent company and by industry. The allocation of firms by industry is based upon their main products as listed by *Fortune* (non-United States enterprises) and by various market guides. Some of the firms whose activities cover a particularly wide spectrum were allocated to one or other of two 'widely diversified' groups. These are 'widely diversified [1]' which includes firms predominantly based in chemicals, textiles, and food processing; and 'widely diversified [2]' covering firms more oriented to the engineering, mining, and capital goods industries. Industry grouping and nationality of ownership are treated as independent influences on sourcing policy.

Our investigation of the relationship between internal exports and R&D proceeds as follows: Research intensive industries are those which in the mid 1960s had research and development expenditures of 2% or more of total sales, or where the number of scientists and engineers employed in R&D activities was 1% or more of total employ-

10

ment. On this basis 6 industries were classified as research intensive—all firms in these 6 industries were thus designated research intensive. This procedure avoids the difficulties of obtaining any reasonably comprehensive and comparable data on the research intensity of individual firms. R&D intensity is used as an alternative to industry classification as a determinant of sourcing policy.

We describe sourcing policy in terms of four sets of key variables. These are:

**KEY VARIABLES**

1. the degree of multinationality of production,
2. the degree of multinationality of sales,
3. export behavior, including the extent of commitment to internal exports,
4. two sourcing ratios.

This section presents the data on each set of variables in tabular form, classified by country and industry. Next, each variable is subjected to regression analyses to identify significant differences according to country and industry characteristics and to research intensity.

The Degree of Multinationality of Production is defined as the ratio of foreign production to total group sales; i.e., b/a. This ratio is conventionally used as the most important indicator of a firm's multinationality. Our sample of 156 firms was broken down by nationality of parent and by industry. Both a weighted (by sales) average version of the index and an unweighted (simple average) calculation of the index were made for each group. The differences between these two indicators thus illustrate the influence of firm size.

**1. The Degree of Multinationality of Production**

The results of the breakdowns of the sample by nationality of ownership show that Swiss (91.6%), Benelux (70.7%), and 'Joint and other' (69.7%) national groups have a significantly higher than average (unweighted 35.6%) proportion of production outside their parent country. The small size of the home market and lack of available inputs in the parent country are important here. This has induced an outlook of much greater multinational orientation in firms of such nationalities. Japan (2.4%) and France (8.0%) have significantly lower than average degree of production multinationality; firms of these nationalities rely on domestic production plus exporting.

Naturally, there are wide industry variations, with oil (57.0%) in particular, but also tobacco (51.8%) and diversified [1] (53.9%) exhibiting greater than average overseas production ratios. The location of basic raw materials is the motivation for overseas production in some of these industries and the predominant form of overseas investment is vertical (chiefly backward: toward source of supply of crucial inputs) integration. Horizontal overseas investment does not, in any industry, command this proportion of resources, although market oriented investment is important when grouped according to nationality as in the Swiss case.

Industries which are below average multinationality are par excellence aircraft[6] (no overseas production facilities in our sample), iron and steel (1.6%), and other metals (13.4%). Aircraft and iron and steel are characterized by economies of scale at plant level, which inhibit overseas production and encourage exporting from one optimum sized plant,[7] and both industries are subject to political and strategic constraints in their location policies. These industries are inhibited by high transport costs of intermediate products from locating different stages of production in different countries. It is notable, however, that the Japanese iron and steel industry exhibits a higher degree of production multinationality than that of other source countries.[8]

A final point of note, before moving on to regression analysis, is the importance of the size of firm. This is illustrated by the differences between the sales weighted average (35.6%) against the simple average (22.0%). Thus, even among the world's largest firms, scale is an influence on the importance of overseas production. In the national ownership groups this scale factor is most marked in Benelux, 'Joint and other,' and United States firms. Among industries, large oil, food products, and diversified [1] firms

11

carry out a much greater proportion of production overseas than their smaller competitors.

Table 1 shows the regression analysis of the Degree of Multinationality of Production.[9] Throughout, the purpose of the regressions is to show the degree to which our independent variables can explain the various aspects of sourcing policy decisions.

As Table 1 shows, firm size (as measured by total group sales) is an important determinant of production multinationality. When combined with country and industry effects, 61.5% of the variance in the dependent variable is explained.

Several points are to be borne in mind in the interpretation of our regression results. The country and industry dummy coefficients are differences from one 'standard' variable taken arbitrarily as the U.S.A. in country studies and 'other' in industry studies.[10] Thus significance here implies 'significantly different from the standard variable'; that is to say, from the United States result and the 'other' industries result. The research intensity dummy takes a value of 1 for research intensive industries, 0 otherwise.

The interpretation of these results therefore is that the United Kingdom, Benelux, and Swiss firms, with 'joint' slightly less so, are significantly more multinational in production than United States firms. Japanese firms are significantly less multinational in production than the sample United States firms. The tobacco, motor vehicles, and diversified [1] industries have a significantly greater proportion of production overseas than the control industry. We cannot infer from these results that R&D intensity is a major influence on overseas production, although in the case of this dependent variable its influence may be swamped by vertically integrated firms acting according to standard location theory.

TABLE 1
Regression Analysis of Degree of Multinationality of Production

| Equation | Dependent Variable | Independent Variables | Significant Variables | $R^2$ (Degrees of Freedom) |
|---|---|---|---|---|
| 1.1 | Degree of multi-nationality of production i.e. $\dfrac{(b)}{(a)}$ | Size Nationality dummies (10) | Size** U.K.** Japan (−)** Benelux** Switzerland** Joint and other* | 0.6150 (26,129) |
| | | Industry dummies (15) | Motor vehicles* Tobacco* Diversified (1)* | |
| 1.2 | Degree of multi-nationality of production | Size Nationality dummies (10) | Size** U.K.** Japan (−)** Benelux** Switzerland** | 0.4984 (12,143) |
| | | Research Intensity | n.s. | |

**indicates that the variable is significant at the 1% level
*indicates that the variable is significant at the 5% level
n.s. indicates not significant

**2. The Degree of Multinationality of Sales**    Two versions of a degree of multinationality of sales coefficient are presented. These are: version 1—

$$\frac{\text{overseas production} + \text{parent's total exports}}{\text{total group sales}}; \text{ i.e., } \frac{(b) + (d)}{(a)},$$

and version 2 which is the same ratio with intragroup exports removed,

$$\text{i.e., } \frac{(b) + (f)}{(a)}$$

The first ratio may overstate the degree of multinationality of sales since some double counting may occur; thus, partially completed goods sent by a parent to its overseas affiliate may be included at that stage and again as final goods sold by the subsidiary. On the other hand the second measure may understate the ratio by totally excluding completed goods sent by the parent to an overseas subsidiary for resale. Since we cannot be sure of the importance of these deficiencies, both measures are used.

The pattern of multinationality is, of course, altered by the inclusion of exports—all industries and nationality groups are more multinational in sales than in production—those groups with the highest export ratios increase more. However, our results show that Japan (19.4%) is still well below average multinationality (47.99%) on version 1 of this index, while Switzerland (97.1%), Benelux (88.3%), and "Joint and other" (73.3%) are well above it. In terms of the industry distribution, oil (63.8%) and diversified [1] (62.3%) are still significantly greater than average on sales multinationality, while paper products, iron and steel, packaging products (32.4%), other metals (18.1%), and 'other' (miscellaneous) (25.3%) are below average multinationality. It is notable that aircraft (44.0%) no longer appears on this list because of the multinational orientation of sales from the parent company. A final point of note is the difference between research intensive industries (53.6% of total sales accounted for by overseas production or exports) and nonresearch intensive industries (39.7%). We shall follow up this point later; for now we merely note the connection between exporting and research intensity.

On the second version of this index we find an almost identical pattern except that the difference between research intensive industries and others is weakened. This suggests that internal exports are closely connected to research intensity.

Turning to the regression analysis of multinationality of sales, we find that national and industry differences are significant in many cases, together with the research intensity variable, as Tables 2 and 3 show.

Again, size is a very important explanatory variable. The differences according to nationality are also important—they show significant deviations from the United States percentage. The United Kingdom, West Germany, Benelux, Switzerland, and 'Joint and other' variables show up well in all equations. Italy and Sweden drop out when internal exports are removed. It will be noted from Tables 2 and 3 that the United States ratio is relatively unaffected by the removal of internal exports, which are insignificant compared to total sales for that nationality. Therefore, countries where internal exports are important, notably Sweden, lose significance as we move from form (1) to form (2) of the dependent variable. Similarly, when internal exports are excluded, the research intensity adds nothing to the explanatory power of Equation 3.2. It is internal exports, not exports as a whole, which appear to be strongly correlated with research intensity. This hypothesis is more fully examined in the following section.

## 3. Export Behavior and the Role of Internal Exports

In this paper we are only able to examine exports from the parent country. Imports for which the parent company is responsible (including those from its overseas affiliates) cannot be accounted for. Our results therefore show the parent firms' exports as a percentage of parent firm production by country and industry. We find that Benelux (60.1%), Swiss (65.5%), and Swedish (47.1%) firms have a significantly higher than average ratio—reflecting the small home market and considerable foreign market servicing from domestic production exported from the parent. The group, 'Joint and other,' is far less export oriented than overseas production oriented. The figure for United States firms (5.9%) is remarkable; the very low export ratio is the result of both a very large home market and a commitment to service foreign markets by production abroad. The Japanese strategy (although this is gradually changing) is far more that of domestic production plus exports than direct overseas production.

There are, of course, significant differences in exporting behavior across industries from the average of 19.1%. Motor vehicles (47.6%) and aircraft (44.0%) register much higher than average export ratios—both industries are characterized by worldwide demand and important economies of scale even at 'giant firm' level—thus location in the market is of primary importance. Industries where exporting from the parent is unimpor-

TABLE 2
Regression Analysis of Degree of Multinationality of Sales (1)

| Equation | Dependent Variable | Independent Variables | Significant Variables | $R^2$ (Degrees of Freedom) |
|---|---|---|---|---|
| 2.1 | Degree of multi-nationality of Sales (1): $\frac{(b) + (d)}{(a)}$ | Size National dummies (10) | Size** U.K.** Germany** Benelux** Italy* Switzerland** Canada* Sweden** Joint and other* | 0.6463 (26,129) |
| | | Industry dummies (15) | Tobacco* Chemicals* Mechanical Engineering* Diversified (1)* | |
| 2.2 | Degree of multi-nationality of Sales (1): $\frac{(b) + (d)}{(a)}$ | Size Nationality dummies (10) | Size** U.K.** Germany** Benelux** Italy* Switzerland** Canada* Sweden** | 0.5521 (12,143) |
| | | Research intensity | Research intensity* | |

**indicates that the variable is significant at the 1% level
*indicates that the variable is significant at the 5% level

tant are tobacco (5.7%), food products (1.9%), packaging (4.8%), and 'other metals' (5.5%); however, at least in the first two of these, trade in raw materials to the parent will be important. There is also a very noticeable difference between the exporting behavior of R&D intensive industries (23.8%) and that of non-R&D intensive ones (13.0%).

We would expect a priori the role of scale factors to be important in exporting and this is confirmed. Large United Kingdom, Canadian, and 'Joint and other' parent firms export a far greater percentage than their smaller counterparts; however, in some industry groups it is the smaller firms which have higher export ratios (tobacco, chemicals, food products, and packaging).

The regression results with parent's export ratio as dependent variable are shown in Table 4. A high degree of explanatory power is given by our two equations. Overall firm size is used as an independent variable in addition to nationality dummies and either the industry dummies or research intensity.

National differences show up very strongly, much more so than industry differences. In the first equation, where industry variation is fully accounted for by industry dummies, all but one national group (Joint and other) show up as having significantly different behavior from United States firms—which is to be expected, given the very low export proportion of United States firms. Rather surprisingly, industry variations are significant (positive) for chemicals and aircraft only. However, when the industry dummies are replaced by research intensity, size falls in exploratory power suggesting the importance of research intensity as a determinant of exporting behavior and a relationship between size and research intensity.

TABLE 3
Regression Analysis of Degrees of Multinationality of Sales (2)

| Equation | Dependent Variable | Independent Variables | Significant Variables | $R^2$ (Degrees of Freedom) |
|---|---|---|---|---|
| 3.1 | Degree of multi-nationality of Sales (2) $\frac{(b) + (f)}{(a)}$ | Size Nationality dummies (10) | Size** U.K.** Germany** Benelux** Switzerland** Joint and other** | 0.6013 (26,129) |
| | | Industry dummies (15) | Tobacco* Chemicals* Mechanical Engineering* Diversified (1)* | |
| 3.2 | Degree of multi-nationality of Sales (2) $\frac{(b) + (f)}{(a)}$ | Size Nationality dummies (10) Research Intensity | Size** U.K.** Germany* Benelux** Switzerland** Joint and other* n.s. | 0.4723 (12,143) |

** indicates that the variable is significant at the 1% level
* indicates that the variable is significant at the 5% level
n.s. indicates not significant

TABLE 4
Regression Analysis of Parent's Export Ratio

| Equation | Dependent Variable | Independent Variables | Significant Variables | $R^2$ (Degrees of Freedom) |
|---|---|---|---|---|
| 4.1 | Parents Export Ratio i.e. $\frac{d}{c}$ | Size Nationality dummies (10) | Size* U.K.** Japan** France* Germany** Benelux** Italy* Switzerland** Canada** Sweden** | 0.6218 (26,129) |
| | | Industry dummies (15) | Chemicals* Aircraft* | |
| 4.2 | Parents Export Ratio | Size Nationality dummies (10) | Size U.K.** Japan** France** Germany** Benelux** Italy** Switzerland** Canada** Sweden** | 0.5505 (12,143) |
| | | Research Intensity | Research Intensity** | |

**indicates that the variable is significant at the 1% level
*indicates that the variable is significant at the 5% level

Indeed, in both equations 4.1 and 4.2 firm size is not the important explanatory variable it was in equations prefixed 1, 2, and 3. Size is more closely related to overseas production than to parent's exporting capability. In fact the research intensity variable is highly significant, suggesting that exporting behavior is more important in the world's largest research intensive firms than it is for nonresearch intensive ones. Equations 4.1 and 4.2 explain, respectively, over 62% and 55% of the variance in the parent's export ratio.

Internal exports represent, in our data, exports from the parent to other units of the firm overseas. The importance of parent's exports to overseas affiliates can be seen from these indices. We calculate both 'the commitment to internal exports' which is the ratio of internal exports to parent production—i.e., (e)/(c)—and the 'internal export ratio' which is the ratio of internal exports to total parent's exports—i.e., (e)/(d).

The average commitment to internal exports is 7.8%; this varies by nationality from 28.3% for Benelux to 1.4% for Japan and by industry from 26.8% for motor vehicles to zero for aircraft. Internal exports depend on the importance of overseas production and the extent of integration of the firm. The typical multinational with a high volume of internal exports will be one which carries out the final stages of an integrated production run in its overseas subsidiaries within, or close to, the final market. Standard location factors are of primary importance here but their effect will be modified by internalization decisions and by governmental interference with location costs (e.g., tariffs, tax remissions).

Internal exports are closely related to firm size as the difference between weighted and unweighted averages shows. (Interestingly, motor vehicles do not follow this pattern.) National groups with a high commitment to internal exports are West Germany (20.1%), Benelux (28.3%), and Sweden (27.7%), while motor cars are well above the industry average. Perhaps the most striking fact, however, is the difference between research intensive industries, where internal exports account for 12% of parental output, and nonresearch intensive industries, where this proportion is under 2½%.

This pattern can be followed up by reference to the internal export ratio. Although exports in toto account for only 3.2% of United States parent companies' output, internal exports account for 54.8% of exports. This figure is more than matched by Sweden where 58.7% of exports are internal to the firm. In contrast, under 8% of Japanese parents' exports go to overseas affiliates and only 13.2% of French. Japanese firms thus deal directly with the final market. Industry differences are also quite marked, with several industries having very low ratios of internal to total parental exports. The R&D intensity factor again shows up—for research intensive firms 50.5% of exports are internal as against 18.3% for nonresearch intensive ones. These assertions are tested more rigorously by reference to the regression analysis of Tables 5 and 6.

The hypothesis that internal exports are related to R&D intensity is not refuted by the evidence of equation 5.2. In both equations 4.2 and 5.2 the R&D independent variable is significant at the 1% level; however, the t value is greater for R&D in equation 5.2 than in 4.2 (t = 4.1342 against 3.1003). This is supporting evidence for the link between R&D and internal exports.

Clearly, internal exports are related to the size of firm and to its research intensity. National and industry variations are also of some importance. The above results are consistent with the hypothesis derived from the Buckley and Casson theory, illustrating the importance of research intensity, scale, industry, and country specific factors in the process of internalizing markets.

**4. Sourcing Ratios**   Two sourcing ratios are examined. The ratios basically represent the proportion of overseas involvement (exports plus overseas production) which is represented by overseas production. Overseas involvement is a useful aggregate which enables the analyst to measure the overall multinational orientation of the group. Our ratios take two forms: (1) overseas production as a percentage of overseas production plus parent's

TABLE 5

Regression Analysis of Commitment to Internal Exports

| Equation | Dependent Variable | Independent Variables | Significant Variables | R² (Degrees of Freedom) |
|---|---|---|---|---|
| 5.1 | Commitment to Internal Exports: $\frac{(e)}{(c)}$ | Size Nationality dummies (10) | Size** Germany** Benelux** Switzerland** Canada** Sweden** | 0.6452 (26,129) |
| | | Industry dummies (15) | Motor vehicles** Chemicals* Electrical and Electronics* Mechanical Engineering* | |
| 5.2 | Commitment to Internal Exports: $\frac{(e)}{(c)}$ | Size Nationality dummies (10) | Size** U.K.** Germany** Benelux** Switzerland** Canada** Sweden** | 0.5386 (12,143) |
| | | Research Intensity | Research Intensity** | |

\*\*indicates that the variable is significant at the 1% level
\*indicates that the variable is significant at the 5% level

TABLE 6

Regression Analysis of Internal Export Ratio

| Equation | Dependent Variable | Independent Variables | Significant Variables | R² (Degrees of Freedom) |
|---|---|---|---|---|
| 6.1 | Internal Export Ratio $\frac{(e)}{(d)}$ | Size Nationality dummies (10) | Size** Japan (−)** France (−)* Canada* Sweden* | 0.4785 (26,129) |
| | | Industry dummies (15) | Motor vehicles* Chemicals* Electrical Engineering and Electronics** | |
| 6.2 | Internal Export Ratio | Size Nationality dummies (10) | Size** Japan (−)** Canada* Sweden* | 0.3812 (12,143) |
| | | Research Intensity | Research Intensity* | |

\*\*indicates that the variable is significant at the 1% level
\*indicates that the variable is significant at the 5% level

17

total exports; i.e., b/b+d, and (2) overseas production as a percentage of overseas production plus parent's extra group exports, i.e., b/b+f. The second ratio therefore excludes internal exports.

From the first sourcing ratio we can see that for Swiss (94.4%) and 'Joint and other' (95.2%) firms, nearly all overseas involvement is accounted for by overseas production. At the other extreme only 12% of Japanese overseas involvement is production abroad, the remainder being accounted for by extensive exports from the parent. Overall 74% of overseas involvement, on this indicator, is accounted for by production abroad. These figures are, of course, altered by the exclusion of internal exports. When these are removed, over 83% of what we can call 'external involvement' is accounted for by production abroad. Now the overseas activities of Swiss (95.9%), 'Joint and other' (96.8%), and United States (94.3%) firms are nearly totally accounted for by production abroad. (This is another indication of the importance of internal exports—particularly to United States firms.) Nevertheless, still only 13% of Japanese involvement is overseas production and France (23.2%) also is low on this indicator of the relative importance of overseas production.

Turning to the industrial breakdown of the sample we find that food products, tobacco, and oil are heavily oriented to production abroad—the location of raw materials (and the perishable nature of some products) being of paramount importance. Aircraft, with no production abroad, and iron and steel are much more export oriented than the sample as a whole, while motor vehicles are also well below average. Economies of scale are important here. When internal exports are excluded we have very much the same pattern with overseas production increasing in importance relative to external exports—particularly in motor vehicles. One noticeable change is that, when we include internal exports, nonresearch intensive industries are more overseas production oriented than research intensive ones, while the exclusion of internal exports makes research intensive industries more overseas production oriented than nonresearch intensive. This is because the connection is stronger between research intensity and overseas exports than it is between research intensity and overseas production. The results of the regression analysis of the sourcing ratios are shown in Tables 7 and 8.

The regression analysis highlights several important points. First, firm size is an influence on the methods of market servicing. Large firms are more likely to service an overseas market by production in that market than are smaller firms. (Indeed, in all but equation 4.2 firm size is a very significant explanatory variable.) Second, there are very strong influences on market servicing methods deriving from the nationality of the parent firm. All the influences on the regressions are relative to United States firms, and Japanese firms in particular are much more export oriented than United States firms. French, West German, and, to some extent, Swedish and Canadian firms, are more export oriented also, but this may be explained in part by the industrial structure of their foreign investors. There is, however, not so much variation between industries as would be expected, except for the very obvious and strong difference between resource oriented overseas investment and market oriented investments and also the deviation of aircraft and iron and steel from the norm. Finally, there is little discernible difference between research intensive and nonresearch intensive industries in sourcing policies. The regressions again have a high degree of explanatory power. Equations 7.1 and 8.1, using size, industry, and country dummies, explain 55% and 56%, respectively, of the variation in sourcing ratios.

**SUMMARY AND CONCLUSION**

Although sourcing policy is under the control of individual MNEs, this study has isolated a number of important regularities in the policies of the world's largest firms. First, even among the largest firms, size of firm is a major influence on the type of sourcing policy adopted; ceteris paribus the larger a firm, the more likely it is to service foreign markets by production in those markets. Second, there are significant variations in the sourcing policies of firms when grouped according not only to industry, but also to nationality; indeed, for many of the key dependent variables we have examined, national charac-

18

## TABLE 7
### Regression Analysis of Sourcing Ratio (1)

| Equation | Dependent Variable | Independent Variables | Significant Variables | $R^2$ (Degrees of Freedom) |
|---|---|---|---|---|
| 7.1 | Sourcing (Ratio (1)) $\dfrac{b}{b+d}$ | Size Nationality dummies (10) | Size* Japan (−)** Germany (−)* Sweden (−)* | 0.5492 (26,129) |
| | | Industry dummies (15) | Motor vehicles (−)* Tobacco* Aircraft (−)** Iron and Steel (−)* | |
| 7.2 | Sourcing Ratio (1) | Size Nationality dummies (10) | Size** Japan (−)** France (−)** Germany (−)** Canada (−)* | 0.4373 (12,143) |
| | | Research Intensity | n.s. | |

** indicates that the variable is significant at the 1% level
* indicates that the variable is significant at the 5% level
n.s. indicates not significant

## TABLE 8
### Regression Analysis of Sourcing Ratio (2)

| Equation | Dependent Variable | Independent Variables | Significant Variables | $R^2$ (Degrees of Freedom) |
|---|---|---|---|---|
| 8.1 | Sourcing Ratio (2) $\dfrac{b}{b+f}$ | Size Nationality dummies (10) Industry dummies (10) | Size** Japan (−)** France (−)* Germany (−)* Aircraft (−)** | 0.5617 (26,129) |
| 8.2 | Sourcing Ratio (2) | Size Nationality dummies (10) | Size** Japan (−)** France (−)** Germany (−)* Canada (−)* | 0.4585 (12,143) |
| | | Research Intensity | n.s. | |

** indicates that the variable is significant at the 1% level
* indicates that the variable is significant at the 5% level
n.s. indicates not significant

teristics are stronger explanatory variables than are industry groups. Third, the size of internal flows from parent to subsidiary is very clearly connected with the degree of research intensity of the industry in which the firm is competing. The more research intensive the industry, the more likely are internal exports to be of importance. We suggest this is because of the greater incentives to internalizing markets in research intensive products. We are thus able to analyze sourcing policy as a compendium of individual firm characteristics (size, degree of research intensity), industry characteristics, and national traits.

19

Standard location theory remains a most important part of sourcing policy decisions; factors such as input costs and raw material availability remain crucial. However, standard least cost location is modified by the internalization decisions of MNEs. These modifications are likely to be most pronounced in R&D intensive industries and in larger firms.

Finally, it should be noted that sourcing policy is not static. Our analysis has been made at a point in time and such a "snapshot" will of course change over time. Standard locational influences—labor and input costs as interpreted by changing exchange rates, for instance—will alter the comparative costs of alternative production locations. Also, the incentives to internalize markets will change over time, affecting choice of market (internal or external) and optimum location strategy for the firm. The framework we have suggested allows us to trace these changes and to predict the development of sourcing policies in response to these two crucial sets of influences.

FOOTNOTES

1. We ignore licensing because of lack of information—this does not mean that, globally, licensing is unimportant or that it does not form an important strand in the market servicing policies of some companies.
2. Peter J. Buckley and Mark Casson, *The Future of the Multinational Enterprise* (London: Macmillan, 1976).
3. John H. Dunning and R. D. Pearce, *Profitability and Performance of the World's Largest Industrial Companies* (London: E. A. G. Research Study Published by Financial Times, 1975).
4. *Fortune Magazine,* May and September 1973.
5. Categories (a) through (f) are used uniformly throughout the paper.
6. Knowledge of firms not included in our sample strongly supports this conclusion.
7. John H. Dunning and Peter J. Buckley, "International Production and Alternative Models of Trade," *The Manchester School,* December 1977. See also F. M. Scherer, et al., *The Economics of Multi-Plant Operation: An International Comparisons Study* (Cambridge, MA: Harvard University Press, 1975).
8. See also Note 3.
9. Full regression results are available on request from the authors.
10. This is standard practice and is carried out for econometric reasons.

# [20]

## INTRA-FIRM TRADE AND INDUSTRIAL EXPORTS TO THE UNITED STATES*

*By* G. K. HELLEINER AND REAL LAVERGNE

### INTRODUCTION

Most theorising on international trade assumes, explicitly or implicitly, that it is undertaken by unrelated buyers and sellers in world markets. Traditional international economic theory also takes the nation as its principal unit of analysis. The growing importance of multinational companies (MNCs) in the world economy, however, calls both these premises into question. It is increasingly recognized that the international exchange of goods and services takes place both on open markets and partly outside them, through transactions within the MNCs. To use Williamson's (1975) terminology in his theoretical analysis of markets, open market transactions co-exist with 'hierarchical' transactions: in the former decisions are relatively decentralized, while in the latter they tend to be centralized and are frequently imposed by fiat.

Since some 'hierarchical' systems of intra-MNC trade are very large, and exceed in value the trade of many countries, the growth of such systems clearly calls for a re-assessment of conventional models of international exchange. The questions of whether hierarchical exchange relationships are important, and of whether they differ significantly in their nature from open-market relationships, merit further examination. In this paper we address ourselves to the first question, of how important intra-firm trade is in different types of goods, and of why such trade may be of significance. We do not try to establish rigorously because there are not yet enough data whether intra-firm trade behaves differently from arm's length trade.

The data used here are drawn from a new source of information on United States intra-firm imports for 1975–77: The Foreign Trade Division of the US Bureau of the Census now provides detailed statistics of imports from 'related parties'. We cannot generalize from this particular set of data to other countries or to other periods, but the findings are suggestive, and one must start somewhere.

Part I summarizes the available US data. In part II multiple regression analysis is deployed to 'explain' the inter-industry structure of US related-party imports. Part III considers the implications of inter-industry (and inter-country) differences in the importance of related-party trade for the prospects for manufactured exports from developing countries. There follows a brief summary and conclusion.

### I. THE STRUCTURE OF US RELATED-PARTY IMPORTS, 1977

In most countries, data on intra-firm trade are only sporadically collected or reported.[1] The United States, however, now reports very detailed information on 'related-party imports', those which enter the US through importing firms related by ownership (5 per cent of voting equity or more) to the exporting firms in which

---

* We would like to thank Sanjaya Lall for his useful comments on an earlier draft.
[1] In the UK, for example, data for 1973 and 1976 exports appear in UK, Department of Industry, 1978, pp. 90–92. For some other sources see UN, ECOSOC, 1978, pp. 41–44.

297

they originated.  These data are reported quarterly (in document IQ246) at a high level of disaggregation, by individual tariff classifications.  We have converted them into more usable categories for the purposes of this paper.

Table I provides a summary of the 1977 data, distinguishing major product categories and major areas of origin.  These and subsequent data are all in terms of f.o.b. customs values.

TABLE 1

*US Related-Party Imports as Percentage of Total Imports, by Product Class and Origin, 1977*

| | Primary** | | | Semi-Manu-factures** | Manufac-tures** | Total | |
|---|---|---|---|---|---|---|---|
| | Petro-leum | Pri-mary ex-cluding petro-leum | Total pri-mary | | | Total | Total ex-cluding petro-leum |
| | % | % | % | % | % | % | % |
| O.E.C.D.* | 57.2 | 35.9 | 41.3 | 43.4 | 61.1 | 53.7 | 53.6 |
| Centrally Planned* | 0 | 3.2 | 2.8 | 8.9 | 8.1 | 7.7 | 7.8 |
| Third World* | 59.6 | 13.6 | 49.1 | 17.0 | 37.0 | 43.4 | 28.1 |
| Total | 59.4 | 23.5 | 47.3 | 37.6 | 53.6 | 48.4 | 45.2 |

* Country Classifications are according to the *United Nations Standard Country Code*, except that Cuba and Yugoslavia have been included among the Centrally Planned Countries.
** Products classified according to UNCTAD system, reported in 'The Definition of Primary Commodities, Semi-Manufactures and Manufactures', 1965, TD/B/C.2/3.
*Source:* Authors' calculations based on data provided by the Foreign Trade Division, US Bureau of the Census.

In 1977, fully 48.4 per cent of the value of total US imports came from firms which were related by ownership to the importing firms.  If these imports are classified according to their broad level of manufacture, we see that related-party trade rises as a proportion of the total as we move from primary goods (excluding petroleum) to semi-manufactured and manufactured ones.  While only 23.5 per cent of non-petroleum primary product imports was from related parties, 37.6 per cent of semi-manufactures, and 53.6 per cent of fully manufactured products, were imported in this manner.  This general pattern is found for US imports from both the Third World and other OECD members.  It is also found in the (relatively less important) imports from centrally planned economics, although, in this case, related-party imports are marginally more important for semi-manufactures than they are for fully manufactured products.  Thus, other things being equal, we may expect the role of related-party imports in to the US to rise as industrialization proceeds in Third World countries and manufactured goods assume a larger proportion of their total exports.

It is also noteworthy that the relative importance of related-party trade is much greater, in all categories of goods, for imports from other OECD members than for imports from the Third World.  In the case of manufactured products, as much as 61.1 per cent, by value, of US imports from other OECD members enters on a related-party basis, a remarkably high figure for an important segment of world trade.

Table 2 presents similar data at the 2-digit SITC level of aggregation, together

INTRA-FIRM TRADE AND INDUSTRIAL EXPORTS TO THE UNITED STATES **299**

TABLE 2

*US Related-Party Imports as Percentage of Total Imports,*
*By Category, From LDCs and OECD Sources, 1977*

|  |  | OECD % | Percentage LDCs % | Total % | Import Value Total ($ million) | LDCs ($ million) |
|---|---|---|---|---|---|---|
| 00 | Live animals | 16.4 | 3.9 | 12.3 | 254 | 87 |
| 01 | Beverages and tobacco | 26.0 | 16.4 | 19.9 | 1,287 | 291 |
| 02 | Dairy products | 13.7 | 2.6 | 12.9 | 229 | 10 |
| 03 | Fish and fish preparations | 34.5 | 8.8 | 23.1 | 2,047 | 890 |
| 04 | Cereals and cereal preparations | 13.3 | 4.5 | 12.1 | 151 | 19 |
| 05 | Fruit and vegetables | 18.9 | 45.1 | 39.9 | 1,523 | 1,230 |
| 06 | Sugar, sugar preparations | 5.5 | 2.7 | 3.3 | 1,219 | 966 |
| 07 | Coffee, tea, cocoa, spices | 59.0 | 6.3 | 9.0 | 5,538 | 5,238 |
| 08 | Feeding stuff for animals | 14.5 | 22.3 | 16.3 | 95 | 22 |
| 09 | Miscellaneous food | 28.3 | 11.5 | 23.6 | 91 | 23 |
| 11 | Beverages | 23.8 | 16.7 | 23.5 | 1,218 | 40 |
| 12 | Tobacco and manufactures | 10.9 | 8.6 | 8.1 | 373 | 263 |
| 21 | Hides and skins | 1.5 | 0.3 | 1.2 | 219 | 50 |
| 22 | Oil seeds, nuts and kernels | 33.2 | 2.7 | 19.1 | 48 | 21 |
| 23 | Crude rubber (including synthetic) | 86.8 | 27.1 | 37.9 | 794 | 649 |
| 24 | Wood, lumber, cork | 17.9 | 5.1 | 17.2 | 1,996 | 105 |
| 25 | Pulp and waste paper | 41.2 | 9.0 | 41.1 | 1,194 | 2 |
| 26 | Textile fibres | 20.6 | 10.1 | 16.7 | 238 | 67 |
| 27 | Crude fertilizers and minerals | 38.1 | 36.2 | 37.6 | 872 | 162 |
| 28 | Metalliferous ores and metal scrap | 63.4 | 40.7 | 52.3 | 2,024 | 943 |
| 29 | Crude animal and vegetable materials | 17.3 | 12.8 | 13.6 | 499 | 235 |
| 32 | Coal, coke and briquettes | 13.6 | 70.9 | 13.5 | 211 | 1 |
| 33 | Petroleum and petroleum products | 48.8 | 57.7 | 56.8 | 41,285 | 37,597 |
| 34 | Gas, natural and manufactured | 59.0 | 12.1 | 55.0 | 2,499 | 215 |
| 41 | Animal oils and fats | 15.5 | 0.2 | 15.0 | 8 | — |
| 42 | Fixed vegetable oils and fats | 9.1 | 8.7 | 8.7 | 505 | 458 |
| 43 | Animal and vegetable oils and fats, processed | 16.4 | 1.9 | 5.2 | 15 | 11 |
| 51 | Chemical elements and compounds | 44.0 | 40.7 | 43.3 | 3,178 | 367 |
| 52 | Mineral tar and chemicals from coal, petroleum and natural gas | 34.3 | — | 33.7 | 11 | — |
| 53 | Dyeing, tanning and colouring materials | 73.4 | 15.7 | 69.8 | 209 | 11 |
| 54 | Medicinal and pharmaceutical products | 46.7 | 60.3 | 46.9 | 318 | 42 |
| 55 | Essential oils and perfumes, etc. | 41.3 | 2.1 | 26.7 | 239 | 82 |
| 56 | Fertilizers, manufactured | 20.6 | 75.1 | 23.4 | 353 | 19 |
| 57 | Explosives and pyrotechnic products | 14.0 | 4.5 | 8.9 | 39 | 9 |
| 58 | Plastic materials, etc. | 57.6 | 14.4 | 54.9 | 402 | 25 |
| 59 | Chemical materials and products n.e.s. | 53.2 | 5.9 | 48.9 | 329 | 22 |
| 61 | Leather and leather manufactures | 7.0 | 5.0 | 5.8 | 256 | 145 |
| 62 | Rubber manufactures, n.e.s. | 78.0 | 31.6 | 73.3 | 999 | 96 |
| 63 | Wood and cork manufactures | 22.6 | 9.4 | 15.1 | 1,034 | 576 |
| 64 | Paper, paperboard, etc. | 20.0 | 39.8 | 20.6 | 2,404 | 81 |
| 65 | Textile yarn, fabrics, made-up articles | 35.1 | 7.8 | 22.6 | 1,776 | 736 |
| 66 | Non-metallic mineral manufactures | 18.0 | 10.4 | 16.4 | 2,802 | 479 |
| 67 | Iron and steel | 65.9 | 20.4 | 61.8 | 5,982 | 483 |
| 68 | Non-ferrous metals | 43.7 | 16.7 | 33.7 | 3,938 | 1,289 |
| 69 | Manufactures of metal, n.e.s. | 28.0 | 12.4 | 24.9 | 2,499 | 455 |
| 71 | Machinery other than electric | 60.3 | 63.5 | 60.3 | 9,777 | 658 |
| 72 | Electrical machinery, apparatus, appliances | 55.2 | 75.2 | 63.4 | 8,451 | 3,541 |
| 73 | Transport equipment | 84.7 | 32.6 | 83.9 | 18,229 | 304 |
| 81 | Sanitary and other fixtures | 17.3 | 14.2 | 15.8 | 109 | 47 |
| 82 | Furniture | 34.0 | 13.6 | 26.3 | 666 | 169 |
| 83 | Travel goods, handbags, etc. | 28.4 | 10.3 | 13.4 | 309 | 254 |
| 84 | Clothing | 12.0 | 11.5 | 11.3 | 4,049 | 3,221 |
| 85 | Footwear | 11.7 | 4.4 | 7.3 | 1,890 | 1,013 |
| 86 | Professional and scientific instruments, etc. | 50.9 | 51.2 | 50.9 | 2,316 | 488 |
| 87 | Miscellaneous manufactures | 33.4 | 17.1 | 27.6 | 5,394 | 1,825 |

300                                        BULLETIN

with the relevant import values. It is worth remarking on the enormous diversity of experience between different sorts of products in intra-firm transactions: imports of transport equipment (influenced by the U.S.-Canadian Auto Pact) (83.9%), dyeing, tanning and colouring materials (69.8%), petroleum and petroleum products (56.8%) are dominated by related-party transactions, while in some other important categories of trade such transactions are relatively insignificant, e.g. sugar (3.3%) and footwear (7.3%).

Related-party trade, as defined by the US Bureau of the Census, can take many different forms. First, it can be undertaken either by US-based firms or by non-US firms. In this respect the new data are considerably more comprehensive than the better known data on majority-owned foreign affiliate (MOFA) trade published by the US Department of Commerce (Chung, 1977) which relate only to US firms. By drawing on some recent information on the role of foreign investment in the US (US Department of Commerce, 1976) we can estimate the share of total related-party imports to the US which is accounted for by *non-US firms* (see Table 3). In 1974, roughly 48 per cent of total US related-party imports appear to have been undertaken by non-U.S. firms. Table 3 reveals a striking difference between imports from major developed countries and those from developing countries as between US and non-US MNCs. Only 15 per cent of related-party imports from developing countries was accounted for by non-US firms (not necessarily firms from the country from which the imports came), whereas the equivalent percentage for developed countries as a whole was 60 per cent, and for the EEC and Japan 78 and 100 per cent respectively. (Canada's 21 per cent, lowest by far of all the OECD's individual members, places it in a class more similar to the developing countries than to the rest of the OECD.)

Secondly, related-party trade comprises two different sorts of products, which need to be clearly distinguished. It includes products which are inputs into a vertically integrated multinational production structure; this is the usual meaning attached to intra-firm trade, as a part of what Dunning (1973) terms 'international production'. It also includes finished products for resale (or rental) outside the country of origin. The importance of such trade for distribution (or 'wholesale trade') has been noted before (U.N. ECOSOC (1978), page 44); our own data permit some estimates of such imports into the US.

Table 3 shows the importance of 'wholesale trade' in related-party trade. As much as 36 per cent of total related-party imports are undertaken by affiliates of non-US firms in the wholesale trade sector (this figure probably understates the proportion of such trade in finished products, since some of the trade undertaken by petroleum, mining and manufacturing firms is also of this kind). We may note the striking contrast between imports from developed countries and those from less developed countries (plus Canada) in the composition of such imports. Only 4 per cent of total related-party imports from less developed countries is undertaken by non-US MNCs in the wholesale trade sector, while the equivalent figure is 48 per cent for developed countries (and, within these, 89 per cent for Japan and 63 per cent for the EEC and only 11 per cent for Canada). Comparable data for US firms' related-party imports of finished products are not available. The nearest

TABLE 3

*Estimated Composition of US Related-Party Imports, by US and non-US Parent, 1974*

| | Estimated total related-party imports[1] | Related-party imports of non-US firms[2] | | | US imports from MOFAs[3] | | | (2)/(1) | (3)/(1) |
| | | Total | Wholesale trade | | Total | Wholesale trade | | | |
| | (1) ($ m.) | (2) ($ m.) | (3) ($ m.) | (4) % | (5) ($ m.) | (6) ($ m.) | (7) % | (8) % | (9) % |
|---|---|---|---|---|---|---|---|---|---|
| Developed countries of which: | 32,161 | 19,336 | 15,488 | 80.1 | 14,831 | 1,127 | 7.6 | 60.1 | 48.2 |
| Canada | 12,235 | 2,570 | 1,314 | 51.1 | 11,411 | 777 | 6.8 | 21.0 | 10.7 |
| EEC | 9,174 | 7,130 | 5,826 | 81.7 | 2,515 | 296[4] | 11.8 | 77.7 | 63.5 |
| Japan | 8,118 | 8,266 | 7,260 | 87.8 | 127 | 5 | 3.9 | 100.0[5] | 89.4 |
| Less Developed countries | 14,042 | 2,114 | 583 | 27.6 | 14,763 | 341 | 2.3 | 15.1 | 4.2 |
| TOTAL | 44,611[1] | 21,451 | 16,071 | 74.9 | 31,801 | 1,418 | 4.5 | 48.1 | 36.0 |

[1] This was obtained by applying 1975 data (1977 data for Canada, EEC and Japan) on the share of total imports accounted for by related-party trade, since there are none available for 1974, to 1974 figures on general imports, as reported in the US Department of Commerce, *Survey of Current Business*. This procedure results in the fact that the estimated total is not equal to the estimates of its components.

[2] From US Department of Commerce, *Foreign Direct Investment in the United States*, Report to Congress, 1976, Tables E-2, E-8. This figure for imports shipped to US affiliates by affiliated foreign groups includes imports from parent firms which own 10% or more of the US importing affiliate or from other firms related to the parent by at least 50% ownership. *Op. cit.* 5–6. The area or country indicated refers not to the country of ownership of the non-US firms but to the country of origin of the imports.

[3] From William K. Chung, 'Sales by majority-owned foreign affiliates of US companies, 1975', *Survey of Current Business* (US Department of Commerce), 57, 2, February 1977, Table 3. This figure includes imports from sources which are unrelated to the importer.

[4] 1975.

[5] The actual percentage is 101.8, but this has been 'rounded down' to 100.

equivalents are the data on US imports from MOFAs, which are also shown in Table 3. While these are not strictly comparable, the fact that the share of wholesale trading firms in total US MOFA imports is under 5 per cent, as against a 75 per cent share for wholesale trading firms in total non-US related-party imports, suggests that US firms' related-party imports are much less for the distribution of finished goods than are those of non-US firms.

In general, then, US related-party imports from developing countries (and from Canada) are primarily undertaken by US firms engaging in 'international production', whereas a high proportion of those from other developed countries (particularly from Japan) are undertaken by non-US firms engaging primarily in trading rather than production activities.

## II  THE DETERMINANTS OF US RELATED-PARTY IMPORTS

Intra-firm international trade is the reflection in commodity exchange of the existence of multinational corporations. In order to understand *why* it exists it is necessary to consult the literature on direct foreign investment and the MNCs' motivation for vertical or horizontal integration across international boundaries. This is not the place to rehearse that extensive literature. While international intra-firm commodity trade requires MNCs, the converse is not necessarily true. It is quite possible for MNCs to engage in relatively little intra-firm international commodity trade; each plant may instead be relatively autonomous with respect to its international purchases, or integrated, with respect to inputs and markets, into the national economy in which it is located. What then, explains the propensity of MNCs to buy within their international corporate structures?

The US data on related-party imports permit further investigation of the determinants and characteristics of intra-firm international trade in manufactured goods. In an earlier paper (Helleiner (1979)), hypotheses with respect to these characteristics or determinants were tested with some success, by relating the share of total US imports of manufactures of different categories which entered the US on a related-party basis in 1975 to a number of industry characteristics. In that paper it was argued, particularly in respect of international production, 'that intra-firm trade—the internalization of what would otherwise be market transactions—is most likely to be found in industries in which firms possess certain advantages which are a potential source of quasi-rent: e.g. scale economies, technology, skills, product differentiation and advertising.... It is also most likely to be associated with the most dynamic and rapidly growing sectors, where there is most likely to be the greatest capacity to employ modern management and information systems for the operation of complex transnational operations.' (Helleiner, 1979.)

Related-party imports as a percentage of total imports were found to be significantly positively correlated with the average wage, R and D (research and development) expenditures as a percentage of sales, and firm size. These results were taken as partial confirmation of the hypotheses with respect to the role of skills, technology and entry barriers. The results for R and D were also consistent with those derived from similar tests conducted on less disaggregated data on US

INTRA-FIRM TRADE AND INDUSTRIAL EXPORTS TO THE UNITED STATES **303**

MNCs' intra-firm exports (Lall, 1978). Other independent influences which were found *not* to be significantly related (at least to the extent that the statistics employed measured them well) to the relative size of intra-firm exports were scale economies, market concentration, advertising, capital-intensity and growth rate.

We decided to extend this econometric testing in order (a) to consider the possibility that imports from developing countries and imports from OECD members are, to a substantial degree, governed by different factors[2] and (b) to exploit more recent data (for 1977) which were now available. The dependent variable remains the percentage of US imports which originated with related parties, but we now use 1977 as well as 1975 figures.[3] The data are now, however, disaggregated by area of origin: OECD or Third World. Each observation relates to a 3-digit SITC category, of which there are 100 in our sample. Since these data may be of wider interest they are reported in Appendix A. The independent variables in the regressions were:[4]

(1) SIZE: firm size, measured by the proportion of the work force employed in establishments of 250 or more in the relevant US industry. This variable was a proxy for barriers to entry of new competition, and was expected to exercise (see Helleiner (1979)) a positive influence on the dependent variable.

(2) SC: Hufbauer's measure of scale economies in the relevant US industry. Scale economies are a source of quasi-rents and so were expected to be positively related to the dependent variable.

(3) CON: the 4-firm concentration ratio in the US for each industry. This was a different index of entry barriers (with significant correlation with SIZE, as appendix B shows), and was expected to have a positive sign.

(4) AD: the ratio of advertising expenditures to gross sales in the relevant US industry. Advertising, like scale economies, may be a source of quasi-rents and so should have a positive sign. Its influence was expected to be especially strong for imports from developing countries, since the role of MNCs, as compared to developing country exporters, was expected to be stronger in commodities where product differentiation barriers were relatively high.

(5) W: the average wage, a measure of skill intensity. This was also expected to have a positive sign.

(6) RD: technological intensity, measured by research and development expenditures as a percentage of sales. The expected sign was positive: high skills and high technology both have large potential quasi-rents.

[2] Similar analysis was conducted for the relatively small imports from centrally planned economies, but is not reported here.
[3] Note that it is a limited dependent variable with its limits being 0 and 1. This means that the use of ordinary least squares mis-specifies the functional form near the limits, and might call for the use of a logit or probit model. In this case, however, since the values of the dependent variable are not particularly concentrated at the limits, OLS is likely to be quite adequate and indeed perhaps even superior to these alternative approaches.
[4] The sources of these data were as follows: SIZE, CON, W: U.S., Bureau of the Census, *Census of Manufactures*.
SC: Hufbauer, 1970
AD: Comanor and Wilson, 1974.
RD: National Science Foundation, 1975.
The correlation matrix for the independent variables is presented in Appendix B.

304                                      BULLETIN

The estimated multiple regression equations are summarised in Table 4.  For *total* US manufactured imports from all sources, the results for 1977 data are similar to those found when 1975 data were employed.  Related-party imports are a significantly higher proportion of total US imports in industries in which the average wage is high, the proportion of the work force in large establishments is high, and R and D expenditure as a percentage of sales is high.  These results are statistically more significant when 1977 data are employed than they are for 1975 data, in that the relevant $t$-values and the $R^2$s are higher.  None of the other variables achieved statistical significance; indeed, the signs on the coefficients attached to them were often contrary to those expected.

TABLE 4

*Determinants of US Related-Party Imports as a Percentage of US Imports, by Industry: Regression Results*

| Total | Constant | SIZE | SC | CON | AD | W | RD | $R^2(F)$ |
|---|---|---|---|---|---|---|---|---|
| 1975 | 0.0286 | 0.0027 | 0.1100 | −0.0006 | −0.0018 | 0.0248 | 1.2223 | 0.262 |
| | | (2.435)** | (0.429) | (0.427) | (0.300) | (1.663)* | (2.601)** | (5.489) |
| 1977 | 0.0209 | 0.0033 | 0.0298 | −0.0010 | −0.0058 | 0.0285 | 1.5291 | 0.354 |
| | | (3.153)** | (0.122) | (0.732) | (1.018) | (2.003) | (3.402)** | (8.493) |
| 1975– 1977 Growth | 0.1251 | 0.0028 | 0.2493 | −0.0015 | −0.0052 | −0.0079 | 3.7298 | 0.099 |
| | | (0.841) | (0.323) | (0.353) | (0.291) | (0.176) | (2.633)** | (1.697) |
| *OECD* | | | | | | | | |
| 1975 | 0.0209 | 0.0023 | 0.1850 | 0.0001 | 0.0001 | 0.0282 | 0.8551 | 0.185 |
| | | (1.807)* | (0.632) | (0.070) | (0.019) | (1.660)* | (1.594) | (3.526) |
| 1977 | 0.0240 | 0.0030 | 0.0463 | −0.0090 | −0.0042 | 0.0274 | 1.3714 | 0.321 |
| | | (2.895)** | (0.191) | (0.677) | (0.737) | (1.950)* | (3.092)** | (7.323) |
| 1975– 1977 Growth | 0.4626 | −0.0033 | 15.3952 | 0.0880 | −0.0862 | −0.4652 | −15.3021 | 0.059 |
| | | (0.074) | (1.489) | (1.548) | (0.358) | (0.775) | (0.807) | (0.972) |
| *Third World* | | | | | | | | |
| 1975 | 0.0522 | 0.0004 | 0.0908 | 0.0015 | −0.0174 | 0.0096 | 3.1390 | 0.355 |
| | | (0.347) | (0.314) | (0.915) | (2.586)** | (0.572) | (5.918)** | (8.521) |
| 1977 | 0.1267 | 0.0015 | −0.0447 | 0.0002 | −0.0102 | −0.0078 | 2.6912 | 0.289 |
| | | (1.247) | (0.160) | (0.100) | (1.576) | (0.479) | (5.258)** | (6.302) |
| 1975– 1977 Growth | 0.0406 | 0.0023 | 0.2194 | −0.0008 | −0.0036 | 0.0019 | 2.2732 | 0.108 |
| | | (1.072) | (0.449) | (0.287) | (0.321) | (0.067) | (2.539)** | (1.877) |

$t$-values are in brackets. One asterisk indicates significance at the 5% level; two asterisks indicate significance at the 1% level.

For imports from the OECD only, the results are broadly similar to those for total US imports.  Firm size (SIZE), average wage (W), and R and D (RD) are significantly related to the relative size of related-party trade in 1977.  The R and D variable falls only slightly short of significance, while the other two variables are again significant, in 1975.  The results with respect to imports from developing countries, however, are somewhat different.  In the latter case, neither firm size (which at least carries the expected sign on its coefficient) nor the average wage is significantly correlated with the extent of related-party trade.  R and D as a percentage of sales is still strongly correlated, however, more so than in the case of OECD imports.[5]  At the same time, AD appears to be significantly related to such trade in 1975 and nearly significantly so in 1977, but with the wrong sign (this sign

[5] RD was the only independent variable significantly (positively) associated with related-party trade in the case of US imports from centrally planned economies as well.

is found in almost all the regressions, but is not significant for other groups). One may interpret this result as reflecting the capacity of MNCs to move rapidly into the 'newer' areas of developing country comparative advantage where standardization, rather than merely cheap labour, is the characteristic feature of the products concerned. Alternatively, one could see it as reflecting the fact that much of the imports from affiliates in developing countries is of intermediate products, concerning which there may be a lot of exchange of design and other information within the MNCs but very little 'marketing' (Lall, 1978, p. 215). Clearly, this relationship requires further investigation.

Although the period 1975–1977 is a very short one, an attempt was also made to 'explain' through similar regression analysis the *changes* over this period in the percentage of US imports acquired from related parties in various sectors of manufactured goods trade. The percentage of 1975–1977 import *growth* taking place on a related-party basis is significantly ( and positively) related to R and D as a percentage of sales, both in total imports from all sources and in imports from developing countries; but this is not the case with imports from OECD countries, where the sign on the R and D coefficient is reversed, and only market concentration and scale economies even come close to statistical significance. Too much significance should not be attached to these limited results. The apparently increasing role of industries involved in high R and D in intra-firm importing from developing countries is nevertheless striking.

The limited success of these tests is accounted for, at least in part, and particularly in the case of imports from developing countries, by our inability to regress separately upon different *types* of related-party imports. Ideally, one should separate imports by wholesale trade firms from the others since the influences upon their decisions to import at arms-length rather than on an intra-firm basis may well differ. Clearly there is room for further refinements on these tests, and the results presented here should be viewed as no more than a first 'cut' at the new data.

### III   EXPORTS BY DEVELOPING COUNTRIES AND INTRA-FIRM TRADE

Evidently technology-intensive industries are those in which US related-party imports from developing (and other) countries are particularly important. To the extent that related-party imports behave differently, or carry different implications either for the exporting or for the importing country, from those of arm's-length imports, we now have some idea of the sectors in which to expect such differences.

Attention has been drawn to the differences between intra-developed country trade and developed-country imports from the developing world as far as the readjustment possibilities of endangered industries are concerned (e.g. Hughes, 1973, pp. 182–3, 276). It is usual to assume that there is much greater potential for expanded intra-industry trade between developed nations through the exchange of differentiated products which benefit from economies of scale and technical specialisation. Thus the reduction of trade barriers within the EEC led, not so much to increased inter-industry specialization in line with traditional comparative advantage theory, as to expanded intra-industry trade. It was therefore not necessary for industries to 'go under'. But in the case of trade with developing countries, it has been argued, the potential for increased exchange of differentiated products within industries is unfortunately much smaller. The adjustment difficulties created for entire industries in the developed world faced with LDC competition are, therefore, much greater.

The possibilities of intra-firm trade, however, leave rather more room for optimism with respect to the capacity of firms and industries in developed countries to adapt to increasing LDC competition. Where the former can draw less developed countries into exporting manufactured products within the integrated international productive systems over which they preside, through component manufacture, assembly activities, and subcontracting of other kinds, or even through specialised exports of final products, these expanding exports do not 'disrupt' these firms' overall activities. The future expansion of LDC exports is 'managed', as part of the longer-term investment planning of the MNCs, so as to minimise later disruptions or surprises.

The effects of the integration of developing country manufacturing plants into the MNC production systems can, however, pose serious problems for employment in plants, firms, industries and the particularly affected communities in the developed world. If employment readjustment is not planned by the firms concerned, labour will legitimately demand that it be planned instead by governments. Governments could respond to such political pressures by instituting long-term adjustment programmes for workers and communities. The more common response (and in the short run the more dramatically effective one), however, has been for governments to set out to 'manage' trade by erecting trade barriers and 'organizing markets'.

The principal means for the MNCs concerned to prevent such governmental interventions in their intra-firm trade are twofold: (1) direct lobbying for low (or lower) trade barriers on the products of their greatest interest; and (2) the minimization of disruptions for their own employees through programmes of continuing employment, carefully phased change, and co-operation with trade unions in the planning of adjustment. Labour unions may, other things being equal, be expected to oppose firms' efforts of the first kind, but they ought to be warm supporters of the latter. Where the new imports are part of successful multinational production systems there is at least the *potential* for the firm to adopt more enlightened adjustment practices (while undoubtedly at the same time continuing to press for freer trade). Where there is no intra-firm trade, there is no one to 'manage' the trade (or the investment) and so to adjust smoothly, except the government; indeed, protection pressures and policies do seem to be concentrated in those sectors of LDC imports in which intra-firm trade is at a minimum.

Table 5 shows the relative importance of related-party trade in US imports of the 5 largest categories of manufactured products obtained from the more industrialized LDCs. It is quite clear from the table that textiles, clothing and footwear are imported from related parties to a far smaller extent than is machinery (which includes apparatus and appliances, radios, electronic components, etc.); the former industries are, of course, also those in which protectionist pressures have been at their most severe.

INTRA-FIRM TRADE AND INDUSTRIAL EXPORTS TO THE UNITED STATES **307**

TABLE 5

*US Related-Party Imports as a Percentage of Total Imports of Selected Manufactured Products, From Selected Newly Industrializing Countries, 1977*

| | Textiles 65* | Non-electric machinery 71* | Electric machinery 72* | Clothing 84* | Footwear 85* | Total mfg | Total Mfg. Import Value |
|---|---|---|---|---|---|---|---|
| | % | % | % | % | % | % | ($ million) |
| Israel | 18.9 | 32.8 | 62.9 | 14.0 | 0.0 | 18.2 | 168 |
| Portugal | 2.8 | 24.7 | 78.4 | 0.4 | 0.2 | 12.5 | 101 |
| Greece | 3.7 | 52.2 | 99.1 | 5.0 | 0.8 | 7.8 | 58 |
| Ireland | 36.3 | 78.5 | 77.8 | 8.3 | 42.2 | 59.0 | 140 |
| Spain | 1.5 | 36.3 | 32.6 | 3.7 | 10.1 | 24.1 | 696 |
| Yugoslavia | 0.1 | 14.0 | 2.0 | 2.3 | 2.2 | 4.9 | 207 |
| Argentina | 0.5 | 39.1 | 76.1 | 2.9 | 0.8 | 9.2 | 167 |
| Brazil | 9.2 | 59.9 | 95.3 | 18.0 | 0.5 | 38.4 | 755 |
| Colombia | 1.5 | 16.8 | 3.9 | 15.7 | 81.2 | 14.1 | 60 |
| Mexico | 9.6 | 87.8 | 95.6 | 68.0 | 60.9 | 71.0 | 1,798 |
| Taiwan | 13.1 | 19.3 | 58.1 | 1.2 | 3.1 | 20.5 | 3,354 |
| Hong Kong | 4.9 | 68.5 | 43.4 | 3.4 | 3.6 | 18.1 | 2,618 |
| India | 6.1 | 30.5 | 58.7 | 15.8 | 6.1 | 10.1 | 180 |
| South Korea | 5.5 | 64.2 | 67.3 | 7.1 | 1.8 | 19.7 | 2,328 |
| Malaysia | 0.2 | 83.2 | 97.0 | 1.9 | 0.0 | 87.9 | 385 |
| Philippines | 28.9 | 69.7 | 31.7 | 53.4 | 0.0 | 47.5 | 352 |
| Singapore | 4.3 | 90.5 | 97.0 | 0.5 | 0.0 | 83.3 | 630 |
| (Haiti) | 2.9 | 33.7 | 36.5 | 24.8 | 77.2 | 28.4 | 101 |
| Total all Third World | 7.8 | 63.5 | 75.2 | 11.5 | 4.4 | 37.0 | |

\* SITC category

Table 5 also shows that some newly industrializing countries exporting manufactured products to the US do so through intra-firm channels to a much greater degree than others, whatever the product. Countries which, like Mexico and Ireland, are particularly welcoming to foreign investors, have high overall proportions of intra-firm exports to the US across the board, while those which, like Yugoslavia, are more restrictive, have low proportions. At the product level, intercountry differences are less predictable. For instance, the Philippines do above-average intra-firm exporting in textiles and clothing; Colombia and Haiti do so in footwear; and Malaysia and Singapore do so in machinery.

In sum, the evolution of trade policy in the developed countries, together with the rapid growth of MNC production abroad, implies that external influences impart a bias to the structure of LDC manufactured exports: other things being equal, intra-firm exports will tend to be favoured over other exports. This implies, in turn, that exports of particular industries (primarily high-technology ones) will grow faster than others, and that countries which welcome MNCs will expand their exports to developed countries faster than others.

## IV SUMMARY AND CONCLUSION

International trade in manufactured goods looks less and less like the trade of basic economic models in which unrelated buyers and sellers interact freely with one another (on reasonably competitive markets) to establish the volume and prices of traded goods. It is increasingly managed by multinational corporations as part of their systems of international production and distribution. Particularly is this so, according to our statistical results, in technology-intensive products. The pricing, volume, and direction of this trade are not necessarily related to the laws of markets, and there are as yet no established international rules or principles governing these matters. In a world of trade also increasingly 'managed' by governments to minimize disruptions, MNC activity seems likely to impart a bias to the structure of developing country (and other) industrial exports, favouring non-market intra-firm trade. On the present limited evidence, this will favour exports in industries which are technologically advanced, and will particularly favour such countries (as Mexico and Ireland) which welcome foreign companies.

What we still possess very little information or analysis about is the extent to which the behaviour of intra-firm international trade actually differs from that of arm's-length trade, or indeed whether it differs from it at all. At a minimum there is need for data collection on the degree to which international trade takes place on a related-party basis in all sectors of world trade. Only with such data can one begin to assess the potential implications of intra-firm international trade for such matters as the stability of the prices and volumes of trade, the sensitivity of trade to exchange rate variations, the role of restrictive business practices, the management of market-disrupting trade, the international distribution of tax revenues from transnational corporate activities, indeed for the overall efficiency and equity of the emerging system of world trade.

*University of Toronto and*
*Queen Elizabeth House, Oxford.*

## REFERENCES

Chung, W. K., 1977, 'Sales by Majority-owned Foreign Affiliates of U.S. Companies, 1975', *Survey of Current Business*, Vol. 57, no. 2, February.

Comanor, William S. and Wilson, Thomas A., 1974, *Advertising and Market Power*, (Harvard Economic Studies, Vol. 144, Cambridge, Mass.)

Dunning, J. H., 1973, 'The Determinants of International Production', *Oxford Economic Papers*, Vol. 25, no. 3, November.

Helleiner, G. K., 1979, 'Transnational Corporations and Trade Structure: The Role of Intra-firm Trade' in Herbert Giersch (ed.), *Intra-Industry Trade* (J. C. B. Mohr, Paul Siebeck; Tübingen).

Hufbauer, Gary C., 1970, 'The Impact of National Characteristics and Technology on the Commodity Composition of Trade in Manufactured Goods', in Raymond Vernon (ed.), *The Technology Factor in International Trade* (Universities-National Bureau Conference Series, 22, London and New York).

Hughes, Helen (ed.) 1973, *Prospects for Partnership, Industrialization and Trade Policies in the 1980s* (John Hopkins, Baltimore and London).

Lall, Sanjaya, 1978, 'The Pattern of Intra-Firm Exports by US Multinationals', *Oxford Bulletin of Economics and Statistics*, Vol. 40, no. 3, August.

INTRA-FIRM TRADE AND INDUSTRIAL EXPORTS TO THE UNITED STATES **309**

National Science Foundation, 1975, *Research and Development in Industry, 1973* (Washington).

UK, Department of Industry, 1978, *Business Monitor M—4: Overseas Transactions* (Business Statistics Office, HMSO).

UN, ESOSOC, 1978, 'Transactional Corporations in World Development: A Re-Examination' (Commission on Transnational Corporations) (E/C. 10/38).

US, Department of Commerce, 1976, *Foreign Direct Investment In the United States, Report to Congress* (US Government Printing Office, Washington).

Williamson, Oliver E., 1975, *Markets and Hierarchies, Analysis and Antitrust Implications, A Study in the Economics of Internal Organization* (The Free Press, New York).

## APPENDIX A

*U.S. Related-Party Imports as Percentage of Total Imports, By Category and Area of Origin, 1977*

| SITC | | OECD | Developing countries | Total* |
|---|---|---|---|---|
| 13 | Canned, prepared meat | 37.1 | 32.7 | 22.7 |
| 32 | Canned, prepared fish | 27.4 | 4.2 | 17.2 |
| 48 | Cereal preparations | 15.6 | 7.4 | 14.6 |
| 53 | Preserved fruit | 21.6 | 39.7 | 35.2 |
| 55 | Preserved vegetables | 25.0 | 6.1 | 14.8 |
| 61 | Sugar and honey | 1.2 | 2.7 | 2.5 |
| 62 | Sugar confectionery | 22.7 | 1.9 | 18.2 |
| 91 | Margarine, shortening | 0 | — | 0 |
| 111 | Nonalcoholic beverages | 1.8 | 2.6 | 2.0 |
| 112 | Alcoholic beverages | 23.9 | 17.3 | 23.6 |
| 122 | Tobacco manufactures | 12.1 | 23.2 | 18.1 |
| 512 | Organic chemicals | 52.8 | 20.0 | 50.4 |
| 513 | Inorganic chemicals: elements, etc. | 38.1 | 45.1 | 39.0 |
| 514 | Other inorganic chemicals | 51.4 | 53.5 | 51.7 |
| 515 | Radioactive materials | 13.4 | 0 | 12.9 |
| 521 | Mineral tar & crude chemicals from coal, petroleum, natural gas | 34.3 | 0 | 33.7 |
| 531 | Synthetic organic dyestuffs | 87.1 | 17.3 | 84.8 |
| 532 | Dyeing & tanning extracts | 12.6 | 1.1 | 7.7 |
| 533 | Pigments, paints, varnishes | 35.9 | 51.5 | 36.6 |
| 541 | Medicinal & pharmaceutical products | 46.7 | 60.3 | 46.9 |
| 551 | Essential oils, perfumes, flavor materials | 47.8 | 1.0 | 24.8 |
| 553 | Perfumery & cosmetics | 29.3 | 3.9 | 19.8 |
| 554 | Soaps, cleansing, polishing preparations | 42.6 | 7.3 | 40.3 |
| 561 | Manufactured fertilizers | 20.6 | 75.1 | 23.4 |
| 571 | Explosives & pyrotechnic products | 14.0 | 4.5 | 8.9 |
| 581 | Plastic materials | 57.6 | 14.4 | 54.9 |
| 599 | Chemical materials | 53.2 | 5.9 | 48.9 |
| 611 | Leather | 5.2 | 2.1 | 3.3 |
| 612 | Manufactures of leather | 14.5 | 13.3 | 13.8 |
| 613 | Fur skins | 5.4 | 0 | 5.2 |
| 629 | Articles of rubber | 78.0 | 31.6 | 73.3 |
| 631 | Veneers, plywood boards | 36.7 | 9.7 | 19.1 |
| 632 | Wood manufactures, n.e.s. | 7.9 | 8.5 | 8.1 |
| 633 | Cork manufactures | 4.3 | 3.9 | 4.3 |
| 641 | Paper & paperboard | 19.7 | 1.2 | 19.4 |
| 642 | Articles of pulp, paper, paperboard | 28.4 | 56.9 | 40.1 |
| 651 | Textile yarn & thread | 44.4 | 10.4 | 39.6 |
| 652 | Cotton fabrics, woven | 31.9 | 5.1 | 15.5 |

## 310                                   BULLETIN

| SITC | | OECD | Developing countries | Total* |
|------|---|------|------------|--------|
| 653 | Other textile fabrics, woven | 39.7 | 8.8 | 29.4 |
| 654 | Tulle, lace, embroidery | 9.7 | 20.3 | 13.4 |
| 655 | Special textile fabrics | 31.6 | 14.1 | 21.4 |
| 656 | Made-up textile articles | 16.6 | 8.3 | 10.2 |
| 657 | Floor coverings, tapestries | 16.4 | 4.1 | 10.1 |
| 661 | Lime, cement, building materials | 33.4 | 16.8 | 30.5 |
| 662 | Clay construction materials | 21.8 | 25.9 | 23.1 |
| 663 | Mineral manufactures, n.e.s. | 40.3 | 38.8 | 39.9 |
| 664 | Glass | 30.5 | 13.3 | 27.5 |
| 665 | Glassware | 33.3 | 4.5 | 25.9 |
| 666 | Pottery | 28.3 | 8.7 | 25.3 |
| 667 | Pearls, precious stones | 8.5 | 6.8 | 8.2 |
| 671 | Pig & sponge iron, ferro-alloys | 29.9 | 18.6 | 25.0 |
| 672 | Ingots & other primary forms | 47.8 | 0 | 47.4 |
| 673 | Bars, rods, angles, shapes | 61.3 | 44.8 | 60.4 |
| 674 | Universals, plates, sheets | 72.1 | 18.6 | 69.3 |
| 675 | Hoop & strip | 56.7 | 47.3 | 56.4 |
| 676 | Rails & track construction material | 37.5 | — | 37.5 |
| 677 | Wire, excluding wire rod | 55.0 | 23.9 | 54.4 |
| 678 | Tubes, pipes, fittings | 74.3 | 16.7 | 66.9 |
| 679 | Castings & forgings, unworked | 16.4 | 1.0 | 13.2 |
| 691 | Finished structural parts & structures | 40.7 | 47.7 | 41.1 |
| 692 | Metal containers for storage, transport | 18.2 | 7.1 | 17.1 |
| 693 | Wire products & fencing grilles | 61.5 | 15.9 | 55.8 |
| 694 | Nails, screws, nuts, bolts, rivets | 24.5 | 28.4 | 24.3 |
| 695 | Tools for hand or machine | 27.4 | 15.4 | 25.1 |
| 696 | Cutlery | 13.2 | 7.4 | 11.5 |
| 697 | Household equipment | 13.6 | 2.2 | 7.8 |
| 698 | Metal manufactures, n.e.s. | 23.0 | 12.1 | 21.2 |
| 711 | Power generating machinery | 69.9 | 76.1 | 70.2 |
| 712 | Agricultural machinery | 69.6 | 51.8 | 68.4 |
| 714 | Office machines | 74.9 | 80.2 | 75.8 |
| 715 | Metalworking machinery | 43.3 | 18.2 | 40.7 |
| 717 | Textile & leather machinery | 51.0 | 29.5 | 50.3 |
| 718 | Machines for special industries | 52.7 | 47.7 | 52.5 |
| 719 | Machinery & appliances, n.e.s. | 47.7 | 47.6 | 47.6 |
| 722 | Electric power machinery, switchgear | 58.5 | 80.3 | 65.7 |
| 723 | Equipment for distributing electricity | 39.8 | 55.8 | 46.8 |
| 724 | Telecommunications apparatus | 56.4 | 65.2 | 59.6 |
| 725 | Domestic electrical equipment | 33.3 | 29.6 | 32.6 |
| 726 | Electrical apparatus for medical purposes | 71.9 | 93.3 | 72.0 |
| 729 | Other electrical machinery, apparatus | 57.0 | 87.0 | 74.3 |
| 731 | Railway vehicles | 65.7 | 1.0 | 54.3 |
| 732 | Road motor vehicles | 87.0 | 45.5 | 86.5 |
| 733 | Road motor vehicles, nonmotor | 37.0 | 13.7 | 30.5 |
| 734 | Aircraft | 43.8 | 75.1 | 43.9 |
| 735 | Ships & boats | 22.8 | 3.5 | 16.4 |
| 812 | Sanitary, plumbing, heating, lighting fixtures | 17.3 | 14.2 | 15.8 |
| 821 | Furniture | 34.0 | 13.6 | 26.3 |
| 831 | Travel goods, handbags, etc. | 28.4 | 10.3 | 13.4 |
| 841 | Clothing except fur | 12.0 | 11.7 | 11.4 |
| 842 | Fur clothing | 11.8 | 8.8 | 9.3 |
| 851 | Footwear | 11.7 | 4.4 | 7.3 |
| 861 | Scientific, medical, optical instruments | 46.8 | 33.1 | 45.0 |
| 862 | Photographic supplies | 66.0 | 36.3 | 65.2 |
| 864 | Watches & clocks | 51.5 | 61.5 | 56.0 |
| 891 | Musical instruments, sound recorders | 57.6 | 41.6 | 55.2 |
| 893 | Plastic articles | 27.6 | 9.4 | 18.9 |
| 894 | Perambulators, toys, sporting goods | 25.4 | 20.4 | 22.3 |
| 895 | Office & stationery supplies | 51.2 | 6.1 | 48.8 |
| 897 | Jewellery, goldsmiths' wares | 15.2 | 15.6 | 15.2 |
| 899 | Manufactured articles, n.e.s. | 25.4 | 5.0 | 12.0 |

*Including imports from centrally planned economies.

## APPENDIX B

*Correlation Matrix for Independent Variables in Table 4's Regression Equations*

|      | SIZE | SC    | CON   | AD    | W      | RD    |
|------|------|-------|-------|-------|--------|-------|
| SIZE | —    | 0.039 | 0.574 | 0.049 | 0.455  | 0.287 |
| SC   |      | —     | 0.087 | 0.150 | 0.051  | 0.167 |
| CON  |      |       | —     | 0.156 | 0.266  | 0.283 |
| AD   |      |       |       | —     | −0.008 | 0.280 |
| W    |      |       |       |       | —      | 0.219 |
| RD   |      |       |       |       |        | —     |

# [21]

## 12 SOME EVIDENCE ON TRANSFER PRICING BY MULTINATIONAL CORPORATIONS

Donald J. Lecraw

Transfer pricing by multinational enterprises (MNEs) has received considerable attention from academics, host-country governments and international organizations. This research has taken essentially four forms: (1) theoretical analyses of the conditions under which MNEs might find it to their advantage to charge transfer prices that do not reflect market, arm's-length prices (Mathewson and Quirin, 1979, Chapters 4-6; Abdel-Khalik and Lusk, 1974); (2) studies that focus on the transfer pricing practices of one or a small number of MNEs (Tang, 1979, 1980; Arpan, 1972a); (3) studies that use large-sample, often highly aggregate data to draw inferences on the extent of manipulation of transfer prices by MNEs (Vaitsos, 1974); and (4) studies that examine the implications of transfer pricing for management in accounting, marketing, finance, control, personnel evaluation, etc. (Barrett, 1977; Benke and Edwards, 1980; Finnie, 1978: and Merville and Petty, 1978). This paper helps to link the theoretical and the descriptive analyses of the determinants of the *level* at which MNEs set transfer prices. It uses data collected in 1978 on the import and export pricing practices of 111 MNEs that operated 153 subsidiaries in six light manufacturing industries in the five countries of the ASEAN region: Thailand, Malaysia, Singapore, Indonesia and the Philippines.[1] It uses these data to test hypotheses concerning the determinants of the transfer price policies and the extent by which non-market transfer prices differed from market-based prices for imports and exports by the MNEs in the sample.

Whenever an MNE engages in transactions across national boundaries between related units of the firm, the price at which the good or service is transferred may be set such that it does not equal the value that would prevail if the units were independent of each other, i.e. the market price for the good or service. Intra-firm sales of goods and services include exports and imports of final and intermediate products and capital equipment, licencing,

## 224 *Transfer Pricing by Multinational Corporations*

technical service and management fees, and intra-firm loans or credit. An MNE determines the price at which a good or service was transferred between related units of the firm based on many factors: reductions of taxes at home or in one of the host countries in which it operates, reduction of tariff fees, allocation of funds from one unit of the firm to another, avoidance of import or export restrictions, meeting local value-added requirements, and reduction of profits accruing to joint-venture partners. In short MNEs determine transfer prices to maximize the risk-adjusted discounted profits accruing to the firm.[2]

The prices that firms set for intra-firm exports and imports across national boundaries are the subject of continual controversy between MNEs and the governments in the countries in which they operate — for three reasons. First, the prices of intra-firm exports and imports directly affect the impact of MNEs on host and home economies — tax and tariff payments, balance of payments, price levels, etc. — as well as affecting the profitability of MNEs and their ability to allocate resources within the firm. Both MNEs and governments have a high stake in the level at which transfer prices are set. Second, there is often considerable latitude between the transfer price that is optimal for the MNE, the price that is optimal for government, and the market price. Third, an arm's-length, competitive market price often does not exist for the product or service, and hence there is often no benchmark against which transfer prices can be evaluated.

The next section presents some data on the extent of intra-firm trade by the MNEs in the sample to serve as a background for the study and give an indication of the scope of the transfer pricing problem faced by the MNEs in the sample and the host countries in which they operated. Section III reviews the theory of the determinants of an MNE's transfer pricing strategy and Section IV tests the hypotheses that arise from this theory. Section V summarizes the results and draws some of their implications for host-country governments and MNEs.

## II

The potential scope and latitude for an MNE to set transfer prices outside the market depends in part on the quantity of goods and services transferred between related units of the MNE

*Transfer Pricing by Multinational Corporations*   225

across national boundaries. This study focuses on intra-firm exports and imports, often the most important component of intra-firm transfers. The extent of these exports and imports has a direct bearing on the importance of transfer pricing for the firms in the sample and the potential impact of nonmarket-based transfer prices on the host countries. A brief description of intra-firm trade of the firms in the sample is, therefore, useful.

All the countries in the ASEAN region have had policies to encourage firms to increase their exports of manufactured products. Until the mid-1970s, however, only Singapore had much success in its efforts. Prior to 1970, with the exception of Singapore, most of the foreign direct investment (FDI) in the manufacturing sector in the countries in the ASEAN region was made to serve the domestic market. The firms in the sample followed this pattern according to the data collected in 1978. In aggregate they exported only 7.1 per cent of their output

**Table 12.1: Export and Import Intensities Normalized by Host Country and Industry (USA = 100)**

| Home Country | Exports | Imports |
|---|---|---|
| United States | 100 | 100 |
| Europe | 80 | 125 |
| Japan | 39 | 235 |
| LDC | 13 | 74 |

Note: All data for all tables based on 1978 questionnaire.

**Table 12.2: Export Destination by MNE Home Country**

| Export Destination (% of Exports) | MNE Home Country | | | |
|---|---|---|---|---|
| | USA | Europe | Japan | LDC |
| USA | 63 | 21 | 47 | 62 |
| Europe | 21 | 54 | 32 | 15 |
| Japan | 10 | 11 | 14 | 12 |
| LDC | 6 | 14 | 7 | 11 |
| | 100 | 100 | 100 | 100 |

226   *Transfer Pricing by Multinational Corporations*

although there was a wide variation about this average depending
on the MNE, the industry and the host country. Normalizing for
industry and country effects, export intensities were highest for
US-based MNEs, followed by European, Japanese and MNEs
based in other LDCs (Table 12.1).[3] Table 12.2 displays the
destination of exports by home-country group. In general, US-
and Europe-based MNEs exported mostly to their home
countries; Japan- and LDC-based MNEs tended to export to the
United States and Europe rather than to their home-country
markets. Per cent intra-firm exports were highest for Japanese
MNEs and lowest for MNEs based in other LDCs (Table 12.4).

The imported inputs of the MNEs in the sample represented
40.8 per cent of their total inputs in their final products.
Normalized import intensity was highest for Japanese MNEs and
lowest for MNEs based in other LDCs (Table 12.1). All the
MNEs in the sample tended to source their imported inputs in
their home countries rather than from other countries. Japanese

## Table 12.3: Import Source by MNE Home Country

| Import Source (% of imports) | MNE Home Country | | | |
| --- | --- | --- | --- | --- |
| | USA | Europe | Japan | LDC |
| USA | 53 | 12 | 2 | 8 |
| Europe | 12 | 47 | 11 | 3 |
| Japan | 28 | 30 | 73 | 17 |
| LDC | 7 | 11 | 14 | 72 |
| | 100 | 100 | 100 | 100 |

## Table 12.4: Per cent of Exports to and Imports from Related Units of the MNE

| Home Country of the MNE | Exports | Imports |
| --- | --- | --- |
| USA | 68 | 53 |
| Europe | 65 | 57 |
| Japan | 79 | 84 |
| LDC | 23 | 37 |

MNEs tended to source most at home, US-based MNEs the least
(Table 12.3). Japanese MNEs tended to source their imports
from related units of their firm to a greater extent than did the
other MNEs in the sample (Table 12.4). Charging nonmarket
transfer prices on imported inputs and exports can only occur
when these transactions are between units of the same MNE.
Some MNEs in the sample internalized their import and export
transactions even when the ultimate source or destination of the
product was not related to them by routing the transaction
through a wholly-owned sales subsidiary either in a third country
or in the country of origin or destination. The extent of intra-firm
exports and imports of the MNEs in the sample indicates that
there was considerable scope for transfer pricing at nonmarket-
based prices.

## III

Several factors have been suggested in the literature that could
influence the type and level of transfer prices used by MNEs
between related units for their exports and imports.[4] The model
of the MNE presented here is one of constrained optimization at
the firm level. The MNE is viewed as optimizing firm-wide, risk-
adjusted profits given its opportunity set and internal (managerial) and external constraints (Robbins and Stobaugh, 1974). In
general, tax and tariff revenues that accrue to the governments of
the host and home countries in which an MNE operates and
profits which accrue to unrelated joint-venture partners reduce
the profits of an MNE. All else equal, an MNE will determine
transfer prices to minimize payments to those outside the firm.
An MNE's latitude for determining transfer prices is constrained
by the goals, power and expertise of the external agents which
have a claim on its resources.

*Ceteris paribus*, as tariffs on imports increase in the host
country, the MNE has an incentive to charge lower transfer prices
on its imported inputs in order to reduce the amount of duty it
pays. Similarly, as the tariffs facing an MNE's exports increase in
the country of destination, it may lower its export prices to
reduce tariff payments. The higher the profit taxes in the host
country relative to the home country of the MNE, the greater is
the incentive to reduce reported profits in the host country to

## 228   *Transfer Pricing by Multinational Corporations*

avoid profit taxes. An MNE can reduce profits in the host country by increasing the transfer price of imported inputs and reducing the transfer price of exports.[5] An MNE may also use transfer prices to reduce the risk of its operations and increase its flexibility in moving funds from one country to another. A high perceived risk by the MNE for its operations in the host country might increase its propensity to transfer money out of the country via high prices for imported inputs and low export prices.[6] The existence of price controls in the local market might also affect transfer pricing policies. Regulatory agencies often control prices in an industry in relation to the costs and profits of firms in the industry. High prices for imported inputs would reduce profits and increase costs and could be used as a justification for increased prices. Reduced export prices would also lower profits reported in the host country. If the government imposed capital or profit repatriation restrictions on MNEs, these might be avoided by setting transfer prices at a low level for intra-firm exports or a high level for intra-firm imports.

Management control considerations may also influence the use of transfer prices that do not reflect market prices. If the MNE's accounting, control and reward system is decentralized by country, manipulation of transfer prices can wreak havoc with the evaluation, control and reward systems (Barrett, 1977; Petty and Walker, 1972; Robbins and Stobaugh, 1973b). In another article (Lecraw, 1983) a variable was constructed to measure the extent of the centralization of corporate control of the MNEs in the sample. This variable essentially measures the locus of control between the headquarters of the MNE and the subsidiary, i.e. whether control over a set of decision variables rests with the parent or with the subsidiary. An MNE's transfer pricing strategy may be influenced by the degree it centralizes control over decision making, evaluation and rewards. The US-based MNEs in the sample tended to be run on a more decentralized basis than the MNEs based in other home countries (especially Japanese MNEs), so, *ceteris paribus*, US-based MNEs might be expected to use transfer prices that approached market prices to a greater extent than did other MNEs, especially the more centralized Japanese MNEs, in the sample.

If an MNE's subsidiary in the host country is a joint venture with a partner outside the MNE's system, the latitude of its transfer price strategy may be limited. If profits in the host

country are affected by its transfer price strategy and profits
accruing to the joint venture are raised, the MNE will earn a
lower return on its total operations; if profits in the host country
are reduced, the MNE's local partner may object. The presence
of a local partner might, therefore, increase the use of market-
based transfer prices. On the other hand, the presence of a joint
venture partner might motivate the MNE to set transfer prices to
reduce reported profits in the subsidiary, profits which would
partially accrue to the joint venture partner. The influence of a
joint venture partner on transfer prices is uncertain.

Finally, in the ASEAN countries there have been charges
from time to time that Japanese MNEs have a greater tendency
to use nonmarket-based transfer prices to avoid host-country
controls and as competitive weapons than do other MNEs. If this
were true, then ownership (Japanese-other MNEs) would be a
factor in explaining the use of nonmarket-based transfer prices.


## IV

The potential influences on the transfer pricing strategy of MNEs
described in the previous section have been well developed in the
literature. The actual extent to which they influence transfer
pricing strategy is not known, however, since data on transfer
prices (compared to market price) are scarce. The unique feature
of this study is that it uses data on actual prices and methods of
determining transfer prices obtained from the MNEs in the
sample to test the effects of these potential determinants of
transfer pricing strategy. The data were obtained by the author in
1978 during structured interviews with several top managers of
the 153 subsidiaries of the 111 MNEs in the sample in response to
a questionnaire.

Tables 12.5 and 12.6 display the responses to questions
concerning the pricing practices of the MNEs in the sample for
imports and exports from the host country. Striking differences
emerge in the pricing practices of the MNEs when selling to other
units of the MNE (intra-firm sales) and to unrelated firms. Four
pricing practices (at world market price, at the market price in
the country of destination for exports from the host country, at
the market price in the host country for imports into the host
country and at full cost of production plus profit) might serve as

230   *Transfer Pricing by Multinational Corporations*

## Table 12.5: Export Pricing Practices

Question: In general exports were priced:

| Pricing Practices | Type of Buyer | |
|---|---|---|
| | Intra-firm | Unrelated Firm[a] |
| A.   By the subsidiary at: | | |
| 1.   World price | 15 | 16 |
| 2.   Price in country of destination | 17 | 31 |
| 3.   Price in host country (exporting country) | 8 | 4 |
| 4.   Full cost of production (plus profit) | 17 | 12 |
| B.   At the direction of parent: | 45 | 31 |
| 5.   At prices in (1-4) | 8 | 24 |
| 6.   At another price than in (5) | 44 | 7 |
| Number of firms responding | 82 | 94 |

Note: a. The numbers in the columns do not add to the number of exporting firms (82) due to multiple responses since the categories of pricing practices are not mutually exclusive.

## Table 12.6: Import Pricing Practices

Question: In general, imports were priced:

| Pricing Practices | Type of Seller | |
|---|---|---|
| | Intra-firm | Unrelated Firm[a] |
| A.   By the subsidiary at: | | |
| 1.   World price | 20 | 67 |
| 2.   Price in the host country (importing country) | 8 | 28 |
| 3.   Price in the source country (exporting country) | 10 | 40 |
| 4.   Full cost of production, plus profit | 28 | 2 |
| B.   At the direction of the parent: | 112 | 71 |
| 5.   At price (1-4) | 31 | 58 |
| 6.   At another price | 81 | 13 |
| Total number of firms | 142 | 152 |

Note: a. The numbers in these columns do not add to 130, the number of importing firms, due to multiple responses.

reasonable proxies for arm's-length prices.[7] Pricing at a price determined on another basis besides these four such as marginal cost pricing, penetration pricing, etc., would seem to reflect the use of nonmarket-based transfer prices. The data in Table 12.5 show that intra-firm exports tended to be at prices that were generally nonmarket based, while prices for transactions with unrelated firms were generally priced in relation to market prices or full costs.

Data on the pricing practices of the MNEs in the sample for their imports are displayed in Table 12.6. Again the same pattern as for exports emerges: there would seem to have been widespread use of nonmarket-based transfer prices when imported inputs were purchased from other units of the MNE.

Classifying pricing practices #1-#4 in Tables 12.5 and 12.6 as market-based and #5 as a nonmarket-based transfer price, then, as shown in Table 12.7, Japanese MNEs tended to use nonmarket-based transfer prices for both intra-firm imports and exports to a greater extent than did US or European MNEs.[8] This tendency may be due to the more centralized control system employed by Japanese MNEs (See Lecraw, 1983).

Table 12.7: Intra-firm Export and Import Prices (all figures in per cent)

| Home country | Market-based | Nonmarket-based |
|---|---|---|
| USA | 68 | 32 |
| Europe | 65 | 35 |
| Japan | 25 | 75 |
| Other LDC | 45 | 55 |
| Total | 42 | 58 |

In order to test the hypotheses concerning the determinants of the firms' transfer pricing practices, the export pricing behaviour of the MNEs in the sample were classified as 'market based' (MB) or 'nonmarket based' (NMB) as defined above. Multiple discriminant analysis was used to uncover the relationships between the characteristics of the MNEs in the sample, the environment in which they operated and the transfer pricing practices they followed. The use of multiple discriminant analysis allows tests for the relative significance of the effects of these

232    *Transfer Pricing by Multinational Corporations*

variables on transfer pricing and determination of the linear combinations of independent variables that best discriminate among firms that used 'market-based' or 'nonmarket-based' transfer prices. Essentially the multiple discriminant analysis assigned the pricing behaviour of each firm to one of the two classifications so as to minimize the probability that the firm's pricing practice was assigned to the class in which it did not in fact belong.[9]

A discriminant function using the variables tariff level, the relative rates of profits taxes, the existence of price controls and capital-profit repatriation controls, perceived risk of operations in the host country, the degree of centralization of the MNE, the existence of a joint-venture partner, and Japanese-other MNE, was estimated to classify the MNEs in the sample into those using market-based and nonmarket-based transfer prices for their exports. (The same type of analysis was done for pricing strategies for imports as described below.)

The discriminant function was of the form:

$$Z = \sum_{i=1}^{8} \alpha_i X_i$$

where $Z$ is the score of the discriminant function, the $a_i$'s are the weighting coefficients, and the $x_i$'s are the standardized values of the eight discriminating variables used in the analysis. The $x_i$'s are defined as:

$X_1$ = nominal tariff rate in country of destination
$X_2$ = tax rate for the MNE in the host country relative to the home country tax rate
$X_3$ = 1 if price controls, 0 if not
$X_4$ = 1 if restrictions on capital and dividend repatriation were in effect, 0 otherwise
$X_5$ = country risk as perceived by the managers of the subsidiary of the MNE (1 = low, 10 = high)
$X_6$ = 1 if the subsidiary had Japanese-ownership, 0 otherwise
$X_7$ = per cent ownership of the subsidiary held outside the MNE
$X_8$ = degree of centralization of management control
$X_9$ = nominal host country tariff rate.

The results of the discriminant analysis are shown in Table 12.9.
Data to construct these eight variables were obtained from the

questionnaire administered during interviews with managers of the 153 subsidiaries in the sample. The variable $X_5$ is the rating of country risk as perceived by the manager of the subsidiary interviewed ranked 1 (low) to 10 (high). Variable $X_8$ was a composite variable constructed from responses to questions relating to the locus of control (parent MNE or subsidiary) for 21 decision variables of each subsidiary weighted by their perceived importance to the subsidiary's success. (This variable and its construction are discussed at more length in Lecraw, 1983.)

### Table 12.8: Confusion Matrix of the Discriminant Functions for Market Based and Nonmarket Based Import and Export Pricing on Intra-firm Transactions

| | Exports | | |
|---|---|---|---|
| Actual | | Predicted | |
| | Market Based | Nonmarket Based | Total |
| Market based | 30 | 7 | 37 |
| Nonmarket based | 10 | 35 | 45 |
| Total | 40 | 42 | 82 |

Correct classification = 79%

| | Imports | | |
|---|---|---|---|
| | | Predicted | |
| Actual | Market Based | Nonmarket Based | Total |
| Market based | 55 | 8 | 63 |
| Nonmarket based | 9 | 70 | 79 |
| Total | 64 | 78 | 142 |

Correct classification = 88%

The discriminant function correctly classified the export pricing behaviour of 30 of the 37 MNEs whose export pricing was classified as 'market based'. It classified 35 of the 45 firms that used nonmarket-based export prices correctly (Table 12.8).[10] These success rates were significantly above the level for random classification. As can be seen in Table 12.9, the F statistic was significant for the variables: degree of centralization of control over the subsidiary, perceived risk, price controls, capital-profit repatriation restrictions, the degree of centralization of the MNE,

234 *Transfer Pricing by Multinational Corporations*

## Table 12.9: The Discriminant Functions for Market-based and Nonmarket-based Export-Import Pricing

| | Exports $Z_1$ | Imports $Z_2$ |
|---|---|---|
| Nominal tariff in country of destination, $X_1$ | +0.22 (3.75) | N.A. |
| Host country tax rate relative to home country tax rate, $X_2$ | +0.17 (4.32) | +0.22 (3.54) |
| Price controls, $X_3$ | +0.20 (2.75) | +0.15 (3.10) |
| Dividend and capital repatriation restriction, $X_4$ | +0.12 (2.95) | +0.093 (3.15) |
| Perceived country risk, $X_5$ | +0.032 (5.71) | +0.043 (6.75) |
| Japanese subsidiary, $X_6$ | +0.021 (0.67) | +0.052 (0.34) |
| Per cent local ownership, $X_7$ | −0.0035 (4.75) | −0.0047 (6.30) |
| Degree of centralization, $X_8$ | +0.23 (4.15) | +0.19 (7.10) |
| Nominal host country tariff rate, $X_9$ | N.A. | 0.037 (5.42) |

Notes: 1. The numbers in parenthesis are the F statistics. For exports, at the 5 per cent level, the critical value for $F_{(8,73)}$ is 2.10; for imports the critical $F_{(8,133)}$ is 2.02. At the 1 per cent level the critical Fs are 2.78 and 2.63 respectively.
2. Firms with $Z_1 > 2.03$ or $Z_2 > 1.85$ were classified as using nonmarket-based transfer prices on intra-firm exports or imports.

tariffs in the country of destination and relative profit taxes. In the discriminant analysis of pricing strategies for exports the nationality of the MNE (Japanese and non-Japanese) was not a significant discriminating variable when the variable representing the degree of centralization of control of the MNE was included. When the centralization variable was dropped, however, nationality was significant: Japanese MNEs tended to use nonmarket-based transfer prices to a greater extent than did other MNEs. This finding is similar to that of Tang (1979).[11] These statistical results support the hypotheses concerning the determinants of the use of transfer prices not based on market prices for exports.

A similar analysis was carried out for the determinants of prices for intra-firm and inter-firm imports. A discriminant function was estimated to classify the import pricing on intra-firm imports as 'nonmarket based' and 'market based' using variables $X_2$ through $X_8$ and the height of the tariff in the host country, $X_9$. This discriminant classified 88 per cent of the firms to the correct category, 55 of 63 firms that used market-based import prices and 70 of 79 firms that used corporate-based prices. (The confusion matrix and the discriminant function are in Tables 12.8 and 12.9.) As indicated by the F statistic, the significant variables were the nominal tariff in the host country, relative tax rates, price controls and the presence of dividend and capital repatriation restrictions, perceived country risk, per cent local ownership and the degree of centralization of the parent MNE. Japanese ownership was not significant.

To test the determinants of the *extent* by which export prices on inter-firm and intra-firm sales differed, multiple regression analysis was used with

$$\text{PDX} = \frac{|P^x_T - P^x_M|}{P^x_M}$$

the per cent deviation of prices for intra-firm ($P^x_T$) from inter-firm ($P^x_M$) sales of the same product as the dependent variable, using data from the 35 MNEs that exported the same product to related firms and to unrelated firms, and that followed nonmarket-based transfer pricing practices. The price of exports to unaffiliated firms, $P^x_M$, was used as the baseline for the competitive arm's-length value of the product on the export market. The relationship between this baseline price and the intra-firm transfer price may depend on conditions in the local market (profits taxes, price controls, country risk, etc.) and on export markets (tariffs).

*A priori* we predict the following signs of the coefficients of the independent variables.

1. The higher are tariffs in the country of destination, the greater the incentive to price intra-firm exports low relative to inter-firm exports to avoid paying tariffs in the country of destination. The coefficient of $X_1$ should be positive.

2. The greater the difference between local profits taxes and home country taxes, the greater the incentive to under- or overprice intra-firm exports to reduce reported local profits and

## 236  *Transfer Pricing by Multinational Corporations*

the greater the absolute value of the per cent deviation of intra-firm and inter-firm export prices for the same product. The value $|X_2-1|$ was used as the independent variable where $X_2$ is the ratio of the profits tax rate in the host and home countries.[12] The sign of $|X_2-1|$ should be positive.

3. If price controls are in effect in the host country ($X_3 = 1$) the MNE may reduce the price of its intra-firm exports to show low profits in the host country in order to increase its bargaining power in trying to have price increases approved in the host country. The sign of $X_3$ should be positive.

4. Similarly, if capital or dividend repatriation controls were in effect ($X_4 = 1$) or, 5., country risk, $X_5$, were perceived as high, the firm may reduce intra-firm export prices in order to transfer money out of the country. The signs of $X_4$ and $X_5$ should be positive.

6. Japanese MNEs ($X_6 = 1$) are thought to engage in more widespread use of nonmarket-based transfer prices than other MNEs (Tang, 1979). The sign of $X_6$ should be positive.

7. The presence of a local joint venture partner, $X_7$, may reduce the ability of MNEs to set nonmarket-based transfer prices that deviate from market prices. The sign of $X_7$ should be negative.

8. Finally, the more decentralized the decision, evaluation and control system of the MNE, the greater the problems caused by deviations of the transfer price from the market price and the greater the incentive to use market-based transfer prices. The sign of $X_8$ should be positive.

The signs of the independent variables and the regression results are displayed in Table 12.10. All the variables had the predicted sign, but the variable for Japanese MNE ($X_6$) was not significant when $X_8$ was included in the regression equation. The regression equation explained 55 per cent of the variation of PDX. The average value for PDX was 7.8 with a standard deviation of 5.3.[13]

A similar regression analysis of the determinants of the transfer prices for intra-firm imports was performed. The dependent variable was the absolute value of the percentage difference between the price for intra-firm imports, $P_T^l$, and inter-firm imports $P_M^l$ for products from 65 firms in the sample which used nonmarket-based transfer prices on intra-firm imports and imported the same input from both related and unrelated firms,

## Table 12.10: Regression Results for PDX and PDI

|  | PDX Predicted Sign | PDX Coefficient | PDI Predicted Sign | PDI Coefficient |
|---|---|---|---|---|
| Constant | + | 1.3[a] (2.71) | + | 2.5[a] (3.25) |
| Nominal tariff in country of destination, $X_1$ | + | 0.032[a] (3.52) |  | N.A |
| Absolute value of relative host-country tax rate $-1$, $\lvert X_2-1 \rvert$ | + | 3.57[a] (3.05) | + | 2.34[b] (2.51) |
| Price controls, $X_3$ | + | 2.32[b] (2.34) | + | 3.26[b] (2.11) |
| Dividend and capital repatriation restrictions, $X_4$ | + | 3.25[b] (2.17) | + | 4.2[b] (2.10) |
| Perceived country risk, $X_5$ | + | 0.20[b] (2.25) | + | 0.37[b] (1.90) |
| Japanese subsidiary, $X_6$ | + | 1.5 (0.63) | + | 2.3 (0.34) |
| Per cent local ownership, $X_7$ | − | 0.22[b] (2.40) | − | 0.19[a] (2.73) |
| Centralization of control, $X_8$ | + | 0.32[a] (3.15) | + | 0.17 (2.96)[b] |
| Nominal host-country tariff, $X_9$ |  | N.A. | + | 0.056[b] (3.15) |
| $\bar{R}^2$ |  | 0.63 |  | 0.72 |
| N |  | 35 |  | 65 |

Notes: Numbers in parenthesis are the t values.
a = significant at the 99 per cent level.
b = significant at the 95 per cent level.

i.e. PDI $= \lvert\ P_T^l - P_M^m \rvert / P_M^l$. The independent variables were the same as those for the regression analysis of export prices, with the exception that the nominal tariff in the host country replaced the nominal tariff in the country of destination. PDI should increase as the tariff in the host country ($X_9$) increases, as

238    *Transfer Pricing by Multinational Corporations*

the differences between relative tax rate, $|X_2-1|$, increases, if there are price controls ($X_3=1$), if there are restrictions on dividend and capital repatriation ($X_4=1$), as the perceived country risk ($X_5$) increases, as the degree of centralization of control ($X_8$) increases and if the subsidiary has Japanese ownership. PDM should decrease as the extent of local equity increases.

The signs of the coefficients of the independent variables and the actual regression results are in Table 12.10. All the coefficients except Japanese ownership had the predicted sign and were significant at the 95 per cent level. Taken together these variables accounted for 74 per cent of the variance in PDI.[14] The average value of PDI was 12.2.

A similar analysis was performed for the prices of imports and exports for the firms that followed a market-based pricing practice for intra-firm trade. None of the variables was significant. The average values of PDX and PDI were 1.2 per cent and 2.4 per cent respectively. Only 5 per cent of the variance of PDX and 8 per cent of the variance of PDI was accounted for by the independent variables.

In summary, the MNEs in the sample charged nonmarket-based transfer prices for intra-firm imports and exports to reduce duties and profit taxes, allocate capital between countries, reduce risk, and to circumvent government price and capital-profit remittance controls. Local joint venture partners decreased the use and extent of nonmarket-based transfer prices.


V


The results of the analysis in this paper support the position often taken by host governments in LDCs and industrialized countries alike that MNEs engage in a widespread and systematic use of transfer prices that differ from market prices to increase their global profits, reduce risk, move funds across national boundaries and allocate them between subsidiaries.[15] The presence of a local partner tended to reduce both the magnitude and the pervasiveness of the use of nonmarket-based transfer prices. The ability of local joint venture partners in the ASEAN region to influence the transfer pricing practices of the MNE partners, however, may exceed that of firms in most other LDCs. To this extent these conclusions may not be applicable in other LDCs.

Governments in both host and home countries of MNEs are certainly aware of the potential problem of the use of nonmarket-based transfer prices on intra-firm transactions of goods and services. This study indicates that charging nonmarket-based transfer prices is not confined to MNEs based in one country, or operating in one industry, or producing in one host country, but is a general practice used by MNEs.

When government imposes high tariffs on imports, relatively high taxes on profits, price controls and controls on profit and capital movements, it should expect MNEs which are affected by these policies to charge transfer prices to avoid their incidence. Government might direct its attention towards these MNEs in its efforts to bring transfer prices towards the arm's-length, market level. The presence of a local partner also might decrease the incidence and extent of the use of corporate-based transfer prices that differ from market prices. A local partner both may have access to intra-firm data that would allow the assessment of the basis of transfer prices of goods and services and may have the incentive to ensure that intra-firm prices approach the arm's-length level.

## Notes

The research of this study was partially funded by the United Nations Centre on Transnational Corporations and the Centre for International Business Studies, the University of Western Ontario.

1. See Lecraw (1981) for a description of the firms in the sample and the industries in which they operated.
2. The risk associated with these cash flows must be incorporated into their valuation in the discounting process.
3. See Lecraw (1981) for a description of the normalization procedure.
4. This section draws heavily on the work of Mathewson and Quirin (1979). See Vernon and Wells (1981, chapters 3 and 4) for a broader discussion of the relationship between transfer pricing and accounting, control and taxation of MNEs.
5. Mathewson and Quirin (1979) concluded that, in the case of Canada, the effects on transfer prices of host-country profits taxes and import duties largely offset each other.
6. Burns (1980) in a survey of corporate executives found that the internal foreign environment was perceived as the most important determinant of transfer pricing strategy. This variable may subsume risk and government price controls and profit and capital repatriation controls.
7. When this paper was originally presented there was disagreement over whether 'cost-plus profit' should be classified as a 'market-based price'. The point

## 240  *Transfer Pricing by Multinational Corporations*

is well taken since this price is one set internally by the firm. During the interviews, however, many managers stated that they regarded such a price as a fair market price which the firm had to receive in order to trade. This price is also used by several governments in anti-dumping and tariff regulations as an approximation of market price.

8. Those firms which followed a mixed strategy, i.e. set prices in both categories 1-5 *and* #6 were excluded from the analysis. This reduced the sample size from 82 to 63 for exports and from 130 to 118 for importing firms.

9. Discriminant analysis is a well-developed and often-used technique particularly in marketing and the behavioral sciences. Its use is gradually increasing in economic analysis. Green (1978, chapters 4 and 7) gives a thorough review of discriminant analysis.

10. If 'cost-plus profit' were shifted to the 'nonmarket based' classification, the power of the discriminant function declined.

11. Tang (1979) found that the transfer pricing strategies followed by US and Japanese MNEs differed in extent and type.

12. The strength of this relationship may be reduced by the provision for foreign tax credits in the tax laws.

13. Tests were run to determine if there were problems of heteroscedasticity of the residuals or multicollinearity of the variables. Regression of the residuals on the estimated values of PDX yielded no significant relationship. The hypothesis of heteroscedasticity was rejected. The only significant collinearity was between Japanese ownership and centralization of control. Despite this problem, there was sufficient variation in the data to break the deadlock, to the extent that the centralization variable was significant although the ownership variable was not.

14. The same tests for heteroscedasticity and multicollinearity were performed for this regression with similar results (see note 13).

15. The study did not cover the transfer prices of intra-firm debt, management and technical service fees, licencing, etc.

\*  \*  \*

# Part VIII
## Offshore Processing and Internationally Rationalized Production

# [22]

## THE MOTIVATION FOR INVESTMENT IN OFFSHORE PLANTS: THE CASE OF THE U.S. ELECTRONICS INDUSTRY

### RICHARD W. MOXON*

*This paper examines the motivation of U.S. electronics companies in establishing plants in less-developed countries for the manufacture of products to be exported to the United States. The results of an analysis of trade statistics and interviews with executives are reported.*

Most foreign direct investment by U.S. companies has been for the establishment of facilities to produce goods or services for foreign markets or to extract raw materials. Recently, however, many companies have established plants in the less-developed countries for the specific purpose of manufacturing products for sale to the U.S. consumer by the parent company or for providing components and subassemblies to parent company plants. These foreign facilities are commonly referred to as "offshore plants." For purposes of this study, an offshore plant is defined as a U.S.-owned plant located in a less-developed country whose principal mission is to manufacture products to be exported to the United States.

The electronics industry has been a leader in offshore production, and many U.S. companies have facilities in less-developed countries, manufacturing products ranging from semiconductors to television sets for the U.S. market. The purpose of this paper is to provide an analytical framework that may be useful in understanding why U.S. electronics companies have established offshore plants and in assessing the implications of these plants for the nations involved.

### HYPOTHESES

The foreign investment decision process has been studied from many different viewpoints, but these studies converge on a small number of propositions as to the motivations for foreign investments. These ideas are used here as the basis for predicting how companies make decisions regarding the offshore production investments of interest in this study.

Several studies have shown that a foreign investment decision is the result of a multistage process involving many persons in a company and occurring over an extended time period.[1] The offshore production decision process may be described in terms of three stages:

---

*Richard W. Moxon is Assistant Professor of International Business, University of Washington, Seattle, Washington.

1. *The administrative readiness to consider offshore production.* Because of limitations on management time and information, foreign investments often are made in response to significant perceived threats or opportunities, and the nature of the response is often suggested by the source of the pressure. It was therefore hypothesized that offshore production investments often would be made in response to severe competitive pressure in a company's U.S. market.

2. *The measurement of the benefits, costs, and risks of offshore production.* Once having begun considering a foreign investment, companies typically undertake an investigation of the benefits, costs, and risks of this possibility. It was hypothesized that for offshore production investments, companies would consider alternatives such as subcontracting and automation, and that certain product characteristics, such as labor intensity, would determine which products were selected for offshore manufacture.

3. *The evolution of offshore production.* Some studies have suggested that foreign ventures are investments in learning and that as a company gains foreign experience its decision process on further investments becomes more sophisticated. It was hypothesized that in the case of offshore production, the perceptions by managers of the benefits and risks of offshore plants would change over time in predictable ways, and that this would lead to an evolution in the nature of these operations.

## METHODOLOGY

The conceptual model described above was tested for the electronics industry.[2] The method used was to examine the extent to which different products were made offshore (dependent variable) and relate this to certain product characteristics (independent variables). Two methods were used to examine the relationship:

1. A multiple regression analysis comparing U.S. imports from offshore plants in different segments of the electronics industry to certain characteristics of those industry segments.

2. An analysis of the results of interviews with executives in 20 companies representing most major segments of the electronics industry and having offshore plants.[3]

For purposes of the regression analysis, the extent of offshore production was measured using data on imports to the United States under Items 806.30 and 807.00 of the Tariff Schedules. These tariff provisions essentially allow the duty-free import to the U.S. of U.S. components that are sent abroad, assembled, and returned to the U.S. Duty is assessed only on the value added abroad.[4] According to an investigation by the United States Tariff Commission, the great majority of these imports in the electronics industry come from plants owned by United States companies, plants which send a majority of their output back to the United States.[5] This relationship between Items 806.30 and 807.00 imports and offshore plants was tested also by comparing the sites of offshore plants with the sources of such imports, and it was confirmed that there is a close relationship.

To compare the extent of offshore production for different product groups in the electronics industry, an index was computed which compares Items 806.30 and 807.00 imports to United States production for each product group. This index measures the importance of offshore production in the United States market for each product. It was computed as follows:

$$\text{OPP} = \frac{\text{Offshore Production}}{\text{Propensity Index}} = 100 \times \frac{\text{Imports to the U.S. under Items 806.30 and 807.00, 1970}}{\text{U.S. Factory Shipments, 1970}}$$

The import figure includes imports from all countries, but in all cases the imports from less-developed countries account for almost all of the imports. This index is the main variable of interest in this study. The value of this index ranged from 0 to 25 for different segments of the electronics industry.

Two multiple linear regression equations were developed to explain the offshore production propensity index. The results of fitting these equations to the electronics industry data are shown in Tables 1 and 2. Equation 1 used an import competition index as a measure of competitive pressure in the U.S.; Equation 2 used a price trend index. All of the variables are defined in more detail in Table 3, and the intercorrelations among them are given in Table 4.

## TABLE 1

### Characteristics of Regression Equation 1

| Independent Variable | Regression Coefficient | t-Statistic |
|---|---|---|
| Constant | −4.54 | |
| Labor intensity index (LI) | 0.11 | 0.90 |
| Skill level index (SL) | −0.76 | −0.40 |
| Value-to-weight index (VW) | 0.09 | 2.61* |
| Tariff index (T) | −0.09 | −0.31 |
| Import competition index (IC) | 0.25 | 5.08* |
| Sales growth index (SG) | 0.34 | 1.58 |
| Coefficient of Determination ($R^2$) | | 0.75 |

*Significant at 5% significance level.

53

## TABLE 2

### Characteristics of Regression Equation 2

| Independent Variable | Regression Coefficient | t-Statistic |
|---|---|---|
| Constant | 5.15 | |
| Labor intensity index (LI) | 0.53 | 2.26* |
| Skill level index (SL) | −2.01 | −0.71 |
| Value-to-weight index (VW) | −0.19 | −1.21 |
| Tariff index (T) | −0.16 | −0.35 |
| Price trend index (PR) | −12.66 | −1.52 |
| Sales growth index (SG) | 0.09 | 0.25 |
| Coefficient of Determination ($R^2$) | | 0.44 |

*Significant at the 5% significance level.

The variables in the first equation explain 75 percent of the variance in the offshore production propensity index, and for each of the variables the regression coefficient has the expected sign. The second equation does not provide as good an explanation of the offshore production propensity, explaining only 44 percent of the variance in the data, but all but one of the regression coefficients has the expected sign. The total group of independent variables seems to provide considerable explanation of offshore production, but it is difficult to determine which of the variables is most important. This is due to the considerable degree of correlation among the explanatory variables. Using the results of the regression and correlation analysis, plus the interviews with executives, some tentative conclusions on the effects of each variable on the offshore production propensity can be drawn.

## RESULTS

### The Administration Readiness to Consider Offshore Production

It was hypothesized that offshore production investments would tend to be made in response to a competitive environment which threatened a company's U.S. market position, especially if the threat came from low-priced imports. Two measures of price competition were used in the regression analysis, one being an import competition index and the other a price trend index. Neither of the measures is very satisfactory by itself, but together they provide a rough indication of where the pressure to reduce costs is the greatest.

TABLE 3

Definitions of the Independent Variables, and Sources of Data

| Definition | Source |
|---|---|
| LI = Labor Intensity Index = $100 \times \dfrac{\text{Wages of Production Workers}}{\text{Value Added by Manufacture}}$ | U.S. Bureau of the Census, *Census of Manufacturers, 1967* (Washington, D.C., 1970). |
| SL = Skill Level Index = $100 \times \dfrac{\text{Wages of Production Workers}}{\text{Man-Hours of Production Workers}}$ | U.S. Bureau of the Census, *Census of Manufacturers, 1967* (Washington, D.C., 1970). |
| VW = Value-to-Weight Index = $\dfrac{\text{Average Selling Price in Dollars}}{\text{Average Weight in Pounds}}$ | Author's estimates based on data in trade catalogs of electronics manufacturers and distributors. |
| T = Tariff Index = Statutory Tariff Rate (Ad Valorem Percentage) | U.S. Tariff Commission, *Tariff Schedules of the United States Annotated (1970)* (Washington, D.C.). |
| IC = Import Competition Index = $\dfrac{\text{Imports to the U.S., 1970}}{\text{(Excluding Items 806.30 \& 807.00)}}{\text{U.S. Factory Shipments, 1970}}$ | Most shipments data are from U.S. Bureau of the Census, *Current Industrial Reports, Series MA-36N, MA-36M, MA-38B, MA-35R: 1968, 1969, 1970* (Washington, D.C.). Import data are from U.S. Bureau of the Census, *U.S. Imports for Consumption: 1970, FT_246* (Washington, D.C.) |
| PR = Price Trend Index = $\dfrac{\text{Average Unit Price, 1970}}{\text{Average Unit Price, 1960}}$ | Author's estimates are based on various sources. Most estimates are based on aggregate shipments data, with adjustments made for changes in product mix. |
| SG = Sales Growth Index = $\dfrac{\text{Value Added in Manufacture, 1967}}{\text{Value Added in Manufacture, 1958}}$ | U.S. Bureau of the Census, *Census of Manufacturers*, 1967, 1963 and 1958 editions (Washington, D.C.). |

## TABLE 4

### Intercorrelations Among the Variables
### Used in the Statistical Analysis

|     | OPP  | LI    | SL   | VW    | T    | IC   | PR    | SG |
|-----|------|-------|------|-------|------|------|-------|----|
| OPP |      |       |      |       |      |      |       |    |
| LI  | .54* |       |      |       |      |      |       |    |
| SL  | −.35 | −.45* |      |       |      |      |       |    |
| VW  | .19  | .19   | .10  |       |      |      |       |    |
| T   | −.19 | −.11  | −.06 | −.20  |      |      |       |    |
| IC  | .62* | .28   | −.36 | −.48* | −.07 |      |       |    |
| PR  | −.12 | .24   | −.24 | −.77* | .23  | .34  |       |    |
| SG  | .25  | .22   | .13  | .47*  | .05  | −.26 | −.45* |    |

*Significant at the 5% significance level.

Tables 1 and 4 indicate that the import competition index is a very important determinant of the offshore production propensity index for a given product. Table 2 indicates that products made offshore are also likely to be those that have been experiencing rapid price declines, but because the price trend index is so highly intercorrelated with the value-to-weight index, it is impossible to distinguish their separate effects.

Further evidence on the effect of price competition on offshore production decisions was provided by the managers interviewed. Seventeen of the 20 executives mentioned some form of price competition as an important contributing factor in choosing products for offshore manufacture. One particularly significant comment was, "We looked for products most threatened by Japanese competition. There are a lot of labor-intensive products, but for many of those the Japanese aren't bothering us."

An analysis of the three industry segments with the most offshore production -- the television, semiconductor, and core memory industries -- also indicated that initially offshore production has occurred most often in response to competitive pressure, both foreign and domestic, and less frequently as an aggressive move in response to opportunities for opening new markets for a product. Of course once one U.S. manufacturer establishes an offshore plant, this adds to the competitive threat to other companies, and they often follow the first investor offshore.

The apparent importance of import competition and price competition as determinants of offshore production decision confirms the results of other studies that have shown that foreign direct investment tends to be a reaction to competitive pressure. It supports the conclusion that many foreign investments are defensive in nature and that executives need a strong stimulus before they seriously consider a given foreign investment.[6]

## The Measurement of the Benefits, Costs, and Risks of Offshore Production

It was hypothesized that several product characteristics would determine whether a given product is chosen for offshore manufacture. These are discussed below.

*Labor Intensity.* Since labor costs in less-developed countries are much lower than in the U.S., it was hypothesized that labor intensive products would be most likely to be selected for offshore manufacture. The statistical analysis shows that this is probably true. Table 1 shows that the labor intensity index (LI) is positively related to the offshore propensity index. But a change of one standard deviation in LI causes a change of only 0.14 standard deviation in OPP, and the positive relationship is not statistically significant. LI shows a much stronger relationship with OPP in the second regression equation (Table 2). This, plus the fact that there is a significant positive correlation coefficient between LI and OPP in Table 4, may indicate that in Table 1 part of the effect of LI is being taken up by other variables with which it is intercorrelated.

All of the managers interviewed mentioned labor intensity as a very important criterion for selecting products and manufacturing operations for offshore plants. The comments of managers also indicated that they often are searching for specific kinds of labor offshore. Managers from companies making computer memories, for example, often said that in the United States they could not find enough workers willing to do the tedious assembly work required. Such manufacturers need large numbers of workers having good dexterity and eyesight and the right kind of mental attitudes. They cited as reasons for their move abroad the high turnover, poor productivity, and poor quality standards of their U.S. workforce. Similar comments were made by some manufacturers of components and consumer electronics products. All managers interviewed agreed that offshore workers are better suited to these kinds of jobs, are more productive, and are less prone to errors.

*Skill Requirements.* Since skilled workers are in relatively short supply in less-developed countries, it was hypothesized that companies would tend to choose for offshore manufacture those products requiring relatively unskilled labor. The regression analysis does not indicate that skill requirements greatly affect the offshore production propensity index, but because of the correlation between skill levels (SL) and other independent variables, no firm conclusions can be reached. In Table 1, SL is related to OPP in the expected direction, but not strongly. A change of one standard deviation in SL causes a change of only 0.06 standard deviation in OPP, and the relationship is not statistically significant. In the second equation, the relationship is stronger, but still not statistically significant. Nevertheless, the fact that there is a fairly strong correlation of SL with OPP and with labor intensity and import competition suggests that it may contribute more than is indicated in the regression equation.

57

The interviews with executives indicated that skill requirements are an important determinant of what products they select for offshore manufacture. Thirteen of the 20 executives stated that they tried to avoid doing jobs abroad that required skilled workers or technical personnel. They felt that it was difficult to find skilled workers abroad, and training them was expensive. The skills required for most of the production done offshore could be acquired in three months or less. Nevertheless, several firms mentioned that, as they gained experience offshore, they found that they could also save money on skilled workers, particularly technicians. These firms said that as they evolved toward training more people, and as they began to find qualified technical people offshore, they had started to take offshore operations which they originally thought too complicated to do outside the U.S.

*Shipping Costs.* It was hypothesized that shipping costs, as measured by a value-to-weight ratio, would have a significant influence on which products were selected for offshore manufacture. The regression analysis seems to bear this out. In Table 1, a change of one standard deviation in the value-to-weight index (VW) caused a change of 0.44 standard deviation in OPP, and the relationship was statistically significant. The second equation indicated a much weaker relationship between VW and OPP. Nevertheless, because VW is significantly correlated with several other variables, it is difficult to separate out its individual importance.

The comments of executives indicated that shipping costs play an important role in their decisions. Fourteen of the 20 managers interviewed mentioned shipping costs as being an important criterion for selecting products and countries for offshore manufacture. Several said that they restricted their offshore production to small, lightweight subassemblies, but would do much more offshore if shipping costs were lower. And many managers in firms with plants in Mexico said that transport costs played a big part in their decision to locate there instead of in the Far East. Shipping costs discourage the offshore manufacture of not only heavy and bulky products but also products that are subject to damage in shipping or for which rapid delivery is necessary.

*Tariffs.* It was hypothesized that both the level of tariffs and special tariff incentives might affect which products were manufactured offshore; thus two measures of tariff costs were used in this study. First, high U.S. tariffs on a product were expected to inhibit imports of that product, whether they be from offshore plants or foreign-owned plants. In the statistical analysis, however, tariffs do not seem to be an important determinant of which electronics products are made offshore. In Table 1, a change of one standard deviation in the tariff level causes a change of only 0.04 standard deviation in OPP. The second regression equation shows similar results.

Second, a measure of possible cost savings under Items 806.30 and 807.00 was computed for each product. For products with high values on this ratio, it was expected that imports under Items 806.30 and 807.00 would be a large percentage of all imports. This was tested by correlating this index of tariff savings with the percentage of total imports accounted for by imports under Items 806.30 and 807.00. The resulting correlation coefficient of -0.31 (in the opposite direction from that expected) was a further indication that Items 806.30 and 807.00 are of very little importance in the product selection process.

Also, tariff considerations were mentioned by only five of the 20 managers as important in offshore production decisions. Many said that the existence of Items 806.30 and 807.00 of the U.S. Tariff Schedules contributed to the benefits obtainable by offshore production and limited offshore operations mainly to assembly and testing, but infrequently influenced *which* products were made offshore. A couple of cases were mentioned in which government rulings had disallowed the use of these tariff provisions for certain products or parts, making offshore production unfeasible; but such incidents were rare. It should be noted, however, that since tariff levels on electronics products are relatively low, tariffs may be a much more important factor in other industries such as apparel.

*Sales Growth.* It was hypothesized that products experiencing rapid sales growth in the U.S. would be more likely to be made offshore, other things being equal, since the establishment of an offshore facility would then not be likely to require the added costs of closing certain U.S. facilities. In the regression analysis, this variable is related to OPP in the expected way. In Table 1, a change of one standard deviation in sales growth (SG) causes a change of 0.24 standard deviation in OPP, but this is not statistically significant. In the second equation, the relationship is even weaker.

The executives interviewed for this study mentioned growth as an important determinant of offshore production less frequently than many other variables. Only six of the 20 managers mentioned it, but many of the others were conspicuously in companies having very high growth rates. A typical comment of executives mentioning growth as a determinant of offshore production was: "We don't want to put our U.S. workers out of work. If the U.S. market grows, so will our offshore plants." An interesting example of how a sales decline in the United States affected an offshore plant was provided by the experience of a large manufacturer of automobile radios. As U.S. sales declined, the domestic company gave less and less work to the offshore plant in an effort to stabilize the United States work force. Finally the situation became so critical that the offshore plant was completely closed down.[7]

*Standardization of Product and Process.* It was hypothesized that companies would probably produce offshore their most standardized products, as these would require less corporate overhead expense in supervising and controlling the offshore plant. Such corporate outlays are made in large part in order to coordinate the activities of the foreign facility with the company's other operations, and to help remedy problems in the foreign plant. It can be expected that managers will select products for overseas production that the company is confident can be manufactured without such problems.

Two hypotheses emerge from this reasoning. First, delivery, quality, and cost problems are less likely to occur for a product manufactured with a proven production process than if it is made with a relatively recently-developed process. Second, the cost of insuring that the plant is manufacturing products with the correct specifications and in the correct quantities will be lower for products which are standardized than for products which have many models, rapidly changing specifications, and uncertain sales volumes. Therefore, it was hypothesized that products having predictable sales volumes and standard specifications would be made offshore.

No satisfactory measures of product and process standardization appropriate to all segments of the electronics industry were found for this study. These variables were not included, therefore, in the statistical analysis. But the interviews with executives of companies having offshore plants produced evidence of the importance of product and process standardization.

Nineteen of the 20 managers interviewed stressed that they chose simple, standardized, high-volume products for offshore production. A typical comment was that for any but high volume products the setup and production scheduling costs would be so high as to cancel out the savings of offshore production. Related to this, nearly all managers said that custom products, products with frequent engineering changes, and products requiring rapid delivery (short lead times) were made in the United States. Anything on which a close liaison between sales, production, and engineering was required was too difficult to do offshore. A few managers also mentioned that quality requirements were important to consider. To make high reliability products offshore would require providing expensive equipment and personnel in the offshore plant, again increasing overhead costs.

The importance of process standardization also showed up in the interviews. Sixteen of the 20 managers mentioned the importance of doing offshore only those parts of the manufacturing process for which no engineering problems existed. Some typical comments were: "We only do offshore things for which all the engineering and quality problems are solved," and "If something goes wrong in the Far East, you can't run down to a hardware store to get the special bolt or wrench that you need. So you have to have a simple, self-contained production process."

*Risks.* It was hypothesized that a manager's decisions concerning offshore production will be based not only on the expected payoffs but also on the potential risks. If he is risk averse, then he is likely to avoid making products offshore for which the consequences of a failure would be very adverse, or for which the cost of protecting against risks is very high.

60

The major risk associated with offshore production is the possibility of a disruption in the flow of goods from an offshore plant, whether caused by political or labor problems or by natural disasters. It was hypothesized that for some products the costs of insuring against this risk, most likely through the use of a backup facility, would be higher than for others. It was expected that the cost of maintaining a backup position for a product would be positively related to the size of its sales volume. That is, the cost of maintaining excess capacity is related to the amount of that excess capacity. It was also expected that the cost of the backup facility would be high for products with significant economies of scale in production, since maintaining a backup facility producing below capacity would be more costly for such products than for products for which changes in output result in only small changes in unit costs.

It was also expected that the choice among different ways of assuring a fallback source of supply may vary from one product to another. For some proprietary products it will be impossible to rely on outside sources of supply, and firms will be forced to maintain backup production capacity. For high volume products with low scale economies it can be expected that multiple offshore plants will be used. But for products with high scale economies, a pattern consisting of one offshore plant with backup capacity in the U.S. might be more common.

It is difficult to test such hypotheses rigorously, but the comments of executives and the practices of their companies in protecting against risks provide some indication of their validity. Nine of the 20 managers expressed concern about the risks involved in offshore manufacture. The most obvious manifestation of this concern was in their criteria for selecting countries for offshore plants, with many executives indicating that they avoided sites with political and economic instability. The most common method used to insure against disruptions was found to be the use of at least one backup facility for an offshore plant. Some companies use multiple offshore plants for this purpose; others rely on a U.S. backup facility. There seems to exist a common pattern for each segment of the industry, with semiconductor and core memory firms using multiple offshore plants and consumer electronics firms maintaining backup capacity in the U.S. It seems likely that there are two reasons for this. First, semiconductor and computer firms are more vulnerable to disruptions, as they can most economically do offshore only one or two manufacturing operations on *all* their products, and they do very different operations in the U.S.; whereas consumer electronics companies can most economically make a limited number of their products offshore, and they make similar things in the U.S., thus automatically having backup facilities. Second, the much greater commitment of time and money required for the establishment of a television plant argues for one site rather than many.

61

*Alternatives.* It was hypothesized that offshore production would be compared to alternatives such as subcontracting to a foreign manufacturer or automating U.S. production facilities. Automation was mentioned by the managers interviewed as an alternative to offshore production for some products. Most commonly, managers said that the products made offshore were those for which further automation was impossible or uneconomic. But automation is economic for a few high-volume standardized products, and one semiconductor company interviewed now makes a few products in automated U.S. plants that were once made offshore.

It was hypothesized that subcontracting was most likely to be used by a company when (1) the manufacturing involved considerable economies of scale and the company's sales volume was too low to achieve economical production, (2) the product's sales volume fluctuated considerably, and (3) the product and its manufacturing process were relatively standardized. The first two characteristics would motivate a company to subcontract to a foreign manufacturer who could combine the orders of several companies, thereby achieving scale economies and leveling out production volumes. The third characteristic would indicate the probable availability of subcontractors with the required know-how, thus eliminating the need to transfer technology and the fear of losing proprietary technology.

Evidence from the interviews with executives of electronics companies, and from the trade literature, seems to support the above reasoning. Two types of situations were mentioned in which subcontracting was a superior alternative to an offshore plant. The first was when a firm's production of a given product was limited. Scale economics are more important for consumer electronics manufacture than for most other kinds of electronics production, and the limited available evidence suggests that several consumer electronics companies subcontract the manufacture of some product lines to foreign companies, mainly Japanese. Several semiconductor manufacturers also subcontract assembly work, but this is most common for very small manufacturers. As the companies grow, they generally establish their own offshore facilities.

The second case in which subcontracting is used is that of fluctuating production volumes. Several executives of semiconductor companies said that they subcontracted assembly work at peak production periods. There are a number of American-owned firms that do nothing but subcontract work offshore for other offshore plants.

The products or manufacturing operations that are subcontracted are invariably the most simple and standardized ones. For example, in the semiconductor industry, subcontracting is most commonly used for standardized transistors, and only the simple assembly work is done by the subcontractor. For such products and operations very little technology must be transferred between the two companies, and the contracting company is in no danger of disclosing proprietary information to the subcontractor.

## The Evolution of Offshore Production

It was hypothesized that offshore production involved a learning process and that as companies gained experience the kinds of products made offshore would tend to change.

That offshore production involves a learning process seems to be borne out in what executives say and from the way their companies' operations have evolved. First of all, virtually all of the executives interviewed expressed satisfaction with the performance of their offshore plants. In nearly all cases companies had experienced good labor productivity, product quality, and delivery schedules. Although many companies cited problems encountered in establishing and running their offshore plants, these were usually minor in nature. In only two instances among the 20 companies interviewed had offshore plants been shut down, one because of poor labor productivity and the other because of labor union problems; and in both cases they had been moved to other offshore sites. Most of the firms interviewed stated that they planned to increase their offshore activities.

The evidence gathered from companies having offshore plants indicates that they have generally progressed from doing only the simplest manufacturing operations on the most standardized products offshore to becoming involved in much more complex operations and products. Semiconductor companies, for example, typically began offshore operations with assembly (the simplest operation) of diodes and transistors (the most standardized products). Later came the testing of these products and the assembly of integrated circuits. As of 1971 no wafer fabrication (the most complex manufacturing operation) was done abroad, but some companies did most of their testing offshore. This represented a considerable change from the simple assembly operations characteristic of the first offshore plants.

A similar pattern of evolution is evident in other segments of the electronics industry. For example, computer core memory producers typically began offshore operations with simple assembly of core planes, but gradually expanded into testing and core fabrication, both of which are considerably more complex. A similar pattern of offshore production is common in the television industry; operations began with subassemblies of monochrome sets and progressed gradually into the complete assembly of monochrome and some color sets.

The comments of an executive of one large semiconductor manufacturer illustrate some of the reasons for the evolution of offshore production. He stressed the importance of gradually building the capabilities of an offshore facility, both technically and administratively, noting that it takes time to create a capable staff of foreign managerial and technical personnel. In the early stages, he said, the parent company made offshore products not requiring much local expertise. But as the foreign staff improved, more jobs requiring foreign technical and managerial abilities were done offshore.

Another factor which encourages the upgrading of the kinds of jobs done offshore is the interdependency among manufacturing operations for a given product. If extensive feedback is required between one operation and another, it makes sense to have a short and rapid communication link between them. It would be unwise in such a case to have one operation in the United States and the other offshore. As an example, most semiconductor companies originally began offshore with assembly, but little or no testing. However, to maintain satisfactory control over the assembly process, it is important to have rapid feedback from testing to assembly. Therefore, test operations have been gradually moved offshore also, even though they are capital-intensive and very technical.

Another pattern of evolution experienced by some companies involves changing from foreign subcontracting to offshore production. For the electronics industry this seems most common for small semiconductor companies. When such companies are young, the managers often prefer to spend their financial and managerial resources on product design, marketing, and the highly technical wafer fabrication operation. At this stage, they often find it economical to subcontract the assembly work offshore, and set up' their own offshore facility only when their production volume justifies it and when their resources are more substantial. But most electronics companies interviewed skipped the subcontracting stage and moved directly into establishing their own offshore plants.

## IMPLICATIONS

The offshore production phenomenon appears to have important implications for the economies of the United States and of the countries hosting offshore assembly plants.[8] The impact on the U.S. economy of offshore plants has been a subject of controversy, and these so-called "runaway plants" have been a special target of some U.S. unions. The major interest has focused on the effects of such plants on employment and the balance of payments. Widely different conclusions can be reached by making different assumptions as to the motivation for the investments. If it is assumed that the motivation is basically defensive in nature, then the net effects on the United States appear to be positive. If it is assumed that the investments are more aggressive than defensive, then the conclusion is that the U.S. economy suffers from these investments.

It has been argued in this paper that most offshore production investments in the electronics industry appear to be defensive in nature. For most products, imports were already penetrating the United States market before offshore plants were established. If offshore plants had not been established, many companies would have had to either drop the product completely, subcontract its manufacture to a foreign company, or automate its production process in the United States. None of these alternatives is likely to be more beneficial to United States employment and the balance of payments than offshore production, although automation may be more beneficial in the long run because of added employment in the capital goods industry.

There is no doubt that the establishment of offshore plants means that jobs of particular kinds are transferred abroad and that imports of certain products to the United States increase. But for the most part these are job transfers and imports that would have occurred without the establishment of offshore plants, simply by the natural change in competitive position of the United States relative to other countries. Also, the use of offshore production may result in the retention of a certain number of jobs in the U.S. compared with the alternative of importing the entire product from abroad. There remains, nevertheless, the important question of how to cushion the impact on U.S. companies and workers of increased competition from imports. There is evidence that current adjustment assistance is inadequate. And although some companies were reluctant to establish offshore plants if this meant laying off U.S. workers, others may not always be careful to consider these effects of their offshore plants.

Offshore plants also have an important impact on the less developed countries in which they operate. Offshore assembly plants bring resources to less-developed countries in terms of capital, technology, and access to foreign markets. They also mobilize local sources of labor and capital. The evidence available indicates that it is unlikely that foreign resources can be obtained more cheaply or the local resources utilized more efficiently by other means than the offshore plants of foreign companies. It also appears that the balance of payments effects are likely to be positive.

There does seem to be some danger for the less-developed countries in having much of their industry dependent on export markets controlled by foreign companies. Protectionist legislation in the industrial countries, for example, could severely injure a country with many offshore plants. On the other hand, there is evidence that as the offshore electronics industry evolves, several developing countries will establish viable integrated electronics complexes able to compete across a wide range of products. Such a development certainly would help to remove some of the dependence that many such countries feel.

65

## FOOTNOTES

1. See, for example, Yair Aharoni, *The Foreign Investment Decision Process* (Boston: Harvard University, 1966).

2. The electronics industry was defined to include the following SIC categories: 3573, electronic computing equipment; 36112, equipment for testing electric circuits; 3651, radio and television receiving sets; 3662, radio and television communication equipment; 3671, electron tubes, receiving type; 3672, cathode ray picture tubes; 3673, electron tubes, transmitting; 3674, semiconductors; 3679, electronic components not elsewhere classified; 3693, x-ray and electronic therapeutic apparatus.

3. The 20 companies included manufacturers of television and other consumer electronic products, computer equipment, semiconductors, electronic instruments, and various electronic components.

4. For details on these provisions, see U.S. Tariff Commission, *Tariff Schedules of the United States (1970)* (Washington, D.C.).

5. U.S. Tariff Commission, *Economic Factors Affecting the Use of Items 807.00 and 806.30 of the Tariff Schedules of the United States* (Washington, D.C., 1970), pp. 97-105.

6. This point was tested in Robert B. Stobaugh and associates, *U.S. Multinational Enterprises and the U.S. Economy,* published in U.S. Department of Commerce, *The Multinational Corporation* (Washington, D.C., 1971).

7. Reported in a case study published by Harvard Business School, *Systek International (D).*

8. These implications are examined in much more detail in the author's "Offshore Production in the Less-Developed Countries by U.S. Electronics Companies," *The Bulletin,* Nos. 98-99 (New York: New York University, July, 1974).

# [23]

# 7 Multinationals and Intermediate Product Trade

## MARK CASSON

### 7.1 INTRODUCTION

Dunning (1981) suggests that the behaviour of multinational enterprises (MNEs) can be analysed in terms of three groups of factors: ownership advantages, location advantages, and internalisation. Buckley (1983) notes that of these three, location advantages have received least attention in recent years, despite the fact that, historically, location advantages have strongly influenced the growth of international production (Dunning, 1982). This chapter is an attempt to make good this deficiency.

The theory of location developed below has four main objectives:

(1) To provide an integrated analysis of the three main types of international investment and to explain the relation between them; these are (i) import-substituting investment in the high-technology industries of developed countries, (ii) 'export-platform' manufacturing investment in cheap-labour countries, and (iii) agricultural- and raw materials-based investment in land- and mineral-rich countries.
(2) To provide a framework for analysing the post-war growth of intermediate product trade and in particular to explain intra-firm trade in components and semi-processed materials.
(3) To examine the influence of transfer-pricing on the international rationalisation of production within an MNE, and in particular to analyse how the location of production by an MNE will differ from location of production by independent competitive producers in the same industry.

144

(4) To analyse in a comparative static framework the impact of technical progress, trade liberalisation and tax harmonisation on the location of production with an MNE.

The conventional theory of international location is based upon the Heckscher–Ohlin (HO) theory of trade. However attempts to apply the HO theory to the MNE (for example Casson, 1979, Chap. 4) have had only limited success. The HO theory seems to be a blind alley, and there are three main reasons for this:

(1) The HO theory overemphasises the role of factor substitution in the location of production. Factor substitution introduces analytical complications which impede the consideration of other important issues. As a result other influences on location – in particular transport costs and economies of scale – are often assumed away.
(2) The theory focuses upon the specialisation of production between industries rather than on the division of labour within an industry. It is therefore ill-adapted to the analysis of intra-industry intermediate product trade.
(3) The theory takes a very narrow view of technology in general and of technical progress in particular. It ignores the fact that much modern technology is proprietary, with imperfect competition being the norm in markets for new products. The analysis of technical progress also reflects the biases of the theory as a whole: it is preoccupied with the classification of technical progress in terms of factor savings and ignores technical progress which reduces transport costs, stimulates economies of scale and promotes the intra-industry division of labour.

## 7.2 AN ALTERNATIVE TO THE HO THEORY

This paper begins from a standpoint quite different from the HO theory. It is inspired by geographical theories of industrial location, and in particular by Norman (1979). This alternative standpoint may be set out in terms of three broad principles.

(a) *Factor substitution has a very limited role in the location of production.* In the HO theory the inputs to production are immobile factors which are continuously substitutable. Differences between locations in relative endowments of the factors generate differences in comparative cost and these differences in cost govern the location of production. It can be argued, however, that factors are not so immobile

146    *The Economic Theory of the Multinational Enterprise*

as the HO theory assumes, and that substitution possibilities are discontinuous, and in some cases negligible. On these grounds it may be argued that the HO approach is less plausible than the much simpler Ricardian theory of comparative labour cost.

Capital, for example, is not so immobile as alleged by the HO theory (MacDougall, 1960). Post-war capital markets are probably better integrated between the metropolitan centres of different countries than they are between metropolitan and non-metropolitan areas of the same country. Furthermore, the MNEs' ability to bypass exchange controls through transfer-pricing creates an internal market within which the cost of capital is equalised across locations (Rugman, 1981, Chap. 4). The availability of capital at a particular location does not, therefore, directly influence the decision to produce there. Rather the availability of capital to the firm as a whole determines to what extent it is economic to divert capital to a particular location to substitute for other factors with which that location is poorly endowed. It is only in this very limited sense that capital substitution influences the extent to which one location is more attractive than another.

Another point is that in practice opportunities for technical substitution between factors are probably less than is assumed by the HO theory. Historically, the most important immobile inputs to production have been labour and environmental services, where environment includes land, soil-quality, weather, geological features such as mineral deposits and so on. Casual empiricism suggests that technical substitutability between environmental services and other factors is much lower than the substitutability between labour and capital. Thus it may be more reasonable to assume that immobile inputs must be combined in fixed proportions than to assume the existence of a continuum of alternative production techniques.

Next, it can be argued that the margin is of little significance in the supply of environmental services. This is because the environment often has the characteristics of a public good. In many cases – for example, the weather – an environmental service is either not available, or is available in such abundance that environmental capacity far exceeds user demand. If an environmental service is not available then – because of limited substitution possibilities – production which normally requires this service cannot take place at all. If the service is available then its opportunity cost is zero and input requirements for this service exert no influence on the level of output. Thus the local environment determines whether or not production is feasible at a given location, but when production is feasible it does not influence the scale on which production occurs.

It is, of course, often possible to discover a margin which influences production – a margin determined by the level of pollution, for example, or by the depletion of some non-renewable resource. The basic point is not that such margins do not exist, but that they are of secondary importance in the location of international production.

It is a consequence of the propositions above that, given a set of locations at which production is feasible, marginal production cost varies between these locations mainly on account of differences in labour costs. These differences reflect differences between locations in the comparative advantage of labour in different industries. Once the impact of environment on the feasibility of production has been taken into account therefore, the influence of international factor endowments on the location of production can be analysed using the Ricardian theory of comparative labour costs.

To express this conclusion another way, it can be said that if capital is mobile, technical substitution is limited and environmental services have public good characteristics then the only margin of significance is the margin at which labour is allocated between industries. It is the position of this margin at different locations which is crucial to international production.

(b) *Technical progress has more to do with reducing transport costs, stimulating economies of scale and promoting the division of labour than it has to do with conventional factor-saving advances in production technology.*

The HO theory is preoccupied with labour-saving and capital-saving technical progress in production – reflecting the emphasis of the theory on factor substitution. The complications introduced by factor substitution make it necessary to simplify by ignoring transport costs and economies of scale. It is obvious, however, that technical improvements in transport have done much to widen the scope for international trade. The HO theory can analyse easily only the extreme case in which a hitherto untradeable product becomes perfectly tradeable. A satisfactory theory must include transport costs at the outset.

The HO assumption of constant returns to scale in production makes it difficult to analyse the consequences of innovations which alter returns to scale. The most obvious case of this is the introduction of a continuous-flow production technique. Establishing continuous-flow production usually incurs a set-up cost, which affords economies to the

148    *The Economic Theory of the Multinational Enterprise*

length of the production run. More important in the present context is that economies of speed and size in machinery often mean that set-up costs increase less than proportionately to capacity. Furthermore, large size may offer economies not only in set-up costs but in running costs – for example, heat loss per unit throughput diminishes continuously with respect to the size of a boiler, pipeline, etc. Thus with continuous flow technology, marginal set-up cost and marginal running cost normally both diminish with respect to the capacity of the plant and therefore generate long-run economies of scale with respect to the rate of output. The exploitation of these economies is limited only by transport costs and the size of the market.

Another form of technical progress overlooked by the HO theory is an increase in the division of labour within an industry. Each subdivision of a productive activity creates a market for an intermediate product. The resolution of an activity into a sequence of two independent activities creates a market in a semi-processed material linking the first activity to the second. (The sequence may, of course, involve more than two activities, in which case there are several intermediate product markets.) In some cases, the division of labour creates a pyramid of activities in which both vertical and horizontal specialisation occurs; the activities at the bottom of the pyramid produce 'components' which are then combined in an 'assembly' process higher up. In some cases the intermediate products may not be tradeable, in which case the subdivision occurs within the plant and may appear simply as a factor-saving shift in the plant production function. When an intermediate product is tradeable, however, it is possible to separate spatially the activities which it links and so replace a single plant by two different ones.

In certain cases the opportunity for spatial separation may increase overall efficiency even though there is no actual factor-saving in either activity. If each activity makes intensive use of a different immobile input then without division of labour each activity must take place at a location where both the inputs are available. With division of labour each activity can take place at a location where only one of the inputs is available. This reduces the pressure on factor use at well-endowed locations and increases efficiency through international specialisation. Alternatively it may simply allow one of the activities to be moved nearer to the final market, and thereby economise on overall transport costs.

(c) *Technology is normally proprietary and firm-specific at the time of innovation. Access to know-how constitutes an important barrier to entry encouraging monopoly or oligopoly in the supply of new products. It is often advantageous for the monopolist to integrate backward into the supply of inputs or components embodied in the final product. This leads to international production of new products being controlled by vertically integrated monopolistic MNEs.*

Many new products are designed specifically to economise upon transaction costs. For example, the introduction of a versatile good which substitutes for several more specific goods enables buyers to economise on transaction costs in the final product market. The typical versatile good is a multi-component good which can be adapted to different uses by utilising different subsets of components. Each sub-set of components substitutes for some specific good. This allows the buyer of a multi-component good to obtain several different services through a single transaction (Casson, 1982, Chap. 10).

The production of a multi-component good, of course, creates transactions between the component producers and the assembler of the good. The cost of these additional transactions is, however, low compared with the savings that are effected in the final product market. Costs are high in the final product market whenever atomistic buyers with little knowledge of the product make irregular purchases. By contrast, component transactions normally involve regular bulk transactions among a few well-informed parties.

New products are also designed to economise on transport costs. Improvements in product design may reduce the bulk or weight of the product, or make it easier to 'stack' in transit. A final product is normally bulkier than the individual components from which it is assembled. Economies in transport costs can therefore be achieved by moving the point of assembly closer to the final user – for example, the product is shipped in 'kit' or 'knocked-down' form to the wholesaler or retailer – in some cases even to the final purchaser. These economies are achieved by designing the product so that its assembly is relatively trivial. The sophistication of the product is built into its components. The result is that economies of scale are likely to predominate in component production and to be relatively insignificant at the assembly stage.

The designer of a product will normally wish to control the marketing of it. The incentive is greatest when the design cannot be patented, for then licensing is problematic (see Chapter 3). Complexity of the specification also discourages licensing because of the need for accuracy in the claims that are made for the product. Licensing is also more difficult if the final product is easily transported for then it is difficult to

150    *The Economic Theory of the Multinational Enterprise*

prevent licensees from invading one another's markets and reducing the world-wide monopoly rent that is earned.

The designers will also wish to control component production. If component design embodies know-how then the designer will be reluctant to subcontract production for reasons of secrecy (see Chapter 2). Control of component production is also important when the tolerances allowed for components in the assembly process are very tight. This is particularly important when the product is durable, for maintenance costs can them be kept down by using interchangeable replacement parts. Precision is therefore vital in component manufacture and this creates a quality problem. Since the costs of poor quality are borne by the assembler he has a vested interest in supervising production, and one way of exercising supervision is to integrate backward into component production.

## 7.3 A MODEL OF THE LOCATION OF INTERNATIONAL PRODUCTION

This section presents a general equilibrium model of the world economy. In some respects it can be regarded as the development of an intuitive model used by Dunning (1972) in which there are just two consumer products: one product is competitively supplied and the other is monopolised by an MNE. The monopoly good is sold internationally and is produced using an integrated sequence of component manufacture, assembly and marketing. The model allows for both international and inter-regional trade in components and the assembled product. Goods move along paths connecting the nodes of a transport network. The routing of goods is modelled, as well as the origin and final destination of each consignment. Environmental endowments determine the locations at which production of each good is feasible. Within these constraints the exact location of production is determined by comparative labour costs. Profit taxes and tariffs are included to allow scope for transfer-pricing. The analysis takes full account of the distributional implications of wages, profits, taxes and tariffs for the demand side of the economy – though very strong assumptions are made in this respect.

This section outlines the general structure of the model. The profit-maximising MNE location strategy is analysed in Section 7.4. The computation of the general equilibrium is illustrated in Section 7.5. The conclusions are summarised in Section 7.6.

Let there be a fixed number of point locations, indexed $i = 1, \ldots, L$, each of which is a potential site for production and a potential source of demand. The $i$th location has a fixed endowment of homogeneous labour, $N_i \geqslant 0$. Labour is the only variable factor of production and is measured in an internationally standardised efficiency unit (as shown later). Labour is geographically immobile, though perfectly mobile between different industries at the same location.

There are $H + 4$ distinct activities that can, in principle, be carried on at each location. Activity zero is the marketing of a monopolised consumer good produced by a (potential) MNE. Activity 1 is the assembly of the monopolised good from components; the term 'component' designates any tradeable raw material or intermediate product; likewise the term 'assembly' designates any activity which processes one or more of the 'components' to produce the final product. The $H$ activities 2 to $H + 1$ involve the production of different components. It is assumed that each of the foregoing activities, indexed $h = 0, 1, \ldots, H + 1$, are carried on by the same firm; the output of the $h$th activity at location $i$ is $x_{hi} \geqslant 0$. The firm is thus vertically integrated from component production through assembly to marketing, and is horizontally integrated across locations.

The remaining two activities are carried on only by independent competitive producers. One activity is the production of a consumer good which is an imperfect substitute for the monopolised good; output of this good at location $i$ is $y_i \geqslant 0$. The competitive consumer good can be traded costlessly but the monopolised consumer-good and its components cannot. The remaining activity is a transport service, whose output at location $i$ is $t_i \geqslant 0$. The transport service is an intermediate product, hired exclusively by the monopolist for the physical distribution of the components and the assembled product.

Some of the monopolised activities require inputs of non-tradeable environmental services. It is assumed that locations either have abundant endowments of these inputs – in which case they are available free – or none at all. If a location has suitable endowments then production can proceed, otherwise it cannot. The variable $\gamma_{hi}$ assumes a value of unity when the $h$th activity can proceed at location $i$ and zero when it cannot.

The competitive consumer good and the transport service are perfect substitutes in production and are produced under constant returns to scale. At each location labour-productivity in transport is the same constant proportion of labour-productivity in the competitive consumer-good industry. The efficiency unit of labour at each location is

152    *The Economic Theory of the Multinational Enterprise*

set so that one unit of labour generates one unit of the competitive consumer-good. Since the consumer-good is freely tradeable the efficiency unit is standardised across locations. The unit of transport service is chosen so that one efficiency unit of labour generates one unit of the transport service. Thus differences between locations in labour productivity in the two competitive activities are reflected entirely in differences between the locations in their endowments of efficiency units per head of working population.

The production technology for the *h*th monopolised activity may be expressed indirectly using the input demand function

$$n_{hi} = n_h(\eta_{hi}x_{hi}, \gamma_{hi}) \qquad\qquad (h = 0, 1, \ldots, H+1) \qquad\qquad (7.1)$$

where $n_{hi} \geq 0$ is the input of labour to the *h*th activity at the *i*th location and $\eta_{hi} > 0$ is a cost parameter indicating the *comparative disadvantage* of labour at location *i* in the *h*th activity (relative to the production of the competitive consumer good). The input function $n_h(.)$ allows no free production, is twice differentiable and everywhere increasing with respect to output, but is otherwise unrestricted and so is compatible with either increasing, constant or decreasing returns to scale. Aggregate employment in monopoly production at location *i* is

$$n_i = \sum_{h=0}^{H+1} n_{hi} \qquad\qquad (7.2)$$

As already noted, the monopolist's activities embrace three stages: component production, assembly and marketing. Assembly combines components in fixed proportion while marketing requires a unit input from assembly for every unit sold. Let $z_{hi} \geq 0$ be the input of the *h*th component into assembly at location *i*, and let $b_h > 0$ be a fixed input–output coefficient for the assembly process; then

$$z_{hi} = b_h x_{1li} \qquad\qquad (h = 2, \ldots, H+1) \qquad\qquad (7.3)$$

Let $z_{0i}$ be the input of the assembled product to the marketing activity at location *i*. Recalling that $x_{0i}$ is the output of marketing, that is, the quantity sold, we have

$$z_{0i} = x_{0i} \qquad\qquad (7.4)$$

It is assumed that at each location there is a perfectly competitive labour market. Since the two competitive activities operate under constant returns to scale the whole of the income from them accrues to the sole variable factor, labour. Each location is sufficiently well endowed with labour for its specialisation in the marketing, production and transport of the monopoly good and its components to be always incomplete. Thus at each location the monopolist faces an infinitely elastic supply of labour at a unit wage.

It is assumed that the recipients of monopoly profit do not work and that only workers demand the monopoly consumer good. Since full employment wage income in each location is equal to the exogenous endowment of labour efficiency units, the income out of which the monopoly product is purchased is independent of the profit earned by the monopoly. Furthermore because no monopoly shareholders wish to purchase the monopoly good, the real income of the shareholders can be evaluated without reference to the price they must pay at their location as consumers of the monopoly good. Monopoly shareholders are therefore unanimous that management should maximise profit in units of the competitive consumer good.

The monopolist can discriminate between buyers at different locations but not between buyers at the same location. It may be assumed, for example, that the monopolist can costlessly introduce minor differentiations of the product which make it suitable for use at just one particular location. Potential arbitragers can only reverse these differentiations at prohibitive cost. It follows that the monopolist must charge a uniform price at each location but can set prices at different locations quite independently.

Analysing the consumer choice of the typical worker at a given location shows that when his preferences are smooth and strictly quasi-concave his demand for the monopolised product will normally be a continually increasing function of his wage income and a continuously decreasing function of its relative price. Since a worker's wage income is determined by his exogenous endowment of efficiency units, the aggregation of consumer demand across workers poses no problems. Thus for any set of workers' endowments at any location $i$ there exists an aggregate demand $d_i$ for the monopoly product which diminishes continuously with respect to its relative price $p_i$; this may be expressed in the indirect form.

$$P_i = p(d_i, N_i, f_i) \tag{7.5}$$

where $N_i$ is the aggregate endowment of efficiency units and $f_i$ is a paramenter governing the intensity of demand; $f_i$ reflects a complex of factors, including the tastes of the different workers and the distribution of the efficiency units between them. It is assumed for simplicity that an input of marketing services in excess of the minimum prescribed

154     *The Economic Theory of the Multinational Enterprise*

by (7.1) has no effect whatsoever on the intensity of demand. It is
assumed that the monopolist maintains the product market in equilibrium by meeting all the demand forthcoming at the price he has set;
thus

$$d_i = z_{0i} \qquad (7.6)$$

The gross quantity of the $h$th monopoly product ($h = 1, \ldots, H+1$)
shipped from location $i$ to location $j$ is $m_{hij} \geqslant 0$ (the amount produced at
location $i$ for the local market is thus $m_{hii}$). Shipments to a location $i$
include not only consignments destined for customers at $i$ but also
consignments being routed through $i$ to other destinations. Let $x_{hij} \geqslant 0$
be the amount of the $h$th monopoly product consigned from produc-
tion at $i$ to customers at $j$ ($x_{hii} = m_{hii}$), and let $e_{hi}$ be the amount of the $h$th
product routed through $i$ for onward shipment to some other destina-
tion.

It is assumed that monopoly products can be freely disposed of either
at the point of production, or at the point of delivery, but not during
shipment. It is a consequence of this that (i) the total outward
consignment from a location cannot exceed the local production:

$$\sum_{j=1}^{L} x_{hij} \leqslant x_{hi} \qquad (h = 1, \ldots, H+1) \qquad (7.7)$$

(ii) the total inward consignment cannot be less than the local input:

$$\sum_{j=1}^{L} x_{hji} \geqslant z_{hi} \qquad (h = 1, \ldots, H+1) \qquad (7.8)$$

(iii) the total outward shipment is equal to the sum of total outward
consignments and the shipments being routed through the location on
the way to somewhere else:

$$\sum_{j=1}^{L} m_{hij} = \sum_{j=1}^{L} x_{hij} + e_{hi} \qquad (h = 1, \ldots, H+1) \qquad (7.9)$$

(iv) the total inward shipment is equal to the sum of total inward
consignments and the shipments destined for re-export:

$$\sum_{j=1}^{L} m_{hji} = \sum_{j=1}^{L} x_{hji} + e_{hi} \qquad (h = 1, \ldots, H+1) \qquad (7.10)$$

The input of transport services to trade between two locations $i$ and $j$
varies according to the product concerned, but is always directly
proportional to the quantity exported:

$$t_{hij} = a_{hij} m_{hij} \qquad (h = 1, \ldots, H+1) \qquad (7.11)$$

where $a_{hii} = 0$. The size of the parameter $a_{hij} \geqslant 0$ reflects the bulk, weight and fragility of the commodity $h$ and the geographical relation between the locations $i$ and $j$. If direct transit from $i$ to $j$ is difficult, it may be easier to route exports through one or more intermediate locations; for example, if $a_{hij} > a_{hil} + a_{hlj}$ then it is efficient to route exports from $i$ to $j$ via $l$ (as shown later).

Because of the earlier assumption that at each location labour productivity in transport stands in exactly the same constant relation to labour productivity in the consumption good industry, no location has a comparative advantage in the supply of transport services. It is assumed, however, that transport services on a given route can be supplied only from the two terminal locations and that the supply of services must be shared equally between them. Thus the total requirement of transport services at location $i$ is

$$t_i = \tfrac{1}{2} \sum_{h=1}^{H+1} \sum_{j=1}^{L} (t_{hij} + t_{hji}) \qquad (7.12)$$

Locations are distributed across countries – though no fixed pattern is assumed. Each country has a sovereign government which levies tariffs and taxes. Countries may in turn be affiliated to free trade areas, customs areas or to international conferences which attempt to harmonise tariffs or taxes.

Let imports of the $h$th product at location $i$, originating from location $j$, be subject to an *ad valorem* tariff $s_{hji} \geqslant 0 (s_{hii} = 0)$. It is often asserted that the impact of tariffs is analogous to that of transport costs but this is true only in respect of consignments and not in respect of shipments. The reason is that tariffs are not normally levied on goods in transit through a location but only upon goods finally destined for it; goods imported to a location for immediate re-export can normally remain in bond and avoid customs duties. Thus while transport costs are incurred over every segment of a route taken by a consignment, tariffs are levied only at the final destination.

Tariffs are often specified according to country of origin and this clearly affords importers an opportunity for 're-originating' goods for tariff purposes at selected points on their route. This complication will, however, be ignored. It is assumed that tariffs are levied according to origin irrespective of the route, and that importers are honest when declaring origin.

Let $q_{hi}$ be the transfer price for the $h$th product delivered to location $i$. The transfer price is identified with the internal 'invoice price' upon which tariffs are based and upon which the international allocation of

156    *The Economic Theory of the Multinational Enterprise*

profit is calculated. It is assumed that there are upper and lower bounds upon transfer prices based upon what the monopolist thinks the fiscal authorities will tolerate. In assessing these bounds the monopolist must take account of the attitudes of both the importing and exporting countries, as well as the attitude of the country in which the parent company is domiciled. If the lower bound for the $h$th commodity at location $i$ is $Q_{hi}>0$ and the upper bound is $Q_{hi}'\geq Q_{hi}$, then

$$Q_{hi}\leq q_{hi}\leq Q_{hi}' \qquad (h=1,\ldots,H+1) \qquad (7.13)$$

The tariff payments collected at location $i$ are

$$v_i=\sum_{h=1}^{H+1}\sum_{j=1}^{L}s_{hji}q_{hi}x_{hji} \qquad (7.14)$$

and so using equation (7.6), the accounting profit imputed to location $i$ is

$$\pi_i=p_id_i+\left(\sum_{h=1}^{H+1}\sum_{j=1}^{L}q_{hj}x_{hij}-\sum_{h=1}^{H+1}\sum_{j=1}^{L}q_{hi}x_{hji}\right)-n_i-t_i-v_i \qquad (7.15)$$

The first term in (7.15) is the revenue from local sales of the final product, the second term is the imputed revenue of intra-group exports net of the imputed value of intra-group imports, and the third term is the local wage bill. The two remaining terms are transport expenditure and tariff payments. It is assumed that at each location it is always the local subsidiary that hires the local transport services; there is no internal manipulation of payments for transport services. Similarly it is assumed that it is always the local subsidiary that pays the import tariff.

When accounting profit is aggregated across locations the imputed values of intra-group transactions cancels out and gives a global profit

$$\pi=\sum_{i=1}^{L}\pi_i=\sum_{i=1}^{L}(p_id_i-n_i-t_i-v_i) \qquad (7.16)$$

Let profit taxation in location $i$ be levied at a constant proportional rate $\tau_i(0\leq\tau_i<1)$ on the profits of the local subsidiary. Tax revenues and tariff payments collected at each location are distributed to local residents in transfer payments. The payments, it is assumed, accrue to profit-recipients rather than to wage-earners, and so have no distributional impact on the demand for the monopolised product. Profit recipients do not, however, 'endogenise' their income from taxes and tariffs when considering the optimal pricing strategy of the monopoly management.

The monopolist maximises global post-tax profit

$$\pi' = \sum_{i=1}^{L}(1-\tau_i)\pi_i \tag{7.17}$$

which simplifies to

$$\pi' = (1-\tau)\pi \tag{7.18}$$

when tax rates are harmonised

$$\tau_i = \tau \; (i=1, \ldots, L) \tag{7.19}$$

When tax rates are harmonised transfer prices enter into post-tax profit only through the impact of tariff payments on pre-tax profit. Consequently a maximum of post-tax profit $\pi'$ implies a maximum of pre-tax profit $\pi$ and vice versa.

The residents of location $i$ own a fixed proportion $g_i \geq 0$ of the monopoly equity, where

$$\sum_{i=1}^{L}g_i = 1 \tag{7.20}$$

Let $\pi^*$ be the global maximum of profit and let $\pi^*_i$ be the imputation of profit to location $i$ associated with this maximum. Budgetary balance for the residents of location $i$ requires that

$$c_i + p_i d_i = N_i + g_i\pi'^* + \tau_i\pi_i^* + v_i \tag{7.21}$$

which determines $c_i$, the consumption of the competitive consumer good as the balancing item in household budgets. Equilibrium in the labour market at location $i$ requires that

$$y_i + n_i + t_i = N_i \tag{7.22}$$

which determines $y_i$, the production of the competitive good. Comparing (7.21) and (7.22) determines the 'balance of trade' created by the production, transport and consumption of the monopolised goods. The balance is equilibrated by a net import at location $i$ of

$$u_i = c_i - y_i \tag{7.23}$$

units of the competitive consumption good. Since the competitive consumption good can be freely traded, the actual network of trade in the competitive good is indeterminate. However, adding (7.21), (7.22) and (7.23), summing over $i$ and using (7.16), (7.17) and (7.20) shows that

$$\sum_{i=1}^{L}u_i = 0 \tag{7.24}$$

which demonstrates that the trading system as a whole is consistent.

158    *The Economic Theory of the Multinational Enterprise*

## 7.4 MULTINATIONAL LOCATION STRATEGY

The behaviour of the MNE monopolist may be deduced in the usual way from the first order conditions for a maximum of profit. Substituting equations (7.1), (7.2), (7.5), (7.6), (7.11), (7.12), (7.14) and (7.15) into the maximand (7.17) and simplifying the constraints (7.3), (7.4) and (7.7) – (7.10) through the elimination of terms in $e$ and $z$ gives the Lagrangian:

$$
L = \sum_{i=1}^{L} (1 - \tau_i) \left\{ 
\begin{array}{l}
p_i(d_i)d_i + \sum_{h=1}^{H+1}\sum_{j=1}^{L} q_{hj}x_{hij} - \sum_{h=1}^{H+1}\sum_{j=1}^{L} q_{hi}x_{hji} \\[2mm]
- \sum_{h=0}^{H+1} n_{hi}(x_{hi}) - \tfrac{1}{2}\sum_{h=1}^{H+1}\sum_{j=1}^{L}(a_{hij}m_{hij} + a_{hji}m_{hji}) \\[2mm]
- \sum_{h=1}^{H+1}\sum_{j=1}^{L} s_{hji}q_{hi}x_{hji}
\end{array}
\right\}
$$

$$
+ \sum_{h=1}^{H+1}\sum_{i=1}^{L}\xi_{hi}\left(\sum_{j=1}^{L}m_{hji} - \sum_{j=1}^{L}m_{hij} - \sum_{j=1}^{L}x_{hji} + \sum_{j=1}^{L}x_{hij}\right)
$$

$$
+ \sum_{i=1}^{L}v_{1i}\left(\sum_{j=1}^{L}x_{1ji} - d_i\right)
$$

$$
+ \sum_{h=2}^{H+1}\sum_{i=1}^{L}v_{hi}\left(\sum_{j=1}^{L}x_{hji} - b_h x^i_{1i}\right)
$$

$$
+ \sum_{h=1}^{H+1}\sum_{i=1}^{L}\mu_{hi}\left(x_{hi} - \sum_{j=1}^{L}x_{hij}\right) \tag{7.25}
$$

$$
+ \sum_{h=1}^{H+1}\sum_{i=1}^{L}\lambda_{hi}(q_{hi} - Q_{hi})
$$

$$
+ \sum_{h=1}^{H+1}\sum_{i=1}^{L}\lambda_{hi}'(Q_{hi}' - q_{hi})
$$

where $v_{hi}, \xi_{hi}, \mu_{hi}, \lambda_{hi}, \lambda_{hi}'$ are undetermined multipliers whose significance is explained later.

The Kuhn–Tucker necessary conditions for a local maximum (Intriligator, 1971) are as follows:

### (a) **The component production decision**

Let $\mu_{hi}$ be the shadow cost of producing the $h$th monopolised good at location $i$. For each component the shadow cost of production at any location cannot exceed the marginal cost of local production, net of tax relief. If the component is locally produced then the shadow cost of component production is equal to the marginal net cost of local production. Thus for $h = 2, \ldots, H + 1$

$$\mu_{hi} \leqslant (1 - \tau_i) \partial n_{hi} / \partial x_{hi} \tag{7.26}$$

with equality if $x_{hi} > 0$

### (b) The assembly decision

The shadow cost of producing the assembled product at any location cannot exceed the sum of the shadow expenditure on component inputs and the marginal net cost of local assembly, and is equal to this sum if the product is assembled locally. Let $v_{hi}$ be the shadow cost of the $h$th monopoly product at location $i$; then

$$\mu_{1i} \leqslant \sum_{h=2}^{H+1} v_{hi} b_h + (1 - \tau_i) \partial n_{li} / \partial x_{li} \tag{7.27}$$

with equality if $x_{1i} > 0$.

### (c) The routing decision

Let $\xi_{hi}$ be the shadow price of a shipment of the $h$th product at location $i$ and define

$$\varphi_{hij} = \xi_{hj} - \xi_{hi} \tag{7.28}$$

as the shadow value of transport for the $h$th product from $i$ to $j$. It is an immediate consequence of the definition (7.28) that

$$\varphi_{hii} = 0, \ \varphi_{hij} = -\varphi_{hji} \tag{7.29}$$

For all the components, and the assembled product too, the shadow value of transport from $i$ to $j$ cannot exceed the unit transport cost, net of tax relief; if the good is actually shipped from $i$ to $j$ then the shadow value and the unit cost are equal. Thus for $h = 1, \ldots, H+1$

$$\varphi_{hij} \leqslant [1 - \tfrac{1}{2}(\tau_i + \tau_j)] a_{hij} \tag{7.30}$$

with equality if $m_{hij} > 0$.

### (d) The transfer-pricing decision

The shadow value of a transfer price constraint is non-zero only if the constraint itself is binding. When the lower bound on the transfer price

160    *The Economic Theory of the Multinational Enterprise*

for the *h*th product at location *i* is binding then the shadow value of the constraint is equal to the excess of the saving in tariff payments at *i* induced by a marginal lowering of the transfer-price over the additional tax obligations incurred by the reallocation of profit to location *i*. Likewise when the upper bound on the transfer price is binding, the shadow value of the constraint is equal to the excess of the saving in tax obligations incurred by a marginal reallocation of profit from location *i* over the additional tariff liability incurred.

Let $\lambda_{hi}$ be the shadow value of the lower bound on the transfer price of the *h*th commodity at location *i*, and let $\lambda'_{hi}$ be the shadow value of the corresponding upper bound. Define the shadow value of the combined transfer price constraints as

$$\delta_{hi} = \lambda_{hi} - \lambda'_{hi} \qquad (7.31)$$

The lower bound is binding if $\lambda_{hi} > 0$ and the upper bound is binding if $\lambda'_{hi} > 0$. For each component, and for the assembled product, the shadow value of the combined transfer-price constraints at location *i* is

$$\delta_{hi} = (1-\tau_i)\sum_{j=1}^{L} s_{hji} x_{hji} + \sum_{j=1}^{L}(\tau_i - \tau_j) x_{hji} \qquad (7.32)$$

for $h = 1, \ldots, H+1$. Note that in (7.32) the expressions for tariff savings and tax savings are weighted sums of the tariff rates and tax rates, with the weights being the quantities consigned from the different locations.

### (e) The disposal decision

If the shadow cost of production of the *h*th product at the *i*th location is positive then there is no disposal of output, that is, if $\mu_{hi} > 0$ then the output constraint (7.7) is binding. If the shadow value at the *i*th location is positive then there is no disposal of supplies, that is, if $v_{hi} > 0$ then the inward consignment constraint (7.8) is binding.

### (f) The assembly sourcing decision

Consider any assembly point *j* and any potential component source *i*. The shadow cost of the *h*th component at *j* cannot exceed the sum of its shadow cost of production at *i*, the shadow value of its transport from *i*, the tariff payable at *j* and the additional tax attributable to the reallocation of cost from *j* to *i*. If the component is actually consigned from $i$ to $j$ then the shadow cost is equal to this sum. Thus for $h = 2, \ldots,$ $H + 1$

$$v_{hj} \leqslant \mu_{hi} + \varphi_{hij} + [(1 - \tau_i)s_{hij} + \tau_i - \tau_j]q_{hj} \qquad (7.33)$$

with equality if $m_{hij} > 0$.

### (g) The market sourcing decision

The shadow value of the assembled product at any location $j$ cannot exceed the sum of the shadow cost of assembly at any location $i$, the transport and tariff costs incurred in its consignment from $i$ to $j$, the additional tax attributable to the reallocation of profit from $j$ to $i$ and the marginal net cost of marketing at $j$. If the assembled product is actually consigned from $i$ to $j$ then the shadow value of the final product is equal to this sum. Thus

$$v_{1i} \leqslant \mu_{1i} + \varphi_{1ij} + [(1 - \tau_i)s_{1ij} + \tau_i - \tau_j]q_{1j} + (1 - \tau_i)\partial n_{oj}/\partial x_{oj} \qquad (7.34)$$

with equality if $x_{1ij} > 0$.

### (h) The market sales decision

In each market the marginal revenue product cannot exceed the shadow value of the assembled product. When sales are positive the marginal revenue product is equal to the shadow value. Let $\varepsilon_i = -(\partial d_i/\partial p_i)p_i/d_i$ be the price elasticity of demand in the $i$th market; then

$$(1 - \tau_i)[1 - (1/\varepsilon_i)]p_i \leqslant v_{1i} \qquad (7.35)$$

with equality if $d_i > 0$.

The Kuhn–Tucker conditions confirm some intuitively obvious results.

(1) Whenever the unit cost of transport, net of tax relief, is positive there will be no cross-hauling of the product between any pair of locations. It is an immediate consequence of the routing conditions (7.28)–(7.30) that $m_{hij} > 0$ implies $m_{hji} = 0$ for any $j \neq i$.

(2) If for any origin $i$ and any destination $j$ there is a location $l$ such that the unit net cost of transport *via* $l$ is less than the unit net cost of direct shipment from $i$ to $j$ then nothing will be shipped directly from $i$ to $j$. Using (7.28) and (7.30) shows that if

$$[1 - \tfrac{1}{2}(\tau_i + \tau_j)]a_{hij} > [1 - \tfrac{1}{2}(\tau_i - \tau_l)]a_{hil} + [1 - \tfrac{1}{2}(\tau_l - \tau_j)]a_{hlj}$$

then $m_{hij} = 0$.

162    *The Economic Theory of the Multinational Enterprise*

(3) There is no disposal of output. Because, by assumption, there is no free production, the shadow cost of production is positive at any location where production occurs and hence the output constraint is always binding.

(4) In the absence of transfer-pricing there is no disposal of inputs either. Because production is costly and unit transport costs are non-negative, the value of supplies at any location is positive and so there is no disposal of inputs. However when transfer-pricing occurs the disposal of inputs is quite possible. When tax rates differ considerably between two countries and the fiscal authorities are flexible over transfer-pricing it may be profitable to ship a low-cost commodity at a high transfer-price from a high-tax country to a low-tax country even though the commodity has no use at its final destination.

The Kuhn–Tucker conditions can, in principle, be solved for the profit maximising monopolistic strategy. The solution determines the outputs of component production and assembly in each location $x_{hi}$, the prices of the final products, $p_i$, and the corresponding quantities sold, $d_i$, the pattern of international consignments, $x_{hij}$, the corresponding pattern of shipments, $m_{hij}$, the employments, $n_{hi}$, and the transfer prices $q_{hi}$ as functions of the comparative disadvantages of labour in different locations, $\eta_{hi}$, the availability of non-tradeable inputs $\gamma_{hi}$, the input coefficients for components in the assembly process, $b_h$, the aggregate endowment of efficiency units in each location, $N_i$, the intensity of local demand, $f_i$, the unit costs of transport $a_{hij}$, the *ad valorem* tariff rates, $s_{hij}$, the profit taxation rates, $\tau_i$, and the upper and lower bounds on the transfer prices, $Q_{hi}$, $Q'_{hi}$ ($H = 1, \ldots, H+1; i = 1, \ldots, L$).

The monopolist's strategy in turn determines the tariff and tax receipts at each location and, through the equity-ownership parameters $g_i$, the distribution of profit to each location as well. Income at each location then determines the local consumption of the competitive consumer good. The balance between local production and local consumption of this good determines the balance of trade.

## 7.5 A COMPUTABLE MODEL OF MULTINATIONAL LOCATION

This section presents a special case of the basic model, designed for practical computation. The model is well adapted to analysing the way that location adjusts to changes in technology and in market conditions.

On the supply side it is assumed that there are constant marginal returns to expanding production at a given location up to the capacity limit set by the labour endowment. On the demand side it is assumed that in the short run the product price in each market is fixed and the firm is committed to supplying all that is demanded at that price. In the long run the firm faces a demand at each location which diminishes linearly with respect to the product price.

Given these specifications, both the objective function and the feasible region faced by the monopolist are convex, and so the local maximum described by the Kuhn–Tucker conditions is a global maximum too. The short-run equilibrium of the firm can be determined from a linear programme, while the long-run equilibrium can be determined from a quadratic programme. Given the solutions of these programmes, the entire pattern of world trade can be deduced by arithmetic substitution into the equations for the competitive good industry.

The following example shows how the model can be applied to a short-run location problem. The accent is very much on simplicity. Four locations are distinguished: London, Brussels, Frankfurt and Madrid. Each location except Madrid is a potential source of demand for the monopoly product. The product is produced by assembling an engine and a frame. The transport costs for the engine and the frame are shown in Table 7.1. The assembled product is much bulkier than either of its components, and as a result, its unit transport cost is three times greater than for either of its components. The matrix of transport costs is assumed to be symmetric; only the elements to the right of the diagonal are shown in Table 7.1. To begin with tariffs are ignored and the rate of profit taxation is assumed to be the same at all locations.

Engine manufacture and assembly are feasible everywhere, but frame production is possible only in Madrid for example, because only

TABLE 7.1    *Transport costs for engines, frames and assembled products*

| From/To | London | Brussels | Frankfurt | Madrid |
|---------|--------|----------|-----------|--------|
| London | — | 2 | 4.5(4) | 5 |
| Brussels | | — | 2 | 4(3.5) |
| Frankfurt | | | — | 1.5 |
| Madrid | | | | — |

164    *The Economic Theory of the Multinational Enterprise*

Madrid has the non-tradeable raw materials required or a geography suited to the disposal of pollutants. Labour costs (in efficiency units) differ significantly between locations. Table 7.2 shows that Frankfurt has a strong comparative advantage in engine manufacture and Madrid has a strong comparative advantage in assembly. The labour endowments in each location are shown in the final column of Table 7.2. The final demand for the finished product at each location is shown in Table 7.3.

In the short run the MNE's objective is to meet the final demands at minimum cost. It is not always necessary to invoke formal programming methods to solve a short-run location problem of this kind. The logical structure of the problem resolves the calculations into four fairly simple stages.

Because transport costs are linear and there is no capacity limit on the transport network the least-cost route between any two locations is independent of the quantity consigned between them. Thus the least-cost route for each consignment can be determined before the amounts to be consigned have been calculated.

Because production costs are linear, the costs of sourcing each location with an engine, a frame and an assembled product are

TABLE 7.2    *Labour costs*

| Location | Labour cost of | | | | Labour endowment |
|---|---|---|---|---|---|
| | *Engine* | *Frame* | *Assembly* | *Marketing* | |
| London | 16 | — | 10 | 2 | 3000 |
| Brussels | 15 | — | 8 | 2 | 3000 |
| Frankfurt | 10 | — | 8 | 2 | 4000 |
| Madrid | 20 | 6 | 3 | 2 | 1000 |

TABLE 7.3    *Final demands*

| Location | Final demand |
|---|---|
| London | 20 |
| Brussels | 30 |
| Frankfurt | 50 |
| Madrid | 0 |

independent of the quantities supplied – until, of course, the labour endowment at the source is exhausted. When calculating the cost of sourcing, it may be assumed that the least-cost route, determined in the first stage, is always employed. It is then quite straightforward to rank in terms of cost the alternative sources of engine and frames for each destination. (If tax rates differ between locations, however, the calculations are complicated by having to allow for the notional transfer of taxable profit between locations.)

To rank alternative sources of assembled products, it is assumed that each assembly plant is supplied with engines and frames from the lowest-cost sources (subject to capacity constraints). Adding the cost of the engine and the frame (inclusive of transport cost) to the labour cost of assembly makes it possible to rank in terms of cost the alternative sources of the assembled product for each market destination.

In the final stage a trial solution is considered in which each market is sourced from the lowest-cost location. If this allocation of production is feasible then it is also optimal. If some capacity limits are exceeded then the 'bottlenecks' must be relieved by switching some production to the next-lowest cost source. It is sensible to arrange for bottlenecks in assembly to be relieved before tackling bottlenecks in component production. If there are many bottlenecks then this heuristic approach is liable to break down and a formal procedure, for example, the simplex method (Baumol, 1977, Ch. 5) may need to be invoked. The simplex method differs from the heuristic approach in that it confines itself to investigating feasible solutions and it searches systematically across them. The heuristic approach can still be used, however, to provide an 'intelligent' trial solution from which the simplex procedure can commence.

Consider now the determination of the least cost routes. In Table 7.1 the figures without brackets indicate the cost of direct transport between the different locations. Inspection of the table reveals that in two instances it is cheaper to route consignments indirectly. Routing from London to Frankfurt via Brussels reduces the cost from 4.5 units to 4, whilst routing from Brussels to Madrid via Frankfurt reduces the cost from 4 units to 3.5. When these substitutions are made, the table may be reinterpreted as indicating the costs of consignment between the various locations, assuming that the consignment always follows the least-cost route. The least-cost routings are illustrated schematically by the solid lines in Figure 7.1.

Once the minimum costs of consignment have been derived, they can be combined with the data on labour costs in Table 7.2 to evaluate

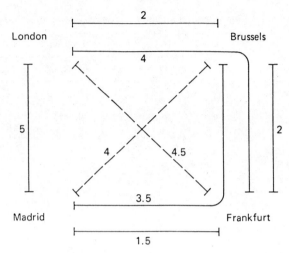

FIGURE 7.1   *Schematic representation of the solution of the least-cost routing problem*

NOTE   Solid lines represent efficient routes

alternative assembly sourcing strategies. The relevant calculations are shown in Table 7.4. Subject to capacity constraints, it is efficient to concentrate all engine production in Frankfurt, irrespective of where assembly takes place.

Given the costs of the assembled product in the different locations, it is a straightforward matter to evaluate the costs of supplying each market from the various assembly points. The cost of supply is equal to the sum of the cost of the assembled product, the cost of transport to the market and the tariff payment (where applicable). The table shows that, subject to capacity constraints, it is efficient to service the London, Brussels and Madrid markets entirely from local assembly and to service the Frankfurt market entirely from Madrid. It follows that all the engines produced in Frankfurt will be exported to assembly plants at the other three locations.

Given the international distribution of final demands shown in Table 7.3, it is readily established that the pattern of specialisation described is compatible with the assumed labour endowment: the assumption of incomplete specialisation of production at each location (Section 7.3) is validated. The resulting matrix of trade flows is shown in Table 7.5. The implications of this matrix for employment at each location are shown in Table 7.6. It can be seen that in Frankfurt a high proportion

TABLE 7.4  *Determination of efficient assembly sourcing strategies*

| | Location of assembly | | | |
|---|---|---|---|---|
| | London | Brussels | Frankfurt | Madrid |
| *Delivered cost of* | | | | |
| *engine from* | | | | |
| London | 16 | 18 | 20 | 21 |
| Brussels | 17 | 15 | 17 | 18.5 |
| Frankfurt | 14* | 12* | 10* | 11.5* |
| Madrid | 24 | 23.5 | 21.5 | 20 |
| Minimum | 14 | 12 | 10 | 11.5 |
| *Delivered cost of* | | | | |
| *frame from Madrid* | 11 | 9.5 | 7.5 | 6 |
| Cost of local assembly | 10 | 8 | 8 | 3 |
| Minimum cost of | | | | |
| assembled product | 35 | 29.5 | 25.5 | 20.5 |
| *Delivered cost of* | | | | |
| *assembled product in* | | | | |
| London | 35* | 35.5 | 37.5 | 35.5 |
| Brussels | 41 | 29.5* | 31.5 | 31 |
| Frankfurt | 47 | 35.5 | 25.5 | 25* |
| Madrid | 50 | 40 | 30 | 20.5* |

NOTE   An asterisk identifies the cost-minimising source.

TABLE 7.5  *Matrix of trade flows for engines, frames and assembled products*

| From/To | | London | Brussels | Frankfurt | Madrid | Total |
|---|---|---|---|---|---|---|
| London | Engine | 0 | 0 | 0 | 0 | 0 |
| | Frame | 0 | 0 | 0 | 0 | 0 |
| | Assembly | 20 | 0 | 0 | 0 | 20 |
| Brussels | Engine | 0 | 0 | 0 | 0 | 0 |
| | Frame | 0 | 0 | 0 | 0 | 0 |
| | Assembly | 0 | 30 | 0 | 0 | 30 |
| Frankfurt | Engine | 20 | 30 | 0 | 50 | 100 |
| | Frame | 0 | 0 | 0 | 0 | 0 |
| | Assembly | 0 | 0 | 0 | 0 | 0 |
| Madrid | Engine | 0 | 0 | 0 | 0 | 0 |
| | Frame | 20 | 30 | 0 | 50 | 100 |
| | Assembly | 0 | 0 | 50 | 0 | 50 |
| Total | Engine | 20 | 30 | 0 | 50 | 100 |
| | Frame | 20 | 30 | 0 | 50 | 100 |
| | Assembly | 20 | 30 | 50 | 0 | 100 |

168    *The Economic Theory of the Multinational Enterprise*

TABLE 7.6    *The international allocation of labour*

| Location | Engine manu-facturing | Frame manu-facturing | Assembly | Marketing | Transport | Competitive production | Total |
|---|---|---|---|---|---|---|---|
| London | 0 | 0 | 200 | 40 | 70 | 2690 | 3000 |
| Brussels | 0 | 0 | 240 | 60 | 100 | 2600 | 3000 |
| Frankfurt | 1000 | 0 | 0 | 100 | 252.5 | 2647.5 | 4000 |
| Madrid | 0 | 600 | 150 | 0 | 222.5 | 1027.5 | 2000 |

of the labour force is involved in the production, transport and marketing of the monopoly product – in particular in the manufacture of engines, their outward transport to London, Brussels and Madrid, and the transport back of the assembled product from Madrid. Labour is also committed to the transport of frames from Madrid to Brussels, as these are routed through Frankfurt. Madrid is engaged extensively in frame manufacture and assembly, in the import of engines and the export of the frames and the assembled product. Labour in Brussels and London is engaged in assembly, the import of components and the marketing of the final product.

This example illustrates very clearly the three types of investment mentioned in Section 7.1. Import-substituting investment is exemplified by the location of assembly in London. London is the highest-cost location for assembly and is also remote from the manufacture of components in Frankfurt and Madrid. Assembly in London is efficient only because of the very high cost of transporting the assembled product instead of the components. The high cost of transporting the 'output' of assembly relative to its 'inputs' accords assembly a high degree of 'effective protection' (Balassa, 1971). London's 'effective protection' is sufficient to outweigh the labour cost savings that would be achieved by assembling elsewhere.

Export platform investment is exemplified by the specialisation of engine manufacture in Frankfurt. This specialisation accords with comparative advantage, and is exploited fully because of the relatively low transport costs for components and the fairly central position of Frankfurt within the transport network ('centrality' being defined with respect to the transport cost metric). Madrid is, to a lesser extent, an export platform for assembly. Like engine manufacture in Frankfurt, assembly in Madrid is exclusively for export – though for different reasons: all engines are exported from Frankfurt because of vertical specialisation within the component production-assembly sequence, whereas all assembled products are exported from Madrid simply because there is no local final demand for the product.

Raw materials investment is exemplified by the specialisation of frame manufacture in Madrid. Essentially this is an extreme form of comparative advantage in frame manufacture arising from exclusive access to an indispensable resource. Since the advantage is so strong, the fact that Madrid is on the 'periphery' of the transport network does not affect the incentive to locate frame manufacture in Madrid.

It is possible to measure the economies of vertical specialisation by comparing this situation with a situation in which, because of more primitive product design it is not feasible to separate the production of the engines and frames from the assembly of the product. If labour productivity in manufacturing were exactly the same as before but there were either no components, or the components were not trade-able, then all production would have to be carried on in Madrid, where essential inputs to frame-production are located. The product cost would be 29 units (see the bottom line of Table 7.2). This would give a delivered cost in London of 44 units (compared with 35 units with vertical specialisation), in Brussels of 41 units (compared with 29.5), in Frankfurt of 33.5 units (compared with 25), and in Madrid of 29 units compared with 20.5.

As noted above, import substitution is encouraged by high transport costs, and export platforms are encouraged by low transport costs. Since transport costs are normally higher for assembled products than for components, import-substituting investment is most likely at the assembly stage and export-platform investment in component manu-facture. It is a consequence of this that improvements in product design which lower the transport cost of the assembled product relative to that of the component (for example, by trivialising a final stage of assembly in which much of the bulk is created) will reduce the significance of import-substitution. If, for example, the bulk of the assembled product could be reduced by one-third then, with a corresponding saving in transport costs, the model predicts that import-substituting assembly would entirely disappear. Both London and Brussels would cease to assemble the product and assembly would be concentrated completely on Madrid.

Tariffs tend to be levied more frequently upon final products than upon components. It is because a tariff on a final product does not directly inhibit the vertical specialisation of production that a fairly low tariff on a final product can generate a fairly high degree of 'effective

170    *The Economic Theory of the Multinational Enterprise*

protection' for assembly. Thus in the model the imposition by Frankfurt of a 5 per cent tariff on imports of the assembled product from Madrid will be sufficient to switch assembly from Madrid to Frankfurt. The impact of tariffs can, however, be mitigated by transfer-pricing. If the MNE can transfer the assembled product from Madrid to Frankfurt at a notional price of less than 10 units rather than at the true cost of 25 units then the tariff payments will be too small to influence location, and assembly will remain in Madrid.

Suppose now that each location has a linear demand curve for the monopolised consumer-product. As noted in Section 7.3, one of the parameters of demand at each location is the endowment of labour efficiency units. Consistency requires that the demand curve at each location does not, under any circumstances, commit wage-earners to spend more than their labour endowment on the monopolised product. The demand schedules reported in the first column of Table 7.7 all satisfy this constraint. It is assumed that demand in Frankfurt is relatively inelastic, in London reasonably elastic and Brussels very elastic. Demand in Madrid is reasonably elastic too, but the intensity of demand is so low that the market does not warrant any supply.

TABLE 7.7    *The long-run marketing plan for the monopolist*

| Location | Demand | Price | Quantity |
|----------|--------|-------|----------|
| London | $d = 110 - 2p$ | 45 | 20 |
| Brussels | $d = 296 - 8p$ | 33.25 | 30 |
| Frankfurt | $d = 125 - p$ | 75 | 50 |
| Madrid | $d = 15 - 2p$ | 20.5 | 0 |

In the long run the monopolist maximises profits by setting prices in each of the markets so that the marginal revenue in each market is equal to the marginal cost of supply. Under these conditions long-run profit-maximisation generates the short-run final demands specified earlier. In Frankfurt a price of 75 units is charged and the quantity sold is fifty; in London the price is 45 units and the quantity sold is twenty; in Brussels the price is 33.25 units and the quantity sold is thirty. In Madrid the product is priced at cost – 20.5 units – but nothing is sold. The location strategy and the matrix of trade flows is therefore exactly the same as before.

## 7.6 CONCLUSION

This chapter has developed a simple computable model of the behaviour of a vertically- and horizontally-integrated MNE operating a rationalised production system in which different activities are linked through international trade. It has been suggested that the model is well adapted to analysing the impact on trade of changes in technology associated with increased division of labour and of reductions in transport costs. It also extends the results of previous models concerning the impact of tariffs and tax differentials on the location of production.

The model is developed with applications at the firm and industry level very much in mind. It enables the modeller to analyse import-substituting investment, export-platform investment and raw-materials investment within a single framework and to derive predictions through simulation using standard computational techniques.

The model can be extended in a number of ways. The assumption that production at each location is incompletely specialised is crucial in generating simple results. In particular, it means that because capacity constraints are never binding, it is unnecessary – in the context of this model – for the firm to resort to multiple sourcing of components. Each assembly process receives any given component from a single source. Introducing binding capacity constraints into the model would increase the problems of solution quite considerably, but would facilitate a detailed analysis of multiple sourcing. Still greater realism could be achieved by making the capacity constraints stochastic, so that the firm could also engage in diversifying the risk of disruption of supplies through multiple-sourcing.

Another useful extension of the model would be to allow the firm a choice of production technique at each location. To allow a meaningful choice of technique another factor of production would have to be introduced; by increasing the generality of the model in this way, the substitution possibilities analysed by the HO model would appear as a special case. The model therefore has great potentiality, though it is difficult to assess at this stage how far it is useful to pursue the quest for generality alluded to above.

# [24]

Journal of Common Market Studies
Volume XXVI, No. 2 December 1987
0021-9886 $3.00

# The Reorganization of European Industries After Integration: Selected Evidence on the Role of Multinational Enterprise Activities

JOHN CANTWELL

*University of Reading*

## 1. INTRODUCTION

To date, most work on the effects of the creation and enlargement of the EC customs union on multinational enterprise (MNE) activities has concentrated on the consequences for import substituting types of investment within Europe. The effects of both trade creation and trade diversion that result from changes in tariffs might be expected to influence this kind of investment. The existence of a common external tariff encourages non-Community firms to relocate their production to a site within the EC, while the reduction of tariffs between European countries widens the market that can thereby be served from any such individual site.

For US firms, the EC customs union has therefore acted as a stimulus towards the establishment of import substituting investments in Europe, displacing or changing the structure of US exports to Europe. Some attempts have been made to quantify this effect of tariff changes on US foreign direct investment (FDI) in Community countries. (Scaperlanda and Mauer (1969), Schmitz and Bieri (1972), Lunn (1980), Scaperlanda and Balough (1983), and Lunn (1983)) These attempts have, however, been plagued by an identification problem; that is, how to disentangle the effects of economic integration from the various other possible influences on US FDI (see, for example, Taveira, 1986). By definition, import substituting types of investment are market oriented, and it can be shown that the size and rate of growth of EC markets have exercised a significant effect on the inward investment of US MNEs (the earliest work here was that of Bandera and White, 1968). A large overall size of market attracts investment by making it possible to produce locally at an efficient scale, while a fast rate of growth enables foreign affiliates to introduce new innovative products more rapidly. It is also clear that the formation of the EC, by way of trade creation and diversion increased the size of potential market of firms located in each participating country, and by way of the dynamic association between trade and growth helped to raise the rate of expansion of European markets.

However, the rate of growth and the size of the market actually served by firms in Member States may be reduced by the greater force of competition incurred from firms based in other European countries. This counter effect has been important in the UK motor vehicles sector, as is discussed below. An even greater difficulty for quantitative studies in this area is that the dynamic effects that arose from the creation of the customs union in 1958 were not the only factor behind the rapid growth of European markets in the 1960s, and indeed were probably not the most important. The rise in industrial innovation in Europe, which was partly facilitated by technology transfer to the foreign affiliates and licensees of US MNEs (Dunning and Cantwell, 1982), attracted further US FDI to Europe. In recent years, with the emergence of global competition in some industries based on systems of complementary technologies, US MNEs may find production in European countries attractive as a means of extending their own capacity for innovation (Cantwell, 1986).

Such considerations suggest that there are a range of complex and interactive dynamic processes that affect FDI in Europe, and that the realignment of tariffs is one element in a complicated scheme of industrial restructuring. Even matters as apparently straightforward as the impact of a customs union on the level and rate of rise of inward FDI may prove intractable in quantitative analysis given the constraints on the data available. One problem is that there has been a shift away from the import substituting type of FDI and towards rationalized investments, which cannot be treated individually but are part of a globally integrated network of affiliates. Aggregate data on FDI do not allow us to distinguish between the two, but an increase in tariffs will tend to increase the first type of investment, but to reduce the second. Models set up to test the impact of tariff changes on import substituting FDI will provide a misleading picture if they work with total FDI at a time when an increasing amount of such investment is being integrated into a global organization by the MNEs responsible.

One response is to consider explicitly the case of export oriented as well as import substituting types of FDI. This is of interest when looking at the possibility of a relocation of production away from an established EC

Member State in favour of a new entrant when the Community is enlarged (Taveira, 1986; Simões, 1985). In statistical work on a particular country it may be possible to distinguish between industries in which import substituting or export oriented types of FDI predominate, depending upon the trading status of the industry in the country in question. Another instance in which a quantitative approach may prove useful is that of countries which, because of preferential tariff arrangements with the EC, attract an export platform type of FDI (Yannopoulos, 1986). For small developing countries the import substituting component of FDI in this situation is likely to be relatively insignificant, due to the weakness of their domestic markets.

Such approaches are much less feasible when examining MNE activities in the major industrialized countries of Europe. Import substituting, export platform and rationalized types of investment are likely to coexist in most sectors. Indeed, part of the problem is that when MNE activities are associated with industrial change (as is the rule), it is really inappropriate to think in terms of FDI when what is at issue is the international production that is financed by that FDI. MNEs may reorganize the regional division of labour within an integrated economic area, moving production away from some locations and towards others, while changing the range of what is actually produced in any given country. Technological factors as well as changes in relative costs are important here, and help to determine whether MNEs move in the direction of greater or lesser specialization in each part of their overall European network. Some production sites will have an especially prominent role to play in innovation in the network as a whole, and perhaps in these cases affiliates rely upon co-operative relationships with other firms and component suppliers in the country concerned. In any case, the growth and relocation of investment by MNEs within the EC must be seen in the context of a change in productive organization.

This suggests that an industrial case study approach may be more fruitful than cross-industry statistical analysis, and this is the approach adopted here. The emphasis is on the restructuring of European industries by the MNEs that operate within the Community, and consequently especially on rationalized as well as import substituting types of investment. This change of emphasis from some of the earlier literature on economic integration and international production is also found in the work of Pelkmans (1984), who argues in favour of an industrial economics and firm strategic perspective. The present contribution goes further in that it uses an approach that is derived not from the literature on industrial organization, but from work on technological competition and industrial dynamics (a distinction discussed by Carlsson, 1985). The particular theory of industrial dynamics used is considered in Section 2, and it is applied in evidence on the motor vehicles and pharmaceuticals sectors in Europe in Section 3.

## 2. A MODEL OF CUMULATIVE CAUSATION IN THE SPECIALIZATION OF INNOVATIVE ACTIVITY IN AN ECONOMICALLY INTEGRATED REGION

The consequences of operating in an economically integrated region are considered here in the context of a model developed more extensively in Cantwell (1988), and also referred to in Dunning and Cantwell (1988). The basic model incorporates some of the insights of Myrdal (1957) and Kaldor (1985) on cumulative causation in the relationship between international trade and economic growth, and of Hymer (1975) on the geographical dispersion of the different types of activity organised by MNEs in the form of a locational hierarchy. A distinction is drawn between two types of production undertaken by the MNEs of each manufacturing sector. They engage in both research intensive production, which in general is linked to local R&D facilities, and in assembly types of production that need not be supported by local research. For example, in the pharmaceuticals sector there is a distinction between the production of active ingredients which relies heavily upon local R&D, and the manufacture of final drugs incorporating active ingredients which can be carried out in countries that have no indigenous research capacity.

The production of research intensive components and final assembly operations may be locationally separated but integrated through trade within the European market, as a result of the strategic decisions of MNEs. Research intensive production in any sector tends to be attracted to sites of strong innovative activity. By locating new production and R&D facilities in such a site, MNEs can gain access to new and complementary lines of technological development that are specific to the host country and its local firms. As a broad generalization, MNE operations in countries where indigenous firms are strong in the sector in question act as a helpful competitive stimulus and induce an increase in the share of research intensive activity in total local production. A higher proportion of research intensive production in the total is associated with a higher rate of productivity growth, through improving local competitiveness with a higher rate of output growth. Conversely, where indigenous firms are technologically backward they may be further weakened when foreign MNEs establish local production.

The model presented here reflects the view that in any international industry brought into being through international trade, there is a long-run process of cumulative causation at work. That is, in locations where innovation is strong, success breeds success in the form of a virtuous circle, while countries whose firms have a lower capacity for innovation fall further and further behind and are gradually driven out of world markets in a vicious circle of cumulative decline. Although this is only a long-run process, it is argued that it has been greatly speeded up by the modern operations of MNEs which have increased the locational mobility of industry. It is further argued that the process works fastest of all and in its purest form in an economically integrated region in which there are few barriers to trade.

The model of cumulative causation through international trade and production is set out in diagrammatic form in Figures 1 and 2. The procedure followed is to consider the long-run process at work in an international industry before explicitly introducing the effects of MNE activities in an economically integrated region. Figure 1 illustrates a virtuous

Figure 1

*A Virtuous Circle with a Recurring Balance of Trade Surplus*

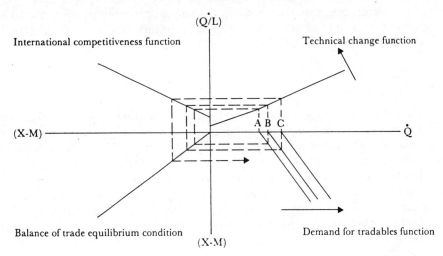

Figure 2

*A Vicious Circle with a Recurring Balance of Trade Deficit*

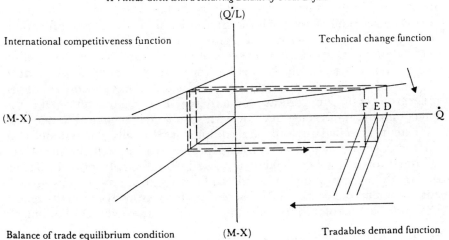

circle such as is likely in a centre of innovative activity in industry, and Figure 2 illustrates a vicious circle. As a location for production, a country is likely to have some industries in which it falls into the first group, some industries in which it falls into the second group, and some industries somewhere between the two.

### The basic model

In the top right hand quadrant of Figures 1 and 2 is the technical change function which relates $\dot{Q}$, the proportional rate of growth of output, to $(\dot{Q/L})$, the proportional rate of growth of productivity.[1] The value of output of the industry in terms of some common international currency unit is denoted by Q, while the number of workers employed in the industry is represented by L. The proportional growth rates are then defined as follows:

$$\dot{Q} = (1/Q)\,(dQ/dt)$$
$$\dot{L} = (1/L)\,(dL/dt)$$
$$(\dot{Q/L}) = \dot{Q} - \dot{L}$$

The technical change function reflects the stylised facts of industrial growth and innovation; that is, higher rates of growth of industry output are associated with higher rates of growth of productivity. This is because faster growth of output is linked to fuller capacity utilization and more rapid technological progress, so that employment growth does not rise by as much as output growth. The greater the research capabilities of the local industry, the steeper will be the slope of the technical change function, as the growth of output is achieved to a greater extent through innovation. The analogous relationship at a macroeconomic level is known as 'Okun's Law', which suggests that for an economy as a whole a 3 per cent rise in output is in general accompanied by a 1 per cent rise in employment. It is here supposed that there is some autonomous component of productivity growth even in a static industry, so that the function does not pass through the origin.

In the top left hand quadrant is the international competitiveness function. This suggests that a higher rate of productivity growth is associated with a larger balance of trade surplus (exports minus imports, X − M), or with a smaller balance of trade deficit (M − X). Two assumptions are implicit in the derivation of this schedule. Firstly, it is assumed that the value of capital per worker grows at the same rate as productivity (output per worker), so that the capital–output ratio is constant. The reason is that technological change is to some extent embodied in new capital equipment. Secondly, it is assumed that while the wage rate rises faster with faster productivity growth, the increase in the growth of wages lags behind the rise in productivity growth. Taken together, these assumptions mean that a higher rate of productivity growth leads to a fall in unit costs, and an increase in international competitiveness.

A simple balance of trade equilibrium condition is placed in the bottom left

[1]Dots are used to indicate proportional rates of growth.

hand quadrant ($X - M = X - M$, or $M - X = M - X$). In the bottom right hand quadrant is the demand function for domestically produced tradable output. As international competitiveness rises export demand increases, and so does domestic demand as imports fall off. The gradual rise in demand encourages optimistic entrepreneurial expectations of future demand, generating a further rise in investment and hence in the growth of output. The function is drawn to show that higher net export demand is associated with higher investment and a faster growth of output (and vice versa).

However, this is not the end of the story. A more rapid rate of growth of output occasioned by more favourable demand conditions leads to an increased requirement for imported component parts. In other words, in the case depicted by Figure 1 a higher rate of growth of output leads to an increased demand for imports to support faster rising domestic production, and this pushes the balance of trade backward towards equilibrium. This is represented by an outward or rightward shift in the net export line of Figure 1, as imports begin to rise at the new rate of growth of output. The increase in imports of components, catching up with buoyant markets for the export of final goods, is likely to be slow where the industry is not very highly internationalized and its various activities are located close to one another.

It is now clear how a trend towards cumulative causation in an internationally trading industry can become established. Let us suppose that the local circumstances of an industry in a particular country are those of Figure 1, and that it begins with a rate of growth of output at point A. This is associated with a sufficient rate of innovation and productivity growth so that the sector is internationally competitive, and it begins to build up a balance of trade surplus as a result. The rate of growth of output rises to a level equivalent to B, and with this imports begin to rise and the tradables demand function shifts to the right. However, the faster rate of growth of output is associated with a still faster rate of growth of output, at C, and a virtuous circle sets in. In the opposite case of an industry illustrated by Figure 2, cumulative causation operates in the reverse direction, and it moves from D to E to F as the growth of domestic production slows down and balance of trade deficits become larger and larger.

Apart from the lack of speed in the shift in the tradables demand function, there are two major factors that constrain this process. Firstly, in the case of a virtuous circle, supplies of (suitably skilled) labour may begin to dry up, causing the wage rate to begin to rise faster than the growth of productivity. Secondly, this quicker rise in wages may induce a more labour saving type of technological change such that capital per worker starts to rise faster than productivity, and the capital-output ratio rises. Moreover, as innovation along the prevailing 'technology paradigm' (Dosi, 1983) becomes increasingly difficult, productivity growth falls below the rate of growth of capital per worker for this reason as well. Both these factors can be represented by an upward shift in the international competitiveness function

*Multinational Corporations*

134	THE REORGANISATION OF EUROPEAN INDUSTRIES

in Figure 1, which has the effect of slowing down the upward spiral of activity, and ultimately of shutting it off altogether. The same arguments can be applied in reverse to explain the stemming of a vicious circle, when for instance excess supplies of labour cause real wages to fall back, and the international competitiveness function of Figure 2 shifts down.

The overall conclusion to be drawn from the basic model is that, as a long run process, an internationally trading industry will gradually become increasingly divided into some dynamic and some stagnant production locations. The former will be characterized by a high proportion of research intensive activity and a relatively steep technical progress function, the latter by a low proportion of research linked production and a comparatively shallow technical progress function.

## The role of MNEs

The activities of MNEs accelerate the process of cumulative causation between competing locations. They do so by increasing the general international mobility of industrial production, and by making more likely the geographical separation of the research intensive and assembly types of production. Their activities have the effect of raising the slope of the technical progress function in dynamic locations while lowering it in stagnant production sites, and of increasing the speed with which the tradables demand function is capable of shifting. Both these effects serve to reinforce the operation of virtuous and vicious circles in different countries. In short, the research intensive production of MNEs is attracted to the major sites of innovation in an international industry, but this in turn serves to strengthen innovation and the growth of production in the countries in question (as well as the competitive position of the MNEs themselves). This secondary spiral of cumulative causation strengthens the primary spiral associated with the existence of international trade, converting a long-run process into a rather more immediate one.

Host countries attract inward MNE investment where they have innovative domestic industries, and the MNEs concerned also establish local R&D facilities to support research intensive forms of production, and to gain further access to local scientific and technological experience, and methods of work. In doing so, foreign MNE entry increases local research capacity, and may also increase the extent of technological dissemination to local suppliers and customers. By increasing the technological competition faced by indigenous firms in the same sector, local rivals may be spurred on to a higher rate of innovation. The combined effect is to raise the local technical progress function, thereby increasing the size of the local trade surplus and output growth. This type of sector is as a rule home to MNEs of its own, and their outward investment plays a similar role to the inward investment of foreign MNEs in this respect. By locating research intensive production in other important centres of innovation abroad, and assembly and allied outlets in other countries, the firms of the most dynamic countries sustain more effectively the global basis for increased research activity at home. They are able to integrate complementary foreign technologies, and to devise more broadly-based technological systems in their domestic innovation.

By contrast, inward MNE investment in declining local sectors is likely to be in assembly types of production, importing research-intensive component parts. The markets of less innovative local firms are then directly threatened, with an implied threat to their existing R&D capaciy. Meanwhile, foreign MNEs may use their increased local sales to help finance an increased level of R&D within their parent companies, and in doing so they become increasingly competitive. Local firms lack the technological and other resources to become MNEs themselves, and are consequently compelled to cut back their own R&D spending. This has the effect of pulling down the technical progress function in countries whose firms are relatively weak in the relevant industry, thereby compounding a vicious circle.

The notion of a vicious circle needs qualification, to the extent that the firms of a country whose technological capacity in an industry is low or declining no longer compete effectively with the MNEs of the strongest countries. In this case the inward investment of foreign MNEs may help to stem a vicious circle by raising the technical progress function through MNE network linked effects rather than indigenous research. Local innovation then takes the form of the development of local skills, incremental process improvement, better production engineering, new quality control techniques and so forth, even though fundamental research capacity is located abroad.

## The effects of economic integration

The geographical dispersion of research intensive and other production in global MNE networks is further reinforced when operations are located in an economically integrated region. When trade barriers between countries are lowered this increases the incentives to organize an international division of labour in which productive activity in each country becomes more highly specialized. This implies that when a customs union is created or extended, industries in the region will be gradually restructured in the following period. For any given industry, countries that are homes to strongly innovative firms will find that local research is further encouraged as local firms increase their market shares elsewhere in the region (through exports and international production), and foreign MNEs find it a more attractive location for their research intensive production. In countries in which local technological capacity is weak, it will be further undermined as indigenous firms lose domestic market shares, both from increased imports from more dynamic parts of the region, and from the local assembly activities of foreign affiliates that are linked up with MNE networks elsewhere in the region.

This suggests that, following the economic integration of a region in any particular industry, the investments of MNEs from outside the region will have beneficial competitive effects in some countries, and damaging anti-competitive effects in others. In countries in which local firms have reserves of technological strength in the industry in question, new MNE entry may act as a catalyst, helping to set in motion a virtuous circle of an increasing proportion of research intensive activity and a faster growth of output. In other cases it is likely to drive out local firms and set in motion a vicious circle of increasing dependency on external sources of supply and technology. Much depends upon the initial technological capacity of local enterprise in the sector concerned, and this influences the motive underlying the MNE investment and hence the form that it takes. Models that embody an implicit assumption that foreign MNE entry is either inherently competitive (Knickerbocker, 1976) or anti-competitive (Hymer, 1976) are misleading or at best tell only part of the story; these two opposite effects in different locations are interdependent with one another.

There may, however, be industries in which MNEs from outside the region are especially strong relative to firms from within the region. In the European Community electronics is a case in point, US and Japanese firms being world leaders. Where this happens research may remain quite highly centralised in the parent companies, except perhaps in certain specialized sub-sectors. It is then possible that a country within the region whose own firms have little innovative capacity in the relevant sector may act as a regional centre for foreign MNEs. In these circumstances the choice of country depends upon the skills of the local work force, wage rates, the provision of government incentives and the like. Where local firms are technologically weak, this kind of foreign entry may have beneficial production and employment effects, even if it is not associated with a (restoration of) fundamental research capacity.

The existence of an economically integrated region strengthens the trend towards a joint determination of production decisions in different countries by MNEs operating within the region. Many MNEs have moved closer to a regionally integrated strategy in their European activities. The creation and enlargement of the EC has played some part in increasing specialization in innovation and production between European countries. In each European industry there are centres of innovation, and there is a tendency for them to attract an increasing amount of the research intensive and allied production of MNEs. The next section considers evidence on this aspect of European industrial restructuring in the pharmaceuticals and motor vehicles sector, as a means of demonstrating the applicability of the model.

3. INCREASING SPECIALIZATION IN THE PHARMACEUTICALS AND MOTOR VEHICLES SECTORS IN THE EC: THE EVIDENCE

The pharmaceuticals and motor vehicles sectors have been chosen as they both illustrate patterns of cumulative causation in the location of technological activity by MNEs in the United Kingdom, as part of their European operations. The UK pharmaceuticals industry has been caught up in a virtuous circle encouraged by the expanding UK research facilities of foreign MNEs, and by the United Kingdom's entry into the EC in 1973. By contrast, the UK motor vehicles sector has undergone a rapid decline since the 1960s in which local technological capacities have fallen further and further behind those of the major centres of innovation abroad, and the integration of British plants into the European networks of MNEs has been given further impetus by UK entry into the EC. These are two cases of cumulative causation in the location of research intensive production in Europe strengthened by the existence of the EC, one of which has been beneficial, and one damaging for the United Kingdom.

*Pharmaceuticals*

*The specialization of innovation in Europe.* In terms of the industrialized world as a whole, Europe remains strong in the pharmaceuticals industry relative to Japan, and in competition with the United States. The countries of high technological capacity are West Germany, the United Kingdom, Switzerland, the United States, and to a lesser extent France (Burstall and Senior, 1984). Countries of medium technological capacity include Italy, the Netherlands, and Belgium in the EC, as well as Japan.

The position of the strongest countries and firms in the industry has been largely sustained since the 1950s, although the United Kingdom has gained somewhat and France has slipped back (Burstall, Dunning and Lake, 1981). The leading four countries are home to 27 of the 32 largest pharmaceutical firms, and the leading five are home to 29. Of the 32 major pharmaceutical producers in 1980, 16 were American, 4 West German, 4 British, 3 Swiss and 2 French (Rigoni, Griffiths and Laing, 1985).

The research facilities of MNEs in the industry have been increasingly decentralized, and many drugs are now developed through the combined efforts of co-ordinated research in establishments located in different countries (Burstall and Dunning, 1985). Only the Japanese firms have so far avoided being drawn into this internationalization of R&D. The main reason for carrying out R&D outside the home country is to gain access to foreign science and technology, and to potential new avenues of innovation complementary to those already established by the firm. Interviews with pharmaceutical companies for various studies confirm the overwhelming

138          THE REORGANISATION OF EUROPEAN INDUSTRIES

importance of this consideration.[2] Taking the four highest capacity countries, MNEs from each of them have set up R&D facilities in each of the others, with just one exception. The only case in which cross-research activity is at a low level is that of the MNEs of West Germany and Switzerland, presumably because of the already close links that exist between research in these two countries.

Turning to Table 1, it can be seen that since the early 1960s there has been an increase in the share of R&D expenditure for which the three high capacity countries of the EC are responsible. This is in line with the predictions of the model of cumulative causation. However, it seems that the positions of Britain and West Germany would be even stronger were it not for French government pressure and regulations that have tied companies' ability to win market shares to the establishment of local R&D facilities (Burstall and Dunning, 1985). This means that looking below the aggregate figures on total R&D spending, a lower proportion of the research carried out in France is of a fundamental kind, by comparison with Britain and West Germany. Of the 30 largest pharmaceutical companies in 1982, 23 have R&D facilities in the US, 16 in the United Kingdom, 11 in France, 7 in West Germany and 7 in Italy. It is the United Kingdom which has gained the most from the foreign location of research by MNEs. West Germany has suffered relative to France due to the high cost of its local research, and the non-interventionist policy of its government. Of the 48 major MNE R&D establishments with fundamental research capacity, 31 per cent are in Britain, 13 per cent in West Germany, and 6 per cent in France (Brech and Sharp, 1984).

Table 1

*The share of total R&D expenditure in the pharmaceutical industry in the six largest EC countries, 1964–82 (%)*

|  | 1964 | 1982 |
|---|---|---|
| W. Germany | 31.9 | 33.5 |
| UK | 23.1 | 25.1 |
| France | 22.3 | 25.1 |
| Italy | 12.0 | 9.6 |
| Netherlands | 7.2 | 3.8 |
| Belgium | 3.6 | 2.9 |
| Total (6 countries) | 100.0 | 100.0 |

*Source*: Burstall, Dunning and Lake (1981); Burstall and Dunning (1985).

[2] See Burstall and Dunning (1985) and Brech and Sharp (1984). For a discussion of the significance of this factor in the growth of intra-industry production in Europe (involving the cross investments of MNEs in the same sector) see Cantwell (1986).

*National shares of EC production and exports.* As the model of cumulative causation suggests, those countries that hold the strongest position in research also tend to have built up the strongest position in research intensive production and exports. However, this process has been hampered in the case of pharmaceuticals by the strict national differentiation of markets, the safety standards that the industry is required to meet, and the social customs towards which it must tailor its drugs. Because of the system of separate national regulations, international production has become very important relative to exports, and in general MNEs maintain some production facilities wherever there are markets. In the most innovative countries, the research intensity of production rises relative to others, but this is not always reflected in their share of total production or exports, as the fruits of research must often be exploited through foreign production facilities.

At first glance Table 2 shows that national shares of pharmaceutical production in the EC have undergone little change sine the 1960s. West Germany, France and Italy seem to have gained a little, while the United Kingdom and the Netherlands have lost a little. Closer inspection suggests a rather more complicated picture. West Germany gained most in the early

Table 2

*The share of production of pharmaceuticals of the largest six EC countries, 1960–82 (%)*

|  | 1960–70* | 1970 | 1982 |
|---|---|---|---|
| W. Germany | 28.6 | 34.0 | 29.1 |
| France | 27.2 | 25.5 | 27.4 |
| UK | 20.2 | 14.8 | 19.2 |
| Italy | 17.1 | 17.7 | 18.6 |
| Belgium | 2.7 | 3.3 | 2.8 |
| Netherlands | 4.1 | 4.7 | 2.8 |
| Total (6 countries) | 100.0 | 100.0 | 100.0 |

*Source*: Burstall, Dunning and Lake (1981); Burstall and Senior (1984).

*Average of shares of 1960, 1965 and 1970.

days of the EC, up to the start of the 1970s, before its most powerful competitor as a research centre, the United Kingdom, joined. By comparison, Britain has made a spectacular recovery since the early 1970s. There may well be a significant effect related to economic integration here. This impression is reinforced by the fact that, after joining the EC, Britain has gained as a production base in part at the expense of the Netherlands, whose patterns of pharmaceutical consumption are said to be similar.

140      THE REORGANISATION OF EUROPEAN INDUSTRIES

Table 3 reveals that the EC as a whole is in a strong trading position with
the outside world, to the tune of a substantial surplus of $3,114m in 1982.
Although France's share of the exports of EC countries has risen at the
expense of West Germany and the United Kingdom, the French share of
total imports has also risen since the early 1960s. Calculated as the share of
pharmaceuticals in total manufacturing exports relative to their share for the
industrialized world as a whole, the UK's revealed comparative advantage
in the sector has increased and is the highest of any EC country. The United
Kingdom, West Germany and France are all clearly surplus countries, and
Britain and France have become very much more so since the mid-1960s.
The rankings of countries according to the size of their trade surpluses more
or less corresponds to their rankings in research. Jointly considering the
evidence it remains true that countries with the greatest research capacity
enjoy the healthiest production and export positions.

Table 3

*The trading positions of the EC (10) countries in pharmaceuticals, 1965–82 and 1982*

|  | Export Share 1965, % | Export Share 1982, % | RCA* 1982 | Trade Balance 1965, $m | Trade Balance 1982, $m |
|---|---|---|---|---|---|
| Germany | 30.4 | 27.0 | 1.05 | 164 | 932 |
| UK | 25.3 | 22.0 | 1.56 | 156 | 1,052 |
| France | 15.9 | 20.0 | 1.49 | 55 | 858 |
| Italy | 8.2 | 8.9 | 0.83 | 2 | 37 |
| Other EC | 20.1 | 22.2 | 1.04 | −8 | 235 |
| Total (10 countries) | 100.0 | 100.0 | 1.18 | 369 | 3,114 |

*Source*: Burstall, Dunning and Lake (1981), Burstall and Senior (1984).

*Relative to all developed countries.

*The local research base of UK production.* The United Kingdom has succeeded in
attracting more fundamental research activity in the local affiliates of foreign
MNEs than any other European country. While Britain only has 3.5 per cent
of world pharmaceutical production, it has 11.5 per cent of R&D expenditure, and its research is responsible for over 17 per cent of the 100 leading
products in world sales (Brech and Sharp, 1984). Royalty receipts earned
abroad on its technology, which in the 1960s were less than payments to
foreigners (as Britain had a deficit on its technological balance of payments
with the United States), now clearly exceed payments.
    Firms from all the other high capacity countries carry out R&D in the
United Kingdom, and the quality of British science appears to be the
predominant factor. For their part, UK MNEs have helped to contribute to
the standards of indigenous R&D facilities through their own global

JOHN CANTWELL 141

research programme. The top four British firms have all been rising in world pharmaceutical company rankings since the early 1970s. The major UK firms, like those from West Germany, not only carry out substantial R&D outside their home territory, but are also able to draw on a larger and more diversified technological experience than is available to smaller firms, thus increasing their capacity to innovate.

*The role of the UK affiliates of US MNEs.* The investments of US MNEs in the United Kingdom since the 1960s have exercised a favourable competitive influence (Lake, 1976), and are largely responsible for helping to get a virtuous circle in the industry under way. Research and production in Britain has constituted an important part of the total operations of US multinationals, which have tended to introduce new chemical entities (which compete in the production of the same drug or of different drugs with the same therapeutic effects) into the United Kingdom earlier than in the United States. In this way they have often led technological development in Britain. This has had the effect of inducing a competitive response on the part of indigenous firms, who had the scientific resources needed to increase their own rate of innovation. The R&D of local UK firms has risen tremendously, and the research environment thereby created has encouraged the entry of other European MNEs. The overall technological capacity located in Britain, and the share of research intensive production in the UK total, have been enlarged accordingly.

*The consequences of EC membership.* It has been noted above that British membership of the EC may have significant influence on its ability to increase its share of European production and trade, especially relative to the Netherlands and West Germany. However, the feeling remains that this effect, predicted by the model of cumulative causation, is still weak by comparison to what it might have been in another industry. This is a result of the greater national separation of national markets in pharmaceutical products, and the comparatively limited importance of trade relative to production. Within the EC there are various barriers to trade which, to a substantial extent, divide the Community into separate national markets. This inhibits the ability of MNEs to rationalize the production of their European networks, despite the international co-ordination of their research activity. The two most important barriers are government controls over the registration of new products, and controls over prices (Burstall and Senior, 1984).

Contrary to what one would normally expect in a customs union, the price of pharmaceutical products diverges widely between EC countries. Drugs are expensive in West Germany, the Netherlands and Denmark, less expensive in the United Kingdom and Ireland, and cheap in France, Italy and Belgium. This in itself does not prevent trade, but companies must negotiate the prices at which they trade (which need bear no relationship to domestic prices, or indeed to the prices at which they are exporting to other countries). Governments have proved to be willing to treat companies selling from local production facilities more favourably in agreeing to higher prices and profit margins. Sometimes, as in France, this is also linked to a requirement to carry out some minimum level of local research.

As a result of the weaker role of trade by comparison with other industries in the EC, the increase in the research intensity of UK production has not been reflected in as large an improvement in her trade performance as might otherwise have been expected. Nevertheless, in 1980, 47 per cent of the world trade in final drugs, and 35 per cent of the trade in intermediates or active ingredients took place within Europe (Burstall and Senior, 1984). That the United Kingdom has the largest trade surplus of any EC country is, thus, still an impressive record.

*The composition of UK output.* Allied to the growth of the research base that supports UK production has been an upgrading in the quality of output. The best evidence of the research intensity of production in the two highest capacity European countries within the EC, is that it is only Britain and West Germany which are clearly net exporters of intermediates or active ingredients.

The strengths of the British and West German pharmaceutical industries, though, are rather different. The traditions of technological accumulation in West Germany have emphasized chemical research, from which work on pharmaceuticals has been a by-product. By contrast, the comparative advantage of the United Kingdom lies in food products and biological research, and R&D in pharmaceuticals has often been allied to this. The United Kingdom is a centre for scientific work in molecular biology, and has clear potential in the new fields of biotechnology. The shift in emphasis within the pharmaceutical industry in recent years, away from chemical and towards biological research, has been an important element in the success of Britain vis-à-vis West Germany in attracting the R&D of foreign MNEs.

*The European strategies of MNEs.* MNEs have achieved a greater integration of their European research programmes than of their European production. This having been said, while the local pharmaceutical production of foreign owned affiliates exceeds imports in the case of Britain and West Germany, France and Italy, imports are greater for the Netherlands and Belgium. The affiliates of American and Swiss companies are particularly prone to export from the former group of countries. Relative to the industry norm, the European affiliates of US MNEs have a high propensity to export (Burstall, Dunning and Lake, 1981).

So far as integration has taken place, the European market tends to be sub-divided into groups of countries. Due to accepted social customs and medical traditions, the pattern of drug consumption is similar in Britain, the Netherlands, Denmark and Ireland, and follows a different but similar pattern in France, Italy, Belgium and Greece (Burstall and Senior, 1984). Through its research, production and exports, the United Kingdom has consequently become a centre for servicing a particular segment of EC countries, whose medical practices and preferences most resemble its own. By comparison to the pharmaceutical industry outside the EC, the integration of MNE operations has made more ground in Europe than elsewhere, to the benefit of the more dynamic research based economies such as the United Kingdom.

## Motor Vehicles

*The specialization of innovation in Europe.* In recent years the centre of innovation in the motor vehicle industry has been Japan. Europe retains some advantage in product technology while the main Japanese strength lies in process technology. Labour productivity in the sector has been rising roughly twice as fast in Japan as in Europe. Static scale economies associated with rising production levels have played their part in this, but dynamic scale economies through innovation have led the way. This has been accomplished through the automation of production based on electronics and robotics technologies, and the better co-ordination of the various stages of production through new managerial and organizational techniques.

Much of this innovation has depended upon close links with the component suppliers that remain independent in Japan, and whose subcontracted work accounts for a much higher proportion of value added than is the case in Europe. The close but flexible arrangements with suppliers has faciliated production planning (the 'just in time system'), production efficiency, product development (through the upstream and downstream diffusion of technology), and quality control (OECD, 1983). The rate of innovation in the European motor vehicle sector, although being overtaken by the Japanese, did not slow down as much as in the United States. However, with the increasing importance of electronics related technologies, America may be able to put a stop to its decline relative to Europe, even if slipping still further behind the productivity growth of Japanese industry. Most of the largest motor vehicle producers have now established links with electronics companies who supply them with micro-processors to monitor and control car functions.

Within Europe, in line with the expectations of the model of cumulative causation, the technologically strong West German industry has forged ahead at the expense of the technologically weak United Kingdom. Table 4 shows that the West German share of EC company patenting in the United States rose from just over 40 per cent in the 1960s to nearly 60 per cent by the early 1980s. The UK share of motor vehicle patents granted to EC firms in

144            THE REORGANISATION OF EUROPEAN INDUSTRIES

Table 4

*The share of patents granted in the US in motor vehicles and motor vehicle equipment to residents of the 6 largest EC countries, 1963–83 (%)*

|                    | 1963–69 | 1977–83 |
|--------------------|---------|---------|
| Germany            | 43.1    | 58.1    |
| UK                 | 28.9    | 18.9    |
| France             | 21.6    | 15.6    |
| Italy              | 4.1     | 5.1     |
| Netherlands        | 1.4     | 1.7     |
| Belgium            | 0.9     | 0.7     |
| Total (6 countries)| 100.0   | 100.0   |

*Source*: US Office of Technology Assessment and Forecast, unpublished data.

the United States fell back by 10 per cent. The French vehicle producers dropped below 20 per cent of European patenting as well, but by 1983 they had recovered some of their lost ground, and their share of R&D expenditure in the EC did not fall at all (see Jones, 1983). The Italian industry has survived in technological competition, due to Fiat's strength in automated process technology through its subsidiary Comau and its links with the traditionally strong Italian machine tool industry.

*National shares of EC production and exports.* The European country with the strongest research record, West Germany, occupies first place in its shares of EC production and exports. Its share of car production has risen since 1960, and it has also increased its substantial trade surplus (Tables 5 and 6). At the other extreme in the process of cumulative causation, the declining research

Table 5

*The share of production of passenger cars of the 6 largest EC countries, 1960–82 (%)*

|                    | 1960  | 1982  |
|--------------------|-------|-------|
| Germany            | 35.2  | 38.5  |
| France             | 22.8  | 28.5  |
| Italy              | 11.6  | 13.3  |
| Belgium            | 3.8   | 9.7   |
| UK                 | 26.2  | 9.1   |
| Netherlands        | 0.4   | 0.9   |
| Total (6 countries)| 100.0 | 100.0 |

*Source*: Dicken (1986).

JOHN CANTWELL 145

Table 6

*The share of passenger car exports and the trade balance of the major EC producing countries,*
*1963–82*

| | Export Share 1963, % | Export Share 1982, % | Trade Balance 1963, '000 | Trade Balance 1982, '000 |
|---|---|---|---|---|
| Germany | 43.4 | 41.3 | 1,084 | 1,354 |
| France | 18.9 | 27.6 | 388 | 474 |
| Belgium | 5.2 | 17.0 | 90 | 440 |
| Italy | 10.4 | 8.2 | 101 | −468 |
| UK | 22.0 | 5.9 | 568 | −630 |
| Total (5 countries) | 100.0 | 100.0 | 2,231 | 1,170 |

*Source*: Dicken (1986).

effort of the UK motor vehicle sector is reflected in a catastrophic fall in its share of EC production, from 26 per cent in 1960 to 9 per cent in 1982 (even without considering the rise in output from Spain). This has been associated with a move from a once healthy trade surplus to a sizeable trade deficit.

The national shares of total European production and trade in the industry are of course also heavily influenced by the location of assembly type activity. Within the EC, Belgium has gained in production and trade since the early 1960s for precisely this reason.

The sector is no longer the powerful force for industrial growth that it once was. Since the early 1970s, motor vehicle output has been rising more slowly than GDP in West Germany and France, and has actually fallen in Britain and Italy (Jones, 1981). Between 1974 and 1984, 150,000 jobs were lost in the UK motor vehicles industry, 130,000 in Italy, and 55,000 in France (Dicken, 1986). In Germany, domestic employment has recovered after a fall in the mid-1970s, through the increasing research strength of the German car companies (Volkswagen and Daimler Benz in co-operation with one another), and the improved links with their component suppliers including the electronics component manufacturer Bosch.

*The local research base of UK production.* The local research base of UK production has been disastrously weakened as foreign MNEs have moved research away from the United Kingdom, and British Leyland has lost market share so rapidly that it has been unable to sustain substantial and diversified technological activity. At a time when the intensity of technological competition has been rising, Britain has not only seen its share of R&D fall, but even the absolute level of R&D expenditure in real terms has been falling (OECD, 1983). The British industry suffers from shortages of the skilled labour that it needs, and is now regarded as a low wage, low productivity location for European production.

146       THE REORGANISATION OF EUROPEAN INDUSTRIES

Ford has relied on research in West Germany and the United States, while British Leyland's R&D has been very low. In 1974 Ford's labour productivity in Britain was the highest of any local company (with British Leyland the lowest), but even this was below that of every other European producer except Fiat (Church, 1986). It is, consequently, hardly surprising that, with the rationalization of European production in Europe in the 1970s, between 1973–83 the local content of Ford's UK cars fell from 88 per cent to 22 per cent, and those of Vauxhall from 98 per cent to 22 per cent (Jones, 1985). Whereas in 1973 US MNEs in Britain had net exports of 200,000 cars, by 1984 they had net imports of 350,000 as British production was cut back and redirected to the assembly and export of kits (Church, 1986).

At the same time as General Motors reduced its UK (Vauxhall) production and removed it from the export market, it built a major new engine plant in Austria to supply global operations, and a new automatic transmission plant in Germany (Dicken, 1986).

*The role of the UK affiliates of US MNEs.* In the UK motor vehicle industry foreign MNEs and especially US MNEs have a major role, unlike in France or Italy where foreign MNEs have no local production, or West Germany where a balance has been maintained between domestic and foreign firms. Around half of Ford's global production is in Europe (Dicken, 1986), and Ford Europe was formed in 1967 within which the significance of British operations has been gradually reduced. About a quarter of General Motors' world production is in Europe, and the West German subsidiary Opel accounts for nearly 90 per cent of this (Dicken, 1986), with, again, production slipping slowly away from the United Kingdom.

British Leyland has been less and less able to compete with the integrated European operations of US MNEs and imports from the innovative Japanese. Since the late 1960s when the rationalization of MNE production in Europe began, the investments of MNEs have had an anti-competitive effect on the only major surviving British producer. British Leyland has also suffered from having no international investments of its own, and indeed, as part of its decline, selling off its Spanish and Italian affiliates.

*The consequences of EC membership.* After the UK entered the EC in 1973, the affiliates of foreign MNEs increased their degree of integration with their European networks, leading indigenous producers to face up to more effective competition. The increased pressure on British Leyland was due partly to increased imports of cars, partly to the greater overall European strength of MNE networks through an improved division of labour, and partly a result of the stronger long-run bargaining position that MNEs thereby gained with the UK labour force (by making clear the locational mobility of industry within Europe). Free trading arrangements within the EC gave MNEs far greater flexibility to take advantage of static scale economies through increased specialization, with each plant responsible for a certain stage of production of European cars.[3] It also meant that production was likely to shift away from low productivity locations such as the United Kingdom.

Church (1986) concludes that whereas Ford's relative strength and its historical base in the United Kingdom checked Britain's decline in the industry up until the mid-1960s, the formation of Ford Europe in 1967 and Britain's entry into the EC reversed this role. The advent of global competition, which was spurred on in Europe by the existence and enlargement of the EC, and the move towards international sourcing by MNEs, meant that indigenous UK enterprise was driven out of markets. After integration into Europe, the strength of Ford in the UK market had an adverse effect on British output and employment, both directly as operations shifted to continental Europe and indirectly as British car firms were undermined.

British firms were further opened up to increased competition from West German and French firms, and, without being MNEs themselves, their survival was threatened by the gradual weakening of their home base. Whereas West German and French companies had sufficiently similar levels of strength that the creation of the EC did not seriously disturb their stable oligopolistic division of markets, British firms were sufficiently weaker than their rivals that, on UK entry, their market shares came under attack (see Cowling, 1985, who also develops his ideas in the context of cumulative causation).

*The composition of UK output.* The proportion of UK output in the motor vehicle sector that is research intensive is relatively low and has declined for two reasons. Firstly, as already described, US MNEs have moved research and related production away from Britain to other locations in Europe. Secondly, the UK component suppliers, who are more productive and innovative than the car producers, have shifted production abroad rapidly since the mid-1970s in response to the decline in domestic demand due to the demise of British Leyland and the switch of production by US MNEs. Vertical integration in the UK motor vehicle sector is much lower than is typical in Europe, but without the kind of innovative linkages between companies that exist in Japan. The British component suppliers have established international production elsewhere in the EC and in the United States to exploit their particular advantage in front wheel drive technology which US car firms have been keen to introduce (Jones, 1981).

The other aspect of the contraction of UK research is that innovation in the industry in Britain has taken a form that is not primarily research linked.

---

[3]For a discussion of intra-firm trade, specialization and scale economies in the European motor vehicle industry see Foreman-Peck (1986).

148            THE REORGANISATION OF EUROPEAN INDUSTRIES

It is an organizational rather than a scientific type of innovation that is associated with a steady tightening of managerial control (Willman and Winch, 1985). British Leyland have attempted to raise productivity and profits through the use of bonus incentive payments and the weakening of trade union organization.

*The European strategies of MNEs.* Whereas General Motors has developed a global strategy grounded on research and production in the United States, Ford is dependent upon its integrated research in West Germany and production in Europe. These US firms have gone furthest in the direction of the integrated production of a 'world car', with the Japanese at the other end of the spectrum relying on close relationships with local component suppliers in each production location (OECD, 1983). Recently, the US companies have retreated a little from the 'world car' concept, but integration remains strong within Europe, to the benefit of West Germany as a research intensive production base.

The Ford Fiesta was conceived of as a 'European car', a standardized model range for the European market with the production of components and vehicles allocated to plants in different European countries and integrated through trade. Ford's share of the British market rose from the early 1970s onwards (for the first time since the early 1950s), and this was entirely attributable to an increase in tied imports, with its UK exports tailing right off (Church, 1986). The decline in the British share of EC car exports, from 22 per cent in 1963 to under 6 per cent in 1983 (Table 6) is largely attributable to the strategic decision of foreign MNEs operating in the United Kingdom (Ford, General Motors and Peugeot) to service export markets from other production sites. The newly rationalized structure of the European industry has worked to the disadvantage of the United Kingdom.

4. PROSPECTS FOR THE LOCATION OF JAPANESE INVESTMENT IN EUROPE, AND HOW ITS IMPACT IS LIKELY TO VARY ACROSS SECTORS

Japanese investment in Europe, although still small by the standards of US MNEs, has been rising rapidly in the last ten years.[4] This seems likely to continue, in part as a means of tapping into European innovation in those sectors in which the MNEs of both regions are particularly strong, thus enhancing global competition (Cantwell, 1986). It is also, of course, a response to trade barriers against Japanese imports, and in some cases (such as the motor vehicle industry) a response to overtures to establish more co-operative arrangements with European firms.

The tendency of the European research and production of US MNEs to help set in motion a process of cumulative causation in the EC was

[4]For a survey of the rise of Japanese investment in the UK and its early impact see Dunning (1986).

illustrated in the previous section. For any EC country, the US MNE affiliate presence and its integration into a European network may contribute to a virtuous circle in some sectors and a vicious circle in others, depending upon the initial technological capacity of local enterprise.

The same general rules are likely to apply when considering the future impact of a growth in the European investment of Japanese MNEs. In a healthy local industry it will act as a beneficial competitive stimulus, while in a declining sector it is liable to further undercut local research. However, since there are differences in the industrial characteristics of US and Japanese technological strengths (vis-à-vis Europe), the impact of Japanese MNEs on the reorganization of European industries is likely to show a different pattern of sectoral variation.

When looking at US investment in Europe, the pharmaceutical and motor vehicle sectors are interesting case studies since they are examples of industries in which the major US and European firms have a balance of technological strengths. The equivalent cases for Japanese investments will involve other industries; compared to the leading European and US firms, Japan is relatively strong in motor vehicles and weak in pharmaceuticals (although she has made some advances in biotechnology).

In a case such as motor vehicles, research is likely to remain quite highly centralized in the Japanese parent companies, while European production is of an import substituting kind aimed at supplying the European market at lower tariff and transport costs. Being more akin to the assembly type than research intensive production, affiliates are more likely to be located in countries which have some reserves of skilled labour, infrastructure, and adaptable component suppliers, rather than in (higher wage) centres of research activity. So far, Japanese car companies have been attracted to the United Kingdom and Spain rather than West Germany as export platforms for EC markets. In the medium and longer term this may have positive effects on production and employment in those host countries, but it is not likely to lead to the creation or return of a fundamental research capacity in the sector.

In dealing with specific cases such as pharmaceuticals or motor vehicles the model of cumulative causation needs some refinement to accommodate real world circumstances such as government regulation of an industry. It is, however, a powerful explanatory device when examining the dynamics of the restructuring of European industries by MNEs operating in the EC.

## REFERENCES

Bandera, V. and White, J. (1968), "US direct investments and domestic markets in Europe", *Economia Internazionale*, Vol. 21, No. 1, February, pp. 117–133.

Brech, M. and Sharp, M. (1984), *Inward Investment: Policy Options for the United Kingdom* (London: Routledge and Kegan Paul).

150        THE REORGANISATION OF EUROPEAN INDUSTRIES

Burstall, M. L. and Dunning, J. H. (1985), "International Investment in innovation", in Wells, N. E. J. (Ed.), *Pharmaceuticals Among the Sunrise Industries* (London: Croom Helm), pp. 185–197.

Burstall, M. L., Dunning, J. H. and Lake, A. (1981), *Multinational Enterprises, Governments and Technology: The Pharmaceutical Industry* (Paris: OECD).

Burstall, M. L. and Senior, I. (1984), *The Pharmaceutical Industry of the European Community: Concentration, Competition and Competitive Strength*, Report submitted to the Commission of the European Communities, June.

Cantwell, J. A. (1986), "Technological competition and intra-industry production in Europe", *University of Reading Discussion Paper in International Investment and Business Studies*, No. 106.

Cantwell, J. A. (1988), *Technological Innovation and Multinational Corporations* (Oxford: Basil Blackwell), forthcoming.

Carlsson, B. (1985), "Reflections on 'Industrial Dynamics': the challenges ahead", presidential address to the Annual Conference of the European Association for Research in Industrial Economics, Cambridge, September.

Church, R. (1986), "The effects of American multinationals on the British motor industry: 1911–83", in Teichova, A., Lévy-Leboyer, M., and Nussbaum, H. (Eds.), *Multinational Enterprise in Historical Perspective* (Cambridge: Cambridge University Press), pp. 116–130.

Cowling, K. (1985), "The internationalization of production and deindustrialization", *Warwick Economic Research Paper* No. 256, February.

Dicken, P. (1986), *Global Shift: Industrial Change in a Turbulent World* (London: Harper and Row).

Dosi, G. (1983), "Technological paradigms and technological trajectories", in Freeman, C. (Ed.), *Long Waves in the World Economy* (London: Butterworths), pp. 78–101.

Dunning, J. H. (1986), *Japanese Participation in UK Manufacturing Industry* (London: Croom Helm).

Dunning, J. H. and Cantwell, J. A. (1982), "Inward direct investment from the US and Europe's technological competitiveness", *University of Reading Discussion Paper in International Investment and Business Studies* No. 65, September.

Dunning, J. H. and Cantwell, J. A. (1988), "The changing role of multinational enterprises in the international creation, transfer and diffusion of technology", in Arcangeli, F., David, P. A. and Dosi, G. (Eds.), *Technology Diffusion and Economic Growth: International and National Policy Perspectives* (Oxford: Oxford University Press), forthcoming.

Foreman-Peck, J. (1986), "The motor industry", in Casson, M. C. *et al, Multinationals and World Trade: Vertical Integration and the Division of Labour in World Industries* (London: Allen and Unwin), pp. 141–173.

Hymer, S. (1975), "The multinational corporation and the law of uneven development", in Radice, H. (Ed.), *International Firms and Modern Imperialism* (Harmondsworth: Penguin Books), pp. 37–62.

Hymer, S. (1976), *The International Operations of National Firms: A Study of Direct Investment* (Cambridge: Mass.: MIT Press).

Jones, D. T. (1981), *Maturity and Crisis in the European Car Industry: Structural Change and Public Policy*, Brighton: University of Sussex European Research Centre Paper No. 8.

Jones, D. T. (1983), "Technology and the UK automobile industry", *Lloyds Bank Review*, No. 148, April, pp. 14–27.

Jones, D. T. (1985), "The import threat to the UK car industry", *University of Sussex Science Policy Research Unit Research Report*.

Kaldor, N. (1985), *Economics Without Equilibrium* (Cardiff: University College Cardiff Press).

Knickerbocker, F. T. (1976), "Market structure and market power consequences of foreign direct investment by multinational companies", *Center for Multinational Studies Occasional Paper* No. 8, Washington.

Lake, A. (1976), "Foreign competition and the UK pharmaceutical industry", *National*

*Bureau of Economic Research Working Paper* No. 155, November.

Lunn, J. (1980), "Determinants of US direct investment in the EEC: further evidence", *European Economic Review*, Vol. 13, No. 1, January, pp. 93–101.

Lunn, J. (1983), "Determinants of US direct investment in the EEC: revisited again", *European Economic Review*, Vol. 21, No. 3, May, pp. 391–393.

Myrdal, G. (1957), *Economic Theory and Underdeveloped Regions* (London: Duckworth).

OECD (1983), *Long-Term Outlook for the World Automobile Industry* (Paris: OECD).

Pelkmans, J. (1984), *Market Integration in the European Community* (The Hague: Martinus Nijhoff).

Rigoni, R., Griffiths, A. and Laing, W. (1985), "Pharmaceutical multinationals: polemics, perceptions and paradoxes", *IRM Multinational Report* No. 3, January–March (Chichester: John Wiley and Sons).

Scaperlanda, A. E. and Balough, R. S. (1983), "Determinants of US direct investment in the EEC: revisited", *European Economic Review*, Vol. 21, No. 3, May, pp. 381–390.

Scaperlanda, A. E. and Mauer, L. J. (1969), "The determinants of US direct investment in the EEC", *American Economic Review*, Vol. 59, No. 3, September, pp. 558–568.

Schmitz, A. and Bieri, J. (1972), "EEC tariffs and US direct investment", *European Economic Review*, Vol. 3, pp. 259–270.

Simões, V. C. (1985), "Portugal", in Dunning, J. H. (Ed.), *Multinational Enterprises, Economic Structure and International Competitiveness* (Chichester: John Wiley and Sons), pp. 337–378.

Taveira, E. M. F. (1986), "Portugal's accession to the EEC and its impact on foreign direct investment", *University of Reading Discussion Paper in International Investment and Business Studies* No. 92, January.

Willman, P. and Winch, G. (1985), *Innovation and Management Control: Labour Relations at BL Cars* (Cambridge: Cambridge University Press).

Yannopoulos, G. N. (1986), "Patterns of response to EC tariff preferences: an empirical investigation of non-ACP associates", *University of Reading Discussion Paper in Economics* No. 174, June.

# Part IX
# Marketing,
# Implicit Contracts,
# and the Service Sector

# [25]

## 11

# Internationalisation in Industrial Systems — A Network Approach

Jon Johanson and Lars-Gunnar Mattsson

### 11.1 INTRODUCTION

The theme of the book suggests that international interdependence between firms and within industries is of great and increasing importance. Analyses of international trade, international investments, industrial organisation and international business behaviour attempt to describe, explain and give advice about these interdependencies. The theoretical bases and the level of aggregation of such analyses are naturally quite varied.

In this chapter we discuss explanations of internationalisation of industrial firms with the aid of a model that describes industrial markets as networks of relationships between firms. The reason for this exercise is a belief that the network model, being superior to some other models of 'markets', makes it possible to consider some important interdependencies and development processes on international markets. The models that we have selected for some comparative analyses are the transaction cost based 'theory of internalisation' for multinational enterprise and the 'Uppsala Internationalization Process Model' emphasising experiential learning and gradual commitments. While the former is a dominating theoretical explanation of multinational enterprise (Buckley and Casson, 1976), the latter seems to be the most cited explanation of a firm's foreign market selection and mode of international resource transfer over time (Bilkey, 1978; Johanson and Vahlne, 1977).

We will first present some empirical data in support of some basic assumptions of the network model. We will then describe this model, commenting especially on the investment nature of marketing activities. Internationalisation of the firm and of the network is also given a conceptual interpretation. We are

287

JON JOHANSON & LARS-GUNNAR MATTSSON

then in a position to analyse four cases concerning internationalisation of the firm and of the network: The Early
Starter, The Lonely International, The Late Starter, and The
International Among Others. Finally, we will comment on some
research issues raised by our analysis.


## 11.2  CUSTOMER–SUPPLIER RELATIONSHIPS IN
## INDUSTRIAL MARKETS: SOME EMPIRICAL FINDINGS

A number of studies in industrial marketing and purchasing
have demonstrated the existence of long-term relationships
between suppliers and customers in industrial markets (e.g.
Blois 1972; Ford, 1978; Guillet de Monthoux, 1975; Håkansson & Östberg, 1975; Levitt, 1983; Wind, 1970). It has also
been emphasised by a leading marketing scholar that 'for strategic purposes, the central focus of industrial marketing should
not be on products or on markets, broadly defined, but on
buyer-seller relationships' (Webster 1979: 50). Such relationships have also been noted in studies of contractual relations
(Macneil, 1978; Williamson, 1979) and in studies of technical
development (von Hippel, 1978).
     In an extensive international research project, industrial
customer-supplier relationships were investigated. Interviews
were made with industrial suppliers in Germany, France,
Britain, and Sweden about the relations to their most important
customers in the four countries and in Italy. Interviews were
conducted with managers who had personal experience of the
customers (Håkansson, 1982). Business transactions with
important customers generally took place within well-
established relationships. The average age of the 300 relations
investigated was around 13 years (Hallén, 1986). The relationships were important to the two parties involved. In export
relationships the suppliers were 'main supplier' — in the sense
that they provided at least half of the customer's needs for the
products concerned — in about half of the cases. In the domestic relationships the suppliers were more often main suppliers —
in around 80 per cent of the relationships.
     The customers were also important to the suppliers. In the
German sub-sample in which data about the customer's share of
the supplier's sales are available, the average share of the
customers investigated was 5.5 per cent. If we (somewhat

INTERNATIONALISATION IN INDUSTRIAL SYSTEMS

arbitrarily) define a relationship as important to the customer if the supplier provides at least half of the need, and important to the supplier if the customer purchases at least 1 per cent of the supplier's sales, then 35 per cent of the relationships are classified as mutually important, 25 per cent as important to the supplier only, 18 per cent as important to the customer only, and 22 per cent as not important.

One of the reasons for the existence of long-term relationships is that suppliers and customers need extensive knowledge about each other if they are to carry on important business with each other. They need knowledge not only about price and quality, which may be very complex and difficult to determine; they also need knowledge about deliveries and a number of services before, during and after delivery. Much of that knowledge can in fact only be gained after transactions have taken place. Besides, they need knowledge about each others' resources, organisation and development possibilities. Knowledge about all these issues is seldom concentrated in one person in the firms. Not only marketers and purchasers, but also specialists in manufacturing, design, development, quality control, service, finance, and so on may take part in the information exchange between the companies. Contacts on several levels in the organisational hierarchies may be required. Such contacts may include personnel on the shop floor, top management and, of course, middle and lower management. The average total number of interacting persons in the relationships is between seven and eight from each party. Such contacts take time to establish: it takes time to learn which persons in a company possess certain types of knowledge, and which have the potentiality to influence certain conditions. On many occasions direct experience is the only possible way to learn so much about each other that the information exchange between the parties works efficiently. Such experiences certainly take time to acquire, and the parties invest in knowledge about each other.

Around 40 per cent of the relationships include contacts on the general management level. Specialists from manufacturing are involved on the customer side in 60-70 per cent of the relationships. Specialists on design and development take part in about 50 per cent of the relationships, and in both cases the supplier side is most involved. On the whole there are quite complex contact and interaction patterns in the relationships

JON JOHANSON & LARS-GUNNAR MATTSSON

between the firms. Another aspect of the relationships is that significant business transactions require that the parties have confidence in each others' ability and willingness to fulfil their commitments. It takes time and effort to build such levels of confidence. The perceived social distance to the customers indicates the investments in confidence in the relationships. In 60-70 per cent of the relationships the respondent considered the relation as involving 'close personal relations' or 'friendly business relations' rather than more 'formal business relations'. Evidently these important relationships are also usually rather close, implying that they result from investments in the relationships.

Suppliers and customers are also often linked to each other through various types of technical and administrative arrangements. They may adapt products, processes, scheduling, delivery routines and logistical systems to the needs and capabilities of the specific counterpart. In the German sub-sample some data are available about this type of investment in customer-supplier relationships. In the eight German customer relationships investigated, on average 2.5 inter-firm production system adaptations were made. In almost every relationship some adaptation of this kind was made. The adaptations were somewhat more common in domestic than they were in export relationships.

Against the background of this type of evidence, we assume that firms in industrial markets are linked to each other through long-lasting relationships. The parties in the relationships are important to each other; they establish and develop complex, inter-firm information channels, and they also develop social and technical bonds with each other. Generally, domestic relationships seem to be more developed and stronger than export relationships. However, many export relationships are also important and long-lasting. We assume that the relationships are important for the functioning of industrial markets and for the market strategies of industrial firms.

## 11.3 MARKETS AS NETWORKS — A GENERAL DESCRIPTION

The network approach in the form described in this section has been developed by a group of Swedish researchers whose back-

INTERNATIONALISATION IN INDUSTRIAL SYSTEMS

ground is research on distribution *systems*, internationalisation *processes* of industrial firms, and industrial purchasing and marketing behaviour as *interaction* between firms (Mattsson (1985) describes this background). The approach is developed in a general way in Hägg and Johanson (1982) and Hammarkvist, Håkansson and Mattsson (1982). This section builds on those publications, and on Johanson and Mattsson (1985, 1986).

The industrial system is composed of firms engaged in production, distribution and use of goods and services. We describe this system as a network of relationships between the firms. There is a division of work in the network which means that the firms are dependent on each other, and their activities therefore need to be co-ordinated. Co-ordination is not brought about through a central plan or an organisational hierarchy, nor does it take place through the price mechanism as in the traditional market model. Instead, co-ordination occurs through interaction between firms in the network, where price is just one of several influencing conditions (cf. Lindblom, 1977). The firms are free to choose counterparts and thus 'market forces' are at play. To gain access to external resources and make it possible to sell products, however, exchange *relationships* have to be established with other firms. Such relationships take time and effort to establish and develop, processes which constrain the firms' possibilities to change counterparts. The need for adjustments between the interdependent firms in terms of the quantity and quality of goods and services exchanged, and the timing of such exchange, call for more or less explicit co-ordination through joint planning, or through power exercised by one party over the other. Each firm in the network has relationships with customers, distributors, suppliers, and so on (and sometimes also directly with competitors), as well as indirect relations via those firms with suppliers' suppliers, customers' customers, competitors, and so on.

The networks are stable *and* changing. Individual business transactions between firms usually take place within the framework of established relationships. Evidently, some new relationships are occasionally established and some old relationships are disrupted for some reason (e.g. competitive activities), but most exchanges take place within earlier existing relationships. However, those existing relationships are continually changing through activities in connection with transactions made within

291

JON JOHANSON & LARS-GUNNAR MATTSSON

the relationship. Efforts are made to maintain, develop, change and sometimes disrupt the relationships. As an aspect of those relationships, *bonds* of various kinds are developed between the firms. We distinguish here between technical, planning, knowledge, social, economic, and legal bonds. These bonds can be exemplified by, respectively, product and process adjustments, logistical co-ordination, knowledge about the counterpart, personal confidence and liking, special credit agreements, and long-term contracts.

We stress complementarity in the network. Of course, there are also important competitive relations. Other firms want to obtain access to specific exchange possibilities either as sellers or as buyers, and co-operating firms also have partially conflicting objectives. The relationships imply that there are *specific inter-firm dependence relations* which are of a different character compared with the general dependence relations to the market in the traditional market model. A firm has direct and specific dependence relations to those firms with which it has exchange relationships. It has indirect and specific dependence relations with those firms with which its direct counterparts have exchange relationships — that is, the other firms operating in the network in which it is engaged. Because of the network of relationships the firms operate in a complex system of specific dependence relations which is difficult to survey.

To become established in a new market — that is, a network which is new to the firm — it has to build relationships which are new both to itself and its counterparts. This is sometimes done by breaking old, existing relationships, and sometimes by adding a relationship to already-existing ones. Initiatives can be taken both by the seller and by the buyer. A supplier can become established in a network which is new to the firm, because a buying firm takes the initiative.

This model of industrial markets implies that the firm's activities in industrial markets are *cumulative processes* in which relationships are continually established, maintained, developed, and broken in order to give satisfactory, short-term economic return, and to create positions in the network, securing the long-term survival and development of the firm. Through the activities in the network, the firm develops relationships which secure its access to important resources and the sale of its products and services.

Because of the cumulative nature of the market activities, the

292

market *position* is an important concept. At each point in time the firm has certain positions in the network which characterise its relations to other firms. These positions are a result of earlier activities in the network both by the firm and by other firms, and constitute the base which defines the development possibilities and constraints of the firm in the network. (see Mattsson (1985) for an analysis of the position concept and its use in a discussion of market strategies.) We distinguish here between *micro-positions* and *macro-positions*. A micro-position refers to the relationship with a specific individual counterpart: A macro-position refers to the relations to a network as a whole or to a specific section of it. A micro-position is characterised by:

(1) the role the firm has for the other firm:
(2) its importance to the other firm; and
(3) the strength of the relationship with the other firm.

A macro-position is characterised by:

(1) the identity of the other firms with which the firm has direct relationships and indirect relations in the network;
(2) the role of the firm in the network;
(3) the importance of the firm in the network; and
(4) the strength of the relationships with the other firms.

The macro-positions are also affected by the interdependencies in the whole network as well as by the complementarity of the micro-positions in the network. Thus, in the context of the whole network, the macro-position is not an aggregation of micro-positions.

*Example: Firm A's micro-position in relation to firm B.* (1) It is a secondary supplier of fine paper and of knowhow about printing processes. (2) The sales volume is 100, A's share of B's purchases of fine paper is 30 per cent and A is an important source of technical information. (3) The knowledge bonds are strong, but social bonds are rather weak due to recent changes in personnel in both A and B.

*Example: Firm A's macro-position.* (1) Lists exist of suppliers, customers, competitors and other firms in the network to whom the firm is directly or indirectly related. (2) It has the role as a full line distributor of fine paper in southern Sweden. (3) Its market share is 50 per cent, making it the market leader. (4) It enjoys strong knowledge, planning and social bonds to its major customers, and strong economic and

JON JOHANSON & LARS-GUNNAR MATTSSON

legal bonds to its suppliers.

The positions describe the firm's relations to its industrial environment and thereby some important strategic possibilities and restrictions. All the other firms in the network have their own positions and likewise have future objectives regarding those positions. Desired changes or defence of positions thus describe important aspects of the firm's strategy. The strategies of firms can be complementary to each other, or competitive, or both. Important dimensions of the network structure are related to the set of positions of the organisations that are established there. The *degree of structuring* of the network is the extent to which positions of the organisations are interdependent. In tightly structured networks, the interdependence is high, the bonds are strong, and the positions of the firms are well defined. In loosely structured networks, the bonds are weak and the positions are less well defined.

The global industrial network can be partitioned in various ways. Delimitations can be made concerning geographical areas, products, techniques, and so on. We use the term 'net' for specifically defined sections of the total network. When the grouping is made according to national borders we distinguish between different 'national nets'. Correspondingly we refer to 'production nets' when the grouping is made on the basis of product areas. A production net contains relationships between those firms whose activities are linked to a specific product area. Thus, it is possible to distinguish a 'heavy truck net' including firms manufacturing, distributing, repairing and using heavy trucks. This heavy truck net differs from the corresponding 'industrial branch' as it also comprises firms with complementary activities, whereas the individual branch comprises firms with similar, mostly competing, activities. The firms in the net are linked to each other and have specific dependence relations to each other.

Within the framework of a product area with its production nets, different national production nets can be distinguished. Thus, in the heavy truck field we can speak of a Swedish, a Danish, a West German, an Italian, etc. heavy truck net, comprising the firms or operations in each country engaged in manufacture, distribution service and use of heavy trucks.

To sum up: we have described markets as networks of relationships between firms. The networks are stable *and* changing. Change and development processes in the networks are

INTERNATIONALISATION IN INDUSTRIAL SYSTEMS

cumulative and take time. Individual firms have positions in the networks, and those positions are developed through activities in the network and define important possibilities and constraints for present and future activities. Marketing activities in networks serve to establish, maintain, develop and sometimes break relationships, to determine exchange conditions and to handle the actual exchange. Thus, important aspects of market analyses have to do with the present characteristics of the positions, the relations and their development patterns, in relevant networks for the firm. Important marketing problems for both management and for researchers are related to *investments*, since activities are cumulative; to *timing* of activities, because of interdependencies in the network; to *internal coordination* of activities, since 'all' the firm's resources are involved in the exchange and since the micro-positions are interdependent; and to *co-operation* with counterparts, since activities are complementary.

## 11.4 INVESTMENTS IN NETWORKS

Investments are processes in which resources are committed to create, build or acquire assets which can be used in the future, assets which can be tangible or intangible. Examples of the former are plants and machinery, while examples of the latter are production and marketing knowledge, and proprietary rights to brand names. We call these assets *internal assets*: they are controlled by the firm and are used to carry out production, marketing, development and other activities.

A basic assumption in the network model is that the individual firm is dependent on resources controlled by other firms. The firm gets access to these external resources through its network positions. Since the development of positions takes time and effort, and since the present positions define opportunities and restrictions for the future strategic development of the firm, we look at the firm's positions in the network as partially controlled, intangible '*market assets*'. Market assets generate revenues for the firm and serve to give the firm access to other firms' internal assets. Because of the interdependencies between firms, the use of the asset in one firm is dependent on the use of other firms' assets. Thus, in addition the investment processes, including their consequences, are interdependent in the

JON JOHANSON & LARS-GUNNAR MATTSSON

network. (The reasoning in this section is developed at greater length in Johanson and Mattsson, 1985.)

## 11.5 INTERNATIONALISATION ACCORDING TO THE NETWORK APPROACH

According to the network model, the internationalisation of the firm means that the firm establishes and develops positions in relation to counterparts in foreign networks. This can be achieved (1) through establishment of positions in relation to counterparts in national nets that are new to the firm, i.e. *international extension*; (2) by developing the positions and increasing resource commitments in those nets abroad in which the firm already has positions, i.e. *penetration*; and (3) by increasing co-ordination between positions in different national nets, i.e. *international integration*. The firm's degree of internationalisation informs about the extent to which the firm occupies certain positions in different national nets, and how important and integrated are those positions. International integration is an aspect of internationalisation which it seems motivated to add to the traditional extension and penetration concepts, against the background of the specific dependence relations of the network model. Since position changes mean, by definition, that relationships with other firms are changed, internationalisation will according to the network model direct attention analytically to the investments in internal assets and market assets used for exchange activities. Furthermore, the firm's positions before the internationalisation process begins are of great interest, since they indicate market assets that might influence the process.

    The network model also has consequences for the meaning of internationalisation of the market (network). A production net can be more or less internationalised. A high degree of internationalisation of a production net implies that there are many and strong relationships between the different national sections of the global production net. A low degree of internationalisation, on the other hand, means that the national nets have few relationships with each other. Internationalisation means that the number and strength of the relationships between the different parts of the global production network increase.

296

INTERNATIONALISATION IN INDUSTRIAL SYSTEMS

It can also be fruitful to distinguish between the internationalisation of production nets, implying more and stronger links between the national sections of the global production net; and the internationalisation of national nets, implying that they are becoming increasingly interconnected with other national nets. The difference is a matter of perspective: in the former case, attention is focused on a production net, in the latter on a national net. The distinction is interesting, because there may be important differences between the degree of internationalisation of different national nets. In one country the production net may be highly internationalised, whereas the corresponding net may not be very internationalised in another country. The distinction is also interesting, because in some situations internationalisation of the global production net affects all the national sections of the global production net. In other situations only some specific national nets with their production nets are internationalised. This may be the case when two or more national economies are integrated.

## 11.6 AN APPLICATION OF THE NETWORK MODEL TO ANALYSES OF THE INTERNATIONALISATION OF INDUSTRIAL FIRMS

What are the reasons explaining why firms internationalise their activities? Let us assume that the driving forces for increased internationalisation are that the firm wants to utilise and develop its resources in such a way that its long-run economic objectives are served. Firms then internationalise if that strategy increases the probability of reaching the general objectives. According to the network model, the firm's development is to an important extent dependent on its positions: it can use its market assets in its further development. Thus, the internationalisation characteristics of both the firm and of the market influence the process. The firm's market assets have a different structure if the firm is highly internationalised than they do if it is not. Furthermore, the market assets of the other firms in the network have a different structure if the market has a high or low degree of internationalisation. We will therefore make a comparative analysis of four different situations, as set out in Figure 11.1.

The analysis of the four situations thus concerns internation-

JON JOHANSON & LARS-GUNNAR MATTSSON

**Figure 11.1**: Internationalisation and the network model: the situations to be analysed

|  |  | Degree of internationalisation of the market (the production net) | |
|---|---|---|---|
|  |  | Low | High |
| Degree of internationalisation of the firm | Low | The Early Starter | The Late Starter |
|  | High | The Lonely International | The International Among Others |

alisation processes in the three dimensions, extension, penetration and integration; and how these processes can at least partially be explained by reference to the network model. After this exercise we will make a comparison with what the internalisation model and the internationalisation model offer in the same types of situations.

### 11.6.1 The Early Starter

The firm has few and rather unimportant relationships with firms abroad. The same holds for other firms in the production net. Competitors, suppliers and other firms in the domestic market, as well as in foreign markets, have few important international relationships. In this situation the firm has little knowledge about foreign markets and it cannot count upon utilising relationships in the domestic market to gain such knowledge. As ventures abroad demand resources for knowledge development and for quantitative and qualitative adjustments to counterparts in the foreign markets, the size and resourcefulness of the firm can be assumed to play an important role. The strategy, often found in empirical studies, that internationalisation begins in nearby markets using agents rather than subsidiaries can be interpreted as (1) minimisation of the need for knowledge development; (2) minimisation of the demands for adjustments; and (3) utilisation of the positions in the market occupied by already-established firms. The firm can utilise the market investments that the agent in the foreign market has made earlier, thereby reducing the need for its own investment and risk taking. As the volume sold in the foreign market increases, the increase in the market assets may justify investment in production facilities in the foreign market.

The alternative strategy, to start with an acquisition or greenfield investment, would require a greater investment in the short run, but might perhaps enhance the long-term possibilities for knowledge development and penetration in the market. This is a strategy which is possible mainly for firms which have already become large and resourceful in the home market before internationalisation.

The importance of agents and other middle men is reinforced by the presumptive buyers' lack of experience of international operations. If those buyers happened to be at all conscious of foreign supply alternatives, they would probably be somewhat reluctant. This means that the supplier must let some third party — an agent — guarantee the firm's delivery capability, or itself invest in confidence-creating activities — for example, getting 'reference customers', keeping local stocks, building a service organisation or even a manufacturing plant in the foreign market. This means further market investments.

Initiatives in the early internationalisation of the firm are often taken by counterparts — that is, distributors or users in the foreign market. Thus, the foreign counterpart uses its own market assets to establish a new firm within its own network. Whether the firm, with this introduction as base, can develop its position in the market is very uncertain, and may depend on the degree of structuring of the network and on the positions of the 'introducer'. If the 'introducer' is a leading distributor in a tightly structured network, the conditions are favourable for rapid penetration by the firm, given that the adjustments to the network are made. An obstacle may be that the demands for quantities become so high that the production capacity of the firm is too small. This may require increased engagement in the market through the establishment of production units. To reduce the risk of overcapacity, the parties may have to enter into long-term supply contracts, a process which is quite consistent with a tightly structured network.

As already discussed, the need for resource adjustment may become quite heavy in connection with a first step abroad. Such adjustments can be assumed to imply investments and it must be important to minimise the resource adjustment requirement in connection with early steps abroad. This holds for quantitative resource adjustments in connection with the capacity increases

JON JOHANSON & LARS-GUNNAR MATTSSON

which the added market may demand, and it also holds for qualitative resource adjustments which may be required because of the possibility of new market needs deviating from earlier ones. Obviously, it may be possible to complement the resources through external sources. To the extent that such resource completions are made in the domestic market, they probably imply the same type of problems. They mean commitments which may be difficult to fulfil if the foreign engagement is a failure. On the other hand, they are probably risk reductions if they can be made in the actual foreign market. It is, however, not likely that a firm which has no experience of foreign operations would have qualifications for organising resource completions in the foreign market — that is, to establish positions in relation to local suppliers.

Another problem is that some resource adjustments can be made possible by giving up control over the operations in exchange for the flexibility needed to reduce risk taking in connection with foreign ventures. Such ventures may be carried out if the old owner transfers control of the firm to someone who is able to complement the firm's resources. In the absence of internationalisation of the environment, the extension to additional foreign markets will also be determined in general by the need for knowledge development and the need to create, or use already-existing, market assets. If conditions in markets which are new to the firm are similar to the conditions in the home market (and/or in the foreign markets in which the firm began its internationalisation), then there is a greater likelihood that these markets will be the next ones. If, however, the network is tightly structured, or if there is a lack of effective 'introducers' on the foreign market that is 'next in line', from a knowledge and adjustment point of view we expect to find extension patterns with other characteristics.

As the firm becomes more internationalised, it changes from an Early Starter situation to becoming a Lonely International.

### 11.6.2 The Lonely International

How is the situation changed if the firm is highly internationalised while its market environment is not? To start with, in this situation the firm has experience of relationships with and in foreign countries. It has acquired knowledge and means to

300

handle environments which differ with respect to culture, institutions, and so on, and failures are therefore less likely. The knowledge situation is more favourable when establishing the firm in a new national net.

The second advantage is that the international firm probably has a wider repertoire of resource adjustments. The need for resource adjustments is likely to be more marginal and less difficult to handle. This holds for both quantitative and qualitative adjustments even if the former are perhaps more strongly affected by the greater size which attends internationalisation than they are by the internationalisation *per se*. In particular it is easier for the international firm to make various types of resource completions in the foreign markets. This is a special case of the general advantage of international firms, because of much greater resource combination possibilities. Note that resource combinations also include those external resources to which the positions give access. The firm which is highly internationalised may also use its market investments to get a rapid diffusion of its new products. It may use its positions partially to control the internationalisation moves of competitors, but may also involuntarily stimulate such moves (see below).

With regard to the structuring of the national nets, it can be assumed that the international firm will experience less difficulties than others in entering tightly structured nets. It already possesses good knowledge about many kinds of national markets. Further extension is not so dependent on similarities between markets as it is for the Early Starter. Experience and resources give the firm a repertoire which allows it to make the heavy market investments which are required to enter a tightly structured production net. It also has better possibilities for taking over firms with positions in the structured net or establishing relationships with such firms. It can also give its counterparts access to other national nets: for example, the international firm has greater possibilities than others to engage in barter trade.

Initiatives for furthering internationalisation do not come from other parties in the production nets, since the firm's suppliers, customers and competitors are not internationalised. On the contrary, the Lonely International has the qualifications to promote internationalisation of its production net, and consequently of the firms engaged in it. The firm's relationships both with and in other national nets may function as bridges to those

JON JOHANSON & LARS-GUNNAR MATTSSON

nets for that firm's suppliers and customers. Perhaps they have a similar effect on competitors (cf. Knickerbocker, 1973). Firms which are internationalised before their competitors are fore-runners in the internationalisation process and may enjoy advantages for that reason, in particular in tightly structured nets, because they have developed network positions before the competitors.

To exploit the advantages of being a Lonely International, the firm has to co-ordinate activities in the different national nets. International integration is therefore an important feature in the development of the highly internationalised firm. However, the need to co-ordinate is probably less than for the International Among Others.


### 11.6.3 The Late Starter

If the suppliers, customers and competitors of the firm are inter-national, even the purely domestic firm has a number of indirect relations with foreign networks. Relationships in the domestic market may be driving forces to enter foreign markets. The firm can be 'pulled out' by customers or suppliers, and in particular by complementary suppliers, e.g. in 'big projects'. Thus, market investments in the domestic market are assets which can be utilised when going abroad. In that case it is not necessary to go from the nearby market to more distant markets and the step abroad can already be rather large in the beginning. In addition, nearby markets may be tightly structured and already 'occupied' by competitors. Thus, the extension pattern will be partly explained by the international character of indirect relations and the existence of entry opportunities.

Is the market penetration process of the firm affected by the degree of internationalisation of the production network where it is operating? The need for co-ordination is greater in a highly internationalised production net, which implies that establish-ment of sales subsidiaries should be made earlier if the firm is a Late Starter than if it is an Early Starter. The size of the firm is probably important: for example, a small firm going abroad in an internationalised world probably has to be highly specialised and adjusted to problem solutions in specific sections of the production nets. Starting production abroad probably is a matter of what bonds to the customers are important. If joint planning with customers is essential it may be necessary to start local production early. Similarly, if technical development requires close contacts with the customers, it may be advantageous to manufacture locally. On the other hand, it may be better to use relationships with customers in the domestic market for development purposes, especially if these customers are internationalised (as they to some extent are, by definition, in the Late Starter case). However, such customers also have access to alternative, internationally based counterparts for their own development processes which might reduce the importance of their domestic suppliers.

The situation is different for large firms. As firms which have become large in the domestic market often are less specialised than small firms, their situation is often more complex than in the case of the small firm. One possibility is that of becoming established in a foreign production net through acquisition or joint venture. Of course, this is associated with great risks to a firm without experience of foreign acquisitions or joint ventures, particularly if other firms in the production net are internationalised. In general, it is probably more difficult for a firm which has become large at home to find a niche in highly internationalised nets. Unlike the small firm, it cannot adjust in a way which is necessary in such a net, nor has it the same ability as the small firm to react on the initiatives of other firms — which is probably the main road to internationalisation in a net in which other firms are already international.

The Late Starter has a comparative disadvantage in terms of its lesser market knowledge as compared with its competitors. Furthermore, as suggested above, it is often difficult to establish new positions in a tightly structured net. The best distributors are, for example, already linked to competitors. More or less legally, competitors can make the late newcomer unprofitable, by means of predatory pricing. In addition in comparison with the Early Starter the Late Starter probably has a less difficult task with regard to trust. Firms in the foreign markets already have experience of suppliers from abroad.

In a highly internationalised world the firms are probably more specialised. Consequently, a firm which is a Late Starter has to have a greater customer adaptation ability or a greater ability to influence the need specifications of the customers. However, the influence ability of a Late Starter is probably rather limited. The comparison between the Early Starter and

303

JON JOHANSON & LARS-GUNNAR MATTSSON

the Late Starter illustrates the importance of timing as a basic issue in the analysis of strategies in networks.

### 11.6.4 The international among others

In this case both the firm and its environment are highly internationalised. A further internationalisation of the firm only means marginal changes in extension and penetration, which, on the whole, do not imply any qualitative changes in the firm. It is probable, however, that international integration of the firm can lead to radical internationalisation changes.

Both with regard to extension and penetration the firm has possibilities to use positions in one net for bridging over to other nets. A necessary condition for such bridging is that the lateral relations within the firm are quite strong. Some kind of international integration is required, not only in the 'vertical', hierarchical sense, but also in the lateral, decentralised sense (Galbraith, 1973). As extension takes place in a globally interdependent network, the driving forces and the obstacles to this extension are closely related to this interdependence. Models of global oligopolies fit the argument here. Entries are made in those sections of the global production net which the competitors consider their main markets in order to discourage the competitor from making threatening competitive moves in other markets. In such a situation the entry may meet some resistance, but it is difficult for the competitors to use predatory pricing.

For the Early Starter, penetration through production in a foreign market was mainly a result of a need to bring about a balance between internal resources and external demands and possibilities in the specific market. For the International Among Others, the situation is different. The operations in one market may make it possible to utilise production capacity for sales in other markets. This may lead to production co-ordination by specialisation and increased volumes of intra-firm international trade. When the markets are expanding, it is possible in that case to put off capacity increases in one market, while capacity increases are made in another market before the positions in that market motivated such expansion. The surplus capacity could be linked to the wider international network, and this requires strong international integration of the firm.

304

INTERNATIONALISATION IN INDUSTRIAL SYSTEMS

Establishment of sales subsidiaries is probably speeded up by high internationalisation, as the international knowledge level is higher and there is a stronger need to co-ordinate activities in different markets. The need for co-ordination places heavy demand on the organisation. The competitors can utilise weaknesses in one market if they are not likely to met counterattacks in markets in which the firm is strong. Co-ordination gains in procurement, production and R&D are more likely than if the internationalisation of the firm and of the network is low. National differences are smaller, innovations are diffused more rapidly, and indirect business relations via the 'third country' become more important to utilise. The market investments in one country will probably be more important as the external resources to which the relationships give access are more dispersed internationally.

The many positions which the International Among Others occupies in internationally linked networks give it access to, and some influence over, external resources. This means that the possibility for 'externalisation' increases. The international manufacturing firm may thus increasingly tend to purchase components, sub-assemblies, etc. rather than do the manufacturing itself. Such subcontracting is sometimes required by host governments, but may also be a way to make the multinational enterprise more effective. Since important customers or joint-venture partners in one country are also by definition international, the International Among Others is faced with opportunities for further extension or penetration in 'third countries'. Thus, a Swedish firm might increase its penetration in a South American market because of its relationship in Japan with an internationalising Japanese firm. Other examples of such international interdependence are 'big projects' in which design, equipment supply, construction, ownership and operation can all be allocated to firms of different national origin, but with internationally more or less dispersed activities. In such production nets, further internationalisation is probably predominantly dependent on the firm's configuration of network positions and on its ability not only to co-ordinate its own resources in different parts of the world, but also to influence, through its market assets, the use of resources owned by other firms.

The advantage of being able to co-ordinate operations in international networks is still more evident when changes take place in the environment. Assume that such changes spread

305

JON JOHANSON & LARS-GUNNAR MATTSSON

from country to country: the international firm is then likely to have better possibilities to discover such changes as well as better opportunities to take advantage of them. A third advantage may be that the international firm can dominate and influence the international diffusion process and thus affect the development — but this probably requires size as well. Changes also occur in the localisation of economic activity. The internationally co-ordinated firm has better opportunities to detect and adjust to such changes. It can, for example, use its earlier established positions in an expanding national market to increase its penetration in that market and perhaps also its extension to other national markets within an expanding region of such markets. A driving force for further internationalisation by the International Among Others is to increase its ability to adjust to (or perhaps to influence) the geographical reallocation of activities in the production net.

The International Among Others predominantly faces counterparts and competitors who are themselves internationally active and markets that are rather tightly structured. This means that major position changes in this situation will increasingly take place through joint ventures, acquisitions and mergers, in contrast with the other three cases that we have analysed. If, finally, we compare with the Early Starter situation, internationalisation for the International Among Others will be much less explicable by reference to the need for knowledge development and the similarities between the foreign markets and the home market. Instead, the driving forces and the restrictions are related to the strategic use of network positions.

## 11.7 THE NETWORK APPROACH COMPARED WITH TWO OTHER MODELS

### 11.7.1 The theory of internalisation

The theory of internalisation (Buckley and Casson, 1976; Rugman, 1982) currently seems to be generally accepted as an explanation of multinational enterprise. The theory assumes that a multinational enterprise has somehow developed a firm-specific advantage in its home market. This is usually in the form of internally developed, intangible assets giving the firm

306

INTERNATIONALISATION IN INDUSTRIAL SYSTEMS

some superior production, product, marketing and/or management knowledge. If this asset cannot be exploited and safeguarded effectively through market (or contractual) transactions, an 'internal market' has to be created. Expansions outside the firm's domestic market, given that local production is advantageous, will then take place through horizontal and/or vertical integration. The firm either establishes or buys manufacturing plants outside its home market. Thus, the multinational enterprise exists because of 'market failures' or high 'contracting costs'. The firm wants to protect its intangible assets and to be able to control the price others pay for the use of these assets. There are, however, also costs of internalising in the form of internal administrative systems and risk-taking. These costs of internalisation will be lower, the less different the foreign market is from the home market. Thus, the internalisation model will predict that internalisation starts in 'nearby' markets (Caves 1982: chapter 1). It should be noted that the internalisation model is not intended to explain processes: rather, it tries to explain a specific economic institution, the multinational enterprise. It does say something, however, about the driving forces for internationalisation and the modes of international resource transfer.

We believe that the explanatory power of the internalisation model is greater in the situations in which the environment is not internationalised. The application of the model to the Early Starter situation is somewhat less than straightforward, though, since in the beginning the Early Starter is not a muitinational enterprise and it exports products rather than manufacturing them abroad. However, we might extend the reasoning underlying the internationalisation model to include not only manufacturing, but also marketing activities. Given such an interpretation, if the advantages of local manufacturing are small, then it seems reasonable to expect the firm to export its intangible assets 'embedded in products,' and that the marketing activities in the foreign market are carried out by a sales subsidiary rather than by an independent agent (unless the contracting costs are less than the cost of internalising). The internationalisation model could be used to explain why firms enter a market using a sales subsidiary and not an independent agent, while the internationalisation model discussed below could be used to explain why agents precede sales subsidiaries. While the first model emphasises the need for exploiting and protecting

307

JON JOHANSON & LARS-GUNNAR MATTSSON

internally created intangible assets, the second model emphasises the need for gradual development of market knowledge and the need to learn from interaction with other firms during the process.

In addition, the further expansion into the Lonely International case seems to fit with basic assumptions in the internalisation approach. The intangible assets constitute a firm-specific advantage that can be exploited in many markets through the operations of a multinational enterprise. However, if it takes a long time from the beginning of the internationalisation process to the status of Lonely International, the question arises as to how the firm can further develop its firm-specific advantage and not merely preserve and exploit it. It seems to be an implicit assumption in the internalisation approach that the firm's development activities are 'internal'. In the network approach, development activities are to an important extent dependent on the relationships with other firms, and thus on the network positions of the firm. Since internationalisation is a process by which network positions are established and changed, internationalisation as such influences the further development of the products, production processes, marketing behaviour, etc.

We said earlier that firms in networks invest in relationships with other firms. The positions thus created are in this chapter regarded as market investments, or in other words, as a form of intangible assets. These assets give partial access to external resources. Thus, the multinational enterprise increasingly enjoys direct relationships with customers and users in foreign markets rather than the indirect relations through agents or licensee's enjoyed by the less internationalised firm, operating only in its home market. This leads to a further observation linked to the network model. The highly internationalised firm may use its network positions effeciively to '*externalise*' some of its activities, without losing control of its crucial intangible assets. The manufacturing value added by multinational industrial firms might decrease because of increased 'subcontracting'. We believe that this is especially true in the International Among Others case.

If both the firm and its environment are highly internationalised, it seems that a model which aims to explain multinational enterprise loses some of its relevance for analysis of further internationalisation. We might, of course, still be helped by the transaction cost approach in our attempts to understand just what institutional form penetration, expansion and integration actually take. However, the approach does not consider the cumulative nature of activities, the use of external assets, the development potential of network relationships, or the interdependence between national markets.

## 11.7.2 The (Uppsala) Internationalisation Model

The internationalisation process described as a gradual step-by-step commitment to sell and to manufacture internationally as part of a growth and experimental learning process is a model that is associated with the research on the internationalisation of Swedish manufacturing industry that has been carried out at the University of Uppsala (see, for example, Hörnell *et al.*, 1973; Johanson and Wiedersheim-Paul, 1974; and Johanson and Vahlne, 1977). Focusing especially on export behaviour Bilkey (1978) conceptualised, and found evidence for, the exporting process as a sequential learning process by which the firm goes through stages of increasing commitment to foreign markets. This 'stage model' has lately come under some criticism, even if its general acceptance in the research community as a valid description seems to be high. Reid (1983) argues that the model is too deterministic and general: according to him, the firm's choice of entry and expansion modes are more selective and context-specific, and can be explained by heterogeneous resource patterns and market opportunities. Firms will therefore use multiple modes of international transfers. Reid suggests that a transaction cost approach is superior to the experiential learning model. Hedlund and Kverneland (1984: 77) also critisise the model, concluding that the 'experiences of Swedish firms in Japan suggest that establishment and growth strategies on foreign markets are changing towards more direct and rapid entry modes than those implied by theories of gradual and slow internationalisation processes'.

We believe that the internationalisation model is less valid in situations in which both the market and the firm are highly internationalised. The firms which started their internationalisation during the early twentieth century were usually in the Early Starter situation. The studies of Swedish industrial firms, on which the Uppsala model is based, describe and explain this situation and its transition to the Lonely International stage.

JON JOHANSON & LARS-GUNNAR MATTSSON

There is no explicit consideration in the model of the internationalisation of the firm's environment. We would therefore expect the internationalisation model to be most valid in the Early Starter case and least valid in the International Among Others stage. Both the network approach and the internationalisation model stress the cumulative nature of the firm's activities. The latter, however, is a model focusing on the internal development of the firm's knowledge and other resources, while the network approach also offers a model of the market and the firm's relations to that market.

In the Late Starter situation, we therefore expect the internationalisation model to be less valid than the network model because of the importance of indirect international relations in the home market and because of the probably quite heterogeneous pattern of entry opportunities when foreign markets are compared. In the International Among Others case, the internationalisation model seems to lose much of its relevance. Reid's, and Hedlund and Kverneland's arguments seem to be valid. Since by definition the firm and its counterparts and competitors have positions in a large number of markets, penetration and integration aspects of internationalisation seem to be more important strategic moves than further extension. In such a global perspective, specific national market differences will likely have less explanatory power.

To sum up: we believe that both the internalisation and the internationalisation models leave out characteristics of the firm and the market which seem especially important in the case of 'global competition' and co-operation in industrial systems.


## 11.8 SOME CONCLUDING REMARKS CONCERNING RESEARCH ISSUES

Against the background of the above discussion, we believe that more research in two, closely related, fields will serve to increase knowledge about the internationalisation of business: firstly, network internationalisation processes; and secondly, use of market assets in international competition.


### 11.8.1 Network internationalisation

Studies of network internationalisation may focus on inter-

310

nationalisation of national nets or of production nets. Such studies should describe and analyse the roles of different types of industrial actors in the process. They should also investigate the implications of the cumulative nature of network processes. More specifically, we advocate research into foreign market entry strategies in different situations with regard to network internationalisation. According to the network we can distinguish entry strategies which differ with regard to the character and number of relationships the entry firm seeks to establish with other firms in the network. We can also study which of the actors in the network take initiative in different entry processes and in networks which are more or less internationalised. Furthermore, the entry strategies may differ with regard to the ambitions of the entry firm in adopting or influencing the network structure in the entry market.

The network approach also implies that the strategic discretion is constrained by the character of the network in which the firm is operating or into which it intends to enter. This indicates that during the internationalisation of a network, the timing of the operations of a firm is important. It can also be expected that, because of the cumulative nature of network processes, the sequential order of activities in international markets is important and should be given more attention in research. Perhaps, however, the problem of timing is next to impossible to solve. From a strategic point of view the most interesting research issue, then, is that of analysing how to build preparedness for action when the time is ripe. Presumably, preparedness is largely a matter of having relationships with other parties.

This view on industrial markets implies that there are strong interdependencies between different sections, i.e. national nets, of the global networks: hence, integration of operations is important. At the same time, the view implies that action has to be taken close to other actors in the market, often in response to their actions. Strategies can probably not be planned and designed by remote headquarters, and their implementation requires some kind of lateral relation between organisational units operating in different national nets. Research about the organisation problem of integrating operations in international networks is required.

JON JOHANSON & LARS-GUNNAR MATTSSON

## 11.8.2 Use of market assets in international competition

We have emphasised the strategic importance of market assets and suggest research about their use in international competition. In particular, there is scope for work on the use of the market assets of one country as they affect competition with other countries. We think it would be interesting to study how market assets in one country are used when entering other country markets. Such studies should concern not only the use of domestic market assets in the first step abroad, but also the use of foreign market assets when entering third-country markets. They could focus on different types of market assets, or the country of the assets utilised — in terms of networks — or the target markets.

Another interesting research issue is the use of market assets in global competition. Such research could focus on the use of relationships with more or less multinational companies in global competition. Relationships with suppliers, customers, distributors or consultants are of different importance when competing in various types of production nets and national nets.

Finally, the strategic importance of market assets implies that fruitful research can be made about control of foreign market assets. Whereas internal assets are usually controlled hierarchically with ownership as the base, control of market assets must have other bases. Research has demonstrated that such factors as access to critical resources, information or legitimacy are often important as bases of control. The significance of those factors may differ considerably in different contexts. Both conceptual and empirical research is required.

## REFERENCES

Bilkey, W.J. (1978) An attempted integration of literature on the export behavior of firms. *Journal of International Business Studies,* Spring, 93-8

Blois, K.J. (1972) Vertical quasi-integration. *Journal of Industrial Economics, 20* (3), 253-72

Buckley, R.J. and Casson, M.C. (1976) *The future of multinational enterprise.* Macmillan, London

Caves, R.E. (1982) *Multinational enterprise and economic analysis.* Cambridge University Press, Cambridge

Ford, J.D. (1978) Stability factors in industrial marketing channels. *Industrial Marketing Management, 7*(6), 410-22

INTERNATIONALISATION IN INDUSTRIAL SYSTEMS

Galbraith, J. (1973) *Designing complex organizations.* Addison-Wesley, Reading, Mass.

Guillet de Monthoux, P. (1975) Organizational mating and industrial marketing conservatism — some reasons why industrial marketing managers resist marketing theory. *Industrial Marketing Management,* 4(1), 25-36

Hägg, I. and J. Johanson (eds) (1982) *Företag i nätverk,* SNS, Stockholm

Håkansson, H. (ed.) (1982) *International marketing and purchasing of industrial goods: an interaction approach.* Wiley, Chichester

—— and C. Östberg, (1975) Industrial marketing — an organizational problem? *Industrial Marketing Management 4,* 113-23

Hallén L. (1986) A comparison of strategic marketing approach. In P.W. Turnbull, and J.P. Valla (eds), *Strategies for international industrial marketing: a comparative analysis,* Croom Helm, London

Hammarkvist, K.-O., Håkansson, H. and L.-G. Mattsson *Marknadsföring för konkurenskraft.* Liber, Malmö

Hedlund, G. and Å. Kverneland. Investing in Japan — the experience of Swedish firms. Institute of International Business, Stockholm School of Economics

Hörnell, E., Vahlne, J.-E. and F. Wiedersheim-Paul (1973) *Export och utlandsestableringar.* Almqvist & Wiksell, Uppsala

Johanson, J. and L.-G. Mattsson, Marketing investments and market investments in industrial networks. *International Journal of Research in Marketing* 2(3), 185-95

—— and —— (1986) International marketing and internationalization processes — A network approach. In S. Paliwoda and P.N. Turnbull (eds), *Research in international marketing,* Croom Helm, London

Johanson, J. and J.-E. Vahlne (1977) The internationalization process of the firm — a model of knowledge development and increasing foreign market commitments. *Journal of International Business, 8* (Spring-Summer), 23-32

—— and F. Widersheim-Paul (1974) The internationalization of the firm — four Swedish case studies. *Journal of Management Studies, 3* (October), 305-22

Knickerbocker, F.T. (1973) *Oligopolistic reaction and multinational enterprise.* Division of Research, Harvard Graduate School of Business Administration, Cambridge, Mass.

Levitt, T. (1983) *The marketing imagination.* The Free Press, New York

Lindblom, C.-E. (1977) *Politics and markets.* Basic Books, New York

Macneil, I.R. (1978) Contracts: adjustment of long-term economic relations under classical, neoclassical, and relational contract law. *Northwestern University Lay Review, 72*(6), 854-905

Mattsson, L.-G. (1985) An application of a network approach to marketing: defending and changing market positions. In N. Dholakia and J. Arndt (eds), *Alternative paradigms for widening marketing theory,* JAI Press, Greenwich CT

Reid, S. (1983) Firm internationalization, transaction costs and strate-

JON JOHANSON & LARS-GUNNAR MATTSSON

gic choice. International Marketing Review, Winter, 44-56

Rugman, A.M. (ed.) (1982) *New theories of the multinational enterprise.* Croom Helm, London

Webster Jr., F.E. (1979) *Industrial marketing strategy.* Wiley, New York

Von Hippel, E. (1978) Successful industrial products from customer ideas. *Journal of Marketing, 42,* 39-49

Williamson, O.E. (1979) Transaction cost economics: the governance of contractual relations. *Journal of Law and Economics,* 233-61

Wind, Y. (1970) Industrial source loyalty. *Journal of Marketing Research, 8,* 433-6

314

# [26]

## Agency Contracts, Institutional Modes, and the Transition to Foreign Direct Investment by British Manufacturing Multinationals Before 1939

### STEPHEN NICHOLAS

This paper analyzes the transition from agents to branch selling as alternative institutional modes for transacting abroad by pre-1939 British manufacturing multinationals. A model to explain the shift between alternative modes is specified in terms of transaction costs. Agent opportunism and contract monitoring costs are the major transaction costs. Besides transaction costs, the frequency of transactions and the accumulation of market-specific knowledge by the principal were found to be important variables.

ECONOMIC historians have only recently become interested in multinational enterprise.[1] The interest was stimulated by the literature on the evolution of the large corporation and by new estimates of aggregate foreign direct investment, which found that over 40 percent of British overseas investment in the Third World and South America by 1914 was direct.[2] According to John Dunning, by 1914 company investment abroad reached £14 billion, representing as much as 35 percent of the long-term capital stake and by 1939 there were well over 350 British manufacturing multinational enterprises.[3] The studies reveal that British multinational enterprises acted as an important but neglected mechanism for transferring technology, products, management skill, and know-how abroad.

The analysis of British multinational enterprises has been largely directed to explaining the reasons firms transact abroad. Utilizing a sample of British multinational enterprises, I discovered that 50 percent had technology advantages and 45 percent selling advantages; 32

*Journal of Economic History*, Vol. XLIII, No. 3 (Sept. 1983). © The Economic History Association. All rights reserved. ISSN 0022-0507.

The author is Lecturer in Economics, University of New South Wales, Kensington, New South Wales, Australia, 2033. He would like to thank Mark Casson, Diane Mort, Donald N. McCloskey, and two referees for assistance. The usual disclaimer on errors applies.

[1] John Stopford, "The Origins of British Based Multinational Manufacturing Enterprises," *Business History Review*, 48 (Autumn 1974), 303–45; D. Paterson, *British Direct Investment in Canada, 1870–1914* (Toronto, 1976); S. J. Nicholas, "British Multinational Investment Before 1939," *Journal of European Economic History*, 11 (Winter 1982), 605–30; Peter J. Buckley and Brian Roberts, *European Direct Investment in the U.S.A. Before World War I* (London, 1982).

[2] Peter Svedberg, "The Portfolio: Direct Composition of Private Foreign Investment in 1914 Revisited," *Economic Journal*, 88 (Dec. 1978), 690–722.

[3] John Dunning, "Changes in the Level and Structure of International Production: The Last 100 Years," mimeographed (1982), pp. 4, 31.

percent integrated abroad to secure raw materials and 31 percent to avoid tariffs.[4] From eight case studies of European investment in the United States, Buckley and Roberts found that the three dominant motives for making a foreign direct investment were the desire to avoid American tariffs, the opportunity to exploit "patents," and the need for local production to satisfy local demand.[5] To explain pre-1939 foreign direct investment, Dunning emphasized the technological capacity of international firms.[6] Patented technology and special skills in selling are knowledge created inside a firm but nonappropriable because of transaction costs in the international market.[7] By nonappropriable I mean that the firm is unable to capture the value to society of the knowledge. All the studies argue that the internalization of the functions of the market within the firm was the point of direct investment.[8] The firm economized on transaction costs by providing an institution for appropriating technology and selling knowledge and transferring property rights in goods.

The uniformity of approach by economic historians reflects the consensus by economists that internalization explains foreign direct investment.[9] The roots of the notion are found in Coase's work on the nature of the firm.[10] Coase derived the dictum that the firm will "tend to expand until the cost of organizing an extra transaction within the firm becomes equal to the cost of carrying out the same transaction by means of exchange in the open market."[11] Recent theoretical work has replaced the Coasian firm-market dichotomy by a "comparative institutional analysis" distinguishing institutions (such as markets, intermediate cooperative modes—agents, licensing, franchising, and other long-term contracts—and the hierarchical firm) all of which economize on transaction costs.[12] The comparative institutional analysis recognizes

---

[4] Nicholas, "Multinational Investment," p. 10.

[5] Buckley and Roberts, *European Direct Investment*, p. 119.

[6] Dunning, "International Production," pp. 4.26–4.65.

[7] See Peter J. Buckley and Mark Casson, *The Future of the Multinational Enterprise* (London, 1976), pp. 10–30; Mark C. Casson, *Alternative to the Multinational Enterprise* (London, 1979), pp. 31–43; Harry G. Johnson, "The Efficiency and Welfare Implications of the International Corporation" in *The International Corporation*, ed. Charles P. Kindleberger (Cambridge, Massachusetts, 1970), pp. 35–39; Steven P. Magee, "Technology and the Appropriability Theory of the Multinational Corporation" in *The New International Economic Order*, ed. J. Bhajwati (Cambridge, Massachusetts, 1976), pp. 319–21.

[8] See Buckley and Roberts, *European Direct Investment*, pp. 8–9; Nicholas, "Multinational Investment," pp. 9–10; Dunning, "International Production," pp. 4-24, 4-34.

[9] For a review of the literature see A. K. Calvet, "A Synthesis of Foreign Direct Investment Theories and Theories of the Multinational Firm," *Journal of International Business Studies*, 12 (Spring/Summer 1981), 43–57.

[10] R. H. Coase, "The Nature of the Firm," *Economica*, n.s. 4 (1937), 381–405.

[11] Ibid., p. 397.

[12] A. Alchian and H. Demsetz, "Production, Information Costs and Economic Organization," *American Economic Review*, 62 (Dec. 1972), 777–95; C. J. Dahlman, "The Problem of Externality," *Journal of Law and Economics*, 22 (April 1979), 141–62; O. Williamson, "The Modern Corporation: Origins, Evolution, Attributes," *Journal of Economic Literature*, 19 (Dec. 1981), 1545–50.

## *Foreign Investment by British Multinationals* 677

that nonmarket organizations do not simply duplicate the allocative results of a price system. They are chosen because they lead to a different allocation of resources.[13]

But the comparative institutional analysis is static. The transition between alternative institutions remains unexplained. The historical evidence shows British and American multinational enterprises passing through stages of overseas involvement from exporting with merchants and the firm's salesmen to the so-called agency system, thence to the foreign direct investment as a sales subsidiary, and finally to direct investment in foreign production.[14] For example, in a study of British multinational enterprises, 88 percent of the firms entered into agency agreements before making an initial direct investment in a sales branch abroad, and few British multinational enterprises began overseas production without first establishing sales subsidiaries.[15] In part, the static analysis of the comparative institutional approach arises from the failure to distinguish between the reasons firms transact abroad and the reasons they choose a particular form. The same arguments used to explain the decision to transact with foreign countries have been used to explain the choice of the mode of transacting.[16] I offer here a dynamic model to explain the transition from selling through an agency system to selling through a hierarchical sales subsidiary between 1870 and 1939. Using agent-principal theory, a transaction cost model is developed to explain the choice of mode.

### THE PRINCIPAL'S PROBLEM

The theory of the agent and the principal concerns long-term contracts for repeat sales. The repeat sales are between the producer (the principal) and the seller of the product (the agent). The principal will often have exported through his salesmen or merchant houses, but the appointment of an agent indicates that the principal's knowledge of the market is limited. The agent knows the language, local customs, and laws, and lives in the country where the product is sold. The principal has knowledge of the product, which is imperfectly transferred to the agent.[17] Conflicts tend to develop between agent and principal over holding stocks in the good, promotional effort, discretionary pricing, and "reasonable" levels of service.[18]

---

[13] John C. McManus, "The Costs of Alternative Economic Organizations," *Canadian Journal of Economics*, 8 (Nov. 1975), 335–50.

[14] Nicholas, "Multinational Investment," pp. 14–16. See also Mira Wilkins, *The Emergence of Multinational Enterprise* (Cambridge, Massachusetts, 1970), pp. 207–13; Mira Wilkins, *The Maturing of Multinational Business* (Cambridge, Massachusetts, 1979), pp. 417–22, 432–37; Buckley and Roberts, *European Direct Investment*, pp. 44, 65, 87, 91–92.

[15] Nicholas, "Multinational Investment," p. 15.

[16] For a similar point see Calvet, "Synthesis," p. 56.

[17] Magee, "Technology," p. 31ᵥ.

[18] This problem has been examined by the marketing channel literature. See L. W. Stern, B. Sternthal, and C. S. Craig, "Managing Conflict in Distribution Channels: A Laboratory Study,"

678                          *Nicholas*

Contractual arrangements between agent and principal are essentially decision problems under uncertainty.[19] The principal tells the agent what to do. The more accurate the principal's knowledge of the agent and the lower the costs of monitoring his behavior, the lower the risks. The risks in the agent-principal problem are that the agent will make a bad decision, hurting the principal. Even if he promises not to, the agent may have incentives to cheat the principal.[20] The contract will be drawn to attenuate such opportunism. Nevertheless, there are costs of monitoring the agent, especially when he provides a service dependent on the energy he devotes to the task and when he is distant from the principal.

A commission on sales is both a control and incentive system. As a control system, commissions meter the agent's performance, allowing the principal to identify and punish bad performers. As an incentive system, commissions discourage opportunism. Having made a promise to sell vigorously, the salesman has less incentive to renege if he is on commission. The posting of a bond by the agent is another control device. Bonding includes investments by the agent in physical capital such as warehouses, or human capital such as knowledge of the product, which locks the agent into the contractual relationship.[21] The more idiosyncratic to the principal's products is the agent's specialized capital investment the greater the lock in effect of bonding. Government or legal enforcement is a third control device, used sparingly because of its great cost. Overwhelmingly, principals rely on the threat of dismissal or the withdrawal of future business for contract enforcement.[22] The

---

*Journal of Marketing Research*, 10 (May 1973), 169–79; M. Pearson and J. Monoly, "The Role of Conflict and Co-operation in Channel Performance," in *Marketing: 1776–1976 and Beyond*, ed. K. L. Bernhardt (Chicago, 1976), pp. 240–44; L. J. Rosenberg and L. W. Stern, "Conflict Measurement in the Distribution Channel," *Journal of Marketing Research*, 8 (Nov. 1971), 437–42.

[19] M. C. Jensen and W. H. Meckling, "Theory of the Firm: Managerial Behaviour, Agency Costs and Ownership Structure," *Journal of Financial Economics*, 3 (Nov. 1976), 305–11; Stephen Ross, "The Economic Theory of Agency: The Principal's Problem," *American Economic Review*, 63 (May 1973), 134–49; Stephen Ross, "On the Economic Theory of Agency and the Principal of Similarity," in *Essays on Economic Behaviour Under Uncertainty*, ed. M. Balch, D. McFadden, and S. Wu (Amsterdam, 1974), pp. 215–20.

[20] Oliver Williamson, *Markets and Hierarchies: Analysis and Antitrust Implications* (New York, 1975), pp. 26–37; David J. Teece, *Vertical Integration and Divestiture in the U.S. Oil Industry* (Stanford, 1976), p. 31; Oliver Williamson, "Transaction-Cost Economics: The Governance of Contractual Relations," *Journal of Law and Economics*, 22 (Oct. 1979), p. 233. Of course, the principal could also act opportunistically. The paper, however, is concerned with the principal establishing branch selling rather than the agent's contractual problems with the principal.

[21] B. Klein, R. Crawford, and A. Alchian, "Vertical Integration, Appropriable Rents, and the Competitive Contracting Process," *Journal of Law and Economics*, 11 (Oct. 1978), 297–326; B. Klein, "Transaction Cost Determinants of 'Unfair' Contractual Arrangements," *American Economic Review*, 70 (May 1980), 356–62; B. Klein and K. Leffler, "The Role of Market Forces in Assuring Contractual Performances," *Journal of Political Economy*, 89 (Aug. 1981), 615–41; Williamson, "Transaction Cost Economics," p. 234, 238–45; Klein, " 'Unfair' Contractual Arrangements," pp. 358–59; Klein, Crawford, and Alchian, "Competitive Contracting Process," pp. 302–7; Klein and Leffler, "Role of Market Forces," pp. 618–25.

[22] Klein, Crawford, and Alchian, "Competitive Contracting Process," p. 303; Klein and Leffler, "Role of Market Forces," pp. 616–20.

## Foreign Investment by British Multinationals 679

model predicts a transition to branch selling when monitoring costs incurred by the principal outweigh the agency's benefits relative to branch selling. The transition from agency agreements to foreign direct investment in a selling branch by pre-1939 British multinational enterprises provides a testing ground for the model.

### TESTING THE MODEL

A nonrandom sample of 21 British multinationals was selected on the basis of archival availability and access.[23] All the sample firms met the United Nations definition of multinationals, as enterprises that control assets, either factories, mines, or sales facilities, in two or more countries.[24] The sample included a range of firm sizes. The four agricultural machinery firms were among the ten best known and largest in the 1870–1939 period, and Huntley Palmer, Reading, and Peak Frean, London, were the two largest biscuit firms in the pre-1939 period. Other firms (for example, Harvey & Co. and Blackie Sons Ltd.) were medium-sized firms. The basic agency contract was fairly standard across sizes of firms, specifying exclusive sales areas, sole agency requirements, and specific arrangements for performance, holding stocks of the good, and promotional effort. As far as it is possible to determine, the agency contracts for the firms in the sample correspond to agency agreements for nonsample firms.[25]

Agency contracts focused on the selling of goods and the payment for them. In every agency contract, vague (and unenforceable) provisions required the agents to "push the sale" of the principal's products.[26] Such promises to behave nonopportunistically involved monitoring by

---

[23] The firms, by industrial groups, were Huntley Palmer and Peak Frean in food; Bentall, Ransomes, Marshall and Fowler in agricultural machinery; A. W. Smith and Mirrlees Watson in sugar-crushing machinery; Alexander Cowan and Blackie Sons Ltd. in paper and publishing; in steel products and cutlery, Osborn Steel, Spear and Jackson, and George Wostenholm & Sons; in engineering, the pump makers, Weir, and Harvey & Co.; Gourock Rope Company in rope; Morton (Sundour) and Linen Thread Company Ltd. in textiles; and Beardmore in shipbuilding and iron and steel. The merchant houses, Anthony Gibb, London, and John Finlay, Scotland, acted as agents when they signed exclusive agreements to represent British firms abroad.

[24] United Nations, *Transactional Corporations in World Development: A Re-Examination*, E.78 II A5 (New York, 1978). This definition is also used by the Group of Eminent Persons in their report, United Nations, *The Impact of Multinational Corporations on Development and on International Relations*, E.74 II A5 (New York, 1974), p. 25; and by John Dunning, *International Production and the Multinational Enterprise* (London, 1981), p. 3. Further, 13 of the firms subsequently made an investment in assembly and manufacturing in the period.

[25] D. Coleman, *Courtalds: An Economic and Social History* (Oxford, 1969), vol. 1, p. 193. I would like to thank Robert Kirk for information on Platt Bros. agency contracts.

[26] For example, Spear and Jackson's agent promised to "deligently and faithfully service the market to the best of his ability and judgment" (Spear and Jackson, Agreements, SJ65 3/7/29, Sheffield Public Libraries Archives). Gourock's agent agreed "to take steps to introduce and sell to local customers" (Gourock, Agency Agreements, UGD42/163/3, 22/1/31, University of Glasgow Archives [where page numbers are not available the date of the reference is given]).

the principal. Agents could sit back and wait for orders. The demand for the principal's products, coming from investments in brand names, good will, product differentiation, and advertising, created an appropriable rent that the agent could capture at the cost of rudimentary paperwork. The scope for opportunistic behavior obviously increased when agents received some payment irrespective of the level of sales. By replacing the salary or guaranteed income with a commission the principal reduced the possibility of opportunistic behavior.[27]

One attempt to strengthen vague performance clauses and to ensure service quality was to write into the contract specific input requirements covering the amount of traveling, advertising, and showing the agent was required to do. The requirements were a form of bonding, involving investments by the agent, which locked the agent into the contractual relationship. To ensure a competent sales staff, principals required agents to invest in engineers or special salesmen with specific technical knowledge of the principal's product. For example, the 1898 agreement between Platt Bros. and N. Wadia & Sons, Bombay, stated "The Agents should at their own cost employ and retain the services of duly qualified representatives."[28] Even with such requirements, however, principals could not be sure that sales performance was adequate. One common practice was to share the expense of a technical representative or salesman, particularly when knowledge of the product was concentrated in the principal. The sugar mill machinery firm, A. W. Smith, shared the £300 salary plus expenses of a technician with their Indian agents, Martin & Co.[29] Many firms, particularly in engineering, provided a technical salesman or mechanic who lived with the agent. By 1920 five textile machinery firms, Asa Lees, Tweedale & Smalley, Platts, Dobson and Barlow, and Howard and Bullough, had one technical man at their expense based at the office of their Indian agents.[30] Having one of the principal's employees inside the agency reporting back to the principal was an effective if costly monitoring mechanism.

Perhaps the most important bonding and monitoring arrangement was the requirement that agents carry stock of the good to be sold. Stocks were vital to ensure prompt delivery, and also served as advertising when displayed in offices and showrooms. Idiosyncratic investment in machines, offices, warehouses, and showrooms effectively locked the agent into the contract. Stocks for sale purchased by the agent,

[27] Spear and Jackson, Agency Correspondence, Alex Vox, Paris, SJC65, 26/4/27, 1/6/27, 3/7/29, Sheffield Public Libraries Archives.

[28] Platt, Agreement, DDPSL 1/109/1, Lancashire Record Office, Preston. Also Fowler, Toepffer Agreement, CO1/9, Institute for Agricultural History, University of Reading; and Bentall, Agreements, DF1/16 1924, Essex Record Office.

[29] A. W. Smith, Directors' Minute Book, UGD118/13/1, 19/2/69, p. 5, University of Glasgow Archives.

[30] S. M. Rutnager, *Bombay Industries: The Cotton Mills* (Bombay, 1927), pp. 643–46. I would also like to thank Robert Kirk for information on this point.

## *Foreign Investment by British Multinationals*     **681**

however, tended to be carried at less than the optimum level, while consignment goods, which earned the agent commission but remained the principal's property, tended to be overstocked. Nearly all firms accepted that their agents would hold mainly consignment stock, since most agents lacked the capital resources to purchase stock.[31] Moreover, consignment stock allowed the principal to advance credit to customers and assured prompt delivery.

Provisions for consignments in the contract were supplemented by a range of monitoring mechanisms. Stocks were monitored by weekly, monthly, or half-yearly stocklists provided by the agents.[32] Alternatively, agents might be required to send terms of each sale to the principal.[33] The arrangements were given teeth by rights to inspect the stock, to inspect the agent's books on demand, and to appoint the agent's bookkeeper or storekeeper.[34] Nevertheless, stocks were a source of principal-agent conflict. For example, when Marshall's found that Johannes Donalsen, their Swedish agents, kept consignment stocks above the four engines and three thrashers stipulated in their 1883 agreement, a new 1889 contract specified that three engines and two thrashers could be stocked.[35] The contract encouraged vigorous selling by moving consignment stock to the sales account after 12 months and making it immediately payable to the agents.[36] Spear & Jackson's contract with Aktu Mokuzai Kaisha, Tokyo, although allowing the agent to keep consignment stock, required the agent to purchase stock valued at £1,000 per year.[37]

A large part of the costs of agency agreements involved regulating sales behavior and stock levels. The most effective monitoring mechanism was to send directors or the firm's traveling representatives to check agents. For example, after accumulating high stocks with little evidence of increasing sales activity, directors of Osborn Steel visited B. M. Jones in the United States, replacing the consignment stock agency with a purchasing or sales agency in 1909.[38] In 1911 Osborn's decided that stockholding of their Warsaw agents was not justified and sent a salesman to Warsaw to review the agency and report to the

---

[31] In 1929 Fowler's stocked machinery valued at £15,297 with their Italian agents and £16,956 with their German agents. Fowler, Memorandum on Branches, AC9/63, 31/12/29, Institute for Agricultural History.

[32] Marshall, Agency Term Book No. 1, pp. 238–40, Institute for Agricultural History; Gourock, Agency Agreements, UGD42/103/3, 22/10, 31, University of Glasgow Archives; Smith, Minute Book, UGD118/13/1, 17/8/14, p. 114, University of Glasgow Archives.

[33] Ransomes, Agency Book, AD7/48, p. 7, Institute for Agricultural History.

[34] Ibid., pp. 36–42; Marshall, Agency Term Book No. 1, pp. 239–40, Institute for Agricultural History; Fowler, Toepffer Agreement, CO1/9, Institute for Agricultural History.

[35] Marshall, Agency Term Book No. 1, pp. 165–68, 183, Institute for Agricultural History.

[36] Ibid., p. 274.

[37] Spear and Jackson, Agreements, SJC65 10/2/20, Sheffield Public Libraries Archives.

[38] Osborn, Letter Book, Osb. 17, pp. 220, 230, 397, 421, Sheffield Public Libraries Archives.

Board.[39] Frequent trips by directors and traveling representatives were undertaken by every firm with an agency network. William Mackie, a director with A. W. Smith, traveled to monitor agents in India in 1920, 1935, 1937, South Africa in 1927, South America in 1931, 1932, and the West Indies in 1933 and 1937, in addition to yearly visits by their American and European salesmen.[40] One of Ransomes's representatives made 81 trips abroad between 1890 and 1900 including 5 to France, 18 to Germany, and 8 to Russia, while directors traveled regularly to Europe and the Americas.[41]

The second major area open to opportunism was the payments system. Of course, stock monitoring and the right to inspect the books also allowed the principal to monitor payments. Such methods were superfluous when the principal insisted on direct execution of orders to customers. Spear & Jackson and Gourock Rope Company, for example, specified that the principal would bill directly.[42] But the agent, by misinforming the principal, could collect a commission by passing orders of noncreditworthy customers. As a result, contracts specified that the agent should take every precaution to pass orders only of creditworthy customers, or to advise the principal whether credit should be given.[43] Peak Frean, the London biscuit firm, required the agent to share the loss from customers' bad debts.[44] Contracts explicitly allowed principals to refuse orders or to make the final approval of orders.[45] Despite such safeguards bad debts were common under the agency system. There were also risks in receiving payment for stock on consignment when customers paid agents for goods that were the property of the principal. A common arrangement was the requirement that agents pay by bill of exchange or letters of credit drawn on a London or European merchant house.[46] In these cases the draft or credit letter guaranteed the principal payment but involved the agent in the expense of a commission to the financial house.[47] Principals also encouraged payment through charging interest on outstanding payments

[39] Osborn, Works Meeting Minutes 1907–24, Osb. 142 9/10/11, 11/12/11, Sheffield Public Libraries Archives.

[40] A. W. Smith, Directors' Minutes No. 1, UGD118/17/2a, pp. 11, 149; Directors' Minutes No. 2, UGD118/17/2b, pp. 102, 104, 127, 232–34, 275, University of Glasgow Archives.

[41] G. Palmer, "The History of the Orwell Works," p. SP1/1HS, Institute for Agricultural History.

[42] Spear and Jackson, Agreements, SJC65 3/7/29, Sheffield Public Libraries Archives; Gourock, Agency Agreements, UGD42/103/3 1/12/27, University of Glasgow Archives.

[43] Gourock, Agency Agreements, UGD42/103/3 1/8/14; 1/12/27.

[44] Peak Frean, *Carr Agency Records*, PK13/4 1/7/01, University of Reading Library Archives.

[45] Spear and Jackson, Agreements, SJC65 12/3/19, 3/7/29, Sheffield Public Libraries Archives.

[46] Ransomes, Agency Book, AD7/49, pp. 68–79, Institute for Agricultural History; Gourock, Agency Agreement, UGD42/103/3 1/6/26, 4/22, University of Glasgow Archives.

[47] Gibb, General Records: Macfarlaine Strong Co. 1889, Ms 11,668/1, London Guildhall Archives; E. J. Perkins, *Financing Anglo-American Trade: The House of Brown, 1800–1880* (Cambridge, Massachusetts, 1978), pp. 5–8; P. Cottrell, "Commercial Enterprise," in *The Dynamics of Victorian Business*, ed. Roy Church (London, 1980), p. 240.

## Foreign Investment by British Multinationals     683

and offering a discount—usually 2½ or 3 percent—for cash within one to three months of the sale. The provisions, however, did not always work. Osborn's in 1905 demanded that their American agents, B. M. Jones, reduce their outstanding credit of £23,000. When the next six months witnessed the dispatch of goods valued at £11,000 but payment of only £9,600, a director's investigation of the agency resulted.[48] Sales representatives or directors also were used as a monitoring and enforcement mechanism to encourage payment. When Ransomes's agent in Rumania in 1882, F. Freund, "never completed payments within specified times," Ransomes's director visited Freund in 1883 to sort out discounts, payment, and the size of the trade.[49] Ransomes's found that Freund was "perfectly honest."[50] A Fowler's director sent to sort out a similar problem at the Societa Anonime La Penetrazione Roma concluded that "the main trouble is that Fowler's are completely in the hands of the Italians who are as cute as can be."[51]

The ultimate enforcement device was the termination of the contract. The standard nonrenewal clause required three to twelve months notice after the contract had run a specific duration, usually two years but on occasion as many as ten. Additional termination conditions including "failure to carry out provisions," "termination at any time," or "termination at the pleasure of the principal" favored the principal.[52] Many principals followed Spear & Jackson's contracts, which provided for termination due to "misconduct or incapacity," and in fact, most terminations were for fraud or concealment by the agents.[53] The option of termination in midcourse was, however, rarely used. Most agency agreements ended by nonrenewal. For example, Burn & Co. were appointed by A. W. Smith as their Indian agents in 1932 and immediately ran into trouble over nonfulfillment of the agency contract. Rather than terminating the agency, Smith's decided in June 1935 to await payment by Burn before ending the agreement. By September a further recommendation saw nonrenewal replace termination "due to the threat of a lawsuit which would freeze money in India."[54]

### FREQUENCY AND NATURE OF TRANSACTING AND LEARNING

A solution to costs resulting from monitoring and opportunism is vertical integration. There is evidence that shifts from an agency system

[48] Osborn, Letter Book, Osb. 17, pp. 222–30, 397, 421, Sheffield Public Libraries Archives.
[49] Ransomes, Agency Book, AD7/48, p. 8, Institute for Agricultural History.
[50] Ibid.
[51] Fowler, Packet: Societa Anonime La Penetrazione Roma, AD6/8, Institute for Agricultural History.
[52] Marshall, Agency Term Book No. 1, pp. 47–48, 235–37, Institute for Agricultural History; Peak Frean, Special Agencies, PF14/2, University of Reading Library Archives.
[53] Spear and Jackson Agreements, SJC65 3/7/29, Sheffield Public Libraries Archives.
[54] A. W. Smith, Directors' Minute Book, UGD118/13/2, pp. 213–14, 221–27, 275, University of Glasgow Archives.

684                              *Nicholas*

to a selling subsidiary occurred in order to economize on such costs. The shifts seem commonly to occur as direct investment in response to a crisis, where the collapse of the agency triggers investment in a selling branch by the principal. For example, John Dickinson, papermakers, Cape Asbestos, Harvey & Co., engineers, Thomas Fenner, makers of leather belts for machinery, all established sales branches as a response to crisis.[55] Nevertheless, it would be misleading to see crisis investment as the typical case of the transition between agency and branch selling. Most firms who made a foreign direct investment in branch selling were not reacting to an immediate contractual breakdown, but were investing abroad after an agency nonrenewal. To construct the theory of foreign direct investment solely on the basis of transaction costs disregards the cooperative nature of contracts. What really happened is that the principal gradually gained information about the market, including the name of customers through direct sales data, regular stocklist, and sales reports by the agent. The monitoring of the agency relationship, by which directors and travelers visited the agents, inspected books and stock, and provided skilled mechanics and representatives, meant an accumulation of knowledge within the firm on the servicing of a particular overseas market. Learning by the principal made the agent unnecessary, even occasionally when sales were few.

There was, however, a minimum sales volume or transaction frequency before a foreign direct investment could be undertaken. For example, Ransomes calculated that a £10,000-a-year trade would be required before a Paris depot could economically compete with an agency trading on less than £2,000 per year.[56] The costs of running branch sales offices were not insignificant, as the 1929 cost of Fowler's Budapest branch of £11,593 and George Wostenholm's New York City branch of £15,700 per year show.[57] The wholly-owned sales subsidiary incurred higher fixed transaction costs but a lower marginal cost of extending sales relative to employing an agent.[58] Furthermore, the larger the number of sales the greater were the monitoring costs of the agency system. Thus, the propensity to establish branch sales was greater the larger were the number of sales, the more complex the product, the greater the

[55] J. Evans, *The Endless Web: John Dickinson & Co. 1804–1954* (London, 1955), pp. 138–41; *Cape Asbestos: The Story of Cape Asbestos Co. Ltd., 1894–1953* (private, 1953); Harvey, Johanesberg Branch: Hosken's Account, DDH/85, Cornwall County Record Office, Truro; E. Vale, *The Harvey's of Hayle* (private, 1960), p. 44; R. Davies, *Twenty One and a Half Bishops Lane: A History of J. H. Fenner & Co. Ltd.* (private, 1961).
[56] Palmer, "Orwell Works," p. SPA/1F54C, Institute for Agricultural History.
[57] Fowler, Branch Reports, AC7/63, Institute for Agricultural History; Wostenholm, New York Office, WosR12(b), Sheffield Public Libraries Archives.
[58] Peter Buckley and M. Casson, "The Optimal Timing of a Foreign Investment," *Economic Journal*, 91 (March 1981), 75–87; M. Casson, "Forward," in *Inside the Multinationals: The Economics of Internal Markets*, A. Rugman (London, 1981), pp. 15–21; Buckley, "New Theories of International Business," pp. 2.12–15.

## *Foreign Investment by British Multinationals*      **685**

idiosyncratic investment in specialized capital and brand name by the principal, and the greater the appropriable rents from opportunism by agents. In part, this explains the sophisticated sales and stock level monitoring arrangements utilized by the agricultural and engineering firms.

Clearly, then, the timing of the transition between modes depended on the frequency and nature of sales, the size of the opportunities for cheating, and the extent of the firm's knowledge of the market. Knowledge of markets was most easily gained by taking over the agent. Fowler's asked their South Africa agent W. A. McLaren in March 1904 to investigate the establishment of branch selling.[59] "The only advantageous way to work our business in South Africa is to work it ourselves," McLaren argued, since there was a "business to work up which needed a lot of energy and special knowledge of machines."[60] McLaren argued that a branch would give people confidence that the firm was not composed of "itinerant bagmen who may never be seen again."[61] In 1905 a South African branch managed by McLaren was opened. Similarly, in 1939 Cowan's took the advice of Conmon Thompson and Thomas Steed, their Argentinian agents, to establish a warehouse, and the agents became full-time company employees.[62] When Cowan's took over their Brisbane agents the staff, including five salesmen, some motormen, warehousemen, office boys, clerks, and typists, were all continued.[63] The establishment of most selling branches did not involve the take-over of former agents, but it did require learning about the market.

### CONCLUSION

The agency system was a unique institution, in which information on markets and products was exchanged between agent and principal. For the principal the exchange of information was a learning experience about servicing a distant market. Market-specific knowledge shifted down the costs functions for branch selling relative to the agency. The greater the frequency of transactions and the more complex the nature of transactions the higher the costs of agency contracting and the relatively cheaper was branch selling. The accumulation of country-specific knowledge of markets, and some minimum transaction frequency were key variables in the timing of the transition to a foreign direct

---

[59] Fowler, South African Branch Correspondence, AD6/11 3/04, Institute for Agricultural History.
[60] Ibid.
[61] Ibid.
[62] Cowan, Reports: Argentina 1938, UGD311/7/34, University of Glasgow Archives.
[63] Cowan, Reports: Australia, UGD311/7/34, University of Glasgow Archives.

investment in a selling organization by British pre-1939 multinational enterprises. Of course, opportunism and monitoring costs were not totally eliminated: they occurred within the firm-owned selling branch itself. Within the firm, however, the organization could be more effectively audited and the machinery of resolving disputes within the firm replaced termination and nonrenewal as enforcement mechanisms. The firm-owned selling branch reflected the growing institutional and organizational maturity of British multinational enterprise in the years before World War II. The shift from one institution to another was dynamic and historical, a matter of learning by doing.

# [27]

Journal of International Economic Studies (1987) No. 2, 1–14
© 1987 The Institute of Comparative Economic Studies, Hosei University

## THE FIRM-SPECIFIC ADVANTAGES OF CANADIAN MULTINATIONALS

Alan M. RUGMAN

*Professor, Centre for International Business Studies, Dalhousie University*

Canada's largest multinational enterprises have developed a successful value-added chain in the harvesting, processing and marketing of resource-based products and services. They have secured competitive advantages by the effective management of a set of entry and exit barriers. These include either timber leases or mineral resource rights, vertical integration, cheap energy inputs, marketing skills, brand name products and customized production. The precise set of firm-specific advantages varies by firm, but the great majority of Canada's multinationals do not rely solely on a technological advantage. The marketing skills of Canada's mature, resource-based multinationals provide an interesting stategic contrast to the mainly technological advantages of traditional large multinationals from other nations.

## 1. Introduction

This paper has as its focus an interesting, indeed unique, set of multinational enterprises (MNEs) based in a small, open economy, Canada. The structure and performance of the largest Canadian industrial MNEs is analyzed and from this research the special firm-specific advantages (FSAs) of each of the MNEs are identified.

It is discovered that the great majority of the Canadian MNEs have FSAs in the production, distribution and trading of resource based products. Indeed, only two of the MNEs possess the knowledge or technologically based FSAs of the typical U.S., European or Japanese MNEs. Thus the Canadian FSAs are related to the country-specific advantage (CSA) of Canada in resources. Yet, since these MNEs are engaged in foreign direct investment (FDI) rather than exporting or licensing it is apparent that significant environmental constraints determine FDI as the foreign entry mode. The reasons for FDI and the manner in which the CSAs are internalized by the Canadian MNEs is studied in the paper, as are the implications for strategic planning of these MNEs in a world of increasing global competition.

This paper is organized in the following manner. Following the Introduction, in Section 2 the largest Canadian-owned MNEs are identified and their recent financial performance is reviewed. The nature of their international operations is examined. In Section 3 some generalizations are drawn about the FSAs of four groups of Canadian MNEs; those active respecitvely in the pulp and paper industry, the bever-

* The author thanks John McIlveen, Research Associate at the Dalhousie Centre for International Business Studies for his collaboration on this project. Research assistance has also been supplied by Greg Ross, Mark Godin, Gary Hierlihy and Thane Sinclair.

Alan M. RUGMAN

ages and spirits industry, the mining industry, and a miscellaneous group of MNEs. Several key FSAs of these MNEs are identified and their strength relative to foreign rival MNEs is assessed. In Section 4 there is a more detailed examination of the individual corporate structure and strategies of these Canadian MNEs.

The theoretical background for this work comes from a combination of two areas of analysis of the corporate enterprise. First, the work of Rugman (1980, 1981) on the theory of internalization is used as a basis for identification of the FSAs of each MNE. In this work it has been shown that each MNE has internalized, i.e. secured property rights over, a special differential advantage. Frequently this is in the form of a knowledge advantage (based on R and D expenditures which have generated a technological edge), but it may also occur due to marketing advantages, as in the possession of a well-established and respected distribution network, or even in more intangible aspects of the skills of the company management. The second strand of theory used is the work by Michael Porter (1980) on competitive analysis, which is readily applicable in an international dimension. Here his emphasis on entry and exit barriers and the analysis of competitive forces as they influence the strategic planning of the corporation is applied in a global context.

In Porter's model the firm needs to assess the environment in which it operates, especially the industry or industries in which it competes. Competition in the industry depends on five competitive forces; rivalry among existing firms, the threat of new entrants, the threat of substitution, and the bargaining power of suppliers and buyers. The goal of competitive analysis is to assess the strength of such competitive forces in order to determine the best strategy to adopt.

Insight as to the strength of each force is available through analysis of entry and exit barriers in the industry. The key entry barriers are: scale economies whereby existing firms enjoy production and cost advantages over new entrants; product differentation as rivals must break the barrier of existing brand loyalties; huge capital requirements involved in entering a new industry; switching costs necessary to change suppliers; access to distribution channels where established firms already have control of the distributors; and government regulation which may bar entry or impose licensing requirements on a new firm.

Exit barriers include: the existence of equipment which is of such a highly technical nature that it has low marketability; fixed costs associated with settlements of contractual arrangements with workers and low productivity once it is known that liquidation will take place; strategic barriers if the business is fundamental to the firm's strategy and image; informational barriers where the absence of clear and accurate information makes it impossible to assess performance; emotional barriers associated with managerial pride in the company and the fear of loss of status; and government which may prevent a firm from exiting in order to preserve jobs or for other social reasons.

## 2. Identification of the Canadian Multinationals

The 24 largest Canadian-owned companies are identified in Table 1. The firms are an inclusive set from the 1982 *Fortune* International 500, a listing of the world's largest non-U.S. industrial firms. Ten foreign-owned subsidiaries also make the *Fortune* list but are excluded from Table 1. A Canadian MNE is defined as a firm

THE FIRM-SPECIFIC ADVANTAGES OF CANADIAN MULTINATIONALS

with a foreign operating subsidiary in at least one foreign country and a minimum foreign to total sales ratio (F/T) of 25 percent. These criteria reduced the set to a group of 16 MNEs, as shown in Table 2.

Canadian Pacific, the largest industrial corporation in Canada, is deleted since it is a holding company. Instead one of its subsidiaries, AMCA International is

Table 1
The 24 Largest Canadian-Owned Companies – 1982

| Fortune Rank | Firm Name | 1982 Sales (billions Cdn. dollars) [1] |
|---|---|---|
| 36 | Canadian Pacific | 12.288 |
| 102 | Alcan Aluminium | 5.729 |
| 145 | Canada Development Corp. | 4.001 |
| 165 | NOVA, AN ALBERTA CORP. | 3.501 |
| 172 | Petro-Canada | 3.329 |
| 191 | Hiram-Walker Resources | 3.085 |
| 198 | Northern Telecom | 3.035 |
| 201 | Canada Packers | 3.019 |
| 208 | Dome Petroleum | 2.929 |
| 211 | International Thomson | 2.879 |
| 219 | Noranda Mines | 2.793 |
| 239 | Massey Ferguson | 2.539 |
| 255 | Seagram | 2.364 |
| 261 | Moore | 2.279 |
| 289 | Stelco | 2.020 |
| 311 | John Labatt | 1.864 |
| 315 | MacMillan Bloedel | 1.843 |
| 331 | Genstar | 1.761 |
| 339 | Domtar | 1.686 |
| 351 | Abitibi-Price | 1.635 |
| 365 | Molson | 1.578 |
| 377 | Inco | 1.525 |
| 389 | Dofasco | 1.485 |
| 398 | Consolidated-Bathurst | 1.424 |

Note 1. Converted from U.S. dollars at $1.2337 Cdn.: U.S.
Source: "The Fortune International 500", *Fortune*, August 22, 1983.

included. AMCA (formerly Dominion Bridge) is the largest multinational subsidiary of Canadian Pacific and its sales are large enough to have it included on the *Fortune* listing were it not a subsidiary. AMCA is a diversified MNE engaged in manufacturing, engineering and construction.

The 16 Canadian MNEs are almost all resource based. The industrial mix is as

Alan M. RUGMAN

Table 2
The 16 Largest Canadian Industrial Multinationals 1978–1982

| Firm | Average Sales 1978–1982 (billions) | F/T | S/T | ROE | S.D. |
|------|------|------|------|------|------|
| Alcan | 5.169 | na[2] | 77 | 11.5 | 7.7 |
| Seagram | 2.991 | 92 | 92 | 10.4 | 2.8 |
| Massey-Ferguson | 2.688 | 93 | 93 | 6.5 | 6.5 |
| Noranda | 2.578 | 60 | 28 | 13.1 | 8.6 |
| Hiram Walker | 2.565 | na | 47 | 11.7 | 2.5 |
| Northern Telecom | 2.214 | 61 | 48 | 14.9 | 5.8 |
| MacMillan Bloedel | 2.135 | 88[1] | 39[1] | 8.9 | 7.6 |
| Moore | 1.991 | 90 | 90 | 17.3 | 1.9 |
| NOVA | 1.990 | na | 34 | 12.1 | 2.2 |
| Inco | 1.636 | 82 | 42 | 9.7 | 7.6 |
| Genstar | 1.584 | na | 52 | 14.4 | 5.6 |
| Domtar | 1.568 | 29[1] | 8[1] | 12.6 | 7.5 |
| Abitibi-Price | 1.505 | 66 | 14 | 13.4 | 5.5 |
| AMCA | 1.403 | na | 78 | 15.8 | 2.8 |
| Consolidated-Bathurst | 1.323 | 54 | 20 | 16.6 | 7.7 |
| Molson | 1.235 | na | 27 | 15.5 | 2.1 |
| Mean | 2.161 | 72 | 49 | 12.8 | 5.3 |

1. 1981.
2. not available.

Source: Corporate Annual Reports.

Notes:  a)  F/T is defined as the rate of foreign (F) to total (T) sales.
             S/T is defined as the rate of sales by subsidiaries (S) to total sales.
             The difference between F and S is exports (E) from the home country nation.
       b)  ROE is the mean return on equity, i.e. the ratio of net income after tax and before
             extraordinary items divided by the average net worth (value of shareholder's
             equity).
       c)  S.D. means standard deviation.

follows: pulp and paper – 4; mining and metal manufacturing – 3; beverages – 3 and six other single industry categories. The special cases include: NOVA, a petroleum resource MNE; Massey-Ferguson, the farm machinery manufacturer; Moore, the world's largest producer of business forms; Genstar, a vertically integrated construction materials and mining resource MNE; and AMCA, the steel related equipment manufacturer specializing in resource extraction and processing equipment. The only non-resource based Canadian MNE is Northern Telecom. It is the second largest manufacturer of telecommunications equipment in North America and is

THE FIRM-SPECIFIC ADVANTAGES OF CANADIAN MULTINATIONALS

widely considered to have the most technologically advanced telephone switching equipment available.

In terms of sales, the Canadian MNEs are smaller than their U.S. or European counterparts. The average size (from Table 2, converted to U.S. dollars) is $1.752 billion. The largest 50 U.S. and European MNEs by contrast have average sales of $16 and $12.4 billion respectively (Rugman 1983).

The Canadian MNEs financial performance as measured by the return-on-equity (ROE) over the last ten years is 12.8 percent compared to 14.3 and 8.5 for U.S. and European MNEs respectively. The ROE for European MNEs is biased downward by the significant presence of state-owned enterprises, see Rugman (1983). The risk of these returns as proxied by one standard deviation (S.D.), is 5.3, 3.6 and 5.2 respectively for Canadian, U.S. and European MNEs. In short, the Canadian MNEs earn comparable returns to U.S. MNEs but at greater risk, while earning higher returns at the same risk level relative to European MNEs.

## 3. Firm-Specific Advantages of Canadian Multinationals

The special nature of the FSA of Canadian MNEs is that it is usually based upon Canada's country-specific advantage in resources. As a relatively small nation of 25 million people spread out across one of the largest land masses in the world, Canada has an abundance of resources, ranging from timber, minerals, and fish to energy sources based on hydroelectric power, oil and natural gas. Traditionally, Canada has been able to market its resources by exports, especially to its close neighbor, the United States. The interesting question is why does Canada now need to service foreign markets by FDI rather than by exporting? There are two answers to this question, based on the analysis of the determinants of FDI in Rugman (1981).

First, there are "natural" market imperfections which make it necessary for firms to retain knowledge about their FSA within the network of the MNE rather than risk its dissipation on open markets. This by now classic explanation of the need for internalization is, however, somewhat weak in the Canadian context since relatively few Canadian MNEs have an FSA in production know-how. Indeed, only Northern Telecom has the typical knowledge-based FSA of most of the U.S., European, and Japanese MNEs. Yet, when the concept of internalization is extended to include control over the marketing function, as well as over production, then it becomes clearer that many of the Canadian MNEs benefit from such control. The brand name products marketed by Seagram and other beverage-based MNEs, the long-established clients of the pulp and paper MNEs and the distribution network of Massey-Ferguson, all serve to illustrate the critical value of internal ownership of the marketing function.

Second, there are "unnatural" market imperfections, that is, regulations and controls imposed by governments. These serve to increase the cost of exporting. Sometimes exports from Canada are restricted, as when there are tariffs. Since tariffs on resource imports, especially by the United States, are minimal, it is necessary to look to non-tariff barriers to understand why trading is being replaced by FDI. In recent years a veritable galaxy of federal, state and municipal regulations have arisen, often for good reasons of their own, to protect domestic workers and industries threatened by trade. To break down these barriers to trade Canadian firms

Alan M. RUGMAN

**Table 3**
**Firm-Specific Advantages of Canadian MNEs**

| Firm | Firm-Specific Advantage |
| --- | --- |
| Abitibi-Price | World leader in newsprint sales; timberland leases; good and long-standing customer relationships. |
| Consolidated-Bathurst | Experience in the production, management and marketing of diversified pulp and paper products; vertical integration; timberland leases. |
| Domtar | Product diversification; long-term leases and holdings of natural resources. |
| MacMillan Bloedel | Access to and control over high quality coastal timber; vertical integration. |
| Seagram | Internationally recognized brand name products; marketing; network of affiliated dealers. |
| Hiram Walker | Internationally recognized brand name products; well-established marketing relationships with agents; ownership of oil and gas resources. |
| Molson | Brand names in beverage production; marketing expertise; product diversification. |
| Alcan | Vertical integration; ownership of cheap hydroelectric power. |
| Inco | Quality, location and size of proprietary mineral holdings; experience and market knowledge; cheap hydro-electric power. |
| Noranda | Ownership of mineral resources; product diversification; vertical integration. |
| Massey-Ferguson | World-wide distribution, sales and service network; well-known standardized products. |
| AMCA (Dominion Bridge) | Experience and expertise in the design, engineering and marketing of resource-related equipment; product diversification; vertical integration. |
| Genstar | Vertical integration in construction; diversification. |
| NOVA | Provincial monopoly over gas transmission; expertise and experience; vertical integration; financial strength. |
| Northern Telecom | R&D technology in digital telephone switching equipment using semiconductors; aggressive world-wide marketing; efficient production; protected home market with Bell Canada. |
| Moore | Marketing network; innovative and adaptive to changing technology in office support systems; corporate culture; financial strength. |

THE FIRM-SPECIFIC ADVANTAGES OF CANADIAN MULTINATIONALS

have turned to FDI to substitute for exporting.

Together, the natural and unnatural market imperfections have acted as a strong incentive for Canadian MNEs to develop and replace exporting. In the process, the Canadian firms have often become more sophisticated in their international operations, and more aware of the need for strategic planning in the face of rivalry from powerful global competitors.

The special characteristics of each key MNE, or group of Canadian MNEs, is now examined and their FSAs are identified. Table 3 is a summary of the FSAs of the largest 16 Canadian MNEs, arranged by industry group. Following this there is a section in which the nature of the FSA is related to the organizational structure and strategic planning of each of these MNEs.

## 4. Entry and Exit Barriers of Canadian Multinationals

### a) Canadian Pulp and Paper Multinationals

The ability of the largest Canadian forest products companies to internalize Canada's CSA in timber resources is a major reason why these firms are competitive in domestic and global markets. The majority of Canada's timber resources are owned by the provincial governments. Generally, Canadian forest product companies control and manage these timber resources on the basis of long-term leases from provincial governments. These leases, and a feeling of nationalism, provide Canadian pulp and paper MNEs with a sufficient supply of secure resources to compete in global markets. While the leases themselves are not formal entry barriers to foreign competition, the Canadian system is sufficiently different from that of the United States to deter foreign competition for Canada's timber resource. American rivals prefer the security which accompanies private ownership of the forest.

Canadian pulp and paper MNEs also benefit from vertical integration which facilitates the development of manufacturing and marketing expertise, most notably in the production and marketing of newsprint. These advantages enable them to compete effectively in foreign markets, especially in the vital nearby U.S. market. The Canadian firms have established long-standing relationships with major customers which act as switching barriers to entry for rivals. Recently, to avoid environmental and political risks they have entered into joint ventures with purchasers (newspaper companies) which further helps to strengthen the degree of vertical integration.

An important exit barrier for the largest Canadian pulp and paper MNEs is the specialized assets which they control, again the most important of which is the vast timber reserves of Canada. Furthermore, many of their production facilities are highly capital-intensive and these specialized investments also represent significant entry and exit barriers. A final exit barrier is the dependence of many of these firms on the U.S. market. Once the pulp and paper firms establish production facilities in the United States the scale of their U.S. operations tends to lock the firms into this market. Since the U.S. market is ten times the size of that in Canada, a Canadian MNE finds investment in the United States to be a larger entry and exit barrier than would a U.S. firm investing in the relatively smaller Canadian market.

Alan M. RUGMAN

### b) Liquor and Beer Multinationals

In the liquor industry, where scale economies, capital requirements and government regulations are relatively insignificant barriers to entry, Seagram and Hiram Walker have used strong FSAs to effectively restrict competition. Potential rivals may have only limited difficulty in financing entry into the industry and subsequently achieving scale economies in production, especially if they are able to acquire an established operation. However, rivals are unable to compete effectively without access to distribution channels.

Seagram and Hiram Walker have both established extensive networks of distributors, agents and affiliates which enable the firms to maintain market shares and respond quickly to market changes and opportunities. Control over these networks amounts to a tremendous entry barrier to potential and existing rivals. It also creates high switching costs. Internationally recognized brand names facilitate product differentiation and are instrumental in retaining loyalty in the distribution network.

Both MNEs have also attempted portfolio diversification strategies. Recent activities on the part of Hiram Walker to diversify into oil and gas and lessen its dependence on liquor are evidence of relatively low exit barriers. Hiram Walker has gone as far as to contract out many of its distilling and aging operations in the United States. This move is also evidence of confidence in its brand reputation and distribution networks. Hiram Walker has thus used its liquor operations as a cash cow to finance diversification into oil (Home Oil) and gas (Consumers' Gas).

Seagram, although also diversifying, continues to concentrate on its liquor businesses due to strong strategic and emotional exit barriers. The liquor business is fundamental to the firm's strategy and image as Seagram attempts to be the world leader in most brands. The long-standing Bronfman family association also reinforces the commitment of the company to the business. Management at Hiram Walker, on the other hand, does not have such a strong emotional commitment to the liquor business.

Molson's FSA in marketing experience and expertise has resulted in a high entry barrier in that its brand names are well-differentiated and enjoy high market acceptance. This is a strong barrier in the mature and competitive brewing industry. Through brand diversification Molson has enhanced its already significant barriers to entry. Potential rivals would have to make a tremendous capital investment, not only to achieve the economies of scale enjoyed by Molson, but also to enter the many regional markets as government regulation prohibits the interprovincial sale of beer. With established facilities in each of the regional markets Molson has been able to distribute its brands nationally and effectively shield itself from new national competition.

Like the liquor multinationals, Molson faces significant exit barriers. Strategic and emotional barriers are the key deterrents to exiting. While government and social interests and specialized assets are normally exit barriers, the competitive nature of the industry would render the assets highly marketable and stifle government and social objections as few jobs would be lost.

### c) Mining Multinationals

An increasing level of world competition in the 1970s and early 1980s is partial

THE FIRM-SPECIFIC ADVANTAGES OF CANADIAN MULTINATIONALS

evidence of a shortage of effective barriers to entry in world mineral resource markets. In the past, Canadian mining multinationals have enjoyed a competitive advantage due to economies of scale and ownership of the mineral resource. The small size of the domestic market necessitates global competition for these firms. The capital intensity of the business, the immense size of the required investment and the lack of known resource deposits were at one time sufficient entry barriers. However, the discovery and subsequent development of rich ore deposits in third world nations has helped to erode these barriers. Government sponsorship and state ownership have all but eliminated capital cost and scale economies as barriers for rivals in such nations.

The increase in worldwide productive capacity has led to an oversupply of both ores and processed products. The increase in the availability of raw materials and smelted metals means that potential entrants no longer face huge capital investments which were once necessary in order to achieve scale economies in extraction and smelting. New rivals may now proceed directly into fabrication. Competition is now at an intense level with cost and efficiency the key factors.

Canadian mining MNEs retain some competitive advantages, however, and their FSAs have resulted in new entry barriers. Vertical integration in extraction, processing and marketing yield a cost advantage. The firm-specific advantages of Alcan, Inco and Noranda in experience and expertise in extraction and processing also help to promote cost efficiency. New rivals initially lack such knowledge. Vertical integration through the ownership of natural resources also ensures stable supplies, thereby reducing the bargaining power of suppliers and reliance on the cyclical primary and speculative secondary markets.

Through extension to the marketing function, vertical integration in mining helps to stabilize demand and reduce the bargaining power of buyers. It also creates a barrier by closing markets to rivals and creating switching costs. The related FSAs in marketing experience and market knowledge help to close distribution channels. Switching costs are created as the Canadian firms benefit from long-standing relationships and long-term contracts with customers.

An important firm-specific advantage and barrier to entry is inexpensive hydroelectric power, particularly for Alcan and, to a lesser extent, Inco. Smelting and processing are very energy intense. Thus, through ownership of the hydroelectric generating facilities and access to relatively cheap Canadian energy, Canadian mining MNEs enjoy a significant cost advantage independent of scale.

These barriers have not been very effective in barring competition from plastic, carbon fibre and new alloy substitutes. Nor have they been effective against competitors who merely fabricate smelted metal purchased on the open market. Consequently, Alcan, Inco and Noranda have all intensified R and D and product and market development. They have also expanded fabrication and concentration on market niches in order to combat substitute competition.

While entry barriers are only moderately high, exit barriers are very strong. The presence of specialized assets, coupled with overcapacity in the industry, reduces the firm's value and marketability. There are also high fixed costs associated with liquidation and tremendous government and social barriers as these firms are the key employers in many regions of Canada. Strategic exit barriers and emotional barriers are also quite powerful.

Alan M. RUGMAN

### d) Other Multinationals

#### Massey-Ferguson

Massey-Ferguson at one time benefitted from FSAs in the efficient production of tractors and combines. In recent years the absence of technological innovation in farm machinery, coupled with relatively low entry barriers in this mature and competitive industry, have forced Massey-Ferguson to rely on its well-established international marketing and distribution network. Today this is still its main FSA. The standardization of farm machinery products has resulted in little product differentiation and brand loyalty. Consequently, there are low switching costs as many distributors carry the lines of many manufacturers. Capital requirements and scale economies are not necessarily restrictive, especially to an established company diversifying into farm machinery by concentrating on a market niche.

Massey-Ferguson's marketing and distribution network creates switching costs and prevents new rivals from gaining access to the distribution network. Toyota was forced to join with Massey-Ferguson in order to market and distribute a line of small tractors. This FSA also reduces the bargaining power of buyers. Exit barriers are quite significant; otherwise Massey-Ferguson might well have left the business during its crisis years early in the 1980s. While the presence of specialized assets may have been partly responsible for this decision, strategic, emotional, social and government exit barriers were also very important.

#### AMCA and Genstar

AMCA and Genstar are each involved in several industries. However, they have differentiated themselves in that they are two of the few firms who can complete turnkey commercial and industrial projects. They also have FSAs in design and engineering expertise and vertical integration in all aspects of a project. Thus, rivals are faced with high switching costs, huge capital requirements and scale economies in attempting to compete with them. Vertical integration reduces the bargaining power of both suppliers and buyers and rivalry from both potential entrants and established competitors. AMCA and Genstar face high exit barriers in the ownership of specialized assets, the high fixed costs of liquidation and strategic and emotional barriers.

#### NOVA

NOVA's most important FSA is its government-granted monopoly over gas transmission in the province of Alberta. NOVA used the related experience, expertise and cash flows to expand its transmission business and to diversify into petrochemicals and petroleum. Vertical integration in all three of its main businesses reduces the bargaining power of buyers and suppliers and ensures stability of markets and supplies. NOVA faces strong exit barriers, particularly provincial legislation which specifically outlines its authorized businesses. Strategic exit barriers are also present along with highly specialized assets.

#### Northern Telecom

Nortel's FSA is based upon R and D and proprietary technology in telephone switching equipment. It is dependent upon one product line (and its variants) for most of its revenues, but is still able to expand sales into new markets as the product line has not yet matured. There are few entry barriers in the industry, thus FSAs

THE FIRM-SPECIFIC ADVANTAGES OF CANADIAN MULTINATIONALS

must be guarded from potential dissipation. Recent regulations in both Canada and the United States have created an opportunity for new competition. There are many firms who are presently engaged in silicon chip technology and a new discovery could quickly destroy Nortel's technological advantage. Furthermore, many high-tech firms possess both the financial strength and the ability to achieve the necessary scale economies once the technology is acquired.

Nortel has other FSAs which help deter competition. Its agressive worldwide marketing creates switching costs and differentiates its product. Its association with Bell Canada protects its home market from competition. Nortel also creates switching costs in that it sells a total system, whereas new and existing rivals are often unable to do so. Nortel needs to expand its product lines and diversify into other areas of information processing and communications due to the shortage of significantly high entry barriers. Exit barriers are relatively low, but they do exist. Strategic and emotional barriers are significant and the government takes great pride in promoting Canadian high-tech.

### Moore

Moore's primary FSA is its extensive world-wide marketing network which allow it to monitor and respond to the changing needs of business and industry and the latest innovations in office systems. Thus, Moore is both innovative and adaptive. Moore has used its FSAs to create strong entry barriers for anyone wishing to compete on a global basis. The strength of these barriers is evidenced by a complete absence of global competition.

Rivals are faced with tremendous capital requirements in trying to emmulate Moore's distribution network and corporate culture. Moore also has vast financial resources capable of withstanding or initiating intense price and/or marketing and service competition. Market knowledge and customer service have differentiated Moore's products and services and created switching costs for rivals. The main exit barriers confronting Moore are strategic and emotional. However, these barriers loss most of their impact due to the limited scope of global competition.

## 5. Conclusions: Lessons for Stategic Management

In today's world of increasing global competition, large U.S., European and Japanese multinationals compete aggressively for market share and profits in every corner of the world. The battles are fought over product lines that shift quickly as the tides of technological innovation ebb and flow between rival corporations. Yet, Canadian multinationals have been surprisingly successful global competitors despite the intensity of competition and the relatively small size of the open Canadian economy.

In this paper, analysis of the sixteen largest Canadian multinationals suggests a variety of reasons for this success. Three important implications for the strategic management of international business in Canada are generated.

First, successful multinationals need not be in the traditional American, Japanese and European mold, i.e. with advantages in proprietary knowledge and the embodiment of high technology. The Canadian pulp and paper, mining and liquor multinationals are non-traditional, yet successful multinationals. Furthermore,

Alan M. RUGMAN

Moore Corporation is an example of a Canadian firm which developed FSAs to complement high technology rather than to rely upon it, as did Northern Telecom. Competitive analysis can lead to strategies which foster the growth of Canadian multinationals, whereas participation in high-tech industries in, of and by itself need not guarantee success.

Second, Canadian multinationals demonstrate that the FSA of the multinational can be in marketing and experience. The efficient marketing of resource-based product lines is the primary strength of many Canadian MNEs. Seagram, Moore and Massey-Ferguson are examples of the critical importance of marketing and distribution. Each has an extensive distribution network which given it a distinct advantage over its competitors. In Massey-Ferguson's case, it is one of the few advantages which the firm continues to enjoy. These relationships help to reduce the environmental costs, especially the political risk, which is part and parcel of any foreign involvement. Effective distribution networks, market knowledge and experience result in favourable barriers to entry and the reduction of competitive forces. Switching costs, product differentiation and control of the distribution channels are effective even when cost, scale and government barriers do not exist.

Third, the FSAs of Canadian multinationals often build upon Canada's country-specific advantages (CSAs). The firms either own mineral deposits, have established long-term leases for timber rights, or own energy resources which are cheap and abundant relative to foreign rivals. In short, Canadian multinationals have internalized Canada's CSAs in resources, which in turn leads to special firm-specific advantages. The only non-resource based Canadian multinational in the top 16 is Northern Telecom and, perhaps, Moore. FSAs which build upon CSAs can form formidable barriers to entry. Such FSAs give Canadian multinationals access not only to important sources of raw materials, but also to cheap Canadian hydroelectric power. Nationalism can also be of importance since favoured Canadian firms may receive preferential access to the resource from the responsible governments. Canadian multinationals also benefit from links with provincial governments which reduce information costs and political risk.

The Canadian MNEs studied in this paper are an object lesson for strategic managers. They demonstrate the success of managerial strategies aimed at the marketing end of the business rather than on the production end. Canadian MNEs are successful because they build on the resource strength of their home nation but process and distribute product lines in an aggressive manner on a world-wide basis. The Canadian MNEs are examples of the fallacy of over-reliance on technological strength. Resource-based MNEs are just as good, if not better, than high tech MNEs.

## References

Alcan Aluminium Limited (1982), *Alcan Facts 1982,* Montreal.
Alcan Aluminium Limited (1978), *Alcan, Its Purpose, Objectives and Policies,* Montreal.
Barnett, John H. and Sweitzer, Robert W. (1980), *The Joseph E. Seagram and Sons, Ltd.,* A case study, Faculty of Administrative Studies, Dalhousie University.
*Business Week,* "Europe: Farm Equipment Sales. The Rut Gets Deeper", June 29,

THE FIRM-SPECIFIC ADVANTAGES OF CANADIAN MULTINATIONALS

1981.

*Business Week*, "Ailing Harvester Turns to New Doctors", May 17, 1982.

Cameron, John I. (1980), "Nickel" Vol. II, in: Carl E. Beigie and Alfred O. Hero, Jr. (eds.) *Natural Resources in U.S.-Canadian-Relations*, Westview Press, Boulder.

Canada (1971), *Report of the Royal Commission on Farm Machinery*, Information Canada, Ottawa.

*Canadian Business*, "Canada's Top 500 Companies," July, 1983.

*Canadian Business*, "Moore Corp. versus the electronic age", September, 1978.

Canadian Pulp and Paper Association (1980), Forests for the Future, in: the proceedings of the Canadian Forest Congress, September.

Cook, Peter (1981), *Massey at the Brink*, Collins Publishers, Don Mills, Ontario.

Corporate Annual Reports, various 1970–1983.

Corporate 10K Forms, various 1970–1983.

Dorr, André L. and Tilton, John E. (1980), Bauxite and Aluminum, in: Carl E. Beigie and Alfred O. Hero, Jr. (eds.), *Natural Resources in U.S.-Canadian Relations*, Vol. II, Westview Press, Boulder.

*Financial Post*, "More for Moore Corp. in Asia", September 18, 1976,

*Financial Post*, "Financial Post 500," June, 1983.

*Financial Times*, "Moore Prospects Look Bright", January 16–22, 1978.

*Financial Times*, "High-tech profits from old-fashioned paper", March 9, 1981.

*Financial Times*, "A Century of Growth", September 27, 1982.

*Forbes*, "The $20,000 Razor", June 21, 1982.

*Fortune*, "Alcan Shakes the Aluminum Market", Andrew C. Brown, February 21, 1983.

Foster, Peter (1982), *The Sorcerer's Apprentices*, Collins Publishers, Don Mills.

Foster, Peter (1983), *Other People's Money*, Collins Publishers, Don Mills.

Goldenberg, Susan (1983), *Canadian Pacific: A Portrait of Power*, Methuen Publications, Agincourt and Facts on File, Inc., New York.

Kraar, Louis, (1981), Seagram Tightens its Grip on Dupont, *Fortune*, November 16.

Litvak, I.A. and Maule, C.J. (1981), *The Canadian Multinationals*, Butterworth and Company, Toronto.

Mackay, Donald, (1982), *Empire of Wood*, University of Washington Press, Seattle.

May, Sherry J. (1981), Massey-Ferguson 1980–1981: A case-study in International Marketing, in: *Proceedings of the Atlantic Schools of Business Annual Conference.*

Mikesell, Raymond F. (1978), *The World Copper Industry*, The Johns Hopkins University Press, Baltimore.

The Mining Association of Canada (1983), *Challenges and Opportunities: Canada's Mining Industry in the Future*, Ottawa.

The Mining Association of Canada (1983), *Mining in Canada: Facts and Figures*, Ottawa.

The Mining Association of Canada (1984), *The Mineral Industry and Canadian Economic Growth*, Ottawa.

The Mining Association of Canada (1984), *Policy Statement*, Ottawa.

*Moody's International Manual, 1982* (1983), Moody's Investor Service, New York.

Nappi, Carmine (1984), *Structural Changes in the International Aluminium Industry:*

Alan M. RUGMAN

*The Situation in Canada*, preliminary draft, École des Hautes Études Commercials, Montreal.

Neufeld, E.P. (1969), *A Global Corporation*, University of Toronto Press, Toronto.

Newman, Peter C. (1981), *The Acquisitors*, McClelland and Stewart Ltd., Toronto.

Newman, Peter C. (1978), *The Bronfman Dynasty*, McClelland and Stewart-Bantam Limited, Toronto.

Newman, Peter C. (1975), *The Canadian Establishment*, McClelland and Stewart-Bantam Ltd., Toronto.

Newman, Peter C. (1982). *The Establishment Man*, McClelland and Stewart-Bantam Limited, Toronto.

Pearse, Peter (1980), Forest Products, in: Carl E. Beigie and Alfred O. Hero, Jr. (eds.), *Natural Resources in U.S.-Canadian Relations*, Vol. II, Westview Press, Boulder, Colorado.

Porter, Michael E. (1980), *Competitive Strategy: Techniques for Analyzing Industries and Competitors*, Free Press, Macmillan Publishers, New York.

*Pulp and Paper Canada*, "GATT: What Effect on Pulp and Paper," Oct. 10, 1979.

*Pulp and Paper Canada*, "C-B Purchases English Mill", September 1981.

*Pulp and Paper Canada*, "Companies Strive to Keep Up with the Times", June 1981.

*Pulp and Paper Canada*, "MB Sells Fine Paper Mill to Fraser", March 1983.

Pye, Charles H. (1981), *Profitability in the Canadian Mineral Industry*, Centre for Resource Studies, Kingston.

Rugman, Alan M. (1980), Internalization as a General Theory of Foreign Direct Investment: A Reappraisal of the Literature, *Weltwirtshaftliches Archiv*, 116:2, pp. 365-379.

Rugman, Alan M. (1981), *Inside the Multinationals: The Economics of Internal Markets*, Croom Helm, London and Columbia University Press, New York.

Rugman, Alan M. (1983), The Comparative Performance of U.S. and European Multinational Enterprises, 1970–79, *Management International Review*, 23:2, pp. 4-14.

Stuckey, John A. (1983), *Vertical Integration and Joint Ventures in the Aluminium Industry*, Harvard University Press, Cambridge.

Urquhart, Elizabeth (1978), *The Canadian Non-ferrous Metals Industry: An Industrial Organization Study*, Centre for Resource Studies, Kingston.

The Value Line Investment Survey (1983), *Alcan Aluminium Limited: Investor Profile*, Arnold Bernhard and Co., Inc., New York.

Whitney, John W. (1980), Copper, in: Carl E. Beigie and Alfred O. Hero, Jr. (eds.), *Natural Resources in U.S.-Canadian Relations*, Vol. II, Westview Press, Boulder.

## Notes on Sources and Acknowledgements

While much of the analysis used here is based on the above published sources, especially company Annual Reports, 10Ks, company histories and press reports, additional vital information was provided by leading company executives. Interviews were conducted with officers involved in corporate planning or other aspects of strategic decision making in each of the multinationals. The interpretation and analysis made of information from these interviews is the sole responsibility of the author and statements in this study should not be attributed to these executives. The author gratefully acknowledges the contribution of these experts to this research project.

# [28]

# SERVICE MULTINATIONALS:
# CONCEPTUALIZATION, MEASUREMENT AND THEORY

J.J. Boddewyn*
*Baruch College*

Marsha Baldwin Halbrich**
*Baruch College*

and

A.C. Perry***
*The American University*

**Abstract.** The application of MNE definitions, measurements and theories to international services is still in its infancy, despite the considerable size and growth of this sector. There are problems in defining, classifying, measuring, comparing and explaining service MNEs, but they do not require special definitions and theories. Still, research to date suggests: (1) delinking the concepts of multinational enterprise and foreign direct investment under certain conditions, and (2) qualifying the nature of ownership, internalization and location advantages in FDI theory, as far as service MNEs are concerned.

*J.J. Boddewyn is Professor of International Business at the Baruch College of the City University of New York, and a Fellow of the Academy of International Business.

**Marsha Baldwin Halbrich (MBA, Baruch College) is a consultant with Susan Horowitz & Associates and with Ibero-American Productions, both in New York City.

***A.C. Perry is an Assistant Professor of International Business at The American University in Washington, DC. An appendix reviewing the domestic literature on the nature of services can be obtained by writing to either Professor Boddewyn or Perry.

This is a revised version of a paper presented at the Annual Meeting of the Academy of International Business, Cleveland Ohio, October 1984. Helpful comments and suggestions were provided by J.N. Behrman (North Carolina), P.J. Buckley (Bradford), Mark Casson (Reading), Kang Rae Cho (Pennsylvania State), H. Peter Gray (Rutgers), Robert Grosse (Miami), B. Herman (Netherlands Economic Institute), Howard Perlmutter (Wharton), C.P. Kindleberger (MIT, Brandeis), A.M. Rugman (Dalhousie), Kenneth Simmonds (London Business School), Helmut Soldner (Augsburg), J.M. Stopford (London Business School), Raymond Vernon (Harvard), A.F. Weinstein (Massachusetts at Boston), L.T. Wells (Harvard) and Mira Wilkins (Florida International) as well as by three anonymous reviewers. Betty Appelbaum and Thomas Quinlan (Baruch College) extended valuable copy-editing help.

Received: January 1985; Revised: May, August & December 1985; Accepted: January 1986.

42 JOURNAL OF INTERNATIONAL BUSINESS STUDIES, FALL 1986

Many international service firms are already household words around the world: American Express, McDonald's, Avis, Thomas Cook, Merrill Lynch, Citibank, Club Med, Pan Am, McKinsey, Arthur Andersen, Barclay's, Dun & Bradstreet and Hilton, among others.[1] Yet, conceptual and theoretical analysis has not kept pace with the size and growth of this sector.[2]

Therefore, this critical essay integrates recently available definitions and theories to answer the following questions: (1) when is a firm in "international services;" (2) what problems are encountered in locating, measuring and comparing international service firms; (3) do the criteria used to categorize an international company as a "multinational enterprise" (MNE) apply to those dealing in services; and (4) are the prevalent theories of foreign direct investment (FDI) relevant to understanding them? It will be argued that newer MNE/FDI definitions and theories are applicable to such firms, provided important characteristics of international services and their providers are kept in mind when researching them.

## THE NATURE OF INTERNATIONAL SERVICES

In the general literature on services, many criteria are used to define them: intangibility (a telephone call), perishability (a plane ride), customization (an engineering plan for a factory), simultaneity of production and consumption (a bank loan), consumer participation in production (remote computer data-processing), and use without ownership (a car rental). Actually, every one of these criteria *by itself* has been found lacking in fully differentiating a "service" from a "non-service." In this analysis, emphasis is placed on those services satisfying at least one of two criteria, namely, intangibility and/or dependence on a customer's participation or input (his person or assets) in the service's production.

When services cross borders, they can be classified in a threefold manner.[3] The *foreign-tradeable service* generates a product that is separable from the production process itself as well as transportable across national boundaries from the site of production to the location of consumer receipt or use — for example, financial loans. On the other hand, a *location-bound service* is tied to the service's production location because its production's time and space constraints are shared by producer and consumer, as in hotel accommodations.[4]

In *combination services*, part of the production process is location-bound and another part is capable of producing a foreign-tradeable product. Thus, in remote computer data-processing, the customer's participation in production can take place at a national site different from the producer's location. The foreign-tradeable elements between these two locations are the semi-processed information from the customer's terminal and the final information from the producer's mainframe, but a location-bound quality is also present because the site of the customer's final use or receipt of the product is tied to his production participation when he provides and receives information on line at his terminal or printer.

This classification is not an idle exercise in typology but has serious research implications. For example, a comparison of exporting vs. foreign direct investment is not appropriate in the cases of location-bound and combination services - as could be surmised from the international-product-lifecycle theory [Vernon 1966] which implies a possible choice between exporting and foreign direct investment, and a progressive evolution from the former toward the latter under certain conditions. In fact, some services require foreign direct investment or alternative non-equity forms of international product *from the very beginning*, when part of the production-delivery-use chain must be performed abroad (see below for further elaboration of these implications).

## LOCATING, MEASURING AND COMPARING INTERNATIONAL SERVICES

Additional problems are encountered in locating, measuring and comparing international service firms.

### *Center-periphery Allocation*

Determining the existence and magnitude of international services is more problematic than may be assumed, particularly when service investments and revenues are spread over several countries. For example, how should investments in communication links between mainframe and user locations — land lines, microwave relay paths, underwater cables, satellite links and communication computers — that are necessary for data transmission within a global system be assigned between one country and another? A similar question arises in apportioning assets in the air-transport industry where capital equipment in airplanes far outweighs sales and support-operations equipment. This industry offers a core service that is produced and consumed largely across national borders and even over international waters so that these assets cannot simply be attributed to the home-country parent organization that made the investment. Besides, revenue allocation between home and abroad is difficult, thereby complicating the determination of the foreign component of a service firm [Herman and van Holst 1984].

### *Difficult Comparisons*

Most studies have dealt with only a single service industry and are not comparative in nature, but further research is bound to extend to more industries and involve comparisons.[5] One major comparative problem centers on *size*. Thus, the *Fortune's* "Service 500" directory [1985] divides its firms into seven categories, each with a primary ranking criterion for measuring that category's relative size and growth: (1) different types of assets are used for ordering diversified-financial, commercial-banking, life insurance and utilities firms; (2) diversified services and retailing are ranked by sales, and (3) transportation companies are compared in terms of operating revenues. These rankings also rest on different types of income: sales, fees, commissions, interest charges, etc.

Consequently, it is difficult to compare one group of service MNEs with another as well as service with non-service firms in terms of size. For instance, contrasting the revenues and assets of a manufacturer and a bank is unrealistic. The latter's income is composed of net interest receipts, fees, commissions and other revenues that cannot be compared to those received by the manufacturer in the form of sales; while its assets include huge deposits at interest, which bear little resemblance to the manufacturer's assets. Yet, a ranking of the 100 largest U.S. multinationals in terms of "foreign revenue" mixes both service and non-service firms [Curtis 1984]. While this problem is also encountered outside of service MNEs, it is certainly magnified in the latter's case.

### Cut-off Points

MNE definitions use some minimum amount of international involvement as a cutoff point — for example, in terms of number of host countries, size and percentage of worldwide revenues, assets, production and personnel related to foreign operations [e.g., Stopford 1982, p. xii]. However, service operations run the gamut from "equipment-based" (e.g., airlines) to "people-based" (e.g., management consulting) firms [Thomas 1978]; and service production is being "industrialized" through hard, soft and hybrid technologies [Levitt 1976]. Therefore, using a standard formula (e.g., X percent of foreign revenues or assets) across service industries to select a sample of service MNEs will prove as arbitrary as in the case of non-service firms, if not more so.

### DEFINING SERVICE MULTINATIONALS

Various problems have been encountered in applying older MNE definitions to services. On the other hand, new conceptualizations of the multinational enterprise raise intriguing questions about what types of international service firms belong to the MNE category.

### Can Service Firms Be MNEs?

Most conceptualizations of the multinational enterprise have dealt only with industrial and extractive firms, or they have been presented as applying to all types of enterprises, including services, without further differentiation. On the other hand, a few scholars (e.g., Behrman) have excluded services producers from the ranks of MNEs as defined in their models.

Building on Perlmutter's [1969] distinction between the ethnocentric, polycentric and geocentric orientations of international firms, Behrman [1974] has formulated a definition of MNEs that effectively excludes international service organizations. According to him, there are three types of international firms. The "classical investor" invests overseas to secure export markets for home-country production or to supply home-country facilities and markets from abroad. An "international holding company" (IHC), on the other hand, produces in each country in a polycentric manner to supply that specific market only; and production efforts are duplicated in each country-market location because they are highly independent of the parent organization and other subsidiaries. Finally, Behrman's geocentric-like "multinational enterprise" is intended to supply the world market through integration and coordination of its production facilities in a number of countries. True MNE production is characterized by flexibility in siting subsidiaries; each subsidiary's contribution to the global system is capable of change, and the MNE produces highly standardized products under conditions of least-cost efficiency.

Services are largely absent from Behrman's MNE category. He states that "services industries are, by nature, highly locally-oriented (p. 5)," and he confines them to illustrations of the polycentric IHC (e.g., hotels) and, in the case of trade-facilitating services (e.g., international trading companies), to the ethnocentric classical-investment type.

Behrman is correct in stressing that many services are significantly location-oriented, but some services also require that the consumer participate to varying degrees in the production process. In other words, they are also location-bound, as was seen above. This location-*boundedness* in the case of services, however, does not imply a solely or even significantly local *orientation* since such services can also be provided to non-residents. Thus, a consumer service that is not foreign tradeable (such as a hotel accommodation) must be produced and ultimately delivered within a particular geographic area even though the original sale of that service may have taken place in another country where the consumer purchased his reservation.

If the international hotel chain that Behrman lists in his IHC category provides a fairly standardized service, the parent organization must have more control over its foreign hotels than would be expected from Behrman's characterization of the IHC. Yet, such hotel chains cannot enter Behrman's MNE category because hotel-service production is unavoidably location-bound and inflexible in its ability to alter its contribution to the global production system.

How does Behrman's classification accommodate a high-technology service such as remote data-processing? Unlike computer manufacturing, this service demands customer locations that are bound to the latter's participation in the product's production and in its receipt and use. Let us assume that one mainframe location serving a great number of foreign user locations is the most efficient arrangement, and that user input into the system is controlled and standardized to an extent that ensures acceptance by the mainframe operation. In such a case, these remote-processing operations cannot be considered polycentric because: (1) part of the multistage production process is located outside the user country, and (2) each user-country production component is under the control of the parent organization which has established a fairly standardized form of user participation.

Can remote data-processing operations then be considered as a form of ethnocentric/classical investment? Raw data from abroad feed the main-frame operations that yield the final product (that is, ordered information) at home. This final product is transported back through the system to the data-originating market. Is this process comparable to the export of wood in one direction and the import of furniture using that wood in the other direction? No, because in the case of data-processing, the service customer's use-location is bound to his production-participation location. As defined by Behrman, such production operations are therefore neither polycentric/IHC nor ethnocentric/classical; and they are not MNE production operations either because the customer production component is necessarily duplicative and inflexible in its country location-boundedness and in its contribution to the entire production system.

Consequently, Behrman's classification cannot accommodate the location-bound service (e.g., hotels) nor the combination service (e.g., remote data-processing), despite its usefulness for other purpose.

### When Are International Service Firms MNEs?

Answering this question requires a review of older and newer MNE definitions. Although no definite agreement exists or is likely, there has been a fairly general consensus that: (1) a multinational enterprise is involved in foreign direct investment, and (2) foreign direct investment means (a) the transfer or formation overseas of all or some of the necessary factors of production (the "ownership" or "equity" dimension), and (b) some element of "control" over their use abroad.[6] If these conditions are not met, a firm will simply be called something like an "international company" engaging either in portfolio investment or in foreign trade.

*New MNE Definitions.* It is interesting to observe the evolution at the United Nations which first defined the multinational corporation (MNC) as covering "all enterprises which *control* assets — factories, mines, sales offices and the like — in two or more countries [1973, p. 5]." A more recent U.N. exercise defines a transnational corporation (its new term for MNC) as "an enterprise (a) comprising entities in two or more countries, regardless of the legal form and fields of activity of those entities, (b) which operates under a system of decision-making permitting coherent policies and a common strategy through one or more decision-making centers, (c) in which the entities are so linked, *by ownership or otherwise*, that one or more of them may be able to exercise a *significant influence* over the activities of the others, and, in particular, to share knowledge, resources and responsibilities with others" [1984, p. 2]. Observe that the word "control" has disappeared from the second definition which also does not require equity ("by ownership or otherwise"). The definitions by Buckley [1983a], Casson [1982] and Dunning and McQueen [1982] have evolved in the same direction of ignoring equity as a criterion (see below).

Some international service companies clearly fit the more traditional definitions. For example, a bank with retail-banking branches in many countries as well as a Japanese trading company with parent-owned offices in major centers around the world would indisputably be termed a "multinational enterprise." On the other hand, no one would care to apply the label "multinational" to mere exporters selling services to many countries but with no offices overseas. However, "new forms of international investment" [Oman 1984] such as licensing and management contracts present problems in applying older definitions to international service firms while the newer definitions encompass such forms much more readily.

*Problems Associated with Licensing and Management Contracts.* A major definition problem arises when licensing, franchising[7] and/or management-contracting are involved. In their pure forms, they do not involve any equity since only technology or management skills are sold to another party [Buckley 1983b]. Besides, they use the "external market" rather than "internalization" within the international firm as a mode of transfer [Buckley and Casson 1985, p. 51]. Therefore, *they cannot be considered forms of foreign direct investment.*

In particular, international licensing must be considered service *trade* rather than investment because the actual use of the factors transferred overseas is *controlled by the licensee.* The fact that a licensing agreement contains restrictions and obligations applying to the licensee does not mean that the latter is "controlled" in the common meaning used to differentiate "foreign direct investment" from "foreign portfolio investment." After all, even foreign trade in tangible goods (e.g., computers) may involve restrictions and obligations (e.g., not to resell the computers to certain countries) but the latter are not sufficient to transform "trade" into "investment" which requires ownership in any case.

For the same reasons, entering into a management contract with a foreign firm to administer the latter's assets is also a form of service *trade.* A service (that is, management) has been sold, but this factor of production is not "controlled," in the FDI sense, by a parent company located in some home country; and no equity investment is necessary on the part of the contract's seller. It is the buyer of the management contract who ultimately owns and "controls" the use of that factor of production, just as he owns and controls his land, labor and capital, while the management-contract's seller "controls" operations only in a delegated manner (see note 10).

A further relevant touchstone is that foreign direct investment normally involves the earning of *profits* on some foreign-based equity whereas trade is associated only with collecting sales, commissions, fees, interest charges, etc. In the cases of international licensing and management-contracting, it is such gross revenues[8] that apply, rather than return on foreign-based equity — a criterion that demonstrates again that one is dealing with trade rather than investment.

The key question then becomes: Can an international service firm based in one country, that only collects licensing and management-contract revenues from other countries but does not own or control assets overseas, still be considered a multinational enterprise even though it is not engaged in foreign direct investment? The answer has to be affirmative if one accepts the following syllogism developed by adding to the above discussion what some researchers (particularly Dunning, McQueen, Buckley and Casson) have advanced:

1. An international firm does not need foreign equity tobecome a multinational enterprise, but can do sothrough licensing and management contracts (see belowfor support of this assertion).

2. "Non-equity" licensing and management-contracting areforms of trade involving the market as a mode of entry(see above).

3. Therefore, international trade firms using only licensing and management contracts are multinational enterprises (assuming that the other criteria regarding size have been satisfied).

On the first point, Dunning and McQueen [1982, p.98] state, "It is our reading of the situation in the hotel sector that, in general, [equity-based] control is not necessary to advance the benefits of global integration and to ensure that the best interests of the parent company are promoted" — the very purposes of "control."[9] Casson confirms this view: "The MNE does not need to be a foreign direct investor since all resources (except possibly inventories) in the foreign location can be hired rather than owned outright. This reflects the fact that the definition employs an income or value-added concept of production rather than a capital or asset concept, as do some other definitions" [1982, p. 36].[10]

Let us assume that, after extrapolating recent developments to a plausible ending, Exxon Corporation has finally relinquished all ownership in foreign oil wells, refineries and gas stations and has come to use other companies to transport, refine and retail the oil products it bought overseas. Should one then say that Exxon is no longer a multinational corporation? The answer would have to be affirmative if Exxon buys foreign oil only to resell it abroad and at home (where it may have kept its refineries and gas stations), but it would have to be negative if Exxon retains licensing and management-contract arrangements with foreigners.

Let us take another limit case where the relaxation of U.S. banking regulations and the improvement of telecommunications have allowed Citicorp to conduct all of its international borrowing and lending from its International Banking Facility unit in New York City, after closing its offshore centers, but with its international-banking officers "jetting" and "telexing" around the world to close such deals. We would then have to say that Citicorp is no longer a multinational enterprise because it no longer has foreign equity, and because licensing and management contracts are not used in this kind of business services [Dunning and Norman 1983].[11]

Altogether, the new definitions of the multinational enterprise dictate that some forms of pure foreign trade (that is, licensing, franchising and management contracting), which do not involve foreign equity or control as conventionally defined in the literature, be brought into the MNE category.

## APPLYING FDI-MNE THEORY TO SERVICES

Mainstream theories of foreign direct investment and the multinational enterprise have recently been extended to several international service industries, mainly hostelry, banking, and a range of business services. A brief review of these theories is appropriate, prior to introducing necessary qualifications as far as international services are concerned.[12]

### Mainstream Theories

Buckley and Casson [1976 and 1985] have conceptualized the MNE as an enterprise responding to imperfect intermediate-product markets by developing "internal markets" across national boundaries. Their views have widened the focus of international activities from the production of final services and goods to include such intermediate products as semi-processed materials, knowledge and expertise, managerial and marketing skills, and technology. Because intermediate-product markets are difficult to organize due to various imperfections, there is an incentive to bypass them and to bring the activities of producing and marketing *within* the organization's ownership and control, that is, to "internalize" them.

Casson [1982] has added to this theory of internalization by demonstrating that buyer uncertainty is a significant transaction cost, especially in consumer goods and services. This cost creates a sufficient condition for the MNE to internalize its ownership advantage(s) when quality control is crucial and when international communication between buyer and producer is best achieved under control of the enterprise (see below).

While also emphasizing "internalization," Rugman [1981] views a (monopolistic) firm-specific advantage in "knowledge" (p. 61) as the key characteristic of the MNE. This advantage, which leads to foreign direct investment when there are imperfect good or factor markets, replaces or complements the country-specific advantages that support trade; and it prompts the creation of an internal market to retain control over firm-specific advantages [Rugman 1981, p. 39].

Dunning's [1980] "eclectic model" of international production (foreign production based on FDI) integrates these and other views. It rests on three simultaneous conditions: ownership-specific, internalization-specific and location-specific advantages. If the enterprise possesses only the first two advantages, it will export domestic production. On the other hand, the MNE must find it profitable to combine its assets with factor endowments located in foreign countries for international production to take place.

### Corroboration of Mainstream Theories

The above theories have been able to accommodate several international service industries. International banking, in particular, has lent itself well

50 JOURNAL OF INTERNATIONAL BUSINESS STUDIES, FALL 1986

to explanation by both the internalization and eclectic theories. Thus, Rugman [1981] has concluded that: "In the same way that the multinational enterprise creates an internal market to overcome imperfect world good and factor markets, so does the multinational bank use internalization to overcome imperfections in international financial markets" (p. 89). Similarly, Yannopoulos has reasoned that Dunning's eclectic theory of international production can successfully explain the growth of transnational banking [1983, p. 251]. Gray and Gray [1981],[13] Cho [1983], Grubel [1977], Pecchioli [1983] and Wells [1983] have reached fairly identical conclusions.

### Necessary Qualifications and Elaborations of Mainstream Theories

Still, studies of other service industries (particularly of the international hotel industry and of foreign branches of business service companies) suggest some qualifications and/or elaborations regarding the nature of ownership, internalization and location advantages.

*Ownership Advantages.* Dunning, Norman, McQueen and Casson have identified some *intangible* advantages associated with international service firms, that compare with the more tangible ones of non-service firms. Thus, Dunning and Norman [1983] illustrate these intangible advantages for foreign branches providing a variety of *business* services:

> If the possession of product, process or materialtechnology is one of the foundations of ownershipadvantages in manufacturing industry, then that ofinformation and management, organizational and marketingtechnology, is the key to success in the provision ofbusiness services. Comparable to the exclusive orprivileged access to raw materials in resource-processingindustries is access to information in the office sector; comparable to the market provided by parent companies to their manufacturing affiliates, auditing, accounting andother business-service affiliates may find a ready-made market for their output from firms that normally deal with parent companies at home; comparable to the spreading of fixed capital and research-and-development overheads that enable large firms in high-technology industries to export such benefits to their affiliates at low marginal costs, so in office activities the tremendous reservoir of organizational and managerial expertise that has been built up over the years can provide branch offices with information at a cost very much lower than a de novo indigenous firm would have to incur; comparable to trademarks which explain why some firms in the tobacco, confectionery, toilet preparations and detergent industries have advantages over others, so there is an identifiable image perceived by purchasers of the services supplied by enterprises like McKinsey's, Foster Wheeler, Peat Marwick, Arthur Andersen, Chase Manhattan Bank, etc., that give these enterprises an important advantage over their lesser-known competitors (pp. 678-679).

In Dunning and McQueen's [1982] study of a *consumer* service, the hotel product is described as: (1) on-premises "room" services; (2) the provision or arrangement of "before, at-the-time or after off-premises services" such as transportation to and from the hotel, tours and reservations at restaurants and other hotels, and (3) a "trademark of guarantee" that the consumer will receive the services contracted. The hotel chain's ownership advantages include experience in serving the market (primarily international business travelers) in other locations, product differentiation, and brand-image marketing of the hotel "experience" good. Training is likened to manufacturing R&D in its contribution to maintaining a brand image (p. 103). Again, these are all intangible advantages.

Casson interprets Dunning and McQueen's hotel study as demonstrating that international hotel chains address quality-conscious markets, do not necessarily depend on product-differentiation advantages, serve mostly international travelers rather than local customers, utilize brand names and, by using international reservations systems, integrate producer and consumer markets [1982, p. 39]. There is "something of value" that allows such international hotel chains to distinguish themselves from their host-country competitors — what Casson calls "quality" [1982, p.38].

This discussion stresses that the analysis of the ownership advantages of service MNEs must be focussed on the intangibility of their offerings even though one can raise the intriguing question of whether service and non-service firms differ at all conceptually in this respect. As Raymond Vernon put it in a private communication: "Inasmuch as the transmission of knowledge can usually be substituted for the transmission of goods, a serious discussion of manufacturing MNEs entails exploring some of the same considerations [as with service MNEs]." In other words, if ownership advantages can be reduced to "knowledge" of various kinds (hard or soft, patentable or not, externally diffusible or not, etc.), one can postulate that *all MNEs are service MNEs.*

Such a view is compatible with Buckley's recent definition of the multinational enterprise as "a firm which adds value by producing in more than one national economy" [1983a, pp. 34-35]. Since all economic activity is about "adding value," and since to add value is to provide a "service," everything that happens in firms — extractive, industrial, commercial, financial, etc. — is essentially a "service." Therefore, all firms are "service" firms and all MNEs are ultimately "service MNEs" in some respects.

While this is an extreme view, it suggests that *we examine carefully, on a case-by-case basis, the ownership advantages proper to each service and non-service industry, rather than assume significant differences between the two types a priori.*

*Internalization Advantages.* Two issues arise here: (1) explaining internalization in service industries that are typically not R&D-intensive and thus rely mostly on "low technology" as the basis for their firm-specific advantages, and (2) accounting for "non-equity FDI" in services — a topic already broached above.

Regarding the first problem, Casson [1982, pp. 24-25] suggests that the non-R&D-intensive MNE is best explained by extending the scope of internalization theory. This can be done by taking account of additional sources of market imperfections that generate "transaction costs" incurred to overcome these obstacles through "market-making activities" (p. 25). He stresses that buyer uncertainty is a significant transaction cost, especially in *consumer* goods and services. The incidence of this cost creates a sufficient condition for the existence of an MNE, even one with low or soft technology which includes a wide range of marketing skills. The recent strategic literature on MNEs adds weight to this argument by emphasizing more intangible advantages such as global distribution networks and brands rather than "high" or "hard" technology advantages considered to be fleeting and more readily copiable and displaceable [Hamel and Prahalad 1985; Ohmae 1985].

Casson illustrates his transaction-cost theory with the banana and hotel industries, demonstrating that the consumer-product MNE comes into existence when quality control is crucial. It can integrate backward to control production; it can reduce international buyers' transaction costs by offering its services in multiple locations, and t can produce some parts of the market-making service (contact-making, specification and negotiation) elsewhere, thereby reducing buyer risks in international communication. It can also generate and transmit market-making skills via the enterprise's internal market.

Four reasons for market-making production to occur in many different country markets are identified by Casson: (1) major production economies of scale exist so that it is efficient to supply and integrate several country markets from one production location; (2) internationally mobile consumers encourage the replication of market-making production in different country markets; (3) consumers want to place orders in one country location for supply in a different one, and/or (4) the enterprise has an internationally transferable absolute advantage in market-making production. [1982, pp. 36-38].

Casson's first category is illustrated by the banana industry, but this class can also accommodate the linkages between many location-bound data-production sites and a mainframe computer-service facility located in the home or some third production country. One mainframe facility serves many integrated consumer production and use locations, and thus offers major economies of scale in the production of the ordered-information product.

Casson's second and third categories are represented by the location-bound international hotel chain and its reservation system but these two categories can also be applied to non-location-bound (i.e., foreign-tradeable) services such as some types of international banking services. For example, banks provide financial information across national borders to other MNEs, and they intermediate in transactions involving parties located in different countries — all non-R&D-intensive activities. Regarding this fourth category of absolute advantage, Casson acknowledges that it fits in with "the orthodox theory of the MNE" and, as such, does not raise any special problem of applicability to service MNEs of all types. *Therefore, no major problem is encountered in applying the central MNE concept of internalization to "low-technology" service firms.*

Regarding the second issue associated with internalization, several studies have explained the existence of "non-equity" FDI in both business and consumer services. On the one hand, equity-based FDI is common in the case of *business* services such as accountancy, finance, consulting and advertising because quality control is difficult to achieve through the licensing or franchising of such services [Dunning and Norman 1983]. Besides, foreign direct investment in offices generally requires lower initial outlays (for example, in real-estate property) than are needed to buy or build a hotel of international standard, so that internalization is the preferred mode for exploiting ownership advantages in such business services (p. 680).

On the other hand, the quality-control problem is more surmountable in *consumer* services where franchising is common (e.g., fast foods). Thus, the high frequency of management contracts in the international hotel industry has been well explained by Dunning and McQueen on the basis of what they call "contract-based control" [1982, p. 91]:

> The owners of the hotel may have little knowledge of hotel operations and employ a professional management company to operate the hotel. The management company in turn will only become involved if they can protect their ownership advantage, and in practice this may require a large degree of control of the assets. The hotel-management company, however, may be un-willing to invest in the ownership of the hotel either because it regards itself as having little expertise in property development, or because it regards ownership as a high-risk venture, or because expansion would be reduced by the need to borrow large sums of capital. We therefore often find that it is to the mutual advantage of both parties for de jure control to be with the hotel owners but de facto control to be established through contracts. These contracts are more easily arranged because of the characteristics of the industry, in the sense that unlike manufacturing, there is no need for a policy of market sharing by the affiliates to maximize the global profits of the MNE, nor is there any production specialization, while there exist ample opportunities to appropriate the economic rent from the MNE's activities (pp. 104-105).

Similarly, Buckley points out, "It is through the use of internal markets in capital, labor management, technology and intermediate goods that effective control of foreign subsidiaries is exercised, rather than through equity ownership"[1983b, p. 202], and, "it is not necessary to own a production process to control it" [1983a, p. 41]. *Therefore, international services can readily be accommodated by internalization theory even in the absence of equity investment although this accommodation applies only in the case of consumer services.*

54          JOURNAL OF INTERNATIONAL BUSINESS STUDIES, FALL 1986

*Location Advantages.* The matter of where the services are provided has already been discussed. Foreign-tradeable services obviously exhibit great mobility. On the other hand, location-bound services present problems: "As in the case of some primary products, the location of hotels is country-specific since they have to be situated where the tourists want to be" [Dunning and McQueen 1982, p. 88]. If the hotel product is to be consumed in Paris, it must be produced there even if Lyon or Marseille were more efficient locations.

Beyond that, common variables such as size of the market, quality of local resources, government policies and political climate affect location choices as in any other type of foreign trade or investment (see Dunning and McQueen [1982] and Dunning and Norman [1983] for further elaboration of these factors).[14] *Therefore, international services encounter no special problems in terms of the locational requirements of FDI/MNE theory, except in the case of location-bound services* since the choice of host countries is dictated by consumer requirements in the latter's case.

## CONCLUSION

The applicability of FDI/MNE definitions, measurements and theories to international service firms is finally receiving some well-deserved attention although not in proportion to services' fast-growing share of international business nor in relation to their long history which predates that of industrial and extractive foreign direct investment [Kindleberger 1983].

Comparisons will always be difficult on account of the variety of size measurements that must be applied to various types of service firms, and also when comparing the latter to industrial firms. Therefore, specific analyses of each service subsector should prove more fruitful than the creation of a general category of "service MNEs" in view of the heterogeneity of this group.

Besides, no special FDI-MNE theories for international service firms are necessary. The existing ones can be readily accommodated through relatively simple qualifications and elaborations while we wait for the initiation and results of more international service studies. Such research is very much needed in view of the reasonable anticipation that, by the year 2000, more than half of the world's multinational enterprises will be in services.

## NOTES

1. *Fortune* has published an annual list of the U.S. "Service 500" since 1983 [1985]; and a similar compendium of foreign service companies is included in *Fortune* and *Forbes* lists of large overseas firms [The International 500, 1985; Curtis 1984].

2. The size and growth of international services and the multinationalization of service enterprises are not considered here. Furthermore, it is assumed that service producers "go international" and become MNEs for the same reasons that producers of tangible goods do. Some corroboration for this assumption is provided by Weinstein's study of multinational advertising agencies [1977]. He demonstrated that their services, whose production alternatives include production for export, foreign direct investment and contractual arrangements, are motivated by offensive, defensive, client-service, and executive-interest considerations significantly similar to those identified for manufacturing

enterprises. For similar conclusions applying to multinational banking, see Gray and Gray [1981] and Pecchioli [1983].

3. This classification resembles Daniels' [1982] differentiation between "footloose" and "tied" services, distinguished from one another by their operations' "location dependence" between: (1) product use or receipt, and (2) production or product origin. Footloose services (found primarily among producer, professional and business services) are those that can be provided with equal effectiveness from different locations, whereas tied services (found primarily among consumer services) can originate in only one location. Gray [1983] provides a fivefold categorization: (1) services that are derivative from international trade in tangible goods (e.g., freight transportation of all kinds, insurance and related financing); (2) services where location-specific attributes are dominant (e.g., tourism); (3) services that are location-joining (e.g., passenger transportation and communications); (4) services usually provided in all nations, consumed anywhere and by anyone and provided anywhere and by anyone (e.g., insurance and banking, professional services and intranational communications), and (5) services that derive from intra-firm relationships usually conducted on the basis of hierarchical rather than arm's-length pricing (p. 378).

4. Unlike financial paper that represents production results on a customer's assets/goods and therefore the product so produced (e.g., a stock or bond), a hotel reservation or airplane ticket is a pre-production scheduling and commitment device. Neither is a usable proxy for the product which exists only within the time and space constraints of production in which the consumer must participate in order to use the product, that is, the room or the flight.

5. The Office of the U.S. Trade Representative [1983] has dealt with a dozen service industries; and Herman and van Holst [1984] identified as least 81 service sectors in the Netherlands, of which 56 had products considered to be in the foreign-tradeable class. See also Riddle [1986].

6. A third condition refers to minimum number of foreign countries involved and to minimal proportions of revenues, assets, production and personnel located overseas. These size criteria, however, have already been discussed and are not relevant here. For enlightening critiques of MNE definitions, see Aharoni [1971], Behrman [1974] and United Nations [1973].

7. Since franchising is a form of licensing, it will not be further discussed as a separate type of foreign business involvement.

8. The fact that such gross revenues may be calculated as a percentage of the profits earned by the foreign licensee or the buyer of the management-contract service is irrelevant. However, for a different and well-articulated view that points to the difficulties encountered in distinguishing between a "sale" and an "investment," see Oman [1984, pp. 18-25].

9. Gabriel's [1966] admonition that MNEs should reduce or eliminate their foreign equity and replace it by licensing and management contracting really amounted to urging mining and manufacturing MNEs to become service multinationals.

10. Actually, Casson's definition of a multinational enterprise ("an MNE is any firm which owns outputs of goods or services originating in more than one country" [1982, p. 36]) is ambiguous because of the combined use of the words "owns" and "originating" — at least in the context of this paper. The international hotel chain that uses management contracts "owns" and sells management skills but the latter do not necessarily "originate" in more than one country. In a private communication, Mark Casson clarified his concept as follows: "If a hotel chain operates purely through management contracts so that when a customer pays his bill, he pays not the hotel chain, but the franchise operators themselves, I would say that the franchise operator is in fact a pure exporter of management skill through its management contracts. If, on the other hand, the customer pays his bill to the hotel chain which, as part of its management contract, collects the customer's fees, then the multinational enterprise does own the 'hotel service' being supplied. It is an unfortunate aspect of my definition that in this case it hinges on the legal entity to which the customer pays his bill, but I think what this tells you is not that the definition was ambiguous, but that it may not be particularly useful in this context."

11. An alternative justification for including international service firms relying exclusively on licensing and management contracts in the MNE category, would be to reason that it is not a case of foreign *trade* (as argued above) but one of foreign *investment* after all because: (1) factors of production have been transferred overseas (technology, information, access to markets, management, quality control, reputation, image, etc.) [Dunning and Norman 1983]; (2) these firms' profits are derived at least in part from the output of the foreign licensee or contractee [Oman 1984, p. 23], and (3) some influence over their use by the foreign licensee or management-contractee has been retained by the licensor or contractor — what Dunning and McQueen [1982] call "quasi-internalization." This third condition, however, requires further analysis of the true nature of "control" or "influence" over licensees and contractees — something that shall not be attempted here, but see Brooke [1985].

12. This section discusses only what might be called the "conditions" (that is, prerequisites) associated with foreign direct investment, leaving out "motivations" and "precipitating circumstances" [Boddewyn 1985].

13. This is particularly true when the bank's foreign subsidiaries operate in *national* foreign financial markets. However, Gray and Gray [1981] argue that the same conditions do not necessarily apply when a bank chooses to operate in *supranational* markets such as the Eurocurrency market because "*net* ownership-specific advantages are not needed since there are no indigenous banks in a supranational market"(p. 53). In effect, Gray and Gray's objection amounts to a redefinition of "location-specific advantages" which are not necessarily limited to a specific country but can also be applied to non-national (stateless) markets.

14. The reason why some countries and not others are involved in the provision of international services is a separate issue not discussed here (but see Dunning and McQueen 1982, pp. 87-88).

## REFERENCES

Aharoni, Yair. On the Definition of a Multinational Corporation. *Quarterly Review of Economics and Business*, 2, Autumn 1971, pp. 27-37.

Behrman, J.N. *Decision Criteria for Foreign Direct Investment in Latin America*. New York: Council of the Americas, 1974.

Boddewyn, J.J. Theories of Foreign Direct Investment and Divestment: A Classificatory Note. *Management International Review*, 25, 1/1985, pp. 57-65.

Brooke, M.Z. *Selling Management Service Contracts in International Business*. New York: Holt, Rinehart and Winston, 1985.

Buckley, P.J. New Theories of International Business: Some Unresolved Issues. In *The Growth of International Business*, edited by M.C. Casson. London: George Allen and Unwin, 1983a, pp. 34-50.

Buckley, P.J. New Forms of International Industrial Cooperation. *Aussenwirtschaft*, 38, 1983b, pp. 195-222.

Buckley, P.J. and Mark Carson. *The Future of Multinational Enterprise*. London: Macmillan, 1976, pp. 32-67 (A Long-run Theory of the Multinational Enterprise).

————. *The Economic Theory of the Multinational Enterprise*. New York: St. Martin's Press, 1985.

Casson, M.C. Transaction Costs and the Theory of the Multinational Enterprise. In *New Theories of the Multinational Enterprise*, edited by A.M. Rugman. New York: St. Martin's Press, 1982, pp. 24-43.

Casson, Mark. General Theories of the Multinational Enterprise: A Critical Examination. Reading, UK: University of Reading Discussion Papers in International Investment and Business Studies, No. 77, January 1984.

Cho, Kang Rae. A Study on Multinational Banks (MNBs): Their Identities and Determinants. Ph.D. Dissertation, University of Washington. Ann Arbor, MI: University Microfilms International, 1983.

Curtis, C.E. The Year of Living Dangerously. *Forbes*, 2 July 1984, pp. 116ff. See the update ("The Forbes 500") in *Forbes*, 29 April 1985, pp. 158ff.

Daniels, Peter. *Service Industries: Growth and Location*, edited by Alan R.H. Baker and Colin Evans. Cambridge, England: Cambridge University Press, Cambridge Topics in Geography, Second Series, 1982.

Dunning, J.H. Toward an Eclectic Theory of International Production. *Journal of International Business Studies*, 11, Spring/Summer 1980, pp. 9-31.

Dunning, J.H. and Matthew McQueen. The Eclectic Theory of Multinational Enterprise and the International Hotel Industry. In *New Theories of the Multinational Enterprise*, edited by A.M. Rugman. New York: St. Martin's Press, 1982, pp. 79-106.

Dunning, J.H. and George Norman. The Theory of the Multinational Enterprise: An Application to Multinational Office Location. *Environment and Planning A*, 1983, pp. 675-692.

Gabriel, Peter. *The International Transfer of Corporate Skills*. Cambridge, MA: Harvard University Press, 1966.

Gray, H. Peter. A Negotiating Strategy for Trade in Services. *Journal of World Trade Law*, 17, September-October 1983, pp. 377-388.

Gray, J.M. and H.P. Gray. The Multinational Bank: A Financial MNC?, *Journal of Banking and Finance*, 10, 1981, pp. 33-63.

Grubel, H.G. A Theory of Multinational Banking. *Banca Nazionale del Lavoro Quarterly Review*, 30, December 1977, pp. 349-363.

Hamel, Gary and C.K. Prahalad. Do You Really Have a Global Strategy? *Harvard Business Review*, July-August 1985, pp. 139-148.

Herman, B. and B. van Holst. International Trade in Services: Some Theoretical and Practical Problems. Rotterdam: Netherlands Economic Institute, 1984.

The International 500. *Fortune*, 19 August 1985, pp. 165ff.

Kindleberger, C.P. International Banks as Leaders or Followers of International Business. *Journal of Banking and Finance*, 7, 4 (1983), pp. 583-595.

Office of the United States Trade Representative. *U.S. National Study on Trade in Services*. Washington, DC, December 1983.

Ohmae, Kenichi. *Triad Power*. New York: Free Press, 1985.

Oman, Charles. *New Forms of International Investment in Developing Countries*. Paris: Organization for Economic Cooperation and Development, 1984.

Pecchioli, R.M. *The Internationalization of Banking; The Policy Issues*. Paris: Organization for Economic Cooperation and Development, 1983.

Perlmutter, Howard. The Tortuous Evolution of the Multinational Enterprise. *Columbia Journal of World Business*, 14, January-February 1969, pp. 9-18.

Riddle, D.I. *Service-led Growth: The Role of the Service Sector in World Development*. New York: Praeger, 1986.

Rugman, A.M. *Inside the Multinationals: The Economics of Internal Markets*. New York: Columbia University Press, 1981.

The Service 500. *Fortune*, 13 June 1983, pp. 152ff.; 11 June 1984, pp. 153ff. and 10 June 1985, pp. 175ff.

Stopford, J.M. *The World Directory of Multinational Enterprise. 1982-1983, Vol. I*. Detroit, MI: Gale Research, 1982.

*Thomas, D.R.E. Strategy Is Different in Service Industries. Harvard Business Review*, July-August 1978, pp. 158-165.

United Nations, Department of Economic and Social Affairs. *Multinational Corporations in World Development*. New York, ST/ECA/190, 1973.

United Nations, Economic and Social Council, Commission on Transnational Corporations. *Work Related to the Definition of Transnational Corporations; Question of the Definition of Transnational Corporations; Report of the Secretariat*. New York, E/C.10/1984/17, 6 February 1984.

Vernon, Raymond. International Investment and International Trade in the Product Cycle. *Quarterly Journal of Economics*, May 1966, pp. 190-207.

Weinstein, Arnold K. Foreign Investments by Service Firms; The Case of Multinational Advertising Agencies. *Journal of International Business Studies*, 8, Spring/Summer 1977, pp. 83-91.

Wells, L.T. Nonmanufacturing Investments. In *Third World Multinationals*. Cambridge, MA: MIT Press, 1983, pp. 117-135.

Yannopoulos, G.N. The Growth of Transnational Banking. In *The Growth of International Business*, edited by Mark Casson. London: George Allen and Unwin, 1983, pp. 236-257.

# Part X
# Comparative Organization and Performance

## 29

# EUROPEAN AND NORTH AMERICAN MULTINATIONALS, 1870–1914: COMPARISONS AND CONTRASTS

By MIRA WILKINS

In the late nineteenth century and early twentieth centuries, the world shrank in its physical dimensions, as steamships, railroads, telegraph, and cables compressed distances. In Europe and North America, economic conditions changed. This was a time of substantial technological advance, with new products, processes, and forms of business organisation, challenging the older order. Because of improvements in transportation and communications, innovations spread rapidly throughout the industrialising world. One crucial conduit was business itself.

British businesses led in the process of multinational expansion. They were, however, not alone and companies headquartered in Continental Europe, the United States, and Canada also extended their activities over borders, making foreign direct investments, defined as those business investments that were or had the potential to be controlled or at least influenced in a significant manner from a headquarters in the United Kingdom, Germany, France, Belgium, Switzerland, Sweden, or other European countries or the United States or Canada.[1] Typically, the phrases 'multinational enterprise' and 'foreign direct investment' have been considered as synonymous, but it is more appropriate to see the relationship as follows: multinational enterprises make foreign direct investments – and carry on other tasks as well. The investments, the capital flows, are only part of the activities of a multinational enterprise. These companies must have a business association with the foreign operations.

British business historians can learn from looking at the experiences of British multinational enterprise, but they learn even more through comparisons. Thus, this article will cover British business overseas, but it will also deal with continental European and North American enterprise. In the conclusion, I will stress the insights that British business historians can obtain by virtue of such comparisons.

Some companies that did business across borders in the pre-1914 years did so in only a single foreign country; others by 1914 already had operations in several or even numerous lands and were truly multinational. The late nineteenth and the early twentieth century was the first period in world history when, owing to the transportation and communications innovations, it became possible to have meaningful business coordination, control, and influence over distance and for our purposes over country frontiers. The new products, processes, and forms of business organisation were integral to this development. Higher per capita income was also critical, placing more individuals in a market economy and providing disposable income for the purchase of a myriad of goods and services. For these reasons, 1870–1914 was the initial era of the modern multinational enterprise.

Because the late nineteenth and early twentieth centuries witnessed great economic change and growth, in considering modern multi-national enterprise I am not merely concerned with the beginnings, but with the subsequent course of the institution. In the years prior to 1914, a firm with business abroad in only one foreign country might be starting in the direction of expanding into other countries as well. Yet, no determinism, no inevitability, existed – and the process might be truncated. The business might fail (domestically and internationally), or alternatively a business might succeed but shed its multinational character, becoming a national enterprise in a host country or in the home country, or as a fourth possibility, a purely bi-national relation-ship might persist over a long period, with no broad multinational spread. The paths in multinational enterprise growth might start from different origins and involve diverse strategies. No simple, single, neat model fits every case. It is important, however, in studying the evolving institution to look at both beginnings and growth.

My definition of multinational enterprise, for purposes of this article, is comprehensive. I include any company that has a head-quarters in one country (a home) and that operates in at least one foreign country (the host). 'Foreign' is defined as synonymous with abroad, that is, not in the home country; it could be within or outside an overseas Empire. A company that crossed a border and made business (operating) investments in only one foreign country was by this defini-tion a multinational enterprise; so, too, I will include a firm with operating investments in many foreign lands. 'Operations' could be in the production of goods or services: a trading company, a bank, a public utility, and an owned sales outlet that produced services are included under the rubric 'operations'. In short, I do not limit myself to manufacturing firms – either at home or abroad.

Multinational enterprise involves *cross-border* control, or potential for control, or, at least, influence. An enterprise run by expatriates or immigrants frequently did not represent an ongoing foreign invest-ment, much less a foreign *direct* investment. If there was no head-quarters at home, there was *no* multinational enterprise. This is very important. A Britisher or German who migrated to the United States (for example) and set up business in this nation, if he had no obligation to any investor in the home country, there was no ongoing foreign investment, or foreign direct investment. (To call Andrew Carnegie's steel business in America a British investment is bizarre). Likewise, Swedes and Germans resident in Russia or Britishers resident in Argentina, who retained no headquarters abroad, are not foreign direct investors.[2]

10                                                    THE END OF INSULARITY

Mark Casson in his latest book has argued that 'the modern theory of
the MNE [multinational enterprise] has the potential to become a
general theory of the enterprise in space, and as such, to embrace
theories of the multi-regional and multi-plant firm'.[3] How can the
comparative study of the history of multinational enterprise contribute
to the efforts of the theoretician? I believe that the way to do so is to
present our findings as we inquire into the development of such
companies.

The rise of multinational enterprise is receiving substantial attention.
Scholars know a great deal about the history of American, British,
German, and Swedish multinationals.[4] We know far less about the
history of French, Belgian, and Swiss business abroad.[5] In this essay, I
seek synthesis. What is known, what is absent? What can the British
business historian learn from the comparisons? What appear to be the
common features in the historical experiences? If not neat nor simple,
is there none the less an 'ideal type' – a model? Does the evidence fit
into the emerging theory of multinational enterprise? What is distinctive
to multinationals of Great Britain and of other particular home
countries; can the special features be ordered in any discernable
pattern? How was the rise of multinational enterprise associated with
the changing national and world economies, 1870–1914? Or, is
generalisation impossible, and regional (or host country) differences
so vast as to nullify attempts to find patterns?[6] What are the new
frontiers for research? How will they help the British business historian
in furthering his search for an understanding of British business
overseas?

I am not considering the years after 1914, because of space
constraints, but also because I am convinced that 1914–18 (the period
of the First World War) forms a watershed[7] and that a post-First World
War analysis requires a greatly expanded treatment. Yet, as indicated
earlier, it is possible to study entries and growth, as well as retreats and
frustration in the pre-1914 years. In short, what follows is a look at an
institution, the multinational enterprise, that seeks private profit
through managed business abroad (in 1870–1914 there were few
government-owned multinational enterprises).[8]

*Influences at Home on Multinational Enterprise*

All companies with business investments abroad are and have been
shaped by economic and other conditions in their homeland, and only
subsequently, by economic and other conditions in the countries
abroad in which they did business. In each home country circumstances
differed from one another, and in addition there were regional
differences *within* home countries (in a short article it is impossible to
inquire whether there were systematic differences between London
and Glasgow-headquartered companies as they operated abroad, or
between New York and Chicago ones, or more obviously Vevey and

*Multinational Corporations*

Basle ones – yet we accept the proposition that such differences existed).[9] In each headquarters nation unique national characteristics had an impact on the nature and extent of firms' foreign direct investments. The galaxy of influences include factor costs, level and pace of industrialisation, areas of technological expertise, size and nature of the domestic market, relationships between banking and industrial units at home, national endowments of and requirements for natural resources, the availability of professional education, national status as exporter or importer of capital, government policies, geographical position, trade patterns (exports and imports), emigration, and undoubtedly such vague imponderables as culture and taste.[10]

Factor costs are helpful in explaining what advantage a company might have *vis-à-vis* companies with head offices in other nations. For a company to venture abroad, it had to have some expected (anticipated) advantage – for otherwise there was no rationale for the expansion and no hope of persistence.[11] It has often been pointed out that American costs of labour were high; thus, Americans substituted machines for labour; American business tended to have advantages abroad in businesses that were capital intensive, in mass production industries.[12] An analysis of British multinationals in 1870–1914 in terms of factor costs would stress the relative cheapness of capital. A recent study suggests that British firms had a comparative disadvantage in goods that were intensive in the use of human capital.[13] Factor costs by themselves, however, seem inadequate as a complete explanation of differences between and among multinationals from different nations. Relatively high labour costs in Canada did not make Canadian development similar to that of the United States. Canadian business abroad varied in numerous ways from its south of the border counterpart. Likewise, I find it very difficult to explain the huge differences between German and French multinational enterprise solely or even fundamentally in terms of factor costs.

The more industrialised, the more economically advanced the country, *ceteris paribus*, the more likely for it to be a headquarters for business abroad. While the match is imperfect, we would predict more German enterprise abroad than Spanish headquartered business over borders and our prediction would in fact be fulfilled. So, too, the large number (in relative terms) of British multinationals fits well under this explanatory rubric. Britain was after all the 'first industrial nation'.

Often technological advantage has been behind specific business enterprise expansion into foreign lands. The explanation is especially helpful *vis-à-vis* many US and German multinationals, but it is by no means adequate as an all-encompassing rationale. Moreover, there have been identified a number of Swedish cases of business abroad based on technology obtained in Germany (a third country) and British cases of business overseas to obtain (to pull in) technology from abroad. Technological advantage is also often inadequate in explaining an enterprise's backward integration into resource development.

12                                                    THE END OF INSULARITY

The size and nature of the domestic market (including the number of customers, disposable income, and geographical dispersion) shaped business at home and became a significant influence on the characteristics of both domestic business and business abroad.[14] It had impact on the shift from family firm to managerial enterprise.[15] Yet, the size-of- and nature-of-market impacts were not always consistent. Swedish and Swiss firms with geographically and demographically small domestic markets, but relatively high income ones, made substantial foreign direct investments, while Danish and Norwegian companies did not. The 'heterogeneous' American market (with consumers from different cultural backgrounds, with extremes in climate, and with other substantial regional variations) offered an excellent learning experience for American managers abroad; the more homogenous British domestic market had a limiting effect on operating companies' managerial training.[16] Business abroad required managing enterprises over distance. This was in no way a given. Coping with the problems of a long span of managerial control often made the difference between success and failure of the ventures.

In most European and North American countries, banks seem not to have been of major importance *vis-à-vis* the vast quantity of their nationals' foreign business operations,[17] but in Germany and Sweden, banks were highly instrumental.[18] And, the foreign direct investments made by British and to a lesser extent, Canadian banks were a significant type of pre-1914 multinational enterprise.[19]

Lack of natural resources at home – when there was a domestic demand for such resources – stimulated some businesses to extend their operations abroad, although the absence of (or alternatively high cost of) a particular raw material did not by definition mean a foreign direct investment in obtaining it (French business invested abroad in phosphate production; I have no evidence that Swiss companies did).

British professional education came later than that in America and Germany; educational systems seem to have had influence on the multinationals of the respective nations.

Operations in foreign countries were embarked on by companies in home countries that were net importers of capital (Russian insurance companies had multinational business) as well as by firms in countries such as Great Britain that were net capital exporters; creditor versus debtor nation status had an impact in shaping business abroad.

Home government policies had a complex collection of effects on business abroad, from those associated with imperial policies, antitrust policies, to tax policies, for instance. Empire created a familiar political infrastructure overseas that in general served to encourage nationals to invest in these countries, for uncertainty was reduced. Thus, British investment in Malaya and India exceeded that from continental Europe or the United States; Dutch companies had a relatively greater significance than any others in the Dutch East Indies. Antitrust policies (or their absence) altered the strategies of foreign investors: that restraint of trade agreements were illegal in the United States had substantial effects on American business abroad. Tax policies began to affect companies' investment tactics (if not strategies) by the early twentieth century; this is a subject about which we know very little; my own research, however, suggests that in the first decade of the twentieth century British taxes may well have influenced the path of British business abroad.[20] It has long been accepted that French taxes redirected French portfolio investment (much of which was done through Switzerland to avoid taxes); yet, whether taxation had a similar impact on French foreign *direct* investment is a subject that as far as I know has never been explored.

The geographical position of the home country seems crucial to an understanding of where a nation's companies invested abroad, when they went abroad, as well as important in understanding their relationships with firms in neighbouring lands. Yet, sometimes, being 'politically', 'culturally', or 'linguistically' nearby was more important that geographical proximity. Directions of trade gave enterprises greater familiarity with certain areas – and a clear connection exists between the extension of business investment abroad and a nation's commerce, albeit there was never a perfect correlation (and, at any particular time, thwarted trade – because of tariffs – might be an incentive to raise foreign direct investment). So, too, often (but not always) there existed a positive relationship between emigration and the locales for foreign direct investment. Once, again, migration served to provide information flows and lower uncertainty costs.

I included the impact of culture, with reluctance, since it seems an amorphous concept. I am not sure that there was one American or German 'culture' that has shaped foreign direct investments, although it is easy to note proto-typical national characteristics and attribute them to culture. The 'American frontier spirit' and 'German aggressiveness' are examples. As a Frenchman explained (in 1915), 'the German is industrious, a remarkably hard worker, who sets about his task with diligence and energy … Germany is disciplined'.[21] 'Taste' must sometimes be resorted to as a sole explanatory factor. How else is it possible to understand the sizeable British foreign direct investments in tea and German multinationals' involvements in coffee. (Is perhaps taste a sub-set of culture?).

In sum, we can itemise crucial variables in a home country that have impact, but such a roster is merely a start. It is the combinations of these economic, demographic, political, social and cultural impacts that form the basis for our discussion and for the marked differences country-by-country in the development of European and North American multinationals.

*British Business Abroad*

Of all nations, the one with the greatest foreign direct investment and

14                                                        THE END OF INSULARITY

the greatest number of overseas operations (1870–1914) was clearly Great Britain.[22] Vying for second place in this period were Germany and the United States, both of which nations headquartered numerous companies with business abroad.[23] After these three leaders, it is difficult to establish which country would rank fourth. Candidates include France and Sweden. Belgium is also a possibility for fourth place. Switzerland ranks high on the list, as does Holland.[24] Lower down on the tabulation are Canada, Austria-Hungary, Italy, Russia, and Bulgaria.

British business in 1870–1914 spanned the globe. Britain had in these years slower growth rates at home than did the United States and Germany. Its enterprises were, however (or as a consequence in some cases), very active abroad. The extent of British *business* overseas is just becoming known; many ventures were shortlived. For this article, I made a very rough count of British headquartered enterprises that I could document as having built or acquired manufacturing plants *in the United States* before 1914. The number of parent companies ran in excess of 100. Many had multiplant businesses in America. They owned roughly 255 manufacturing plants. But, approximately a third of these factories had shut down, or were no longer British-owned by 1914.[25]

British firms that operated overseas were of two basic varieties. First, and foremost, there were what I have called 'free-standing' companies.[26] Second, there were companies that did business in Britain and then expanded overseas, extending their existing operations.[27] There were many more free-standing companies than any other type of British foreign direct investment. The companies were registered in the United Kingdom and were established to do business typically in a single country abroad. Thus, there were Anglo-Argentine, Anglo-Australian, Anglo-Russian firms. Each usually operated in a single economic activity overseas, but together they covered the economic spectrum; they were in agriculture, manufacturing, and services (including public utilities, transportation, and banking services). The enterprises were both 'market-oriented' (to serve the host country markets) and 'supply-oriented' (to provide for British, or less often, third country needs). Their founders hoped to unite the abundant capital in Great Britain with the potentially or actually profitable opportunity abroad. Each had a board of directors in Britain, charged with managing the overseas business. The British headquarters was, however, at least at origin usually limited to the part-time board of directors and possibly one full-time secretary. In short, the head office did not amount to very much.

There were literally thousands of British free-standing companies. They attracted British capital, but also French, German, Belgian, and other foreign investors. The firms, however, were the investors abroad. The free-standing companies were frequently grouped in loose clusters – clusters that were often overlapping. A single firm might be classified in a handful of different clusters. The principals in the clusters provided a range of services to the free-standing companies.[28]

There were British free-standing companies in many different activities from rubber in Malaya to copper mining in Russia, from cattle ranches in the United States to nitrate mines in Chile, from railroads in Brazil to hotels in Egypt, from mortgage companies in Australia to meat-packing in Argentina. The variety was extraordinary.

In addition, there were in Britain many companies that first developed their business operations with the home market preeminent and then invested abroad to pursue added markets and to obtain sources of supply. Such businesses included 'industrials', but also numerous British producers of services (trade, shipping, insurance, accounting, engineering, and so forth). The British producers of goods that invested abroad in the years before 1914 appear to have been heavily concentrated in the consumer products sector (soap, thread, and patent medicines are excellent examples).[29] All were trademarked. If the companies made producer goods, the home industries were often related to textiles (Bradford Dyers, United Alkali, H & G Bullock). There seem to have been very little British overseas business based on advanced technology. The crucible steel makers – which had major technical advantages – appear to have had their advantage in long experience rather than especially new developments.[30] Four examples of British 'high-technology' companies that did invest abroad in this era are: (1) Courtaulds (rayon); (2) Burroughs & Wellcome (drugs); (3) Brunner, Mond (alkalies); and (4) Marconi (radio installations). The first case was in synthetic textiles (and the technology here was developed in part outside Britain or with the aid of foreign ideas); the second was of a company founded by Americans, which sold patent medicines as well as ethical drugs; the third was a firm that was part of a Belgian multinational enterprise (and it was the latter rather than the British one that was at the centre of the multinational business behaviour); and the fourth was a company founded by a man with an Italian father and a British mother (it was not a 'purely' British enterprise), and moreover, although radio was new, economic historian Hugh Aitken could write of the 'technological conservatism' of the Marconi organisation and that the technological leadership Marconi once held was already 'shaky' by 1914; 'confident in its technical supremacy, it [the Marconi organisation] had failed to mount a sustained research program'.[31]

It has often been assumed by American students of multinational enterprise that textile companies did not become multinationals. Yet, the largest British textile enterprises were engaged in overseas direct investments. By 1914 J. & P. Coats had mills in the United States, Canada, and Russia.[32] English Sewing Cotton Co. produced through affiliated companies in the United States, France, and Russia. Linen Thread Co., Ltd., had factories in the United States and France.[33] The Fine Cotton Spinners' & Doublers' Association acquired around the

16                                    THE END OF INSULARITY

turn of the century 'a dominant interest' in its most prominent French competitor, La Société Anonyme des Filatures Delebart Mallet Fils.[34] Bradford Dyers had a major plant in the United States and one in Germany. Nairn Linoleum (linoleum is made of jute or burlap – and thus can be classified as a textile) had factories in the United States, France, and Germany.[35] This is only a small sample of the British textile plants abroad. The host country list – the United States, Canada, France, Germany, Russia – is, however, worth noting.

British businesses also integrated backward to obtain needed raw materials, from cotton seed and palm oil (by Lever) to crude oil (by the 'Shell' Transport and Trading Co.), to iron ore (by Consett and Dowlais).[36] It was apparently even more common for British enterprises to use the free-standing firm for investments in basic inputs and other agricultural products.

Prominent among the 'service' sector multinationals were trading companies.[37] Often trading houses set up free-standing companies (combining the two forms). Likewise, men involved in overseas shipping frequently were associated with free-standing units.[38] So, too consulting and managing engineers had responsibility for managing free-standing mining companies.[39] As yet we know little about the role of the British overseas banks in assisting the expansion of British business abroad.[40] We do know that British banks abroad were a significant aspect of British business overseas.[41] We also know that many of the British international and imperial banks began as free-standing companies.[42]

In my *Economic History Review* article, I outline ten cluster sets that united British free-standing companies. These clusters and others need more attention. While most, as indicated, involved a very tenuous coupling of companies – joined by a functional service provided to the enterprise (promotion, engineering, accounting, services) – some cluster sets could be tighter and then we move to a description of the pivotal service firm as a multinational enterprise.[43] We need to think about the nature of influence and control, influence that is specific to particular functions (finance, construction, engineering, purchasing, marketing) and control (which determines or has the potential to establish overall administrative direction).[44] Faithful and effective performance in a single function might be simpler for a British business to achieve than full internalisation.

While the two basic forms of British overseas business before 1914 appear to have been the free-standing company and the enterprise that evolved from a home base, two other variants in origin have been identified. The first is what Geoffrey Jones has called the migrating multinational.[45] This is a company that began with a headquarters in one country, invested in Britain, and then became over time a British-headquartered multinational. The second variant is more difficult for me to incorporate in my frame of reference. This is a firm established abroad (with no UK registration) that attracted both British capital and

*Multinational Corporations*

British management. It is not, by my definition, a free-standing firm, since it did not have a legal headquarters in Britain; it was not a *company* investing over borders. Yet, some have felt this type of activity should be included under the category of British business abroad.[46] Frequently, companies set up abroad became free-standing ones with British registration and then the free-standing company was dissolved, to be again replaced by a local firm. Sometimes, a free-standing company was set up anew and then the place of incorporation migrated abroad. My research suggests (tentatively) that when the last step occurred, the administrative control from Britain either weakened substantially, or terminated; what was once a direct investment became a portfolio one.[47] The 'British' management was by immigrants or expatriates – if it persisted. Some overseas-registered companies seem to have been established by British trading houses that provided their management and arranged their financing. Can it be said that such companies are part of a multinational enterprise in which the trading house provides the administrative guidance? The trading house, in turn, had the UK head office.

If we were able to identify a company *registered* abroad, with a concentrated ownership in the United Kingdom that provided a British 'head office' and assumed a 'managerial role' but had no 'operations' by the unincorporated head office – I would be prepared to call this a 'free-standing firm – variant I'.[48] More research needs to be done on the distinctions between British- and locally-registered firms and the management of the business institution.[49]

One significant British multinational captured aspects of three of the four categories, but, none the less, could be classified in one of them. Borax Consolidated, Ltd., by 1914 was a major British multinational – with a headquarters in London and operations in Britain, North and South America, and Europe. It was a vertically and horizontally integrated international enterprise with a legal and administrative headquarters in the United Kingdom.

Its genesis was when an American went to England – seeking markets and monies. He met a Britisher. What evolved was a merger of the British Redwood and Sons and the American's far more extensive operation. A headquarters was established in the United Kingdom, as was a British holding company. For Redwood this was backward vertical integration. I am prepared to call the new holding company, a *British* multinational enterprise. Yet, even though the legal and administrative head office was in Britain, the largest stockholding in the parent company was by the American. The parent was to integrate operations (uniting the British and American businesses), but also to raise capital in Britain for the entire business. While the new British enterprise was clearly not a free-standing one, it bore resemblances to many such companies. It had a prestigious chairman of the board – brought in to encourage Britishers to invest. And, when another British 'free-standing company' shifted its headquarters from London

18                                                      THE END OF INSULARITY

to New York, the principal American stockholder in the borax company suggested that it follow suit. It did not. London remained the headquarters for not only the British and American, but the firm's newly-acquired worldwide business operations. Eventually, in 1913, the American was forced out of the business (and sold his shareholdings).[50] It could be argued (although I do not want to do so) that this was a migrating multinational; clearly, however, the insights and recognition of the existence of migrating multinationals helps us understand this British business abroad.

The idea of the migrating multinational provides even more insights into the activities of another giant British multinational enterprise (albeit I would argue that this firm did not become a *British* multinational until the 1920s). The British–American Tobacco Co. (BAT) came into being in 1902, as a part of a division of market agreement that followed American Tobacco's aggressive attempt to penetrate the British market. BAT at origin was owned two-thirds by American Tobacco and one-third by Imperial Tobacco, and had operations worldwide; it could not sell in the United States nor in the United Kingdom, but had export-related activities in both countries, and most important, it had a London headquarters. At the start, its top management seems to have been American. In 1902, it was an American business abroad. In time, the American stock ownership was reduced, the American management cut back, the home office well established in London, and this company became a British multinational (a migrating multinational enterprise).[51]

I am less sure that when a free-standing registered company shifted to foreign registration (as was often the case) that there was retained British direct investment characteristics. Thus, Otis Steel, an American company, was acquired by a British free-standing company. For years it was a British direct investment in the United States. In time, however, the British headquarters had seemed superfluous. The British-registered company was dissolved. A British accountant joined the US board of directors, presumably representing British investors. When the British registered company was dissolved, I would suggest that the *company* that had made the direct investment was also out-of-the-picture; now the individual British investors had portfolio rather than direct investment stakes (despite the accountant who represented their interests).[52]

In considering British business abroad, we must have a flexibility in evaluating what we find. We need to inquire why was the British free-standing company more common than the British enterprise that developed its operations abroad out of an existing business in Britain? What happened to the free-standing companies through time? How did they deal with the problems of managing business overseas? Why did consumer goods industries predominate in those British businesses that went abroad? Why was the textile industry so visible in British business abroad? To what extent was there foreign direct investment in

EUROPEAN AND NORTH AMERICAN MULTINATIONALS, 1870–1914　　19

raw materials and foodstuff production? Why did the trading company take such a key role in diffusing British business abroad? What exactly was the role of banking institutions? What insights does the paradigm of the cluster set provide? What do the discoveries of migrating multinationals tell us about British business activities? Is the transfer of registration overseas an aspect of the migration of business head-quarters? What insights are cast on British managerial performance overseas?

The home country influences outlined earlier in this paper help us to start to answer some of these questions. Factor costs: British capital was abundant; the relative cheapness of capital meant that the British had the opportunity (the incentive) to invest it elsewhere around the world where the returns were higher than at home. Free-standing companies were the institutional device to maintain control. Britain was industrialised; it had been the first industrial nation. Britain used its technological advantage in textiles abroad – and on occasion British multinationals borrowed abroad to overcome technological deficien-cies. There was a high income domestic market in which consumer goods had been sold; the textile industry had grown first and foremost in that market. Many British investments abroad were designed to provide for the domestic market. But, the geographically small British domestic market was inadequate as a training ground for managers. The family firm without a well-developed managerial structure persisted in Britain. British companies had problems operating abroad. The free-standing firm was a compromise and may in many cases have substituted for British firms that apparently found the extension of management internationally a difficult proposition.[53]

Since Britain did not have 'universal' banks, it was often 'the investment group', with a trading company at the centre that assisted British business abroad.[54] Britain was a small island, dependent on international trade, which meant the emergence of well-developed and numerous trading companies with important roles in developing British business abroad.

Lack of certain basic natural resources (plus demand for them) encouraged not only trade, but also British business investment abroad. The investment, however, was highly selective and more needs to be done on the institutional structure and management of British mining and agricultural investments abroad and especially on the management of the marketing of the output.[55] Many British direct investments in railroads were associated with primary product procurement.

Scots abroad often ran British overseas investments from Burma to Canada to Chile. The overseas Scot provided the British company with a familiar dependable representative abroad. Culturally, Britain is frequently perceived as 'insular', and smug. A number of years ago, however, Charles Wilson pointed out that Unilever and Imperial Chemical Industries in the 1920s had involved a merging of multi-

national founders.[56] So did Royal Dutch-Shell much earlier. The more
one deals with the British international business community, the more
cosmopolitan it seems.[57] It is a paradox that contrasts with the stereo-
type – although it has long been recognised that British business
innovation was promoted by 'outsiders' rather than by those in the
mainstream of British life.[58] None the less, the insularity does appear to
have created in many instances constraints on British management
abroad,[59] constraints that the many Scots abroad could only partially
rectify.

### German and American Multinationals

The differences between British and German multinationals were
vivid, yet, as we will see, there were similarities. There was not the
same mix of the two (or four) varieties of German and British business abroad. There seem to have been few (or certainly far fewer
than the British, in relative terms) German free-standing companies
that operated in foreign countries – at least this is my present view
– though the subject needs more investigation, especially as relates
to public utilities, transportation, and raw material procurement (some
of the German investments in US phosphate mining, for example,
seem to have been by free-standing companies). Migrating multinationals do not appear to have been a particularly important feature
in the origins of German multinationals (albeit could the Rheinische
Stahlwerke AG be seen in these terms – it was established in 1869
by Frenchmen and Belgians and headquartered in Paris;[60] and what
about Allgemeine Elektrizitäts Gesellschaft? could it be considered
a migrating multi-national? its predecessor was part of an American
business abroad).[61] I have not been able to identify *independent*
German companies registered in the host country, with German capital
*and* management direction *from* Germany (there were, however,
numerous firms established by German immigrants and registered
in the host country, but these either fit into the category of German
multinational enterprise – where the immigrant represented a parent
firm abroad – or were separate businesses of the immigrant and
*not* part of a German business abroad, not a foreign direct investment). We need more study, however, of third-country registrations
– London-registered companies that operated in Argentina (for
example) – that were German-owned and probably (in the host
country) German-managed. The London-registration seems to have
been to aggregate capital, to have a convenient operating framework, but where was the real 'headquarters'? In a German city?
I do not know, but that would be my hypothesis. If so, this might
well be part of a German multinational enterprise expansion.

There were many German companies that began to do business in
Germany and then based on their advantage at home, extended their
business abroad, typically to reach foreign markets and to obtain raw

materials.[62] Such investments included many in public utilities, designed to *sell* German electrical equipment. There were also numerous German trading companies – mercantile houses – that had outlets throughout Europe and in addition appear in locales from Guatemala to Turkey.[63] Especially important were the German metal traders.[64] And then there were the German banks active in Europe, North and South America, Asia, and Africa, encouraging and representing German business abroad.[65]

The extent of German-managed enterprise in foreign countries in the pre-First World War years is just being deciphered; there are studies of German foreign direct investment in the United States, in Great Britain, and elsewhere.[66] What seems evident is that unlike the British ones, German multinationals were particularly active abroad in 'high technology' products – especially in the chemical and in the electrical industries.[67] German companies also operated abroad in iron and steel manufactures.[68] They were involved in capital goods industries. German industrial enterprise took the initiative in world markets – exporting, setting up marketing organisations abroad, and establishing foreign manufacture, and foreign companies that would buy German output.

The British – as we have seen – excelled in trademarked consumer products. The Germans also used the trademark as an important property right in their business abroad. Yet, the use may have been different. In the United States Bayer, for example, sold aspirins, which it would claim was its trademarked product. The drug was sold through prescriptions; however, increasingly *before 1914*, consumers bought it over-the-counter and decided on 'self-medication'. Bayer advertised widely, *but* to physicians and to the trade, rather than to the final consumer. Ultimately (in 1921), Bayer would lose the trademark Aspirin in America; the reason the court gave was that before 1915, the company had let the retail druggist (or the manufacturing chemist, who bottled or transformed powder into tablets) sell to the consumer *without* the Bayer name on the product. Thus, in the trademark case, the court ruled that for the consumer the word had passed into the public domain.[69] Germans invested abroad in chocolates – a consumer product. Here again, the product was trademarked, but once again, Stollwerck in many instances sold not to the ultimate buyer, but as a cooking chocolate to other producers.[70]

Actually, there were a surprising number of trademarked German consumer products.[71] The A.W. Faber pencil was one. The German Faber firm by the 1870s was a multinational enterprise, with its main factory in Stein (near Nürnberg); a large slate facility at Geroldsgrun, Bavaria; branches in Paris and London; an agency in Vienna; and a pencil factory in Brooklyn, New York. In the early twentieth century, the American subsidiary, A.W. Faber, was advertising that the German company had manufactories in Germany, France, and the United States. The idea that there were no (or few) German consumer goods manufactured by German multinationals abroad is false.[72]

Like the British, there were some important German textile invest-ments in foreign countries – in woollens and silk (not the textiles most typically associated with British overseas business) – albeit some scholars have found that German textile producers were not active abroad.[73]

Certain German industrial firms integrated backward to obtain raw materials. This was true of German iron and steel manufacturers.[74] Trading companies also appear to have made investments in producing activities abroad. Metallgesellschaft is an excellent example.[75]

German banks were ubiquitous abroad, aiding industrial enterprises in numerous manners. They were active, for example, in relation to the German search abroad for oil – in Romania and in the Middle East.[76]

Like the German multinationals, US multinationals often invested abroad to sell and to make goods, based on new technology and typically trademarked products (whether sold to producer or consumer).[77] In some of the same industries, American and German business both expanded abroad, but, in the main, the industries were different. The US-registered free-standing company existed (in Cuban sugar, for example), although it was of little significance in American business abroad in the pre-1914 years. Again, while I can identify some migrating multinationals (W.R. Grace started in Peru, and then became a US-headquartered business), that pattern was atypical. In both the American and German cases, the prototype multinational was a firm that started at home and then expanded over borders – either to reach markets or to obtain sources of supply. Yet, in the German evolution of multinational enterprise, the role of the giant banks was key, whereas in the United States, to be sure private banks had London and Paris outlets (principally to encourage the flow of European monies to America), but US national banks could not branch abroad until after the passage of the Federal Reserve Act (1913). Thus, not only did the United States have virtually nothing comparable to the numerous British overseas banks (the International Banking Corpora-tion established in 1902 is the one possible exception), it had nothing that was anywhere near equivalent to the Deutsche Bank or the other great German banks.[78]

Here again, home country characteristics help explain why the German and American multinational enterprise pattern differed from that of the British. Clearly, in each case, factor costs were different. German enterprise could draw on an abundance of skilled workers and professionals; in products that were skill- and research-intensive, German business excelled and expanded at home and abroad. This was especially relevant in the dyestuff sector of the German chemical industry, where literally thousands of products were produced in small batches by large companies, heavily manned with skilled and often university educated personnel. Americans found labour costs high and substituted capital for labour. Mass production techniques used unskilled labour. American companies expanded abroad in sewing machines, harvesters, and mass produced automobiles. America had abundant oil; new refineries had large throughput; the country became a large exporter of refined oil, and Standard Oil became a major multinational enterprise.[79] Differences in factor costs in part accounted for the differing German and American advantages. In Alfred Chandler's terms, economies of scope and economies of scale created differences in cost advantages.[80] By 1914, Germany ranked second and the United States ranked first in world manufacturing (Britain was third). The growth of industrialisation spurred new enterprises that quickly expanded over national frontiers. It was often in the newest and most technologically advanced products that German and US businesses invested abroad. Technologically innovative enterprises abounded, and it was these companies that introduced the new processes and products abroad (through foreign direct investments).

German and US firms sold first at home and then abroad. In both Germany and the United States, administrative hierarchies in business organisation emerged more rapidly than in Britain. In Germany, however, the family firm seems to have lingered longer in sizeable enterprise (and in business abroad) than was the case in the United States. If family members went abroad, they often supported German business expansion (George Merck in America, for example). The Germans, like the British, and far more than Americans, found business over borders very difficult. The German electrical companies' problems in controlling their business investments in the United States are a case in point.[81] In the United States, where scale economies were key, the huge and heterogeneous US market offered a superb training arena for business managers who would move abroad. The ever-present German bank in domestic business reflected itself in the international scene.

US and American states' banking laws sharply restricted American banks in their expansion at home (and abroad). We need more information on German business abroad and natural resource procurement; there were many German foreign direct investments in production of primary products. The Germans had little oil – and German companies, accordingly, desired to fill domestic needs. By contrast, the US international oil industry began based on abundant oil and refined oil exports. The evolution of the German and US (and for that matter the British) international oil companies was entirely different. By 1914, one American tyre company (US Rubber) had begun to invest in rubber plantations in Sumatra; the British, Dunlop had invested in rubber estates in Malaya; did the leading German tyre company have similar investments? Many of the products required for the German economy – but not produced there – were obtained through German importing firms.

German professional education – the scientific training – had immense impact on German advantage in world markets. American education was more practical, more engineering-oriented. This seems to have had an influence on the firms in America that had advantages and that moved abroad. The connections in the German case are very specific; in the American one more general.

Germany was a net exporter of capital, but its growth at home absorbed substantial investment. None the less, that it was a net capital exporter may help explain the important role of banks in its international expansion. The United States before 1914 was a net importer of capital. Its portfolio investments abroad (1870–1914) were very small compared with its foreign direct investments. US companies moved abroad not to locate better financial returns, but to reach markets and to obtain sources of supply. When we compare American and British business abroad, this difference is vivid. In Britain, there was substantial surplus capital and rates of return were higher overseas. The evidence in the British case indicates that foreign portfolio investments were larger than foreign direct investments. The free-standing company served to direct and to monitor the use of passive investors' capital abroad. Since America was a net importer of capital, there was generally little need for the free-standing company form. Business abroad grew out of the requirements of business at home.

In Germany, because cartels were perfectly acceptable, there existed some foreign direct investments by cartel representatives to encourage exports.[82] Cartels may have also deterred some foreign direct investment. The restraint of trade rules in America encouraged mergers; domestic conditions required integration of operations; integrated business abroad was a natural extension.

German business crossed over into neighbouring countries; Austria–Hungary – especially the Austrian part, where the language was German – was especially attractive. In some ways, Austria–Hungary may have been to German enterprise rather like Canada to US business, with German business 'spilling over' the border. Likewise, there were sizeable German investments in other nearby countries; transportation and communication links within Europe had by 1870–1914 become very easy – and enterprising German businessmen often made their presence felt – from France to Switzerland, and in many other European countries. But German businesses made their greatest direct investments in United States (in part because that was where there was the major German immigration). American business abroad went first and foremost to nearby countries (geographically nearby such as Canada, Mexico, and the Caribbean) and culturally nearby (such as Canada and the United Kingdom). German emigrants were very significant in developing German business abroad. There were German settlers from China to Russia. (Odessa in 1910, for example, had a German community of 12,000).[83] There was nothing at all similar with American emigrants; the United States was a country of immigrants not emigrants. Germans abroad created familiar conditions for German business in foreign lands and helped overcome some of the difficulties of doing business in strange lands. (As noted earlier, American businessmen learned at home how to deal with 'foreigners' in the domestic markets, since American business was already selling at home to a nationally diverse population).

Clearly, 'the culture' of economic growth influenced German and American businesses in their expansion over borders. There was a vitality in the German and American people that reflected itself in the spread of business abroad. Whereas in Britain at least some of the business activities overseas (particularly those of the free-standing companies) involved a conscious reallocation of resources – at least capital resources – from domestic to international use; in the German and US cases, business abroad was more typically complementary to that at home.

### French, Swedish, Belgian, Swiss, and Dutch Business Investments Abroad

French business abroad was extensive in the years 1870 to 1914; while substantial work has been done on French finance, we are slowly learning about the institutional mechanisms by which French industry extended itself over borders.[84] The St. Gobain glassworks as early as the 1850s had built a branch plant in Germany; by 1900 it was a multi-plant enterprise in that country.[85] Before the First World War, St. Gobain was also manufacturing in Italy, Belgium, Holland, Spain, and Austria–Hungary.[86] (How aggressive it seems compared with Pilkington; that British firm had manufacturing abroad in only one country – Canada).[87] The French family firm, Michelin, had by 1914 factories in the United States, Italy, and Great Britain (its rival, Dunlop, in 1914 manufactured in Germany, France, and Japan; no German nor US tyre company had three foreign manufacturing plants in 1914).[88] French car companies also had a collection of business investments abroad.[89]

Most extensive, however, were the international operations of Société Schneider et Cie. Claude Ph. Beaud has done remarkably well in deciphering its business abroad – from Italy to Chile to England (all disappointing ventures). Often the firm's participations were minority ones, but they were designed for business purposes – that is, to obtain orders for Schneider. In Morocco, Schneider set up a diversified group of companies, associated with Moroccan development – from mining companies to gas and electric ones. In Argentina, it made major investments, with the hope of obtaining orders from the newly-established firms. It invested in iron-mines in Lorraine and collieries in Belgium. In 1911 it participated in developing the Russian armaments industry.[90]

I have found a surprising number of French businesses that operated in the United States;[91] more operated in Russia; Spain was attractive to French businessmen (often operating through London-registered companies).[92] French free-standing companies seem to have existed, albeit the extent of them is unknown.[93] French trading companies need investigation,[94] as do French banks.[95] John McKay's 'The House of Rothschild (Paris) as a Multinational Industrial Enterprise, 1875–1914', breaks new ground in the study of French business abroad.[96] Where ever there was gold, French businessmen were interested; thus, students of British business in South Africa have encountered French (and German) involvements.

The French always complained that German business had grabbed, in international business, what was French technology (in silk, for example). The French were the innovators in rayon – but initially the prominent multinational in rayon was the British-headquartered Courtaulds. The Héroult process in aluminium was a French one – and yet, American, German-Swiss, and to a far lesser extent British companies took precedence over French business abroad in this new industry. In a number of different industries where the French excelled, we know little about why or how French business enterprises took, or failed to take, the initiative in business abroad. Often, in the French case we are talking about family firms, not publicly-owned companies. Yet, France was a large capital exporter in the years before 1914 (second only to Great Britain) and it does seem that some (and perhaps much) of this foreign investment was in the form of direct investment (business investment), probably more than is generally assumed.[97]

Ragnhild Lundström has documented the remarkable expansion of Swedish business abroad. Swedish companies (often based on German technology) spread internationally – seeking new markets, setting up plants abroad. Banks played a crucial role, in assisting Swedish international business and Swedish entrepreneurs who went abroad. Swedes established operations in Russia; they financed these ventures in European capital markets; often, the Swedes settled in Russia. Can this be called 'Swedish' business abroad, or Swedish direct investment? Once the migration took place, should this not be described as a Russian business, financed by European (portfolio) investment? Such activities bear resemblance to the Britisher, who went abroad, set up business in a country overseas, and then called on home capital for financing. It appears frequently that in neither case was there a real European head office administering operations. The investment from Europe seems to have been pure finance. Here, again, family associations must be traced.[98]

Lundström identified a hybrid-type operation. A man went abroad to do business, set up a manufacturing company, and got full equity financing from the Enskilda Bank. Is this a foreign direct investment by the Bank? The bank had control. Yet, the initiative came from the trusted entrepreneur, who was in a business abroad that had nothing to do with banking. How common was such a pattern?[99]

There were numerous Belgian businesses in foreign lands that are very well known – from Leopold's extensive activities in the Congo to

Solvay & Cie.'s international business.[100] Belgium had heavy industry. Société Générale de Belgique made direct investments in Spain, Italy, France, Austria, Russia, China, Mexico, Brazil, Argentina, and of course, the Congo, in railroad construction, to help secure markets for Belgian industry. The Société Générale also invested in an extensive chain of banks that did business outside of Belgium.[101] There were formidable Belgian foreign direct investments in tramways, especially those of the Empain group.[102] Individual Belgian entrepreneurs had many direct investments abroad.[103] The complex Belgian direct investments in the Russian iron and steel industry have been well documented by Ulrich Wengenroth.[104] More modest investments were those of Gevaert, an Antwerp maker of photographic paper. His production began in 1892 and by the eve of the First World War, Lieven Gevaert had opened branch distribution depots in Paris, Vienna, Berlin, Milan, Moscow, London, Buenos Aires, and Rio.[105] If Solvay & Cie.'s and Gevaert's business abroad seem comfortable in the conventional model of multinational enterprise, many of the other Belgian businesses outside the country do not conform as neatly. Robert Liefmann, many years ago, concluded that the big banks in Belgium 'have had a greater influence upon the initiation and financing of enterprises [at home and abroad] than in any other country'.[106] By all accounts, Belgian-managed business over borders was extensive. How and where did banks find managers that were appropriate to the task to be performed abroad? We need more studies on how the managerial structure emerged. Likewise, we require more evidence on where Belgian business went; from all appearances, Belgian enterprise was truly multinational; yet Solvay & Cie. excepted, it was conspicuously absent in the United States before the First World War.[107] Is the reason, that Belgian industrial advantages were not advantages in the United States?

Swiss multinational enterprise, likewise, requires far more attention. Many Swiss businesses invested abroad – in silk, cotton, wool and embroidery, canned goods, chocolates, pharmaceuticals, electrotechnical and electrochemical industries, machinery, and so forth.[108] By 1914, there were five Swiss hotel companies that ran hotels in Italy, France, and North Africa.[109] The common feature of all Swiss investments was always quality goods and services.[110] If Ernest Himmel's figures on 77 Swiss companies are to be trusted, in 1913 they had the most invested in France, followed by 'North America' (principally the United States), Germany, and then Italy.[111]

According to an obituary of Robert Schwarzenbach (1839–1904), this Swiss pioneer in silk power looms had by 1904 established silk manufacturing plants not only in Switzerland, but in the United States, Italy, France, and Germany.[112] When in 1900, Nestlé built its American factory in Fulton, New York, a local town directory announced that 'The milk received at the Fulton factory is subjected to the same high test as has been observed for 30 years and more at the Swiss factories of

Henri Nestlé at Vevey, Bercher and Payerne, as well as at the Norwegian factory at Christiania, and those at Edlitz, Austria, and Tutbury, England'.[113] Brown, Boveri & Co. – one of the largest manufacturers in Switzerland – had by 1914 'branches' in Italy, France, and Norway.[114] This is merely a small sample of Swiss multinational enterprises, in different industries. Where did the Swiss find management for all these businesses abroad? How often were family connections significant? How were these plants administered over borders? What role did Swiss banks play? There are many unanswered questions. Throughout the period Himmel studied (1898–1919), the Swiss businesses he monitored had greater investments *outside* Switzerland than at home.[115]

Whereas in the case of Switzerland, I identified very few 'free-standing companies', by contrast, this form is prevalent in the case of Dutch foreign direct investment.[116] Dutch finance has captured substantial attention, as have certain Dutch businesses abroad (The Royal Dutch Company and its successor, Royal Dutch-Shell, for example). Yet, we require more information on the nature of Dutch business abroad (1870–1914).[117] In Holland, private banks set up administrative trusts to hold American railroad securities, which securities were, in turn, owned by Dutch small investors. The effect was concentrated ownership that gave the banks a say in the conduct of the business abroad, at least *vis-à-vis* the financial function. Was this, therefore, foreign direct investment? The railroads in the United States were American-incorporated, American-administered, but the Dutch bankers often had more influence (at least on financial matters) than a typical 'portfolio' investor.[118] How does the student of multinational enterprise view such investments? This brings us to the matter of influence and control, and 'functional' relationships to which I will return in the conclusion.

In short, France exempted, all these contestants for fourth rank as homes to foreign direct investors were geographically small, relatively high income countries. In each case the nature of domestic business operations shaped business abroad. There seem to have been identifiable business elites (sometimes cosmopolitan in nature) that can be tracked in connection with the business abroad; some, but certainly not by any means all, of these business elites had banking connections. All of these countries except Holland and Switzerland appear to have looked more east than west in their investments and had larger direct investments in Russia than in the United States. Beyond this, it is difficult to generalise about this very diverse group of home countries, and I will leave that for future researchers. How many – aside from the Swiss – had greater investments abroad than at home?

*The Other Multinationals*

Canadian business abroad went typically across the border into the

United States, albeit it did extend further into the Caribbean and Latin America. In public utilities particularly there was a marked expansion of Canadian business abroad.[119]

Austro-Hungarian businesses across Empire borders were few and isolated, but there were some important ones. The Austrian Hermann Schmidtmann, with his direct investments in Germany and the United States, provides a good case in point.[120] Often, multi-plant Austro-Hungarian enterprises became 'international', after the break-up of the Empire! Fiat was exceptional among the modern Italian businesses in this period to invest abroad; it had manufacturing branches in Austria, the United States, and Russia by 1913.[121] Russian and Bulgarian fire insurance companies were before 1914 multinational enterprises. 'Bulgaria', First Bulgarian Insurance Co. of Roustchouk, Bulgaria, in 1913 operated in England, Germany, Belgium, Bulgaria, France, Holland, Spain, Turkey, and the United States.[122]

In sum, such debtor countries and Empires as Canada, the Austro-Hungarian Empire, Italy, Russia, and Bulgaria were homes to multinational enterprise.[123] The business abroad that was headquartered in these places tended, in the case of Canada, to be very limited as to where it went abroad, and in all these 'homes' tended to be quite restricted in terms of the economic sectors represented.

## The Host Countries

Of all the hosts to foreign direct investment, the United States was in 1914 by far the most important. It was a high income market, surrounded by a high tariff wall; it was rich in natural resources; and the opportunities for profit seemed immense. I will not give rankings beyond this, for I believe that any attempt to try to give the standing of host countries is at this stage premature.[124] Part of the problem in ranking hosts to foreign multinational enterprise is the lack of consensus on what is to be included as 'foreign direct investment'. In this article, I have tried to indicate what I believe should and should not be included. Until there is consensus in definition, however, country ranking will lead to nothing but frustration. This, however, is only part of the problem: each region or country has been studied separately, without comparative evaluations (scholars are trained as experts in European history, Chinese history, South African history, and so forth).

Without question, wherever a European or North American multinational enterprise invested, circumstances in the host country influenced its behaviour. It is, however, doubtful that each host country was so distinctive as to transform or to homogenise the foreign business, though over time, host country consumers might not be aware they were buying products of a foreign-owned firm.[125]

The evidence suggests that since a foreign direct investment by definition has a headquarters in the home country, the strategies of the

30                                              THE END OF INSULARITY

firm (at least initially) can be said to be more shaped by home rather than host country considerations, albeit clearly both play an important role and it goes almost without saying that the characteristics of the host country – from size of market to resources available, to political conditions (including tariff policies) – determine at the start whether a company will invest, in what sectors it will invest, and the legal forms of the investment. These matters also shaped the pace and the course of the expansion (or contraction, in some cases) of the business. A number of business investments of this era were 'joint-ventures' of one type or another – and the joint-venture relationships varied substantially, based on host country considerations.

Such comments accepted as a given, none the less, it seems to me that there are comparisons that can be made and that if one begins with the firm and its investments, there are patterns that transcend host country and regional impacts. One of the virgin territories for students of multinational enterprise relates to how companies of different nationalities performed differently in a host country.[126]

More is needed on the relationships between trade and emigration patterns in considering why particular investors chose to invest in particular host countries. As I study European-headquartered firms, I find myself asking many questions about 'partial' relationships – how these 'groupings', clusters, functional ties, reflected themselves in the management of business abroad in different countries; this seems to need more scrutiny.

## Conclusions

While substantial research has been done on the history of multi-national enterprise, much more is clearly required. The general, comparative research is particularly important to the British business historian, for it poses new questions and presses the historian toward a recognition of what is and what is not distinctive about the British experience. Research has made it evident that it is useful to look at the behaviour of business over borders. Too often there have been two constraints. The first is the assumption that the findings on the history of American business abroad (the American model) can be rigidly applied to business headquartered in Great Britain, Continental Europe and Canada. The second is that multinational enterprise and foreign direct investment are identical.

Let us look at each in turn. The application of the American model has provoked exciting new research. British business historians have been particularly active in this respect. Often, there is congruence in the behaviour of multinationals from different countries. However, the newer research shows considerable differences in the development of multinational enterprise in the pre-1914 years from one country to the next. The British experience is not exactly coincident with the American one. The modes used (free-standing enterprise versus operating base for example; involvement of banks, as another example) were different.[127] Whereas in the American case, by 1870–1914, it was the large-scale enterprises with administrative organisations that were the innovators in business abroad,[128] in the case of many British and continental European companies we are often describing family firms and kinship rather than corporate linkages over borders. Even in the German instance, where certain of the electrical and chemical companies had huge domestic employment and hierarchical managerial organisations,[129] at the same time, there were many family firms with business both at home and abroad.

These differences reflected themselves in motives. Because America was a net importer of capital, because profitable opportunities were available at home, in 1870–1914, only in the rarest instance was the motive for foreign direct investment purely financial. In countries, particularly Great Britain, where there were 'free-standing' companies often the reason for a specific business investment abroad was purely and simply a higher return in the foreign country, albeit the investment was designed as a managed business abroad. Some free-standing companies were established by promoters that arranged the business investment abroad with the sole purpose of their own quick personal financial gain. Free-standing companies aside, the other rationales do not seem to vary. Thus, companies made foreign direct investment to obtain better representation abroad, to be closer to (and thus more responsive to) customers, to save on transportation costs, to get behind tariff walls (and on rare occasions other host government barriers to trade), to assure sales to an enterprise abroad, and to complement existing foreign direct investments. Some products do not travel well and must be made near the customer (for example, explosives, products that get stale, and beer in this period). Still other foreign direct investments were made to develop or to secure sources of supply. Some foreign direct investments were designed to obtain information. While these motives did not vary by home country, what varied was the relative importance of particular motives – and that needs further study.

One major difference between and among countries was the extent of the business abroad *vis-à-vis* domestic operations. American business at home was always larger than its firms' foreign direct investments. If Himmel is correct, by contrast, Swiss business investments abroad were greater than those at home; are there other geographically small countries that fit this pattern? British business historians need to ask of companies engaged in business abroad, what percentage of their assets, sales, and employment were at home and what percentage abroad?

America was a country receiving immigrants. While there were individual Americans who went abroad to establish businesses, by 1870–1914 this was not the principal pattern and the 'American model' of multinational enterprise correctly excludes such activity. In the case

32                                    THE END OF INSULARITY

of Great Britain (and some continental European countries), there was
a dispersion – a worldwide spread – of business entrepreneurs. This has
posed major problems for students of British multinational enterprise.
British-born individuals spanned the globe; they went to the United
States, Canada, Argentina, to Sicily, India, Hong Kong – and so forth.
Some times they brought capital with them; sometimes, they established businesses using monies they had earned abroad. Sometimes
they used locally available capital; sometimes they tapped British
capital markets for their overseas businesses. I have argued in the
introduction to this article (and elsewhere as well) that to fit the
definition of multinational enterprise there must be *cross-border*
control, or potential for control. The problem lies in defining 'home', in
deciding, was there a *cross-border* activity? The Britisher who went to
the United States and, in many instances, Canada settled in these
countries. There was no ongoing foreign direct investment. Likewise,
the Britisher who went to Argentina typically settled, but he often
thought of Britain 'as home'. Since he actually settled, and if there was
no British home office or British legal registration, I cannot (as
indicated in the introduction to this article) refer to his managed
business in Argentina as a British foreign direct investment. The matter
gets far more difficult with the expatriate rather than the emigrant –
with businesses in Sicily, India, and Hong Kong. Take the case of
Benjamin Ingham, who spent most of his life in Sicily, but who kept his
bank account in the United Kingdom and saw the United Kingdom 'as
home'. In real terms, the United Kingdom was home for Ingham, even
though his trading business was managed from his base in Sicily.
What of British 'expatriates' in India and Hong Kong? They were
conspicuously 'British' – white men in a non-white world. 'Home' was
Britain: their children were educated there. Hong Kong was frequently
a base for business elsewhere in the Far East, especially in China. How
should the businesses of these expatriates (as distinct from emigrants)
be treated by students of multinational enterprise? This question is
important for several reasons: (1) how we define such business affects
our statistics on 'British' capital abroad and particularly on British
foreign direct investment; (2) in many cases, the expatriates in India
and Hong Kong did seek capital in the United Kingdom. It seems to me
that if there was no UK home office, the 'British' capital (the cross-
border capital) invested in these expatriate ventures must be referred
to as British portfolio investments; (3) even more important, from an
institutional standpoint, what happened to these enterprises through
time? When the individual entrepreneur died or went back 'home' to
Great Britain, how were these ventures sustained? If there was some
means of replenishing management through time in the United Kingdom, perhaps that can define a 'real' head office. The discussion of
multinational enterprise pushes us to look not merely at the individual
entrepreneur, but at the continuing managerial structure through time.
The answers to these fundamental questions may help us in determin-

ing whether the business can legitimately be classified as a 'British' multinational enterprise. In any case, the operating characteristics and the administration of such expatriate businesses – as distinct from ones clearly headquartered in the United Kingdom – need further investigation.

An additional difference that emerges from the comparisons is associated with the 'partial' or functional relationships. Frequently, I found British and Continental European firms (or individuals joined with those companies) participated in business investments abroad, designed not to control the foreign enterprise, but nonetheless to capture a business opportunity. The business motive could be general, such as obtaining insider knowledge on how the foreign firm performed and whether there would be security of supply of a raw material, or it could be highly specific, such as an arrangement to handle the company's financing (the sale of a service) or a contract to sell goods or other particular services to the firm, or one to market the firm's output. Do such 'partial' relationships fit into the category of foreign direct investments? And if so in what manner? The investor often exercised influence (or even control) over a key function, yet in no way sought to run or even had the potential to manage or to control the entire foreign business. Such business investments usually have been dealt with in the literature as foreign direct investments and put in the context of joint-ventures, which seems reasonable.[130] And, what of the trading company – especially the British trading company – with an investment in a particular productive activity (beyond trade) abroad? Its earnings often came from the management contract (a sale of an important service), assured by the investment. It did have the potential to control the overseas enterprise, through the management contract. It seems to this author that the management contract may well be different from the purely functional relationships; in this case, the entire business of the 'joint-venture' is controlled, though the 'owners' of the business presumably had the power to void a management contract.[131]

The industries of key importance from one home country to the next were different. British business historians must ask why British business abroad was concentrated in particular industries *and* why certain companies in those same industries showed little interest in overseas business. So, too, the locales where investments were made differed by home country. The 'American model' would hypothesise that the firm goes first to the 'nearby' – defined not merely in geographical, but in cultural, linguistic, and political terms. Dr Geoffrey Jones has suggested to me that whereas American business went abroad initially to geographically nearby regions: Canada, Mexico, and the Caribbean (it also went to 'culturally nearby' ones: Canada and the United Kingdom), British business tended to favour the linguistically (the United States, but also Canada, Australia, and South Africa) and politically (imperial) 'nearby'. This needs more

34                                                    THE END OF INSULARITY

verification with added research on British business investments on the
geographically nearby European continent.

The performance of management abroad also differed by home
country, and in a way that may well be amenable to systematic
treatment. Indeed, I believe that the distinctive British and other home
country characteristics – an inquiry into the home environment – can be
used to explain not only many of the differences in the way (including
'the why') firms moved abroad and how they behaved once there,
which firms went abroad, but in addition how they performed in foreign
lands.

On the second and related matter, multinational enterprise and
foreign direct investments are not the same. To repeat what I wrote at
the beginning of this article, multinational enterprises make foreign
direct investments – and they also do other things as well *vis-à-vis* a
business abroad. Management of such a business (just as at home)
involved financial decisions; it also calls for operating ones: hiring
workers, supervisors, and managers; making choices on technology;
selecting appropriate machinery; finding suppliers and purchasing (as
needed) raw materials, parts and components, and other supplies, as
well as the capital goods; deciding what should be bought and what
should be made; and developing relationships with suppliers.

None of these decisions on inputs is 'one-time': management consists
(among other things) of training those who are hired, altering technology choices as appropriate and as the learning process goes forward,
maintaining as well as buying machines, changing 'make-buy' decisions, and educating suppliers. It involves coordinating and administering the inputs once acquired, organising work, assigning tasks.
There is, thus, not only management of the purchasing functions, but of
the labour relations, the engineering, and the production activities.

And then there are output decisions. Some of these relate to how
much of a process will be done by the firm: does a mining company own
a concentrator, a smelter, and a refinery as well? does a plantation
company do any further processing? All of these new activities must be
managed. And, then if the output is not used or further processed
within the firm, how is the product to be marketed? does the company
integrate forward into the marketing activity? the management of the
marketing function is again not a given. All of these (and many more)
management requirements accompany the establishment and development of business abroad. Financing the operation, the foreign direct
*investment*, is but one facet (a single function) of what a business does
abroad. Thus, students of the history of multinational enterprise must
consider and ask questions about how a business abroad is managed,
how managers perform; it must separate overall management from the
'partial' functional relationships. British business historians have only
begun their task when they identify foreign direct investments.

A study of the history of multinational enterprise needs to look at
firms extending a specific business over borders. We must ask of the

origins, why, which, how, and where did a firm invest? What were its options? A firm grows over time, and I find myself fully in sympathy with Mark Casson and others who view the multinational enterprise in terms of the theory of the firm.[132] As the firm moves over borders, we must look not merely at the basis for the entry, but the subsequent choices and strategies pursued. The dynamics are critical. We have figures on numbers of British companies in particular regions (the materials are not as rich on other nationalities), but we have far less information on how the business abroad was pursued and managed over time. How and where was the output marketed? In the British case, the void is particularly evident in relation to the free-standing firm.[133]

A crucial subject is the relation between trade and foreign direct investment. British business historians need to ask the relationship between both British exports and imports and foreign direct investment. In many instances, foreign direct investment encouraged further exports of goods and services; in other instances it substituted for exports; and in still others it encouraged imports. The effects on trade need to be systematically studied by home country, through time; were there differences by home country?[134]

We need more discussion of performance and measures of success. Geoffrey Jones has suggested that British business abroad was often unsuccessful in its performance. Comparative studies help British business historians pinpoint some of the problems British enterprise had as it moved overseas.

We are by training comfortable in dealing with national behaviour and while it is now relatively easy to write about the international operations of national firms,[135] it is far harder to deal with some of the more complex multinational relationships. Regrettably, I do not have space here to discuss the cooperative ventures over borders that disclose the cosmopolitan nature of pre-1914 investment patterns – yet these must be analysed, particularly in relationship to the management of the cross-border participations.[136]

Comparative research on the pre-1914 years is probably simpler than for the post-1914 ones, because in the years 1880–1914 there was little fluctuation in foreign exchange values and also some of the greater complexities that developed later had not yet emerged. It ought to be possible to put together legitimate comparative figures, not significantly distorted by exchange variations. Before, however, the number game is played and the definitions are fixed in stone, the first step for British business historians is to establish the institutional dimensions of their nation's business over borders. This effort is greatly aided by the comparative approach that stimulates new questions. There seems no doubt that the business institution, controlling operations outside its home country, served as a key conduit of capital and also of production methods and new products, of personnel, technology, marketing arrangements, and managerial expertise. How it carried forth all these

36                                          THE END OF INSULARITY

functions within the firm – and using outside contractors – needs still to be charted. How it succeeded in its own terms (profits to the business) and in social terms (as an assister in economic growth and development at home and abroad) requires additional investigation. The research – while it explores home, and host country, circumstances – must concentrate on the business enterprise per se. A good start has been made, but the opportunities for further research are legion.

*Florida International University*

NOTES

I owe a great debt to Alfred D. Chandler and Geoffrey Jones in the development of the ideas in this article. Likewise, I am grateful to Rondo Cameron for including me in his 'Bellagio group', which has broadened my horizons.

1.  For statistical purposes, the US Department of Commerce uses a ten per cent equity interest to qualify. A ten per cent interest is always adequate for 'influence'; it may not, in fact – as this article will indicate – be enough for 'control'.
2.  Such settlers are often referred to as 'foreign' investors. I believe that it is inappropriate to refer to their activities as a foreign direct investment, if there was no financial obligation to a headquarters in Sweden, Germany, or Great Britain.
3.  Mark Casson, *The Firm and the Market* (Cambridge, MA, 1987), p.1.
4.  Much of the huge 1977–84 literature on the history of European multinationals is summarised in Mira Wilkins, 'The History of European Multinationals: A New Look', *The Journal of European Economic History*, Vol.15 (1986), pp.483–510. An immense amount has been published subsequent to 1984. While Geoffrey Jones (ed.), *British Multinationals: Origins, Management and Performance* (Aldershot, 1986) greatly advances our knowledge of the history of British multinationals, there is still no comprehensive history. Stephen Nicholas has one in process, albeit it will be confined to industrial enterprises. Charles A. Jones, *International Business in the Nineteenth Century* (Brighton, 1987), provides an excellent introduction to the network of trading companies that evolved in nineteenth-century Britain. Likewise, S.D. Chapman's 'British-Based Investment Groups Before 1914', *Economic History Review*, 2nd series 38 (1985), pp.230–51, has stimulated new perspectives on British business abroad. While the work of Peter Hertner and others has greatly enlarged what we know of German multinational enterprise, there is once again no overall history. Likewise, although Ragnhild Lundström, 'Swedish Multinational Growth before 1930', in Peter Hertner and Geoffrey Jones (eds.), *Multinationals: Theory and History* (Aldershot, 1986), pp.135–56, covers the history of Swedish multinational enterprise, there is no book-length synthesis. Alfred D. Chandler's forthcoming history of modern managerial enterprise will be immensely helpful on the rise of the major British and German multinationals.
5.  Harm Schröter is doing research on multinationals with headquarters in small European countries. There are also many firm-, industry-, and host-country-specific studies of French, Belgian and Swiss business abroad.
6.  Robert Vicat Turrell and Jean Jacques Van-Helten, 'The Investment Group: The Missing Link in British Overseas Expansion before 1914?' *Economic History Review*, 2nd series 40 (1987), p.269, scold Chapman for his generalisations and write 'In view of the historical specificity of economic developments in Africa and Asia ... it would have been more profitable to emphasise the different paths of

EUROPEAN AND NORTH AMERICAN MULTINATIONALS, 1870–1914        37

development of business enterprise'.

7. Because of (1) the breakdown of the international gold standard; (2) the loss of the clear primacy of Great Britain as the great creditor nation in the world; (3) the defeat of Germany and its effect on German business abroad; and (4) the shift of the United States from debtor to creditor country in international accounts.

8. Albeit there were some: For the Russian government's business investments in China, see C.F. Remer, *Foreign Investments in China* (1933; reprint, New York, 1968), pp.89, 558–9. The Russian bank in Persia was owned by the Russian state bank after 1894: Geoffrey Jones, *Banking and Empire in Iran* (Cambridge, 1986), p.56.

9. There is a large literature on Scottish overseas investments, as distinct from the broader literature on 'British' overseas investments, which usually includes both Scottish and English business abroad. However, the *Dictionary of Business Biography* – now the standard work on businessmen in 'Britain' – omitted business leaders based in Scotland, in deference to a project being carried out in Glasgow. The first volume of the *Dictionary of Scottish Business Biography*, edited by A. Slaven and S. Checkland, was published in 1987.

10. I began to identify crucial features of the home environment in Wilkins, 'The History of European Multinationals'. For some preliminary early testing, see Mira Wilkins, 'Japanese Multinational Enterprise before 1914', *Business History Review*, 60 (1986), pp.199–231.

11. Until recently this has been universally accepted among students of multinational enterprise (MNE). Casson, however, suggests that the high benefits of internalisation (integrating operations) offset the costs of such integration over borders and thus the theorist does not have to find an additional advantage. Casson, *The Firm and the Market*, pp.32, 34. He recognised, however, that the success (persistence) of MNEs does depend on some advantage, but stresses that this advantage may lie in internalisation, that is, in managing resources within the firm. Casson wants to separate choice (entry decisions) and performance. Ibid., pp.35–6. My problem with this analysis is that it does not explain which firms make the choice to go abroad; some do and some do not. The choice, it seems to me, must entail at least a perception of advantage.

12. This view is the accepted one. Professors Raymond Vernon, John Dunning, Lawrence Franko, and others have all made this point.

13. N.F.R. Crafts and Mark Thomas, 'Comparative Advantage in UK Manufacturing Trade 1910–1935', *Economic Journal* 96 (1986), pp.629–45.

14. I found this particularly true of American business abroad. Mira Wilkins, *The Emergence of Multinational Enterprise* (Cambridge, MA, 1970). See also Alfred D. Chandler, *The Visible Hand* (Cambridge, MA, 1977).

15. Professor Chandler has made this point in a number of places.

16. Wilkins, 'The History of European Multinationals'.

17. A forthcoming book edited by Rondo Cameron and V.I. Bovykin, *International Banking, Investment, and Industrial Finance, 1970–1914*, explores some of these relationships.

18. Ibid. See also J. Riesser, *The German Great Banks and Their Concentration* (1911; reprint, New York, 1977).

19. A.S.J. Baster, *The Imperial Banks* (1929; reprint, New York, 1977) and idem., *The International Banks* (1935; reprint, New York, 1977). Geoffrey Jones is in the process of preparing the basic work on British overseas banks since 1890. See also his two volumes on The British Bank of the Middle East: Jones, *Banking and Empire in Iran* and idem., *Banking and Oil* (Cambridge, 1987). F.H.H. King, *The History of the Hongkong and Shanghai Banking Corporation* (Cambridge, 1987), Vol.I, covers 1864–1902. (Volumes 2–4 are forthcoming, scheduled for 1988). For Canadian banks' extension into the United States, see Mira Wilkins, *The History of Foreign Investment in the United States to 1914*, forthcoming.

20. For example, because of new taxes imposed during the Boer War, Eastman Kodak, Ltd. changed from a legal British to an American headquarters. Carl W.

Ackerman, *George Eastman* (Boston, MA, 1930), pp.173–4. Other examples of tax motivated decisions are provided in Wilkins, *The History of Foreign Investment in the United States*.

21. Carl N. Degler's presidential address to the American Historical Association was entitled 'In Pursuit of an American History'. *American Historical Review*, 92 (1987), pp.1–12. Degler argues that there were significant national attributes, some of which he seems to define in terms of 'culture'. The quotation is from a chapter, entitled 'Qualities of the Germans', in Henri Hauser, *Germany's Commercial Grip on the World* (New York, 1918), p.9. This is a translation from the French. Hauser was a professor at Dijon University; the first edition of this work, in French, appeared in 1915.

22. I agree with Geoffrey Jones in this conclusion. Lawrence Franko, *The European Multinationals* (Stamford, CT, 1976), p.10, put the United States in first place as a home country, based on data collected by James Vaupel and Joan Curhan. These statistics – which are constantly reprinted – have been superseded by more recent research. They were, moreover, based on companies *still in existence* when the research was undertaken, which created a bias on the low side.

23. This is my own conclusion, based on my own research and my reading of the work of other students of the history of multinational enterprise. John H. Dunning, 'Changes in the Level and Structure of International Production: The Last One Hundred Years', in Mark Casson, *The Growth of International Business* (London, 1983), p.87, presents estimates on the level of foreign direct investment by country of origin in 1914. He ranked the United Kingdom first, and far out front, followed by the United States in clear second place, and then came France; he put Germany in fourth place. I think he has greatly underestimated the activities of German business abroad.

24. Franko, *European Multinationals*, the first book that dealt with the history of European multinationals – and one that holds up very well over time – never makes an attempt to rank continental European home countries.

25. Based on data provided in Wilkins, *The History of Foreign Investment in the United States*. Franko, in *The European Multinationals*, p.10, using the Vaupel and Curhan data, was able to identify only 60 UK 'manufacturing subsidiaries established or acquired' by UK parents before 1914 *worldwide*! Only nine were in the United States. See breakdown in Dunning, 'Changes in the Level and Structure', p.90. But, Dunning elsewhere in the same article did recognise that the UK was 'far and away' the largest source of foreign direct investment in 1914. See ibid., pp.86–7, and note 23 above.

26. Wilkins, 'The Free-Standing Company, 1870–1914: An Important Type of British Foreign Direct Investment', *Economic History Review*, 2nd series 41 (1988). I first used the term 'free-standing' firm at a conference in Florence in 1983. Wilkins, 'Defining a Firm', in Hertner and Jones (eds.), *Multinationals*, pp.84–7.

27. On these companies, see Jones (ed.), *British Multinationals, passim*.

28. I give more details on the clusters in 'The Free-Standing Company'. The theoretical literature on multinational enterprise has dealt with 'modes' of operations – direct investment, licensing, and market – or direct investment, contract, and market. The loosely-coupled groupings of the free-standing companies represent a mode of handling business abroad that the theoretical literature has failed to consider (because this institutional path is just coming to be understood). The British free-standing company could invest abroad directly or serve as a holding company, owning the securities of a locally-incorporated company. It made a difference.

29. On patent medicines, see the work of T.A.B. Corley, for example, 'Interactions between British and American Patent Medicine Industries', *Business and Economic History*, forthcoming.

30. The authority on crucible steel is Geoffrey Tweedale, *Sheffield Steel and America* (Cambridge, 1987).

31. Hugh G.J. Aitken, *The Continuous Wave* (Princeton, NJ, 1985), pp.317, 357–8.

32. Wilkins, *The History of Foreign Investment in the United States*.

33. US Federal Trade Commission, *Report on Cooperation in American Export Trade*, 2 vols. (Washington, 1916), I, pp.252, 254.
34. Ibid., I, p.250.
35. Wilkins, *The History of Foreign Investment in the United States*.
36. Consett and Dowlais were joint-venture partners with Krupp in Orconera Iron Ore Co., Ltd., that carried on mining in Spain. Ulrich Wengenroth, 'Iron and Steel', in Cameron and Bovykin (eds.), *International Banking*.
37. See Shin'ichi Yonekawa and Hideki Yoshihara (eds.), *Business History of General Trading Companies* (Tokyo, 1987), for fascinating material on British trading companies. See also Stephanie Jones, *Two Centuries of Overseas Trading. The Origins and Growth of the Inchape Group* (London, 1986); Charles Jones. *International Business*; and Chapman, 'British-Based Investment Groups'.
38. See, for example, Andrew Porter, *Victorian Shipping, Business and Imperial Policy: Donald Currie, the Castle Line and Southern Africa* (Woodbridge and New York, 1986).
39. John Taylor & Sons, for instance, were in 1907 managers of 45 companies around the world. Charles Harvey and Peter Taylor, 'Mineral Wealth and Economic Development: Foreign Direct Investment in Spain, 1851–1913', *Economic History Review*, 2nd series 40 (1987), p.189 n.22. See also Wilkins, *History of Foreign Investment in the United States*.
40. Geoffrey Jones's new research will rectify that.
41. Baster, *International Banks*, p.248, indicated that in 1910 24 British international banks had 308 foreign branches, while Baster, *Imperial Banks*, p.269, states that in 1915, 18 imperial banks had 1,169 branches and sub-branches overseas. According to Oliver Pastré and Anthony Rowley (in 'The Multinationalisation of British and American Banks', in Alice Teichova, *et al., Multinational Enterprise in Historical Perspective* (Cambridge, 1986), p.233), who cite no source, in 1914, 36 banking companies in Britain had 2,091 branches 'in the world', and in addition, there were 3,538 colonial banks (surely, colonial bank branches and agencies?). It is hard to reconcile Pastré and Rowley's numbers with those of Baster.
42. The Imperial Bank of Persia, for example. See Jones, *Banking and Empire in Iran*.
43. Some of the trading companies at the centre of cluster sets were clearly multinational enterprises.
44. Questions about control are, for example, posed in Turrell and Van-Helten, 'The Investment Group'.
45. Jones (ed.), *Multinationals*, p.7.
46. Discussions with Geoffrey Jones and Charles Jones.
47. In the case of British investment in America, this appears to have happened immediately. See text of this article. But take the case of the New Gellivara Co. Ltd. with mines in Sweden. In 1882, it was transformed into a Swedish Company (Gellivara Aktiebolog), which was 100 per cent owned by Sir Giles Loder, London. When the latter died, in 1889, his heirs lost all of their concessions. Wengenroth, 'Iron and Steel'. The suggestion was that control could no longer be maintained.
48. The description is theoretical. At present, I have no candidates that fit this model.
49. In this connection, host country policies were often crucial. In 1908, a Court in Alexandria ruled that a company formed to do business in Egypt, must be considered Egyptian, and a Khedivial decree was required before it could be legally constituted. The Court ruling, however, specifically stated that no restriction was placed on the operations in Egypt of a bona-fide branch of a foreign company with headquarters abroad. The Court's decision 'referred only to companies whose operations, headquarters and sole "raison d'être" were in Egypt'. A.E. Crouchley, *The Investment of Foreign Capital in Egyptian Companies and Public Debt* (Cairo, 1936), p.63.
50. The best history of Borax Consolidated is Norman J. Travis and E.J. Cocks, *The Tincal Trail* (London, 1984). See also Wilkins, *History of Foreign Investment in the United States*.

51. Wilkins, *The Emergence*, pp.91–3; Jones (ed.), *British Multinationals*, p.7.
52. Had the ownership been concentrated, perhaps control might have been maintained.
53. I make this last point in 'The Free-Standing Company'.
54. On investment groups, see Chapman, 'British-Based Investment Groups'. On the absence of 'universal' banks, see P.L. Cottrell's forthcoming paper on British banking in Cameron and Bovykin (eds.), *International Banking*.
55. Harvey and Taylor, 'Mineral Wealth', provide rich information on British companies producing lead, iron ore and pyrites (sulphur and copper) in Spain. The article, however, tells us little about the extent to which these mining operations were part of integrated enterprises – in the United Kingdom, France, or Germany. Were the spectacular profits of the Orconera Co., for example, related to the intra-company pricing arrangements made by its three parent companies? On its parents, see note 36 above.
56. Charles Wilson, 'Multinationals, Management, and World Markets: A Historical View', in Harold F. Williamson (ed.), *Evolution of International Management Structures* (Newark, DE, 1975), p.193.
57. In this connection, see the fascinating Editor's Introduction (by Maryna Fraser) of Lionel Phillips, *Some Reminiscences* (Johannesburg, 1986), pp.11–30, on 'British' business in South Africa. See also D.C.M. Platt, *Britain's Investment Overseas on the Eve of the First World War* (New York, 1986), pp.31–6.
58. In this connection, see Everett E. Hagen, *On the Theory of Social Change* (Homewood, IL, 1962), pp.294–309.
59. Geoffrey Jones has found many cases where British management had severe difficulties in operating abroad.
60. Rondo Cameron, *France and the Economic Development of Europe* (Princeton, NJ, 1961), p.396; on the important Belgian role, see Wengenroth, 'Iron and Steel'.
61. Wilkins, *The Emergence*, pp.52–9.
62. Peter Hertner has written extensively on German business abroad. For a start, see his excellent 'German Multinational Enterprise before 1914: Some Case Studies', in Hertner and Jones (eds.), *Multinationals*, pp.113–34. See also W. Feldenkirchen, 'The Export Organisation of the German Economy', in Yonekawa and Yoshihara (ed.), *Business History*. Chandler's new book will consider the international extension of German business.
63. The German trading house, Schuchardt and Schutte, for example, was probably 'the most prestigious distributor of machine tools in Europe'; it had 'outlets' in Germany, Austria, Belgium, and Russia. Charles W. Cheape, *Family Firm to Modern Multinational: Norton Company, a New England Enterprise* (Cambridge, 1985), p.50. See also, Feldenkirchen, 'The Export Organisation' on export houses. The firms in Guatemala and Turkey were more active in providing imports into Germany than in selling exports from Germany. Schuchardt and Schutte handled some American exports as well as German ones.
64. See Wilkins, *History of Foreign Investment in the United States*.
65. Richard Tilly, 'International Aspects of the Development of German Banking, 1870–1914', in Cameron and Bovykin (eds.), *International Banking*.
66. My *History of Foreign Investments in the United States* has a sizeable amount on German business investments in the United States. Geoffrey Jones, 'Foreign Multinationals in Britain before 1945', *Economic History Review*, forthcoming, has much on German business in the United Kingdom. It has long been known that there were large German investments in Latin America – from railroads in Colombia to nitrate mines in Chile, but the nature of the management of such investments is still ambiguous. The reviews of Walther Kirchner, *Die Deutsch Industrie und die Industrialisierung Russlands 1815–1914* (St. Katharinen, F.R.G., 1986), indicate that it covers the activities of German multinationals in Russia.
67. Every basic history of the chemical industry, covering 1870–1914, deals with the German direct investments abroad (as well as at home). On the electrical industry,

EUROPEAN AND NORTH AMERICAN MULTINATIONALS, 1870–1914      41

see, for example, Peter Hertner, 'Financial Strategies and Adaptation to Foreign Markets: The German Electro-Technical Industry and Its Multinational Activities', Teichova, *et al., Multinational Enterprise*, pp.145–59, and Albert Broder, 'The Multinationalisation of the French Electrical Industry 1880–1914; Dependence and its Causes', in Hertner and Jones (eds.), *Multinationals*, pp.178–80, 184–5. According to Feldenkirchen, 'The Export Organisation', p.325 n.91, Siemens had in 1913, 17 plants in nine European countries.

68. On the foreign marketing organisation of the principal German iron and steel companies, see Feldenkirchen, 'The Export Organisation', pp.310–11. On Bochumer Verein, Mannesmann, and Rheinische Stahlwerke's major foreign investments, see ibid., pp.318–19, and Wengenroth, 'Iron and Steel', on the last two.

69. Bayer Co., Inc. v. United Drug Co., 272 Fed. 505 (SDNY, 1921).

70. Wilkins, *History of Foreign Investment in the United States*.

71. Here my conclusions depart from Franko, *European Multinationals*, p.22, who was struck by the fact that 'continental European' enterprises rarely had advantages in marketing and advertising.

72. Data on the Faber firm in the 1870s are based on an undated (probably 1872–73) newspaper article, provided to me by Eberhard Faber, Wilkes-Barre, Pennsylvania. See also A.W. Faber's US colour advertisement (in English), reprinted in L. Fritz Gruber, 'Das Bleistift Schloss', *Frankfurter Allgemeine Zeitung*, 13 Feb. 1987. My thanks go to Richard Tilly for directing my attention to this. The parent company became Faber-Castell in 1900. Peter Hertner describes Kathreiner's Malzkaffee-Fabriken, as having direct investments in manufacturing plants in Austria–Hungary, Sweden, Russia, and Spain by 1914. It marketed and advertised a consumer product, malt coffee. Hertner, 'German Multinational Enterprise', 118–19.

73. Compare Wilkins, *History of Foreign Investment in the United States*, with Feldenkirchen, 'The Export Organisation', p.317.

74. Franko, *European Multinationals*, p.50, and Wengenroth, 'Iron and Steel'.

75. On its interests in American Metal Company, see Wilkins, *The History of Foreign Investment in the United States*. Franko, *European Multinationals*, p.50, on other of its foreign direct investments.

76. For the involvements in Romania, see M. Pearton, *Oil and the Rumanian State* (Oxford, 1971) and Fritz Seidenzahl, *100 Jahre Deutsche Bank, 1870–1970* (Frankfurt, 1970), pp.205–24. For German oil activities in the middle east, see ibid., pp.224–7, and Marian Kent, *Oil & Empire* (London, 1976).

77. My *The Emergence of Multinational Enterprise*, published in 1970, provided a history of American business abroad in the years before 1914. Subsequently, there have been many studies of the history of US businesses abroad. Among the recent contributions are Fred V. Carstensen, *American Enterprise in Foreign Markets. Studies of Singer and International Harvester in Imperial Russia* (Chapel Hill, NC, 1984); Lawrence A. Clayton, *Grace. W.R. Grace & Co. The Formative Years 1850–1930* (Ottawa, IL, 1985); and Cheape, *Family Firm to Modern Multinational*.

78. On I.B.C., see Wilkins, *The Emergence*, p.107.

79. See Alfred D. Chandler, *The Visible Hand*; his 'Technological and Organisational Underpinnings of Modern Industrial Multinational Enterprise: The Dynamics of Competitive Advantage', in Teichova, *et. al., Multinational Enterprise*, pp.30–54; and his forthcoming book.

80. Ibid. Sometimes economies of scale and scope are viewed as part of an advantage – based on factor costs. More recently, new developments in trade theory have looked at economies of scale (and scope) as separate from traditionally-defined comparative advantages; trade (and, in turn, investments) arise directly from such economies. See Paul R. Krugman, 'Is Free Trade Passé?', *Economic Perspectives*, Vol.1 (1987), p.133. The distinction is between what is endogenous to the firm and exogenous. Yet, the achievements of economies of scope and scale (albeit

42                                            THE END OF INSULARITY

endogenous) were based, I firmly believe, on conditions in the home country.
81. Wilkins, *History of Foreign Investment in the United States*.
82. The Potash Cartel, for example, had a sales company in the United States. See ibid.
83. P. Chalmin, 'The Rise of International Commodity Trading Companies in Europe in the Nineteenth Century', in Yonekawa and Yoshihara (ed.), *Business History*, p.290.
84. Some of the best work on this subject remains that in Rondo Cameron's 1960 book, *France and the Economic Development*.
85. Ibid., pp.397–400. On St. Gobain's German factories, see Jean-Pierre Daviet, 'Un Processus de Multinationalisation de Longue Duree: L'Exemple de Saint-Gobain (1853–1939)', unpublished paper (1984). This paper has been published (in Italian) in Peter Hertner, *Per La Storia delli' impresa multinazionale in Europa* (Milan, 1987). Daviet completed a 1793-page doctoral dissertation at the Sorbonne in 1983.
86. Daviet, 'Un Processus'.
87. Theo Barker, 'Pilkington', in Jones (ed.), *Multinationals*, p.185.
88. Wilkins, *History of Foreign Investment in the United States*, on Michelin. On Dunlop, Geoffrey Jones, 'The Growth and Performance of British Multinational Firms before 1939: The Case of Dunlop', *Economic History Review*, 2nd series 37 (Feb. 1984), p.36. In addition, Dunlop had licensing agreements with companies in Canada, Australia, and Russia. Ibid., p.39.
89. Patrick Fridenson, 'The Growth of Multinational Activities in the French Motor Industry, 1890–1979', in Hertner and Jones (eds.), *Multinationals*, pp.157–9.
90. Claude Ph. Beaud, 'Investments and Profits of the Multinational Schneider Group: 1894–1943', in Teichova, *et al.*, *Multinational Enterprise*, pp.87–102. See also idem., 'La Schneider in Russia (1896–1914)', in Hertner, *Per La Storia*, pp.101–48.
91. Wilkins, *History of Foreign Investment in the United States*.
92. French investors often appear to have used British-registered companies for investments abroad – not only in Spain. I found this to be true of some French investments in the United States, principally in mining. Beaud found that Schneider (and other French investors) used the Bolivian Rubber and General Enterprise, Ltd., registered in London, for its investments in Bolivia. Beaud, 'Investments and Profits', p.90.
93. Robert L. Tignor, *State, Private Enterprise and Economic Change in Egypt, 1918–1952* (Princeton, NJ, 1984), pp.19–20, found that in the pre-First World War years 'French businessmen experienced great difficulty in maintaining managerial control over French firms in Egypt. French investment was widely dispersed, and small French shareholders took little interest in the management of companies so long as dividend payments continued to arrive. Hence, small groups of organised shareholders on the ground could gain control of companies, even though holding only a fraction of the shares.' This sounds like some of the problems faced by British free-standing companies. I suppose one could call the Suez company a free-standing firm. See Hubert Bonin, *Suez* (Paris, 1987).
94. On French trading companies (and French banks), see Chalmin, 'The Rise', especially pp.289–91. Chalmin argues that 'the first disease of French trade [was] the determination of the [French] industry to do its marketing itself' – and it was always a job badly done. The 'second disease' was that the French concentrated on quality and luxury products – perfumes, cognac, champagne, and fashion, which sold themselves. Thus there was no need to bother to have representatives abroad. He believes, however, that French trading houses were more efficient on the import than on the export side. On the large French West African chartered company, see Hubert Bonin, *La Compagnie Française d'Afrique Occidentale* (Paris, 1987).
95. Geoffrey Jones is planning a conference on 'banks as multinationals'. It will be extremely useful to compare the role of French banks with those of other

nationalities. For one recent contribution on French banking abroad, which despite its title does cover the pre-1914 years, see Yasuo Gonjo, 'La Banque de l'Indochine devant l'interventionisme (1917–1931)', *Le Mouvement Social*, 142 (Jan.–March, 1988), pp.45–74.

96. John McKay, 'The House of Rothschild (Paris)', in Teichova, *et. al, Multinational Enterprise*, pp.74–86.
97. Cameron found this to be true. See *France and the Economic Development*. Maurice Lévy-Leboyer's work also suggests this.
98. The footnotes in Lundström, 'Swedish Multinational Growth', bear witness to the large literature on Swedish multinationals. Since her article was written, the synthesis volume on Swedish Match and its predecessors has been published, Karl-Gustaf Hildebrand, *Expansion Crisis Reconstruction, 1917–1939* (Stockholm, 1985). Lundström's contributions to Cameron and Bovykin's forthcoming book add further material on Swedish business abroad.
99. Data from Lundström on Empire Cream Separator Co. See also Wilkins, *History of Foreign Investment in the United States* on this company.
100. There is a history of Solvay & Cie. J. Bolle, *Solvay, L'Invention, L'homme, L'entreprise Industrielle* (Brussels, 1963).
101. This is all from Herman Van der Wee and Martine Goosen's splendid contribution, 'International Factors in the Formation of Banking Systems – Belgium', forthcoming in the Cameron and Bovykin volume.
102. Ibid. and John McKay, *Tramways and Trolleys* (Princeton, NJ, 1976), pp.149, 244 (on the Belgian role).
103. Van der Wee and Goosen, 'International Factors'.
104. Wengenroth, 'Iron and Steel'; see also John P. McKay, *Pioneers for Profit* (Chicago, 1970).
105. Lutz Alt, 'The Photochemical Industry' (Ph.D. dissertation MIT, 1986), pp.71–9.
106. Robert Liefmann, *Cartels, Concerns, and Trusts* (London, 1932), p.269.
107. Wilkins, *History of Foreign Investment in the United States*, and Van der Wee and Goosen, 'International Factors'.
108. For a list of Swiss companies engaged in international business, see Ernst Himmel, *Industrielle Kapitalanlagen der Schweiz im Auslande* (Langensalza, 1922), pp.116–37.
109. Ibid., pp.132–3.
110. Every Swiss company history – and they are numerous – attests to this.
111. Himmel, *Industrielle Kapitalanlagen*, Recapitulation, no page number. But see also Urs Rauber, *Schweizer Industrie in Russland* (Zurich, 1985). Rauber believes Himmel underestimated Swiss industrial investments in Russia. (Rauber's book sent me to Himmel, albeit I have had difficulty matching Rauber's numbers with Himmel's. The data in my text are from Himmel).
112. Silk Association of America, *Annual Report 1905*, pp.60–61.
113. *Fulton, New York 1901*, p.65.
114. Federal Trade Commission, *Cooperation*, I, p.145.
115. Himmel, *Industrielle Kapitalanlagen*, Recapitulation.
116. Based on my own research.
117. See F.C. Gerretson, *History of the Royal Dutch Company*, 4 vols. (Leiden: E.J. Brill, 1953–57). K.D. Bosch, *Nederlandse Beleggingen in De Verenigde Staten* (Amsterdam, 1948), is invaluable on Dutch investment in the United States.
118. See Wilkins, *History of Foreign Investment in the United States*, and Augustus J. Veenendaal, Jr. 'The Kansas City Southern Railway and the Dutch Connection', *Business History Review*, Vol.61 (1987), pp.291–316. Often, the Dutch delegated their authority to Americans; such delegation, however, would not by definition bar such stakes from the category of foreign direct investment.
119. Wilkins, *History of Foreign Investment in the United States*; Christopher Armstrong and H.V. Nelles, 'A Curious Capital Flow: Canadian Investment in Mexico, 1902–1910', *Business History Review*, Vol.58 (1984), pp.178–203.

120. Wilkins, *History of Foreign Investment in the United States*. Geoffrey Jones has directed my attention to the Hungarian Bank for Commerce and Industry of Pest's controlling interest in the Romanian oil company, Steaua Romana, from 1892–1902. See Pearton, *Oil and the Rumanian State*, pp.23–31. Three large Hungarian banks were owners of the Transatlantic Trust Co., New York, founded in 1912. Wilkins, *History of Foreign Investment in the United States*.
121. Fridenson, 'The Growth', p.157.
122. *Best's Insurance Report – Fire and Marine, 1914*.
123. There were, in addition, some non-European, non-North American head-quartered multinational enterprises. See, for example, Wilkins, 'Japanese Multinational Enterprise before 1914'.
124. It is my own conclusion that the United States ranked first. For my forthcoming *History of Foreign Investment in the United States*, I prepared a ranking of debtor nations in 1914; this included, however, both foreign portfolio and direct investments and does not offer a legitimate ranking for direct investment alone. Dunning, 'Changes in the Level and Structure', p.88, made estimates and provided a 1914 ranking that is not broken down by country in Latin America (32 per cent of the world's foreign direct investment), but which, excluding Latin America, suggests the following leading recipients: the United States (10.3 per cent), China (7.8 per cent), Russia (7.1 per cent), Canada (5.7 per cent). These were, as Dunning recognizes, 'estimates'. In Latin America, Argentina, Brazil, Mexico, Chile, Peru, and Cuba would figure as the most important recipients of foreign direct investment in 1914. All of Europe – excluding Russia, the UK (a mere 1.4 per cent), and 'Southern Europe' (2.8 per cent) – had by Dunning's reckoning, 9.2 per cent of the total.
125. This was true of aspirins in the United States (made by Bayer) and sewing machines in Germany (made by Singer) in this period.
126. For some thoughts on this matter, see Mira Wilkins, 'Efficiency and Management: A Comment on Gregory Clark's "Why Isn't the Whole World Developed?"' *Journal of Economic History*, Vol.47 (Dec. 1987), pp.981–3.
127. Since this article has space constraints, I have not discussed the pre-1914 licensing activities of multinationals as a separate 'mode'. However, the comparative evidence on the amount of licensing done by companies headquartered in different home countries seems too lean – at present – for anything but the most superficial conclusions. If joint-ventures are to be considered a 'mode', there were a large number of such by multinationals of all nationalities – although the exact nature of the shared relationships is still ill-defined and it would be impossible to choose say 1914 and to rank the prevalence of joint ventures by home country of the multinationals.
128. America had lots of small companies that had nothing but local business.
129. Professor Alfred D. Chandler has been important in pointing out to me how very large employers some of the pre-1914 German enterprises actually were, when compared with their American counterparts.
130. I found in my research on *American* business abroad a number of such 'partial' relationships, but they seem far more conspicuous in the European context – especially in connection with primary product production – agriculture, or mineral extraction.
131. Porter, *Victorian Shipping*, noted that the dividends paid by the Castle Line were not impressive; yet, Donald Currie, who had a management contract to run the line, emerged as a very wealthy man. He obviously obtained his returns from the management contract, *assured* by his equity holdings. Whenever management contracts exist, the scholar must check the account books carefully. Sometimes, a British agency house abroad could have a negligible (or even no) investment and still have a management contract that provided it good returns – whether there were or were not profits.
132. See Mira Wilkins, *The Maturing of Multinational Enterprise* (Cambridge, MA, 1974), pp.414, 565 ns.8–9; Chandler, *The Visible Hand*; O.E. Williamson, 'The

*Multinational Corporations*

Modern Corporation: Origins, Evolution, Attributes', *Journal of Economic Literature*, Vol.19 (1981), pp.1537–68; Wilkins, 'Defining a Firm', and most recently, Casson, *The Firm and the Market*, p.1. There has been some dispute as to who first applied the ideas of R.H. Coase to the theory of multinational enterprise. The first two published applications were in 1970 by Stephen Hymer, 'The Efficiency (Contradictions) of Multinational Corporations', *American Economic Review*, Vol.60 (1970), pp.441–8, and Robert Z. Aliber, 'A Theory of Direct Foreign Investment', in Charles Kindleberger (ed.), *The International Corporation* (Cambridge, MA, 1970), p.20. In 1974 I picked up on the idea (in a footnote which no one ever read). Wilkins, *The Maturing*, p.565 n.9.

133. I consider that my *Economic History Review* article poses more questions than it answers. For some of the applications, see Wilkins, 'Efficiency and Management'.

134. Kiyoshi Kojima has described US multinationals as trade-destroying, while Japanese ones were trade-creating. Kojima, *Japanese Direct Foreign Investment* (Tokyo, 1978) and idem., *Japan and a New World Economic Order* (Tokyo, 1977). I do not think that in 1870–1914, American multinationals were trade-destroying; in fact, I believe that all the multinationals of 1870–1914 were trade creating – albeit to different extents. It is very important to study exports and imports separately in this context.

135. Note that this was the title of Stephen Hymer's seminal Ph.D. dissertation (1960).

136. For example, when parent entrepreneurs have 'homes' in three countries and operate in a host nation, say South Africa, how does one decipher a 'home' or headquarters? I believe one must close one's eyes to 'nationality' and look at administrative and legal institutional relationships. Was Alusuisse, for instance, a German or a Swiss aluminium company – or a truly co-operative venture?

# [30]

## Chapter 1

## External and Internal Functioning of American, German, and Japanese Multinational Corporations: Decisionmaking and Policy Issues*

*Anant R. Negandhi†*

The quest of multinational corporations for global reach has led them to rationalize and unify their production, financial, research and developmental, and marketing activities. To facilitate such unification in strategies and policies, the American multinational corporation (MNC) has changed its organizational structure for managing international business from a mere export department to an international division, to a multinational structure with area and/or product concentration, to a matrix organizational form, and eventually to a transnational enterprise structure.[1]

A similar trend for European and Japanese multinational corporations has been predicted by Franko[2] and Yoshino.[3]

Although the global rationalization concept has been advocated

---

*This chapter is part of the large-scale study undertaken in 16 countries with 158 subsidiaries and 39 headquarters of American, British, German, Japanese, and Swedish multinational companies. The research is being supported by the International institute of Management, Science Center Berlin, and the Institute of International Business of the Stockholm School of Economics, Sweden. The research team consisted of A. R. Negandhi (University of Illinois); Ram Baliga (Texas Tech University); Anders Edstrom, Gunnar Hedlund, and Lars Otterbeck (Stockholm School of Economics); and Martin Welge (Fernuniversität Hagen, West Germany).

†University of Illinois at Urbana–Champaign.

21

*22  /  Behavioral and Organizational Aspects*

and is being implemented, the real attributes, such as the nature of decisionmaking, levels of centralization-decentralization in specific areas, the relative influence of headquarters and overseas subsidiaries and the resulting effectiveness or tensions in their relationships, and the impact on the MNC-nation-states relationships have not been explored systematically by many researchers.

The purpose of this chapter is to examine some of the components of the global rationalization processes that are being adopted by the American, German, and Japanese multinational companies. More specifically, the following elements are examined in more detail:

1. Levels of formalization of policies and practices.
2. Degree of centralization-decentralization and the relative influence of the headquarters and subsidiaries in decision-making.
3. Headquarters-subsidiary relationships and the nature of the critical issues and problem areas between them.
4. Nature of the external problems encountered by the three types of multinationals in the countries studied.
5. Implications of global rationalization processes on internal efficiency and the maintenance of effective external relationships with the host countries.

Prior to the analysis and discussion of the results of this study, a word about research methodology and sample may be in order.

## THE RESEARCH METHODOLOGY AND SAMPLE

The project was conceived in a comparative vein; we endeavored to study American, German, British, Japanese, and Swedish multinationals and their subsidiares. Our aim was to collect detailed information on many aspects of multinational operations, both at headquarter and subsidiary levels. Subsidiaries of 158 American, British, German, Japanese, and Swedish multinationals operating both in Europe (West Germany, United Kingdom, Spain, Portugal, Belgium, and the Netherlands), and in the United States, Mexico, Brazil, India, Iran, and their respective 39 headquarters were studied. Our sample was restricted to firms that were engaged in some form of manufacturing activity. Hence, firms in travel, banking, and other service sectors were omitted from consideration. Firms that were studied were selected from various investment directories and listings provided by the Chambers of Commerce, governmental agencies, and trade associations.

It is appropriate to make some remarks on the type of sample that was utilized in the analysis. Ideally, in order to have some confidence (statistically) in the results, the sample needed to be large enough and drawn randomly. Matching was impossible as the historical patterns of American, British, German, Japanese, and Swedish investments are all quite different; with Japanese multinationals being a much more recent phenomenon. Accordingly, a conscious, random sampling procedure was not feasible. In order to increase the generalization and external validity of the study, considerable supplemental information was obtained concerning the activities of the multinational corporations in these countries. Despite these efforts, the reader is cautioned to bear the limitations of the sample in mind when reading through the analyses and discussions.

In-depth interviews were conducted with the chief executive officers and other managerial personnel from all firms that had agreed to participate in the study. A semistructured interview guide was utilized to conduct the interviews. Each interview lasted an average of between four and eight hours; and in most cases included luncheon and dinner sessions. These sessions proved to be extremely valuable as the executives tended to relax, and, in narrating episodes related to the organizational functioning, they revealed significant, although subtle, aspects of their operations.

This chapter analyzes the results of the study conducted with 120 subsidiaries of American, German, and Japanese multinational corporations. The characteristics of these companies are given in Table 1.1.

## INTERNAL FUNCTIONING OF THE MULTINATIONAL CORPORATIONS

We first examine the level of formalization of policies and practices, degree of centralization-decentralization, and the relative influence of the headquarters and the subsidiaries in decisionmaking, the headquarter-subsidiary relationships, and the nature of the critical problems between them. As noted earlier, our aim of examining these elements was to assess the extent of the global rationalization strategies utilized by the three types of multinational corporations, namely, American, German, and Japanese.

In the next section, we examine the implications of these practices on the effectiveness of the firm at both the internal and the external levels.

## 24 / *Behavioral and Organizational Aspects*

Table 1.1   Profile of the Companies Studied

|  | Country of Origin | | |
|---|---|---|---|
|  | *United States* *(N = 34)* | *Germany* *(N = 45)* | *Japan* *(N = 41)* |
| *Type of Industry* | | | |
| Heavy engineering | 12 | 14 | 2 |
| Light engineering | 5 | 6 | 14 |
| Chemical and pharmaceutical | 7 | 21 | 4 |
| Electrical and electronics | 0 | 2 | 6 |
| Automobile | 6 | 2 | 2 |
| Tires and rubber products | 3 | 0 | 0 |
| Foods | 1 | 0 | 1 |
| Mixed—diversified trading companies with manufacturing investments | 0 | 0 | 12 |
| *Ratio of Equity* | | | |
| Wholly owned | 32 | 44 | 31 |
| Majority ownership | 2 | 0 | 1 |
| 50-50 ownership | 0 | 1 | 5 |
| Minority ownership | 0 | 0 | 4 |
| *Size: Number of Employees* | | | |
| 5000 and more | 5 | 6 | 2 |
| 1001 to 4999 | 11 | 11 | 2 |
| 501 to 1000 | 4 | 9 | 4 |
| 201 to 500 | 4 | 4 | 9 |
| 101 to 200 | 3 | 8 | 3 |
| 100 or fewer | 1 | 3 | 5 |
| Information inadequate | | 26 | |

## LEVEL OF FORMALIZATION

To assess the level of formalization in the American, German, and Japanese multinational companies, three aspects are examined:

1. The dependence of the subsidiaries on the manuals, policies, and procedures supplied by the headquarters;
2. utilization of these policies and procedures for decisionmaking; and;
3. the nature and the frequency of reporting required by headquarters.

Table 1.2 shows the extent to which the subsidiaries of the American, the German, and the Japanese multinational companies depended upon the written policies of the headquarters. An overwhelmingly large number of the American subsidiaries (88 percent) relied on

## American, German, and Japanese Multinational Corporations / 25

Table 1.2   Extent to which Subsidiaries Depend on the Written Policies
from Headquarters

| MNC Ownership | Great Deal (%) | To Some Extent (%) | Very Little to Not at All (%) |
|---|---|---|---|
| American (N = 33) | 88 | 6 | 6 |
| German (N = 44) | 32 | 20 | 48 |
| Japanese (N = 40) | 12 | 22 | 66 |

Level of significance = 0.0001.
Number of missing observations = 3.
Total number of observations = 120.

policies of headquarters. Approximately one-third of the German subsidiaries did so, while merely 12 percent of the Japanese subsidiaries utilized the policies supplied by their headquarters. Conversely, only 6 percent of the American, 48 percent of the German, and 66 percent of the Japanese subsidiaries indicated very negligible influence on strategic and policy decisions affecting their operations.

A similar picture emerges when we examine the influence of the written policies and procedures (whether supplied by the headquarters and/or modified by the subsidiaries) on actual strategic and policy-level decisions (see Table 1.3).

One can also evaluate the relative influences of headquarters on the subsidiaries' operations by examining the nature and frequency of reporting required of the managers of the subsidiaries.

As can be seen in Table 1.4, almost all of the American subsidiaries and approximately two-thirds of the German and Japanese subsidiaries were required by their respective headquarters to provide up-to-date information on balance sheet, profit and loss figures, production output, market share, cash and credit positions, inventory levels, and sales per product. The frequency of reporting was greater for the

Table 1.3.   Extent to which Subsidiaries Depend on Manuals, Policies, and
Procedures for Strategic and Policy-Level Decisions

| MNC Ownership | Great Deal (%) | To Some Extent (%) | Very Little to Not at All (%) |
|---|---|---|---|
| American (N = 33) | 88 | 3 | 9 |
| German (N = 44) | 32 | 16 | 52 |
| Japanese (N = 40) | 10 | 32 | 58 |

Level of significance = 0.0001.
Number of missing observations = 3.
Total number of observations = 120.

Table 1.4. Nature and Frequency of Reporting by the Subsidiaries to the Headquarters in Various Areas

| Type of Report | American (N = 33) | | | | German (N = 44) | | | | Japanese (N = 40) | | | |
|---|---|---|---|---|---|---|---|---|---|---|---|---|
| | Weekly | Monthly | Quarterly | Ad Hoc Yearly | Weekly | Monthly | Quarterly | Ad Hoc Yearly | Weekly | Monthly | Quarterly | Ad Hoc Yearly |
| Balance sheet | | 97 | 24 | — | 5 | 49 | 32 | 14 | 2 | 42 | 24 | 32 |
| Profit and loss statements | 6 | 91 | 3 | — | — | 49 | 35 | 16 | — | 42 | 32 | 26 |
| Production output | 6 | 94 | — | — | 13 | 50 | 29 | 8 | 6 | 47 | 25 | 22 |
| Market share | 3 | 70 | 24 | 3 | 2 | 48 | 29 | 21 | 3 | 31 | 33 | 33 |
| Cash and credit statement | — | 100 | — | — | 2 | 41 | 36 | 21 | 2 | 39 | 27 | 32 |
| Inventory levels | 3 | 88 | 9 | — | 5 | 46 | 26 | 23 | 5 | 38 | 23 | 34 |
| Sales per product | 3 | 88 | 9 | — | 2 | 37 | 26 | 35 | 5 | 44 | 19 | 32 |
| Performance review of personnel | 3 | 9 | 3 | 85 | — | 15 | 5 | 80 | — | 2 | — | 98 |
| Report on local economic and political conditions | 6 | 33 | 6 | 55 | 5 | 32 | 17 | 46 | 5 | 12 | 7 | 76 |

*American, German, and Japanese Multinational Corporations / 27*

American (usually monthly) than for the German and the Japanese subsidiaries.

It is revealing to note from this table that the only items with which the subsidiaries were less bothered were the performance reviews of their personnel and local socioeconomic and political conditions. In other words, stress is placed more on aspects that affect the short-run financial picture of the company rather than on factors that affect the firm's long-term survival and growth.

The analyses of the above three aspects of formalized reporting clearly indicate the increasing levels of formalization being introduced by American MNCs. Although the German MNCs seem to be catching up with the Americans, the Japanese companies, however, are still relying on their informal network of reporting.

## THE RELATIVE INFLUENCE ON DECISIONMAKING

Centralization versus subsidiary autonomy is a perennial and conflicting issue for most multinational companies. On the one hand, increasing competition in the world market requires some measure of rationalization of production and marketing processes at a global level, thus requiring a higher degree of centralization of decision-making at the headquarter and/or regional headquarter levels. On the other hand, however, satisfying the increasing demands from the host as well as the home countries of the multinationals necessitates some measure of subsidiary autonomy in strategic decisionmaking.

To assess the relative influence of the headquarters and subsidiaries in decisionmaking, we examined the following factors:

1. Training programs for local employees
2. Laying off operating personnel
3. Use of expatriate personnel
4. Appointment of a chief executive
5. Maintenance of production facilities
6. Determining aggregate production schedules
7. Pricing decisions
8. Expansion of production capacity
9. Use of a local advertising agency
10. Servicing of products sold
11. Introduction of a new product for the local market
12. Choosing a public accountant
13. Extension of credit to major customers
14. Use of cash flow by the subsidiary
15. Borrowing from local banks

## 28 / Behavioral and Organizational Aspects

Tables 1.5 and 1.6 provide the raw score and difference in means between the influences of the subsidiary and headquarters on decision-making. Here again, as can be seen from the tables, American subsidiaries have the least autonomy, the Japanese the most with the German subsidiaries in the middle.

However, the picture of greater automony for the subsidiaries changed when we compared the role of strategic versus routine decisions. As shown in Table 1.7, the relative score becomes negative for all three types of subsidiaries when measuring the influence of strategic decisions.

To probe further, we computed an overall delegation index by assigning different weights to strategic versus routine decisions. Strategic decisions were weighted three times as much as routine

Table 1.5.  The Relative Influence of Subsidiaries in Decisionmaking[a]

|  | Mean Scores | | |
|---|---|---|---|
|  | United States | Japan | Germany |
| Personnel training program for your subsidiary | 3.8 | 4.6 | 4.5 |
| Layoffs of operating personnel | 4.4 | 4.9 | 4.4 |
| Use of expatriate personnel from headquarters | 2.7 | 3.6 | 2.4 |
| Appointment of chief executive of your subsidiary | 1.5 | 2.8 | 1.7 |
| Maintenance of production facilities at subsidiary | 3.3 | 4.3 | 4.8 |
| Determining aggregate production schedule | 3.2 | 4.2 | 4.3 |
| Expansion of your production capacity | 2.5 | 3.5 | 2.7 |
| Use of local advertising agency | 3.9 | 4.7 | 4.5 |
| Servicing of products sold | 4.4 | 4.7 | 4.7 |
| Pricing on products sold on your local market | 3.0 | 4.5 | 4.0 |
| Introduction of a new product on your local market | 2.6 | 4.1 | 3.1 |
| Choice of public accountant | 2.7 | 4.6 | 4.4 |
| Extension of your credit to one of your major customers | 3.7 | 4.5 | 4.3 |
| Use of cash flow in your subsidiary | 3.2 | 4.2 | 3.4 |
| Your borrowing from local banks or financial institutions | 3.2 | 3.6 | 3.4 |
| Average (means) | 3.21 | 4.19 | 3.77 |

*Source:* Authors' interviews.

[a]The responses were precoded from "1" for "Very Little to No Influence" to "5" for "Very High Influence."

*American, German, and Japanese Multinational Corporations / 29*

Table 1.6.   Relative Influence over 15 Decision Areas:
Mean Score Differences[a]

|  | Differences in Means | | |
|---|---|---|---|
|  | United States | Japan | Germany |
| Personnel training . . . | 1.1 | 3.1 | 2.4 |
| Layoffs . . . | 2.6 | 3.3 | 2.7 |
| Expatriates . . . | −0.7 | 0.2 | −1.7 |
| Appointment of CEO . . . | −3.0 | −1.6 | −3.0 |
| Maintenance . . . | 0.1 | 1.8 | 2.4 |
| Production Schedule . . . | −0.1 | 1.2 | 1.9 |
| Expansion . . . | −1.4 | −0.2 | −1.2 |
| Advertising . . . | 1.4 | 2.7 | 2.7 |
| Servicing . . . | 2.5 | 2.9 | 3.1 |
| Pricing . . . | −0.5 | 1.9 | 1.3 |
| New Products . . . | −1.2 | 0.8 | −0.6 |
| Choice of CPA . . . | −0.5 | 1.8 | 2.4 |
| Credit to Customers . . . | 1.2 | 2.4 | 2.5 |
| Use of Cash Flow . . . | 0.1 | 1.7 | 0.3 |
| Borrowing from Banks . . . | 0.1 | 0.5 | 0.1 |
| Average (means) | 0.11 | 1.50 | 1.02 |

*Source:* Authors' interviews.
[a]The figures in the table represent the differences in means between the rated *subsidiary* and *HQ* influence for each of the decision items, the means taken over the companies in the identified country category. A positive number implies a relatively greater influence on the part of the subsidiary, while a negative number indicates greater HQ influence.

decisions. The weighting factor reflected the approximate ratio of feedback time for strategic decisions as compared to routine decisions. Table 1.8 presents the findings for the overall delegation index and the extent of delegation provided to the subsidiary management along with a set of decisions.

As can be seen from Table 1.8, the overall delegation index is fairly low in absolute terms. Despite the acknowledgement of head-

Table 1.7.   Relative Influence over 15 Decision Areas:
Selected Strategic Decisions

| Item | Overall | United States | Japan | Germany | Sweden | United Kingdom |
|---|---|---|---|---|---|---|
| Appointment of CEO | −2.1 | −3.0 | −1.6 | −3.0 | −0.4 | −1.7 |
| Expansion | −0.8 | −1.4 | −0.2 | −1.2 | −0.5 | −0.2 |
| New Products | −0.2 | −1.2 | −0.8 | −0.6 | −0.4 | 0.4 |
| Mean | −1.3 | −1.87 | −0.33 | −1.6 | −0.17 | −0.50 |

*Source:* Authors' interviews.

Table 1.8. Comparison of Delegation in the Various Areas for U.S., German, and Japanese MNCs

| | United States (N = 34) | | Germany (N = 45) | | Japan (N = 41) | | United States (N = 34) | | Germany (N = 45) | | Japan (N = 41) | |
|---|---|---|---|---|---|---|---|---|---|---|---|---|
| | Mean | S.D. | Mean | S.D. | Mean | S.D. | Mean | S.D. | Mean | S.D. | Mean | S.D. |
| Overall delegation index | -1.68 | 4.33 | 0.14 | 3.72 | 2.89[a] | 3.38 | -1.68 | 4.33 | 0.14 | 3.72 | 2.89[a] | 3.38 |
| Local personnel decisions | 2.40 | 1.46 | 2.85 | 1.24 | 3.51[b] | 0.93 | 2.40 | 1.46 | 2.85 | 1.24 | 3.51[b] | 0.93 |
| Expatriate personnel decisions | -2.10 | 1.67 | -2.49 | 1.60 | -0.65[b] | 2.00 | -2.10 | 1.67 | -2.49 | 1.60 | -0.65[a] | 2.00 |
| Routine production decisions | -0.04 | 2.63 | 2.59[a] | 1.43 | 2.24 | 1.84 | -0.04 | 2.63 | 2.59[a] | 1.43 | 2.24 | 1.84 |
| Strategic production decisions | -1.78 | 2.21 | -1.54 | 2.21 | 0.07[b] | 2.26 | -1.78 | 2.21 | -1.54 | 2.21 | 0.07[b] | 2.26 |
| Routine marketing decisions | 1.27 | 1.62 | 2.42[a] | 1.19 | 2.85[a] | 1.11 | 1.27 | 1.62 | 2.42 | 1.19 | 2.85 | 1.11 |
| Strategic marketing decisions | -1.58 | 2.14 | -0.83 | 2.42 | 1.14[a] | 2.35 | -1.58 | 2.14 | -0.83 | 2.42 | 1.14[a] | 2.35 |
| Financial decisions | 0.30 | 2.00 | 1.61[a] | 1.50 | 1.90[a] | 1.00 | 0.30 | 2.00 | 1.61 | 1.50 | 1.90[b] | 1.00 |

Key:

| -4 | 0 | +4 |
|---|---|---|
| maximum HQ influence | equal influence | maximum subsidiary influence |

[a] $p \leq 0.001$
[b] $p < 0.05$

*American, German, and Japanese Multinational Corporations / 31*

quarters of a less than perfect understanding of the subsidiary's operation and its environment, the subsidiary's influence on strategic
decisionmaking is minimal.

## CRITICAL PROBLEMS BETWEEN
## HEADQUARTER AND SUBSIDIARY
## OPERATIONS

During interviews with the senior executives of both headquarters and the subsidiaries, we probed into some of the critical
problems encountered in headquarters–subsidiary relationships.
Besides examining the nature and intensity of focal issues between
headquarters and the subsidiaries, we also attempted to assess the
relative influence of headquarters and the subsidiaries in resolving
these issues.

Approximately half of the subsidiaries of the American, German,
and Japanese multinational companies studied indicated that there
were no serious problems in their relationships with headquarters. Of
the 48 critical issues narrated by the executives of the subsidiaries,
roughly a third were concerned with the lack of the subsidiary's
autonomy in dealing with their problems in the host countries and
approximately a quarter were concerned with capital investment
decisions. Table 1.9 shows the range of problems between headquarters and the subsidiaries.

In measuring the relative influence of headquarters and the subsidiaries in resolving issues, our results indicated that in approximately
half of the cases, headquarters made the final decisions whereas in
less than a third of the cases the subsidiaries' viewpoint prevailed.
Among the three types of subsidiaries studied, the German and
Japanese seem to have greater influence in resolving issues.

## IMPACT OF SPECIFIC FACTORS OF
## THE FIRM AND COUNTRY ON
## DECISIONMAKING AND THE
## CONSEQUENCES OF AUTONOMY

Both in organizational theory and international business, it
has been shown that specific factors of the firm, such as size, technology, and type of industry, as well as specific factors of the country,
such as levels of industrial and economic development, market and
other economic conditions prevailing in a given country, and the
level of government control on industry, may affect not only the

Table 1.9. Nature of Critical Issues Existing Between Headquarters and Subsidiaries

| Ownership of MNC | Capital Investment $N/q_0^1/q_0^2$ | Sales and Financial $N/q_0^1/q_0^2$ | Home Country Policies $N/q_0^1/q_0^2$ | Host Country Policies $N/q_0^1/q_0^2$ | Organizational Autonomy $N/q_0^1/q_0^2$ | No Issues $N/q_0^1/q_0^2$ | Total |
|---|---|---|---|---|---|---|---|
| United States | 3/10.3/27.3 | 2/6.9/22.2 | 1/3.4/14.3 | 1/3.4/16.7 | 5/17.2/33.2 | 17/58.6/27.9 | 29 |
| Germany | 5/12.2/45.5 | 3/7.3/33.3 | 2/4.9/28.6 | 2/4.9/33.3 | 8/19.5/53.3 | 21/51.2/34.4 | 41 |
| Japan | 3/7.7/27.3 | 4/10.3/44.4 | 4/10.3/57.1 | 3/7.7/50.0 | 2/5.1/13.3 | 23/59.0/37.7 | 39 |
| Column Total | 11 | 9 | 7 | 6 | 15 | 61 | 109 |

*Source:* Authors' interviews.

Key: $q_0^1$ refers to row percentages.
$q_0^2$ refers to column percentages

Chi square = 6.35    10 D.f.    Significance = 0.78

*American, German, and Japanese Multinational Corporations / 33*

centralization decisions, but also the impact of these decisions on the firm's efficiency.[4]

At the present time my colleagues collaborating in this project and I are analyzing our composite data further to examine the effects of these factors on the subsidiary's autonomy and the consequences of autonomy on the firm's efficiency.

Our preliminary analysis suggests the following trends:*

1. When there is a large amount of intercompany transfer of technology, raw materials, and semifinished and finished goods with a high degree of interdependence between headquarters and the subsidiary, there is a lower level of subsidiary autonomy.
2. Subsidiaries located in the developing countries tend to have somewhat lower autonomy.
3. Subsidiaries operating in competitive markets tend to have higher autonomy.
4. The size of the subsidiary does not affect the level of autonomy.
5. The nature of the product lines has a very marginal effect on the subsidiary's autonomy.
6. Subsidiary autonomy has some effect, although it is not very significant, on the firm's profits, growth, and other performance criteria. Tightly controlled subsidiaries are relatively better performers, financially, than the autonomous subsidiaries. However, a subsidiary with higher autonomy has a more positive impact on the host country's acceptance of its operation, thereby improving its eventual growth and survival potential.

This last finding thus provides support to the advocates of the processes of rationalization and unification for MNCs. However, at the same time it raises an intriguing question about the utility of such centralization processes under rapidly changing socioeconomic and political conditions in industrialized as well as in developing countries. To explore this question further, we first examine the changing conditions in the industrialized countries and then discuss the implications of such changes on MNC strategies, policies, and structure.

## FAST-CHANGING CONDITIONS IN INDUSTRIALIZED COUNTRIES

Although many of the industrialized countries are operating as "free and open markets" and are generally very congenial to foreign

*The summary results are drawn from the twin papers of Johnny K. Johansson et al., "Autonomy of Subsidiaries in Multinational Corporations," in *The Management of Headquarter-Subsidiary Relationships in Multinational Corporations*, edited by Lars Otterbeck (London: Gower, 1982).

*34 / Behavioral and Organizational Aspects*

investors, recently they, too, have begun to question the utility of unchecked foreign investment. In other words, the governmental decisionmakers as well as other public groups (e.g., labor unions, consumer advocates, and environmentalists) are discovering that national needs, ambitions, and objectives can be at variance with the objectives, goals, and strategies of MNCs.

The range, nature, and intensity of these issues, of course, differ considerably from country to country, depending upon the prevailing political climate and economic conditions (e.g., unemployment, inflation, or balance of payments position) and the level of industrial and economic development. For example, in a study of MNCs in developed countries, Fry[5] reported that the issue of worker participation ("Mitbestimmung") was most prominent in West Germany, and the traditional issues, such as providing new techonology, employment, upgrading wages, and developing local resources, were considered secondary by the governmental officials.

In contrast, in Belgium the major issues pertaining to MNC activities were related to employment capabilities, potential effect on the balance of payments position, research and development activities (or lack of), development and utilization of local resources, and worker participation in management. Simultaneously, however, MNCs emphasized their importance in terms of increasing the entrepreneurial spirit, providing new technology, and producing consumer goods at lower prices. These differences in expectations between the host government and MNC priorities are clearly highlighted in Table 1.10.

Especially since the oil crisis of 1973 most of the industrialized nations have experienced a downturn in their economic growth and prosperity, which in turn has created considerable hostility, not only toward foreign multinationals but also among the opposing groups in a given society (e.g., management against labor, domestic multinationals against foreign multinationals, and multinationals against their own subcontractors). For example, when faced with declining sales of U.S. automobiles, the three largest U.S. auto companies (General Motors, Ford, and Chrysler) began to denounce auto imports from Japan and the European countries asked the U.S. Congress and the President to help them. At the same time, their own subcontractors have publicly accused the auto companies of being "double talkers" by asserting that "it is not just imported cars, it's imported parts that are causing problems."[6] The growing complaints over Detroit's policies of importing parts for domestically assembled cars have now reached Washington. Consequently, congressional proposals that were originally designed to limit imports of autos are being amended to also place restrictions on imported parts.[7]

*American, German, and Japanese Multinational Corporations / 35*

Table 1.10. Expectation Differences Between Multinational
Corporations and Nation-States

| Impact | Government Wants More | Firms Give More |
| --- | --- | --- |
| *Germany* | | |
| Worker participation | X | |
| Increased competition | | X |
| Capital inflows | | X |
| Increased skilled employment | | X |
| Create entrepreneurial spirit | | X |
| | | |
| *Belgium* | | |
| Increased general employment | X | |
| Increased skilled employment | X | |
| Balance of payment effects | X | |
| Increased R&D efforts | X | |
| Develop local resources | X | |
| Worker participation | X | |
| Increased quality of consumer services | X | |
| Social and cultural values | | X |
| Increased entrepreneurial spirit | | X |
| Provide new technology | | X |
| Create lower prices | | X |

*Source:* David E. Fry, "Multinational Corporations–Host Government Relationships: An Empirical Study of Behavioral Expectations," D.B.A. dissertation, Kent State University, 1977.

The results of our own large-scale study, reported in Table 1.11, illustrate the nature of demands made by MNCs in West Germany, the United Kingdom, Spain, Portugal, and France.

As can be seen from this table, economic stagnation, triggered by the oil crisis, has generated traditional economic demands even in the more industrialized nations of the world. However, except in the case of Spain and Portugal, the European countries, in which this field research was undertaken, have not yet legislated these demands.

However, one thing appears clear: the less economically developed a country, and/or the more intensive its economic problems, the greater are the demands placed on MNCs and the more willing is the country to legislate these expectations.

Table 1.12 shows the nature of the problems faced by the American, German, and Japanese MNCs in various industrialized countries. The labor force seems to be the source of almost half the problems faced by the multinationals. However, U.S. and German subsidiaries have, proportionately, more labor problems than Japanese companies. The underlying theme of labor–management problems is, however, quite different in the various countries. In Germany, for instance, industry representatives were involved in challenging the constitutional

36 / *Behavioral and Organizational Aspects*

Table 1.11.  Nature of Demands Made on Multinational Corporations
in Selected Industrialized Countries[a]

| | Germany (N/%) | United Kingdom (N/%) | Spain (N/%) | Portugal (N/%) | France (N/%) | Total |
|---|---|---|---|---|---|---|
| Technology transfer | 0/0.0 | 2/21.4 | 0/0.0 | 0/0.0 | 0/0.0 | 3/5.3 |
| Exports | 0/0.0 | 1/7.1 | 0/0.0 | 0/0.0 | 1/12.5 | 2/3.5 |
| Employment | 0/0.0 | 2/14.3 | 0/0.0 | 0/0.0 | 0/0.0 | 2/3.5 |
| Economic development | 3/23.1 | 5/35.7 | 10/90.9 | 9/81.8 | 7/87.5 | 34/59.6 |
| Ambivalent | 1/7.7 | 0/0.0 | 0/0.0 | 0/0.0 | 0/0.0 | 1/1.8 |
| No specific demands | 9/69.2 | 3/21.4 | 1/9.1 | 2/2.18 | 0/0.0 | 15/26.3 |
| | 13/22.8 | 14/24.6 | 11/19.3 | 11/19.3 | 8/14.0 | 57/100 |

*Source:* Interview data collected by the authors.
[a] Raw chi square = 43.19530 with 20 degrees of freedom. Significance = 0.0019.

validity of the "codetermination" laws as well as influencing the election of representatives who were against the codetermination laws. The U.S. multinational subsidiaries, owing to stipulations about the size of the workforce in the law, were most susceptible to the laws. Given the confrontational nature of management–labor relations in the United States, American multinationals initially had a difficult time accepting the collaborative philosophy.

Except in Germany and a few other countries, all multinationals, especially the larger U.S. and German MNCs, have been the target of leftist-oriented labor unions. This has been particularly true of Spain and Portugal, where rising nationalistic expectations have made these issues even more difficult to handle. Japanese multinationals appear to have avoided serious problems with labor, to some extent, by their smaller size and their willingness to enter into joint ventures with either government organizations or private entrepreneurs. This finding is interesting in the light of the fact that, despite being involved in joint ventures or minority holdings in the developing countries, Japanese organizations have had considerable problems with labor.[8] These problems have stemmed mainly from efforts made by the Japanese to impose their management style, and—in South and Southeast Asia—from animosities rooted in recent history. Apparently the Japanese MNCs have learned from their experience in the developing countries of Asia and South America and therefore have restricted the use of a Japanese management style (such as lifetime employment and demanding loyalty to the company) in the industrialized countries.

Japanese subsidiaries were involved, however, in conflicts with the EEC Commission. Problems were centered around charges of

Table 1.12. Problems Faced by the Multinationals in Industrialized Countries

| | Host Government (N/%) | Labor (N/%) | Political Groupings (N/%) | Local Competitors (N/%) | Multiple Sources (N/%) | No Problems (N/%) | Regional Economic Grouping (N/%) | Total |
|---|---|---|---|---|---|---|---|---|
| U.S. MNCs | 1/25.0 | 11/40.7 | 1/100.0 | 1/100.0 | 1/100.0 | 8/38.1 | 0/00.0 | 23/100 |
| | 1/4.3 | 11/47.8 | 1/4.3 | 1/4.3 | 1/4.3 | 8/34.8 | 0/0.0 | |
| German MNCs | 0/0.0 | 12/44.4 | 0/0.0 | 0/0.0 | 0/0.0 | 3/14.3 | 0/0.0 | 15/100 |
| | 0/0.0 | 12/80.0 | 0/0.0 | 0/0.0 | 0/0.0 | 3/20.0 | | |
| Japanese MNCs | 3/75.0 | 4/14.8 | 0/0.0 | 0/0.0 | 0/0.0 | 10/47.6 | 2/100.0 | 19/100 |
| | 3/15.7 | 4/21.0 | 0/0.0 | 0/0.0 | 0/0.0 | 10/52.6 | 2/10.5 | |
| Total | 4/100 | 27/100 | 1/100 | 1/100 | 1/100 | 21/100 | 2/100 | 57/100 |
| | 4/7.0 | 27/47.4 | 1/1.8 | 1/1.8 | 1/1.8 | 21/36.8 | 2/3.5 | 57/100 |

*38 / Behavioral and Organizational Aspects*

"dumping" by Japanese organizations, despite the fact that the accused Japanese companies had manufacturing subsidiaries in the EEC countries. The Japanese organizations responded by adopting a legalistic stance while simultaneously emphasizing their local manufacturing activities in efforts to make the dumping charge untenable.

As noted earlier, although the industrially developed countries have, thus far, constrained themselves in enacting limiting legislation against foreign private investments and multinational corporations, the public debates and discussions are moving closer to this end at a faster speed than would have been anticipated. For example, the recent establishment of the Foreign Investment Review Agency in Canada[9] and their pronouncements about expected corporate behavior, as seen in Table 1.13, come very close to what the developing countries have been demanding from foreign investors during the last two decades.

In turning to the United States, it is apparent that unemployment and inflation continue to undermine the people's confidence in national economic conditions, the legislators both at the state and national levels have begun to introduce legislation to curb the activities of foreign investors and multinational companies. For example, in the last few years approximately half of the 50 states have introduced legislation to restrict foreign investment in agricultural land. At a lesser end, as mentioned earlier, the subcontractors of U.S. automobile companies as well as the labor unions have begun to question the virtue of multinational investments and their general strategies of global rationalization.

Our results, on the other hand, clearly show the increasing trend toward global rationalization and centralization in decisionmaking. Thus, the question must be asked whether the German and Japanese multinationals are flexible enough to turn the tide and maintain their flexible structures and responses, as they have been able to do in the developing countries, once circumstances demand that they do so in the industrialized countries.

Even the American multinationals, champions in evolving progressive organizational structures for managing expanding international business (from export departments to international divisions, regional structure, worldwide product setup, and the matrix system) have been warned about the swiftly changing environmental conditions in both the developed and the developing countries.

Business International,[10] a reputed consulting firm in international business, recently identified some of the major economic and political changes that will affect the need for changes in present organizational forms utilized by American and other multinational companies.

American, German, and Japanese Multinational Corporations / 39

Table 1.13.  Canada's 12 Good Corporate Behavior Principles
(as They Relate to Alleged Objectionable U.S.
Subsidiary Policies)

| Guiding Principle Summary | Alleged Objectionable Practices |
|---|---|
| 1. Full realization of the company's growth and operating potential in Canada. | 1. U.S.-based corporate planners institute expansion and cutback plans without regard for Canada's plan and aspirations. |
| 2. Make Canadian subsidiary a self-contained, vertically integrated entity with total responsibility for at least one productive function. | 2. The Canadian subsidiary is primarily an assembler of imported parts or distributor of goods produced elsewhere so operations can be easily shut down or transferred. |
| 3. Maximum development of export markets from Canada. | 3. Filling export orders to third-country markets from the U.S. country stock earns credits for U.S. balance of payments rather than Canada's. |
| 4. Extend processing of Canada's raw materials through maximum number of stages. | 4. Have as few as possible materials-processing stages in Canada to minimize political leverage. |
| 5. Equitable pricing policies for international and intracompany sales. | 5. Negotiated or spurious prices by Canadian U.S. subsidiaries are designed to get around Canadian income taxes. |
| 6. Develop sources of supply in Canada. | 6. Preference for U.S. or third-country sources for purposes of corporate convenience or political leverage. |
| 7. Inclusion of R&D and product development. | 7. The concentration of R&D and product design in the United States means Canada can never develop these capabilities. |
| 8. Retain substantial earnings for growth. | 8. Profits earned in Canada do not remain to finance Canadian expansion. |
| 9. Appointment of Canadian officers and directors. | 9. Use of U.S. officers and directors to prevent development of local outlook in planning and execution. |
| 10. Equity participation by Canadian investing public. | 10. Creation of wholly owned subsidiaries denies policy determination and earnings to Canadians. |
| 11. Publication of financial reports. | 11. Consolidation of Canadian operating results into parent company statement or failure to publish any relevant information. |
| 12. Support of Canadian cultural and charitable institutions. | 12. Failure locally to support such causes as the United Appeal where parent corporations give generously to comparable U.S. campaigns. |

Source: David J. Ashton, "U.S. Investments in Canada: Will the Other Shoe Drop?"
Worldwide P & I Planning (September–October 1968): 57.

40 / *Behavioral and Organizational Aspects*

### DECLINING OR STAGNANT
### ECONOMIC GROWTH IN
### INDUSTRIALIZED COUNTRIES

On the average, Canada, France, West Germany, Japan, the United States, and the United Kingdom will experience their real growth in GNP drop from about 3 percent in 1979 to 1 percent in 1980. The U.S. GNP growth may drop from 2 percent in 1979 to 1.25 percent in 1980; Japan from 6 percent to 4.75 percent; West Germany from 3 percent to 2 percent; Canada from 2.75 percent to 1.5 percent; and the United Kingdom from 0.5 percent to 2 percent.[11] While growth rates in major industrialized countries are declining, inflation continues to soar. Thus, the poorer future outlook and the higher inflation rates are likely to reinforce protectionist forces in the United States and other developed countries.[12]

Given such changing economic and political conditions, Business International warns that multinational corporations will have to create a responsive organizational structure that could combine the centralization of strategies and policies with the increasing decentralization of subsidiary operations.[13]

Whether the German and Japanese companies, in their quest for adopting the American model of global rationalization, will be able to achieve a marriage between the centralization of strategies and policies (as required by the global rationalization concept) and the needed decentralization or higher autonomy of the subsidiary operations is an open question awaiting the attention of the academic scholars as we move into the 1980s.

### NOTES

1. Stopford, John, and Wells, Louis. *Managing the Multinational Enterprise.* London: Longmans, 1972.
2. Franko, Lawrence. "The Move Toward a Multi-Divisional Structure in European Organizations." *Administrative Science Quarterly*, 19 (1974): 493-506.
3. Yoshino, Michel. *Japan's Multinational Enterprise.* Cambridge, Mass.: Harvard University Press, 1976.
4. Pugh, Derek, et al. "The Context of Organization Structures." *Administrative Science Quarterly* 14 (1969): 91-114. For international aspect see Vernon Raymond, *Storm Over the Multinationals: The Real Issues.* Cambridge, Mass.: Harvard University Press, 1979, especially chapters 1 and 2, pp. 1-33.
5. Fry, David E. *Multinational Corporations-Host Government Relationships:*

## American, German, and Japanese Multinational Corporations / 41

*An Empirical Study of Behavioral Expectations.* DBA dissertation, Kent State University, 1977.

6. *Wall Street Journal* LX, 149 (May, 14, 1980), p. 1.
7. Ibid.
8. Negandhi, Anant R., and Baliga, B. R. *Quest for Survival and Growth: A Comparative Study of American, European and Japanese Multinationals.* Königstein, West Germany: Athenäum, and New York: Praeger, 1979.
9. Safarian, A. E., and Bell, Joel. "Issues Raised by the National Control of the Multinational Enterprise." In *Multinational Corporations and Governments: Business–Government Relations in an International Context,* edited by Patrick M. Boardman and Hans Schollhammer, p. 74. New York: Praeger, 1975.
10. Business International. "Pressures on Management Call For Coordination and Innovative Twists." *Business International* (January 4, 1980), pp. 1, 7, 8.
11. Ibid.
12. Ibid.
13. Ibid.

# [31]

## THE DETERMINANTS OF MULTINATIONAL ENTERPRISE:

## A COMPARATIVE STUDY OF THE US, JAPAN, UK,

## SWEDEN AND WEST GERMANY

### INTRODUCTION

Modern theory argues that an integrated approach is required to study the international operations of multinational enterprises (MNEs) and, by extension, those of countries. To date only a few empirical studies have analysed both trade and production generated by direct foreign investment (DFI) _pari passu_ whilst distinguishing the country-specific features of the results. Such a methodology is, however, imperative according to the eclectic theory (Dunning, 1977; 1981) and the internalisation approach (Buckley and Casson, 1976).

This enquiry takes the need for an integrated framework as its starting point, and extends the empirical analysis in two ways. Firstly through the inclusion of international non-affiliate licensing, and secondly through a comparative investigation of the determinants of outward and inward competition in manufacturing, for five major developed countries over the period 1965-75.

### HYPOTHESES

Data allow the testing of a range of leading ownership hypotheses. Locational hypotheses, represented in their orthodox form as measures of impediments to trade, however, do not appear in the statistical analysis. While theoretically important, locational variables can rarely be measured with sufficient accuracy in aggregative studies, as evidenced by their highly chequered performance. Nevertheless, the methodology employed here permits some appreciation of the influence of locational variables on the development of international competition.

Hypotheses are constructed for both outward and inward involvement,
though employing the same set of explanatory characteristics.  Accordingly
the two methods of interpreting the exogenous variables are quite distinct.
For outward equations the exogenous variables represent source country/owner-
ship advantages.  For inward equations they represent those of host firms, and
interpretation is more problematic.  In principle, high host advantages will
repel inward competition, per contra the identity of foreign firms' ownership
advantages can be inferred from the characteristics of those industries in
which inward competition is highest.  However, this only applies if international competition is inter-industry in nature; if it is significantly intra-
industry this will lead to an observed positive relationship between host
advantages and foreign entry.  Interpretation could be further clouded by
internationally shared characteristics, including those arising from the
existing colonisation of domestic industry by foreign MNEs.  Industrial aggregation acts both so as to exacerbate and to dilute these problems.

Because we anticipate country-specific differences between the equations
to be estimated for the five countries, a large number of specific hypotheses
are generated.  Below are outlined some essential considerations underlying
the hypotheses.

Technology Intensity

The general hypothesis provided by theory is of a positive relationship
between technology (or research) intensity and each route of international
market servicing, both outward and inward.  Only early Japanese DFI abroad
is thought to be based on alternate explanations.

The existence of a substituting relationship between US outward/direct
foreign production (DFP) and exports was first identified by Horst (1972),
where total involvement in the Canadian market was better explained than either
route taken separately.  Here we expect to produce a similar result, while
extending the analysis to licensing, and to the other source countries.

For a country with a comparative advantage in technology-intensive products, the quasi location-specific nature of novel technology will cause
research intensity to explain exports more strongly than direct foreign production (Lall, 1980).  However this is only necessarily true for first-time
DFI; where firms already produce abroad a curtailment of the product cycle
(PC) model is tenable (Vernon, 1979).  For the US alone the initial effect
is thought still to dominate.

The intra-industry nature of technology-based competition is argued to
guarantee a positive association for inward competitive routes and research
intensity.  This would break down only where there is a general indigenous
technological superiority, causing inter-industry type inward DFI; this is
proposed for the US,following Lall and Siddarthan (1982).

Host research will reduce the transaction costs of inward licensing and
accordingly generate a positive association (Oshima, 1973; Buckley and Casson,
1981).

Capital Intensity

In theory the savings on the deferral of fixed capital expenditure abroad
renders capital a location-specific advantage which favours exports, until
such time as DFI is warranted by foreign market size (Buckley and Casson,
1981).  This would apply, in the PC model, to newly foreign-investing
countries; coupled with DFI as a response to rising domestic labour costs,

such DFI would be labour-intensive in character.  However, for source
countries identified with large capital-endowed firms (often existing MNEs)
capital represents an ownership advantage, given an imperfect capital market,
enabling the firm to better cover the fixed costs of DFI.  For this second
group of countries, which includes the US and UK, capital intensity should
then favour DFP; moreover, for these two countries
DFP should be favoured over licensed foreign production (LFP).  Arguably, the
other three countries might reveal a stronger association for LFP because of
the capital saving this mode offers.  Exports will remain capital-intensive
for all countries, except where its structural assocation with natural
resource intensity strongly suggests otherwise.

As a host-country characteristic, capital intensity might be interpreted
normally as an entry barrier; however it is in precisely such industries that
MNEs generally predominate, thus arguing for a positive relationship with
inward DFP.  Imports are argued to be less capital-intensive, when measured
by host-industry capital intensity, while this same variable should also
represent existing domestic capacity, thus lowering the transfer costs of
inward licensing.


Skills

As developed countries, all exports are expected to be intense in human skills.
The non-transferability of production worker (operative) skills to foreign
plant, as opposed to managerial and professional (non-operative) skills, has
been argued by Lall (1980).  Accordingly operative skills should promote
exports, but relate negatively to DFP.  Conversely, non-operative skills
should explain, and favour, DFP over exports.  This latter hypothesis fur-
nishes an interesting explanation for the extension of DFI abroad in the

absence of technological advantages, while transferable managerial skills
should lower the cost of setting up and running DFI, thus reducing recourse
to licensing.

Developed-country MNEs will seek high skills abroad as dictated by
their own production functions. If the source and host country share a comparable industry structure and average level of skills, then entry will be
positively related to host skills intensity. If, however, the host's average
skills are significantly higher, the reverse is argued to apply. In the
absence of suitable partner-country data, only the US is anticipated to reveal
this latter relationship, which will be confined to operative skills.

Analogous reasoning to that offered for capital intensity is applied to
explain the expected positive relationship for managerial skills and inward
DFI, while as a host characteristic such skills are also hypothesised to
facilitate the assimilation of new technology via licensing. Operative skills
are expected similarly to represent existing productional competence, and so
to promote inward licensing.


Complexity of Management

This is an hypothesis considered by Caves (1974) to be theoretically weak,
although he pointed out that it is perhaps better suited to cross-country
analysis, as here.

Measured by the proportion of managerial staff, it captures the level of
investment in managerial and production-coordinating infrastructure rather
than skills. Accordingly it is argued to favour DFP over exports, in addition
to increasing the capacity for DFI and therefore diminishing the usage of
licensing abroad.

With the exception of Japan, there is a very close correspondence in the degree of managerial complexity between countries, suggesting that entry via DFI will generally follow an intra-industry pattern. This host variable may also encourage inward licensing, as it captures indigenous firms' assimilative capacity.

This variable is found to correlate positively with advertising intensity, using US data (Lall, 1980) - an ownership hypothesis excluded from this study. It is possible that this measure may behave similarly to an omitted advertising variable for other countries as well.

THE CONSTRUCTION OF THE VARIABLES AND STATISTICAL METHODOLOGY

## The Data

The statistical data are drawn from both official and private surveys conducted for the five countries.[1]

Trade statistics are already recorded as output values; however to render the data comparable, where necessary, output values have been estimated from the DFI position, using the domestic output-to-capital ratio for each industry and country. Raw licensing statistics represent the transaction values of payments and receipts for technological rights. As these occur primarily on a royalty-rate basis, we follow Buckley and Davies (1981) in multiplying these values by a factor of twenty, assuming an average royalty rate of five per cent. The data for all variables are classified to nine industry groups[2].

## The Endogenous and Exogenous Variables

The data are divided by the value of domestic gross output in order to standardise for the size of industry, and so generating the endogenous vari-

ables, which are expressed as follows:

| | |
|---|---|
| INTPRODOUT | the sum of exports plus direct foreign production abroad plus licensed foreign production abroad, divided by domestic industrial production (in the source country). |
| EXP | exports divided by domestic industrial production. |
| DFPOUT | direct foreign production abroad divided by domestic industrial production. |
| LFPOUT | licensed foreign production abroad divided by domestic industrial production. |
| INTPRODIN | the sum of imports plus inward direct foreign production plus inward licensed foreign production divided by domestic industrial production (in the recipient country). |
| IMP | imports divided by domestic industrial production. |
| DFPIN | inward direct foreign production divided by domestic industrial production. |
| LFPIN | inward licensing foreign production divided by domestic industrial production. |

The exogenous variables are also standardised appropriately for the size of

industry, and are expressed as follows:

| | |
|---|---|
| RDEXP | research and development expenditure divided by domestic industrial production, as a proxy for the degree of innovation and creation of technological ownership advantages. |
| NTFA | net tangible fixed assets at book value per employee, as a measure of capital intensity. |
| WSOP | wages and salaries per operative, measuring the skill level of production workers. |
| WSNONOP | wages and salaries per non-operative, measuring the skill quality of managerial manpower. |
| NONOP | non-operatives as a proportion of total employment, as a proxy for the complexity of management. |

These data are compatible across countries, with the possible exception

of that on non-operatives in Japan, where the definition of this class is

appreciably wider than elsewhere.  Otherwise there is no reason to anticipate

any attendant problems of multicollinearity.

Statistical Methodology

As concurrent methods of market servicing, theory requires that for each
country each endogenous variable be regressed on the full set of exogenous
variables in the model.  Therefore the equations for each country are in the
form of Zellner's Seemingly Unrelated Regressions (Zellner, 1962), and as
they are run with the full model, classical linear regression is optimal.
The fact that the disturbances are correlated contemporaneously across equations allows us later to investigate the possible influence of omitted variables.

   The regressions are run on three pooled cross-sectional sets of data,
for 1965, 1970 and 1975.  All relevant data were rendered into constant (1970)
dollars, and the variables entered in natural logarithmic form, a consequence
of which is that the estimated coefficients are elasticities.  Additional
regressions were run to test formally the stability of the model, both between
countries and over time.[3]

   Tables 1 and 2 summarise the hypotheses for each of the five countries.
The uncertain signs for INTPRODOUT and INTPRODIN arise mainly because of their
summational nature.

STATISTICAL FINDINGS

Outward Equations

Of the hundred regression  coefficients, excluding the constants, forty-seven
are significant, although not all of these are as anticipated.  The varied
pattern of significance highlights the country-specific nature of the results.

   It can be seen from Table 3 that the research intensity hypotheses are
the most consistently supported, despite the partial exceptions of Japan and

TABLE 1    *The expected directions of the relationships between the dependent and independent variables, outward equations*

|            | RDEXP | NTFA | WSOP | WSNONOP | NONOP |
|------------|-------|------|------|---------|-------|
| *USA*      |       |      |      |         |       |
| INTPRODOUT | +     | +    | ?    | ?       | ?     |
| EXP        | +     | +    | –    | +       | +     |
| DFPOUT     | +     | +    | –    | +       | +     |
| LFPOUT     | +     | +    | ?    | –       | –     |
| *Japan*    |       |      |      |         |       |
| INTPRODOUT | ?     | ?    | ?    | ?       | ?     |
| EXP        | +     | –    | +    | +       | –     |
| DFPOUT     | –     | –    | –    | +       | +     |
| LFPOUT     | +     | +    | ?    | --      | --    |
| *UK*       |       |      |      |         |       |
| INTPRODOUT | +     | ?    | ?    | ?       | ?     |
| EXP        | +     | ?    | +    | +       | --    |
| DFPOUT     | +     | +    | –    | +       | +     |
| LFPOUT     | +     | +    | ?    | –       | +     |
| *Sweden*   |       |      |      |         |       |
| INTPRODOUT | +     | ?    | ?    | ?       | ?     |
| EXP        | +     | +    | +    | +       | –     |
| DFPOUT     | +     | –    | –    | +       | +     |
| LFPOUT     | +     | +    | ?    | –       | –     |
| *FGR*      |       |      |      |         |       |
| INTPRODOUT | +     | ?    | ?    | ?       | ?     |
| EXP        | +     | +    | +    | +       | –     |
| DFPOUT     | +     | –    | –    | +       | +     |
| LFPOUT     | +     | +    | ?    | –       | –     |

TABLE 2    *The expected directions of the relationships between the dependent and independent variables, inward equations*

|           | RDEXP | NTFA | WSOP | WSNONOP | NONOP |
|-----------|-------|------|------|---------|-------|
| *USA*     |       |      |      |         |       |
| INTPRODIN | ?     | ?    | ?    | ?       | ?     |
| IMP       | +     | ?    | –    | ?       | ?     |
| DFPIN     | ?     | +    | –    | +       | +     |
| LFPIN     | +     | +    | +    | +       | +     |
| *Japan*   |       |      |      |         |       |
| INTPRODIN | +     | ?    | ?    | ?       | ?     |
| IMP       | +     | ?    | –    | ?       | ?     |
| DFPIN     | +     | +    | +    | +       | +     |
| LFPIN     | +     | +    | +    | +       | +     |
| *UK*      |       |      |      |         |       |
| INTPRODIN | +     | ?    | ?    | ?       | ?     |
| IMP       | +     | ?    | –    | ?       | ?     |
| DFPIN     | +     | +    | +    | +       | +     |
| LFPIN     | +     | +    | +    | +       | +     |
| *Sweden*  |       |      |      |         |       |
| INTPRODIN | +     | ?    | ?    | ?       | ?     |
| IMP       | +     | ?    | –    | ?       | ?     |
| DFPIN     | +     | +    | +    | +       | +     |
| LFPIN     | +     | +    | +    | +       | +     |
| *FGR*     |       |      |      |         |       |
| INTPRODIN | +     | ?    | ?    | ?       | ?     |
| IMP       | +     | ?    | –    | ?       | ?     |
| DFPIN     | +     | +    | +    | +       | +     |
| LFPIN     | +     | +    | +    | +       | +     |

TABLE 3 *Multiple regression results for the outward equations*

| | RDEXP | NTFA | WSOP | WSNONOP | NONOP | Constant | $R^2$ | F. Stat. |
|---|---|---|---|---|---|---|---|---|
| **USA** | | | | | | | | |
| INTPRODOUT | 0.512 | 0.568 | −1.850 | −0.604 | 0.064 | 4.232 | 0.764 | 13.590ᵃ |
| | (3.784)ᵃ | (2.768)ᵃ | (−1.626)ᶜ | (−0.282) | (0.110) | (1.271) | | |
| EXP | 0.473 | 0.284 | −0.853 | 0.032 | −0.308 | −0.472 | 0.680 | 8.920ᵇ |
| | (2.814)ᵃ | (1.116) | (−0.604) | (0.012) | (−0.422) | (−0.114) | | |
| DFPOUT | 0.479 | 0.735 | −2.320 | −0.372 | 0.406 | 4.073 | 0.701 | 10.027ᵃ |
| | (2.935)ᵃ | (2.974)ᵃ | (−1.693)ᶜ | (−0.144) | (0.574) | (1.015) | | |
| LFPOUT | 0.848 | 0.516 | −1.265 | −1.569 | −1.149 | 2.508 | 0.688 | 9.260ᵇ |
| | (3.467)ᵃ | (1.393)ᶜ | (−0.615) | (−1.615)ᶜ | (−1.083) | (0.417) | | |
| **Japan** | | | | | | | | |
| INTPRODOUT | −0.063 | −0.762 | 3.205 | −1.867 | −2.968 | −4.313 | 0.709 | 10.229ᵃ |
| | (−0.537) | (−3.290)ᵃ | (3.088)ᵃ | (−1.616)ᶜ | (−4.901)ᵃ | (−3.652)ᵃ | | |
| EXP | 0.293 | −0.988 | 5.842 | −5.272 | −4.828 | −2.914 | 0.762 | 13.434ᵃ |
| | (1.822)ᵇ | (−3.100)ᵃ | (4.088)ᵃ | (−3.314)ᵃ | (−5.790)ᵃ | (−1.791)ᵇ | | |
| DFPOUT | −0.749 | −0.803 | 0.390 | 2.675 | 0.378 | −8.885 | 0.764 | 13.636)ᵃ |
| | (−3.982)ᵃ | (−2.155)ᵇ | (0.234) | (1.438)ᶜ | (0.388) | (−4.673)ᵃ | | |
| LFPOUT | 1.170 | 0.618 | 3.705 | −3.940 | −0.277 | −0.060 | 0.739 | 11.913ᵃ |
| | (4.384)ᵃ | (1.169) | (1.562)ᶜ | (−1.493)ᶜ | (−0.200) | (−0.022) | | |
| **UK** | | | | | | | | |
| INTPRODOUT | 0.080 | 0.165 | −1.170 | 2.100 | 0.361 | −1.954 | 0.350 | 2.264 |
| | (0.950) | (1.109) | (−1.173) | (1.461)ᶜ | (0.776) | (−1.493)ᶜ | | |
| EXP | 0.298 | −0.237 | 0.146 | 1.511 | −0.416 | −2.933 | 0.528 | 4.698ᶜ |
| | (2.837)ᵃ | (−1.281) | (0.118) | (0.834) | (−0.718) | (−1.798)ᵇ | | |
| DFPOUT | −0.141 | 0.442 | −3.430 | 4.628 | 1.049 | −4.330 | 0.394 | 2.730 |
| | (−0.949) | (1.681)ᶜ | (−1.946)ᵇ | (1.821)ᵇ | (1.277) | (−1.872)ᵇ | | |
| LFPOUT | 0.145 | 0.403 | −4.195 | 3.905 | 2.701 | −1.220 | 0.296 | 1.768 |
| | (0.513) | (0.806) | (−1.251) | (0.807) | (1.727)ᵇ | (−0.277) | | |
| **Sweden** | | | | | | | | |
| INTPRODOUT | 0.716 | −0.294 | 1.317 | −0.539 | −1.122 | 0.343 | 0.513 | 4.430ᶜ |
| | (2.953)ᵃ | (−0.753) | (0.575) | (−0.218) | (−0.921) | (0.129) | | |
| EXP | 0.709 | −0.294 | 1.951 | −1.062 | −1.795 | −0.910 | 0.440 | 3.296ᶜ |
| | (2.820)ᵃ | (−0.726) | (0.822) | (−0.415) | (−1.422)ᶜ | (−0.331) | | |
| DFPOUT | 0.796 | −0.036 | 0.634 | 0.789 | 0.158 | −1.164 | 0.622 | 6.919ᵇ |
| | (2.770)ᵃ | (−0.078) | (0.234) | (0.269) | (0.110) | (−0.370) | | |
| LFPOUT | 0.583 | −0.199 | −5.054 | 3.641 | 0.497 | −0.389 | 0.441 | 3.310ᶜ |
| | (1.760)ᵇ | (−0.373) | (−1.614)ᶜ | (1.078) | (0.298) | (−0.107) | | |
| **Federal Republic of Germany** | | | | | | | | |
| INTPRODOUT | 0.287 | −0.408 | 0.491 | 0.738 | −0.289 | −1.384 | 0.867 | 27.395ᵃ |
| | (6.335)ᵃ | (−2.404)ᵇ | (0.590) | (0.849) | (−0.855) | (−1.567)ᶜ | | |
| EXP | 0.305 | −0.658 | 1.870 | −0.708 | −0.664 | −1.167 | 0.811 | 17.985ᵃ |
| | (5.184)ᵃ | (−2.984)ᵃ | (1.731)ᵇ | (−0.628) | (−1.512)ᶜ | (−1.019) | | |
| DFPOUT | 0.272 | 0.114 | −3.437 | 5.327 | −0.431 | −6.731 | 0.709 | 10.255ᵃ |
| | (3.021)ᵃ | (0.339) | (−2.079)ᵇ | (3.087)ᵃ | (−0.642) | (−3.841)ᵃ | | |
| LFPOUT | 0.921 | 0.023 | −0.319 | 0.572 | −0.526 | −1.709 | 0.717 | 10.619ᵃ |
| | (5.485)ᵃ | (0.037) | (−0.103) | (0.178) | (0.178) | (−0.522) | | |

NOTES: Figures in parentheses are *t* statistics.
Significance levels are denoted by: a(1%), b(5%) and c(10%).

the UK, these latter for which DFPOUT is, respectively, negatively related
and unrelated to research intensity.

Capital intensity, in its naive product cycle interpretation (favouring exports over DFPOUT) is rejected by all our results. As hypothesised for
the USA and UK, this variable is found to promote DFPOUT, supporting the
contention that indigenous firms do enjoy advantaged access to capital,
whatever the source of this advantage might be. This positive association
extends to LFPOUT for the US alone, indicating that US firms' technology is
characteristically capital-intensive in orientation.

Japanese technology licensing is consistent with high operative skills
industries, as well as being characteristically research-intensive, unlike
Japanese outward DFP. Such a pattern might reflect the allure of more sophisticated product markets, which cannot be serviced from Japan.

The hypotheses for WSNONOP gain some support, although the pattern of
significance is erratic. The relative promotion of DFPOUT over EXP is supported other than for the US and Sweden, as is that for DFPOUT and LFPOUT
with the exception of Sweden, and where NONOP attains significance it also
favours DFPOUT over EXP (for Japan, Sweden and Germany).

On the internalisation hypothesis, only the UK returns a significant
result which runs counter to expectations for the other countries. One reasons
why LFPOUT may be positively related to NONOP is if this variable were capturing UK
marketing advantages (brand names and trade marks) transferred by contract.
Otherwise the UK equations are singularly lacking in significance, for DFPOUT
and even LFPOUT with respect to research intensity, indicating that an
alternate model is indeed required for the UK.

The conclusion of Horst (1972) regarding the partial substitutability
of US DFI and exports is extended here to licensing, as the significance of

the total equation, INTPRODOUT, is the highest.  This result also applies
to Germany, but not the other countries.

The finding that research intensity favours US exports over DFP (Lall,
1980) is not quite reproduced, possibly as a consequence of the inclusion of
two additional years.  Nevertheless, the coefficients obtained are not
greatly at variance with those supporting Lall's interpretation of the product cycle.

Japan's early DFI is known to have been in standardised-technology and
labour-intensive products, and the equations estimated here give confirmation
of this, although this cannot extend to the Kojima hypothesis (Kojima, 1973;
1978; 1982) other than as an historical account.

A significant role for research intensity is endorsed by the Swedish
equations, but surprisingly not for skills, which have been viewed as par-
ticuarly central to Swedish firms' competitiveness abroad (Swedenborg, 1979),
although a total skills variable (not reported) does just attain significance
at ten per cent as a promoter of outward DFP.  The cause of this conflict
might be the aggregation of firms to the industry groups used here, in which
case the highest skills may be more characteristic of the smaller foreign
investors.

Consistent with expectations, the German equations do suggest a meaningful distinction between managerial and operative skills, with the latter positively related to exports and negatively to DFPOUT and the former positively
related to DFPOUT, confirming some differential international transferability
between the two.

International Differences in Competition

Here formal tests are made of the differences in the outward models between

TABLE 4   *Chow tests of international stability in the outward equations*

Tests in the total outward production equations (INTPRODOUT)

| | All countries | US | Japan | UK | Sweden |
|---|---|---|---|---|---|
| *All countries* | 5.906[a] | | | | |
| *US* | | | | | |
| *Japan* | | 7.612[a] | | | |
| *UK* | | 4.144[a] | 6.545[a] | | |
| *Sweden* | | 3.554[a] | 2.251[c] | 2.913[b] | |
| *FGR* | | 13.719[c] | 4.851[a] | 5.979[a] | 1.226 |

Tests in the export equation (EXP)

| | All countries | US | Japan | UK | Sweden |
|---|---|---|---|---|---|
| *All countries* | 8.227[a] | | | | |
| *US* | | | | | |
| *Japan* | | 5.129[a] | | | |
| *UK* | | 2.401[b] | 5.248[a] | | |
| *Sweden* | | 7.923[a] | 1.981[c] | 0.594 | |
| *FGR* | | 18.994[a] | 5.601[a] | 1.063 | 0.684 |

Tests in the outward direct foreign production equations (DFPOUT)

| | All countries | US | Japan | UK | Sweden |
|---|---|---|---|---|---|
| *All countries* | 7.763[a] | | | | |
| *US* | | | | | |
| *Japan* | | 7.042[a] | | | |
| *UK* | | 2.824[b] | 8.520[a] | | |
| *Sweden* | | 2.659[b] | 4.002[a] | 6.220[a] | |
| *FGR* | | 3.232[b] | 5.829[a] | 9.450[a] | 3.209[b] |

Tests in the outward licensed foreign production equation (LFPOUT)

| | All countries | US | Japan | UK | Sweden |
|---|---|---|---|---|---|
| *All countries* | 2.245[a] | | | | |
| *US* | | | | | |
| *Japan* | | 2.360[b] | | | |
| *UK* | | 1.356 | 2.709[b] | | |
| *Sweden* | | 0.883 | 3.131[b] | 0.886 | |
| *FGR* | | 0.930 | 0.757 | 1.996[c] | 0.870 |

NOTES: Values shown are F ratios.
Significance levels are denoted by: a(1%), b(5%) and c(10%).

countries, so extending the observations made above. Table 4 presents Chow
tests for the hypothesis of equality between the set of coefficients in
pairs of equations.

In thirty-four of the forty-four tests the hypothesis is rejected; no
common equation exists for all five countries, while few of the bilateral tests
find equality either. Of the ten cases of equality, six are for the outward
licensing equations. DFPOUT is the one model where no similarity is found
at all, endorsing those researchers who recognised the idiosyncratic nature
of single-country studies.

Dummy variables testing for the equality of individual coefficients
represent more searching tests of international differences. Those in Table
5 report these for countries as compared with the US (and can be viewed as a
more detailed breakdown of the 'all countries' cell in the Chow tests) while
those in Table 6 present the instances of significance in bilateral tests.

The strength of the research intensity hypothesis in explaining outward
competition is clearly lowest for the UK and Japan. US exports are found to
be significantly more capital-intensive than those of the other countries,
thus agreeing with the traditional factor-proportions stylisation of US trade,
although to a certain extent a similar contrast applies to UK imports. The
same variable is confirmed as especially characteristic of US and UK outward
DFP, but as least so for Japan and Sweden. It also transpires that German
outward DFP, while not itself capital-intensive, is placed least behind the
US and UK.

The low incidence of significant differences across the skills and
managerial complexity variables is largely a consequence of insignificant
coefficients in the original regressions. Nonetheless, skills may provide an
alternate foundation for DFI, and in tests for international equality in a
total skills variable (not reported) both DFPOUT and EXP are found to be

## 15

TABLE 5  *Tests of international stability in the coefficients for the outward equations*

Test of the total outward production equation (INTPRODOUT)

|        | RDEXP | NTFA | WSOP | WSNO-NOP | NONOP | Constant |
|--------|-------|------|------|----------|-------|----------|
| *Japan*  | −2.505[a] | −3.329[b] | 2.554[a] | −0.408 | −2.790[a] | −1.910[b] |
| *UK*     | −2.119[b] | −1.238 | 0.349 | 0.818 | 0.308 | −1.362[c] |
| *Sweden* | 0.913 | −2.481[a] | 1.602[c] | 0.021 | −1.147 | −0.868 |
| *FGR*    | −1.215 | −2.604[a] | 1.197 | 0.442 | −0.386 | −1.269 |

Test of the export equation (EXP)

|        | RDEXP | NTFA | WSOP | WSNO-NOP | NONOP | Constant |
|--------|-------|------|------|----------|-------|----------|
| *Japan*  | −0.680 | −2.762[a] | 2.933[a] | −1.485[c] | −3.607[a] | −0.473 |
| *UK*     | −0.745 | −1.390[c] | 0.444 | 0.388 | −0.097 | −0.470 |
| *Sweden* | 0.915 | −1.442[c] | 1.230 | −0.309 | −1.246 | −0.085 |
| *FGR*    | −0.787 | −2.179[c] | 1.207 | −0.215 | −0.337 | −0.136 |

Test of the outward direct foreign production equation (DFPOUT)

|        | RDEXP | NTFA | WSOP | WSNO-NOP | NONOP | Constant |
|--------|-------|------|------|----------|-------|----------|
| *Japan*  | −3.838[a] | −2.765[a] | 0.983 | 0.706 | −0.018 | −2.079[b] |
| *UK*     | −2.182[b] | −0.648 | −0.408 | 1.086 | 0.479 | −1.328[b] |
| *Sweden* | 1.018 | −1.594[c] | 1.073 | 0.271 | −0.172 | −0.839 |
| *FGR*    | −0.802 | −1.189 | −0.410 | 1.348[c] | −0.656 | −1.752[b] |

Test of the outward licensed foreign production equation (LFPOUT)

|        | RDEXP | NTFA | WSOP | WSNO-NOP | NONOP | Constant |
|--------|-------|------|------|----------|-------|----------|
| *Japan*  | 0.666 | 0.121 | 1.192 | −0.364 | 0.381 | −0.273 |
| *UK*     | −1.636[c] | −0.166 | −0.713 | 0.786 | 1.898[b] | −0.390 |
| *Sweden* | −0.564 | −0.978 | −0.911 | 0.806 | 0.756 | −0.307 |
| *FGR*    | 0.187 | −0.625 | 0.230 | 0.335 | 0.323 | −0.453 |

NOTES: Values shown are *t* statistics.
Significance levels are denoted by: a(1%), b(5%) and c(10%).

TABLE 6 Bilateral tests of the international stability in the outward equations

### INTPRODOUT

(a) Compared with Japan

| | RDEXP | NTFA | WSOP | WSNO-NOP | NONOP | Constant |
|---|---|---|---|---|---|---|
| UK | 0.993 | 3.375c | -3.040a | 2.149b | 4.367a | 1.338c |
| Sweden | 2.832a | 0.934 | -0.750 | 0.481 | 1.314c | 1.610 |
| FGR | 2.958a | 1.244 | -2.045b | 1.818b | 3.997a | 2.005b |

(b) Compared with the UK

| | RDEXP | NTFA | WSOP | WSNO-NOP | NONOP | Constant |
|---|---|---|---|---|---|---|
| Sweden | 2.675a | -1.155c | 1.004 | -0.840 | -1.196 | 0.750 |
| FGR | 2.246b | -2.468a | 1.278 | -0.834 | -1.144 | 0.368 |

(c) Compared with Sweden

| | RDEXP | NTFA | WSOP | WSNO-NOP | NONOP | Constant |
|---|---|---|---|---|---|---|
| FGR | -2.096b | -0.252 | -0.342 | 0.498 | 0.727 | -0.642 |

### EXP

(a) Compared with Japan

| | RDEXP | NTFA | WSOP | WSNO-NOP | NONOP | Constant |
|---|---|---|---|---|---|---|
| UK | 0.025 | 2.081b | -3.012a | 2.795a | 4.405a | -0.008 |
| Sweden | 1.372a | 1.261 | -1.403b | 1.385b | 1.960a | 0.629 |
| FGR | 0.074 | 0.864 | -2.220b | 2.367b | 4.619a | 0.888 |

(b) Compared with the UK

| | RDEXP | NTFA | WSOP | WSNO-NOP | NONOP | Constant |
|---|---|---|---|---|---|---|
| Sweden | 1.609b | -0.132 | 0.678 | -0.762 | -1.035 | 0.615 |
| FGR | 0.060 | -1.428c | 1.047 | -1.071 | -0.344 | 0.899 |

(c) Compared with Sweden

| | RDEXP | NTFA | WSOP | WSNO-NOP | NONOP | Constant |
|---|---|---|---|---|---|---|
| FGR | -1.841b | -0.749 | -0.031 | 0.129 | 0.921 | -0.089 |

### DFPOUT

(a) Compared with Japan

| | RDEXP | NTFA | WSOP | WSNO-NOP | NONOP | Constant |
|---|---|---|---|---|---|---|
| UK | 2.501a | 2.684a | -1.571b | 0.626 | 0.521 | 1.529c |
| Sweden | 4.433a | 1.211 | 0.076 | -0.540 | -0.124 | 2.108b |
| FGR | 4.872a | 1.824b | -1.628c | 1.045 | -0.682 | 0.832 |

(b) Compared with the UK

| | RDEXP | NTFA | WSOP | WSNO-NOP | NONOP | Constant |
|---|---|---|---|---|---|---|
| Sweden | 3.031a | -0.925 | 1.262 | -0.940 | -0.553 | 0.796 |
| FGR | 2.408a | -0.757 | -0.003 | 0.230 | -1.420c | -0.833 |

(c) Compared with Sweden

| | RDEXP | NTFA | WSOP | WSNO-NOP | NONOP | Constant |
|---|---|---|---|---|---|---|
| FGR | -1.956b | 0.254 | -1.287 | 1.352c | -0.393 | -1.584c |

### LFPOUT

(a) Compared with Japan

| | RDEXP | NTFA | WSOP | WSNO-NOP | NONOP | Constant |
|---|---|---|---|---|---|---|
| UK | -2.484a | -0.273 | -1.913b | 1.480b | 1.361c | -0.229 |
| Sweden | -1.367b | -1.047 | -2.230b | 1.760b | 0.353 | -0.073 |
| FGR | -0.715 | -0.712 | -1.030 | 1.070 | -0.126 | -0.384 |

(b) Compared with the UK

| | RDEXP | NTFA | WSOP | WSNO-NOP | NONOP | Constant |
|---|---|---|---|---|---|---|
| Sweden | 0.992 | -0.817 | -0.187 | -0.045 | -0.958 | 0.146 |
| FGR | 2.397a | -0.466 | 0.850 | -0.581 | -1.620c | -0.090 |

(c) Compared with Sweden

| | RDEXP | NTFA | WSOP | WSNO-NOP | NONOP | Constant |
|---|---|---|---|---|---|---|
| FGR | 0.908 | 0.269 | 1.077 | -0.657 | -0.490 | -0.270 |

NOTES: Values shown are t statistics.
Significance levels are denoted by: a(1%), b(5%) and c(10%).

significantly more intensive in skills for the other countries as compared

with the US.


Inward Equations

Table 7 presents the inward equations, which record generally lower levels of

significance than their outward counterparts, reflecting the diminished

robustness of using industrial data as host rather than home-country variables

- a fact which might invite problems of multicollinearity.  Of the hundred

regression coefficients, excluding the constants, thirty-four are significant,

although again, not always as anticipated.

     The basic research-intensity hypothesis for inward DFP is confirmed for

Japan, the UK and Germany.  The finding of no relationship for the US supports

that of Lall and Siddarthan (1982) while the negative result for Sweden con-

flicts with that of Samuelsson (1977).  In the present study we infer that

MNEs enter where they are technologically advantaged and, with respect to the

negative signs on operative skills, where they face the least adaptation

costs.  Because US and Swedish average research and operative skills levels

are the highest, this generates characteristically inter-industry type inward

DFI.  The contradiction with the earlier Swedish study may arise because of

the aggregation of source countries in the current investigation in which case the

negative relationship exists with respect to European rather than to US DFI

into Sweden.

     Capital intensity is found to explain inward DFP only for the USA, and

LFP with the addition of Sweden.  This leads to the conclusion that capital

access is a distinguishing advantage of MNEs entering the US, while US and

Swedish industries are founded on capital-intensive technologies.

     Operative skills promotes inward licensing in Japan and Germany, reflect-

ing the role of production workers' assimilative capacity in the acquisition of

TABLE 7 *Multiple regression results for the inward equations*

| | RDEXP | NTFA | WSOP | WSNONOP | NONOP | Constant | $R^2$ | F. Stat. |
|---|---|---|---|---|---|---|---|---|
| **USA** | | | | | | | | |
| INTPRODIN | 0.119 | 0.814 | −2.634 | 1.798 | −0.001 | −2.895 | 0.539 | 4.917[b] |
| | (0.966) | (4.364)[a] | (−2.546)[a] | (0.924) | (−0.001) | (−0.956) | | |
| IMP | 0.035 | 0.202 | −1.127 | 1.760 | −0.426 | −5.904 | 0.216 | 1.154 |
| | (0.207) | (0.783) | (−0.788) | (0.654) | (−0.577) | (−1.410)[c] | | |
| DFPIN | −0.205 | 1.812 | −8.735 | 5.385 | 2.641 | −0.979 | 0.446 | 3.386[c] |
| | (−0.480) | (2.806)[a] | (−2.440)[b] | (0.799) | (1.430)[c] | (−0.094) | | |
| LFPIN | 0.825 | 1.422 | −2.259 | −3.679 | −1.052 | 5.590 | 0.548 | 5.097[b] |
| | (2.952)[a] | (3.357)[a] | (−0.962) | (−0.832) | (−0.868) | (0.828) | | |
| **Japan** | | | | | | | | |
| INTPRODIN | 0.741 | 0.012 | −0.506 | 0.388 | 1.179 | 2.087 | 0.744 | 12.189[a] |
| | (5.851)[a] | (0.048) | (−0.450) | (0.310) | (1.797)[b] | (1.630)[c] | | |
| IMP | 0.256 | 0.136 | −0.231 | 0.103 | 1.674 | −0.877 | 0.262 | 1.490 |
| | (1.618)[c] | (0.433) | (−0.164) | (0.066) | (2.042)[b] | (−0.548) | | |
| DFPIN | 1.419 | 0.434 | −1.021 | −0.090 | 3.322 | 5.849 | 0.741 | 12.027[a] |
| | (6.597)[a] | (1.019) | (−0.534) | (−0.042) | (2.979)[a] | (2.689)[a] | | |
| LFPIN | 1.586 | −1.029 | 8.040 | −7.959 | −3.539 | 4.406) | 0.800 | 16.752[a] |
| | (5.550)[a] | (−1.818)[b] | (3.166)[a] | (−2.816)[a] | (−2.389)[b] | (1.062) | | |
| **UK** | | | | | | | | |
| INTPRODIN | 0.061 | 0.073 | 0.380 | 1.162 | 0.034 | −3.052 | 0.423 | 3.082 |
| | (0.814) | (0.547) | (0.427) | (0.904) | (0.082) | (−2.608)[a] | | |
| IMP | −0.259 | 0.016 | −1.161 | 2.534 | 0.533 | −4.720 | 0.371 | 2.473 |
| | (−2.607)[a] | (0.091) | (−0.986) | (1.492)[c] | (0.971) | (−3.054)[a] | | |
| DFPIN | 0.411 | 0.220 | 1.657 | 0.501 | −0.517 | −3.801 | 0.636 | 7.341[b] |
| | (3.716)[a] | (1.125) | (1.264) | (0.265) | (−0.847) | (−2.210)[b] | | |
| LFPIN | 0.022 | 0.041 | −3.020 | 1.807 | 3.326 | 0.729 | 0.418 | 3.013 |
| | (0.108) | (0.113) | (−1.228) | (0.510) | (2.902)[a] | (0.226) | | |
| **Sweden** | | | | | | | | |
| INTPRODIN | 0.448 | −0.135 | −6.182 | 6.782 | −0.734 | −3.606 | 0.761 | 13.341[a] |
| | (3.394)[a] | (−0.636) | (−4.958)[a] | (5.042)[a] | (−1.108) | (−2.496)[b] | | |
| IMP | 0.588 | −0.242 | −6.040 | 6.622 | −1.496 | −3.942 | 0.741 | 12.006[a] |
| | (3.810)[a] | (−0.975) | (−4.145)[a] | (4.212)[a] | (−1.932)[b] | (−2.334)[b] | | |
| DFPIN | −0.366 | 0.560 | −11.530 | 13.290 | 3.578 | −9.640 | 0.625 | 7.010[b] |
| | (−1.367)[c] | (1.297) | (−4.555)[a] | (4.867)[a] | (2.660)[a] | (−3.286)[a] | | |
| LFPIN | 0.574 | 0.681 | −4.150 | 3.801 | 0.138 | −3.858 | 0.706 | 10.084[a] |
| | (3.564)[a] | (2.626)[a] | (−2.729)[a] | (2.316)[a] | (0.170) | (−2.189)[b] | | |
| **Federal Republic of Germany** | | | | | | | | |
| INTPRODIN | 0.068 | −0.056 | −0.444 | 1.470 | −0.389 | −3.320 | 0.710 | 10.276[a] |
| | (1.980)[b] | (−0.433) | (−0.698) | (2.216)[b] | (−1.508)[c] | (−4.928)[a] | | |
| IMP | −0.048 | −0.233 | −0.818 | 1.749 | −0.688 | −4.745 | 0.505 | 4.286[c] |
| | (−1.089) | (−1.419)[c] | (−1.019) | (2.086)[b] | (−2.108)[b] | (−5.571)[a] | | |
| DFPIN | 0.144 | 0.014 | 1.589 | −0.362 | 0.676 | −2.005 | 0.693 | 9.469[b] |
| | (1.974)[b] | (0.051) | (1.186) | (−0.259) | (1.244) | (−1.412)[c] | | |
| LFPIN | 0.534 | 0.086 | 5.458 | −6.094 | 1.713 | 3.281 | 0.737 | 11.768[a] |
| | (4.522)[a] | (0.195) | (2.516)[b] | (−2.692)[a] | (1.945)[b] | (1.427)[c] | | |

NOTES: Figures in parentheses are *t* statistics.
Significance levels are denoted by: a(1%), b(5%) and c(10%).

technology. The managerial skills hypotheses, however, receive support only
for Swedish inward DFP and licensing, while those for complexity of management
are supported for the US, Sweden and Japan, although the latter's data remain
suspect as noted earlier.

Technology, rather than capital, appears to enable inward DFI into
Japan, testifying to the regulation and guidance of inward investment in
technology-intensive sectors by the host government. In the UK regressions
only the DFPIN equation attains any significance, with the dependent variable,
as hypothesised,. is positively related to research intensity. Neither skills
hypothesis is supported, although if combined to one variable (not reported)
this does attain a positive significance (at five per cent) implicating some
problems of multicollinearity.

In general Germany's inward and outward competition are both characterised
by research intensity. As with the UK, only research intensity is significant
in the DFPIN equation, while the skills variables also have to be combined
before any significance is attained. Inward licensing, however, is found to
associate with operative skills-intensive industries, signifying the infusion
of foreign technology into those already sophisticated domestic industries
where assimilative capacity is highest. The positive signs of NONOP in both
the UK and German LFPIN equations may result from a hidden relationship with
marketing intensity, but this can only be speculation.

## International Differences in Competition

The Chow tests presented in Table 8 reveal an even lower degree of concordance
than those for the outward equations, a fact which may be partly attributable
to the more extensive governmental regulation of inward competition. In all
but six equations the hypothesis of equality is rejected, and of these
licensing accounts for only two.

TABLE 8 *Chow tests of international stability in the inward equations*

Tests in the total inward production equations (INTPRODIN)

| | All countries | US | Japan | UK | Sweden |
|---|---|---|---|---|---|
| All countries | 23.063ᵃ | | | | |
| US | | | | | |
| Japan | | 7.664ᵃ | | | |
| UK | | 8.174ᵃ | 11.125ᵃ | | |
| Sweden | | 22.450ᵃ | 4.622ᵃ | 9.202ᵃ | |
| FGR | | 34.439ᵃ | 6.769ᵃ | 1.763 | 8.381ᵃ |

Tests in the import equations (IMP)

| | All countries | US | Japan | UK | Sweden |
|---|---|---|---|---|---|
| All countries | 16.488ᵃ | | | | |
| US | | | | | |
| Japan | | 1.534 | | | |
| UK | | 4.596ᵃ | 8.109ᵃ | | |
| Sweden | | 17.571ᵃ | 7.420ᵃ | 9.015ᵃ | |
| FGR | | 13.413ᵃ | 3.970ᵃ | 3.071ᵇ | 9.716ᵃ |

Tests in the inward direct foreign production equations (DFPIN)

| | All countries | US | Japan | UK | Sweden |
|---|---|---|---|---|---|
| All countries | 11.557ᵃ | | | | |
| US | | | | | |
| Japan | | 6.065ᵃ | | | |
| UK | | 5.012ᵃ | 12.251ᵃ | | |
| Sweden | | 1.575 | 6.381ᵃ | 10.116ᵃ | |
| FGR | | 9.273ᵃ | 9.479ᵃ | 1.035 | 14.256ᵃ |

Tests in the inward licensed foreign production equations (LFPIN)

| | All countries | US | Japan | UK | Sweden |
|---|---|---|---|---|---|
| All countries | 6.926ᵃ | | | | |
| US | | | | | |
| Japan | | 9.924ᵃ | | | |
| UK | | 2.732ᵇ | 7.902ᵃ | | |
| Sweden | | 7.375ᵃ | 6.564ᵃ | 1.055 | |
| FGR | | 5.968ᵃ | 6.886ᵃ | 1.887 | 3.152ᵇ |

NOTES: Values shown are F ratios.
Significance levels are denoted by: a(1%), b(5%) and c(10%).

The more detailed tests for individual coefficients are reported in Tables 9 and 10. These highlight the distinctive capital intensity of US inward DFI and licensing; however the general lack of significance in the US skills variables precludes any compelling international comparisons. Nevertheless, it does appear that, bar Sweden (which resembles the US), the other countries received inward DFI in industries where the host's operative skills were highest.

The low significance of the UK equations permits only the observation that UK inward DFP ranks second only to Japan in terms of the role of research intensity, a feature which probably reflects the attraction the UK has exerted on US MNEs.

Swedish imports, while research-intensive, are the least capital-intensive (in host terms) which may reflect their low natural resource content, Sweden being relatively abundant in natural resources. In view of the earlier discussion on Swedish DFPIN it is likely, from Tables 9 and 10, that European rather than US DFI into Sweden is in the least research-intensive industries. The equations obtained for Germany, it appears, are not strongly idiosyncratic, occupying the middle ground in these findings.

Evolution of International Competition Over Time

The methodology adopted in this paper requires that the time stability of the equations be tested in order to justify the pooling procedure. While a general rejection of the stability assumption would be a serious matter, any limited changes may provide valuable insights into the dynamics of international competition.

There are only three equations where general instability is indicated by Chow tests, two of which are for the US (DFPOUT and IMP) although a close inspection of these two does not permit any meaningful conclusions to be drawn,

22

TABLE 9 *Tests of international stability in the coefficients for the inward equations*

Test of the total inward production equation (INTPRODIN)

| | RDEXP | NTFA | WSOP | WSNO-NOP | NONOP | Constant |
|---|---|---|---|---|---|---|
| Japan | 3.672ᵃ | −2.723ᵃ | 1.457ᶜ | −0.617 | 1.472ᶜ | 1.510ᶜ |
| UK | −0.382 | −3.089ᵃ | 2.093ᵇ | −0.261 | 0.049 | −0.047 |
| Sweden | 1.997ᵇ | −3.704ᵃ | −2.433ᵃ | 2.200 | −0.961 | −0.215 |
| FGR | −0.369 | −3.148ᵃ | 1.518ᵃ | −0.146 | −0.575 | −0.130 |

Test of the import equation (IMP)

| | RDEXP | NTFA | WSOP | WSNO-NOP | NONOP | Constant |
|---|---|---|---|---|---|---|
| Japan | 0.713 | −0.265 | 0.218 | 0.657 | 2.755ᵃ | 0.905 |
| UK | −2.509ᵃ | −0.311 | 0.738 | 0.293 | 1.374ᶜ | −0.033 |
| Sweden | 2.024ᵇ | −2.292ᵇ | 0.223 | 1.154 | −0.513 | 1.233 |
| FGR | −1.975ᵇ | −1.837ᵇ | 1.002 | 1.230 | 0.482 | −0.164 |

Test of the inward direct foreign production equation (DFPIN)

| | RDEXP | NTFA | WSOP | WSNO-NOP | NONOP | Constant |
|---|---|---|---|---|---|---|
| Japan | 4.281ᵃ | −2.088ᵇ | 2.359ᵃ | −1.070 | 0.379 | 0.924 |
| UK | 1.827ᵇ | −2.961ᵃ | 3.222ᵃ | −0.894 | −1.984ᵇ | −0.376 |
| Sweden | −0.438 | −2.181ᵇ | −0.856 | 1.557ᶜ | 0.548 | −1.169 |
| FGR | 1.138 | −2.904ᵃ | 3.195ᵃ | −1.146 | −1.299ᶜ | −0.140 |

Test of the inward licensed foreign production equation (LFPIN)

| | RDEXP | NTFA | WSOP | WSNO-NOP | NONOP | Constant |
|---|---|---|---|---|---|---|
| Japan | 2.018ᵇ | −3.735ᵃ | 3.167ᵃ | −0.841 | −1.393ᶜ | −0.221 |
| UK | −2.394ᵃ | −2.581ᵃ | −0.237 | 1.010 | 2.765ᵃ | −0.655 |
| Sweden | −0.685 | −1.296ᶜ | −0.582 | 1.482 | 0.700 | −1.296ᶜ |
| FGR | −0.956 | −2.168ᵇ | 2.402ᵃ | −0.484 | 1.837ᵇ | −0.331 |

NOTES: Values shown are *t* statistics.
Significance levels are denoted by: a(1%), b(5%) and c(10%).

**TABLE 10** *Bilateral tests of the international stability in the inward equations*

### INTPRODIN
(a) Compared with Japan

|        | RDEXP     | NTFA   | WSOP    | WSNO-NOP | NONOP    | Constant |
|--------|-----------|--------|---------|----------|----------|----------|
| UK     | -4.752[a] | 0.222  | 0.620   | 0.422    | -1.511   | -2.930[a]|
| Sweden | -1.596[c] | -0.442 | -3.379[a]| 3.474[a] | -2.041[b]| -2.952[a]|
| FGR    | -5.877[a] | -0.248 | 0.049   | 0.781    | -2.420[a]| -3.826[a]|

(b) Compared with the UK

|        | RDEXP     | NTFA   | WSOP    | WSNO-NOP | NONOP    | Constant |
|--------|-----------|--------|---------|----------|----------|----------|
| Sweden | 2.636[a]  | -0.849 | -4.299[a]| 2.901[a] | -1.005   | -0.294   |
| FGR    | 0.092     | -0.658 | -0.752  | 0.223    | -0.884   | -0.205   |

(c) Compared with Sweden

|        | RDEXP     | NTFA   | WSOP    | WSNO-NOP | NONOP    | Constant |
|--------|-----------|--------|---------|----------|----------|----------|
| FGR    | -3.221[a] | 0.304  | 4.127[a]| -3.598[a]| 0.523    | 0.185    |

### IMP
(a) Compared with Japan

|        | RDEXP     | NTFA   | WSOP    | WSNO-NOP | NONOP    | Constant |
|--------|-----------|--------|---------|----------|----------|----------|
| UK     | -2.716[a] | 0.031  | 0.776   | 0.376    | -1.540[a]| -1.356[c]|
| Sweden | 1.498[b]  | -0.940 | -2.869[a]| 2.937[a] | -2.806[a]| -1.318[b]|
| FGR    | -2.118[b] | -1.070 | -0.365  | 0.947    | -2.908[a]| -2.184[b]|

(b) Compared with the UK

|        | RDEXP     | NTFA   | WSOP    | WSNO-NOP | NONOP    | Constant |
|--------|-----------|--------|---------|----------|----------|----------|
| Sweden | 4.718[a]  | -0.861 | -2.611[a]| 1.724[b] | -2.168[a]| 0.337    |
| FGR    | 2.090[b]  | -0.975 | 0.240   | -0.437   | -1.958[b]| -0.015   |

(c) Compared with Sweden

|        | RDEXP     | NTFA   | WSOP    | WSNO-NOP | NONOP    | Constant |
|--------|-----------|--------|---------|----------|----------|----------|
| FGR    | -4.532[a] | 0.031  | 3.157[a]| -2.775[a]| 1.031    | -0.437   |

### DFPIN
(a) Compared with Japan

|        | RDEXP     | NTFA   | WSOP    | WSNO-NOP | NONOP    | Constant |
|--------|-----------|--------|---------|----------|----------|----------|
| UK     | -4.374[a] | -0.487 | 1.161   | 0.200    | -3.143[a]| -3.414[a]|
| Sweden | -5.150[a] | 0.200  | -3.312[a]| 3.847[a] | 0.145    | -4.251[a]|
| FGR    | -6.156[a] | -0.845 | 1.123   | -0.108   | -2.254[a]| -3.070[a]|

(b) Compared with the UK

|        | RDEXP     | NTFA   | WSOP    | WSNO-NOP | NONOP    | Constant |
|--------|-----------|--------|---------|----------|----------|----------|
| Sweden | -2.861[a] | 0.749  | -4.661[a]| 3.563[a] | 2.891[a] | -1.670[c]|
| FGR    | -2.009[b] | -0.615 | -0.036  | -0.366   | 1.458[c] | 0.804    |

(c) Compared with Sweden

|        | RDEXP     | NTFA   | WSOP    | WSNO-NOP | NONOP    | Constant |
|--------|-----------|--------|---------|----------|----------|----------|
| FGR    | 2.116[b]  | -1.022 | 4.610[a]| -4.518[a]| -2.150[a]| 2.413[a] |

### LFPIN
(a) Compared with Japan

|        | RDEXP     | NTFA     | WSOP    | WSNO-NOP | NONOP    | Constant |
|--------|-----------|----------|---------|----------|----------|----------|
| UK     | -4.428[a] | 1.588[c] | -3.129[a]| 2.153[b] | 3.666[a] | -0.769   |
| Sweden | -3.133[a] | 2.912[a] | -4.121[a]| 3.627[b] | 2.227[b] | -2.331[b]|
| FGR    | -3.542[a] | 1.564[c] | -0.775  | 0.518    | 3.120    | -0.213   |

(b) Compared with the UK

|        | RDEXP     | NTFA   | WSOP    | WSNO-NOP | NONOP    | Constant |
|--------|-----------|--------|---------|----------|----------|----------|
| Sweden | 1.973[b]  | 1.370  | -0.388  | 0.540    | -2.189[b]| -1.275   |
| FGR    | 2.197[b]  | 0.076  | 2.585[a]| -1.915[b]| -1.126   | 0.652    |

(c) Compared with Sweden

|        | RDEXP     | NTFA   | WSOP    | WSNO-NOP | NONOP    | Constant |
|--------|-----------|--------|---------|----------|----------|----------|
| FGR    | -0.177    | -1.192 | 3.611[a]| -3.503[a]| 1.248    | 2.414[a] |

NOTES: Values shown are *t* statistics.
Significance levels are denoted by: a(1%), b(5%) and c(10%).

24

TABLE 11 *Selected tests of time stability in the coefficients of Japanese equations*

Outward direct foreign production (DFPOUT)

| | RDEXP | NTFA | WSOP | WSNO-NOP | NONOP | Constant |
|---|---|---|---|---|---|---|
| 1975 and 1965 | 2.816ʰ | 1.488ᶜ | − 0.944 | − 0.157 | 0.917 | 2.464ʰ |
| 1970 | 0.964 | 1.057 | − 1.058 | 0.559 | 0.824 | 0.729 |
| 1975 and 1970 | 1.565ᶜ | 0.285 | 0.169 | − 0.565 | 0.044 | 1.494ᶜ |
| 1970 and 1965 | 1.271 | 1.394 | − 1.396 | 0.738 | 1.087 | 0.962 |

Inward licensed foreign production (LFPIN)

| | RDEXP | NTFA | WSOP | WSNO-NOP | NONOP | Constant |
|---|---|---|---|---|---|---|
| 1975 and 1965 | − 2.299ʰ | 1.508 | − 2.793ʰ | 2.279ʰ | 2.651ʰ | − 0.687 |
| 1970 | − 1.982ʰ | 0.920 | − 1.581ᶜ | 1.448ᶜ | 1.451ᶜ | − 0.932 |
| 1975 and 1970 | − 0.691 | 1.670ᶜ | − 2.984ʰ | 2.048ʰ | 3.567ᵃ | 0.685 |
| 1970 and 1965 | − 1.653ᶜ | 0.768 | − 1.319 | 1.208 | 1.210 | − 0.778 |

NOTES: Values shown are *t* statistics.
Significance levels are denoted by: a(1%), b(5%) and c(10%).

602 *Multinational Corporations*

25

and so they are not reported. More rewarding is an investigation into the Japanese LFPIN equation, presented in Table 11, together with tests on the DFPIN equation, within which a limited instability is recorded.

The relaxation of governmental control over the industrial allocation of licensing contracts is witnessed by the decline in the role of research intensity in the LFPIN equation. This inference is supported by the increasing coefficients on managerial skills and complexity, capital intensity and the decline in operative skills.

There is evidence that DFPOUT has become more technology-intensive, both in 1975 and 1970 and over the period as a whole; coupled with this, the increase in capital intensity demonstrates that Japanese MNEs as a group have become more research and capital-intensive in their DFI. Such findings falsify the hypothesis on which Kojima's theory of Japanese DFI is based.

Locational and Country-Specific Factors: Insights from the Correlation of the Residuals

The theoretically important variables omitted from this study are locational and country-specific in nature. Some inference on their identity and importance can be made from an inspection of correlations between the residuals, and from the industries involved.

Table 12 reports the results for the outward equations. The positive US DFPOUT and EXP correlation arises mainly from high-technology products, possibly caused by the US country-specific advantage (demand leadership) as argued in the PC model, causing different generations of products to raise both exports to and DFI in Europe and Canada as their markets expand. The similar Japanese correlation derives from low indigenous locational and country-specific ownership advantages in resource-intensive sectors, coupled with the staged migration of maturing and obsolescent industries from Japan to South-East Asian hosts.

Low exports caused by UK locational disadvantages are linked with low

TABLE 12 *Correlations of the residuals between outward equations*

|  | EXP | DFPOUT | LFPOUT |
|---|---|---|---|
| **USA** | | | |
| EXP | 1.000 | | |
| DFPOUT | 0.480[b] | 1.000 | |
| LFPOUT | 0.202 | −0.055 | 1.000 |
| **Japan** | | | |
| EXP | 1.000 | | |
| DFPOUT | 0.410[b] | 1.000 | |
| LFPOUT | 0.115 | 0.153 | 1.000 |
| **UK** | | | |
| EXP | 1.000 | | |
| DFPOUT | −0.254 | 1.000 | |
| LFPOUT | 0.326[c] | 0.227 | 1.000 |
| **Sweden** | | | |
| EXP | 1.000 | | |
| DFPOUT | 0.625[a] | 1.000 | |
| LFPOUT | 0.418[b] | 0.769[a] | 1.000 |
| **FGR** | | | |
| EXP | 1.000 | | |
| DFPOUT | −0.221 | 1.000 | |
| LFPOUT | 0.250 | 0.129 | 1.000 |

NOTES: Values shown are *t* statistics.
Significance levels are denoted by: a(1%), b(5%) and c(10%).

TABLE 13 *Correlations of the residuals between inward equations*

|  | IMP | DFPIN | LFPIN |
|---|---|---|---|
| **USA** | | | |
| IMP | 1.000 | | |
| DFPIN | −0.105 | 1.000 | |
| LFPIN | −0.160 | 0.311 | 1.000 |
| **Japan** | | | |
| IMP | 1.000 | | |
| DFPIN | 0.457[b] | 1.000 | |
| LFPIN | 0.279 | 0.129 | 1.000 |
| **UK** | | | |
| IMP | 1.000 | | |
| DFPIN | 0.305 | 1.000 | |
| LFPIN | 0.480[b] | 0.192 | 1.000 |
| **Sweden** | | | |
| IMP | 1.000 | | |
| DFPIN | 0.077 | 1.000 | |
| LFPIN | 0.606[a] | 0.569[a] | 1.000 |
| **FGR** | | | |
| IMP | 1.000 | | |
| DFPIN | −0.393[c] | 1.000 | |
| LFPIN | 0.130 | 0.226 | 1.000 |

NOTES: Values shown are *t* statistics.
Significance levels are denoted by: a(1%), b(5%) and c(10%).

licensing for two types of industry - those with low ownership advantages and those with ownership advantages exploited abroad primarily by DFI. For Sweden also a central, though positive, role is played by locational factors - being the only country for which the residuals are cross-correlated. Here it is argued that Swedish natural resource advantages have generated trade and country-specific ownership advantages specialised in particular industrial sectors, causing simultaneously high international orientation in all three routes of international competition.

Table 13 reports the correlations for the inward equations, where the first finding is for Japan's IMP and DFPIN. Here the causal locational and country-specific factors appear to apply to two key sets of industries - those high-technology sectors both for which natural resources are lacking and inward DFI is high owing to governmental guidance, and those where high indigenous ownership advantages and trade restrictions deflect both imports and DFI.

The strong presence of foreign marketing-orientated MNEs attracted by the UK market may partly induce the correlation of IMP and LFPIN, together with high residuals for those technology-intensive sectors for which UK locational advantages have declined and in which UK firms are increasing their technological dependence.

Sweden's specialised competitive strengths, noted above, appear to repel inward competition in its major industries, here resulting in positive correlations for all but IMP and DFPIN. Lastly, an import-substituting relationship is revealed for Germany's inward DFP. Moreover, as the German market can be serviced from elsewhere within the European Community (EC) at zero tariff costs, this relationship testifies principally to the attractiveness of Germany itself as a production base within the EC. The industries this applies to are mainly food et al., and transport equipment especially in the earlier period.

CONCLUSIONS

At least up to the mid-1970s national characteristics played a leading role in the international competition of firms and countries. Of the outward routes direct foreign investment feels the greatest impact.

Omissions from the model employed provided some clues as to why this might be, pointing to a possible causal link between locational and country-specific ownership factors, rendering the latter endogenous (Dunning, 1979). The product cycle account of US trade and DFI was itself predicated upon such a class of argument and while it is extended here to licensing, no other country shares the same structure of competition. Indeed, skills feature more prominently in the equations of countries other than the US.

Sweden's natural resources and small size have focused national specialisation, causing unusually high orientation via 'learning by doing' in each route of outward competition. For the US and UK, rather than capturing country-specific differences in savings ratios, the earlier internationalisation of their MNEs may explain better the capital intensity of outward DFI, consistent with the predominance of UK DFI in mature industries. A corollary is that MNEs from other countries will follow a similar path to the US and UK; one example is provided by the increase in capital and research intensity of Japanese MNEs, confirming the conclusion that the Kojima account represents only the static and not the dynamic pattern of Japanese DFI abroad. Of all the countries Germany revealed the least idiosyncratic pattern of competition.

The increased weight given to all types of host factors was thought to generate the greater dissimilarity prevalent among the inward equations. The markedly high (operative) skills levels in the US and Sweden were argued to deflect inward DFI, causing an inter-industry type of entry, intensified by a comparable finding for research intensity. Entry into the US may be instead

based on the capital advantages of foreign MNEs, as enjoyed by those from
the UK, which constitute leading investors.  By contrast Germany is an attractive production location within the EC precisely for technology-intensive products.

The scope for government intervention on inward DFI is very limited.
While beginning in an era of lower economic interdependence, Japan's management of the nature of inward DFI and licensing has given way to a perceptible
liberalisation in licensing.

This formal investigation of countries' equations and international contrasts has supported the theoretical framework adopted.  Even so it is clear
that more inclusive models are required, especially for the UK, where an
alternate model with sales promotional variables appears essential, all of
which highlights the challenge of capturing the full diversity of influences
on international competition.

30

## Notes

1 The main sources of data are: USA - Department of Commerce, National Science Foundation and US Tariff Commission; Japan - Ministry of International Trade and Industry, Ministry of Finance and Bureau of Statistics; UK - Department of Trade and Industry; Sweden - Industriens Utrednings-institut and Statistiska Centralbyrån; Germany - Deutsche Bundesbank, Stiftenverband für die Deutsche Wissenschaft and Statistisches Bundesamt. Other sources include OECD, IMF and UN publications. For further details see Appendices A and B in Clegg (1987).

2 The industrial groups used are: Food, drink and tobacco; Chemicals and allied products; Primary and fabricated metals; Mechanical and instrument engineering; Electrical engineering; Transportation equipment; Textiles, leather, clothing and footwear; Paper, printing and publishing; Other manufacturing industries.

3 For a more extensive discussion of the statistical issues see Clegg (1987, Ch. 4).

## Bibliography

Buckley, P.J. and Casson, M.C. (1976) The Future of the Multinational Enterprise, London: Macmillan.

Buckley, P.J. and Casson, M.C. (1981) 'The Optimal Timing of a Foreign Direct Investment', Economic Journal, 91, March, pp.75-87, reprinted in Buckley, P.J. and Casson, M.C. (1985) The Economic Theory of the Multinational Enterprise, London: Macmillan.

Buckley, P.J. and Davies, H. (1981) 'Foreign Licensing in Overseas Operations: Theory and Evidence from the UK', in Hawkins, R.G. and Prasad, A.J. (eds), Research in International Business and Finance, vol. 2, pp.75-89, Greenwich, Conn.: JAI Press.

Caves, R.E. (1974) 'Multinational Firms, Competition and Host-Country Markets', Economica, 41, May, pp.176-93.

Clegg, J. (1987) Multinational Enterprise and World Competition: A Comparative Study of the USA, Japan, the UK, Sweden and West Germany, London: Macmillan.

Dunning, J.H. (1977) 'Trade, Location of Economic Activity and the MNE: a search for an eclectic approach', ch. 12 in Ohlin, B., Hesselborn, P.-O. and Wijkman, P.M. (eds), The International Allocation of Economic Activity, London: Macmillan.

Dunning, J.H. (1979) 'Explaining changing patterns of international production: in defence of the eclectic theory', Oxford Bulletin of Economics and Statistics, Special Issue: The Multi-National Corporation, 4., no. 4, November, pp.255-67.

Dunning, J.H. (1981) International Production and the Multinational Enterprise, London: Allen & Unwin.

Horst, T. (1972) 'The Industrial Composition of US Exports and Subsidiary Sales to the Canadian Market', American Economic Review, 62, March, pp.37-45.

Kojima, K. (1973) 'A Macroeconomic Approach to Foreign Direct Investment', Hitotsubashi Journal of Economics, 14, June, pp.1-21.

Kojima, K. (1978) Direct Foreign Investment: A Japanese Model of Multinational Business Operations, London: Croom Helm.

Kojima, K. (1982) 'Macroeconomic Versus International Business Approach to Direct Foreign Investment', Hitotsubashi Journal of Economics, 23, no. 1, June pp.1-19.

Lall, S. (1980) 'Monopolistic Advantages and Foreign Involvement by US Manufacturing Industry', Oxford Economic Papers, 32, no. 1, pp.105-22, reprinted in Lall, S. (1980) The Multinational Corporation, London: Macmillan.

Lall, S. and Siddarthan, N.S. (1982) 'The Monopolistic Advantages of Multinationals: Lessons from Foreign Investment in the US', Economic Journal, 92, September, pp.668-83, reprinted in Lall, S. (1983) Multinationals, Technology and Exports, London: Macmillan.

Oshima, K. (1973) 'Research and Development and Economic Growth in Japan', in Williams, B.R. (ed.) Science and Technology in Economic Growth, New York: Wiley.

32

Samuelsson, H.F. (1977) Utlandska directa investeringar i sverige. En ekonometrisk analys av bestamningsfaktorerna (Foreign Direct Investments in Sweden - an Econometric Analysis), Stockholm: Industriens Utredningsinstitut.

Swedenborg, B. (1979) The Multinational Operations of Swedish Firms. An Analysis of Determinants and Effects, Stockholm: Industrial Institute of Economic and Social Research.

Vernon, R. (1979) 'The Product Cycle Hypothesis in a New International Environment', Oxford Bulletin of Economics and Statistics, Special Issue: The Multi-National Corporation, 41, no. 4, November, pp.255-67.

Zellner, A. (1962) 'An Efficient Method of Estimating Seemingly Unrelated Regressions and Tests for Aggregation Bias', Journal of the American Statistical Association, 57, no. 298, June, pp.348-68.

# Name Index

Abdel-Khalik 352
Acocella, N. 3
Ahnström, L. 275
Aho, C.M. 88
Albin, E. 229
Alchian, A.A. 109, 142
Aliber, R.Z. 76
Arditti, F. 203
Arpan 352
Arrow, K. 185–6

Bailey, E.L. 317, 322
Balassa 413
Balough, R.S. 417
Bandera, V. 418
Barrett 352, 357
Batra, N. 63
Baumol, W.J. 410
Beamish, P.M. 161
Beaud, C.P. 536
Behrman, J.N. 277, 284, 502–4
Benke 352
Berrill, K. 186
Bieri, J 417
Bilkey, W.J. 445
Blois, K.J. 446
Blomström, M. 234
Boddewyn, J.J. 499
Bradbury, F.R. 274
Brash, D.T. 230
Brech, M. 428, 430
Bruce Wallace, R. 233
Buckley, P.J. 3, 76, 106, 116, 141, 159, 164, 325, 445, 464, 474, 504–7, 511, 578, 580, 583
Burstall, M.L. 427–33

Cantwell, J.A. 3, 418, 420, 438
Carlsson, B. 419
Carter, W.H. 53
Casas, F. 63
Casson, M.C. 3, 6, 76, 141, 159, 164, 390, 394, 445, 464, 504–10, 521, 546, 578, 580
Caves, R.E. 63, 76, 78, 89, 91, 106, 108, 141, 229–31, 233, 273, 285–6, 290, 293, 296, 465, 582
Chandler, A. 4, 534

Cho, K.R. 508
Chow, G.C. 197
Chung, W.K. 340
Church, R. 436–8
Coase, R.H. 3, 5, 10–11, 18, 24, 76, 141, 474
Comanor, W.S. 322
Cordell, A.J. 273, 276
Cory, P.F. 231
Cowling, K. 437
Crawford, R.G. 109
Creamer, D. 275–6
Curtis, C.E. 502

Daniels, J. 101
Davidson, W.H. 146
Davies, H. 583
Demsetz, H. 142
Dicken, P. 435–6
Dixit, A.K. 107
Dosi, G. 423
Dunning, J.H. 3, 141, 207, 210–11, 213, 218, 220, 222, 389, 395, 418, 420, 427–30, 432, 473, 504, 506–8, 511–12, 578, 605

Edwards 352
Edwards, C.D. 102

Faith, N. 101
Farmer, D. 150
Fernlund, I. 277
Finnie 352
Fischer, W.A. 277, 284
Ford, J.D. 446
Franko, L.G. 161, 557
Freeman, C. 186, 273

Galbraith, J. 462
Globerman, S. 229–30, 233
Gorecki, P.K. 229
Granstrand, O. 277
Gray, H.P. 508
Gray, J.M. 508
Griffiths, A. 427
Grubel, H.G. 508
Guillet de Monthoux, P. 446

Hägg, I. 449